American Social and
Political Thought

AMERICAN SOCIAL AND POLITICAL THOUGHT

A READER

Edited by
Andreas Hess

EDINBURGH UNIVERSITY PRESS

Selection and editorial material
© Andreas Hess, 2002. The texts are
reprinted by permission of other
publishers; the acknowledgements on
pp. xi–xvi constitute an extension of this
copyright page.

Edinburgh University Press Ltd
22 George Square, Edinburgh

Typeset in Sabon and Gill Sans
by Bibliocraft Ltd, Dundee, and
printed and bound in Great Britain by
MPG Books Ltd, Bodmin, Cornwall

A CIP record for this book is available from
the British Library

ISBN 0 7486 1528 8 (hardback)
ISBN 0 7486 1529 6 (paperback)

The right of the contributors to be
identified as authors of this work
has been asserted in accordance with the
Copyright, Designs and Patents Act 1988.

CONTENTS

ACKNOWLEDGEMENTS

Grateful acknowledgement is made to the following sources for permission to reproduce material in this book previously published elsewhere. Every effort has been made to trace copyright holders, but if any have been inadvertently overlooked the publisher will be pleased to make the necessary arrangement at the first opportunity.

1. *Reconstructing America: The Symbol of America in Modern Thought* by James W. Ceaser, Yale University Press, 1997.
2. From *Anti-Intellectualism in American Life* by Richard Hofstadter, copyright © 1962, 1963, by Richard Hofstadter. Used by permission of Alfred A. Knopf, a division of Random House, Inc.
3. *Letters from an American Farmer* by J. Hector St. John de Crèvecoeur (Oxford: Oxford University Press 1997).
4. *The Frontier in American History* by Frederick Jackson Turner, New York: Dover Publications, 1996.
5. *The Influence of Sea Power upon History* by Alfred Thayer Mahan, New York: Dover Publications, 1987.
6. *The Thomas Paine Reader* edited by Michael Foot and Isaac Kramnick, Penguin, 1987.
7. *Democracy in America* by Alexis de Tocqueville, edited by J. P. Mayer, Fontana (part of HarperCollins Publishers), 1994.
8. *American Exceptionalism – A Double-Edged Sword* by Seymour Martin Lipset (New York/London: W. W. Norton, 1996).

9. From *From Max Weber: Essays in Sociology* by Max Weber, edited by H. H. Gerth and C. Wright Mills, translated by H. H. Gerth and C. Wright Mills, copyright 1946, 1958 by H. H. Gerth and C. Wright Mills. Used by permission of Oxford University Press, Inc.

10. *Democracy in America* by Alexis de Tocqueville, edited by J. P. Mayer, Fontana (part of HarperCollins Publishers), 1994.

11. *The Thomas Paine Reader* edited by Michael Foot and Isaac Kramnick, Penguin, 1987.

12. *Writings* by Thomas Jefferson, The Library of America, 1984.

13. *Redeeming American Political Thought* by Judith N. Shklar, edited by Stanley Hoffman and Dennis F. Thompson, University of Chicago Press, 1998 © Judith Shklar.

14. Reprinted by permission of the publisher from *The New England Mind: From Colony to Province* by Perry Miller, Cambridge, MA: The Belknap Press of Harvard University Press, Copyright © 1953 by the President and Fellows of Harvard College, Copyright © 1981 by Elizabeth W. Miller.

15. This piece consists of excerpts from throughout the book *American Jeremiad* by Sacvan Bercovitch © 1978. Reprinted by permission of The University of Wisconsin Press.

16. From *Protestant–Catholic–Jew* by Will Herberg, copyright © 1955 by Will Herberg. Used by permission of Doubleday, a division of Random House, Inc.

17. *The Machiavellian Moment* by J. G. A. Pocock. Copyright © 1975 by Princeton University Press. Reprinted by permission of Princeton University Press.

18. Joyce Appleby: *Liberalism and Republicanism in the Historical Imagination* (Cambridge, MA: Harvard University Press: 1992).

19. *On Revolution* by Hannah Arendt, Faber and Faber, 1963, reproduced by permission of Faber and Faber Ltd.

20. *The Federalist Papers* by James Madison, Alexander Hamilton and John Jay, Penguin, 1987.

21. 'Montesquieu and the New Republicanism' by Judith Shklar from *Machiavelli and Republicanism* by Gisela Bock, Quentin Skinner and Maurizio Viroli (eds), Cambridge University Press, 1990. Copyright © Cambridge University Press.

22. *A Passion for Democracy* by Benjamin Barber. Copyright © 1998 by Princeton University Press. Reprinted by permission of Princeton University Press.

23. Wolin, Sheldon, *The Presence of the Past: Essays on the State and the Constitution*, © 1990 Sheldon Wolin. Reprinted by permission of the Johns Hopkins University Press.

24. Excerpts from *The Liberal Tradition in America: An Interpretation of American Political Thought Since the Revolution*, copyright © 1955 and renewed 1983 by Louis Hartz, reprinted by permission of Harcourt, Inc.

25. From *Reconsidering American Liberalism* by James P. Young. Copyright © 1995 by Westview Press. Reprinted by permission of Westview Press, a member of Perseus Books, LLC.
26. From *Political Liberalism* by John Rawls, copyright © 1993 Columbia University Press. Reprinted by permission of the publisher.
27. 'The Liberalism of Fear' by Judith N. Shklar. Extracts reprinted by permission of the publisher from *Liberalism and the Moral Life* edited by Nancy Rosenblum, Cambridge, MA: Harvard University Press, Copyright © 1989 by the President and Fellows of Harvard College.
28. 'Precommitment and the Paradox of Democracy' by Stephen Holmes from *Constitutionalism and Democracy* by J. Elster and R. Slagstad (eds), Cambridge University Press, 1988, © Cambridge University Press.
Stephen Holmes from *Responsibility, Rights, and Welfare* edited by Donald Moon, Westview Press, 1988.
The version reproduced here appeared in *Passions and Constraint* by Stephen Holmes, University of Chicago Press, 1995.
29. *Essays and Lectures* by Ralph Waldo Emerson, The Library of America, 1983.
30. 'What Pragmatism Means' from *Pragmatism: A New Name for Some Old Ways of Thinking* by William James, Longmans, Green & Co., 1907, as reprinted in *Pragmatism: A Contemporary Reader* edited by Russell B. Goodman, Routledge, 1995.
31. Extracts from The *Public and its Problems* by John Dewey (Swallow Press, 1980). Reprinted with the permission of Ohio University Press/Swallow Press, Athens, Ohio.
32. From *The Power Elite*, new edition by C. Wright Mills, copyright © 1956, 2000 by Oxford University Press, Inc. Used by permission of Oxford University Press, Inc.
33. This piece consists of excerpts from throughout the book *The American Evasion of Philosophy* by Cornel West. © 1989. Reprinted by permission of The University of Wisconsin Press.
34. Richard Rorty, 'Objectivity, relativism, and truth', Cambridge University Press, 1988. Reproduced by permission of Cambridge University Press and Richard Rorty.
35. From *Social Origins of Dictatorship and Democracy: Lord and Peasant in the Making of the Modern World* by Barrington Moore, Jr. (Viking, 1966) copyright © Barrington Moore, Jr, 1966. From *Social Origins of Dictatorship and Democracy* by Barrington Moore, Jr. Copyright © 1966 by Barrington Moore, Jr. Reprinted by permission of Beacon Press, Boston.
36. From *The Power Elite*, new edition by C. Wright Mills, copyright © 1956, 2000 by Oxford University Press, Inc. Used by permission of Oxford University Press, Inc.
37. *A Preface to Democratic Theory* by Robert A. Dahl, University of Chicago Press, 1956, reproduced by permission of the University of Chicago Press.

38. *Who Governs? Democracy and Power in an American City* by Robert A. Dahl, Yale University Press, 1961.

39. Reprinted by permission of the publisher from *Democracy and Disagreement* by Amy Gutmann and Dennis Thompson, Cambridge, MA: The Belknap Press of Harvard University Press, Copyright © 1996 by the President and Fellows of Harvard College.

40. *Strong Democracy: Participatory Politics for a New Age* by Benjamin Barber, University of California Press. Copyright © 1984 The Regents of the University of California.

41. From *Democracy and Capitalism* by Samuel Bowles and Herbert Gintis. Copyright © 1986 by Basic Books, Inc. Reprinted by permission of Basic Books, a member of Perseus Books, LLC.

42. *Habits of the Heart: Individualism and Commitment in American Life* by Robert N. Bellah, Richard Madsen and William M. Sullivan, University of California Press, Copyright © 1985, 1996 Regents of the University of California.

43. *Essays on Theory and Democracy* by Sheldon S. Wolin. Copyright © by Princeton University Press. Reprinted by permission of Princeton University Press.

44. Reprinted by permission of the publisher from *A Theory of Justice* by John Rawls, Cambridge, MA: The Belknap Press of Harvard University Press, Copyright © 1971, 1999 by the President and Fellows of Harvard College.

45. *Understanding Rawls* by Robert P. Wolff. Copyright © 1977 by Princeton University Press. Reprinted by permission of Princeton University Press.

46. From *Spheres of Justice: A Defense of Pluralism and Equality* by Michael Walzer. Copyright © 1983 by Basic Books, Inc. Reprinted by permission of Basic Books, a member of Perseus Books, LLC.

47. Ronald Dworkin: *Sovereign Virtue – The Theory and Practice of Equality* (Cambridge, MA: Harvard University Press 2000).

48. Reprinted by permission of the publisher from *American Citizenship: The Quest for Inclusion* by Judith N. Shklar, Cambridge, MA: The Belknap Press of Harvard University Press, Copyright © 1991 by the President and Fellows of Harvard College.

49. From *W. E. B. Du Bois: A Reader*, edited by David Levering Lewis, © 1995 by David Levering Lewis. Reprinted by permission of Henry Holt and Company, LLC.

50. Reprinted by permission of the publisher from *We Are All Multiculturalists Now* by Nathan Glazer, Cambridge, MA: Harvard University Press, Copyright © 1997 by the President and Fellows of Harvard College

51. *Multiculturalism and the Politics of Recognition* by Charles Taylor. Copyright © 1994 by Princeton University Press. Reprinted by permission of Princeton University Press.

52. Michael Walzer: *What it Means to be an American* (New York: Marsilio, 1996).

53. *Color Conscious* by K. Anthony Appiah & Amy Gutmann. Copyright © 1996 by Princeton University Press. Reprinted by permission of Princeton University Press.

54. bell hooks: *killing rage: ending racism* (London: Penguin, 1995).

55. From *Loose Canons: Notes on the Cultural Wars* by Henry Louis Gates, Jr., copyright © 1992 by Henry Louis Gates, Jr. Used by permission of Oxford University Press, Inc.

56. *Civil Society and Political Theory* by Jean L. Cohen and Andrew Arato, The MIT Press, 1992, reproduced by permission of The MIT Press.

57. Jeffrey C. Isaac, 'Democracy in Dark Times' from *Political Theory* 23, November 1995, copyright © 1995 by Jeffrey C. Isaac. Reprinted by permission of Sage Publications, Inc.

58. Jeffrey C. Goldfarb from *Civility and Subversion*, Cambridge University Press, 1998, reproduced by permission of Cambridge University Press and Jeffrey C. Goldfarb.

59. Jean Bethke Elshtain: 'Antigone's Daughters', in: Anne Phillips (ed.): *Feminism and Politics* (Oxford: Oxford University Press, 1998).

60. Mary G. Dietz 'Citizenship with a Feminist Face' from *Political Theory* 13/1, February 1985, copyright © 1985 by Mary G. Dietz. Reprinted by permission of Sage Publications, Inc.

61. 'Gender and Public Access' by Mary P. Ryan from *Habermas and the Public Sphere* edited by Craig Calhoun, The MIT Press, 1992, reproduced by permission of The MIT Press.

62. Reprinted by permission of Sage Publishing Ltd. From *Real Civil Societies* by Jeffrey C. Alexander, © 1998 by Jeffrey C. Alexander.

63. Reprinted by permission of the publisher from *Democracy's Discontent: America in Search of a Public Philosophy* by Michael J. Sandel, Cambridge, MA: The Belknap Press of Harvard University Press, Copyright © 1996 by Michael J. Sandel.

64. 'Fusion Republicanism' by Nancy L. Rosenblum from *Debating Democracy's Discontent: Essays on American Politics, Law and Public Philosophy* edited by Anita K. Allen and Milton C. Regan, Jr., Oxford University Press, 1998. Reprinted by permission of Oxford University Press.

65. 'A Defense of Minimalist Liberalism' by Richard Rorty from *Debating Democracy's Discontent: Essays on American Politics, Law and Public Philosophy* edited by Anita K. Allen and Milton C. Regan, Jr., Oxford University Press, 1998. Reprinted by permission of Oxford University Press.

66. 'And for the Pursuit of the Common Good' by Richard Sennett. This review first appeared in the *Times Literary Supplement*, 18 October 1996 © Times Supplements Ltd.

67. *Whose Keeper? Social Science and Moral Obligation* by Alan Wolfe, University of California Press. Copyright © 1989 Regents of the University of California.

68. *Essays in Trespassing* by Albert O. Hirschman, Cambridge University Press, 1981, reproduced by kind permission of the author.
69. From *The Company of Critics: Social Criticism and Political Commitment in the 20th Century* by Michael Walzer. Copyright © 1988 by Michael Walzer. Reprinted by permission of Basic Books, a member of Perseus Books, LLC.

Extract from *The Company of Critics* by Michael Walzer, Peter Halban Publishers 1989, copyright 1988 by Basic Books, Inc.
70. C. L. R. James: *Mariners, Renegades and Castaways* (Detroit: Bewick/ ED, 1978).

INTRODUCTION

Since the events of 11 September 2001, there has been an even greater necessity to understand what makes the United States 'tick' and what the United States represents. In order to come to a better understanding, there could be no less want to do so than to study the American intellectual tradition and the contributions that American intellectuals have made in the course of more than two hundred years of independent existence.

A closer look reveals that what is so unique about the US and distinguishes it from other societies is in fact the debate on the democratic nature of that society itself. After all, it was the United States that did not confine the process of enlightenment to lofty intellectual circles, but rather applied it practically and put in place unique political and social processes and institutions. From this, a dialectic relationship developed, whereby institutions created by intellectual design also had an impact and continued to shape the American political tradition. Today, one may stand back and observe the development of such a genuine American tradition of social and political thought.

However authentic this tradition may be, it should be added here that the ideas that played a major role in the American tradition are not limited to the American realm. Social and political thought has always bounced back and forth between particularistic aspects of what is unique to certain social and political circumstances and more universalistic aspects of what is common and can be applied to all circumstances. The central point is that it is only by looking at particular circumstances that one can be in a position to suggest that something is universal, and it is only through discussing the universal aspects that the unique and the particular aspects stand out. Accordingly, this *Reader* is informed by the idea that one can gain a better understanding of American democracy and its appeal by looking at how intellectuals concerned with America have themselves tried to understand and explain it. Beyond that, it is also hoped that the *Reader* will enable the student to imagine and understand social and political thought beyond the boundaries of the United States. In this respect American democracy can serve as an example of how to interpret and act upon the issues and challenges posed to modern democracy worldwide.

In the past, social and political thinkers made every effort to learn from the experience of others. In actual fact, the entire history of social and political conceptualisation could be written from a perspective of intercultural and international (sic) exchange and learning. Such a history could not only be looked at in terms of individual learning processes but also looked at as collective processes where nations and/or cultures learn from each other's experiences and insights. Prominent names and events come to mind: Hobbes, Locke, Machiavelli, Montesquieu, Kant, Hegel, Marx, Burke and Paine, the French and American Revolutions, to name just the most prominent examples. However, mutual learning presupposes the will to learn from each other and, if we look at the intellectual relationship between Europe and the United States, for example, this is exactly what has happened over the last four centuries. However, the relationship and the mutual learning process between the two continents were not always easy. As a matter of fact, they have often been troubled by war, revolutions and/or diplomatic rifts and disagreements. Nevertheless, it would be justified to say that in the past Europe and the United States had a mutual interest in each other's affairs and intellectual history, and even in troubled times the learning process through dialogue was bound to continue in one way or another. Such a process would be especially encouraged by two factors: 'intellectual' journeys, mainly on a voluntary basis, and the 'forced' experience of exiles. This last 'experience' needs further qualification, particularly since it was more one-directional. The European exiles who came to America learned from their sanctuary, and very often they would report back to Europe, while exiles going the other way around, - that is, Americans seeking refuge in Europe – are almost unheard of unless one cites upper-crust figures such as Henry James.

My contention is that as we enter the twenty-first century the experience of exile is now less influential than it used to be. This is mainly due to long-term positive developments in the 'Old World'. In a changed European environment, particularly after World War II, the stream of exiles leaving Europe for the United States has declined. Furthermore, Europe is now discussing its own future with more self-confidence than ever before – and it does so by relying on democratic means and institutions. Thus, we can expect a situation in which Europe concentrates more on its own affairs.

The other experience, that of voluntary intellectual interchange in the context of travelling and visiting, is much harder to grasp. There is plenty of interchange between European and American intellectuals, not least because there are also plenty of official exchange programmes which allow for such communication. However, in the more recent past a problematic view has come into fashion. I am referring here to an intellectual view of the world that deals rather with the symbols of America than with its real structures and events. Such a view has its origins in French and German social and political thought, but increasingly it has captured the minds of others as well. In connection with other symbolic messages – mainly stemming from the media – it seems that there exists now an entire world-view that knows the United States *only* by its symbols. Such a view can lend itself easily to prejudice, particularly when it begins to dominate all perception.

In Europe particularly there seems to be a *habitus* developing, which pretends that there is nothing more to learn from the experience of the United States. Two recent discussions come to mind. There is, firstly, the idea that while Europe faces enlargement and reform it has to find its own 'European' solution. The notion of the federal 'United States of Europe' is rejected instantly. However, the prospects for the other, so-called 'more realistic' European alternative of a federation of nation-states, a model that has gained much more support, looks rather bleak. This is partly because a federation of nations would have to deal with the historical container that is the nation-state. With more than twenty nation-states in the new European Union and the individual European nation-states still alive and well, there could easily be a problem in terms of democratic means and ends. The Nice summit has already provided a glimpse of such a future. In such a context a closer look at the American experience might not provide all the answers that the new Europe faces; however, it could teach Europe a lesson on how to have a large territory, democratic accountability and functioning institutions at the same time. For such an intercontinental learning process it would be necessary to engage in honest intellectual debate – something that is far from being the norm in Europe.

In the said context – and this is the second discussion I am referring to – it is deeply troubling that particularly after the events of 11 September 2001 there is now an increasingly worrying tendency amongst European intellectuals to no longer engage with American ideas at all. This tendency has certainly always existed, but with 11 September and the intellectual reactions towards it, it has become clear that there is not only a reluctance to engage in intercontinental dialogue but open and frank Anti-Americanism. It is, for example, openly stated that the victim is guilty and that America is somehow responsible for the attacks, or deserved it somehow. To speak merely of *Schadenfreude* would underestimate the significance and seriousness of this change in attitudes. In such a highly politicised environment this *Reader* is a modest attempt to engage again with ideas that represent some of the best arguments for an intellectual exchange between America and Europe.

On a more practical level, the main purpose of this *Reader* is to function as a companion to *American Social and Political Thought: A Concise Introduction*.

The aim of the *Reader* is to provide substantial extracts from the core texts used in this latter *Introduction*. It allows easy access to the material and pays closer attention to the content of the original texts themselves. The *Reader* consists of two parts, or layers. The first is entitled 'Thinking the Political: The Main Modes and Traditions of American Social and Political Thought'. It deals mainly with the basic political foundations and building blocks of the American intellectual tradition: 'Exceptionalism', 'Political Theology', 'Republicanism', 'Liberalism' and 'Pragmatism'. Part I aims at preparing the ground for the second part, entitled 'Theorising the Social: Modern Applications of American Social and Political Thought'. This second part is more concerned with how differentiated American social and political thought became in the course of the twentieth century. It consists of the following sections: 'Democracy and Power', 'Justice and Injustice', 'Pluralism and Multiculturalism', 'Civil Society, Social Theory and the Task of Intellectuals' and 'Social and Political Thought at the Dawn of the Twenty-first Century'.

The logic or the specific order of the proposed readings could of course be questioned, and there are surely other ways to order them. As an editor, I can only say that it was a matter of making difficult choices. I took the decision to be highly selective in terms of the sources, knowing that less can sometimes be more. I decided to include at least one classic in each field or topic and I have sought contributions that would be reactions to, or discussions of, the original contributions or any given pioneering work. However, my main hope is that the two-part mosaic-like approach will give an impression of the overall picture of American social and political thought. The book will have served its purpose and will have achieved its aim if the reader has gained a better understanding of what it is that makes American society function.

GENERAL SECTION

In his book *Reconstructing America* the political scientist James W. Ceaser voices his discontent vis-à-vis past and present attempts to construct a 'metaphysical' or 'symbolic' America. The problem with these 'Amerika' approaches is not only their deep ideological bias towards actually existing American society and its reality, but, having originally been 'invented' in France and Germany, these metaphysical ideas have now spread to the East, to Africa and Latin America – and have even made it back to the United States. However, as Ceaser reminds us, such a view is a distorted view, one which is ignorant about most of the findings of one of America's oldest and finest disciplines – political science.

Richard Hofstadter's classic *Anti-Intellectualism in American Life* is also a history of intellectual life in America and, within this intellectual life, the relationship between knowledge and power. In the final chapter of his study Hofstadter discusses the various American intellectual streams and what separates modern thought from those of earlier times. Here he distinguishes between the eighteenth-century intellectuals in America where there was little differentiation – intellectuals and people in power were almost undistinguishable – and twentieth-century conditions, where knowledge and power have become differentiated and where we speak now of 'critics' and 'associates of power'. As Hofstadter is ready to acknowledge, such differentiation calls for a new response from intellectuals that avoids the extremes of critics who are completely detached and powerful men using their intellect solely for the purpose of staying in power or serving the powerful.

I

RECONSTRUCTING AMERICA – THE SYMBOL OF AMERICA IN MODERN THOUGHT

James W. Ceaser

In a line of development that can be traced back more than two hundred years, some of the most illustrious thinkers of Europe have seized on the word 'America' and made it into something more than a place or country. They have converted it into a concept of philosophy and a trope of literature. From Hegel to Heidegger in Germany (with passages through Spengler and Jünger) and from Buffon to Baudrillard in France (with passages through de Maistre and Kojève), a new America has been born. I shall refer to this America as the 'metaphysical America' or the 'symbolic America'. And I shall try to distinguish it, so far as I can, from the real America, by which I mean the country where we live, work, struggle, and pray, and where we have forged a system of government that has helped to shape the destiny of the modern world.

The symbolic America is not, of course, identical for every thinker. But all have worked from the same concept, successively modifying and amending it with the previous meanings in mind, I could provide scores of examples illustrating the content of the symbolic America ... But I will spare my readers for the moment the pain of such a litany and confine myself here to a nice passage from the French writer Henry de Montherlant:

> One nation that manages to lower intelligence, morality, human quality on nearly all the surface of the earth, such a thing has never been seen before in the existence of the planet. I accuse the United States of being in a permanent state of crime against humankind.[1]

From: James W. Ceaser, *Reconstructing America: The Symbol of America in Modern Thought* (New Haven and London: Yale University Press, 1997).

Writers on America do not simply speak of the United States; they have also constructed the concept of 'Americanism' or 'Americanization', which refers to such fundamental developments of modernity as cultural homogenization, democratization, and degeneration. America so conceived may exist outside of the United States and involve no actual Americans. Once this point is reached, it becomes clear that the real America is no longer at issue: an idea or symbol called 'America' has taken over. No other nation, so far as I know, has attained in anything like the same degree this status of a pure abstraction. No one, for example, speaks of New Zealandism or Venezuelanization. Yet for all this, the real nation remains the object of the symbol, and 'America' always points back to the United States. In this respect America differs from other well-known geographical symbols where the object designated is not a political entity or society but a spiritual or intellectual activity, as is the case with 'Jerusalem' (the biblical religion), 'Athens' (philosophy), and 'Rome' (the Catholic faith).

The symbolic or metaphysical America must be distinguished from the various images of America that circulate around the world today. Mass opinion, which generally holds a more favorable picture of America, derives from sources that are partly independent of the thoughts of philosophers and the musings of poets – a fact that no doubt accounts for some of the intellectual hostility toward America. The influence of America on public opinion comes from political events (above all, American participation in the world wars), from America's status today as the world's preeminent economic and military power, from America's identification with the idea of modern democracy, and from America's supremacy in the realms of popular entertainment, advertising, mass media, and computer language. The ascendancy of America in so many realms, which by accident happens to have followed upon Great Britain's reign as the world's foremost empire, has also elevated the English language – or 'American', as many in the world now call it – to the status of the universal medium of communication in business, science, and diplomacy and on the Internet.

The spread of popular images about America in our era of globalization has made America into the nearest thing ever to an object of universal reference. America is spoken of with greater frequency and carries more meaning to more people than any other image in recorded time, including the biblical God or our own Madonna. From Mogadishu to Tbilisi and from Bogotá to Minsk, almost everyone has an impression of or an opinion about America. People may either love or hate America, but they almost never ignore it. The penetration of America into the consciousness of other peoples is well captured by the title of a recent book in France, *L'Amérique dans les têtes*, which, to take advantage of a colloquialism of our youth today, may be translated as *America Getting Inside Your Head*.[2] Foreign intellectuals and journalists often lament this preoccupation with America, but they still seem to underestimate its depth; for after delivering themselves of some weighty assessment about the meaning of America, they often work a conversation around to asking what the

American perspective is on their nation's politics and culture – on the assumption that as they have a view about America, so too must Americans have a view of them. For the most part, however, there is no American view of France or Canada or Germany or England or Honduras in the same way that there is a French, Canadian, German, English, or Honduran view of America. This fact is less a manifestation of Americans' well-documented ignorance of foreign things than it is a reflection of the current asymmetry in the position of the nations of the world. Because America has a significant bearing on just about everyone else, yet because no other nation has this same effect on America, Americans have less need to build elaborate images of other countries.

Mass opinion about America, as noted, is not quite the same thing as the metaphysical or symbolic America. A congruence between the two would be impossible, if only because the foundations of the symbolic America were laid two centuries ago, well before the United States achieved its current status. The symbolic America has nevertheless exercised a significant, although indirect, effect on public thinking. Anchored in the works of some of the major thinkers of our age, the symbol continually impresses itself on the educated strata and on opinion makers, who in turn transmit bits and pieces of it to the public at large. Because the ideas of philosophers and writers have a staying power that cannot be matched by the evanescent images generated in the modern mass media, the influence of the symbolic America on public consciousness is sure to persist.

Irrespective of its impact on public opinion, however, the symbolic America is important in its own right and has become a central concept of contemporary thought. Open any book of modern intellectual history, and you are apt to see an allusion to America as the primary reference for such fundamental themes as technology (and rationalist thought or 'logocentrism'), the end of history, political homogenization, cultural banalization, and (while it was still a respectable theme of intellectual thought) racial and ethnic homogenization ('mongrelization'). Whoever says 'America' may mean any one of these things. Today America may not have a status equivalent to God in medieval thought or Being in classical thought, but it rivals any modern symbol for dominance in our time. In considering the symbolic America, a window is opened on modern thought itself.

NOTES

1. Henry de Montherlant, '*Le chaos*' et '*La nuit*' (Paris: Gallimard, 1963), p. 265. Translation of Jean-Philippe Mathy, *Extrême-Occident* (Chicago: University of Chicago Press, 1993), p. 18.
2. *L'Amérique dans les têtes*, Denis Lacorne, Jacques Rupnik and Marie-France Toinet (eds) Paris: Hachette, 1986).

2

ANTI-INTELLECTUALISM IN AMERICAN LIFE

Richard Hofstadter

The dislike of involvement with 'accredited institutions' exhibited by the prophets of alienation bespeaks a more fundamental dislike of the association of intellect with power. The frightening idea that an intellectual ceases altogether to function as an intellectual when he enters an accredited institution (which would at one stroke eliminate from the intellectual life all our university professors) may be taken as a crude formulation of a real problem: there is some discord between the imperatives of a creative career and the demands of the institution within which it takes place. Scholars have long since had to realize that the personal costs of working within institutions are smaller than the costs of living without institutional support. Indeed, they have no real choice: they need libraries and laboratories – perhaps even pupils – which only an institution can provide.

For imaginative writers this problem is more serious. The amenities and demands of academic life do not accord well with imaginative genius, and they make the truly creative temperament ill at ease. Moreover, the conditions of academic life are such as to narrow unduly the range of one's experience; and it is painful to imagine what our literature would be like if it were written by academic teachers of 'creating writing' courses, whose main experience was to have been themselves trained in such courses. It would be a waste, too, if poets with primary gifts were to spend time as members of committees on the revision of the freshman composition course – hummingbirds, to resurrect an image of

From: Richard Hofstadter, *Anti-Intellectualism in American Life* (New York: Vintage Books, 1963).

Mencken's, immersed in *Kartoffelsuppe*. Still, the partial or temporary support offered by the academy to writer and artist has proved helpful in many careers, and very often the alternative to such support is the creation of a frustrated cultural *lumpenproletariat*.

However, for intellectuals in the disciplines affected by the problem of expertise, the university is only a symbol of a larger and more pressing problem of the relationship of intellect to power: we are opposed almost by instinct to the divorce of knowledge from power, but we are also opposed, out of our modern convictions, to their union. This was not always the case: the great intellectuals of pagan antiquity, the doctors of the medieval universities, the scholars of the Renaissance, the philosophers of the Enlightenment, sought for the conjunction of knowledge and power and accepted its risks without optimism or naïveté. They hoped that knowledge would in fact be broadened by a conjunction with power, just as power might be civilized by its connection with knowledge. I have spoken of the terms on which knowledge and power were related in the days of the Founding Fathers as being consonant with this ideal: knowledge and power consorted more or less as equals, within the same social circles, and very often within the same heads. But this was not simply because, as some modern critics seem to imagine, the Founding Fathers were better than we are, though they probably were better. It is not simply that Jefferson read Adam Smith and Eisenhower read Western fiction. The fundamental difference is that the society of the eighteenth century was unspecialized. In Franklin's day it was still possible for a man to conduct an experiment of some scientific value in his woodshed, and for the gifted amateur in politics to move from a plantation to a law office to a foreign ministry. Today knowledge and power are differentiated functions. When power resorts to knowledge, as it increasingly must, it looks not for intellect, considered as a freely speculative and critical function, but for expertise, for something that will serve its needs. Very often power lacks respect for that disinterestedness which is essential to the proper functioning of the expert – the governor of a great state once called several distinguished sociologists into conference to arrange a public-opinion poll on a controversial, current issue, and then carefully outlined for them what this poll was to find.

If the typical man of power simply wants knowledge as an instrument, the typical man of knowledge in modern America is the expert. Earlier I observed that it has been largely the function of expertise which has restored the intellectual as a force in American politics. But the pertinent question is whether the intellectual, as expert, can really be an intellectual – whether he does not become simply a mental technician, to use the phrase of H. Stuart Hughes, working at the call of the men who hire him. Here, as in the case of the university and other accredited institutions, I think the answer is not easy or categorical, and a true answer will almost certainly not be apocalyptic enough to please the modern intellectual sensibility. The truth is that much of American education aims, simply and brazenly, to turn out experts who are not intellectuals or men of culture at all: and when such men go into the service of government or business or the universities themselves, they do not suddenly become intellectuals.

The situation of men of real intellectual accomplishment who may also enter the service of power is much more complicated. Do men distinguished for reflective minds cease to be intellectuals simply because they become ambassadors to India or Yugoslavia or members of the President's staff? No doubt certain intellectual responses are no longer possible for men who look at the world from an angle of vision that is close to power and who assume as given those compromises which have to be made when power is attained. But to me it seems to be a personal choice, one that cannot be squeezed into the terms of the forced morality of alienation, whether one is to sacrifice some of one's range of critical freedom in the hope that power may be made more amenable to the counsels of intellect, or even for the Faustian urge to learn something about the world which cannot be so readily learned from the vantage point of the academy.

The intellectual who has relinquished all thought of association with power understands well – almost too well – that his state of powerlessness is conducive to certain illuminations. What he is prone to forget is that an access to power and an involvement with its problems may provide other illuminations. The critic of power tries to influence the world by affecting public opinion; the associate of power tries directly to make the exercise of power more amenable to the thought of the intellectual community. These functions are not of necessity mutually exclusive or hostile. Each involves certain personal and moral hazards, and it is not possible to make the personal choice of the hazards one cares to run into a universal imperative. The characteristic intellectual failure of the critic of power is a lack of understanding of the limitations under which power is exercised. His characteristic moral failure lies in an excessive concern with his own purity; but purity of a sort is easily had where responsibilities are not assumed. The characteristic failure of the expert who advises the powerful is an unwillingness to bring his capacity for independent thought to bear as a source of criticism. He may lose his capacity for detachment from power by becoming absorbed in its point of view. For American intellectuals, so long excluded from places of power and recognition, there is always the danger that a sudden association with power will become too glamorous, and hence intellectually blinding.

What is at stake for individuals is, as I say, a personal choice; but what is important for society as a whole is that the intellectual community should not become hopelessly polarized into two parts, one part of technicians concerned only with power and accepting implicitly the terms power puts to them, and the other of willfully alienated intellectuals more concerned with maintaining their sense of their own purity than with making their ideas effective. Experts there will undoubtedly be, and perhaps also critics capable of stepping mentally outside their society and looking relentlessly at its assumptions, in sufficient number and with sufficient freedom to make themselves felt. Presumably the possibility of debate between them will continue to exist, and the intellectual community will have within it types of minds capable of mediating between the world of power and the world of criticism. If so, intellectual society will avoid the danger of being cut up into hostile and uncommunicative segments. Our society is sick in many ways; but such health as it has lies in the plurality of the elements composing it and their freedom to interact with each other. It would be tragic if all intellectuals aimed to serve power; but it would be equally tragic if all intellectuals who become associated with power were driven to believe they no longer had any connection with the intellectual community: their conclusion would almost inevitably be that their responsibilities are to power alone.

PART I: THINKING THE POLITICAL: THE MAIN MODES AND TRADITIONS OF AMERICAN SOCIAL AND POLITICAL THOUGHT

SECTION I
EXCEPTIONALISM

Part I opens with the discussion of what has made and still makes America exceptional. It reflects one of the longest debates in America's intellectual history and gathers the main contributions to the Exceptionalism debate. The *Letters from an American Farmer* (1793) written by the French-American farmer Hector St. John de Crèvecoeur had been the first systematic attempt to reflect on the peculiar new conditions in America. He describes Americans as being a new breed, a melded version of different kinds of influences that for the first time had to work together under the same conditions, thereby forming a new American hybrid. Crèvecoeur also touched on topics that would later resurface in other contexts – the role of religious belief and affiliations, economically important attitudes such as self-interest and self-reliance, the importance of local customs and identities, and the unique Frontier experience. It was almost a hundred years later, at the time when the Frontier came to a close, that the American historian Frederick Jackson Turner addressed some of the questions which Crèvecoeur had touched upon earlier in his own book *The Frontier in American History*. Although Turner acknowledged the role of the thirteen original states in the creation of American democracy, he maintains that it was the later Frontier experience that really gave birth to the modern United States. It was the western experience that really put the question of magnitude and related questions such as size and governmentability on the agenda. For Turner it was less a question of how to found a democracy as one of how to maintain democracy in such a vast territory. The West also played a major role in terms of social psychology, that is to say the western experience provided individual citizens with hope. It showed that it was not only possible

---

to dream the American dream but it also provided individual opportunities to realise these hopes and dreams – at least to a certain extent. However, when the Frontier came to a close, new problems had to be addressed. Writing around the same time as Turner, Alfred Thayer Mahan, a former naval officer turned historian, built indirectly on some of Turner's ideas but also went beyond the idea of the Frontier in his study *The Influence of Sea Power upon History*. For Mahan, the United States will only preserve its greatness and democratic character if it uses its territory, particularly its coasts, intelligently as a base to develop into a seafaring nation, interested in peaceful and extensive commerce. Looking back at earlier seafaring nations and taking Portugal and Spain as negative, despotic examples and England and the Netherlands as positive, trade-based experiences, Mahan develops the idea of a direct relationship between democratic systems and modern global trade – a scenario which he suggests the US should pursue.

In terms of developing a new democratic system under modern conditions, the Americans had already been well advised a long time before Turner and Mahan arrived on the scene. It had been the writings of Thomas Paine, the English-American radical, which during the course of the War of Independence and in the early years of the American republic had influenced the consciousness of Americans. In a series of pamphlets – most famously in his *Rights of Man* – which received maximum distribution at the time, Paine outlined the uniqueness of modern revolutions. For the first time the new Republican governments – Paine referred to both the American and the French Revolution – had left behind the old natural order of things as symbolised by the aristocracy, monarchy and Church, and had attributed a new, popular sovereignty to the nation as a whole. Also, the idea of modern representation was mentioned in Paine, but it was left to the French statesman and political theorist Alexis de Tocqueville to develop this idea more thoroughly in his *Democracy in America*. In contrast to France, where the idea of the sovereignty of the people had been perverted by the part derailment of the French Revolution, the American Revolution had been quite successful. The experience of the terror and the reign of revolutionary virtue was something that Americans escaped. With the help of a uniquely developed model of federalism, a constitution including a bill of rights, a democratic government based on checks and balances, all in conjunction with a distinct political culture, the Americans were better equipped to put the idea of the sovereignty of the people into practice. More than 200 years after the founding of the American republic and more than 170 years after Tocqueville visited America, we can now look back and see both the possible achievements and the failures of the American exceptionalist path to modernity. The political sociologist Seymour Martin Lipset provides an updated version of Tocqueville's exceptionalism thesis in his book *American Exceptionalism – A Double-Edged Sword*. Looking back over the past two centuries Lipset is less optimistic than Tocqueville and Paine. As Lipset shows, the ambivalence of the American creed based on liberty, egalitarianism, individualism, populism, and laissez-faire had indeed results that cut both ways, depending on one's viewpoint and the empirical evidence.

3

LETTERS FROM AN AMERICAN FARMER

J. Hector St. John de Crèvecoeur

What then is the American, this new man? He is neither a European, nor the descendent of a European: hence that strange mixture of blood, which you will find in no other country. I could point out to you a family, whose grandfather was an Englishman, whose wife was Dutch, whose son married a French woman, and whose present four sons have now four wives of different nations. He is an American, who, leaving behind him all his antient prejudices and manners, receives new ones from the new mode of life he has embraced, the new government he obeys, and the new rank he holds. He becomes an American by being received in the broad lap of our great *alma mater*. Here individuals of all nations are melted into a new race of men, whose labours and posterity will one day cause great changes in the world. Americans are the western pilgrims, who are carrying along with them that great mass of arts, sciences, vigour, and industry, which began long since in the east. They will finish the great circle. The Americans were once scattered all over Europe. Here they are incorporated into one of the finest systems of population which has ever appeared, and which will hereafter become distinct by the power of the different climates they inhabit. The American ought therefore to love this country much better than that wherein either he or his forefathers were born. Here the rewards of his industry follow, with equal steps, the progress of his labour. His labour is founded on the basis of nature, *self-interest*: can it want a stronger allurement? Wives and children, who before in vain demanded of him a morsel of bread,

From: J. Hector St. John de Crèvecoeur, *Letters From an American Farmer* (Oxford: Oxford University Press, 1997).

now, fat and frolicsome, gladly help their father to clear those fields whence exuberant crops are to arise, to feed and to clothe them all, without any part being claimed, either by a despotic prince, a rich abbot, or a mighty lord. Here religion demands but little of him; a small voluntary salary to the minister, and gratitude to God: can he refuse these? The American is a new man, who acts upon new principles; he must therefore entertain new ideas and form new opinions. From involuntary idleness, servile dependence, penury, and useless labour, he has passed to toils of a very different nature, rewarded by ample subsistence – this is an American.

British America is divided into many provinces, forming a large association, scattered along a coast of 1500 miles extent and about 200 wide. This society I would fain examine, at least such as it appears in the middle provinces; if it does not afford that variety of tinges and gradations which may be observed in Europe, we have colours peculiar to ourselves. For instance, it is natural to conceive that those who live near the sea must be very different from those who live in the woods: the intermediate space will afford a separate and distinct class.

Men are like plants. The goodness and flavour of the fruit proceeds from the peculiar soil and exposition in which they grow. We are nothing but what we derive from the air we breathe, the climate we inhabit, the government we obey, the system of religion we profess, and the nature of our employment. Here you will find but few crimes; these have acquired as yet no root among us. I wish I were able to trace all my ideas. If my ignorance prevents me from describing them properly, I hope I shall be able to delineate a few of the outlines, which is all I propose.

Those who live near the sea feed more on fish than on flesh, and often encounter that boisterous element. This renders them more bold and enterprising: this leads them to neglect the confined occupations of the land. They see and converse with a variety of people. Their intercourse with mankind becomes extensive. The sea inspires them with a love of traffic, a desire of transporting produce from one place to another; and leads them to a variety of resources, which supply the place of labour. Those who inhabit the middle settlements, by far the most numerous, must be very different. The simple cultivation of the earth purifies them; but the indulgences of the government, the soft remonstrances of religion, the rank of independent freeholders, must necessarily inspire them with sentiments very little known in Europe among a people of the same class. What do I say? Europe has no such class of men. The early knowledge they acquire, the early bargains they make, give them a great degree of sagacity. As freemen they will be litigious. Pride and obstinacy are often the cause of law-suits; the nature of our laws and governments may be another. As citizens, it is easy to imagine that they will carefully read the newspapers, enter into every political disquisition, freely blame, or censure, governors and others. As farmers, they will be careful and anxious to get as much as they can, because what they get is their own. As northern men, they will love the cheerful cup. As Christians, religion curbs them not in their opinions: the general indulgence leaves everyone to think for themselves in spiritual matters. The law inspects our actions; our thoughts are left to God. Industry, good living, selfishness, litigiousness, country politics, the pride of freemen, religious indifference, are their characteristics. If you recede still farther from the sea, you will come into more modern settlements: they exhibit the same strong lineaments in a ruder appearance. Religion seems to have still less influence, and their manners are less improved.

Now we arrive near the great woods, near the last inhabited districts. There men seem to be placed still farther beyond the reach of government, which, in some measure, leaves them to themselves. How can it pervade every corner, as they were driven there by misfortunes, necessity of beginnings, desire of acquiring large tracks of land, idleness, frequent want of œconomy, antient debts. The re-union of such people does not afford a very pleasing spectacle. When discord, want of unity and friendship, when either drunkenness or idleness prevail in such remote districts, contention, inactivity, and wretchedness must ensue. There are not the same remedies to these evils as in a long-established community. The few magistrates they have are, in general, little better than the rest. They are often in a perfect state of war; that of man against man; sometimes decided by blows, sometimes by means of the law: that of man against every wild inhabitant of these venerable woods, of which they are come to dispossess them. There men appear to be no better than carnivorous animals, of a superior rank, living on the flesh of wild animals when they can catch them, and, when they are not able, they subsist on grain. He who would wish to see America in its proper light, and to have a true idea of its feeble beginnings and barbarous rudiments, must visit our extended line of frontiers, where the last settlers dwell, and where he may see the first labours of settlement, the mode of clearing the earth, in all their different appearances. Where men are wholly left dependent on their native tempers and on the spur of uncertain industry, which often fails when not sanctified by the efficacy of a few moral rules. There, remote from the power of example and check of shame, many families exhibit the most hideous parts of our society. They are a kind of forlorn hope, preceding, by ten or twelve years, the most respectable army of veterans which come after them. In that space, prosperity will polish some, vice and the law will drive off the rest, who, uniting again with others like themselves, will recede still farther, making room for more industrious people, who will finish their improvements, convert the log-house into a convenient habitation, and, rejoicing that the first heavy labours are finished, will change, in a few years, that hitherto-barbarous country into a fine, fertile, well-regulated district. Such is our progress, such is the march of the Europeans toward the interior parts of this continent. In all societies there are off-casts. This impure part serves as our precursors or pioneers. My father himself was one of that class; but he came upon honest principles, and was therefore one of the few who held fast. By good conduct and temperance he transmitted to me his fair inheritance, when not above one in fourteen of his contemporaries had the same good fortune.

Forty years ago this smiling country was thus inhabited. It is now purged. A general decency of manners prevails throughout, and such has been the fate of our best countries.

Exclusive of those general characteristics, each province has its own, founded on the government, climate, mode of husbandry, customs, and peculiarity of circumstances. Europeans submit insensibly to these great powers, and become, in the course of a few generations, not only Americans in general, but either Pennsylvanians, Virginians, or provincials under some other name.

4

THE FRONTIER IN AMERICAN HISTORY

Frederick Jackson Turner

Most important of all has been the fact that an area of free land has continually lain on the western border of the settled area of the United States. Whenever social conditions tended to crystallize in the East, whenever capital tended to press upon labor or political restraints to impede the freedom of the mass, there was this gate of escape to the free conditions of the frontier. These free lands promoted individualism, economic equality, freedom to rise, democracy. Men would not accept inferior wages and a permanent position of social subordination when this promised land of freedom and equality was theirs for the taking. Who would rest content under oppressive legislative conditions when with a slight effort he might reach a land wherein to become a co-worker in the building of free cities and free States on the lines of his own ideal? In a word, then, free lands meant free opportunities. Their existence has differentiated the American democracy from the democracies which have preceded it, because ever, as democracy in the East took the form of highly specialized and complicated industrial society, in the West it kept in touch with primitive conditions, and by action and reaction these two forces have shaped our history.

In the next place, these free lands and this treasury of industrial resources have existed over such vast spaces that they have demanded of democracy increasing spaciousness of design and power of execution. Western democracy is contrasted with the democracy of all other times in the largeness of the tasks to which it has set its hand, and in the vast achievements which it has wrought

From: Frederick Jackson Turner, *The Frontier in American History* (New York: Dover Publications, 1996).

out in the control of nature and of politics. It would be difficult to over-emphasize the importance of this training upon democracy. Never before in the history of the world has a democracy existed on so vast an area and handled things in the gross with such success, with such largeness of design, and such grasp upon the means of execution. In short, democracy has learned in the West of the United States how to deal with the problem of magnitude. The old historic democracies were but little states with primitive economic conditions.

[...]

American democracy is fundamentally the outcome of the experiences of the American people in dealing with the West. Western democracy through the whole of its earlier period tended to the production of a society of which the most distinctive fact was the freedom of the individual to rise under conditions of social mobility, and whose ambition was the liberty and well-being of the masses. This conception has vitalized all American democracy, and has brought it into sharp contrasts with the democracies of history, and with those modern efforts of Europe to create an artificial democratic order by legislation. The problem of the United States is not to create democracy, but to conserve democratic institutions and ideals. In the later period of its development, Western democracy has been gaining experience in the problem of social control. It has steadily enlarged the sphere of its action and the instruments for its perpetuation. By its system of public schools, from the grades to the graduate work of the great universities, the West has created a larger single body of intelligent plain people than can be found elsewhere in the world. Its political tendencies, whether we consider Democracy, Populism, or Republicanism, are distinctly in the direction of greater social control and the conservation of the old democratic ideals.

To these ideals the West adheres with even a passionate determination. If, in working out its mastery of the resources of the interior, it has produced a type of industrial leader so powerful as to be the wonder of the world, nevertheless, it is still to be determined whether these men constitute a menace to democratic institutions, or the most efficient factor for adjusting democratic control to the new conditions.

Whatever shall be the outcome of the rush of this huge industrial modern United States to its place among the nations of the earth, the formation of its Western democracy will always remain one of the wonderful chapters in the history of the human race. Into this vast shaggy continent of ours poured the first feeble tide of European settlement. European men, institutions, and ideas were lodged in the American wilderness, and this great American West took them to her bosom, taught them a new way of looking upon the destiny of the common man, trained them in adaptation to the conditions of the New World, to the creation of new institutions to meet new needs; and ever as society on her eastern border grew to resemble the Old World in its social forms and its industry, ever, as it began to lose faith in the ideals of democracy, she opened new provinces, and dowered new democracies in her most distant domains with her material treasures and with the ennobling influence that the fierce love of freedom, the strength that came from hewing out a home, making a school and a church, and creating a higher future for his family, furnished to the pioneer.

She gave to the world such types as the farmer Thomas Jefferson, with his Declaration of Independence, his statute for religious toleration, and his purchase of Louisiana. She gave us Andrew Jackson, that fierce Tennessee spirit who broke down the traditions of conservative rule, swept away the privacies and privileges of officialdom, and, like a Gothic leader, opened the temple of the nation to the populace. She gave us Abraham Lincoln, whose gaunt frontier form and gnarled, massive hand told of the conflict with the forest, whose grasp of the ax-handle of the pioneer was no firmer than his grasp of the helm of the ship of state as it breasted the seas of civil war. She has furnished to this new democracy her stores of mineral wealth, that dwarf of those of the Old World, and her provinces that in themselves are vaster and more productive than most of the nations of Europe. Out of her bounty has come a nation whose industrial competition alarms the Old World, and the masters of whose resources wield wealth and power vaster than the wealth and power of kings. Best of all, the West gave, not only to the American, but to the unhappy and oppressed of all lands, a vision of hope, and assurance that the world held a place where were to be found high faith in man and the will and power to furnish him the opportunity to grow to the full measure of his own capacity. Great and powerful as are the new sons of her loins, the Republic is greater than they. The paths of the pioneer have widened into broad highways. The forest clearing has expanded into affluent commonwealths. Let us see to it that the ideals of the pioneer in his log cabin shall enlarge into the spiritual life of a democracy where civic power shall dominate and utilize individual achievement for the common good.

5

THE INFLUENCE OF SEA POWER UPON HISTORY

Alfred Thayer Mahan

If sea power be really based upon a peaceful and extensive commerce, aptitude for commercial pursuits must be a distinguishing feature of the nations that have at one time or another been great upon the sea. History almost without exception affirms that this is true. Save the Romans, there is no marked instance to the contrary.

All men seek gain and, more or less, love money; but the way in which gain is sought will have a marked effect upon the commercial fortunes and the history of the people inhabiting a country.

If history may be believed, the way in which the Spaniards and their kindred nation, the Portuguese, sought wealth, not only brought a blot upon the national character, but was also fatal to the growth of a healthy commerce; and so to the industries upon which commerce lives, and ultimately to that national wealth which was sought by mistaken paths. The desire for gain rose in them to fierce avarice; so they sought in the new-found worlds which gave such an impetus to the commercial and maritime development of the countries of Europe, not new fields of industry, not even the healthy excitement of exploration and adventure, but gold and silver. They had many great qualities; they were bold, enterprising, temperate, patient of suffering, enthusiastic, and gifted with intense national feeling. When to these qualities are added the advantages of Spain's position and well-situated ports, the fact that she was first to occupy large and rich portions of the new worlds and long remained without a

From: Alfred Thayer Mahan, *The Influence of Sea Power upon History* (New York: Dover Publications, 1987).

competitor, and that for a hundred years after the discovery of America she was the leading State in Europe, she might have been expected to take the foremost place among the sea powers. Exactly the contrary was the result, as all know. Since the battle of Lepanto in 1571, though engaged in many wars, no sea victory of any consequence shines on the pages of Spanish history; and the decay of her commerce sufficiently accounts for the painful and sometimes ludicrous inaptness shown on the decks of her ships of war. Doubtless such a result is not to be attributed to one cause only. Doubtless the government of Spain was in many ways such as to cramp and blight a free and healthy development of private enterprise; but the character of a great people breaks through or shapes the character of its government, and it can hardly be doubted that had the bent of the people been toward trade, the action of government would have been drawn into the same current. The great field of the colonies, also, was remote from the centre of that despotism which blighted the growth of old Spain. As it was, thousands of Spaniards, of the working as well as the upper classes, left Spain; and the occupations in which they engaged abroad sent home little but specie, or merchandise of small bulk, requiring but small tonnage. The mother-country herself produced little but wool, fruit, and iron; her manufactures were naught; her industries suffered; her population steadily decreased. Both she and her colonies depended upon the Dutch for so many of the necessaries of life, that the products of their scanty industries could not suffice to pay for them. 'So that Holland merchants,' writes a contemporary, 'who carry money to most parts of the world to buy commodities, must out of this single country of Europe carry home money, which they receive in payment of their goods.' Thus their eagerly sought emblem of wealth passed quickly from their hands. It has already been pointed out how weak, from a military point of view, Spain was from this decay of her shipping. Her wealth being in small bulk on a few ships, following more or less regular routes, was easily seized by an enemy, and the sinews of war paralyzed; whereas the wealth of England and Holland, scattered over thousands of ships in all parts of the world, received many bitter blows in many exhausting wars, without checking a growth which, though painful, was steady. The fortunes of Portugal, united to Spain during a most critical period of her history, followed the same downward path; although foremost in the beginning of the race for development by sea, she fell utterly behind:

> The mines of Brazil were the ruin of Portugal, as those of Mexico and Peru had been of Spain; all manufactures fell into insane contempt; ere long the English supplied the Portuguese not only with clothes, but with all merchandise, all commodities, even to salt-fish and grain. After their gold, the Portuguese abandoned their very soil; the vineyards of Oporto were finally bought by the English with Brazilian gold, which had only passed through Portugal to be spread throughout England.

We are assured that in fifty years, five hundred millions of dollars were extracted from 'the mines of Brazil, and that at the end of the time Portugal had but twenty-five millions in specie' – a striking example of the difference between real and fictitious wealth.

The English and Dutch were no less desirous of gain than the southern nations. Each in turn has been called 'a nation of shopkeepers'; but the jeer, in so far as it is just, is to the credit of their wisdom and uprightness. They were no less bold, no less enterprising, no less patient. Indeed, they were more patient, in that they sought riches not by the sword but by labor, which is the reproach meant to be implied by the epithet; for thus they took the longest, instead of what seemed the shortest, road to wealth. But these two peoples, radically of the same race, had other qualities, no less important than those just named, which combined with their surroundings to favor their development by sea. They were by nature business-men, traders, producers, negotiators. Therefore both in their native country and abroad, whether settled in the ports of civilized nations, or of barbarous eastern rulers, or in colonies of their own foundation, they every-where strove to draw out all the resources of the land, to develop and increase them. The quick instinct of the born trader, shopkeeper if you will, sought continually new articles to exchange; and this search, combined with the industrious character evolved through generations of labor, made them neces-sarily producers. At home they became great as manufacturers; abroad, where they controlled, the land grew richer continually, products multiplied, and the necessary exchange between home and the settlements called for more ships. Their shipping therefore increased with these demands of trade, and nations with less aptitude for maritime enterprise, even France herself, great as she has been, called for their products and for the service of their ships. Thus in many ways they advanced to power at sea. This natural tendency and growth were indeed modified and seriously checked at times by the interference of other governments, jealous of a prosperity which their own people could invade only by the aid of artificial support – a support which will be considered under the head of governmental action as affecting sea power.

The tendency to trade, involving of necessity the production of something to trade with, is the national characteristic most important to the development of sea power.

[...]

It must be noted that particular forms of government with their accompany-ing institutions, and the character of rulers at one time or another, have exer-cised a very marked influence upon the development of sea power. The various traits of a country and its people which have so far been considered constitute the natural characteristics with which a nation, like a man, begins its career: the conduct of the government in turn corresponds to the exercise of the intelligent will-power, which, according as it is wise, energetic and perserving, or the reverse, causes success or failure in a man's life or a nation's history.

It would seem probable that a government in full accord with the natural bias of its people would most successfully advance its growth in every respect; and, in the matter of sea power, the most brilliant successes have followed where there has been intelligent direction by a government fully imbued with the spirit of the people and conscious of its true general bent. Such a government is most certainly secured when the will of the people, or of their best natural exponents, has some large share in making it.

6

THE RIGHTS OF MAN

Thomas Paine

From the revolutions of America and France, and the symptoms that have appeared in other countries, it is evident that the opinion of the world is changed with respect to systems of government, and that revolutions are not within the compass of political calculations. The progress of time and circumstances, which men assign to the accomplishment of great changes, is too mechanical to measure the force of the mind, and the rapidity of reflection, by which revolutions are generated: all the old governments have received a shock from those that already appear, and which were once more improbable, and are a greater subject of wonder, than a general revolution in Europe would be now.

When we survey the wretched condition of man under the monarchical and hereditary systems of government, dragged from his home by one power, or driven by another, and impoverished by taxes more than by enemies, it becomes evident that those systems are bad, and that a general revolution in the principle and construction of governments is necessary.

What is government more than the management of the affairs of a Nation? It is not, and from its nature cannot be, the property of any particular man or family, but of the whole community, at whose expense it is supported; and though by force or contrivance it has been usurped into an inheritance, the usurpation cannot alter the right of things. Sovereignty, as a matter of right, appertains to the Nation only, and not to any individual; and a Nation has at all times an inherent indefeasible right to abolish any form of government it finds

From: Michael Foot and Isaac Kramnick (eds), *The Thomas Paine Reader* (London: Penguin Books, 1987).

inconvenient, and establish such as accords with its interest, disposition, and happiness. The romantic and barbarous distinction of men into Kings and subjects, though it may suit the condition of courtiers, cannot that of citizens; and is exploded by the principle upon which governments are now founded. Every citizen is a member of the Sovereignty, and, as such, can acknowledge no personal subjection; and his obedience can be only to the laws.

When men think of what government is, they must necessarily suppose it to possess a knowledge of all the objects and matters upon which its authority is to be exercised. In this view of government, the republican system, as established by America and France, operates to embrace the whole of a Nation; and the knowledge necessary to the interest of all the parts, is to be found in the centre, which the parts by representation form. But the old governments are on a construction that excludes knowledge as well as happiness; government by monks, who know nothing of the world beyond the walls of a convent, is as consistent as government by Kings.

What were formerly called revolutions, were little more than a change of persons, or an alteration of local circumstances. They rose and fell like things of course, and had nothing in their existence or their fate that could influence beyond the spot that produced them. But what we now see in the world, from the revolutions of America and France, are a renovation of the natural order of things, a system of principles as universal as truth and the existence of man, and combining moral with political happiness and national prosperity.

> 1. *Men are born and always continue free, and equal in respect of their rights. Civil distinctions, therefore, can be founded only on public utility.*
> 2. *The end of all political associations is the preservation of the natural and imprescriptible rights of man; and these rights are liberty, property, security, and resistance of oppression.*
> 3. *The Nation is essentially the source of all Sovereignty; nor can any* INDIVIDUAL, *or* ANY BODY OF MEN, *be entitled to any authority which is not expressly derived from it.*

In these principles, there is nothing to throw a Nation into confusion by inflaming ambition. They are calculated to call forth wisdom and abilities, and to exercise them for the public good, and not for the emolument or aggrandizement of particular descriptions of men or families. Monarchical sovereignty, the enemy of mankind, and the source of misery, is abolished; and sovereignty itself is restored to its natural and original place, the Nation. Were this the case through Europe, the cause of wars would be taken away.

[...]

The only forms of government are the democratical, the aristocratical, the monarchical, and what is now called the representative.

What is called a *republic*, is not any *particular form* of government. It is wholly characterisical of the purport, matter, or object for which government ought to be instituted, and on which it is to be employed, RES-PUBLICA, the public affairs, or the public good; or, literally translated, the *public thing*. It is a word of a good original, referring to what ought to be the character and business of government; and in this sense it is naturally opposed to the word *monarchy*, which has a base original signification. It means arbitrary power in an individual person; in the exercise of which, *himself*, and not the *res-publica*, is the object.

Every government that does not act on the principle of a *republic*, or in other words that does not make the *res-publica* its whole and sole object, is not a good government. Republican government is no other than government established and conducted for the interest of the public, as well individually as collectively. It is not necessarily connected with any particular form, but it most naturally associates with the representative form, as being best calculated to secure the end for which a nation is at the expense of supporting it.

Various forms of government have affected to style themselves a republic. Poland calls itself a republic, which is an hereditary aristocracy, with what is called an elective monarchy, Holland calls itself a republic, which is chiefly aristocratical, with an hereditary stadtholdership. But the government of America, which is wholly on the system of representation, is the only real republic in character and in practice, that now exists. Its government has no other object than the public business of the nation, and therefore it is properly a republic; and the Americans have taken care that THIS, and no other, shall always be the object of their government, by their rejecting everything heredi-tary, and establishing government on the system of representation only.

Those who have said that a republic is not a *form* of government calculated for countries of great extent, mistook, in the first place, the *business* of a government, for a *form* of government; for the *res-publica* equally appertains to every extent of territory and population. And, in the second place, if they meant anything with respect to *form*, it was the simple democratical form, such as was the mode of government in the ancient democracies, in which there was no representation. The case, therefore is not that a republic cannot be extensive, but that it cannot be extensive on the simple democratical form; and the question naturally presents itself, *What is the best form of government for conducting the* RES-PUBLICA, *or the* PUBLIC BUSINESS *of a nation, after it becomes too extensive and populous for the simple democratical form?*

It cannot be monarchy, because monarchy is subject to an objection of the same amount to which the simple democratical form was subject.

It is possible that an individual may lay down a system of principles, on which government shall be constitutionally established to any extent of territory. This is no more than an operation of the mind, acting by its own powers. But the practice upon those principles, as applying to the various and numerous circumstances of a nation, its agriculture, manufacture, trade, commerce and so on, requires a knowledge of a different kind, and which can be had only from the various parts of society. It is an assemblage of practical knowledge, which no one individual can possess; and therefore the monarchical form is as much limited, in useful practice, from the incompetency of knowledge, as was the democratical form, from the multiplicity of population. The one degenerates, by extension, into confusion; the other, into ignorance and incapacity, of which all the great monarchies are an evidence. The monarchical form, therefore, could not be a substitute for the democratical, because it has equal inconveniences.

Much less could it when made hereditary. This is the most effectual of all forms to preclude knowledge. Neither could the high democratical mind have voluntarily yielded itself to be governed by children and idiots, and all the motley insignificance of character, which attends such a mere animal system, the disgrace and the reproach of reason and of man.

As to the aristocratical form, it has the same vices and defects with the monarchical, except that the chance of abilities is better from the proportion of numbers, but there is still no security for the right use and application of them.

Referring, then, to the original simple democracy, it affords the true data from which government on a large scale can begin. It is incapable of extension, not from its principle, but from the inconvenience of its form; and monarchy and aristocracy, from their incapacity. Retaining, then, democracy as the ground, and rejecting the corrupt systems of monarchy and aristocracy, the representative system naturally presents itself; remedying at once the defects of the simple democracy as to form, and the incapacity of the other two with respect to knowledge.

Simple democracy was society governing itself without the aid of secondary means. By ingrafting representation upon democracy, we arrive at a system of government capable of embracing and confederating all the various interests and every extent of territory and population; and that also with advantages as much superior to hereditary government, as the republic of letters is to hereditary literature.

It is on this system that the American government is founded. It is representation ingrafted upon democracy. It has fixed the form by a scale parallel in all cases to the extent of the principle. What Athens was in miniature, America will be in magnitude. The one was the wonder of the ancient world; the other is becoming the admiration and model of the present. It is the easiest of all the forms of government to be understood, and the most eligible in practice; and excludes at once the ignorance and insecurity of the hereditary mode, and the inconvenience of the simple democracy.

It is impossible to conceive a system of government capable of acting over such an extent of territory, and such a circle of interests, as is immediately produced by the operation of representation. France, great and populous as it is, is but a spot in the capaciousness of the system. It adapts itself to all possible cases. It is preferable to simple democracy even in small territories. Athens, by representation, would have outrivalled her own democracy.

7

DEMOCRACY IN AMERICA

Alexis de Tocqueville

The immigrants who came at different times to occupy what is now the United States were not alike in many respects; their aims were not the same, and they ruled themselves according to different principles.

But these men did have features in common, and they all found themselves in analogous circumstances.

Language is perhaps the strongest and most enduring link which unites men. All the immigrants spoke the same language and were children of the same people. Born in a country shaken for centuries by the struggles of parties, a country in which each faction in turn had been forced to put itself under the protection of the laws, they had learned their political lessons in that rough school, and they had more acquaintance with notions of rights and principles of true liberty than most of the European nations at that time. At the time of the first immigrations, local government, that fertile germ of free institutions, had already taken deep root in English ways, and therewith the dogma of the sovereignty of the people had slipped into the very heart of the Tudor monarchy.

That was the time of religious quarrels shaking Christendom. England plunged vehemently forward in this new career. The English, who had always been staid and deliberate, became austere and argumentative. These intellectual battles greatly advanced education and a more profound culture. Absorption in talk about religion led to chaster mores. All these general characteristics of the

From: Alexis de Tocqueville (ed. J. P. Mayer), *Democracy in America* (London: Fontana Press, 1994).

nation were more or less the same among those of its sons who sought a new future on the far side of the ocean.

Moreover, one observation, to which we shall come back later, applies not to the English only, but also to the French, Spaniards, and all Europeans who came in waves to plant themselves on the shores of the New World; all these new European colonies contained the germ, if not the full growth, of a complete democracy. There were two reasons for this; one may say, speaking generally, that when the immigrants left their motherlands they had no idea of any superiority of some over others. It is not the happy and the powerful who go into exile, and poverty with misfortune is the best-known guarantee of equality among men. Nonetheless, it did happen several times that as a result of political or religious quarrels great lords went to America. Laws were made there to establish the hierarchy of ranks, but it was soon seen that the soil of America absolutely rejected a territorial aristocracy. It was obvious that to clear this untamed land nothing but the constant and committed labor of the landlord himself would serve. The ground, once cleared, was by no means fertile enough to make both a landlord and a tenant rich. So the land was naturally broken up into little lots which the owner himself cultivated. But it is land that is the basis of an aristocracy, giving it both roots and support; privileges by themselves are not enough, nor is birth, but only land handed down from generation to generation. There may be huge fortunes and grinding poverty in a nation; but if that wealth is not landed, one may find rich and poor, but not, using words strictly, an aristocracy.

Hence there was a strong family likeness between all the English colonies as they came to birth. All, from the beginning, seemed destined to let freedom grow, not the aristocratic freedom of their motherland, but a middle-class and democratic freedom of which the world's history had not previously provided a complete example.

But within this general picture there were some very pronounced nuances which need to be mentioned.

There were two main branches of the great Anglo-American family which have, so far, grown up together without completely mingling – one in the South, and the other in the North.

Virginia was the first of English colonies, the immigrants arriving in 1607. At that time Europe was still peculiarly preoccupied with the notion that mines of gold and silver were the basis of the wealth of nations. That was a fatal notion that did more to impoverish the European nations deluded by it and cost more lives in America than were caused by war and all bad laws combined. It was therefore gold-seekers who were sent to Virginia,[1] men without wealth or standards whose restless, turbulent temper endangered the infant colony[2] and made its progress vacillating. Craftsmen and farm laborers came later; they were quieter folk with better morals, but there was hardly any respect in which they rose above the level of the English lower classes[3] No noble thought or conception above gain presided over the foundation of the new settlements. The colony had hardly been established when slavery was introduced.[4] That was the basic fact destined to exert immense influence on the character, laws, and future of the whole South.

Slavery, as we shall show later, dishonors labor; it introduces idleness into society and therewith ignorance and pride, poverty and luxury. It enervates the powers of the mind and numbs human activity. Slavery, combined with the English character, explains the mores and social condition of the South.

In the North the English background was the same, but every nuance led the opposite way. Of this some detailed explanation is required.

It was in the English colonies of the North, better known as the states of New England,[5] that the two or three main principles now forming the basic social theory of the United States were combined.

New England principles spread first to the neighboring states and then in due course to those more distant, finally penetrating everywhere throughout the confederation. Their influence now extends beyond its limits over the whole American world. New England civilization has been like beacons on mountain peaks whose warmth is first felt close by but whose light shines to the farthest limits of the horizon.

The foundation of New England was something new in the world, all the attendant circumstances being both peculiar and original.

In almost all other colonies the first inhabitants have been men without wealth or education, driven from their native land by poverty or misconduct, or else greedy speculators and industrial entrepreneurs. Some colonies cannot claim even such an origin as this; San Domingo was founded by pirates, and in our day the English courts of justice are busy populating Australia.

But all the immigrants who came to settle on the shores of New England belonged to the well-to-do classes at home. From the start, when they came together on American soil, they presented the unusual phenomenon of a society in which there were no great lords, no common people, and, one may almost say, no rich or poor. In proportion to their numbers, these men had a greater share of accomplishments than could be found in any European nation now. All, perhaps without a single exception, had received a fairly advanced education, and several had made a European reputation by their talents and their knowledge. The other colonies had been founded by unattached adventurers, whereas the immigrants to New England brought with them wonderful elements of order and morality; they came with their wives and children to the wilds. But what most distinguished them from all others was the very aim of their enterprise. No necessity forced them to leave their country; they gave up a desirable social position and assured means of livelihood; nor was their object in going to the New World to better their position or accumulate wealth; they tore themselves away from home comforts in obedience to a purely intellectual craving; in facing the inevitable sufferings of exile they hoped for the triumph of *an idea*.

[...]

Any discussion of the political laws of the United States must always begin with the dogma of the sovereignty of the people.

The principle of the sovereignty of the people, which is always to be found, more or less, at the bottom of almost all human institutions, usually remains buried there. It is obeyed without being recognized, or if for one moment it is brought out into the daylight, it is hastily thrust back into the gloom of the sanctuary.

'The will of the nation' is one of the phrases most generally abused by intriguers and despots of every age. Some have seen the expression of it in the bought votes of a few agents of authority, others in the votes of an interested or frightened minority, and some have even discovered it in a people's silence, thinking that the *fact* of obedience justified the *right* to command.

But in America the sovereignty of the people is neither hidden nor sterile as with some other nations; mores recognize it, and the laws proclaim it; it spreads with freedom and attains unimpeded its ultimate consequences.

If there is one country in the world where one can hope to appreciate the true value of the dogma of the sovereignty of the people, study its application to the business of society, and judge both its dangers and its advantages, that country is America.

I have already said that from the beginning the principle of the sovereignty of the people was the creative principle of most of the English colonies in America.

But it was far from dominating the government of society then as it does now.

Two obstacles, one external and the other internal, checked its encroachments.

It could not be ostensibly proclaimed in the laws, as the colonies were then still bound to obey the motherland; it had therefore to lie hidden in the provincial assemblies, especially that of the township. There it spread secretly.

American society at that time was by no means ready to accept it with all its consequences. In New England, education, and south of the Hudson, wealth long exercised a sort of aristocratic influence which tended to keep the exercise of social power in a few hands. It was far from being the case that all public officials were elected and all citizens electors. Everywhere voting rights were restricted within certain limits and subject to some property qualification. That qualification was very low in the North but quite considerable in the South.

The American Revolution broke out. The dogma of the sovereignty of the people came out from the township and took possession of the government; every class enlisted in its cause; the war was fought and victory obtained in its name; it became the law of laws.

[...]

The state of Maryland, which had been founded by great lords, was the first to proclaim universal suffrage[6] and introduced the most democratic procedures throughout its government.

Once a people begins to interfere with the voting qualification, one can be sure that sooner or later it will abolish it altogether. That is one of the most invariable rules of social behavior. The further the limit of voting rights is extended, the stronger is the need felt to spread them still wider; for after each new concession the forces of democracy are strengthened, and its demands increase with its augmented power. The ambition of those left below the qualifying limit increases in proportion to the number of those above it. Finally the exception becomes the rule; concessions follow one another without interruption, and there is no halting place until universal suffrage has been attained.

In the United States in our day the principle of the sovereignty of the people has been adopted in practice in every way that imagination could suggest. It has been detached from all fictions in which it has elsewhere been carefully wrapped; it takes on every possible form that the exigencies of the case require. Sometimes the body of the people makes the laws, as at Athens; sometimes deputies, elected by universal suffrage, represent it and act in its name under its almost immediate supervision.

There are countries in which some authority, in a sense outside the body social, influences it and forces it to progress in a certain direction.

There are others in which power is divided, being at the same time within the society and outside it. Nothing like that is to be seen in the United States; there society acts by and for itself. There are no authorities except within itself; one can hardly meet anybody who would dare to conceive, much less to suggest, seeking power elsewhere. The people take part in the making of the laws by choosing the lawgivers, and they share in their application by electing the agents of the executive power; one might say that they govern themselves, so feeble and restricted is the part left to the administration, so vividly is that administration aware of its popular origin, and so obedient is it to the fount of power. The people reign over the American political world as God rules over the universe. It is the cause and the end of all things; everything rises out of it and is absorbed back into it.

NOTES

1. The charter granted by the English Crown in 1609 contained, among other clauses, a provision that the colonists should pay a fifth of the output of gold and silver mines to the Crown. See Marshall's *Life of Washington*, Vol. I, pp. 18–66.
2. According to Stith's *History of Virginia*, a large proportion of the new colonists were unruly children of good family whose parents sent them off to escape from ignominy at home; for the rest there were dismissed servants, fraudulent bankrupts, debauchees and others of that sort, people more apt to pillage and destroy than to consolidate the settlement. Seditious leaders easily enticed this band into every kind of extravagance and excess. For the history of Virginia see the following works:
   History of Virginia from the First Settlements in the Year 1624, by Smith.
   History of the First Discovery and Settlement of Virginia, by William Stith.
   History of Virginia from the Earliest Period, by Beverley, translated into French in 1807.
3. It was only later that some rich landowners came to settle in the colony.

4. Slavery was first introduced about the year 1620 by a Dutch ship, which landed twenty Negroes on the banks of the James River. See Chalmer.
5. The states of New England are those states which lie east of the Hudson, and there are now six of them: Connecticut, Rhode Island, Massachusetts, Vermont, New Hampshire and Maine.
6. Amendments introduced into the constitution of Maryland in 1801 and 1809.

8

AMERICAN EXCEPTIONALISM – A DOUBLE-EDGED SWORD

Seymour Martin Lipset

The idea of American exceptionalism has interested many outside the United States. One of the most important bodies of writing dealing with this country is referred to as the 'foreign traveler' literature. These are articles and books written by visitors, largely European, dealing with the way in which America works as compared with their home country or area. Perhaps the best known and still most influential is Alexis de Tocqueville's *Democracy in America*.[1] The French aristocrat came here in the 1830s to find out why the efforts at establishing democracy in his native country, starting with the French Revolution, had failed while the American Revolution had produced a stable democratic republic. The comparison, of course, was broader than just with France; no other European country with the partial exception of Great Britain was then a democracy. In his great book, Tocqueville is the first to refer to the United States as exceptional – that is, qualitatively different from all other countries.[2] He is, therefore, the initiator of the writings on American exceptionalism.

The concept could only have arisen by comparing this country with other societies. Tocqueville looked at the United States through the eyes of someone who knew other cultures well, particularly that of his native country, but also to some considerable degree Great Britain. *Democracy in America* deals only with the United States and has almost no references to France or any other country, but Tocqueville emphasized in his notes that he never wrote a word about

From: Seymour Martin Lipset, *American Exceptionalism – A Double-Edged Sword* (New York and London: W. W. Norton & Co., 1996).

America without thinking about France. A book based on his research notes, George Pierson's *Tocqueville and Beaumont in America*, makes clear the ways in which Tocqueville systematically compared the United States and France.[3] At one point, he became sensitive to the fact that America was a very decentralized country, while France was reputed to be the opposite. Tocqueville commented that he had never given much thought to what centralization in France meant since as a Frenchman, he did what came naturally. He then wrote to his father, a prefect of one of the regional administrative districts, and asked him to describe the concentration of political power in France. His father apparently sat down and wrote a lengthy memorandum dealing with the subject.

When Tocqueville or other 'foreign traveler' writers or social scientists have used the term 'exceptional' to describe the United States, they have not meant, as some critics of the concept assume, that America is better than other countries or has a superior culture. Rather, they have simply been suggesting that it is qualitatively different, that it is an outlier. Exceptionalism is a double-edged concept. As I shall elaborate, we are the worst as well as the best, depending on which quality is being addressed.

The United States is exceptional in starting from a revolutionary event, in being 'the first new nation', the first colony, other than Iceland, to become independent. It has defined its *raison d'être* ideologically. As historian Richard Hofstadter has noted, It has been our fate as a nation not to have ideologies, but to be one.[4] In saying this, Hofstadter reiterated Ralph Waldo Emerson and Abraham Lincoln's emphases on the country's 'political religion', alluding in effect to the former's statement that becoming American was a religious, that is, ideological act. The ex-Soviet Union apart, other countries define themselves by a common history as birthright communities, not by ideology.

The American Creed can be described in five terms: liberty, egalitarianism, individualism, populism, and laissez-faire Egalitarianism, in its American meaning, as Tocqueville emphasized, involves equality of opportunity and respect, not of result or condition. These values reflect the absence of feudal structures, monarchies and aristocracies. As a new society, the country lacked the emphasis on social hierarchy and status differences characteristic of post-feudal and monarchical cultures. Postfeudal societies have resulted in systems in which awareness of class divisions and respect for the state have remained important, or at least much more important than in the United States. European countries, Canada, and Japan have placed greater emphasis on obedience to political authority and on deference to superiors.

Tocqueville noted, and contemporary survey data document quantitatively, that the United States has been the most religious country in Christendom. It has exhibited greater acceptance of biblical beliefs and higher levels of church attendance than elsewhere, with the possible exception of a few Catholic countries, such as Poland and Ireland, where nationalism and religion have been interwoven. The American religious pattern, as Tocqueville emphasized in seeking to account for American individualism, is voluntary, in other words, not state-supported. All denominations must raise their own funds, engaging in a constant struggle to retain or expand the number of their adherents if they are to survive and grow. This task is not incumbent upon state-financed denominations.

The United States is the only country where most churchgoers adhere to *sects*, mainly the Methodists and Baptists, but also hundreds of others[5] Elsewhere in Christendom the Anglican, Catholic, Lutheran, and Orthodox *churches* dominate. The churches are hierarchical in structure and membership is secured by birthright. Parishioners are expected to follow the lead of their priests and bishops. Sects, by contrast, are predominantly congregational; each local unit adheres voluntarily, while the youth are asked to make a religious commitment only upon reaching the age of decision. Churches outside of the United States historically have been linked to the state; their clergy are paid by public authorities, their hierarchy is formally appointed or confirmed by the government, and their schools are subsidized by taxes.

American Protestant sectarianism has both reinforced and been strengthened by social and political individualism. The sectarian is expected to follow a moral code, as determined by his/her own sense of rectitude, reflecting a personal relationship with God, and in many cases an interpretation of biblical truth, one not mediated by bishops or determined by the state. The American sects assume the perfectibility of human nature and have produced a moralistic people. Countries dominated by churches which view human institutions as corrupt are much less moralistic. The churches stress inherent sinfulness, human weakness, and do not hold individuals or nations up to the same standards as do the sectarians who are more bitter about code violations.

The strength of sectarian values and their implications for the political process may be seen in reactions to the supreme test of citizenship and adherence to the national will, war.[6] State churches have not only legitimated government, for example, the divine role of kings; they have invariably approved of the wars their nations have engaged in, and have called on people to serve and obey. And the citizens have done so, unless and until it becomes clear their country is being defeated. Americans, however, have been different. A major anti-war movement sprang up in every conflict in which the United States has been involved, with the notable exception of World War II, which for the country began with an attack. Americans have put primacy not to 'my country right or wrong', but rather to 'obedience to my conscience'. Hence, those who opposed going to war before it was declared continued to be against it after Congress voted for war.

Protestant-inspired moralism not only has affected opposition to wars, it has determined the American style in foreign relations generally, including the ways we go to war. Support for a war is as moralistic as resistance to it. To endorse a war and call on people to kill others and die for the country, Americans must define their role in a conflict as being on God's side against Satan – for morality, against evil.[7] The United States primarily goes to war against evil, not, in its self-perception, to defend material interests. And comparative public opinion data reveal that Americans are more patriotic ('proud to be an American') and more willing to fight if their country goes to war than citizens of the thirty or so other countries polled by Gallup.

The emphasis in the American value system, in the American Creed, has been on the individual. Citizens have been expected to demand and protect their rights on a personal basis. The exceptional focus on law here as compared to Europe, derived from the Constitution and the Bill of Rights, has stressed rights against the state and other powers. America began and continues as the most anti-statist, legalistic, and rights-oriented nation.

The American Constitution intensifies the commitment to individualism and concern for the protection of rights through legal actions. The American Bill of Rights, designed to protect the citizenry against the abuse of power by government, has produced excessive litigiousness. It has fostered the propensity of Americans to go to court not only against the government, but against each other. The rights of minorities, blacks and others, women, even of animals and plants, have grown extensively since World War II through legal action.

The American disdain of authority, for conforming to the rules laid down by the state, has been related by some observers to other unique American traits, such as the highest crime rate, as well as the lowest level of voting participation, in the developed world. Basically, the American revolutionary libertarian tradition does not encourage obedience to the state and the law. This point may be illustrated by examining the results when the American and Canadian governments tried to change the system of measurements and weights to metric from the ancient and less logical system of miles and inches, pounds and ounces. A quarter century ago, both countries told their citizens that in fifteen years, they must use only metric measurements, but that both systems could be used until a given date. The Canadians, whose Torymonarchical history and structures have made for much greater respect for and reliance on the state, and who have lower per capita crime, deviance, and litigiousness rates than Americans, conformed to the decision of their leaders and now follow the metric system, as anyone who has driven in Canada is aware. Americans ignored the new policy, and their highway signs still refer to miles, weights are in pounds and ounces, and temperature readings are in Fahrenheit.

An emphasis on group characteristics, the perception of status in collectivity terms, necessarily encourages group solutions. In Europe, the emphasis on explicit social classes in postfeudal societies promoted class-consciousness on the part of the lower strata and to some extent *noblesse oblige* by the privileged. The politics of these countries, some led by Tories such as Disraeli and Bismarck, and later by the lower-class-based, social democratic left, favored policies designed to help the less affluent by means of state solutions such as welfare, public housing, public employment, and medical care. Americans, on the other hand, have placed greater stress on opening the door to individual mobility and personal achievement through heavy investment in mass education.

The cross-national differences are striking. This country has led the world by far in the proportion of people completing different levels of mass education from early in the nineteenth century, first for elementary and high schools, later for colleges and graduate institutions.

While America has long predominated in the ratio of those of college and university age attending or completing tertiary education, the numbers and proportions involved have been massive since World War II. A report on the proportion of 20- to 24-year-olds in higher education, as of 1994, indicates that it is almost double, 59 per cent in the United States to that in most affluent European countries and Japan: the Netherlands (33 per cent), Belgium (32 per cent), Spain (32 per cent), France (30 per cent), Germany (30 per cent), Japan (30 per cent), and Austria (29 per cent).[8] And America spends a greater proportion of its gross domestic product (GDP) on education, 7.0 per cent, than does the European Union, 5.3 per cent, or Japan, 5.0 per cent.[9]

Conversely, European countries have devoted a much larger share of their GNP, of their public funds, to bettering the living conditions of their working classes and the less privileged generally. The European social democrats have had frequent opportunities to hold office since the 1930s. To transform the situation of the working class, they have emphasized group improvement policies, such as public housing, family allowances and state medicine. Until recently, however, they preserved a class-segregated educational system with elite high schools and failed to focus on the expansion of university education.

American values were modified sharply by forces stemming from the Great Depression and World War II. These led to a much greater reliance on the state and acceptance of welfare and planning policies, the growth of trade unions and of class divisions in voting. While these changes continue to differentiate the contemporary United States from the pre-Depression era, the prosperous conditions which characterized most of the postwar period led the population to revert in some part to the values of the founders, especially distrust of a strong state. Support for diverse welfare entitlement policies has declined; trade union membership has dropped considerably, from a third to a sixth of the employed labor force; and class-linked electoral patterns have fallen off. Americans remain much more individualistic, meritocratic-oriented, and anti-statist than peoples elsewhere. Hence, the values which form the context for public policy are quite different from those in other developed countries, as the results of the 1994 congressional elections demonstrated.

These differences can be elaborated by considering the variations between the American Constitution and those of 'most other liberal democracies ... [which contain] language establishing affirmative welfare rights or obligations'.[10] Some writers explain the difference by the fact that except for the American, almost all other constitutions were drawn up since World War II and, therefore, reflect a commitment to the welfare state, to upgrading the bottom level. But as Mary Ann Glendon has emphasized,

> The differences long predate the postwar era. They are legal manifestations of divergent, and deeply rooted, cultural attitudes toward the state and its functions. Historically, even eighteenth- and nineteenth-century continental European constitutions and codes acknowledged state obligations to provide food, work, and financial aid to persons in need. And continental Europeans today, whether of the right or the left, are much more likely than Americans to assume that governments have affirmative duties ... By contrast, it is almost obligatory for American politicians of both the right and the left to profess mistrust of government.[11]

In much of the writing on the subject, American exceptionalism is defined by the absence of a significant socialist movement in the United States. This again is a comparative generalization, emphasizing that socialist parties and movements have been weaker in the United States than anywhere else in the industrialized world, and also that the membership of trade unions has been proportionately smaller than in other countries. Analysts have linked those facts to the nature of the class system as well as to attitudes toward the state. Where workers are led by the social structure to think in fixed class terms, as they are in postfeudal societies, they have been more likely to support socialist or labor parties or join unions. But class has been a theoretical construct in America. The weakness of socialism is undoubtedly also related to the lower legitimacy Americans grant to state intervention and state authority.

NOTES

1. Alexis de Tocqueville, *Democracy in America*, Vols I and II (New York: Alfred A. Knopf, 1948).
2. Ibid., II, pp. 36–7. For a sophisticated critique which emphasizes external influences on America, see Lon Tyrell, 'American Exceptionalism in an Age of International History', *American Historical Review*, 96 (October 1991), pp. 1031–55. For a detailed reply, see Michael McGerr, 'The Price of the "New Transnational History"', *American Historical Review*, 98 (October 1991), pp. 1056–67.
3. George Wilson Pierson, *Tocqueville and Beaumont in America* (Gloucester, MA: Peter Smith, 1969).
4. Quoted in Michael Kazin, 'The Right's Unsung Prophet'. *The Nation*, 248 (20 February 1989), p. 242.
5. For a brilliant analysis of the religious background of the United States, see David Fischer, *Albion's Seed. Four British Folkways in America* (New York: Oxford University Press, 1989).
6. See Seymour Martin Lipset, *Revolution in the University* (Chicago: University of Chicago Press, 1971), pp. 12–14.
7. See Fischer, *Albion's Seed*, passim.
8. Charles Hampden-Turner and Alfons Trompenaars, *The Seven Cultures of Capitalism* (New York: Doubleday, 1993), p. 245.
9. 'The European Union', *The Economist*, 22 October 1994, Survey, p. 4.
10. Mary Ann Glendon, 'Rights in Twentieth Century Constitutions', in Geoffrey R. Stone, Richard A. Epstein, and Cass R. Sunstein (eds), *The Bill of Rights in the Modern State* (Chicago: University of Chicago Press, 1992), p. 521.
11. Ibid., pp. 524–5. See also Gerhard Casper, 'Changing Concepts of Constitutionalism: 18th to 20th Century', *Supreme Court Review*, 311 (1989), pp. 318–19.

SECTION 2
POLITICAL THEOLOGY

The readings under the heading Political Theology discuss the long-lasting and complex relationship between religious thought and the broader aspects of American culture and politics. In 1904 the German sociologist Max Weber visited the United States. The result was a larger essay entitled 'The Protestant Sects and the Spirit of Capitalism', in which Weber discussed the links between religious affiliation, middle-class ascendancy and American political culture. For Weber the Protestant sects – mainly late formations of Puritan history – provided the infrastructure for the entrepreneurial class and it functioned as a kind of test run for local democracy. In other words, while looking at the Protestant Spirit, Weber hinted at the various levels of interconnectedness between capitalism and democracy. Of course, Weber had a predecessor in Alexis de Tocqueville, who had been the first one to point out that in America there was and still continued to be a genuine relationship between the spirit of religion and the spirit of freedom. The missing link that Tocqueville referred to in *Democracy in America* was mores. It was the moral conduct of daily life, taught in the multitude of Protestant sects, churches and congregations that helped to develop a certain habit and create early American political culture.

However, as Tom Paine's famous pamphlet *The Age of Reason* together with Thomas Jefferson's letters reveal, not all American revolutionaries were followers of a sect or church, or a member of a religious group. Most of the early American intellectuals and founders were actually Deists, that is they believed in a higher being but were appalled by what they saw as repressive and mainly European forms of religious affiliation of either the Catholic or the Anglican sort. The exact relationship between religious belief systems and habits and political philosophy in early American democratic thought is nowhere better explained than in an essay by the political scientist Judith N. Shklar, entitled 'The Boundaries of Democracy' (published in her essay collection *Redeeming American Political Thought*). Interesting in this article is the analysis of the relations that existed between certain Puritan practices – how the settlers reacted to the challenges that the early New England conditions posed – together with political philosophy (Hobbes, Locke) and radical thought (Paine).

To understand this late merger, it is useful to go even further back in history. In his investigation of the emergence of *The New England Mind* the Harvard historian Perry Miller looks at the development of the Puritan settlements. Miller tells the story of how they started out as a colony and how their earlier ideas and hopes were set on reporting back to Europe on their religious experiments in the New World. He further tells the story of how they came to stay and how the settlers genuinely turned the colony into a province – an American province in which the inhabitants would no longer report back to the Old World but had their minds fully set on the conditions of the New World. Particularly important in this respect is the emergence of the metaphor of the errand and the Jeremiad, a related biblical figure of speech. For Miller the word 'errand' can have multiple meanings. It can refer to somebody sent out to convey a message; but it can also refer to the conscientious intention or content of the message itself. The Jeremiad was the appropriate figure of speech that would allow for a ritual in which original intentions were reaffirmed under social conditions that had changed.

Sacvan Bercovitch follows Perry Miller in his main assumptions but also elaborates on a theme. In his *The American Jeremiad*, a study of the relationship between American culture and intellectual discourse, he sees a generalization of the Jeremiad. By no means does Bercovitch see the speech figure of the Jeremiad as limited to the religious realm. Rather he sees the entire American intellectual discourse as being fuelled by such speech figures. For Bercovitch the Jeremiad has become *the* symbol of American intellectual discourse.

The chapter on Political Theology closes with an except from another modern classic written by a sociologist of religion, Will Herberg. In his *Protestant – Catholic – Jew* Herberg sets out to analyse the peculiarities of American religion – thus referring back to Tocqueville's earlier statement about *mores* and the relationship between religion and democracy. However, Herberg is interested in the actual links that exist between religion and democracy, thus proving that Tocqueville's main argument still holds under modern conditions – conditions that saw a further differentiation between religious groups and beliefs.

9

THE PROTESTANT SECTS AND THE SPIRIT OF CAPITALISM

Max Weber

Admission to the congregation is recognized as an absolute guarantee of the moral qualities of a gentleman, especially of those qualities required in business matters. Baptism secures to the individual the deposits of the whole region and unlimited credit without any competition. He is a 'made man'. Further observation confirmed that these, or at least very similar phenomena, recur in the most varied regions. In general, *only* those men had success in business who belonged to Methodist or Baptist or other *sects* or sectlike conventicles. When a sect member moved to a different place, or if he was a traveling salesman, he carried the certificate of his congregation with him; and thereby he found not only easy contact with sect members but, above all, he found credit everywhere. If he got into economic straits through no fault of his own, the sect arranged his affairs, gave guarantees to the creditors, and helped him in every way, often according to the Biblical principle, *mutuum date nihil inde sperantes.* (Luke vi:35)

The expectation of the creditors that his sect, for the sake of their prestige, would not allow creditors to suffer losses on behalf of a sect member was not, however, decisive for his opportunities. What was decisive was the fact that a fairly reputable sect would only accept for membership one whose 'conduct' made him appear to be morally *qualified* beyond doubt.

It is crucial that sect membership meant a certificate of moral qualification and especially of business morals for the individual. This stands in contrast to

From: Max Weber (ed. H. H. Gerth and C. Wright Mills), *Max Weber: Essays in Sociology* (New York: Oxford University Press, 1946).

membership in a 'church' into which one is 'born' and which lets grace shine over the righteous and the unrighteous alike. Indeed, a church is a corporation which organizes grace and administers religious gifts of grace, like an endowed foundation. Affiliation with the church is, in principle, obligatory and hence proves nothing with regard to the member's qualities. A sect, however, is a voluntary association of only those who, according to the principle, are religiously and morally qualified. If one finds voluntary reception of his membership, by virtue of religious *probation*, he joins the sect voluntarily.

[...]

Today the kind of denomination [to which one belongs] is rather irrelevant. It does not matter whether one be Freemason,[1] Christian Scientist, Adventist, Quaker, or what not. What is decisive is that one be admitted to membership by 'ballot', after an *examination* and an ethical *probation* in the sense of the virtues which are at a premium for the inner-worldly asceticism of protestantism and hence, for the ancient puritan tradition. Then, the same effect could be observed.

Closer scrutiny revealed the steady progress of the characteristic process of 'secularization,' to which in modern times all phenomena that originated in religious conceptions succumb. Not only religious associations, hence sects, had this effect on American life. Sects exercised this influence, rather, in a steadily decreasing proportion. If one paid some attention it was striking to observe (even fifteen years ago) that surprisingly many men among the American middle classes (always outside of the quite modern metropolitan areas and the immigration centers) were wearing a little badge (of varying color) in the buttonhole, which reminded one very closely of the rosette of the French Legion of Honor.

When asked what it meant, people regularly mentioned an association with a sometimes adventurous and fantastic name. And it became obvious that its significance and purpose consisted in the following: almost always the association functioned as a burial insurance, besides offering greatly varied services. But often, and especially in those areas least touched by modern disintegration, the association offered the member the (ethical) claim for brotherly help on the part of every brother who had the means. If he faced an economic emergency for which he himself was not to be blamed, he could make this claim. And in several instances that came to my notice at the time, this claim again followed the very principle, *mutuum date nihil inde sperantes*, or at least a very low rate of interest prevailed. Apparently, such claims were willingly recognized by the members of the brotherhood. Furthermore – and this is the main point in this instance – membership was again acquired through balloting after investigation and a determination of moral worth. And hence the badge in the buttonhole meant, 'I am a gentleman patented after investigation and probation and guaranteed by my membership'. Again, this meant, in business life above all, tested *credit worthiness*. One could observe that business opportunities were often decisively influenced by such legitimation.

All these phenomena, which seemed to be rather rapidly disintegrating – at least the religious organizations – were essentially confined to the middle classes. Some cultured Americans often dismissed these facts briefly and with a certain angry disdain as 'humbug' or backwardness, or they even denied them; many of them actually did not know anything about them, as was affirmed to me by William James. Yet these survivals were still alive in many different fields, and sometimes in forms which appeared to be grotesque.

These associations were especially the typical vehicles of social ascent into the circle of the entrepreneurial middle class. They served to diffuse and to maintain the bourgeois capitalist business ethos among the broad strata of the middle classes (the farmers included).

As is well known, not a few (one may well say the majority of the older generation) of the American 'promoters', 'captains of industry', of the multi-millionaires and trust magnates belonged formally to sects, especially to the Baptists. However, in the nature of the case, these persons were often affiliated for merely conventional reasons, as in Germany, and only in order to legitimate themselves in personal and social life – not in order to legitimate themselves as businessmen; during the age of the Puritans, such 'economic supermen' did not require such a crutch, and *their* 'religiosity' was, of course, often of a more than dubious sincerity. The middle classes, above all the strata ascending with and out of the middle classes, were the bearers of that specific religious orientation which one must, indeed, beware viewing among them as only opportunistically determined.[2] Yet one must never overlook that without the universal diffusion of these qualities and principles of a methodical way of life, qualities which were maintained through these religious communities, capitalism today, even in America, would not be what it is. In the history of any economic area on earth there is no epoch, [except] those quite rigid in feudalism or patrimonialism, in which capitalist figures of the kind of Pierpont Morgan, Rockefeller, Jay Gould, *et al.* were absent. Only the technical *means* which they used for the acquisition of wealth have changed (of course!). *They* stood and they stand 'beyond good and evil'. But, however high one may otherwise evaluate their importance for economic transformation, they have never been decisive in determining what economic mentality was to dominate a given epoch and a given area. Above all, they were not the creators and they were not to become the bearers of the specifically Occidental bourgeois mentality.

[...]

In the past and up to the very present, it has been a characteristic precisely of the specifically American democracy that it did *not* constitute a formless sand heap of individuals, but rather a buzzing complex of strictly exclusive, yet voluntary associations. Not so long ago these associations still did not recognize the prestige of birth and *inherited* wealth, of the office and educational diploma; at least they recognized these things to such a low degree as has only very rarely been the case in the rest of the world. Yet, even so, these associations were far from accepting anybody with open arms as an equal. To be sure, fifteen years ago an American farmer would not have led his guest past a plowing farmhand (American born!) in the field without making his guest 'shake hands' with the worker after formally introducing them.

Formerly, in a typical American club nobody would remember that the two members, for instance, who play billiards once stood in the relation of boss and clerk. Here equality of gentlemen prevailed absolutely.[3] To be sure, the American worker's wife accompanying the trade unionist to lunch had completely accommodated herself in dress and behavior, in a somewhat plainer and more awkward fashion, to the bourgeois lady's model.

He who wished to be fully recognized in this democracy, in whatever position, had not only to conform to the conventions of bourgeois society, the very strict men's fashions included, but as a rule he had to be able to show that he had succeeded in gaining admission by ballot to one of the sects, clubs, or fraternal societies, no matter *what* kind, were it only recognized as sufficiently legitimate. And he had to maintain himself in the society by proving himself to be a gentleman. The parallel in Germany consists in the importance of the *Couleur*[4] and the commission of an officer of the reserve for *commercium* and *connubium*, and the great status significance of qualifying to give satisfaction by duel. The thing is the same, but the direction and material consequence characteristically differ.

He who did not succeed in joining was no gentleman; he who despised doing so, as was usual among Germans,[5] had to take the hard road, and especially so in business life.

However, we shall not here analyze the social significance of these conditions, which are undergoing a profound transformation. First, we are interested in the fact that the modern position of the secular clubs and societies with recruitment by ballot is largely the product of a process of *secularization*. Their position is derived from the far more exclusive importance of the prototype of these voluntary associations, to wit, the sects. They stem, indeed, from the sects in the homeland of genuine Yankeedom, the North Atlantic states. Let us recall, first, that the universal and equal franchise within American democracy (of the Whites! For Negroes and all mixtures have, even today, no *de facto* franchise) and likewise the 'separation of state and church' are only achievements of the recent past, beginning essentially with the nineteenth century. Let us remember that during the colonial period in the central areas of New England, especially in Massachusetts, full citizenship status in the church congregation was the precondition for full citizenship in the state (besides some other prerequisites). The religious congregation indeed determined admission or non-admission to political citizenship status.[3]

The decision was made according to whether or not the person had *proved* his religious qualification through conduct, in the broadest meaning of the word, as was the case among all Puritan sects. The Quakers in Pennsylvania were not in any lesser way masters of that state until some time before the War of

Independence. This was actually the case, though *formally* they were not the only full political citizens. They were political masters only by virtue of extensive gerrymandering.

The tremendous social significance of admission to full enjoyment of the rights of the sectarian congregation, especially the privilege of being admitted to the *Lord's Supper*, worked among the sects in the direction of breeding that ascetist professional ethic which was adequate to modern capitalism during the period of its origin. It can be demonstrated that everywhere, including Europe, the religiosity of the ascetist sects has for several centuries worked in the same way as has been illustrated by the personal experiences mentioned above for [the case of] America.

When focusing on the religious background[6] of these Protestant sects, we find in their literary documents, especially among those of the Quakers and Baptists up to and throughout the seventeenth century, again and again jubilation over the fact that the sinful 'children of the world' distrust one another in business but that they have confidence in the religiously determined righteousness of the pious.[7]

Hence, they give credit and deposit their money only with the pious, and they make purchases in their stores because there, and there alone, they are given honest and *fixed prices*. As is known, the Baptists have always claimed to have first raised this price policy to a principle. In addition to the Baptists, the Quakers raise the claim, as the following quotation shows, to which Mr. Edward Bernstein drew my attention at the time:

> But it was not only in matters which related to the law of the land where the primitive members held their words and engagements sacred. This trait was remarked to be true of them in their concerns of trade. On their first appearance as a society, they suffered as tradesmen because others, displeased with the peculiarity of their manners, withdrew their custom from their shops. But in a little time the great outcry against them was that they got the trade of the country into their hands. This outcry arose in part from a strict exemption of all commercial agreements between them and others and *because they never asked two prices for the commodities they sold.*[8]

The view that the gods bless with riches the man who pleases them, through sacrifice or through his kind of conduct, was indeed diffused all over the world. However, the Protestant sects consciously brought this idea into connection with this *kind* of religious conduct, according to the principle of early capitalism: 'Honesty is the best policy'. This connection is found, although not quite exclusively, among these Protestant sects, but with characteristic continuity and consistency it is found *only* among them.

The whole typically bourgeois ethic was from the beginning common to all aceticist sects and conventicles and it is identical with the ethic practiced by the sects in America up to the very present. The Methodists, for example, held to be forbidden:

1. To make words when buying and selling ('haggling')
2. To trade with commodities before the custom tariff has been paid on them
3. To charge rates of interest higher than the law of the country permits
4. 'To gather treasures on earth' (meaning the transformation of investment capital into 'funded wealth')
5. To borrow without being sure of one's ability to pay back the debt
6. Luxuries of all sorts

But it is not only this ethic, already discussed in detail,[9] which goes back to the early beginnings of asceticist sects. Above all, the social premiums, the means of discipline, and, in general, the whole organizational basis of Protestant sectarianism with all its ramifications reach back to those beginnings. The survivals in contemporary America are the derivatives of a religious regulation of life which once worked with penetrating efficiency.

NOTES

1. An assistant of Semitic languages in an eastern university told me that he regretted not having become 'master of the chair', for then he would go back into business. When asked what good that would do the answer was: as a traveling salesman or seller he could present himself in a role famous for respectability. He could beat any competition and would be worth his weight in gold.
2. 'Hypocrisy' and conventional opportunism in these matters were hardly stronger developed in America than in Germany where, after all, an officer or civil servant 'without religious affiliation or preference' was also an impossibility. And a Berlin ('Aryan!') Lord Mayor was not confirmed officially because he failed to have one of his children baptised. Only the direction in which conventional 'hypocrisy' moved differed: official careers in Germany, business opportunities in the United States.
3. This was not always the case in the German-American clubs. When asking young German merchants in New York (with the best Hanseatic names) why they all strove to be admitted to an American club instead of the very nicely furnished German one, they answered that their (German-American) bosses would play billiards with them occasionally, however not without making them realize that they (the bosses) thought themselves to be 'very nice' in doing so.
4. Student fraternity, comparable to a 'Greek letter society'.
5. But note above. Entry into an American club (in school or later) is always the decisive moment for the loss of German nationality.
6. Some references from the older literature which is not very well known in Germany may be listed. A sketch of Baptist history is present in Vedder, *A Short History of the Baptists* (2nd ed. London, 1897). Concerning Hanserd Knollys: Culross, *Hanserd Knollys*, vol. II of the Baptist Manuals edited by P. Gould (London, 1891).

   For the history of Anabaptism: E. B. Bax, *Rise and Fall of the Anabaptists* (New York, 1902). Concerning Smyths: Henry M. Dexter, *The True Story of John Smyth, the Se-Baptist*, as told by himself and his contemporaries (Boston, 1881). The important publications of the Hanserd Knollys Society (printed for the Society by J. Hadden, Castle Street, Finsbury, 1846–54) have been cited already. Further official documents in *The Baptist Church Manual* by J. Newton Brown, DD (Philadelphia, American Baptist Publishing Society, 30 S. Arch Street). Concerning the Quakers, besides the cited work of Sharpless: A. C. Applegarth, *The Quakers in Pennsylvania*, ser. X, vol. VIII, IX of the Johns Hopkins University Studies in History and Political Science. G. Lorimer, *Baptists in History* (New York, 1902), J. A. Seiss, *Baptist System Examined* (Lutheran Publication Society, 1902).

Concerning New England (besides Doyle): The Massachusetts Historical Collections; furthermore, Weeden, *Economic and Social History of New England*, 1620–1789, 2 vols, Daniel W. Howe, *The Puritan Republic* (Indianapolis, Bobbs-Merrill Co.).

Concerning the development of the 'Covenant' idea in older Presbyterianism, its church discipline and its relation to the official church, on the one hand, and to Congregationalists and sectarians on the other hand, see Burrage, *The Church Covenant Idea* (1904), and *The Early English Dissenters* (1912). Furthermore, W. M. Macphail, *The Presbyterian Church* (1918); J. Brown, *The English Puritans* (1910). Important documents in Usher, *The Presbyterian Movement*, 1584–9 (Com. Soc., 1905). We give here only an extremely provisional list of what is relevant for us.

7. During the seventeenth century this was so much taken for granted that Bunyan, as mentioned previously, makes 'Mr. Money-Love' argue that one may even became pious *in order* to get rich, especially in order to add to one's patronage; for it should be irrelevant for what reason one had become pious. (*Pilgrims' Progress*, Tauchnitz ed., p. 114.)

8. Thomas Clarkson, *Portraiture of the Christian Profession and Practice of the Society of Friends* (3rd ed. London, 1867), p. 276.

9. In *The Protestant Ethic and the Spirit of Capitalism*.

10

DEMOCRACY IN AMERICA

Alexis de Tocqueville

I have already said enough to put Anglo-American civilization in its true light. It is the product (and one should continually bear in mind this point of departure) of two perfectly distinct elements which elsewhere have often been at war with one another but which in America it was somehow possible to incorporate into each other, forming a marvelous combination. I mean the *spirit of religion* and the *spirit of freedom*.

The founders of New England were both ardent sectarians and fanatical innovators. While held within the narrowest bounds by fixed religious beliefs, they were free from all political prejudices.

Hence two distinct but not contradictory tendencies plainly show their traces everywhere, in mores and in laws.

For the sake of a religious conviction men sacrifice their friends, their families, and their fatherland; one might suppose them entirely absorbed in pursuit of that intellectual prize for which they had just paid so high a price. Yet it is with almost equal eagerness that they seek either material wealth or moral delights, either heaven in the next world or prosperity and freedom in this.

Under their manipulation political principles, laws, and human institutions seem malleable things which can at will be adapted and combined. The barriers which hemmed in the society in which they were brought up fall before them; old views which have ruled the world for centuries vanish; almost limitless opportunities lie open in a world without horizon; the spirit of man rushes

From: Alexis de Tocqueville (ed. J. P. Mayer), *Democracy in America* (London: Fontana Press, 1994).

forward to explore it in every direction; but when that spirit reaches the limits of the world of politics, it stops of its own accord; in trepidation it renounces the use of its most formidable faculties; it forswears doubt and renounces innovation; it will not even lift the veil of the sanctuary; and it bows respectfully before truths which it accepts without discussion.

Thus, in the moral world everything is classified, coordinated, foreseen, and decided in advance. In the world of politics everything is in turmoil, contested, and uncertain. In the one case obedience is passive, though voluntary; in the other there is independence, contempt of experience, and jealousy of all authority.

Far from harming each other, these two apparently opposed tendencies work in harmony and seem to lend mutual support.

Religion regards civil liberty as a noble exercise of men's faculties, the world of politics being a sphere intended by the Creator for the free play of intelligence. Religion, being free and powerful within its own sphere and content with the position reserved for it, realizes that its sway is all the better established because it relies only on its own powers and rules men's hearts without external support.

Freedom sees religion as the companion of its struggles and triumphs, the cradle of its infancy, and the divine source of its rights. Religion is considered as the guardian of mores, and mores are regarded as the guarantee of the laws and pledge for the maintenance of freedom itself.

[...]

Men cannot do without dogmatic beliefs, and even that it is most desirable that they should have them. I would add here that religious dogmas seem to me the most desirable of all. That can clearly be deduced, even if one only considers the interests of this world.

There is hardly any human action, however private it may be, which does not result from some very general conception men have of God, of His relations with the human race, of the nature of their soul, and of their duties to their fellows. Nothing can prevent such ideas from being the common spring from which all else originates.

It is therefore of immense importance to men to have fixed ideas about God, their souls, and their duties toward their Creator and their fellows, for doubt about these first principles would leave all their actions to chance and condemn them, more or less, to anarchy and impotence.

That is therefore the most important question about which all of us need fixed ideas, and unfortunately it is the subject on which it is most difficult for each of us, left to his own unaided reason, to settle his ideas.

Only minds singularly free from the ordinary preoccupations of life, penetrating, subtle, and trained to think, can at the cost of much time and trouble sound the depths of these truths that are so necessary.

Indeed we see that philosophers themselves are almost always surrounded by uncertainties, that at each pace the natural light which guides them grows dimmer and threatens to go out, and that for all their efforts they have done no more than discover a small number of contradictory ideas on which the mind of man has been ceaselessly tossed for thousands of years without ever firmly grasping the truth or even finding mistakes that are new. Studies of this sort are far above the average capacities of men, and even if most men were capable of such inquiries, they clearly would not have time for them.

Fixed ideas about God and human nature are indispensable to men for the conduct of daily life, and it is daily life that prevents them from acquiring them.

The difficulty seems unparalleled. Among the sciences some that are useful to the crowd are also within its capacities; others can be mastered only by the few and are not cultivated by the majority, who need nothing beyond their more remote applications. But the sciences in question are essential to the daily life of all, though their study is out of reach of most.

General ideas respecting God and human nature are therefore the ideas above all others which ought to be withdrawn from the habitual action of private judgment and in which there is most to gain and least to lose by recognizing an authority.

The chief object and one of the principal advantages of religion is to provide answers to each of these primordial questions; these answers must be clear, precise, intelligible to the crowd, and very durable.

Some religions are very false and very ridiculous. Nevertheless, one can say that all those religions which remain within the circle of influence which I have just defined and do not claim to go beyond it (as many religions have tried to do, restraining the free flight of the human mind on every side) impose a salutary control on the intellect, and one must recognize, whether or not they save men's souls in the next world, that they greatly contribute to their happiness and dignity in this.

This is especially true of men living in free countries.

When a people's religion is destroyed, doubt invades the highest faculties of the mind and half paralyzes all the rest. Each man gets into the way of having nothing but confused and changing notions about the matters of greatest importance to himself and his fellows. Opinions are ill-defended or abandoned, and in despair of solving unaided the greatest problems of human destiny, men ignobly give up thinking about them.

Such a state inevitably enervates the soul, and relaxing the springs of the will, prepares a people for bondage.

Then not only will they let their freedom be taken from them, but often they actually hand it over themselves.

When there is no authority in religion or in politics, men are soon frightened by the limitless independence with which they are faced. They are worried and worn out by the constant restlessness of everything. With everything on the move in the realm of the mind, they want the material order at least to be firm and stable, and as they cannot accept their ancient beliefs again, they hand themselves over to a master.

For my part, I doubt whether man can support complete religious independence and entire political liberty at the same time. I am led to think that if he has no faith he must obey, and if he is free he must believe.

The great usefulness of religions is even more apparent among egalitarian peoples than elsewhere.

One must admit that equality, while it brings great benefits to mankind, opens the door, as I hope to show later, to very dangerous instincts. It tends to isolate men from each other so that each thinks only of himself.

It lays the soul open to an inordinate love of material pleasure.

The greatest advantage of religions is to inspire diametrically contrary urges. Every religion places the object of man's desires outside and beyond worldly goods and naturally lifts the soul into regions far above the realm of the senses. Every religion also imposes on each man some obligations toward mankind, to be performed in common with the rest of mankind, and so draws him away, from time to time, from thinking about himself. That is true even of the most false and dangerous religions.

Thus religious peoples are naturally strong just at the point where democratic peoples are weak. And that shows how important it is for people to keep their religion when they become equal.

I have neither the right nor the intention to examine the means by which God inspires a sense of religious belief into the heart of man. At the moment I am only looking at religions from a purely human point of view. I seek to discover how they can most easily preserve their power in the democratic centuries which lie before us.

I have pointed out how in times of enlightenment and democracy the human spirit is loath to accept dogmatic beliefs and has no lively sense of the need for them except in the matter of religion. This shows that, at such times above all, religions should be most careful to confine themselves to their proper sphere, for if they wish to extend their power beyond spiritual matters they run the risk of not being believed at all. They should therefore be at pains to define the sphere in which they claim to control the human spirit, and outside that sphere it should be left completely free to follow its own devices.

[...]

Continuing this line of argument further, I find that, humanly speaking, if religions are to be capable of maintaining themselves in democratic ages, it is not enough that they should simply remain within the spiritual sphere. Their power also depends a great deal on the nature of the beliefs they profess, the external forms they adopt, and the duties they impose.

The preceding observation, that equality leads men to very general and very vast ideas, is especially applicable to religion. Men who are alike and on the same level in this world easily conceive the idea of a single God who imposes the same laws on each man and grants him future happiness at the same price. The conception of the unity of mankind ever brings them back to the idea of the unity of the Creator, whereas when men are isolated from one another by great differences, they easily discover as many divinities as there are nations, castes, classes, and families, and they find a thousand private roads to go to heaven.

One cannot deny that Christianity itself has in some degree been affected by the influence of social and political conditions on religious beliefs.

At the time when Christianity appeared on earth, Providence, which no doubt was preparing the world for its reception, had united a great part of mankind, like an immense flock, under the scepter of the Caesars. The men composing this multitude were of many different sorts, but they all had this in common, that they obeyed the same laws, and each of them was so small and weak compared to the greatness of the emperor that they all seemed equal in comparison to him.

One must recognize that this new and singular condition of humanity disposed men to receive the general truths preached by Christianity, and this serves to explain the quick and easy way in which it then penetrated the human spirit.

The counterpart of this state of things was evident after the destruction of the empire.

The Roman world being then broken up into a thousand fragments, each nation reverted to its former individuality. There soon developed within these nations an infinite hierarchy of ranks. Racial differences became marked, and castes divided each nation into several peoples. In the midst of this communal effort, which seemed bent on subdividing humanity into as many fragments as it is possible to conceive, Christianity did not lose sight of the principal general ideas which it had brought to light, but seemed nonetheless to lend itself, as far as it could, to the new tendencies which came into existence as humanity was broken up. Men continued to worship one sole God, creator and preserver of all things, but each people, each city, and, one may almost say, each man thought he could obtain some particular privilege and win the favor of private protectors before the throne of grace. Unable to subdivide the Deity, they could at least multiply and aggrandize His agents beyond measure. For most Christians the worship of angels and saints became an almost idolatrous cult, and for a time there was room to fear that the Christian religion might relapse into the religions it had conquered.

It seems clear that the more the barriers separating the nations within the bosom of humanity and those separating citizen from citizen within each people tended to disappear, by so much the more did the spirit of humanity, as if of its own accord, turn toward the idea of a unique and all-powerful Being who dispensed the same laws equally and in the same way to all men. In democratic ages, therefore, it is particularly important not to confuse the honor due to secondary agents with the worship belonging to the Creator alone.

Another truth seems very clear to me, that religions should pay less attention to external practices in democratic times than in any others.

In speaking of the philosophical method of the Americans I have made clear that in a time of equality nothing is more repugnant to the human spirit than the idea of submitting to formalities. Men living at such times are impatient of figures of speech; symbols appear to them as childish artifices used to hide or dress up truths which could more naturally be shown to them naked and in broad daylight. Ceremonies leave them cold, and their natural tendency is to attach but secondary importance to the details of worship.

In democratic ages those whose duty is to regulate the external forms of worship should pay special attention to these natural propensities of the human mind in order not to run counter to them unnecessarily.

I believe firmly in the need for external ceremonies. I know that they fix the human spirit in the contemplation of abstract truths and help it to grasp them firmly and believe ardently in them. I do not imagine that it is possible to maintain a religion without external observances. Nevertheless, I think that in the coming centuries it would be particularly dangerous to multiply them beyond measure, indeed that they should be limited to such as are absolutely necessary to perpetuate dogma itself, which is the essence of religions,[1] whereas ritual is only the form. A religion which became more detained, more inflexible, and more burdened with petty observances at a time when people were becoming more equal would soon find itself reduced to a band of fanatic zealots in the midst of a skeptical multitude.

I anticipate the objection that religions with general and eternal truths for their subject cannot thus trim their sails to the changing urges of each century without losing their reputation for certainty in men's eyes. My answer is that one must make a very careful distinction between the chief opinions which form a belief, and are what the theologians call articles of faith, and those secondary notions which are connected with it. Religions are bound to hold firmly to the first, whatever may be the spirit of the time. But they should be very careful not to bind themselves like that to the secondary ones at a time when everything is in flux and the mind, accustomed to the moving pageant of human affairs, is reluctant to be held fixed. Things external and secondary, it would seem, have a chance of enduring only when society itself is static. In any other circumstances I am disposed to regard rigidity as dangerous.

A passion for well-being is, as we shall see, the most lively of all the emotions aroused or inflamed by equality, and it is a passion shared by all. So this taste for well-being is the most striking and unalterable characteristic of democratic ages.

It may be that, should any religion attempt to destroy this mother of all desires, it would itself be destroyed thereby. If it attempted to wean men entirely from thinking of the good things of this world in order to concentrate all their faculties on the contemplation of the next, sooner or later one may be sure that men's souls would slip through its fingers to plunge headlong into the delights of purely material and immediate satisfactions.

The main business of religions is to purify, control, and restrain that excessive and exclusive taste for well-being which men acquire in times of equality, but I think it would be a mistake for them to attempt to conquer it entirely and abolish it. They will never succeed in preventing men from loving wealth, but they may be able to induce them to use only honest means to enrich themselves.

NOTE

1. In all religions there are ceremonies which are inherent in the very substance of belief, and one must take care not to change anything in them. That is especially seen in the Catholic religion, where form and substance are so closely united that they are one.

11

THE AGE OF REASON

Thomas Paine

I believe in one God, and no more; and I hope for happiness beyond this life.

I believe in the equality of man; and I believe that religious duties consist in doing justice, loving mercy, and endeavouring to make our fellow-creatures happy.

But, lest it should be supposed that I believe many other things in addition to these, I shall, in the progress of this work, declare the things I do not believe, and my reasons for not believing them.

I do not believe in the creed professed by the Jewish Church, by the Roman Church, by the Greek Church, by the Turkish Church, by the Protestant Church, nor by any church that I know of. My own mind is my own church.

All national institutions of churches, whether Jewish, Christian or Turkish, appear to me no other than a human inventions, set up to terrify and enslave mankind, and monopolize power and profit.

I do not mean by this declaration to condemn those who believe otherwise; they have the same right to their belief as I have to mine. But it is necessary to the happiness of man that he be mentally faithful to himself. Infidelity does not consist in believing, or in disbelieving; it consists in professing to believe what he does not believe.

It is impossible to calculate the moral mischief, if I may so express it, that mental lying has produced in society. When a man has so far corrupted and prostituted the chastity of his mind as to subscribe his professional belief to

From: Michael Foot and Isaac Kramnick (eds), *The Thomas Paine Reader* (London: Penguin Books, 1987).

things he does not believe he has prepared himself for the commission of every other crime.

He takes up the trade of a priest for the sake of gain, and in order to qualify himself for that trade he begins with a perjury. Can we conceive any thing more destructive to morality than this?

12

LETTER TO DR BENJAMIN RUSH

Thomas Jefferson

In a comparative view of the Ethics of the enlightened nations of antiquity, of the Jews and of Jesus, no notice should be taken of the corruptions of reason among the ancients, to wit, the idolatry & superstition of the vulgar, nor of the corruptions of Christianity by the learned among its professors.

Let a just view be taken of the moral principles inculcated by the most esteemed of the sects of ancient philosophy, or of their individuals; particularly Pythagoras, Socrates, Epicurus, Cicero, Epictetus, Seneca, Antoninus.

1. PHILOSOPHERS

> 1. Their precepts related chiefly to ourselves, and the government of those passions which, unrestrained, would disturb our tranquillity of mind. In this branch of philosophy they were really great.
> 2. In developing our duties to others, they were short and defective. They embraced, indeed, the circles of kindred & friends, and inculcated patriotism, or the love of our country in the aggregate, as a primary obligation: toward our neighbors & countrymen they taught justice, but scarcely viewed them as within the circle of benevolence. Still less have they inculcated peace, charity & love to our fellow men, or embraced with benevolence the whole family of mankind.

II. JEWS

> 1. Their system was Deism; that is, the belief of one only God. But their ideas of him & of his attributes were degrading & injurious.

From: Thomas Jefferson, *Writings* (New York: The Library of America, 1984).

2. Their Ethics were not only imperfect, but often irreconcilable with the sound dictates of reason & morality, as they respect intercourse with those around us; & repulsive & antisocial, as respecting other nations. They needed reformation therefore, in an eminent degree.

III. JESUS

In this state of things among the Jews, Jesus appeared. His parentage was obscure; his condition poor, his education null; his natural endowments great; his life correct and innocent: he was meek, benevolent, patient, firm, disinterested, & of the sublimest eloquence.

The disadvantages under which his doctrines appear are remarkable.

1. Like Socrates & Epictetus, he wrote nothing himself.

2. But he had not, like them, a Xenophon or an Arrian to write for him. On the contrary, all the learned of his country, entrenched in its power and riches, were opposed to him, lest his labors should undermine their advantages; and the committing to writing his life & doctrines fell on the most unlettered & ignorant men; who wrote, too, from memory, & untill long after the transactions had passed.

3. According to the ordinary fate of those who attempt to enlighten and reform mankind, he fell an early victim to the jealousy & combination of the altar and the throne, at about thirty-three years of age, his reason having not yet attained the *maximum* of its energy, nor the course of his preaching, which was but of three years at most, presented occasions for developing a complete system of morals.

4. Hence the doctrines which he really delivered were defective as a whole, and fragments only of what he did deliver have come to us mutilated, misstated, & often unintelligible.

5. They have been still more disfigured by the corruptions of schismatising followers, who have found an interest in sophisticating & perverting the simple doctrines he taught by engrafting on them the mysticisms of a Grecian sophist, frittering them into subtleties, & obscuring them with jargon, until they have caused good men to reject the whole in disgust, & to view Jesus himself as an impostor.

Notwithstanding these disadvantages, a system of morals is presented to us, which, if filled up in the true style and spirit of the rich fragments he left us, would be the most perfect and sublime that has ever been taught by man.

The question of his being a member of the Godhead, or in direct communication with it, claimed for him by some of his followers, and denied by others, is foreign to the present view, which is merely an estimate of the intrinsic merit of his doctrines.

1. He corrected the Deism of the Jews, confirming them in their belief of one only God, and giving them juster notions of his attributes and government.

2. His moral doctrines, relating to kindred & friends, were more pure & perfect than those of the most correct of the philosophers, and greatly more so than those of the Jews; and they went far beyond both in inculcating universal philanthropy, not only to kindred and friends, to neighbors and countrymen, but to all mankind, gathering all into one family, under the bonds of love, charity, peace, common wants and common aids. A development of this head will evince the peculiar superiority of the system of Jesus over all others.

3. The precepts of philosophy, & of the Hebrew code, laid hold of actions only. He pushed his scrutinies into the heart of man; erected his tribunal in the region of his thoughts, and purified the waters at the fountain head.

4. He taught, emphatically, the doctrines of a future state, which was either doubted, or disbelieved by the Jews; and wielded it with efficacy, as an important incentive, supplementary to the other motives to moral conduct.

13

THE BOUNDARIES OF DEMOCRACY

Judith N. Shklar

The origins and end of the formative era of American democratic thought are not easily set. They surely go back as far as New England Puritanism, especially as it altered under the pressure of conflict with England. And it obviously must take us through the works of Tom Paine and Thomas Jefferson. Its end might be seen in that revival of intense democratic sentiment which is rather loosely called the age of Jackson. The tensions that had prevailed in democratic thinking then became overt. As is often the case, the end or the denouement makes manifest the deepest conflicts of a preceding era, and so reveals the implications of much that has now come to a close. On one side there were the radical Jacksonian democrats like O'Sullivan, the editor of *The United States and Democratic Review*, who argued passionately that the nation of futurity must expand to fulfill its destiny to bring democracy to the entire continent, perhaps even to the whole hemisphere.[1] There could be no geographic boundaries to a providential design. Against this vision Albert Gallatin, who had been secretary of the treasury under both Jefferson and Madison, thundered with no less a sense of providential endorsement, 'Your mission is to improve the state of the world, to be the Model Republic, to show that men are capable of governing themselves ... by your example to exert a moral influence most beneficial to mankind at large.' As for the fashionable idea of the 'hereditary superiority' of the Anglo-Saxon race over the Mexicans, Gallatin was sure that democracy must reject such a claim, as it rejects all hereditary claims.[2] What is most curious

From: Judith N. Shklar (ed. Stanley Hoffmann and Dennis F. Thompson), *Redeeming American Political Thought* (Chicago: University of Chicago Press, 1998).

of all is that both O'Sullivan and Gallatin were perfectly convinced that their respective views were those of the Sage of Monticello, whom both revered. Which of the two was the true heir of the original promise of American democracy? Quite possible both were equally entitled to wear the mantle of Jefferson, in whom all the built-in contradictions of democracy found their meeting place.

At the opening of the road to Jefferson stand the New England Puritans, whose 'atrabilious philosophy' he detested and whose descendants loathed him as a second Jeroboam who had turned Israel from the law.[3] They were, nevertheless, democrats – if not in theory, at least in their electoral practices. Not all members of the community could be members of the Congregational Church, but those who were did elect their ministers. And more relevant, magistrates were elected annually by all the freemen. Puritans thought that government was both very important, because it was of God, and very negative, because it was there to punish and restrain us in our fallen and sinful condition. To be a magistrate required a calling, a special fitness for the office, and while election did not prove that a man really had a vocation to govern, it was at least a sign to that effect. A people's refusal to reelect a man was similarly a clear indication of his failure to have been truly summoned to the office. While the freemen who were entitled to participate in these annual elections were not the entire male population, the practice is by any standard very democratic. To insist that magistrates be qualified to exercise their functions is, moreover, a denial of hereditary authority. Merit as it is perceived in the personal qualities of a potential magistrate, rather than in his birth, is the sign of a true calling. The origin of this way of choosing one's governors was not political, but part of the normal rules governing companies, which became part of a polity with the settlement of a territory. Inadvertently the result was democratic. In theory, the clergy took no direct part in governing. In actuality, it was they who decided what the tasks of government were to be, and who could be a member of the community at all. Eventually it was not possible to require voters to be members of the Congregational Church, but for a long time one had to show that one believed what the rest of the community was supposed to believe. It was in short a democracy that was both exclusive and authoritarian.[4]

To guide the magistrates and the people as a whole the clergy delivered particularly political sermons on the yearly election day. These annual sermons were unique to New England and their immediate purpose was to be a 'watch-man upon Jerusalem's walls, whose proper business is to descry dangers, and give seasonable notice thereof, to observe the sins of the times and the awful symptoms of God's departure'.[5] The content of these sermons was a review of the events of the past in terms of biblical hermeneutics. It was not a new interpretive system, but the occasions to which it was applied were highly original. It was assumed that the Bible, especially the Old Testament, contained the 'types', which we would now call archetypes, of all possible political events and experiences. The way to understand one's own world was to relate it to the appropriate biblical type of which it was the antitype. That is how one could understand who one was, what had already happened, and what was likely to occur. The clergy was meant to show the community to what biblical events they were to look in order to discern the meaning of their most recent political conduct. The question 'who are the people' was answered in no uncertain terms. The Puritans were the people of Israel. As such they were apart from every other people. They were, of course, not the natural heirs of the ancient Hebrews, but their replica. The Old Testament was their story as a prophecy to be reenacted. First and foremost, they must attend to the Exodus from Egypt, then to the Babylonian captivity and its end, always a dreadful warning. David's story was naturally significant, but most of all Noah seemed to apply to the early comers, who had also started out anew after crossing a flood of water more awful than the original deluge. Getting across the Atlantic was a terrifying experience and it made the founding of a new settlement in a wild and empty country seem very much like Noah's re-creation of mankind after all the other people had died. It was not difficult to fit themselves into these prophetic molds. It is not a historical way of relating past and present, because it does not involve thinking in terms of sequences or of continuities at all. Events are not connected in a chain. The new people of Israel relived the original biblical experiences exactly as they occurred then. The only obstacle was intellectual, to fully know which were the right reference points. That was the work of the learned clergy, especially in the election sermons. As many historians have noted, the 'errand into the wilderness' which the Puritans undertook was both a real experience of life in a wild country, and a recollection of Isaiah and John the Baptist in its spiritual significance. They had come to the natural wilderness to save the garden of the Church from the wilderness of the world which had not yet fully responded to the Protestant Reformation. The society they would set up in New England would be a beacon that would lead the rest of mankind to a full Reformation, and by setting an example of holy living would bring Protestantism to its realization. They were on an errand for all mankind. This was not just a self-imposed task; they had been chosen. They had covenanted with the Lord, repeating the covenant of Abraham. If they fulfilled it He would reward them, though this was not wholly certain. If they failed in their duty He would punish them. So every public misfortune was a divine penalty inflicted for some wrongdoing. Moreover, because they were the best, the only people of Israel, they failed absolutely when they erred at all. The election sermons therefore had only one subject, declension. There was always a falling away from the covenant, and as the years went by, from the standards of virtue that had prevailed among the first settlers. Only they were truly Noah-like. Since then there had been drubbing, adultery, idleness, and unthriftiness. As their just reward God had sent epidemics and King Philip's War. When the people were obedient God would send them magistrates like Moses or Nehemiah and all would be well. Mostly the election sermons were terrifying warnings, and at the end the people said 'Amen' in a horrifying repetition of the Deuteronomic precedent. Since everything had already happened once before and was constantly being repeated, it was not difficult to know what the boundaries of political life were. Even profane history had its lessons.[6] Classical history also contained types. The corruptions of the Romans had brought their own version of the Babylonian captivity. The clergy had read their Tacitus and Sallust and the relevant pages in St Augustine and they could see that pagan decline had its own awful lesson to teach. The psychological and political decline of the Romans indulging in easy and luxurious living was a natural addition to the sacred history of the people of Israel. It thus made perfectly good sense to speak of Sir Edmund Andros as a second Nero and to see the fall of Rome as a replication of the punishment of Israel. In fact the two are very often juxtaposed. That these awful imprecations and warnings should be addressed on a political occasion to the entire people carries a more than politically democratic meaning. There is implicit in this entire way of defining the people a complete collective responsibility for the fate of the community. Everyone's actions mattered to them all. And if they seem self-absorbed in their recollections and prophecies, they did believe that they were acting for all mankind.

How could this political theology have been integrated with the philosophy of John Locke? Unlikely as it may seem, it did happen, gradually, but surely. First of all there was the great common experience of felt oppression under James II. The idea of a basic social contract was not so alien either. The Puritans had not only taken up the covenant of Abraham with God, but had also contracted with each other to fulfill together the terms of that first covenant. Their society was built on a mutual promise to bear the communal responsibility to fulfill the mission of Israel. To resist tyranny and in any case to watch the magistrates carefully, even as one obeyed them dutifully, was part of the belief system that was no less familiar to Locke than to them. They were therefore quite prepared to accept a secular explanation of their difficulties with England as well as a purely political justification for resistance, as long as these did not interfere with or replace their biblical understanding of their situation. Locke was simply added on to a religious doctrine of government. And New Englanders were ready to hear his message by the eighteenth century. John Wise, a perfectly orthodox preacher, gives us a very good idea of how Locke was taken in as a spiritual lodger in Puritan thinking. Not only did Wise dwell on the social contract as the way Israel had come together for the greater service of God, but self-preservation was also a duty to Him. The instinct for self-preservation was divinely given and a sign from God that He wanted us to preserve His creation. Had not Noah saved himself thus? The Puritans had come to America like Noah to preserve themselves, as he had, for God's sake. Natural rights, the most important point for American democracy, after all, were also not beyond the Puritan embrace. Wise reminded them of their duty, and thus right, to resist tyrannical and specifically papist rulers. Every Protestant Englishman had a right to resist with all his powers an evil as great as a papist king. And as the English government seemed to favor the Catholics of

Quebec more than its Protestant subjects in New England, the latter had every right and duty to resist. Here was a danger against which they had an obvious right to preserve themselves. The great Mr Locke had simply explained to them in immediate terms what they already understood from contemplating the story of Noah. His prescriptions were perfectly compatible with their own sense of their situation.[7]

[...]

It is a great mistake to think of Tom Paine as a marginal figure in American political thinking. He did not take a direct part in building its enduring institutions, but the rhetoric of radical journalism owes him much even now, and he was much read by the Yankee pioneers moving westward. More significantly he certainly impressed Jefferson genuinely and through him became a lasting voice in American democratic discourse. The first effect of his pamphlet was spectacular not only as a unifying force, but also as a revelation of what democratic feeling in America was then, and in some measure would remain. Baptists in Virginia, tired of the Anglican Filmer-like sermons of Jonathan Boucher; Pennsylvanians fed up with Quaker passivity; deistic Virginia gentlemen, even John Adams, who came to hate Paine; all were moved by *Common Sense*. The title itself is a stroke of genius. 'Common sense' means shared and universal understanding. It is everybody's birthright. And it is also the untutored intelligence of every-man. Finally it implies an active, 'can do' attitude, a ready, practical approach to one's problems, efficiency in short. The first thing that Paine did with the notion of common sense was to turn a local squabble into a struggle for the salvation of the world.

> The cause of America is in a great measure the cause of all mankind. Many circumstances hath and will arise, which are not local but universal, and through which the principles of all Lovers of Mankind are affected and in the event of which their affections are interested.[8]

A struggle for freedom is inherently important for everyone who hopes for it anywhere. That was not a new idea for his audience. Even more familiar was his recalling of biblical examples and a pervasive use of sexual imagery in his condemnations. 'Society is a blessing,' but government is 'like dress a sign of our lost innocence,' combines the two. For we do not need much government, and certainly Americans did not need the sort of government the English were inflicting upon them. Paine's state of nature was not quite Locke's. It was more familiar, a natural wilderness to which colonists came and in which they cooperated in order to survive. That certainly corresponded more than the Hobbesian version to the experiences of Americans. It followed that if settlers needed some government, it was merely to supply 'the deficit of virtue,' but it did not seem to be a great debit and would soon be made up. Neither the Puritan sense of sin nor the restraints it called for remained, but even as they listened to old notions, Americans were absorbing a transforming doctrine. All men, not just the children of Israel, were now fit for good government. Frequent elections and limited authority would make the magistrates indistinguishable from their electors. Why had this not always been the case? In Paine's view, it was human pride that urged rulers on to overstep their bounds. And that pride was the supreme sin was no news to Paine's Christian readers. The antecedent biblical type for this political pride was the dreadful story of Jewish royalty. When the people of Israel wanted 'to be like all the other nations,' they acquired kings, like the heathen. Samuel and Gideon warned them against it, and the consequences were known to all of Paine's readers. 'Monarchy is in every instance the Popery of government.' Joined to this religious language was a decidedly secular vocabulary also designed to desacralize and demystify monarchy. Consider the origin of the English kings, 'a French bastard landing with armed banditi'. Unruly descendants of a bastard, acting against the consent of nature, they were surely not chosen by God to govern anyone. To Paine, the kings of England were, in fact, the offspring of the lowest of the low, the criminal classes. And they showed no improvement. They waged war and distributed patronage only to their favorites. They were 'crowned ruffians' and no one should be impressed by them. The parental bond, if it ever existed, was broken by them. Indeed 'even brutes do not devour their young' as the king of England was then attacking Americans. Americans were not, however, children, but adults ready to rule themselves. Above all, and this really was a new thought, they were superior because they were young, not old and senile like the English. Paine was urging Americans and all mankind to stop looking to the past as a guide.

> The sun never shined on a cause of greater worth. 'Tis not the affair of a city, a country, a province or a kingdom, but of a continent, of at least one eighth of the habitable globe. 'Tis not the concern of a day, a year, or an age, posterity are virtually involved in the contest, and will be more or less affected, even to the end of time, by the proceedings. Now is the seed-time of continental union, faith and honor ... By referring the matter from argument to arms, a new era for politics is struck: a new method for thinking has arisen.[9]

Everything was to be new, and new was better. Newest of all was the expectation of a permanent, continental, democratic government. The very size of the new nation made all the old metaphors of politics obsolete. To Paine, the notion of a continental family was absurd. It would be a marketplace where all the nations would meet to exchange goods and ideas, a universe in its very character. The New World had been an asylum for the persecuted lovers of freedom all along; now its vastness would make all who came countrymen. Ancestor worship could mean nothing to such a population and its youth would last. 'Youth is the seed-time of good habits.' Europe may have still believed that old age was the time of wisdom and good counsel, but America knew better. The world must be renewed all the time. That, Paine cleverly noted, was the real meaning of Noah's survival. So the most traditional of memories was brought to bear on the news that 'the birthday of a new day is at hand'.[10] And the revolutionary call went out to all, not just to Americans. They may have been acting as messengers for mankind, but all were asked to come and join the struggle against the past.

> Oh ye that love mankind! Ye that dare oppose, not only the tyranny, but the tyrant, stand forth! Every spot of the old world is over-run with oppression. Freedom hath been hunted round the globe. Asia, and Africa, have long expelled her. Europe regards her like a stranger, and England hath given her warning to depart. Oh! receive the fugitive, and prepare in time an asylum for mankind.[11]

There can be no doubt that for Paine the boundaries of democracy were meant to embrace all those who loved freedom.

America would also be open in another way. It would trade with anybody, without any barriers. Like many other eighteenth-century writers, Paine was convinced that commerce was a source of peace. Every exchange was to be welcome. Wealth and population would mean geographic expansion, of course. The continent would soon contain more people than Europe. There was, after all, room for all. It was really to be the business of the world, or rather of its youth. For America would have no part of the old international order, with its treaties, and balances, and wars. It would be huge, and self-contained. These views were not ignored in Europe, as readers of Felix Gilbert's *To the Farewell Address* know. Well might the English and the Spanish in America tremble.[12] There seemed to be no limits to the power that Paine foresaw for America. He talked as if ships and a whole navy could simply jump out of the trunks of trees. It was all meant to be defensive power, but very threatening, by any standards.

What boundaries, if any, did Paine envision for this huge new democracy? There were to be none between ruler and ruled, citizen and emigrant, old and young. The only wall was ideological. Those who did not reject the past were not real friends of freedom. They had no place here. The American Tory, Paine wrote, was just a traitor. A captured English soldier would be set free or sent home, but the Tory was to be executed. He may not have been a traitor in the old common law, but he was disloyal, and not just to a cause, but to the future. The providential tone as Paine spoke of the 'chain of extraordinary events' must have stirred his readers deeply.[13] And they may also have responded to the hope of a political future free from the corruptions of the old order. There was something here for every republican free from both the religious and social restrictions of Europe, but it was all presented in the language of the oldest of memories. The promise was absolutely dazzling. There was to be power without aggression and a mingling of all the nations without conflict. All this would be possible for young, democratic citizens who needed little government, and who were determined to assert their rights. Those who believed all that were welcome, and those who did not were excluded and not immune from attack. The standard for democratic citizenship was ideological. Anyone who wanted to be a democratic citizen belonged to the people, and those who rejected the ideology of the New World ought to remain in the old and decrepit order of the European past. North America had enough room for them all and it would be strong enough to defend itself against foreign incursions, if it had to do so. But it would do its best to enter into no political relations with other states, all the more so since it wanted no part of their old and disreputable conventions. This came as close as possible to defining the democratic people as mankind in general. It set ideological rather than territorial boundaries, but it did so in the confident belief that the Western Hemisphere could accommodate all democratic people whatever their national origins might be.

For American democratic thought Paine's greatest single achievement was the profound impression that his writings made upon Thomas Jefferson. Jefferson helped with the publication of Paine's later books, and came to his aid when the old radical fell upon hard times. *The Rights of Man*, especially, was very close to Jefferson's deepest beliefs about one set of boundaries, those between generations. Paine argued there that no generation owes anything to another. The world belongs entirely to the living. And from as early as 1784 to as late as 1824, two years before his death, Jefferson repeated over and over again his conviction that there was an absolutely impassable barrier between generations. The newness of Noah's second world, after all, did imply a gulf between past and present, and to perpetually repeat his voyage implied a recurrent rebirth. 'The earth belongs in usufruct to the living. The dead have no rights, the earth belongs to the living.' Each generation must be as self-ruling as every other. 'One generation,' he wrote, 'is to another as one independent nation to another.' There were no natural bonds joining them, and the social distance was as complete as the physical one. Every generation, according to his calculations, lasted for about nineteen years. It followed that all the existing laws should be revoked at the end of twenty years and every generation be as free as its predecessors to create its own society. It was not just a matter of newness – majority government did demand the consent of those who were alive in the present. It was inherent in democracy that the present alone should matter. One could not vote if one was dead or not yet born. And the 'consent of the governed' was not an idle phrase for Jefferson.[14]

The immediate and often repeated occasion for expressing these sentiments was America's foreign debt. In Jefferson's view, America ought not to borrow from foreign bankers and saddle future generations with debts. Moreover no generation should feel obliged to repay debts incurred by their predecessors. They should simply repudiate these impositions to which they had never given their consent. We simply had no right to transmit debts to our progeny. They, however, had every right to refuse to honor them. When James Madison objected that America would lose all its credit, once it was known that it might renege on its debt after nineteen-odd years, Jefferson replied that that was exactly what he hoped for. If no Dutch banker would lend us anything we would avoid indebtedness. The temptation would never arise at all.[15]

It was not only the prospect of international indebtedness that provoked Jefferson to emphasize the independence of generations from each other. In fact he thought that constitutions and all subordinate legislation should be completely revoked every twenty years. A constitution was an agreed precommitment to the structure and limits of governmental authority. Who, however, could be democratically pre-committed? Only the generation that tied its own hands for the sake of its own purposes. It could not bind future generations. That was not consent. Laws simply must be renewed. When James Madison objected to these arguments, he raised only prudential, not philosophical, arguments. Constant change, he pointed out not unreasonably, would be inefficient in the extreme; it would make each generation utterly irresponsible with no regard for their successors, and in any case, people built their lives on expectations of the future. It would be too frustrating and it could not be done.[16]

If Jefferson had been interested, say, in making the trains run on time, he might have agreed, but that was not his aim. He wanted to recognize all the implications of a genuine democracy, not to arrange an easy one. The barriers between generations, between those majorities that could consent and dissent, and those that could not must be absolute. There could be no abridgment of the rights of the living.

NOTES

1. Norman A. Graebner (ed.), *Manifest Destiny* (Indianapolis: Bobbs-Merrill, 1968), pp. 15–29, 135–43.
2. Ibid., pp. 192–3.
3. Henry Adams, *The History of the United States of America during the Administration of Jefferson and Madison*, Ernest Samuels (ed.) (Chicago: University of Chicago Press, 1967), pp. 61–2, 107–8.
4. Edmund S. Morgan (ed.) *Puritan Political Ideas* (Indianapolis: Bobbs-Merrill, 1965), pp. xiii–xlvii.
5. A. W. Plumstead, *The Wall and the Garden: Selected Massachusetts Election Sermons, 1670–1775* (Minneapolis: University of Minnesota Press, 1968), p. 16.
6. Perry Miller, *Errand into the Wilderness* (Cambridge, MA: Belknap Press of Harvard University Press, 1956), pp. 1–47, 141–52. Sacvan Betcovitch, *The Puritan Origins of the American Self* (New Haven: Yale University Press, 1975); and *The American Jeremiad* (Madison, WI: University of Wisconsin Press, 1978), passim.
7. John Wise, 'A Vindication of the Government of New England', in Morgan (ed.), *Puritan Political Ideas*, pp. 252–67.
8. *Common Sense*, Isaac Kramnick (ed.), (London: Penguin, 1976), p. 63.
9. Ibid., p. 82.
10. Ibid., pp. 107, 120.
11. Ibid., p. 100.
12. Princeton, NJ: Princeton University Press, 1970), pp. 36–75, 107–11.
13. Kramnick (ed.), *Common Sense*, pp. 117–18. *The American Crisis: The Writings of Tom Paine*, Moncure Daniel Conway (ed.) (New York: G. P. Putnam, 1902), 1: pp. 170–9, 204–7, 215–17, 250.
14. All references are to Thomas Jefferson, *Writings* (New York: Library of America, 1984). To James Madison, 6 September 1789, pp. 959–64; To John Wayles Eppes, 24 June 1813, pp. 1280–6; To Samuel Kercheval, 12 July 1816, pp. 1395–401; To Major John Cartwright, 25 June 1824, pp. 1490–6.

15. To Archibald Stuart, 25 January 1786, pp. 843–5.
16. Marvin Myers, *The Mind of the Founder: Sources of the Political Thought of James Madison* (Indianapolis: Bobbs-Merrill, 1973); To Thomas Jefferson, 4 February 1790, pp. 229–34.

14

THE NEW ENGLAND MIND – FROM COLONY TO PROVINCE

Perry Miller

The first thanksgiving, held at Plymouth in 1621, has become enshrined in an American institution. In the seventeenth century, New England observed many days of rejoicing, but none in imitation of this original; all were ordered 'pro temporibus et causis,' according to the manner in which providence was dealing with the land. Accordingly, it observed mostly days of humiliation; over the years there were more chastisements than blessings. For the Puritan mind, to fix thanksgiving to a mechanical revolution of the calendar would be folly: who can say that in November there will be that for which thanks should be uttered rather than lamentation? By the time ceremonial gratitude can be channelized into an annual festival, calculated in advance, society is rewarding its own well-doing, not acknowledging divine favor. When this happens, Calvinism is dead; though the society doggedly persists in giving autumnal thanks, it no longer has a mechanism for confessing its shortcomings and seeking forgiveness for its trespasses.

[...]

Hence the one literary type which the first native-born Americans inevitably developed, into which they poured their energy and their passion, was the fast-day sermon. On annual days of election, in the spring, after officers were installed and oaths taken, before turning to business the General Court

From: Perry Miller, *The New England Mind: From Colony to Province* (Cambridge, MA: Belknap Press of Harvard University Press, 1953).

regularly listened to a sermon which, under the circumstances, was bound to be more a review of recent afflictions than an exposition of doctrine; ministers chosen for the occasion would try then to be their most impressive. Thus they developed, amplified, and standardized a type of sermon for which the rules were as definite as for the ode. Where the most characteristic creations of the founders were subtle explorations of the labyrinth of sin and regeneration – employing, as did Shepard and Hooker, a complex psychological doctrine, full of shadow and nuance – for the second generation the dominant literary form, almost the exclusive, is something we may term, for shorthand purposes, a 'jeremiad'. Although the practitioners themselves never quite distinguished it by name from the sermon in general, it quickly became so precise a formula as to be immediately recognizable to the student of types – as, no doubt, it was to the audiences at the time.

The structure of this jeremiad was prescribed by the theory of external covenant. Perforce it addressed mankind not as beings of a complicated psychology, but as creatures governed by a simple calculus. The 'doctrine' must be some proposition that they are pertinaciously pursued for their sins; any of a hundred verses in the Old Testament would supply the text, especially in Isaiah or Jeremiah. The 'reasons' would then become expositions of the national covenant, its terms, conditions, and duties. But the real substance of the discourse came at the end, in the 'applications' or 'uses,' where the preacher spelled out the significance of the situation. Here he enumerated, in as much detail as he had courage for, the provocations to vengeance, proposed a scheme of reformation, and let his imagination glow over the still more exquisite judgments yet in store unless his listeners acted upon his recommendations. A minister's reputation for eloquence came to be based upon the skill with which he could devise prognostications of a mounting disaster, by contrast with which the present suffering dwindled into mere annoyance.

[...]

By calling the jeremiad a literary type I mean that it was more than a rhetorical exercise. Its hold upon the New England mind for four or five generations is an instance of the tyranny of form over thought. But there is a vastly more important consideration: art requires conventions which emphasize the relevant aspects of experience; a new convention, says W. H. Auden, is a revolution in sensibility: 'It appeals to and is adopted by a generation because it makes sense of experiences which previously had been ignored.' For the second and third generations of New England, the jeremiad was the one appropriate convention because it made sense out of their unique experience. After a time, it became stereotyped; after a century we may well call it, in Auden's language, 'reactionary,' but in the beginning it was, however manufactured according to formula, a vision. It was a way of conceiving the inconceivable, of making intelligible order out of the transition from European to American experience.

[…]

The jeremiad would be obliged to comment on the social scene in terms recognizable to those who knew it, but the remarkable fact about the succession of sermons is how stylized became the categories under which defections were grouped and arranged. As with 'arguments' in logic, data were ordered according to Ramist 'method'. The *Result* of the Synod was not so much a fresh survey as a digest of previous inventories. As long as we understand that it was bound to be cast into a now stabilized mold, we may cautiously read it as a description of society. But properly to interpret it, we must remember how the *Magnalia* betrays the actual situation by confessing that the people had not really sunk so far into corruption as in other places; it was only that New England, being under the greatest 'obligations', was to be held criminal for 'omissions' which in other countries were more or less normal 'commissions'! The *Result* must not, therefore be taken too literally, but rather construed as the climax of an emerging ritual. It was not sociological investigation, it was purgation by incantation.

[…]

When delivering jeremiads, a worried clergy were performing, under compulsions they only half understood, a ritual of confession. Hence these ceremonial discourses do provide, taken in sequence, a chronology of social evolution; in them everything the historian pieces together out of records and documents is faithfully mirrored. They tell the story, and tell it coherently, of a society which was founded by men dedicated, in unity and simplicity, to realizing on earth eternal and immutable principles – and which progressively became involved with fishing, trade, and settlement. They constitute a chapter in the emergence of the capitalist mentality, showing how intelligence copes with – or more cogently, how it fails to cope with – a change it simultaneously desires and abhors.

One remarkable fact emerges: while the ministers were excoriating the behavior of merchants, laborers, and frontiersmen, they never for a moment condemned merchandizing, laboring, or expansion of the frontier. They berated the consequences of progress, but never progress; deplored the effects of trade upon religion, but did not ask men to desist from trading; arraigned men of great estates, but not estates. The temporal welfare of a people, said Jonathan Mitchell in 1667, required safety, honesty, orthodoxy, and also 'Prosperity in matters of outward Estate and Liveleyhood'.

In fact, in the ecstasy of denunciation, Jeremiahs enthusiastically indorsed those precepts of pious labor which from the beginning had been central in Calvinism. Merchants, farmers, and shipbuilders increased 'cent per cent', and the consequence appeared to be a decay of godliness, class struggles, extravagant dress, and contempt for learning; New England seemed to be deserting the ideals of its founders, but preachers would have deserted them even more had they not also exhorted diligence in every calling – precisely the virtue bound to increase estates, widen the gulf between rich and poor, and to make usury inevitable.

[...]

Had the founders been uncomplicated Calvinists like the Scotch-Irish Presbyterians, the intellectual history of American Puritanism could be briefly told. But by retaining the scholastic liberal arts, and then by rephrasing Calvinism in the language of the several covenants, New Englanders managed to bring to the wilderness a complex system (which they innocently supposed was simple). As jeremiads multiplied, the complaint mounted that sound conversions were few, and even of these, many were of so insipid a sanctity as to cause doubts of their authenticity. Bit by bit preachers raised a suspicion that the remnant might have become too small any longer to save. It became increasingly imperative, therefore, that prophets urge upon the unconverted no less than upon the converted the necessity of doing something. Since the national covenant demanded an effort by all, mere natural ability gradually was deemed adequate (if commanded by a few saints) for outward compliance. A whole town or colony recorded their vow of reformation on a day of humiliation, but the gesture would remain empty unless everyone did have a power to keep his promise without first having to undergo the elusive rite of regeneration.

15

THE AMERICAN JEREMIAD

Sacvan Bercovitch

We need not discount the validity of this frontier thesis to see what it does *not* explain: the persistence of the Puritan jeremiad throughout the eighteenth and nineteenth centuries, in all forms of the literature, including the literature of westward expansion. Indeed, what first attracted me to the study of the jeremiad was my astonishment, as a Canadian immigrant, at learning about the prophetic history of America. Not of North America, for the prophecies stopped short at the Canadian and Mexican borders, but of a country that, despite its arbitrary territorial limits, could read its destiny in its landscape, and a population that, despite its bewildering mixture of race and creed, could believe in something called an American mission, and could invest that patent fiction with all the emotional, spiritual, and intellectual appeal of a religious quest. I felt then like Sancho Panza in a land of Don Quixotes. Here was the anarchist Thoreau condemning his backsliding neighbors by reference to the Westward errand; here, the solitary singer Walt Whitman, claiming to be the American Way; here, the civil rights leader Martin Luther King, descendant of slaves, denouncing segregation as a violation of the American dream; here, an endless debate about national identity, full of rage and faith, Jeffersonians claiming that they, and not the priggish heirs of Calvin, really represented the errand, conservative politicians hunting out socialists as conspirators against the dream, left-wing polemics proving that capitalism was a betrayal of the country's sacred origins. The question in these latter-day jeremiads, as in their

From: Sacvan Bercovitch, *The American Jeremiad* (Madison, WI: University of Wisconsin Press, 1978).

seventeenth-century precursors, was never 'Who are we?' but, almost in deliberate evasion of that question, the old prophetic refrain: 'When is our errand to be fulfilled? How long, O Lord, how long?' And the answers, again as in the Puritan jeremiads, invariably joined lament and celebration in reaffirming America's mission.

[...]

The newness of New England becomes both literal and eschatalogical, and (in what was surely the most far-reaching of these rhetorical effects) the American *wilderness* takes on the double significance of secular and sacred place. If for the individual believer it remained part of the wilderness of the world, for God's 'peculiar people' it was a territory endowed with special symbolic import, like the wilderness through which the Israelites passed to the promised land. In one sense it was historical, in another sense prophetic; and as Nicholas Noyes explained, in a sermon on the errand three decades after Danforth's, '*Prophesie* is *Historie antedated*; and *Historie* is *Postdated Prophesie*: the same thing is told in both.'[1] For these American Jeremiahs, and all their second- and third-generation colleagues, the ambiguity confirmed the founders' design. They dwelt on it, dissected it, elaborated upon it, because it opened for them into a triumphant assertion of their destiny, migration and pilgrimage entwined in the progress of New England's holy commonwealth.

[...]

Danforth's strategy is characteristic of the American jeremiad throughout the seventeenth century: first, a precedent from Scripture that sets out the communal norms; then, a series of condemnations that details the actual state of the community (at the same time insinuating the covenantal promises that ensure success); and finally a prophetic vision that unveils the promises, announces the good things to come, and explains away the gap between fact and ideal. Perry Miller seems to have understood this form as a triptych, a static three-part configuration in which the centerpiece, considered merely as lament, conveys the meaning of the whole. So interpreted, the New England sermons embody a cyclical view of history: the futile, recurrent rise and fall of nations that sustained the traditional jeremiad. But the rhetoric itself suggests something different. It posits a movement from promise to experience – from the ideal of community to the shortcomings of community life – and thence forward, with prophetic assurance, toward a resolution that incorporates (as it transforms) both the promise and the condemnation. The dynamic of the errand, that is, involves a use of ambiguity which is not divisive but progressive – or more accurately, progressive because it denies divisiveness – and which is therefore impervious to the reversals of history, since the very meaning of progress is inherent in the rhetoric itself.

[...]

I am suggesting that 'the process of Americanization' began not with the decline of Puritanism but with the Great Migration, and that the jeremiad, accordingly, played a significant role in the development of what was to become modern middle-class American culture. I hope that in suggesting this I do not seem to be over-straining the worn links between Puritanism and the rise of capitalism. My point is simply that certain elements in Puritanism lent themselves powerfully to that conjunction, and precisely those elements came to the fore when the Bay emigrants severed their ties with the feudal forms of Old England and set up a relatively fluid society on the American strand – a society that devalued aristocracy, denounced beggary, and opened up political, educational, and commercial opportunities to a relatively broad spectrum of the population.

[...]

These and many similar quantitative differences between Old and New England are symptomatic, I believe, of a sweeping qualitative distinction between America and all other modern countries. In England (and the Old World generally), capitalism was an economic system that evolved dialectically, through conflict with earlier and persistent ways of life and belief. Basically New England bypassed the conflict. This is by no means to say that conflict was avoided altogether. On the contrary: the first century of New England history is a remarkable instance of rapid social change, involving widespread moral, psychic, and political tensions. The emergent structures of a free-enterprise economy did not all at once transform the guild and craft mentality; for a time mercantile capitalism actually helped maintain aristocratic privilege; for an even longer time pre-modern modes of social and familial relationship resisted the commercial revolution underway in the Northern Anglo-American colonies. But by and large the resistance was as ineffectual as it was anachronistic. It signified not a contest between an established and an evolving system, but a troubled period of maturation. The emigrant leaders did not give up their class prerogatives when they landed at Massachusetts Bay, and yet the forms they instituted tended to erode traditional forms of deference. They restricted opportunity in commerce and property ownership, yet social power in the colony increasingly shifted to the commercial and property-owning classes. In all fundamental ideological aspects, New England was from the start an outpost of the modern world. It evolved from its own origins, as it were, into a middle-class culture – a commercially oriented economy buttressed by the decline of European feudalism, unhampered by lingering traditions of aristocracy and crown, and sustained by the prospect (if not always the fact) of personal advancement – a relatively homogeneous society whose enterprise was consecrated, according to its civic and clerical leadership, by a divine plan of progress.

[...]

The European jeremiad developed within a static hierarchical order; the lessons it taught, about historical recurrence and the vanity of human wishes, amounted to a massive ritual reinforcement of tradition. Its function was to make social practice conform to a completed and perfected social ideal. The American Puritan jeremiad was the ritual of a culture on an errand – which is to say, a culture based on a faith in process. Substituting teleology for hierarchy, it discarded the Old World ideal of stasis for a New World vision of the future. Its function was to create a climate of anxiety that helped release the restless 'progressivist' energies required for the success of the venture. The European jeremiad also thrived on anxiety, of course. Like all 'traditionalist' forms of ritual, it used fear and trembling to teach acceptance of fixed social norms. But the American Puritan jeremiad went much further. It made anxiety its end as well as its means. Crisis was the social norm it sought to inculcate. The very concept of errand, after all, implied a state of *un*fulfillment. The future, though divinely assured, was never quite there, and New England's Jeremiahs set out to provide the sense of insecurity that would ensure the outcome. Denouncing or affirming their vision fed on the distance between promise and fact.

[...]

The Puritan jeremiad set out the sacred history of the New World; the eighteenth-century jeremiad established the typology of America's mission. That outlook, to be sure, had become almost explicit by the last decades of the seventeenth century. But the Puritans were careful to make Scripture the basis of their figuralism. They always rooted their exegeses (however strained) in biblical texts, and they appealed to (even as they departed from) a common tradition of Reformed hermeneutics. Because they believed the Reformation was reaching its fulfillment in America, and because they identified themselves primarily in religious terms, they found it necessary to include all the standard landmarks of Protestant historiography. Their Yankee heirs felt relatively free of such constraints. During the eighteenth century, the meaning of Protestant identity became increasingly vague; typology took on the hazy significance of metaphor, image, and symbol; what passed for the divine plan lost its strict grounding in Scripture; 'providence' itself was shaken loose from its religious framework to become part of the belief in human progress. The Yankee Jeremiahs took advantage of this movement 'from sacred to profane' to shift the focus of figural authority. In effect they incorporated Bible history into the American experience – they substituted a regional for a biblical past, consecrated the American present as a movement from promise to fulfillment, and translated fulfillment from its meaning within the closed system of sacred history into a metaphor for limitless secular improvement.

All this was a matter of extension and adaptation, not of transformation. The Puritan clergy had set out to blur traditional distinctions between the world and the kingdom. Their rhetoric issued in a unique mode of ambiguity that precluded the heaven's time and man's. 'Canaan' was a spiritual state for them, as it was for other Christians; but it was also (in another, but not conflicting sense) their country. They spoke of the mutuality (rather than the coexistence) of fact and ideal. By 'church-state' they meant a separation of powers in the belief that in the American Canaan, and there only, the ecclesiastical and the civic order were not really distinct. *By their own contradictions they were made to correspond.*

[...]

One important reason for the success of the American Revolution was that its advocates had inherited a figural mode of consensus that could endorse Lockean universalism and yet exclude from it whatever then hindered the progress of the republic. The *American* was not (like the French *citoyen* or the Latin American *ciudadano*) a member of 'the people'. He stood for an errand that was limitless in effect, because it was limited in fact to a 'peculiar' nation. Thus (in the notorious paradox of the Declaration of Independence) he could denounce servitude, oppression, and inadequate representation while concerning himself least (if at all) with the most enslaved, oppressed and inadequately represented groups in the land. Those groups were part of 'the people', perhaps, but not the chosen people; part of America, but not the America of the Revolution. Through the ritual of the jeremiad, the leading patriots recast the Declaration to read 'all propertied Anglo-Saxon Protestant males are created equal'. Through that ritual, they *bound* and *tamed* the potential excesses of the early republic – on the one hand, the social demands of groups outside their middle-class consensus; on the other hand, the anarchy of unfettered self-interest. In short, they used the jeremiad to confine the concept of revolution to American progress, American progress to God's New Israel, and God's New Israel to people of their own kind. It is no accident that the debate at the turn of the nineteenth century between the Federalists and the Jeffersonians turned on which party was the legitimate heir to the title of the American Israel.[2] Nor is it by accident that under Jefferson's administration the Revolution issued in an increasing violation – for blacks and Indians – of life, liberty, and the pursuit of happiness. Nor is it accidental, finally, that while France and Latin America degenerated into factional pandemoniums, the American republic generated a conformist spirit that foreign observers termed a 'tyranny of the majority'.

Middle-class majority would have been more precise. Nationalism has served elsewhere to unify modern communities, but always by recourse to secular continuities from the past. Even when the national ideal makes universal claims, its basis remains local, historical, and complex. European national heroes, for all their representative qualities, are circumscribed by class and genealogy; the messianic dreams of German and Russian nationalism are rooted in atavistic distinctions of race, religion, and geography. The 'American' community, on the contrary, defines itself by its relation to the Revolution and the promised future; or, more accurately, by a continuing revolution based on '*a conception of the future as the present*'. Especially when its adherents invoke the legend of the fathers, as William Arthur does in his July Fourth oration, 'American' identity obviates the usual distinctions of national history – divisions of class, complexities of time and place – because the very meaning of 'American' involves a *cultural*, not a national, myth of consensus.[3] It is a testament to the power of this myth that our major nineteenth-century writers through Henry James could complain about the lack of history and diversity in the land. 'I have never seen a nation so much alike in my life, as the people of the United States,' wrote Cooper in *Notions of the Americans* (1828). He knew well enough about Indians and blacks, about differences between the urban rich, emigrant laborers, and rural gentry, about the variety of customs in the North, South, and West. So, too, did Hawthorne when in 1860 he described the United States as 'a country where there is no ... antiquity, no mystery, no picturesque and gloomy wrong, nor anything but a commonplace prosperity, in broad and simple daylight.' It was not ignorance or insensitivity that led to these wry complaints. It was merely, astonishingly, that in terms of the myth which Cooper and Hawthorne shared, such differences did not count. *Nation* meant *Americans* for them, *Americans* meant *the people*, and *the people* meant those who, thanks to the Revolution, enjoyed a *commonplace prosperity*: the simple, sunny rewards of American middle-class culture.

[...]

Indeed, the very proliferation of dissidents and reformers – the endless debate during the Middle Period about the true meaning of America – served to confirm the norms of the culture. What higher defense could one offer for middle-class society than an American Way that *sui generis* evoked the free competition of ideas? – and what could make this freedom safer for society than to define it in terms of the American Way? For by the logic of continuing revolution, any term blessed by the adjective American was a positive good; but by the same logic not everything in America was so blessed. Margaret Fuller could represent the American spirit to her supporters insofar as they denied that spirit to her no less representative antagonists. Both Henry Thoreau and William Arthur defined themselves as revolutionary Americans, but for each the definition entailed a rejection of the other. The state of tension that ensued proved an inexhaustible (because self-generating) source of exultation through lament. Under the slogan of continuing revolution, the ritual of the jeremiad spawned an astonishing variety of official or self-appointed committees on un-American activities: 'progressivist societies' for eradicating the Indians, 'benevolent societies' for deporting the blacks, 'Young Americans' for banning European culture, 'populists' obsessed with the spectre of foreign conspiracy, voluntary associations for safeguarding the Revolutionary tradition, male and female 'reform societies' for social regeneration through sexual purification.

In all cases, the ideal of *American* revolution ruled out any basic challenge to the system. In Europe and Latin America, the summons to 'the people', precisely because it was generalized and unbounded, exposed the pretense of unity; there, revolution bared the dialectics of historical change. In the United States, the summons to dissent, because it was grounded in a prescribed ritual form, preempted the threat of radical alternatives. Conflict itself was rendered a mode of control: a means of facilitating process through which process became an aid to socialization. Again, the plight of the mid-nineteenth-century feminists is instructive. On the one hand, it reminds us that the jeremiad has always restricted the ritual of consensus to a certain group within the culture. When William Arthur spoke of 'the American', he was not thinking of people like Margaret Fuller – or for that matter, of Frederick Douglass, Black Hawk, Rabbi Issac Meyer Wise, or John England, the Catholic Bishop of Charleston, South Carolina. But on the other hand, the feminist struggle reminds us that such restrictions were largely a matter of what Plotinus Plinlimmon called 'virtuous expediency'. For the fact is that the American consensus could also absorb feminism, so long as that would lead into the middle-class American Way. Blacks and Indians too could learn to be True Americans, when in the fullness of time they would adopt the tenets of black and red capitalism. John Brown could join Adams, Franklin, and Jefferson in the pantheon of Revolutionary heroes when it was understood that he wanted to fulfill (rather than undermine) the American dream. On that provision, Jews and even Catholics could eventually become sons and daughters of the American Revolution. On those grounds, even such unlikely candidates for perfection as Alaska, Hawaii, and Puerto Rico could become America.

[...]

The ritual of the jeremiad bespeaks an ideological consensus – in moral, religious, economic, social, and intellectual matters – unmatched in any other modern culture. And the power of consensus is nowhere more evident than in the symbolic meaning that the jeremiads infused into the term America. Only in the United States has nationalism carried with it the Christian meaning of the sacred. Only America, of all national designations, has assumed the combined force of eschatology and chauvinism. Many other societies have defended the *status quo* by reference to religious values; many forms of nationalism have laid claim to a world-redeeming promise; many Christian sects have sought, in secret or open heresy, to find the sacred in the profane, and many European defenders of middle-class democracy have tried to link order and progress. But only the American Way, of all modern ideologies, has managed to circumvent the paradoxes inherent in these approaches. Of all symbols of identity, only *America* has united nationality and universality, civic and spiritual selfhood, secular and redemptive history, the country's past and paradise to be, in a single synthetic ideal.

The symbol of America is the triumphant issue of early New England rhetoric and a long-ripened ritual of socialization.

[...]

The symbol took on an entirely different function from that of the religious symbols in which it was rooted. The revelation of the sacred serves to diminish, and ultimately to deny, the values of secular society. The revelation of America serves to blight, and ultimately to preclude, the possibility of fundamental social change. To condemn the profane is to commit oneself to a spiritual ideal. To condemn 'false Americans' as profane is to express one's faith in a national ideology. In effect, it is to transform what might have been a search for moral or social alternatives into a call for cultural revitalization. This had been the purpose of the New England Puritan Jeremiahs as well; but in their case the symbolic mode drew its authority from figural exegesis. Despite the secular-sacred correspondences they asserted, some conflict remained in their rhetoric (if only by sheer force of the tradition they invoked) between *Christian* on the one hand and *New Englander* or *American* on the other. And despite their insistent progressivism, the future they appealed to was necessarily limited, by the very prophecies they vaunted, to the ideals of the past. The American experience for them was a new, last book of Scripture, but Scripture itself was the Book of God, not 'the Bible of the Free'. As I noted earlier, New England Puritan symbology, like the theocracy itself, was a transitional mode, geared toward new forms of thought but trailing what Melville scornfully called the 'maxims of the Past'. For Melville, and all the major writers of the American Renaissance, America as symbol was its own reality, a totalistic bipolar system, sufficient to itself.

I do not mean to blur the differences between these writers, much less to reduce their works to ideology. On the contrary, I invoke them precisely because of their well-known divergence from 'popular culture', in order to indicate the pervasive impact of the American jeremiad. Let me say at once, to avoid all misunderstanding, that all our classic writers (to varying degrees) labored against the myth as well as within it. All of them felt, privately at least, as oppressed by Americanism as liberated by it. And all of them, however captivated by the national dream, also *used* the dream to reach beyond the categories of their culture. To speak of their cultural limitations may be no more than to speak of Chaucer's debt to the medieval world picture. Still, their case seems to me somewhat special. For one thing, critics of American literature have tended to ignore cultural limitations, or else to translate these into quasi-mystical terms, as though the American Renaissance were the embodiment of some New World spirit. Clearly, such terms have their source in the symbol of America – but in this case they seem to derive directly from the great works of our literary tradition. This points to the second, more important reason for insisting that that tradition was the expression of a particular society. Chaucer wrote openly from within his culture. American writers have tended to see themselves as outcasts and isolates, prophets crying in the wilderness. So they have been, as a rule: *American* Jeremiahs, simultaneously lamenting a declension and celebrating a national dream. Their major works are the most striking testimony we have to the power and reach of the American jeremiad.

NOTES

1. Nicholas Noyes, *New-Englands Duty* (Boston, 1698), p. 43.
2. The Federalists, wrote Nathaniel Howe in a typical Jeffersonian attack, were modern 'Pharaohs', seeking to return God's Country to an Old World bondage (*An Oration* [Portland, ME, 1805], p. 6). The characteristic Federalist response was that the Jeffersonians were, like Absalom, rebels in 'the land of promise' (James Sloan, *An Oration Delivered* [Trenton, NJ, 1802], p. 22).
3. This mode of filiopietism, Arthur's oration makes clear, also carries in it a marked ambivalence. The examples of the past do not resolve problems, as in other national or tribal rituals. Instead, they heighten the anxiety of process. Sometimes this leads to a fear of betrayal: the past may prove an outmoded guidebook to the future, as Melville suggests in *Redburn* and other works. Arthur would not agree with Melville that, according to America's 'express dispensation', it is 'the part of wisdom to pay homage to the prospective precedents of the Future in preference to those of the Past' (*White-Jacket; or, The World in a Man-of-War*, Hennig Cohen (ed.) [New York, 1967], pp. 149–50); but this view was latent in the outlook both men inherited from the New England Puritans, with its overriding emphasis on emulation as fulfillment. Charles Sprague's July Fourth dictum, 'In place of the fathers shall be the children' (*Oration* [Boston, 1825], p. 25), may be traced back to Cotton Mather and forward through Emerson into our own time.

16

PROTESTANT – CATHOLIC – JEW

Will Herberg

Americans believe in religion in a way that perhaps no other people do. It may indeed be said that the primary religious affirmation of the American people, in harmony with the American Way of Life, is that religion is a 'good thing', a supremely 'good thing', for the individual and the community. And 'religion' here means not so much any particular religion, but religion as such. 'Our government makes no sense,' President Eisenhower recently declared, 'unless it is founded in a deeply felt religious faith-*and I don't care what it is*' (emphasis added).[1] In saying this, the President was saying something that almost any American could understand and approve, but which must seem like a deplorable heresy to the European churchman. Every American could understand, first, that Mr. Eisenhower's apparent indifferentism ('and I don't care what it is') was not indifferentism at all, but the expression of the conviction that at bottom the 'three great faiths' were really 'saying the same thing' in affirming the 'spiritual ideals' and 'moral values' of the American Way of Life. Every American, moreover, could understand that what Mr Eisenhower was emphasizing so vehemently was the indispensability of religion as the foundation of society. This is one aspect of what Americans mean when they say that they 'believe in religion'. The object of devotion of this kind of religion, however, is 'not God but "religion" ... The faith is not in God but in faith; we worship not God but our own worshiping.'[2] When Americans think of themselves as a profoundly religious people, whose 'first allegiance' is 'reserved ... to the

---

From: Will Herberg, *Protestant–Catholic–Jew* (Garden City, NY: Doubleday & Co., 1955).

kingdom of the spirit',[3] this is, by and large, what they mean, and not any commitment to the doctrines or traditions of the historic faiths.

With this view of religion is associated a closely analogous view of the church. For America, the celebrated dichotomy of 'church' and 'sect,'[4] however pertinent it may be to European conditions, has only a secondary significance. The concept of the church as the nation religiously organized, established socially, if not always legally, has no relevance whatever to American reality; and though America does know sects in the sense of 'fringe' groups of the 'disinherited', it does not understand these groups and their relation to the more conventional churches the way Europe does. An entirely new conception of church and church institutions has emerged in America.

It must be remembered that in America the variety and multiplicity of churches did not, as in Europe, come with the breakdown of a single established national church; in America, taking the nation as a whole, the variety and multiplicity of churches was almost the original condition and coeval with the emergence of the new society. In America religious pluralism is thus not merely a historical and political fact; it is, in the mind of the American, the primordial condition of things, an essential aspect of the American Way of Life, and therefore in itself an aspect of religious belief.[5] Americans, in other words, believe that the plurality of religious groups is a proper and legitimate condition. However much he may be attached to his own church, however dimly he may regard the beliefs and practices of other churches, the American tends to feel rather strongly that total religious uniformity, even with his own church benefiting thereby, would be something undesirable and wrong, indeed scarcely conceivable. Pluralism of religions and churches is something quite axiomatic to the American. This feeling, more than anything else, is the foundation of the American doctrine of the 'separation of church and state', for it is the heart of this doctrine that the government may not do anything that implies the pre-eminence or superior legitimacy of one church over another.

This means that outside the Old World distinction of church and sect America has given birth to a new type of religious structure – the denomination.[6] The denomination as we know it is a stable, settled church, enjoying a legitimate and recognized place in a larger aggregate of churches, each recognizing the proper status of the others.[7] The denomination is the 'non-conformist sect' become central and normative. It differs from the church in the European understanding of the term in that it would never dream of claiming to be *the* national ecclesiastical institution; it differs from the sect in that it is socially established, thoroughly institutionalized, and nuclear to the society in which it is found. The European dichotomy becomes meaningless, and instead we have the nuclear denomination on the one side, and the peripheral sect on the way to becoming a denomination on the other. So firmly entrenched is this denominational idea in the mind of the American that even American Catholics have come to think in such terms; theologically the Catholic Church of course continues to regard itself as the one true church, but in their actual social attitudes American Catholics, hardly less than American Protestants or Jews, tend to think of their church as a denomination existing side by side with other denominations in a pluralistic harmony that is felt to be somehow of the texture of American life.[8]

Denominational pluralism, as the American idea of the church may be called, obviously implies that no church can look to the state for its members or support. Voluntarism and evangelism are thus the immediate consequences of the American idea: for their maintenance, for their very existence, churches must depend on the voluntary adherence of their members, and they are therefore moved to pursue a vigorous evangelistic work to win people to their ranks. The accommodation of the church to American reality extends even to its inner polity. 'As the polity of the Roman church followed the pattern of the Roman empire,' H. Richard Niebuhr points out, 'so the American churches incline to organize themselves [along representative lines] in conformity with the system of state and national legislatures and executives.'[9] Even the Roman Catholic Church, with its fixed hierarchical structure, has not been totally immune to American influence of this kind.[10]

The denominational idea is fundamental to American thinking about religion, but it is not the last word. Americans think of their various churches as denominations, but they also feel that somehow the denominations fall into larger wholes which we have called religious communities. This kind of denominational aggregation is, of course, something that pertains primarily to Protestantism and to a lesser degree to Judaism; both have more or less organized denominations which, taken together, form the religious communities. Catholicism, on the other hand, has no such overt inner divisions, but American Catholics readily understand the phenomenon when they see it among Protestants and Jews. Denominations are felt to be somehow a matter of individual preference, and movement between denominations is not uncommon; the religious community, on the other hand, is taken as something more objective and given, something in which, by and large, one is born, lives, and dies, something that (to recall our earlier analysis) identifies and defines one's position in American society.[11] Since the religious community in its present form is a recent social emergent, its relations to the denominations properly so-called are still relatively fluid and undefined but the main lines of development would seem to be fairly clear.

When the plurality of denominations comprehended in religious communities is seen from the standpoint of the 'common faith' of American society, what emerges is the conception of the three 'communions' – Protestantism, Catholicism, Judaism – as three diverse, but equally legitimate, equally American, expressions of an over-all American religion, standing for essentially the same 'moral ideals' and 'spiritual values'. This conception, whatever may be thought of it theologically, is in fact held, though hardly in explicit form, by many devout and religiously sophisticated Americans. It would seem to be the obvious meaning of the title, *The Religions of Democracy*, given to a recent authoritative statement of the Protestant, Catholic, and Jewish positions.[12] 'Democracy' apparently has its religions which fall under it as species fall under the genus of which they are part. And in this usage 'democracy' is obviously a synonym for the American Way of Life.

[...]

The 'common faith' of American society is not merely a civic religion to celebrate the values and convictions of the American people as a corporate entity. It has its inner, personal aspects as well; or rather, side by side and in intimate relation with the civic religion of the American Way of Life, there has developed, primarily through a devitalization of the historic faiths, an inner, personal religion that promises salvation to the disoriented, tormented souls of a society in crisis.

This inner, personal religion is based on the American's *faith in faith*. We have seen that a primary religious affirmation of the American is his belief in religion. The American believes that religion is something very important for the community; he also believes that 'faith', or what we may call religiosity, is a kind of 'miracle drug' that can cure all the ailments of the spirit. It is not faith in *anything* that is so powerful, just faith, the 'magic of believing'. 'It was back in those days,' a prominent American churchman writes, recalling his early years, 'that I formed a habit that I have never broken. I began saying in the morning two words, "I believe". Those two words *with nothing added* ... give me a running start for my day, and for every day' (emphasis not in original).[13]

The cult of faith takes two forms, which we might designate as introvert and extrovert. In its introvert form faith is trusted to bring mental health and 'peace of mind', to dissipate anxiety and guilt, and to translate the soul to the blessed land of 'normality' and 'self-acceptance'. In earlier times this cult of faith was quite literally a cult of 'faith healing', best expressed in what H. Richard Niebuhr has described as the 'man-centered, this-wordly, lift-yourselves-by-your-own-bootstraps doctrine of New Thought and Christian Science'.[14] Latterly it has come to vest itself in the fashionable vocabulary of psycho-analysis and is offering a synthesis of religion and psychiatry.[15] But at bottom it is the same cult of faith in faith, the same promise that through 'those two words, "I believe", with nothing added,' all our troubles will be dissipated and inner peace and harmony restored.

The cult of faith has also its extrovert form, and that is known as 'positive thinking', 'Positive thinking', thinking that is 'affirmative' and avoids the corrosions of 'negativity' and 'skepticism', thinking that 'has faith', is recommended as a powerful force in the world of struggle and achievement.[16] Here again it is not so much faith in anything, certainly not the theocentric faith of the historic religions, that is supposed to confer this power – but just faith, the psychological attitude of having faith, so to speak. And here too the cult is largely the product of the inner disintegration and enfeeblement of the historic religions; the familiar words are retained, but the old meaning is voided. 'Have faith', 'don't lose faith', and the like, were once injunctions to preserve one's unwavering trust in the God from Whom comes both the power to live and the 'peace that passeth understanding'. Gradually these phrases have come to be an appeal to maintain a 'positive' attitude to life and not to lose confidence in oneself and one's activities. 'To believe in yourself and in everything you do': such, at bottom, is the meaning of the contemporary cult of faith, whether it is proclaimed by devout men from distinguished pulpits or offered as the 'secret of success' by self-styled psychologists who claim to have discovered the 'hidden powers' of man.[17] What is important is faith, faith in faith. Even where the classical symbols and formulas are still retained, that is very often what is meant and what is understood.

Such are some major aspects of the social, cultural, and spiritual environment in which religion in America moves and has its being. And religion in America means the three great religious communities, the Protestant, the Catholic, and the Jewish.

[...]

The outstanding feature of the religious situation in America today is the pervasiveness of religious self-identification along the tripartite scheme of Protestant, Catholic, Jew. From the 'land of immigrants', America has, as we have seen, become the 'triple melting pot', restructured in three great communities with religious labels, defining three great 'communions' or 'faiths'. This transformation has been greatly furthered by what may be called the dialectic of 'third generation interest': the third generation, coming into its own with the cessation of mass immigration, tries to recover its 'heritage', so as to give itself some sort of 'name', or context of self-identification and social location, in the larger society. 'What the son wishes to forget' – so runs 'Hansen's Law' – 'the grandson wishes to remember'. But what he can 'remember' is obviously not his grandfather's foreign language, or even his grandfather's foreign culture; it is rather his grandfather's *religion* – America does not demand of him the abandonment of the ancestral religion as it does of the ancestral language and culture. This religion he now 'remembers' in a form suitably 'Americanized', and yet in a curious way also 'retraditionalized'. Within this comprehensive framework of basic sociological change operate those inner factors making for a 'return to religion' which so many observers have noted in recent years – the collapse of all secular securities in the historical crisis of our time, the quest for a recovery of meaning in life, the new search for inwardness and personal authenticity amid the collectivistic heteronomies of the present-day world.

Self-identification in religious terms, almost universal in the America of today, obviously makes for religious belonging in a more directly institutional way. It engenders a sense of adherence to a church or denomination and impels one to institutional affiliation. These tendencies are reinforced by the pressures of other-directed adjustment to peer-group behavior, which today increasingly requires religious identification and association with some church. Thus a pattern of religious conformism develops, most pronounced, perhaps, among the younger, 'modern-minded' inhabitants of Suburbia, but rapidly spreading to all sections of the American people.

The picture that emerges is one in which religion is accepted as a normal part of the American Way of Life. Not to be – that is, not to identify oneself and be identified as – either a Protestant, a Catholic, or a Jew is somehow not to be an American. It may imply being foreign, as is the case when one professes oneself a Buddhist, a Muslim, or anything but a Protestant, Catholic, or Jew, even when one's Americanness is otherwise beyond question. Or it may imply being obscurely 'un-American', as is the case with those who declare themselves atheists, agnostics, or even 'humanists'. Sidney H. Scheuer, a leading Ethical Culturist, was expressing a genuine concern when he stated recently: 'There is a tendency to regard all people who are not committed to one of the three great faiths as being disloyal to American principles and traditions.'[18] Americanness today entails religious identification as Protestant, Catholic, or Jew in a way and to a degree quite unprecedented in our history. To be a Protestant, a Catholic, or a Jew are today the alternative ways of being an American.

NOTES

1. *The New York Times*, 23 December 1952; see also G. Elson Ruff, *The Dilemma of Church and State* (Muhlenberg, 1954), p. 85.
2. Miller, 'Piety Along the Potomaq'. *The Reporter*, 17 August 1954. Mr. Miller continues: 'If the object of devotion is not God but "religion" ... then the resulting religiosity may become simply the instrument of more substantial commitments'. The most 'substantial' commitment of the American people, to which their 'religiosity' is instrumental, is the American Way of Life.
3. Dwight D. Eisenhower, quoted in Paul Hutchinson, 'The President's Religious Faith', *The Christian Century*, 24 March, 1954.
4. See Ernst Troeltsch, *The Social Teaching of the Christian Churches* (1911; trans. by Olive Wyon, Macmillan, 1931), Vol. I, pp. 331–49, Vol. II, pp. 691–728; also J. Milton Yinger, *Religion in the Struggle for Power* (Duke, 1946), pp. 16–50.
5. Williams speaks of a 'value-consensus in which religious differences are subsidiary to the values of religious liberty' (*American Society*, p. 345).
6. 'The Mormons, the Orthodox Jews, and a few small religious communities are religiously organized peoples, but almost all other religious bodies in the United States, including the Roman Catholic Church, are neither national churches nor sects; they are commonly known as denominations or "communions"' (*Schneider, Religion in 20th Century America*, p. 22). Even the groups Schneider mentions an exceptions, insofar as they have become acculturated to American life, would seem to fall into the same pattern.
7. Since most American denominations emerged from earlier sects, denominations have sometimes been defined as 'simply sects in an advanced stage of development and adjustment to each other and the secular world' (Leopold von Wiese, *Systematic Sociology*, adapted and amplified by Howard Becker [Wiley, 1932], p. 626). There is, of course, a good deal of truth in this definition; its defect, however, is that it regards the denomination as essentially transitional between sect and church, which is emphatically not the case with denominations in the American sense. American denominations have indeed, by and large, developed out of sects, but they represent the final stage of development, rather than a transitional stage to something else ('church' in the European sense). For a more general discussion, see Joachin Wach,

Types of Religious Experience (Routledge and Kegan Paul, 1951), ch. ix, 'Church, Denomination, and Sect'.

8. In a number of European countries (Germany, Holland, Switzerland), Protestant and Catholic churches have reached a kind of balance in which neither can pretend to be 'the' national church. But where this is the case, it is simply a social and historical fact, not the proper and normative condition. In America, on the other hand, the plurality of churches is held to be proper and normative; in this the American situation differs fundamentally from the European, even where the latter seems to resemble it most.

9. H. Richard Niebuhr, *The Social Sources of Denominationalism*, p. 207. Cf. the statement of Franklin Clark Fry, president of the United Lutheran Church of America. 'The polity of our church as a whole is frankly constructed on a secular model. Its prototype is the government of the United States' (quoted in H. E. F., 'Lutherans Centralize', *The Christian Century*, 27 October 1954).

10. Thus McAvoy speaks of the 'practical and parochial character of American Catholicism'; the 'parochial' character he relates to the 'American tradition of disestablishment', while for the 'practical' aspect of American Catholinism, he notes that 'some observers have claimed that [it] is the product of the puritanism dominant in American Protestantism' (Thomas T. McAvoy, 'The Catholic Church in the United States', in Waldemar Gurian and M. A. Fitzsimons, *The Catholic Church in World Affairs* [Notre Dame, 1954], pp. 364, 361).

11. Despite all the instability of American life, fully ninety-six per cent of Americans were found in 1955 still belonging to the religious community of their birth (see *Public Opinion News Service*, 20 March 1955).

12. Louis Finkelstein, J. Elliot Ross and William Adams Brown, *The Religions of Democracy: Judaism, Catholicism, and Protestantism in Creed and Life* (Devin-Adair, 1946). One of the clearest expressions of this conception by a layman was voiced by Admiral William F. Halsey, principal speaker at the fifth annual 'four chaplains award dinner'. 'This picture,' Admiral Halsey declared, 'is symbolic of our national life. Protestant, Catholic, and Jew, each group has given, when called upon, the full measure of devotion in defense of our [American democratic] way of life' (*The New York Times*, 6 February 1955).

13. Daniel A. Poling, 'A Running Start for Every Day', *Parade: The Sunday Picture Magazine*, 19 September 1954.

14. H. Richard Niebuhr, *The Social Sources of Denominationalism*, p. 104. Niebuhr thus describes this type of religiosity in which the old Puritan spirituality has terminated: 'In its final phase, the development of this religious movement exhibits the complete enervation of the once virile force ... the problem of evil [has been] simplified out of existence, and for the mysterious will of the Sovereign of life and death and sin and salvation [has been substituted] the sweet benevolence of a Father-Mother God or the vague goodness of the All. Here the concern for self has been secularized to its last degree; the conflicts of sick souls have been replaced by the struggles of sick minds and bodies; the Puritan passion for perfection has become a seeking after the kingdom of health and mental peace and its comforts' (p. 105).

15. The most celebrated effort along these lines is undoubtedly Joshua Loth Liebman, *Peace of Mind* (Simon and Schuster, 1946).

16. Norman Vincent Peale, *The Power of Positive Thinking* (Prentice-Hall, 1952).

17. A salesman writes to Norman Vincent Peale in the latter's regular question page in *Look*: 'I have lost my faith and enthusiasm. How can I get them back?' To which Dr. Peale replies: 'Every morning, give thanks for the new day and its opportunities. Think outgoingly of every prospect you will call on ... Affirm aloud that you are going to have a great day. Flush out all depressing, negative, and tired thoughts. Start thinking faith, enthusiasm and joy ...' ('Norman Vincent Peale Answers Your Questions', *Look*, 10 August 1954). This may be compared with an advertisement

for a quite 'secular' self-help book in *The New York Times Magazine* for 8 May 1949:

DON'T WORRY
If you don't acknowledge it,
it isn't so!
Develop the Art of Adaptability

18. Sidney H. Scheuer, a vice president of the American Ethical Union, in an address to the annual assembly of that organization, St. Louis, April 1954; reported in *Information Service* (National Council of the Churches of Christ), 30 October 1954.

SECTION 3
REPUBLICANISM

The section on Republicanism begins with the treatment by John G. A. Pocock of the subject in the last part of his study *The Machiavellian Moment – Florentine Political Thought and the Republican Tradition*. In this modern classic of intellectual history, Pocock traced the thinking of most of the founders back to a tradition of political thought that was first coherently conceptualised in the small city republics in northern Italy. From there the tradition migrated to England, where republican ideas were influential but never became so powerful as to influence or shape British institutions for any long period. Generally, republicanism in the British Isles remained a subordinated tradition. However, English oppositional thought finally travelled to the New World, where the thinking about republican virtue became Americanised and achieved political realisation in the period 1776–90. Pocock argues that the republican element played a much larger influential role in America than has been assumed. Joyce Appleby appreciates the new line of investigation that was triggered by Pocock's study, particularly against the approaches that had previously prevailed: in particular, liberalism and Marxism. However, as Appleby also argues in *Liberalism and Republicanism in the Historical Imagination*, there still remains a lot be done. Exactly where the interface is between republicanism and liberalism and where possible clashes between the two lines of thought emerged needs to be determined by further historical research.

Hannah Arendt also discusses American republicanism and how it compares to its French counterpart. In Arendt's influential book *On Revolution* the argument is less informed by historical inquiry and the origins of republicanism than why one republican model – the American – succeeded while the other – the French – failed in terms of establishing free republican institutions? Hannah Arendt's answer here is that the American founders were more inclined to argue about individual rights, political equality and freedom. Theirs was truly a new beginning while the French Revolutionaries got caught up in the European past and were preoccupied with social questions and how to come to terms with class and social inequality.

A look into the *Federalist Papers* reveals how the Founding Fathers thought about these questions. The excerpts that are reprinted here show that James Madison, Alexander Hamilton and John Jay were concerned with the question of how republican and democratic thought – until then only put to practical test in small units and communities such as city states – could be applied to new conditions and changed circumstances in America, that is to a large territory that was still expanding. As Judith N. Shklar explains in an influential essay, entitled 'Montesquieu and the New Republicanism' (published in her essay collection *Political Thought and Political Thinkers*) the Founding Fathers were not only exposed to and influenced by classical republican thought but were also influenced by the French political philosopher Montesquieu, who had already tried to rethink modern government. In order to reform the French government of the time, Montesquieu had argued that the English political system with its insistence on the rule of law and its division of power showed the way to reform. In the end, as Shklar shows, the American founders went even further in their critique of small unit democracy than Montesquieu, but it was the French philosopher's work which had opened the path to the ideas of constitutional government, new forms of representation – and finally federalism.

The remainder of the section on republicanism offers two modern variations on the republican theme. In an essay entitled 'The Compromised Republic' (published in the essay collection *A Passion for Democracy*) the political scientist Benjamin Barber takes issue with the adversary model in the American political system where almost everything comes in twos (federalism, political parties, the legal system). Planned as a system in which checks and balances kept the egoism and interests of the players in place, the increased complexity of the system in modern times had prevented almost any meaningful political initiative from taking off or had brought it to a standstill. Sheldon S. Wolin is of the opinion that the original republican design was flawed or at least ambivalent. It preferred citizens to be above all loyal and thus left little room for the development of a modern multiple civic self. In an essay entitled 'Democracy without the Citizen', from his book *The Presence of the Past*, written to assess the history of 200 years of the American constitution, Wolin argues against a conception of the republic whose ideal of politics is that of a 'politics of management', not a 'politics of citizens'.

17

THE MACHIAVELLIAN MOMENT – FLORENTINE POLITICAL THOUGHT AND THE ATLANTIC REPUBLICAN TRADITION

John G. A. Pocock

If corruption was to be avoided, there must be virtue within equality; and the still largely Christian minds of eighteenth-century civic humanists had sought to ensure this by employing the classical differentiation into one, few, and many to make the people a trinity-in-unity, within which there could be relationship and hence virtue. But this orthodoxy now seemed to be failing. The *materia* was beginning to seem too monophysite and one-dimensional to be given form, and the paradigm of the *zōon politikon* was in danger. There is an audible note of dismay in the American writings of the early 1780s.

Wood traces, through the rich complexity of the utterances of this period – all articulate Americans seem to have been versed in the vocabulary of the sociology of liberty – the emergence of a new paradigm of democratic politics, designed by the masters of Federalist theory to overcome the crisis caused by the failure of natural aristocracy – though whether they intended to replace the last-named, or to restore it, is not always clear. The crucial revision was that of the concept of the people. Instead of being differentiated into diversely qualified and functioning groups, the people was left in so monastic a condition that it mattered little what characteristics it was thought of as possessing; and the various agencies of government – still essentially the legislature, judiciary, and executive of separation theory – were thought of as exercised not immediately, by social groups possessing the relevant capacities, but mediately, by individuals whose title to authority was that they acted as representing the

From: John G. A. Pocock, *The Machiavellian Moment* (Princeton, NJ: Princeton University Press, 1975).

people. All power was entrusted to representatives, and every mode of exercising power was a model of representing the people. If the people were an undifferentiated mass, possessed of infinitely diverse qualities, they possessed also an infinite capacity for differentiating between diverse modes of power and embodying themselves in correspondingly diverse means of representation. They had come a long way from the Florentine *materia*.

There was a distinction between the exercise of power in government, and the power of designating representatives to exercise it; and it could be argued both that all government was the people's and that the people had withdrawn from government altogether, leaving its exercise to a diversity of representatives who, situated as they were where the art of ruling might be learned from experience, took on the characteristics of the old natural aristocracy or specialized Few. Rousseau, with his insistence that the *volonté générale* should never engage in the taking of particular decisions, might have approved of this distinction between a constituent and a governing people; and he might have joined the Federalists in seeing Machiavelli's *ridurre* ensured in the provision that the power of constitutional revision was always in the people and its exercise always potentially imminent.[1] Here, at least, the people as such were active in a fairly immediate sense. What Rousseau would not have approved – and what is no part of the republican tradition as we have studied it – is the universal intervention in government of the relation between represented and representative; and here certainly the character of Federalist thought is medieval rather than classical and sovereign rather than republican – Hobbesian, it might even be added, rather than Lockean.

[...]

In Revolutionary America, the tide had been running strongly in favor of the view that elected representatives were highly corruptible delegates, who must be subject to instruction and recall; but Madison seems to have leaned toward a Burkean position which presented their role as that of a Few, and their ranks as to be filled, if possible, by members of the patrician elites.[2] The crucial question remained, however, that raised by Rousseau. Given that a natural aristocracy had not emerged, and was not expected to emerge, from the electoral process, was the mere act of choosing a representative, the mere relationship between representative and elector, sufficient to ensure virtue? For some Federalists the answer was predetermined. If there was no natural aristocracy, the people could not be virtuous; if none had emerged, the most probable explanation was that the people were already corrupt; government accordingly became a Guicciardinian affair of guiding a people who were not virtuous, or helping them guide themselves, along paths as satisfactory as could be hoped for in these circumstances. This perspective, of course, did not prevent those who adopted it from regarding themselves as members of a virtuous natural aristocracy, Catos of the deserving side. Madison's position, as we shall see, was more complex; but Wood shows that the Federalists talked both as if virtue was to be restored, and as if it had vanished and must be replaced by new paradigms,[3] And it was, as always, difficult to hit upon surrogates for virtue in its classical sense. There was this to be said for Rousseau's critique of representation. Virtue consisted in a particular being's regard for the common good, and was contingent upon his association with other particular beings who regarded the same good through different eyes. The differentiation of Few from Many, of natural aristocracy from natural democracy, was the paradigm case of this association between men of different qualities; and without some theory of qualitative and moral differentiation between individuals, it was hard to see how the relations between citizens that constituted virtue could be established. The act of choosing a person to act for me, one with whom I asserted an artificial identity, could never be the same as that of recognizing a person who acted with me, and with whom I formed a natural association. This was why it was hard to see the relation of representative to represented as one of classical virtue. Neither the Federalists nor their critics employed Rousseau as a tool of analysis,[4] but there are perceptible tensions between their remodeling of the theory of representation and their unwillingness to abandon the paradigm of the republic of virtue.

They sought – so successfully as to bring about something like a paradigmatic revolution – to reconcile the two by developing a theory of multiple representation. Instead of a medieval or Hobbesian identity, natural or artificial, between the representative and the represented as simple entities, they asserted that there was a plurality of modes of exercising power and that every one of these – the quasi-classical executive, judiciary, and legislative were the obvious examples – constituted a separate mode in which the people chose to be represented. The people's representatives taken as individuals formed a plurality of functionally differentiated groups, and to that extent might still be looked upon as a natural aristocracy; the plurality of functions which they exercised ensured the existence between and among them of a system of checks and balances, so that it could be said they were prevented from becoming corrupt, or corrupting the people, by any one's acquiring so much power as to bring the rest into dependence.[5] The rhetoric of the classical tradition, from Aristotle to Montesquieu, thus remained appropriate over wide fields of the phenomena presented by the new government; but beneath it – and accounting for the widespread belief that the concept of representation was the only great discovery in theoretical politics made since antiquity – lay that sharply new perspective which leads Wood to speak of an 'end of classical politics'. The people were still thought of as uncorrupted, but there were important senses in which they need not and could not be said to affirm their virtue in action. They were not differentiated into groups of diverse quality and function, each of which exercised citizenship in its own way and between which there existed the relationships of virtue; nor, since they were not politically active in a diversity of ways functionally differentiated, could it strictly be said that they were directly or immediately engaged in governing at all. They were directly engaged in the choice of representatives, and the multiplicity of the federal structure ensured that this function could be seen as ongoing and perpetual; they were also constituent, directly engaged in the establishment and revision of constitutions, and there are passages of rhetoric which suggest that this too was seen as a continuous activity.[6] Even Machiavelli, the most kinetic of republican theorists, had seen *ridurre* and *ripigliare lo stato* as no more than an affair of exemplary purges at intervals of a few years; even Rousseau had envisaged no more than occasional if frequent assemblies of the sovereign people, for the duration of which any constitution was necessarily suspended. If Federalist theory surpassed tradition at this point too, it is important to understand how.

The decline of virtue had as its logical corollary the rise of interest.[7] If men no longer enjoyed the conditions thought necessary to make them capable of perceiving the common good, all that each man was capable of perceiving was his own particular interest; and to the extent that there survived the very ancient presumption that only perception of the common good was truly rational, perception of one's interest was primarily a matter of appetite and passion and only secondarily of profit-and-loss rational calculation which might extend so far as perception of one's interest as interdependent with that of another's. Non-virtuous man was a creature of his passions and fantasies, and when passion was contrasted with virtue its corruptive potential remained high; but we have already seen how in eighteenth-century theory fantasy and commerce could appear an explosive and transforming force, possessing the dynamism if also the limitations of Machiavellian *virtù*, and rather more than the latter's capacity to transform the natures of men. Interest was both a limiting and an expanding force. As Federalist thought took shape, and the people were less and less seen as possessing virtue in the classical sense, it is not surprising to find, in Madison's writings and those of others – the tenth issue of *The Federalist* is the *locus classicus* – an increasing recognition of the importance, and the legitimacy, in human affairs of the faction pursuing a collective but particular interest,[8] which in older Country and republican theory had figured as one of the most deadly means to the corruption of virtue by passion. Interest and faction are the modes in which the decreasingly virtuous people discern and pursue their activities in politics; but in Madison's thought two consequences soon follow. In the first place, the checks, balances, and separations of powers, to be built into the federal structure, ensure as we have seen that interest does not corrupt, so that the full rhetoric of balance and stability can still be invoked in praise of an edifice no longer founded in virtue, and the very fact that it is no longer so founded can easily be masked and forgotten.[9] In the second place, there are passages which strikingly indicate that the capacity of this structure for absorbing and reconciling conflicting interests is without known limits.[10] There is no interest which cannot be represented and given its place in the distribution of power – only the most peculiar of institutions, it has seemed to historians in the Federalist tradition, was to prove an exception to this rule – and should the growth and change of the people generate new interests, the federal republic can grow and change to accommodate them.

In this 'end of classical politics', Wood detects primarily a partial shift from republicanism to liberalism[11] – from, that is to say, the classical theory of the individual as civic and active being, directly participant in the *res publica* according to his measure, toward (if not fully reaching) a theory in which he appears as conscious chiefly of his interest and takes part in government in order to press for its realization, making only an indirect contribution to that mediating activity whereby government achieves a reconciliation of conflicts which is all the common good there is. In this sense, representative democracy involves a recession, on the part of both individual and 'people', from direct participation in government, of which the 'decline of virtue' is the measure; but it does not involve political quiescence or a lowering of tensions. It also coincides with a vast expansion of party activity and appeal to a highly responsible electorate. Wood further detects in Madison a dimension of thought which is kinetic and romantic. Because 'the people' is now undifferentiated, it is not circumscribed by the definition and distribution of specific qualities. It is of unknown mass and force, and can develop new and unpredicted needs, capacities, and powers. All of these can be received and coordinated within the structure of federalism, so that the classical rhetoric of balance and stability is still appropriate, but this structure can be proclaimed capable of indefinite expansion, since there is no need to insist in advance that the new social elements which will seek representation be those previously conceived as part of the harmonics of virtue. They are not perceived rationally as elements in the architecture of the common good, but as interests conceived and pursued in passion; the federal structure, however, is capable of absorbing new passions and grows by absorbing them. If the people are perpetually constituent, therefore, this is because they and their republic are in perpetual and kinetic growth. The republic of represented interests is a commonwealth for expansion. Something has been lost to virtue, but more has been gained by *virtù*. The liberal structure is not tame or sedate; like archetypal Rome before it, it is at once stable and expansive.

Wood's 'end of classical politics' is at bottom predicated upon an abandonment of the closely related paradigms of deference and virtue. Because natural aristocracy failed the Americans in the moment of classical *rinnovazione*, they had to abandon any theory of the people as qualitatively differentiated, and therefore either virtuous in the classical sense or participant in government in ways directly related to personality; and at the heart of Federalist thought arose something akin to the paradoxes of Rousseau – all government was the people's, and yet the people never directly governed. This price once paid, the advantages of the great restatement of paradigms which accompanied the conservative revolution of 1787–9 were enormous. It permitted the overcoming of the widely accepted limitation which enjoined republics to be of finite size if they would escape corruption; the new federation could be both republic and empire, continental in its initial dimensions and capable of further expansion by means of simple extensions of the federative principle, greatly surpassing the semimilitary complex of colonies and provinces which had extended the Roman hegemony. It permitted the growth of new modes of association in pursuit of particular ends – political parties which, it has been argued by Chambers,[12] were modern in precisely the sense that they were not based on deference, and which mobilized participant energies on a scale undreamed of in ancient republics. It is not surprising, then, that Wood and Chambers tend to speak of deference as the principle of the classical republic, and that republic itself as a subspecies of the closed and stable social hierarchy;[13] though less cautious proponents of this view are (and long have been) open to the criticism that they confound the natural with the hereditary aristocracy.

But our pursuit of the Machiavellian consequences of the republican principle that virtue is active has led us through realms of consciousness in which deference was not passive and the republic was not a hierarchy. We have grown used to thinking of virtue as active in a world of proportionately equal citizens, and the republic as expanding beyond the confines of that world through the exercise of *virtù*. In the Polybian and Machiavellian tradition, the republic was not simply and naturally finite, and the injunction to remain small must not be misread. It faced the dilemma, born of its finitude, that it could escape neither expansion nor the corruption that followed expansion. The American republic proposed from its inception to offer a fresh solution to this ancient problem; the terms of this solution were in some respects dramatically new, but in others a restatement of old. We have further grown used to the existence in British thought of an alternative or 'Court' ideology, which emphasized that men were guided by interest and passion, that factions and parties were necessary rather than illegitimate, and that government must be carried on by a sovereign power, ultimately unchecked but capable of subdivision into self-balancing powers, which ruled men partly by direct authority, partly by appeal to those passions, and partly by conversion of those passions into perception of a common interest. It should be clear by now that important elements of this ideology reappear in Federalist theory at just the points where the latter moves away from virtue and toward interest.

There are, however, some major and obvious differences. Where the Court thesis locates sovereignty in a parliamentary monarchy, self-balanced by the distinction between executive and legislative but held together by the influence which the former wields in the latter, the Federalist thesis locates it in the represented people and maintains the separation of powers with a rigor which is republican rather than merely Country. Once again we are at the point where the full rhetoric of republicanism was entirely appropriate to Federalist purposes, and the extent to which virtue was being abandoned could be masked to speakers as well as audiences. Where the Court thesis appealed to a version of history in which there were pragmatic adjustments and no fundamental principles, the Federalists could and did claim to be founding a republic in an extra-historical and legislative moment – one of *occasione* – in which the principles of nature, including balance and even virtue, were being reaffirmed. Their kinetic and expansive vision was of the future, and carried with it no Machiavellian sense of being part of an already disorderly *saeculum*. Finally, the Court thesis, originating as we have seen in the collisions of war and credit finance with the presumed stability of landed property, entailed a high degree of recognition that credit and commerce formed the expansive principle, the blend of Machiavellian *virtù* and *fortuna*, which doomed men to follow their passions and government to acknowledge and utilize corruption. Whether or not the failure of natural aristocracy in revolutionary America can be attributed to the competition of new merchant and artisan elements with the older patrician elites, there seems little evidence that the thought of the 1780s was responding to a traumatic intrusion of the 'monied interest' like that which so dramatically altered English thinking ninety years before. There was no American Court – as yet; the confrontation between virtue and commerce was not absolute, and once again this furnishes reason to believe that the founders of Federalism were not fully aware of the extent to which their thinking involved an abandonment of the paradigm of virtue. In what follows, it will be argued that Wood's 'end of classical politics' was an end of one guiding thread in a complex tissue, but not a disappearance of the whole web.

[...]

The American apocalypse is not inherently more absurd than those entertained in other cultures, which present themselves as embodying the last stage of some unified scheme of human history and as about to attain utopia through the working out of that scheme's final dialectic. But because the movement of American history has been spatial rather than dialectical, its apocalypse has been early modern rather than historicist; it has been envisaged in the form of a movement out of history, followed by a regenerative return to it, so that there have been perpetuated in American thinking those patterns of messianic and cyclical thought with which this book has been concerned. For if the liberation of Asia should not come about, the partnership of virtue and commerce would have failed and the cycle of history would be closed again. The chosen people would be imprisoned in time for lack of a theater for further expansion and the pursuing forces of commerce would once more turn corruptive, imposing upon them the imperial government desired by Hamilton in the eighteenth century and described as the 'military-industrial complex' by Eisenhower in the twentieth, or the condition of universal dependence feared by Jefferson and analyzed by Tocqueville. When the chosen people failed of their mission, they were by definition apostate, and the jeremiad note so recurrent in American history would be sounded again. It would call for the internal cleansing and regeneration of the 'city on a hill', since the politics of sectarian withdrawal and communal renewal form a standing alternative to those of millennial leadership; 'come out of her, my people' might be heard again in the form of

George McGovern's 'come home, America'; but there would simultaneously be heard a variety of neo-Machiavellian voices offering counsel on the proper blend of prudence and audacity to display in a world where virtue was indeed finite. The fate of Rome began to be invoked by the anti-imperialists of 1898, and has been invoked since.

The twentieth-century intellect distrusts metahistory for many reasons, nearly all of them good, but American culture has been sufficiently pervaded by metahistorical ways of thinking to make the ability to reconstruct eschatological scenarios a useful tool in interpreting it. We can see, in the light of the scheme provided here, why it was necessary, both at the beginnings of the Jeffersonian perspective and as it took further shape, to reject Alexander Hamilton as a false prophet and even a kind of Antichrist; he looked east, not west,[14] saw America as commercial empire rather than agrarian republic, and proclaimed that corruption was inescapable, that the cycle was closed and the end had come, before the covenant was fairly sealed or the experiment in escaping corruption had begun. We can further see why it was that Frederick Jackson Turner adopted the tones of an American Isaiah when proclaiming the closing of the frontier in 1890; one phase in the prophetic scheme, one revolution of the wheel in the struggle between virtue and corruption, was drawing to an end. It is also intelligible that there is now an interpretation of American history since that era, which proposes that after 1890 the choice lay between internal reformation on the one hand and oceanic empire on the other, leading to the liberation of Asia by trade through an Open Door;[15] and that the apparent rejection of America by Asia in the third quarter of the twentieth century is seen as leading to a profound crisis in self-perception, in which the hope of renewed innocence and recovered virtue is felt (once again) to have gone forever and the national jeremiad is sounded in peculiarly anguished terms. The Machiavellian note is audible when Americans reproach themselves, as they have at intervals since at latest 1898, with exercising the 'tyranny of a free people' and imposing the empire of virtue on those who are not to receive full citizenship within it.[16] But it is also significant that the jeremiad has at times taken the form of a quarrel with the Constitution itself, and more recently of a quarrel with a 'Lockean consensus', a politics of pragmatic adjustment and a political science of the empirical study of behavior, all of which are seen – however exaggeratedly – as underlying the edifice of the republic since its beginnings and as contributing to that state of affairs which it is the object of the jeremiad to denounce as corruption. The tensions between political practice and the values to which it must answer sometimes grow so great that Americans lose that delight in both the practice and the contemplation of politics in the Madisonian manner which normally characterizes them. The language of practice has not been republican in the classical sense, but the language of myth and metahistory has ensured the repetition of dilemmas first perceived in the eighteenth century; and what is often stated as a quarrel with Locke is in reality a quarrel with Madison's solution to these dilemmas. American political scientists currently see themselves as passing through a 'post-behavioral revolution'[17] but much of the language of that movement is recognizable as the language of jeremiad; and a post-jeremiad revolution in the field of ideology would in some respects be more drastic still. It would signal the end of the Machiavellian moment in America – the end, that is, of the quarrel with history in its distinctively American form. But what would succeed that perspective is hard to imagine – the indications of the present point inconclusively toward various kinds of conservative anarchism – and its end does not seem to have arrived.

It is notorious that American culture is haunted by myths, many of which arise out of the attempt to escape history and then regenerate it. The conventional wisdom among scholars who have studied their growth has been that the Puritan covenant was reborn in the Lockean contract, so that Locke himself has been elevated to the station of a patron saint of American values and the quarrel with history has been seen in terms of a constant attempt to escape into the wilderness and repeat a Lockean experiment in the foundation of a natural society.[18] The interpretation put forward here stresses Machiavelli at the expense of Locke; it suggests that the republic – a concept derived from Renaissance humanism – was the true heir of the covenant and the dread of corruption the true heir of the jeremiad. It suggests that the foundation of independent America was seen, and stated, as taking place at a Machiavellian – even a Rousseauan – moment, at which the fragility of the experiment, and the ambiguity of the republic's position in secular time, was more vividly appreciated than it could have been from a Lockean perspective.

The foundation of the republic, this interpretation suggests, was not seen in terms of a simple return to nature – Crevecoeur to the contrary notwithstanding – but as constituting an ambivalent and contradictory moment within a dialectic of virtue and corruption, familiar to most sophisticated minds of the eighteenth century. There was indeed a flight from history into nature, conceived by many Americans of the revolutionary and early national periods – and with less excuse by a succession of historians lasting to this day – in terms of a flight from the Old World, from the burden of a priestly and feudal past (Adams's 'canon and feudal laws'); but the analysis of corruption makes it clear that what was involved was a flight from modernity and a future no less than from antiquity and a past, from commercial and Whiggish Britain – the most aggressively 'modern' society of the mid-eighteenth century – no less than from feudal and popish Europe; just as the nature into which Americans precipitated themselves was not simply a Puritan, Lockean, or Arcadian wilderness, but that *vita activa* in which the *zōon politikon* fulfilled his nature, but which since Machiavelli had grown steadily harder to reconcile with existence in secular time. Because the neo-Harringtonian version of the Machiavellian moment was one from which superstition, vassalage, and paper-money speculation could be beheld and condemned at a single glance, the old and new versions of corruption could be telescoped into one; and because the American republic could be seen in terms of *rinnovazione* in a New World, it was natural to see the departure from corruption as a single gesture of departure from a past – which encouraged the illusion that it led toward a nature which was unhistorical because its future was unproblematical. But this entailed much distortion of history, surviving in the determination of American historians writing in this vein, even today, to equate Britain with Europe and the Whig empire with the *ancien régime*.[19] The dialectic of virtue and commerce was a quarrel with modernity, most fully articulated – at least until the advent of Rousseau – within the humanist and neo-Harringtonian vocabularies employed by the English-speaking cultures of the North Atlantic; and it was in those vocabularies and within the ambivalences of those cultures that American self-consciousness originated and acquired its terminology.

[...]

A history could therefore be written – though it cannot be attempted here – of how British thought diverged from American, and from Augustan neoclassicism, in the half-century following the American Revolution. An ironic feature of such a history would surely be the high degree of success with which Victorian parliamentary legislation set about eliminating that corruption and its image which had been to all men, and to Americans remained, such an obsession. In this respect the British could and did feel well rewarded for their adherence, at the price of a disrupted Atlantic and an Anglo-Irish union, to the paradigm of parliamentary sovereignty over that of republican balance; the Americans, having made the republican commitment to the renovation of virtue, remained obsessively concerned by the threat of corruption – with, it must be added, good and increasing reason. Their political drama continues, in ways both crude and subtle, to endorse the judgment of Polybius, Guicciardini, Machiavelli, and Montesquieu in identifying corruption as the disease peculiar to republics: one not to be cured by virtue alone. In the melodrama of 1973, the venality of an Agnew makes this point in one way; an Ehrlichman's more complex and disinterested misunderstanding of the relation between the reality and the morality of power makes it in another.

The Americans, then, inherited rhetorical and conceptual structures which ensured that venality in public officials, the growth of a military-industrial complex in government, other-directness and one-dimensionality in individuals, could all be identified in terms continuous with those used in the classical analysis of corruption, the successive civic-humanist denunciations of Caesar and Lorenzo de' Medici, Marlborough, Walpole, and Hamilton. This language remains in many ways well suited to the purposes for which it is used; the case against the modern hypertrophy of Madisonian adjustive politics can be, and is, admirably made in terms of the Guicciardinian paradigm of corruption; but the historian notes that it serves at the same time to perpetuate the singular persistence of early modern values and assumptions in American culture. While the cult of Spartan and Roman antiquity among French revolutionaries was helping to generate the vision of a despotism of virtue through terror,[20] while German idealism was restating the quarrel between value and history in terms of a vision of reason as the working out of history's contradictions within the self,[21] and while the British were developing an ideology of administrative reform which claimed – in the face of a generally triumphant Burkean counterpoint – to reduce history to a science,[22] the unique conditions of the continental republic and its growth were perpetuating the Augustan tension between virtue and commerce, the Puritan tension between election and apostasy, the Machiavellian tension between virtue and expansion, and in general the humanist tension between the active civic life and the secular time-continuum in which it must be lived. Hence the persistence in America of messianic and jeremiad attitudes toward history; hence also, in part, the curious extent to which the most post-modern and post-industrial values, of societies continues to venerate pre-modern and anti-industrial values, symbols, and constitutional forms, and to suffer from its awareness of the tensions between practice and morality.

Hegel is on record as commenting upon the United States of his time that though a vital and growing political culture, it as yet lacked anything which he could recognize as a 'state'. He resorted, however, to the proto-Turnerian explanation that the safety valve of the frontier accounted for the absence of class conflicts, and the prognosis that when the land was filled urbanization, a standing army, and class conflicts would begin, a true 'state' would be necessitated, and the dialectic of history as he understood it would begin to operate.[23] This prophecy can be very readily transposed into a Marxist key; but it is notorious that it has yet to be fulfilled. Classical Marxist class conflict has been even slower to develop in American than in other advanced industrial societies, and if Herbert Marcuse be accepted as the most significant Marxist theoretician to operate out of an American context, his Marxism is post-industrial, romantic, and pessimistic. The fact is not, as we have seen, that a complacent Lockean liberalism has led American thought to state too narrowly the quarrel of the self with history; it is that this quarrel has been, and has continued to be, expressed in a pre-modern and pre-industrial from, and has never taken the shape of a rigorous Hegelian or Marxian commitment to a dialectic of historical conflict. The St Louis Hegelians, it has recently been shown, were romantic ideologues of a consciousness-expanding urban frontier, inheritors of the geopolitical messianism described by Tuveson and Smith;[24] and the more academic Hegelian philosophers who succeeded them were never ideologues at all. American metahistory has remained the rhetoric of a spatial escape and return, and has never been that of a dialectical process.

In terms borrowed from or suggested by the language of Hannah Arendt,[25] this book has told part of the story of the revival in the early modern West of the ancient ideal of *homo politicus* (the *zōon politikon* of Aristotle), who affirms his being and his virtue by the medium of political action, whose closest kinsman is *homo rhetor* and whose antithesis is the *homo credens* of

Christian faith. Following this debate into the beginnings of modern historicist sociology, we have been led to study the complex eighteenth-century controversy between *homo politicus* and *homo mercator*, whom we saw to be an offshoot and not a progenitor – at least as regards the history of social perception – of *homo creditor*. The latter figure was defined and to a large degree discredited by his failure to meet the standards set by *homo politicus*, and eighteenth-century attempts to construct a bourgeois ideology contended none too successfully with the primary already enjoyed by a civic ideology; even in America a liberal work ethic has historically suffered from the guilt imposed on it by its inability to define for itself a virtue that saves it from corruption; the descent from Daniel Boone to Willy Loman is seen as steady and uninterrupted. But one figure from the Arendtian gallery is missing, curiously enough, from the history even of the American work ethic: the *homo faber* of the European idealist and socialist traditions, who served to bridge the gap between the myths of the bourgeoisie and the proletariat. It is not yet as clear as it might be how the emergence of this figure is related to the European debate between virtue and commerce; but because industrial labor in America conquered a wilderness rather than transforming an ancient agrarian landscape, *homo faber* in this continent is seen as conquering space rather than transforming history, and the American work force has been even less willing than the European to see itself as a true proletariat. The ethos of historicist socialism has consequently been an importation of transplanted intellectuals (even the martyr Joe Hill left word that he 'had lived as an artist and would die as an artist'), and has remained in many ways subject to the messianic populisms of the westward movement.

The quarrel between civic virtue and secular time has been one of the main sources of the Western awareness of human historicity; but at the same time, the continued conduct of this quarrel – largely because it is anchored in a concern for the moral stability of the human personality – has perpetuated a pre-modern view of history as a movement away from the norms defining that stability, and so as essentially uncreative and entropic where it does not attain to millennium or utopia. When we speak of historicism we mean both an attempt to engage the personality and its integrity in the movement of history, and an attempt to depict history as generating new norms and values. The underlying strength of historicism is – or has been, since the astronauts and ecologists are working to close the circle once more – this sense of the secular creativity of history, its linear capacity to bring about incessant qualitative transformations of human life; but the paradox of American thought – on the other hand, the essence of socialist thought – has been a constant moral polemic against the way in the which this happens. On one side of the paradox, the civic ideal of the virtuous personality, uncorrupted by specialization and committed to the social whole in all its diversity, has formed an important ingredient of the Marxian ideal of the same personality as awaiting redemption from the alienating effects of specialization. – On another side, however, the socialist and revolutionary thrust has often ended in failure for the reason – once among others – that it threatens to 'force men to be free', to involve them in history, or in political and historical action, to a degree beyond their capacity for consent. Conservatism involves a denial of activism, a denial that the sphere of the *vita activa* is coterminous with the sphere of societal life. At this point our study of the quarrel between virtue and commerce has a contribution to offer on the conservative side of the ledger, with which a history being completed at a profoundly counter-revolutionary point in time may be permitted, without prejudice, to conclude.

NOTES

1. Gordon Wood, *Creation of the American Republic* (Chapel Hill: University of North Carolina Press, 1969), pp. 613–14.
2. Wood, p. 505.
3. Wood, pp. 474–5, 507–18, 543–7, 562–4.
4. Paul M. Sperlin, *Rousseau in America, 1760–1809* (University of Alabama Press, 1969), indicates that *The Social Contract* was not much read or quoted. Noah Webster is an interesting exception.
5. See for example Wood, pp. 446–3.
6. Wood, pp. 532–6, 599–600, 613–14.
7. There is much semantic confusion on this point. Given that in classical theory each major institution 'represented' a distinct 'order' in society, for example the one, the few, and the many – it was by this time possible to speak of these 'orders' as 'interests'; and radical democrats, speaking still from within the classical tradition, could argue that in the popular assembly individuals, not relatively elitist interests, were what should be 'represented'. But in true interest-group theory, which may be the child of radical individualism, the individual needs to perceive only his interests and the group with which they associate him, and need not practice the 'virtue' of *looking beyond* them.
8. J. R. Pole, *Political Representation in England and the Origins of the American Republic* (New York: St Martin's Press, 1966), pp. 374–5; Wood, pp. 501–6, 576.
9. Wood, pp. 535–47, 559–60.
10. Wood, pp. 605–10, relying largely on *The Federalist*, no. 51.
11. Wood, pp. 562, 606–15.
12. William N, Chambers, *Political Parties in a New Nation: the American Experience, 1776–1809* (New York: Oxford University Press, 1963).
13. See, for example, Wood, p. 606; Chambers, pp. 122–4; Pole, pp. 528–31. Wood in particular presents the republic as an ideal essentially hierarchical and at the same time essentially mobile; pp. 478–9.
14. He spoke of Canada as on 'our left', Florida on 'our right' (Stourzh, p. 195). See also Felix Gilbert, *To the Farewell Address: Ideas of Early American Foreign Policy* (Princeton, NJ: Princeton University Press, 1961, 1970).
15. See, for example, Max Silberschmidt, *The United States and Europe: Rivals and Partners* (New York: Harcourt Brace Jovanovich, 1971). Is it worth remarking that the 'open door' of China policy in the West recalls words on the plinth of the Statue of Liberty in the East?
16. See, for example, William Graham Summer in 1896: 'Our system is unfit for the government of subject provinces. They have no place in it. They would become seats of corruption, which would react on our own body politic. If we admitted the island [Cuba] as a state or a group of states, we should have to let it help govern us.' Cited in Lloyd C. Gardner (ed.), *A Different Frontier: selected readings in the foundations of American economic expansion* (Chicago: Quadrangle Books, 1966),

p. 87. Also Robert L. Beisner, *Twelve Against Empire: the Anti-imperialists, 1898–1900* (New York: McGraw Hill, 1968).

17. David C. Easton, 'The New Revolution in Political Science' (Presidential address to the American Political Science Association), *American Political Science Review* 73, no. 4 (1969), pp. 1051–61. See also Graham and Carey (eds), *The Post-Behavioral Era: Perspectives on Political Science* (New York: David McKay, 1972).

18. David W. Noble, *Historians Against History: The Frontier Thesis and the National Covenant in American Historical Writing since 1830* (Minneapolis: University of Minnesota Press, 1965).

19. Louis Hartz, *The Liberal Tradition in America* (San Diego/New York: Harcourt Brace, 1955).

20. Harold T. Parker, *The Cult of Antiquity and the French Revolutionaries: A Study in the Development of the Revolutionary Spirit* (Chicago: Chicago University Press, 1937).

21. George Armstrong Kelly, *Idealism, Politics and History: Sources of Hegelian Thought* (Cambridge: Cambridge University Press, 1969).

22. Crane Brinton, *English Political Thought in the Nineteenth Century* (New York: Harper and Row, 1962).

23. G. W. F. Hegel, *Lectures on the Philosophy of History*, tr. J. Sibree (New York: Colonial Press, 1900), pp. 85–7.

24. William II. Goetzmann (ed). *The American Hegelians: An Intellectual Episode in the History of Western America* (New York: Alfred A. Knopf, 1973).

25. Hannah Arendt, *The Human Condition* (New York: Viking, 1958), and Peter Fuss, 'Hannah Arendt's Conception of Political Community'. *Idealistic Studies* 3, no. 3 (1973), pp. 252–65.

18

LIBERALISM AND REPUBLICANISM IN THE HISTORICAL IMAGINATION

Joyce Appleby

With the publication of Bernard Bailyn's *The Ideological Origins of The American Revolution*, the study of the American Revolution was itself revolutionized, although curiously the word *republicanism* does not figure prominently in his text. What Bailyn did was to effect that fusion of substantive and theoretical meaning that republicanism has come to represent. In a single study he turned around the entire field working on eighteenth-century America. By joining earlier work on the English Commonwealthmen to a powerful explanation of how ideas enter into the realm of history-making events, he made ideology the central concept in our current accounts of the break with Great Britain. In his analysis of revolutionary rhetoric Bailyn dropped themes into our history which like dye in a vat have permeated and colored our writings on the whole era stretching from the Stamp Act crisis through the Jeffersonian presidencies. More significantly he replaced the tired old notion of intellectual influence with the exciting concept of ideology. Ideas, Bailyn maintained, only influence political action when they are part of a socially created structure. The Cassandras of the British Opposition shaped events in America because their opinions organized attitudes otherwise too vague to be acted upon, because, as he said, they crystallized otherwise inchoate discontent. Ideas, to use Bailyn's metaphor, compose themselves into intellectual switchboards wired so that certain events almost surely will provoke particular reactions. The colonial elite, confronting the Parliamentary reforms of the 1760s, for example, was

From: Joyce Appleby, *Liberalism and Republicanism in the Historical Imagination* (Cambridge, MA: Harvard University Press, 1992).

compelled to interpret the new measures as signs of a tyrannical impulse in England because this unexpected exercise of power tripped existing fears about the unbalancing of the constitutional order which preserved Englishmen in their liberties and estates.[1]

It remained for Bailyn's student Gordon Wood to connect explicitly the conceptual order of the American patriots to the classical republican tradition in England. This he did, in *The Creation of the American Republic*, which carried the story of Americans' engagement with republicanism through the drafting of the Constitution. Concentrating as they did upon the founding acts of independence and constitution-making, Bailyn and Wood left unexamined the genesis of the English ideology they found flourishing in the colonies. Content to explore how classical republicanism organized the consciousness of the most influential generation in American history, they presented the source of the founders' ideology as a kind of grab bag of radical Whig notions about power, rights, and virtue. It was left to J. G. A. Pocock to provide a central nervous system for the new skeleton of American political culture which they had fashioned. And this he did in *The Machiavellian Moment*. A keystone in Pocock's scholarship, *The Machiavellian Moment* completed the arches raised in his *Ancient Constitution* and *Politics, Language and Time*.[2] Like Bailyn, Pocock had simultaneously thought about what eighteenth-century men actually believed as well as how beliefs figure in the historical drama of situation, action, and reaction. Unlike Bailyn, Pocock has pursued these questions as part of a larger enterprise – an investigation of the spiritual crisis that accompanied the birth of the modern world.

In his *Ancient Constitution* Pocock explored the emergence of civic consciousness among those Englishmen centrally involved in their country's century of revolution. Following the twin histories of the common law and Parliament, he showed how the idea of citizenship emerged when the king could no longer count on the unthinking obedience of his subjects. According to Pocock, after the execution of Charles I and the subsequent failure of the Puritans' Elect Nation, Englishmen came face to face with the temporality of their polity. Then they turned to that great theorist of fortune and design, Machiavelli. Although Pocock did not draw from the anthropological work of Clifford Geertz, his findings accord with Geertz's contention that ideologies emerge and take hold at precisely the time when a society begins 'to free itself from the immediate governance of the received tradition'.[3] Only Pocock's English did not so much free themselves as find themselves unhappily free. They are emphatically not like the Parliamentarians who move through Whig history confidently championing a new era of government by the consent of the governed. In Pocock's account, England's leaders reached backward for classical models to teach them how to stay the march of time. At once enamored of their unchanging constitution and deeply aware of the demonic force of rebellion, they looked to the residual wisdom of the past for a theory of how to remain in place. And they found it in the classical writings of Aristotle and Polybius and their Renaissance interpreters.

From Machiavelli's analysis of ancient politics the English gentry, according to Pocock, took the idea of civic virtue. The exercise of civic virtue enabled men to realize their human potential at the same time it imposed form on the flotsam and jetsam of human events. Only men secure in their property could be virtuous, and only through the exertions of such virtuous men could property be made secure.[4] Thus the classical republican outlook of England's ruling class denied a place in the polity for the capitalist carriers of change and made every advance in economic development appear as evidence of fortune's zone of irrationality.[5] Shrewdly aware that both Marxists and liberals drew their intellectual hubris from a common assumption that they understood progress, Pocock removed the place for progress from the Anglo-American worldview. Taken as a whole, his work can be seen as a formidable indictment of the reductionism in liberal and Marxist historiography.

Both Pocock's theoretical assumptions and his findings about English political discourse are essential to his stunning interpretation of how material advance was received in the homelands of capitalism. Theoretically, Pocock says that the conceptual language of a society structures both personality and the world. People do not choose their beliefs so much as they feel an affinity for an explanation of experience which thereafter entails them in its multiple meanings. 'Men cannot do what they have no means of saying they have done,' he has said, 'and what they do must in part be what they can say and conceive that it is.'[6] Social languages thus confine more than they liberate. The precedent-shattering economic innovations did not seem like precedent-shattering economic innovations because there was no conceptual language for understanding them as such. Instead they appeared as threats to that balance of the one, the few, and the many which alone secured order and liberty for Englishmen. Innovation involved change and change evoked fears of the disruption of the constitutional balance. This was especially the case, Pocock says, because the new wealth-generating activities of the late seventeenth century became entangled actually and in men's minds with fiscal schemes which extended the range and size of the king's patronage.[7] The purely economic features of the commercial revolution were subsumed under the political rubric of corruption, since it was a maxim of classical republicanism that only those capable of subordinating their own interests to the well-being of the whole could perform the crucial job of protecting the constitution. English classical republicans could not say that it was otherwise.

Thomas Hobbes and John Locke had provided an alternative way of talking about private men and public policy, but Pocock maintains that Locke's notorious indifference to history rendered him a nugatory influence in his day. Dispensing with Locke in this manner has cut the taproots of the liberal tradition in both England and America, forestalling until a later day the triumph of the natural rights philosophy in America and a bourgeois revolution in England. No Locke, no Marx, it seems, and the shot heard around the world went backward. As Pocock wrote with characteristic audacity, 'an effect of the recent research has been to display the American Revolution less as the first political act of revolutionary enlightenment than as the last great act of the Renaissance'.[8]

The sweep of Pocock's revision is breathtaking. Against the pull of two centuries of unexamined assumptions about the reception of economic progress, he has succeeded in giving us eighteenth-century men firmly planted in their own time, facing an uncertain future with the sensibilities of their predecessors in the foreground and the values of their descendants properly out of sight. As he wrote about his *Machiavellian Moment*, it was concerned with 'ways in which men perceived change in their times, rather than with our endorsement of their perceptions'.[9] Pocock's formidable erudition has contributed to his achievement, but so have his brilliant insights on the functioning of political languages. Here Thomas Kuhn's analysis of how scientists order their research around models of nature offered him an appropriate template for understanding the structuring of political thought.[10] Indeed what Geertz was to Bailyn, Kuhn was to Pocock. Rejecting the liberal treatment of ideas as discrete units which people picked up and dropped according to need and preference, all four scholars maintained that ideas exerted influence as parts of wholes, paradigms in Kuhn's lexicon, and then only because the whole illuminated reality. Those who share a paradigm form a community. Kuhn's scientific practitioners became analogues for Pocock's English gentry. For each group a common language made coherent social action possible. As Pocock explained, social thought involved both linguistic and political processes because any socially organized way of thinking became a means for distributing authority, as well as communicating ideas. Political languages distribute authority as and because they communicate the wisdom of the society. With those who lived by the strictures of classical republicanism only men secure in landed property were free to practice civic virtue. Power thus flowed to those men and away from entrepreneurs and financiers, and everyone understood why. Pocock recognizes that the symbolic and evasionary aspects of rhetoric distinguish the language of politics from the language of a disciplined inquiry. However, their similarities lie in the control implicit in both. As he wrote, 'the individual's thinking may now be viewed as a social event'.[11] Kuhn showed Pocock the way to discomfit both liberal and Marxist historians. The reigning paradigm of classical republicanism denied liberals their forward-moving, freedom-loving makers of history – the innovator as hero – while it confronted Marxists with a ruling class speaking a language which wrote rising capitalists out of the political script.

The republican revisionists have self-consciously reached out for social scientific models to free intellectual history from its distortingly rationalistic assumptions about the life of the mind. In the sympathetic analysis of belief systems done by anthropologists they found the means for studying thought as a social phenomenon. What anthropologists also offered was a concept of ideology which concentrated upon the means rather than the causes or consequences of specific beliefs. Approached as 'systems of interacting symbols, as patterns of interworking meanings', ideology was fashioned into a concept which could integrate social psychology with linguistic analysis, or in the language of historians, motivation with documentation. [12] The anthropologists' concept of ideology was particularly helpful to those studying early America because in presenting what eighteenth-century people actually thought, historians had all too often collapsed the colonial past into the historian's present. The ideological approach encouraged a dispassionate sympathy for those beyond one's ken; it invited scholars to look for structured meaning; and it moved American historiography beyond the filiopietistic evaluation of nation-building acts. As Bailyn commented, it was now possible to understand both the English and the colonial positions in the Revolution.

[...]

The recovery of classical republican modes of thinking in the colonies has changed forever our understanding of early America. Further, because republicanism has been propelled into our consciousness by the engine of ideology we can leave behind that place where, as Louis Hartz put it, the American historian functioned as 'an erudite reflection of the limited social perspectives of the average American',[13] Not the least of the merits of the ideological approach is the possibility it affords of dealing with liberalism as a cultural artifact. When scholars recognize in self-interest as conceptual a notion as classical republicanism's civic virtue, we can be certain that the new insights about the social construction of reality have been absorbed. Like fish unaware of water, we American writers have moved about in a world of invisible liberal assumptions. The clarity with which republicanism has been delineated enables us to detect the elements of liberalism in our own thinking and hence to identify them as they entered into public discourse during the eighteenth century.

Republicanism has become an integrative theme for a vast amount of recent research in social history. In part this is because those historians who have studied the lives of ordinary men and women have found in classical political truths a cluster of values congruent with the lives of early Americans. Although classical republicanism has been traced to the most politically powerful and sophisticated men in the eighteenth century, its emphasis upon virtuous leaders and the subordination of self-interest reflected the popular mentality as well, we are told. The new recognition in intellectual history that human thinking is structured also accords with the social historians' own discovery of social patterning. Since it is largely through charts, graphs, and tables that the historically inaudible have been described, the texts of classical republicanism have been welcomed for their audibility. In the reigning assumptions of classical republicanism, moreover, social historians have found the antidote to the instrumental logic and demystifying rationality of that Lockean liberalism which has dominated historical writing for so long. The presence of republicanism in the American past has provided roots at last for a genuine alternative to the worldview generated by liberal capitalism, a need all the more pressing for those scholars working on periods before industrialization.

While most scholars would agree that the possibility of institutionalizing the civic values extolled in classical republicanism ended with the ratification of the Constitution, the vitality of republican ideals not only persisted but continued to embarrass the progress of liberal values in America. What remains to be sorted out are the circumstances and influences which account for the appeal of different constructions of reality.

Notes

1. Bernard Bailyn, *The Ideological Origins of the American Revolution* (Cambridge, MA, 1967); 'The Central Themes of the American Revolution: An Interpretation', in *Essays on the American Revolution*, Stephen G. Kurtz and James H. Hutson (eds) (Chapel Hill, 1973).
2. J. G. A. Pocock, *The Machiavellian Moment: Florentine Political Thought and the Atlantic Republican Tradition* (Princeton, NJ, 1975); *The Ancient Constitution and the Feudal Law* (Cambridge, MA, 1957); *Politics, Language and Time* (New York, 1960).
3. Clifford Geertz, 'Ideology as a Cultural System', in *The Interpretation of Cultures* (New York, 1973), p. 219.
4. Pocock, *Machiavellian Moment*, p. 184.
5. Ibid., p. 461.
6. J. G. A. Pocock, 'Virtue and Commerce in the Eighteenth Century', *Journal of Interdisciplinary History*, 3 (1972), p. 122.
7. Pocock, *Machiavellian Moment*, pp. 122–6, 426.
8. Pocock, 'Virtue and Commerce', p. 124.
9. J. G. A. Pocock, 'The Machiavellian Moment Revisited: A Study in History and Ideology,' *Journal of Modern History*, 53 (1981), p. 61.
10. Pocock, *Politics, Language and Time*, 14–15; Thomas S. Kuhn, *The Structure of Scientific Revolutions* (Chicago, 1962).
11. Ibid.
12. Geertz, 'Ideology as a Cultural System', p. 207.
13. Louis Hartz, *The Liberal Tradition in America* (New York, 1955).

19

ON REVOLUTION

Hannah Arendt

Nothing could be less fair than to take the success of the American Revolution for granted and to sit in judgment over the failure of the men of the French Revolution. The success was not due merely to the wisdom of the founders of the republic, although this wisdom was of a very high caliber indeed. The point to remember is that the American Revolution succeeded, and still did not usher in the *novus ordo saeclorum*, that the Constitution could be established 'in fact', as 'a real existence ... in a visible form', and still did not become 'to Liberty what grammar is to language'.[1] The reason for success and failure was that the predicament of poverty was absent from the American scene but present everywhere else in the world. This is a sweeping statement and stands in need of a twofold qualification.

What were absent from the American scene were misery and want rather that poverty, for 'the controversy between the rich and the poor, the laborious and the idle, the learned and the ignorant' was still very much present on the American scene and preoccupied the minds of the founders, who, despite the prosperity of their country, were convinced that these distinctions – 'as old as the creation and as extensive as the globe' – were eternal.[2] Yet, since the laborious in America were poor but not miserable – the observations of English and Continental travelers are unanimous and unanimously amazed: 'In a course of 1200 miles I did not see a single object that solicited charity' (Andrew Burnaby) – they were not driven by want, and the revolution was not

From: Hannah Arendt, *On Revolution* (London: Faber, 1963).

overwhelmed by them. The problem they posed was not social but political, it concerned not the order of society but the form of government.

[...]

It would be difficult to find, in the whole body of revolutionary oratory, a sentence that pointed with greater precision to the issues about which the founders and the liberators, the men of the American Revolution and the men in France, parted company. The direction of the American Revolution remained committed to the foundation of freedom and the establishment of lasting institutions, and to those who acted in this direction nothing was permitted that would have been outside the range of civil law. The direction of the French Revolution was deflected almost from its beginning from this course of foundation through the immediacy of suffering; it was determined by the exigencies of liberation not from tyranny but from necessity, and it was actuated by the limitless immensity of both the people's misery and the pity this misery inspired. The lawlessness of the 'all is permitted' sprang here still from the sentiments of the heart whose very boundlessness helped in the unleashing of a stream of boundless violence.

Not that the men of American Revolution could have been ignorant of the great force which violence, the purposeful violation of all laws of civil society, could release. On the contrary, the fact that the horror and repulsion at the news of the reign of terror in France were clearly greater and more unanimous in the United States than in Europe can best be explained by the greater familiarity with violence and lawlessness in a colonial country. The first paths through the 'unstoried wilderness' of the continent had been opened then, as they were to be opened for a hundred more years, 'in general by the most vicious elements', as though 'the first steps [could not be] trod ... [the] first trees [not be] felled' without 'shocking violations' and 'sudden devastations'. But although those who, for whatever reasons, rushed out of society into the wilderness acted as if all was permitted to them who had left the range of enforceable law, neither they themselves nor those who watched them, and not even those who admired them, ever thought that a new law and a new world could spring from such conduct. However, criminal and even beastly the deeds might have been that helped colonize the American continent, they remained acts of single men, and if they gave cause for generalization and reflection, these reflections were perhaps upon some beastly potentialities inherent in man's nature, but hardly upon the political behavior of organized groups, and certainly not upon a historical necessity that could progress only via crimes and criminals.

To be sure, the men living on the American frontier also belonged to the people for whom the new body politic was devised and constituted, but neither they nor those who were populating the settled regions ever became a singular to the founders. The word 'people' retained for them the meaning of manyness, of the endless variety of a multitude whose majesty resided in its very plurality. Opposition to public opinion, namely to the potential unanimity of all, was therefore one of the many things upon which the men of the American Revolution were in complete agreement; they knew that the public realm in a republic was constituted by an exchange of opinion between equals, and that this realm would simply disappear the very moment an exchange became superfluous because all equals happened to be of the same opinion. They never referred to public opinion in their argument, as Robespierre and the men of the French Revolution invariably did to add force to their own opinions; in their eyes, the rule of public opinion was a form of tyranny. To such an extent indeed was the American concept of people identified with a multitude of voices and interests that Jefferson could establish it as a principle 'to make us one nation as to foreign concerns, and keep us distinct in domestic ones',[3] just as Madison could assert that their regulation 'forms the principal task of ... legislation, and involves the spirit of party and faction in the operations of the government'. The positive accent here on faction is note-worthy, since it stands in flagrant contradiction to classical tradition, to which the Founding Fathers otherwise paid the closest attention. Madison must have been conscious of his deviation on so important a point, and he was explicit in stating its cause, which was his insight into the nature of human reason rather than any reflection upon the diversity of conflicting interests in society. According to him, party and faction in government correspond to the many voices and differences in opinion which must continue 'as long as the reason of man continues fallible, and he is at liberty to exercise it'.[4]

The fact of the matter was, of course, that the kind of multitude which the founders of the American republic first represented and then constituted politically, if it existed at all in Europe, certainly ceased to exist as soon as one approached the lower strata of the population. The *malheureux* whom the French Revolution had brought out of the darkness of their misery were a multitude only in the mere numerical sense. Rousseau's image of a 'multitude ... united in one body' and driven by one will was an exact description of what they actually were, for what urged them on was the quest for bread, and the cry for bread will always be uttered with one voice. Insofar as we all need bread, we are indeed all the same, and may as well unite into one body. It is by no means merely a matter of misguided theory that the French concept of *le peuple* has carried, from its beginning, the connotation of a multiheaded monster, a mass that moves as one body and acts as though possessed by one will; and if this notion has spread to the four corners of the earth, it is not because of any influence of abstract ideas but because of its obvious plausibility under conditions of abject poverty. The political trouble which misery of the people holds in store is that manyness can in fact assume the guise of oneness, that suffering indeed breeds moods and emotions and attitudes that resemble solidarity to the point of confusion, and that – last, not least – pity for the many is easily confounded with compassion for one person when the 'compassionate zeal' (*le zèle compatissant*) can fasten upon an object whose oneness seems to fulfill the prerequisites of compassion, while its immensity, at the same time, corresponds to the boundlessness of sheer emotion. Robespierre once compared the nation to the ocean; it was indeed the ocean of misery and the ocean-like sentiments it aroused that combined to drown the foundations of freedom.

The superior wisdom of the American founders in theory and practice is conspicuous and impressive enough, and yet has never carried with it sufficient persuasiveness and plausibility to prevail in the tradition of revolution. It is as though the American Revolution was achieved in a kind of ivory tower into which the fearful spectacle of human misery, the haunting voices of abject poverty, never penetrated. And this was, and remained for a long time, the spectacle and the voice not of humanity but of humankind. Since there were no sufferings around them that could have aroused their passions, no overwhelmingly urgent needs that would have tempted them to submit to necessity, no pity to lead them astray from reason, the men of the American Revolution remained men of action from beginning to end, from the Declaration of Independence to the framing of the Constitution. Their sound realism was never put to the test of compassion, their common sense was never exposed to the absurd hope that man, whom Christianity had held to be sinful and corrupt in his nature, might still be revealed to be an angel. Since passion had never tempted them in its noblest form as compassion, they found it easy to think of passion in terms of desire and to banish from it any connotation of its original meaning, which is παθεῖν, to suffer *and* to endure. This lack of experience gives their theories, even if they are sound, an air of lightheartedness, a certain weightlessness, which may well put into jeopardy their durability. For, humanly speaking, it is endurance which enables man to create durability and continuity. Their thought did not carry them any further than to the point of understanding government in the image of individual reason and construing the rule of government over the governed according to the age-old model of the rule of reason over the passions.

[…]

The men of the French Revolution had no conception of the *persona*, and no respect for the legal personality which is given and guaranteed by the body politic. When the predicament of mass poverty had put itself into the road of the Revolution that had started with the strictly political rebellion of the Third Estate – its claim to be admitted to and even to rule the political realm – the men of the Revolution were no longer concerned with the emancipation of citizens, or with equality in the sense that everybody should be equally entitled to his legal personality, to be protected by it and, at the same time, to act almost literally 'through' it. They believed that they had emancipated nature herself, as it were, liberated the natural man in all men, and given him the Rights of Man to which each was entitled, not by virtue of the body politic to which he belonged but by virtue of being born. In other words, by the unending hunt for hypocrites and through the passion for unmasking society, they had, albeit unknowingly, torn away the mask of the *persona* as well, so that the Reign of Terror eventually spelled the exact opposite of true liberation and true equality;

it equalized because it left all inhabitants equally without the protecting mask of a legal personality.

The perplexities of the Rights of Man are manifold, and Burke's famous argument against them is neither obsolete nor 'reactionary'. In distinction from the American Bills of Rights, upon which the Declaration of the Rights of Man was modeled, they were meant to spell out primary positive rights, inherent in man's nature, as distinguished from his political status, and as such they tried indeed to reduce politics to nature. The Bills of Rights, on the contrary, were meant to institute permanent restraining controls upon all political power, and hence presupposed the existence of a body politic and the functioning of political power. The French Declaration of the Rights of Man, as the Revolution came to understand it, was meant to constitute the source of all political power, to establish not the control but the foundation-stone of the body politic. The new body politic was supposed to rest upon man's natural rights, upon his rights insofar as he is nothing but a natural being, upon his right to 'food, dress, and the reproduction of the species', that is, upon his right to the necessities of life. And these rights were not understood as prepolitical rights that no government and no political power has the right to touch and to violate, but as the very content as well as the ultimate end of government and power. The *ancien régime* stood accused of having deprived its subjects of these rights – the rights of life and nature rather than the rights of freedom and citizenship.

[...]

What always made it so terribly tempting to follow the French Revolution on its foredoomed path is not only the fact that liberation from necessity, because of its urgency, will always take precedence over the building of freedom, but the even more important and more dangerous fact that the uprising of the poor against the rich carries with it an altogether different and much greater momentum of force than the rebellion of the oppressed against their oppressors. This raging force may well nigh appear irresistible because it lives from and is nourished by the necessity of biological life itself. No doubt the women on their march to Versailles 'played the genuine part of mothers whose children were starving in squalid homes, and they thereby afforded to motives which they neither shared nor understood the aid of a diamond point that nothing could withstand'.[5] And when Saint-Just out of these experiences exclaimed, 'Les malheureux sont la puissance de la terre', we might as well hear these grand and prophetic words in their literal meaning. It is indeed as though the forces of the earth were allied in benevolent conspiracy with this uprising, whose end is impotence, whose principle is rage, and whose conscious aim is not freedom but life and happiness. Where the breakdown of traditional authority set the poor of the earth on the march, where they left the obscurity of their misfortunes and streamed upon the market-place, their furor seemed as irresistible as the motion of the stars, a torrent rushing forward with elemental force and engulfing a whole world.

Tocqueville (in a famous passage, written decades before Marx and probably without knowledge of Hegel's philosophy of history) was the first to wonder why 'the doctrine of necessity ... is so attractive to those who write history in democratic ages'. The reason, he believed, lay in the anonymity of an egalitarian society, where 'the traces of individual action upon nations are lost', so that 'men are led to believe that ... some superior force [is] ruling over them'. Suggestive as this theory may appear, it will be found wanting upon closer reflection. The powerlessness of the individual in an egalitarian society may explain the experience of a superior force determining his destiny; it hardly accounts for the element of motion inherent in the doctrine of necessity, and without it the doctrine would have been useless to historians. Necessity in motion, the 'close enormous chain which girds and binds the human race' and can be traced back 'to the origin of the world',[6] was entirely absent from the range of experiences of either the American Revolution or American egalitarian society. Here Tocqueville read something into American society which he knew from the French Revolution, where already Robespierre had substituted an irresistible and anonymous stream of violence for the free and deliberate actions of men, although he still believed – in contrast to Hegel's interpretation of the French Revolution – that this free-flowing stream could be directed by the strength of human virtue. But the image behind Robespierre's belief in the irresistibility of violence as well as behind Hegel's belief in the irresistibility of necessity – both violence and necessity being in motion and dragging everything and everybody into their streaming movements – was the familiar view of the streets of Paris during the Revolution, the view of the poor who came streaming out into the street.

In this stream of the poor, the element of irresistibility, which we found so intimately connected with the original meaning of the word 'revolution', was embodied, and in its metaphoric usage it became all the more plausible as irresistibility again was connected with necessity – with the necessity which we ascribe to natural processes, not because natural science used to describe these processes in terms of necessary laws, but because we experience necessity to the extent that we find ourselves, as organic bodies, subject to necessary and irresistible processes. All rulership has its original and its most legitimate source in man's wish to emancipate himself from life's necessity, and men achieved such liberation by means of violence, by forcing others to bear the burden of life for them. This was the core of slavery, and it is only the rise of technology, and not the rise of modern political ideas as such, which has refuted the old and terrible truth that only violence and rule over others could make some men free. Nothing, we might say today, could be more obsolete than to attempt to liberate mankind from poverty by political means; nothing could be more futile and more dangerous. For the violence which occurs between men who are emancipated from necessity is different from, less terrifying, though often not less cruel, than the primordial violence with which man pits himself against necessity, and which appeared in the full daylight of political, historically recorded events for the first time in the modern age. The result was that necessity invaded the political realm, the only realm where men can be truly free.

NOTES

1. Thomas Paine, *The Rights of Man* (1791), Everyman's Library edition, pp. 48, 77.
2. John Adams, *Discourses on Davila, Works*, (Boston, 1851), vol. VI, p. 280.
3. In a letter to Madison from Paris of 16 December 1786.
4. *The Federalist* (1787), ed Jacob E. Cooke, (Meridian, 1961). no. 10.
5. Lord Acton, *Lectures on the French Revolution* (1910), Noonday paperback edition, 1959, ch. 9.
6. Alexis de Tocqueville, *Democracy in America*, vol. II, ch. 20.

20

THE FEDERALIST PAPERS

James Madison, Alexander Hamilton, John Jay

All that remains within this branch of our inquiries is to take notice of an objection that may be drawn from the great extent of country which the Union embraces. A few observations on this subject will be the more proper as it is perceived that the adversaries of the new Constitution are availing themselves of a prevailing prejudice with regard to the practicable sphere of republican administration, in order to supply by imaginary difficulties the want of those solid objections which they endeavor in vain to find.

The error which limits republican government to a narrow district has been unfolded and refuted in preceding papers. I remark here only that it seems to owe its rise and prevalence chiefly to the confounding of a republic with a democracy, and applying to the former reasonings drawn from the nature of the latter. The true distinction between these forms was also adverted to on a former occasion. It is that in a democracy the people meet and exercise the government in person: in a republic they assemble and administer it by their representatives and agents. A democracy, consequently, must be confined to a small spot. A republic may be extended over a large region.

To this accidental source of the error may be added the artifice of some celebrated authors, whose writings have had a great share in forming the modern standard of political opinions. Being subjects either of an absolute or limited monarchy, they have endeavored to heighten the advantages, or palliate the evils of those forms, by placing in comparison with them the vices and

From: James Madison, Alexander Hamilton and John Jay, *The Federalist Papers* (London: Penguin Books, 1987).

defects of the republican and by citing as specimens of the latter the turbulent democracies of ancient Greece and modern Italy. Under the confusion of names, it has been an easy task to transfer to a republic observations applicable to a democracy only; and among others, the observation that it can never be established but among a small number of people, living within a small compass of territory.

Such a fallacy may have been the less perceived, as most of the popular governments of antiquity were of the democratic species; and even in modern Europe, to which we owe the great principle of representation, no example is seen of a government wholly popular and founded, at the same time, wholly on that principle. If Europe has the merit of discovering this great mechanical power in government, by the simple agency of which the will of the largest political body may be concentered and its force directed to any object which the public good requires, America can claim the merit of making the discovery the basis of unmixed and extensive republics. It is only to be lamented that any of her citizens should wish to deprive her of the additional merit of displaying its full efficacy in the establishment of the comprehensive system now under her consideration.

As the natural limit of a democracy is that distance from the central point which will just permit the most remote citizens to assemble as often as their public functions demand, and will include no greater number than can join in those functions, so the natural limit of a republic is that distance from the center which will barely allow the representatives of the people to meet as often as may be necessary for the administration of public affairs.

[. . .]

What, then, are the distinctive characters of the republican form? Were an answer to this question to be sought, not by recurring to principles but in the application of the term by political writers to the constitutions of different States, no satisfactory one would ever be found. Holland, in which no particle of the supreme authority is derived from the people, has passed almost universally under the denomination of a republic. The same title has been bestowed on Venice, where absolute power over the great body of the people is exercised in the most absolute manner by a small body of hereditary nobles. Poland, which is a mixture of aristocracy and of monarchy in their worst forms, has been dignified with the same appellation. The government of England, which has one republican branch only, combined with an hereditary aristocracy and monarchy, has with equal impropriety been frequently placed on the list of republics. These examples, which are nearly as dissimilar to each other as to a genuine republic, show the extreme inaccuracy with which the term has been used in political disquisitions.

If we resort for a criterion to the different principles on which different forms of government are established, we may define a republic to be, or at least may bestow that name on, a government which derives all its powers directly or indirectly from the great body of the people, and is administered by persons holding their offices during pleasure for a limited period, or during good behavior. It is *essential* to such a government that it be derived from the great body of the society, not from an inconsiderable proportion or a favored class of it; otherwise a handful of tyrannical nobles, exercising their oppressions by a delegation of their powers, might aspire to the rank of republicans and claim for their government the honourable title of republic. It is *sufficient* for such a government that the persons administering it be appointed, either directly or indirectly, by the people; and that they hold their appointments by either of the tenures just specified; otherwise every government in the United States, as well as every other popular government that has been or can be well organized or well executed, would be degraded from the republican character. According to the constitution of every State in the Union, some or other of the officers of government are appointed indirectly only by the people. According to most of them, the chief magistrate himself is so appointed. And according to one, this mode of appointment is extended to one of the co-ordinate branches of the legislature. According to all the constitutions, also, the tenure of the highest offices is extended to a definite period, and in many instances, both within the legislative and executive departments, to a period of years. According to the provisions of most of the constitutions, again, as well as according to the most respectable and received opinions on the subject, the members of the judiciary department are to retain their offices by the firm tenure of good behavior.

On comparing the Constitution planned by the convention with the standard here fixed, we perceived at once that it is, in the most rigid sense, conformable to it. The House of Representatives, like that of one branch at least of all the State legislatures, is elected immediately by the great body of the people. The Senate, like the present Congress and the Senate of Maryland, derives its appointment indirectly from the people. The President is indirectly derived from the choice of the people, according to the example in most of the States. Even the judges, with all other officers of the Union, will, as in the several States, be the choice, though a remote choice, of the people themselves. The duration of the appointments is equally conformable to the republican standard and to the model of State constitutions. The House of Representatives is periodically elective, as in all the States; and for the period of two years, as in the State of South Carolina. The Senate is elective for the period of six years which is but one year more than the period of the Senate of Maryland, and but two more than that of the Senates of New York and Virginia. The President is to continue in office for the period of four years; as in New York and Delaware the chief magistrate is elected for three years, and in South Carolina for two years. In the other States the election is annual. In several of the States, however, no explicit provision is made for the impeachment of the chief magistrate. And in Delaware and Virginia he is not impeachable till out of office. The President of the United States is impeachable at any time during his continuance in office. The tenure by which the judges are to hold their places is, as it unquestionably ought to be, that of good behavior.

The tenure of the ministerial offices generally will be a subject of legal regulation, conformably to the reason of the case and the example of the State constitutions.

Could any further proof be required of the republican complexion of this system, the most decisive one might be found in its absolute prohibition of titles of nobility, both under the federal and the State governments; and in its express guaranty of the republican form to each of the latter.

'But it was not sufficient,' say the adversaries of the proposed Constitution, 'for the convention to adhere to the republican form. They ought with equal care to have preserved the *federal* form, which regards the Union as a *Confederacy* of sovereign states; instead of which they have framed a *national* government, which regards the Union as a *consolidation* of the States'. And it is asked by what authority this bold and radical innovation was undertaken? The handle which has been made of this objection requires that it should be examined with some precision.

Without inquiring into the accuracy of the distinction on which the objection is founded, it will be necessary to a just estimate of its force, first, to ascertain the real character of the government in question; secondly, to inquire how far the convention were authorized to propose such a government: and thirdly, how far the duty they owed to their country could supply any defect of regular authority.

First, in order to ascertain the real character of the government, it may be considered in relation to the foundation on which it is to be established; to the sources from which its ordinary powers are to be drawn; to the operation of those powers; to the extent of them; and to the authority by which future changes in the government are to be introduced.

On examining the first relation, it appears, on one hand, that the Constitution is to be founded on the assent and ratification of the people of America, given by deputies elected for the special purpose; but, on the other, that this assent and ratification is to be given by the people, not as individuals composing one entire nation, but as composing the distinct and independent States to which they respectively belong. It is to be the assent and ratification of the several States, derived from the supreme authority in each State – the authority of the people themselves. The act, therefore, establishing the Constitution will not be a *national* but a *federal* act.

That it will be a federal and not a national act, as these terms are understood by the objectors – the act of the people, as forming so many independent States, not as forming one aggregate nation – is obvious from this single consideration: that it is to result neither from the decision of a *majority* of the people of the Union, nor from that of a *majority* of the States. It must result from the *unanimous* assent of the several States that are parties to it, differing no otherwise from their ordinary assent than in its being expressed, not by the legislative authority, but by that of the people themselves. Were the people regarded in this transaction as forming one nation, the will of the majority of the whole people of the United States would bind the minority, in the same manner as the majority in each State must bind the minority; and the will of the majority must be determined either by a comparison of the individual votes, or by considering the will of the majority of the States as evidence of the will of a majority of the people of the United States. Neither of these rules has been adopted. Each State, in ratifying the Constitution, is considered as a sovereign body independent of all others, and only to be bound by its own voluntary act. In this relation, then, the new Constitution will, if established, be a *federal* and not a *national* constitution.

The next relation is to the sources from which the ordinary powers of government are to be derived. The House of Representatives will derive its powers from the people of America: and the people will be represented in the same proportion and on the same principle as they are in the legislature of a particular State. So far the government is *national*, not *federal*. The Senate, on the other hand, will derive its powers from the States as political and coequal societies; and these will be represented on the principle of equality in the Senate, as they now are in the existing Congress. So far the government is *federal*, not *national*. The executive power will be derived from a very compound source. The immediate election of the President is to be made by the States in their political characters. The votes allotted to them are in a compound ratio, which considers them partly as distinct and coequal societies, partly as unequal members of the same society. The eventual election, again, is to be made by that branch of the legislature which consists of the national representatives; but in this particular act they are to be thrown into the form of individual delegations from so many distinct and coequal bodies politic. From this aspect of the government it appears to be of a mixed character; presenting at least as many *federal* as *national* features.

The difference between a federal and national government, as it relates to the *operation of the government*, is by the adversaries of the plan of the convention supposed to consist in this, that in the former the powers operate on the political bodies composing the Confederacy in their political capacities; in the latter, on the individual citizens composing the nation in their individual capacities. On trying the Constitution by this criterion, it falls under the *national* not the *federal* character; though perhaps not so completely as has been understood. In several cases, and particularly in the trial of controversies to which States may be parties, they must be viewed and proceeded against in their collective and political capacities only. But the operation of the government on the people in their individual capacities, in its ordinary and most essential proceedings, will, in the sense of its opponents, on the whole, designate it, in this relation, a *national* government.

But if the government be national with regard to the *operation* of its powers, it changes its aspect again when we contemplate it in relation to the extent of its powers. The idea of a national government involves in it not only an authority over the individual citizens, but an indefinite supremacy over all persons and things, so far as they are objects of lawful government. Among a people consolidated into one nation, this supremacy is completely vested in the national legislature. Among communities united for particular purposes, it is vested partly in the general and partly in the municipal legislatures. In the former case, all local authorities are subordinate to the supreme; and may be controlled, directed, or abolished by it at pleasure. In the latter, the local or municipal authorities form distinct and independent portions of the supremacy, no more subject, within their respective spheres, to the general authority than the general authority is subject to them, within its own sphere. In this relation, then, the proposed government cannot be deemed a *national* one; since its jurisdiction extends to certain enumerated objects only, and leaves to the several States a residuary and inviolable sovereignty over all other objects. It is true that in controversies relating to the boundary between the two jurisdictions, the tribunal which is ultimately to decide is to be established under the general government. But this does not change the principle of the case. The decision is to be impartially made, according to the rules of the Constitution; and all the usual and most effectual precautions are taken to secure this impartiality. Some such tribunal is clearly essential to prevent an appeal to the sword and a dissolution of the compact; and that it ought to be established under the general rather than under the local governments, or, to speak more properly, that it could be safely established under the first alone, is a position not likely to be combated.

If we try the Constitution by its last relation to the authority by which amendments are to be made, we find it neither wholly *national* nor wholly *federal*. Were it wholly national, the supreme and ultimate authority would reside in the *majority* of the people of the Union; and this authority would be competent at all times, like that of a majority of every national society to alter or abolish its established government. Were it wholly federal, on the other hand, the concurrence of each State in the Union would be essential to every alteration that would be binding on all. The mode provided by the plan of the convention is not founded on either of these principles. In requiring more than a majority, and particularly in computing the proportion by *States*, not by *citizens*, it departs from the national and advances towards the *federal* character, in rendering the concurrence of less than the whole number of States sufficient, it loses again the *federal* and partakes of the *national* character.

The proposed Constitution, therefore, even when tested by the rules laid down by its antagonists, is, in strictness, neither a national nor a federal Constitution, but a composition of both. In its foundation it is federal, not national; in the sources from which the ordinary powers of the government are drawn, it is partly federal and partly national: in the operation of these powers, it is national, not federal; in the extent of them, again, it is federal, not national; and, finally in the authoritative mode of introducing amendments, it is neither wholly federal nor wholly national.

[...]

But the great security against a gradual concentration of the several powers in the same department consists in giving to those who administer each department the necessary constitutional means and personal motives to resist encroachments of the others. The provision for defense must in this, as in all other cases, be made commensurate to the danger of attack. Ambition must be made to counteract ambition. The interest of the man must be connected with the constitutional rights of the place. It may be a reflection on human nature that such devices should be necessary to control the abuses of government. But what is government itself but the greatest of all reflections on human nature? If men were angels, no government would be necessary. If angels were to govern men, neither external nor internal controls on government would be necessary. In framing a government which is to be administered by men over men, the great difficulty lies in this; you must first enable the government to control the governed; and in the next place oblige it to control itself. A dependence on the people is, no doubt, the primary control on the government; but experience has taught mankind the necessity of auxiliary precautions.

This policy of supplying, by opposite and rival interests, the defect of better motives, might be traced through the whole system of human affairs, private as well as public. We see it particularly displayed in all the subordinate distributions of power, where the constant aim is to divide and arrange the several offices in such a manner as that each may be a check on the other – that the private interest of every individual may be a sentinel over the public rights. These inventions of prudence cannot be less requisite in the distribution of the supreme powers of the State.

But it is not possible to give to each department an equal power of self-defense. In republican government, the legislative authority necessarily predominates. The remedy for this inconveniency is to divide the legislature into different branches; and to render them, by different modes of election and different principles of action, as little connected with each other as the nature of their common functions and their common dependence on the society will admit. It may even be necessary to guard against dangerous encroachments by still further precautions. As the weight of the legislative authority requires that it should be thus divided, the weakness of the executive may require, on the other hand, that it should be fortified. An absolute negative on the legislature appears, at first view, to be the natural defense with which the executive magistrate should be armed. But perhaps it would be neither altogether safe nor alone sufficient. On ordinary occasions it might not be exerted with the requisite firmness, and on extraordinary occasions it might be perfidiously abused. May not this defect of an absolute negative be supplied by some qualified connection between this weaker department and the weaker branch of the stronger department, by which the latter may be led to support the constitutional rights of the former, without being too much detached from the rights of its own department?

If the principles on which these observations are founded be just, as I persuade myself they are, and they be applied as a criterion to the several State constitutions, and to the federal Constitution, it will be found that if the latter does not perfectly correspond with them, the former are infinitely less able to bear such a test.

There are, moreover, two considerations particularly applicable to the federal system of America, which place that system in a very interesting point of view.

First. In a single republic, all the power surrendered by the people is submitted to the administration of a single government; and the usurpations are guarded against by a division of the government into distinct and separate departments. In the compound republic of America, the power surrendered by the people is first divided between two distinct governments, and then the portion allotted to each subdivided among distinct and separate departments. Hence a double security arises to the rights of the people. The different governments will control each other, at the same time that each will be controlled by itself.

Second. It is of great importance in a republic not only to guard the society against the oppression of its rulers, but to guard one part of the society against the injustice of the other part. Different interests necessarily exist in different classes of citizens. If a majority be united by a common interest, the rights of the minority will be insecure. There are but two methods of providing against this evil; the one by creating a will in the community independent of the majority – that is, of the society itself; the other, by comprehending in the society so many separate descriptions of citizens as will render an unjust combination of a majority of the whole very improbable, if not impracticable. The first method prevails in all governments possessing an hereditary or self-appointed authority. This, at best, is but a precarious security: because a power independent of the society may as well espouse the unjust views of the major as the rightful interests of the minor party, and may possibly be turned against both parties. The second method will be exemplified in the federal republic of the United States. Whilst all authority in it will be derived from and dependent on the society, the society itself will be broken into so many parts, interests and classes of citizens, that the rights of individuals, or of the minority, will be in little danger from interested combinations of the majority. In a free government the security for civil rights must be the same as that for religious rights. It consists in the one case in the multiplicity of interests, and in the other in the multiplicity of sects. The degree of security in both cases will depend on the number of interests and sects; and this may be presumed to depend on the extent of country and number of people comprehended under the same government. This view of the subject must particularly recommend a proper federal system to all the sincere and considerate friends of republican government, since it shows that in exact proportion as the territory of the Union may be formed into more circumscribed Confederacies, or States, oppressive combinations of a majority will be facilitated; the best security, under the republican forms, for the rights of every class of citizen, will be diminished; and consequently the stability and independence of some member of the government, the only other security, must be proportionally increased. Justice is the end of government. It is the end of civil society.

It ever has been and ever will be pursued until it be obtained, or until liberty be lost in the pursuit. In a society under the forms of which the stronger faction can readily unite and oppress the weaker, anarchy may as truly be said to reign as in a state of nature, where the weaker individual is not secured against the violence of the stronger; and as, in the latter state, even the stronger individuals are prompted, by the uncertainty of their condition, to submit to a government which may protect the weak as well as themselves; so, in the former state, will the more powerful factions or parties be gradually induced, by a like motive, to wish for a government which will protect all parties, the weaker as well as the more powerful. It can be little doubted that if the State of Rhode Island was separated from the Confederacy and left to itself, the insecurity of rights under the popular form of government within such narrow limits would be displayed by such reiterated oppressions of factious majorities that some power altogether independent of the people would soon be called for by the voice of the very factions whose misrule had proved the necessity of it. In the extended republic of the United States, and among the great variety of interests, parties, and sects which it embraces, a coalition of a majority of the whole society could seldom take place on any other principles than those of justice and the general good; whilst there being thus less danger to a minor from the will of a major party, there must be less pretext, also, to provide for the security of the former, by introducing into the government a will not dependent on the latter, or, in other words, a will independent of the society itself. It is no less certain than it is important, notwithstanding the contrary opinions which have been entertained, that the larger the society, provided it lie within a practicable sphere, the more duly capable it will be of self-government. And happily for the *republican cause*, the practicable sphere may be carried to a very great extent by a judicious modification and mixture of the *federal principle*.

21

MONTESQUIEU AND THE
NEW REPUBLICANISM

Judith N. Shklar

The bridge that leads from the republicanism of Machiavelli to that of the French Revolution does not stand alone. There is another one that ends in the United States Constitution of 1787. After a heated debate about the possibility of an extensive republic Americans discovered that they were actually living in such a polity and that they needed to explain it to themselves. That was the task that Alexander Hamilton and James Madison, writing under the name of Publius, accomplished in their celebrated *Federalist Papers*. Their first object, however, was to reply to the numerous critics of the proposed constitutional plan. Many democratically inclined Americans shared Rousseau's fears, and one journalist in Newport, RI, even quoted him correctly to demonstrate that representation on the English model was not freedom, but a charade.[1] Other less original anti-federalists argued, quoting Montesquieu copiously, that no large territory could be a republic, that the government was so remote from the people that it must soon degenerate into a distinct political class, and become despotical. The electoral districts were so large that only the rich and clever could ever be elected to the House of Representatives, and that they would certainly not speak for the general will. The culture of the North, with its industrious traders was wholly unlike that of the slave-owning, idle planters of the South. Had not Montesquieu said all there was to say about the differences created by the climate? No government could possibly suit such diverse populations and one must dominate and oppress the other, soon there would

From: Gisela Block, Quentin Skinner and Maurizio Viroli (eds), *Machiavelli and Republicanism* (Cambridge: Cambridge University Press, 1990).

be Georgian militiamen in New England and Pennsylvania. Finally the separation of powers was not as complete as was required by Montesquieu, nor did the provisions for a safe criminal law and jury trials meet his or their standard for a free government.[2] As we know, half the amendments of the Bill of Rights are about the rights of the accused in criminal cases, so the point was well taken. For us the most relevant issue is, however, about republican government. The radical Pennsylvanians clearly believed that the individual states were small societies in the classical pattern, and that egalitarian virtue could survive only under democratic political arrangements in which the sovereignty of the people expressed itself in fairly direct, participating ways, and the distance between voter and representative was slight. It should be added that there was no trace of martial breast-beating among the Pennsylvanian anti-federalists, some of whom were, of course, Quakers.

Such were the arguments Publius had to answer. He was, however, determined to do more than merely assuage the fears of his opponents; he meant to show that the new constitutional order would be in every way superior to all other republican governments, especially those of classical antiquity. It was intrinsically better because it would offer its citizens stability and freedom such as no city-state had ever known. Moreover, it would be a real republic, not in spite but because of its size. Without a monarch, or a hereditary nobility, or a mixed regime it would be an entirely popular state based on the consent of the governed. The very divergences among its many citizens would, moreover, create a system in which no party would impose its will upon the public to destroy the republic in the suicidal manner of the ancient city-states.[3] To that end Publius had to put the greatest possible distance between modern America and classical antiquity. The illusion that any of the thirteen states resembled republican Rome or Athens was to be dispelled once and for all. They were simply far larger already. However, the old city-states were in any case an unworthy example to follow. Publius had far less affection for them than Montesquieu had displayed. Their main use for him was negative, as awful examples of political failure. The only time Rome is mentioned with full approval in *The Federalist* is to demonstrate that two concurrent taxing authorities are compatible with achieving greatness. The power of both the states and the Federal Government to tax the same citizenry does not, therefore, have to lead to any dire consequences at all.[4] With that exception, the institutions of antiquity were treated as suggestions to be discarded or as examples of everything that was to be avoided.

[...]

When one considers the scorn that Publius heaped upon the endemic disorders of the republics of antiquity, one might suppose that unity was his highest political aim, which would scarcely be compatible with his ardent championship of liberty. That was not the case, however. It was his view that America could overcome the tension between freedom and unity thanks to the practices of representative government. In this it was again ahead of the ancient republics, for although the Athenians had understood representation, they did not use it fully, and so fell prey to personal tyrants.[5] There was far too much direct participation by the entire body of citizens in every branch of the government, and especially in Athens' popular assemblies. 'Had every Athenian citizen been a Socrates, every Athenian assembly would still have been a mob.' Such a crowd is bound to give way to unreasoning passions and is invariably manipulated by some wholly unprincipled leader.[6] In contrast to this lamentable spectacle, 'is it not the glory of the people of America' that 'they have not suffered a blind veneration for antiquity?' Though they have shown 'a decent regard for the opinions of former times', they have now embarked upon 'the experiment of an extended republic' and posterity will be grateful for this innovation. 'Happily for America, happily we trust for the whole human race' they have rejected the past and 'pursued a new and more noble course'.[7] To legislate for one's own needs as they arose and to favour political change, rather than merely to preserve one's institutional patrimony, was clearly one of the greatest departures of Publius from classical political theory and even from Montesquieu's caution. Above all, it reversed the belief that republics had to be bound by ancient mores, rather than by innovative legislation. Publius had, after all, absorbed the lessons of a successful revolution, and if his faith in human nature was not great, he certainly had a lot of confidence in modern science, not least the political science learned from Montesquieu. That science had taught him that freedom and virtue were not necessarily tied to each other. The English, as they make their second appearance in *The Spirit of the Laws*, are presented as selfish, irrational, debauched and devoid of any religious beliefs whatever. Yet they will bear any taxes and give their lives for their freedom.[8] Joined to what he had said about the excellences of the British constitution, Montesquieu's American readers, who thought of themselves as the last true Englishmen, could now understand just how different their world was from that of ancient Sparta and its like. The political qualities that they had to cultivate did not in any way depend on the educative forces of the small, watchful city. They appreciated virtue, but its requirements were not those of Rousseau. A respect for the property and rights of all citizens and a willingness to do one's best for one's constituents was all that was required of those who ruled. Nor should one rely on great men. Even 'enlightened statesmen' were a rarity, and a good constitution was built on their absence or political insignificance. What counts is to get reasonably able representatives into office, and here the larger the constituency, the greater the pool of able people who might be candidates for election. Extensive republics are simply 'more favorable to the election of proper guardians of the public weal'.[9] Moreover, as long as elections are popular the essence of republicanism is preserved, for it is not size or immediacy that counts, but the ultimate source of authority, which remains the people. This was no monarchy or aristocracy, but a republic, that realised the permanent will of the people because both the states and the proposed federal republic had constitutions that were designed to preserve their liberty and property.[10] The new extended republic, unlike the little republics of antiquity would, moreover, be able to protect the public against the local factions that threatened freedom and property precisely because it was both large, powerful and overtly grounded in the consent of the entire American people, 'the only legitimate fountainhead of power'.[11] After all, the constitution Publius was defending does begin with the words. 'We the People' and it did not mean the plebs of Rome or the Commons of England or the Third Estate of France. It was everybody. The mixed constitution had, in fact, died early on in the Convention, when Charles Pinckney got up and said what everyone knew, that there was nothing to mix in America, the difference between the rich and poor was not so great as to require any institutional recognition. Neither Polybius' Roman constitution, nor its equally mixed feudal successor had any relevance. Even England was not to be treated with the reverence that Montesquieu had heaped upon it.[12]

If the mixed constitution was gone, direct democracy and its ethics were even more irrelevant. Modern representative government in an extended republic was a vast improvement because, unlike classical democracy, it has a built-in remedy against the ruinous conflicts of factions. Far from having to crush differences of interest or political and religious opinion, diversity was encouraged to flourish in an extended republic. The greater the multiplicity of religious sects and of more tangible property interests, the more likely these groups are to form changing and flexible electoral coalitions, none of which has a motive for crushing the others.[13] Bargaining replaces the tumult of popular assemblies, as order and freedom are reconciled pre-politically just as among free sects, in society generally. As every group has a chance of being part of a majority at some time, but also in the minority at others, none has an interest in oppressing their opponents. The representatives of the people act according to the same expectations. They can, moreover, deliberate calmly and save the people from occasional follies, and still remain close enough to the electorate to maintain their trust. Any temptation to behave despotically must die as they remember that they must face the voters soon and eventually become ordinary citizens again. With federalism the need for what Montesquieu called 'intermediary powers' is satisfied, and together with the separation of powers, any concentration of authority in too few hands becomes impossible. Indeed the separation of powers in the federal government was greater than Montesquieu, with his English model, had prescribed. Not only was the judiciary given all the independence it needed, the balance of powers was psychologically perfectly equilibrated; 'ambition had been made to counteract ambition'. To be sure, in a republic the legislature must predominate, but in an extensive republic the multiplicity of interests will be reflected there as well, and 'the security for civil rights must be the same as that for religious rights', which were in principle at least fully protected.[14] Finally, as a trump, Publius recalled the military inefficiency of small republics which would now be overcome in a federation that really worked. That was more than all those ancient leagues had been able to do. The latter only showed the costs of smallness, an awful warning to the States.[15]

Turning from the general structure to the specific institutions of the ancient city-states Publius found that they also failed to pass muster. Rome had so feeble an executive that it had to resort to dictators in moments of danger, which was a dangerous expedient.[16] The consuls who made up its plural executive, were often at odds and would have been so more often if, as patricians, they had not been united by their fear of the people.[17] And finally, worst of all, ancient politicians did not really know how to put a constitution together. They had to find individual legislators who were driven to resort to violence and superstition to impose a basic law upon their republics. The men who together had written the proposed constitution of the United States were in every way their intellectual and ethical superiors. They had managed to introduce stability and energy into a limited republican government designed for a free people.[18] And they had done this by 'quitting the dim light of historical research' and following 'reason and good sense'.[19] Antiquity had very little to teach them, except to remind them of its many errors.

This then is the second bridge from Montesquieu to a wholly new notion of republicanism. Clearly Publius used Montesquieu's account of republican government to suit his own purposes. He had to denigrate the old republics far more than Montesquieu was inclined to do, and while the latter did constantly speak of legislators, the very idea of a constitutional assembly writing out a future scheme of government had not occurred to him. Cromwell's failed attempt was, after all, the only predecessor of this American political practice. Nevertheless, the extensive republic, short on virtue and dedicated to securing 'the blessings of liberty' was deeply indebted to him. If Rousseau was able to rescue the virtuous, small republic from the assaults of modern politics, Publius managed to make the expansive republic respectable and to devise a model of government that was neither oppressive nor given to the militaristic Augustan ideologies which Montesquieu set out to unmask and destroy. In either case republicanism survived thanks to him even though in forms that were notably different from the Renaissance version and its classical archetype.

NOTES

1. 'A Newport Man', *Newport Mercury*, 1788, *The Complete Anti-Federalist*, ed. Herbert J. Storing (Chicago, 1981), vol. IV, pp. 250–4.
2. See especially *Essays of John DeWitt* and *Letters of Agrippa* for New England anti-federalism, and for Pennsylvania, *Essay by Montezuma* and, most important of all, *The Address and Reasons of Dissent of the Minority of the Convention of Pennsylvania to their Constituents*, *The Complete Anti-Federalist*, vol. IV, pp. 15–40 and 68–116; vol. III, pp. 53–7 and 145–67.
3. See especially *Federalist*, nos 10, 39 and 51. Because there are so many editions of *The Federalist Papers*, and since the individual papers are so short, I shall cite them only by number.
4. *Federalist*, no. 34.
5. Ibid. no. 63.

6. Ibid. no. 55.
7. Ibid. no. 14.
8. *De l'Esprit des lois*, Bk xix, ch. 27.
9. *Federalist*, no. 10.
10. Ibid. no. 36.
11. Ibid. no. 49.
12. *The Records of the Federal Convention of 1787*, ed. Max Farrand (New Haven, 1966), vol. I, pp. 396–404.
13. *Federalist*, nos 10 and 51.
14. Ibid. no. 51.
15. Ibid. no. 17 and 18.
16. Ibid. no. 69.
17. Ibid. no. 70.
18. Ibid. nos 37 and 38.
19. Ibid. no. 70.

22

THE COMPROMISED REPUBLIC

Benjamin Barber

The American republic was founded at least in part on the political theory of classical republicanism.[1] Although its aims were plural, the motives of its founders complex, and the sources of their rationalizations manifold, the Constitution was conceived and set down in the language of republican thought – a changing but ancient idiom whose history as theory can be traced in various forms through the writings of Rousseau, Montesquieu, Harrington, Machiavelli, and Cicero back to Plato's seminal *Republic* and whose history as praxis has been visible in the living experience of Europe's commercial cities, Switzerland's mountain *Landesgemeinden*, the town republics of Renaissance Italy, as well as Rome's early republic and the *poleis* of ancient Greece. It was an idiom known and used by all of the parties to the American Founding. However little their interests coincided and however much their ideologies collided, Federalists and Anti-Federalists, aristocrats and democrats, mercantilists and agrarians all spoke this common tongue. To some degree they all shared a republican concern for a government of excellence, a citizen body of virtue, a public order defined by fundamental law (the constitution, or *politeia*) and conducive to well-being, and a community of moderation in which the governed would neither be abused nor be permitted to abuse themselves.

The traditional literature of republicanism and the historical practice in which and from which it issued did not, however, treat the republic as an ideal form that could be instituted without regard to condition; the Founders, their

From: Benjamin Barber, *A Passion for Democracy* (Princeton, NJ: Princeton University Press, 1998).

practical eyes fixed as much on American conditions as on European political theory, appreciated this. They understood the republican form of government to be as fragile as it was rare, and they knew it could flourish only under very special conditions. Hamilton had noted the tendency of Europe's city republics to 'perpetual vibration between the extremes of tyranny and anarchy', dangers that Rousseau and Montesquieu had regarded as inevitable when republics were founded in the absence of the proper conditions.[2] These conditions, it was generally agreed included: (1) a small-scale society limited in both population and territory; (2) social and cultural homogeneity, to insure a natural consensus on fundamental values; (3) economic self-sufficiency and (relative) autarky – usually specified in terms of a pastoral or commercial (but certainly *not* an industrial) economy; (4) frugality in life-style and manners and austerity in taste conducive to the cultivation of simple, nonmaterial public virtues; (5) rough economic and political equality of citizens; and (6) a distrust of rapid change that would be more accommodating to nature and stasis than to artifice and progress.

The classical literature argued that such conditions were prerequisite to the promotion of a strong sense of commonality, a clear public identity (the citizen as a public person holding a common moral outlook and sharing common interests), and a spirit of self-government that subordinated the private person to the public citizen no less than the private realm to the public life. Conditions conducive to a public spirit were necessarily hostile to hedonistic privatism and contentious self-interest; they thus served to insulate well-conceived republics from the high-tension privatism to which they seemed so vulnerable. Thus, for example, Rousseau insisted that the founding of a democratic republic pre-supposed:

> first, a very small state, where the people can readily be got together where each citizen can with ease know all the rest; secondly, great simplicity of manners, to prevent business from multiplying and raising thorny problems; next, a large measure of equality in rank and fortune, without which equality of rights and authority cannot long subsist; lastly, little or no luxury – for luxury either comes of riches or makes them necessary; it corrupts at once rich and poor, the rich by possession and the poor by covetousness; it sells the country to softness and vanity, and takes away from the state all its citizens to make them slaves one to another and one and all to public opinion.[3]

The Founders of the American Republic, and perhaps even more importantly, those who had to make good on the Founders' blueprints, faced an ironic dilemma: not only were they eclectics drawing on sources other than the republican tradition, *and* ideologues with varying and contrary interests, *and* skeptics of one kind or another about the desirability, feasibility, and degree of democracy in the republican formula; they were also republican lawgivers to a people lacking almost all of the conditions deemed requisite to the founding of a republic. James Winthrop of Massachusetts wrote with incredulity: 'the idea of an uncompounded republick, on an average one thousand miles in length, and eight hundred in breadth, and containing six millions of white inhabitants all reduced to the same standards of morals, of habits, and of laws, is in itself an absurdity, and contrary to the whole experience of mankind'.[4] Territorially, the new country potentially embraced a continent – a prospect that the Louisiana Purchase made more than merely credible soon after the republic's founding. Patrick Henry looked at that continent and declared that to make it a republic was 'a work too great for human wisdom'.[5] If its territory outreached the wildest ambitions of Europe's empires, let alone Europe's traditional city-states, its people comprised as heterogeneous a lot as had ever lived under a single national roof. Could a people who barely spoke a single tongue, who answered to different mother cultures and worshiped in different churches, who knew either the hammer or the plow, the loom or the baler, but never both – could they live under a single constitution in a continental republic in what Madison, in *Federalist* No. 14, called an 'extended Republic'? Surely, as critics of the Constitution insisted, it was 'impossible for one code of laws to suit Georgia and Massachusetts'.[6] And even were an extended republic somehow to be founded, America's underpopulated land and endless bounty invited growth, expansion, progress, acquisition, and material prosperity – the cardinal sins of republican life against which the Constitutional Convention was repeatedly warned by men like Gouverneur Morris, but which finally seduced even the agrarian democrats and Thomas Jefferson himself (enemy of mercantilism but friend, finally, to expansionism and material growth).[7] Not only was the early American economy heterogeneous and expansionist, but it depended on the two forms least conducive to republican stability: plantation agriculture and mass (manufacturing) industrialism. Moreover, its complexity assured the proliferation of economic orders and competing factions in a fashion completely inimical to the nurturing of a common interest. Quite aside from the two subjugated populations (Black and Indian), differentials among citizens were very great. *Time on the Cross* reports that many urban white workers were poorer than rural black slaves.[8] Sectional interests not only emerged from, but were deeply implicated in, the proceedings of the Constitutional Convention.

In sum, it would be difficult to invent a set of conditions as little conducive to the founding of a democratically tinged republic as the one that described America at the time of its founding. This dilemma presented the Founders and their successors with a virtually unprecedented problem in lawgiving and nation-building: how to serve republican virtue in a land more suited to empire; how to serve empire – economic growth, progress, material well-being, and continental power – without completely surrendering the republican ideal; how, in other words, to take a country whose conditions Montesquieu would have deemed suitable only to empire and Rousseau, to corruption, and give it a constitution of moderation, freedom, and self-government. And to do all of this without falling prey to the inherent deficiencies of either factional democracies ('spectacles of turbulence and contention') or fragmentary republics ('an infinity of little, jealous, clashing, tumultuous commonwealths, the wretched nurseries of unceasing discord').[9]

The constitutional solutions devised to treat with this dilemma were directly responsible for the national purposelessness that has characterized American public life ever since; they enable us to understand both the historical successes and the present failures of purposelessness in our national way of life. Each of these solutions was in part a response to economic and sectional interests, the fruit of a spirit of compromise that itself became integral to the spirit of the new republic; but each also aimed at using the peculiar conditions of America to reinforce in new and novel ways a republican constitution that would normally be undermined by such conditions. The constitutional solution was thus a radical and wholly untested challenge to the traditional wisdom of republican thought, one that turned the nation's early years into an unprecedented historical experiment, and one that could be met only by a people that had, in Madison's bold language, 'not suffered a blind veneration for antiquity, for custom, or for names, to overrule the suggestions of their own good sense, the knowledge of their own situation, and the lessons of their own experience' – that had already managed in the Confederation to 'rear ... the fabrics of governments which have no model on the face of the globe'.[10] For many, many years, in many, many ways, the experiment achieved a remarkable success. Indeed it was successful enough to make its centralist features tolerable to Jeffersonian decentralists, its sectionalist propensities tolerable to Hamiltonian nationalists, and its increasingly democratic tendencies palatable to both. Only recently have its deficiencies emerged clearly; it is this that has led to what is now seen as the crisis in public purpose.

The formula designed by the Founders was anything but monolithic; it incorporated a variety of institutional innovations and procedural compromises that together created a national pluralism flexible enough to accommodate republican virtue *and* material progress *and* imperial power. The critical institutions included federalism, the representative system, presidential government, and the adversary method as the guiding principle of political procedure and political epistemology. Although they often appear as historical compromises, they were less compromises than surrogates for pristine republican institutions that could not function under America's unique conditions. Thus, for example, it might be said that private property became the surrogate for public norms, self-interest binding men to their public obligations no less surely than shared values once did; that procedural consensus became the surrogate for substantive consensus; that representation replaced participation, as accountability replaced self-government, and autonomy was traded for rights.

More concretely, to take the four institutions cited above, federalism was the compromise power negotiated with scale to permit the development of a national imperium that did not entirely destroy regional autonomy and local self-government. The Articles of Confederation had yielded to state sovereignty and state power a prominence 'utterly irreconcilable with the idea of an aggregate sovereignty'.[11] National government required a general license to operate; but powers not delegated to it had, in the words of the Tenth Amendment, 'to be reserved to the States respectively, or to the people'. For purposes of political participation, republican scale, autonomous self-government, and sectional autarky, America was to pass as a nation of semisovereign states. But for purposes of economic development, the security of property and debt, national defense (and imperial offense), and the public weal, it was endowed with all of the centripetal forces of the unitary nation – of, at least *in potentia*, the emerging empire.

Representation was an ingenious device with much the same utility: it used accountability to bridge the widening abyss between participatory self-government and efficient central administration. Like federalism, it permitted a form of self-government (not necessarily democratic) to survive in a land whose scale seemed to preclude self-government. To be self-governed and to be governed by representatives was, to be sure, not the same thing; but even from the skeptical vantage point of later elitist critics of representative democracy like Joseph Schumpeter, it was clear that a people who chose their masters were better off than a people who did not. If the people were to be little trusted – one of the few points upon which the Founders agreed – those who ruled in their name but not by their mandate were to be even less so; this was Jefferson's rather skeptical democratic faith. The representative, then, played two roles. He mediated the divergent interests of heterogeneous constituencies, thereby insuring the 'participation' of sectional and other interests in national decision-making.[12] But he also mediated and thus moderated public passions; for, as Madison (sounding remarkably like Burke) had put it, the representative system could 'refine and enlarge the public views by passing them through the medium of a chosen body of citizens'.[13] Popular control *and* wise government, self-government *and* a national imperium, accountability *and* centripetal efficiency – these were the promises of representative government.

Presidential government was, in one sense, the crowning achievement of the representative system, the One in whom the Many could be safely united: for in the presidency was to be found the source and the symbol of the nation's collective power – the spirit of sovereign nationhood; yet in it too was preserved the right to self-government, initially of the states (through their electors), later of the people themselves – the spirit of sovereign citizenship. The President as Executive Officer and Commander-in-Chief embodied the power of the whole, of The People as a symbolic collectivity. The President as Elected Representative of the semisovereign states, as Chief Tribune, and, later, Party Leader, embodied the power of the parts, of the states and the people as self-governing entities, ruling themselves through their mandated executive representative. The dual accountability of the Presidency – to The People as Nation and to the people as citizens – has remained the source of its strength as a mediator between national power and local citizenship. It is no accident that the mythology of the common man has been more closely associated with the presidency than with any other institution; or that in 1976 Governor Brown of California and Governor Carter of Georgia, like Bryan before them, could lay claim to the presidency in the name of an alienated citizenry as if that office were wholly independent of the governmental bureaucracy against which they railed. Neater solutions to the problem of governmental leadership were to be found in parliamentary or monarchical government, but no more effective solution to the problem of accommodating republican self-government to imperial scale seem conceivable than presidential government.

The adversary method was less an institution than a procedural principle – perhaps *the* procedural principle – that governed the processes in which American institutions manifested themselves. The goal was unity (the republican ideal and the national imperative) through diversity (the democratic ideal and the sectional imperative). It seemed clear that no stubborn search for singular truths or monolithic standards or objective goals or agreed-upon powers could wring from the economic and social heterogeneity of America substantive consensus on anything. The adversary method in effect polarized the *pluribus* of E *pluribus unum* in order to secure a more moderate, centrist *unum*. It transformed market relations into political relations, requiring of every political transaction a buyer and a seller, a purveyor and a client, a complainant and a respondent, an obligation and an interest. Only where there were two sides could there be a reasonable outcome; only where contraries were aired could unity be anticipated.

America has thus been a land of Noah where everything durable comes in twos: the two-house Congress, the two-seat-per-state Senate, the two-sided trial (by prosecutor and defense, not by judge and jury), and, in time, the two-party system and the two-authority legal system (where the Legislature *and* the Supreme Court vie in the conflicting voices of the written Constitution and a Higher Law for the right to give ultimate laws to the nation).[14] And where the system did not create polar opposites, it nonetheless generated adversaries – separating and casting into opposition the major governmental powers (executive, legislative, and judicial), institutionalizing military service rivalries, encouraging the growth of an unofficial representative system (of lobbyists, interest groups, voluntary associations) to challenge, balance, and complement the official representative system, and generally nourishing an understanding of the polity as a public realm within which private forces are encouraged to seek their own advantage – the polity, in short, as a 'pluralist pressure system'. The faith has always been that from the clash of opposites, of contraries, of extremes, of poles, will come not the victory of any one but the mediation and accommodation of them all. The American version of truth and unity, if there was to be one, could never be forged from some ideal form. It would, as Jefferson knew, have to be hammered out on the anvil of debate.

The adversary method also played a secondary role as the functional equivalent of horizontal federalism: in polarizing authority it divided power;

in pluralizing truth it separated powers. Making truth a function of debate, it put force at odds with itself. As Madison had argued in the *Federalist Paper*, 'Ambition must be made to counteract ambition ... [for] in framing a government which is to be administered by men over men ... you must first enable the government to control the governed; and in the next place oblige it to control itself'.[15]

In each of these institutions, then, central power and local control, administrative efficiency and regional autonomy, effective leadership and citizen participation, national planning and individual interest, were assiduously mediated – power (read planning, progress, efficiency, expansion, and prosperity) forever being balanced off against citizenship (read participation, excellence, fellowship, responsibility, and civic virtue). The theory of classical republicanism had been confounded: for a republic (a rather odd sort of republic, but a republic nonetheless) had been devised that would accommodate both democracy (a rather odd sort of democracy, but democracy nonetheless) and imperialism (a rather odd sort of imperialism, but imperialism nonetheless); and if the ancient conditions did not obtain, then the rules had been successfully altered to accommodate the American conditions that did obtain. American exceptionalism – the refusal to follow the historical patterns of the political culture to which America was heir – was thus built into the institutions by which the republic was fashioned; indeed, it was crucial to the initial successes of the experiment.

NOTES

1. See, for example, J. G. A. Pocock, *The Machiavellian Moment: Florentine Political Thought and the Atlantic Republican Tradition* (Princeton, NJ: Princeton University Press, 1975); Bernard Bailyn, *The Ideological Origins of the American Revolution* (Cambridge, MA: Harvard University Press, Belknap Press, 1967); and Cecelia M. Kenyon, 'Men of Little Faith: The Anti-Federalists on the Nature of Representative Government', *William and Mary Quarterly*, 3: 12 (1955).
2. Alexander Hamilton, *The Federalist*, no. 9 (New York: Modern Library, n.d.), p. 47.
3. Jean-Jacques Rousseau, *The Social Contract*, B 3, ch. 4. See also the 'Dedication' to the Republic of Geneva, in *The Discourse on the Origins of Inequality*.
4. *Agrippa* Letters in Paul L. Ford, *Essays on the Constitution of the United States* (Brooklyn, NY: 1892), p. 65.
5. In Jonathan Elliot, *The Debates in the Several State Conventions on the Adoption of the Federal Constitution*, 2nd ed., 5 vols. (Philadelphia, 1896), 3:164.
6. *Agrippa* Letters, in Ford, *Essays*, p. 64.
7. Gouverneur Morris thus warned the Convention in Philadelphia: 'Wealth tends to corrupt the mind and to nourish its love of power, and to stimulate it to oppression. History proves this to be the spirit of the opulent.' Cited by Richard Hofstadter, *The American Political Tradition* (New York: Vintage, 1974), p. 10.
8. R. W. Fogel and S. L. Engerman, *Time on the Cross: The Economics of American Negro Slavery* (Boston: Little, Brown, 1974), 2 vols, 1: 2.
9. James Madison, *The Federalist*, no. 10, p. 58; Alexander Hamilton, *The Federalist*, no. 9, pp. 49–50.
10. Madison, *The Federalist*, no. 14, p. 79.
11. Madison to Randolph (1787), *The Writings of James Madison*, Gaillard Hunt (ed.), 9 vols (New York: 1900–10), 2: 336–40. The debate about the sovereignty and

power of the states that divided nationalists and decentralists in the Constitutional Convention was not settled by the Constitution, as the Tenth Amendment makes clear.

12. Richard Henry Lee had thus suggested in his *Letters of a Federal Farmer* a system redolent of functional representation for example 'a fair representation, therefore, should be so regulated, that every order of men in the community, according to the common course of elections, can have a fair share in it – in order to allow professional men, merchants, traders, farmers, mechanics, etc. to bring a just proportion of their best informed men respectively into the legislature' (in P. L. Ford, *Pamphlets on the Constitution of the United States* [Brooklyn, NY: 1888], p. 288).

13. Madison, *The Federalist*, no. 10, p. 59.

14. Judicial review thus challenged the positivist conception of law as a function of the sovereign will advanced by the Legislature with a conception rooted in natural reason's discovery of a higher law. For a seminal discussion, see Edward S. Corwin, 'The Progress of Constitutional Theory between the Declaration of Independence and the Meeting of the Philadelphia Convention', *American Historical Review* no. 4, 30 (1925).

15. Madison, *The Federalist*, no. 51, pp. 335–41.

23

DEMOCRACY WITHOUT THE CITIZEN

Sheldon S. Wolin

The original constitution embodied two competing notions of power. One was staked out by Madison and Jefferson. It insisted upon binding the powers of the national government by the literal language of the Constitution. The government's powers were limited by the specific objects set out in the Constitution; only those means could be employed that were absolutely essential to the achievement of the specified ends. Or, in Jefferson's words, the point of the Constitution was 'to lace up straitly within the enumerated powers' the powers assigned to the national government.[1] This position viewed power with increasing suspicion the more it was removed from the influence of state governments and the citizens. Its basic assumption was that power was less trustworthy the more it was dissociated from the participatory practices of local politics. Its unstated assumption could be put this way: it could not conceive of a national politics in terms that could be reconciled with the politics of citizens.

The other position was associated with Hamilton. While it accepted the idea that a constitution stood for a conception of limited governmental powers, it did not believe that this restrictive conception formed the starting point for understanding the kind of power society needed. Rather, the starting point was that colonial society desperately lacked a strong central power, a national government that could act assertively and decisively. To be able to do that, the government would have to possess sources of power independent of the

From: Sheldon S. Wolin, *The Presence of the Past: Essays on the State and the Constitution* (Baltimore, MD: Johns Hopkins University Press, 1990).

individual states. The powers to wage war, establish armed forces of its own, levy taxes without having to depend on the states, regulate commerce, establish national standards of money, and control final interpretation of the Constitution all signified an attempt to establish a new power base independent of the states.

But Hamilton was also to make an argument for an expanded conception of power, one that did not depend so closely upon specific provisions of the Constitution but rather was to be determined by the nature of the objects that the new constitution set for the government. Thus, the Constitution authorizes Congress to declare war. According to Hamilton's view, the national government could lay claim to any amount of power that would enable it to wage war successfully as long as it did not violate specific constitutional provisions: 'The government ought to be cloathed with all the powers requisite to the complete execution of its trust.'[2] Thus, the nature of war, rather than the nature of the Constitution, initially defined the magnitude of power which government could justifiably claim.

But in order to legitimate that broad notion of power it had to be accompanied by an appropriate conception of the citizen. How much civic involvement was needed for this new kind of power? What did this kind of power need from the citizen? What had this kind of power to fear from the citizen? Because the Constitution proposed to establish a centered system of power, a national government, it had to create a new type of citizen, one who would accept the attenuated relationship with power implied if voting and elections were to serve as the main link between citizens and those in power. At the same time, if the attenuated relationship were to work, if it were to succeed in conveying enthusiasm as well as material support to the center, it needed a citizen who could identify himself with a power that was remote, abstract, and so distant that, for the most part, it would operate unseen. In other words, because the project involved establishing a form of power which bore certain unfortunate resemblances to the kind of power which the colonists had rejected less than two decades earlier when they had rebelled against the authority of the British Crown and Parliament, the Constitution had to reject the idea of the citizen which the colonists had themselves assumed when they had defended local participatory politics against the distant authority of the British Crown and Parliament.

These earlier controversies left Americans with a conception of citizenship divided within itself and, for that reason, unable to evolve in ways that would meet the challenge of modern power. The civic self was divided between national citizenship, which the original constitution had restricted to the act of voting and had ingeniously prevented from organizing a majority purpose, and local citizenship, which had a busy and active life of frequent elections, officeholding in state legislatures, town councils, and local committees, jury duty, and militia service. In contrast, the civic self designed by the Constitution was not a design of citizenship but of a legitimation process.

Further, it was, as *The Federalist Papers* made clear, a political structure whose purpose was to elevate the presidency as the center of a centralized system and, by the same token, to demote the legislature. The implicit task set by that presidential form was to develop a citizenry that would look at the president in a new and depoliticized way: as a monarch above politics, as a father figure, as an easily accessible symbol of unity (as contrasted with the diversity represented in Congress). In short, a citizenry was conceived in terms that allowed the American political animal to evolve into the domesticated creature of media politics.

But the Constitution also had to contend with a rival form of civic life and a rival conception of the citizen. For there existed in the colonies at that time a flourishing political life that did not depend upon the Constitution but preceded it. The political life-forms of state and local governments and of the voluntary and spontaneous associations of citizens to which Tocqueville later drew attention presented a sharp contrast to the formalistic and abstract politics centering upon the national government. It was a different kind of politics, immediate, direct, and recurrent. It was a politics of experience and based on substance rather than image.

Thus, the actual politics of the country was, as it were, different from and larger than the constitutional definition of it. The actuality of American life then, as well as now, is that American politics in all of its ramifications requires a multiple civic self, one who is required to act the citizen in diverse settings, national, state, city or town, neighborhood, and voluntary association. It is perhaps the most complex conception of citizenship ever devised, and yet we have no coherent conception of it. Instead, we have assumed that the issue could be defined in terms of a simple confrontation between two opposing conceptions: the republican or representative conception of the citizen as an occasional participant through the single act of voting, on the one hand, and the democratic one, which conceived citizenship as direct participation in self-government, on the other.

These notions are inadequate, but in different ways. The republican model is the most dangerous because it wants the citizen to be a loyal subject; that is, to provide a stable basis of support and legitimacy so that those in power can undistractedly concentrate upon exercising power in a dangerous, complex, and changing world. If it didn't need the legitimacy that at the present is primarily supplied by elections, a legitimacy that enables it to extract resources and human labor and skills from society, it would happily dispense with the whole business of electoral politics. For its ideal is a politics of management, not a politics of citizens. Its notion of public politics is what can be distilled through the media. It wants a citizen adapted to the megastate.

It is clearly impossible to impose a democratic conception of the citizen upon the political realities of the megastate. But the democratic conception is also inappropriate because participation in megastate power is difficult. If the politics of the megastate is to be even minimally democratized, however, it will require a citizen who fulfills his or her civic role by doing something other than passively supporting those in authority. It demands a critical, thoughtful citizen who can participate in the form in which megastate politics presents itself: it is abstract, remote, and often technical in character. It demands a citizen who can participate intellectually and passionately in the controversies that surround the megastate, such as nuclear weapons, ecological problems, the actions of public men and women, foreign policy, and much else. The task of the citizen is to insist upon a widened debate in these vital matters: to reclaim public space as a space for deliberation, criticism, and alternatives and to prevent important political matters from being depoliticized and turned into in-house discussions.

The democratic conception of the citizen must be preserved as an ideal form, the measuring rod of what it means to be a citizen. It must be kept alive and reinvigorated at all of the political levels which have not been fully incorporated into the politics of the megastate. Democracy stands for an alternative conception of politics, even a standing criticism of and a living opposition to the megastate and to media politics. The political forms accessible to the democratic citizen are, as suggested earlier, diverse, not only in their substance but also in the degree of active participation they allow. The citizen of a state cannot be as directly involved as the citizen of a town; and the latter cannot be as concerned as the citizen of a neighborhood school district. The value of each of these involvements lies in their coexistence, the fact that they place different demands and offer different experiences. For what democratic politics is about is not simply discussion and cooperation among friends and neighbors but deliberation about differences, not just differences of opinion and interest, but the different modes of being represented in race, culture, ethnicity, religion, gender, and class. The encounter with difference is becoming the most important experience in contemporary America as new populations make their homes here. For difference presents a potential anomaly to the politics of the megastate: it upsets the passivity that is the essential condition of bureaucratic rule and the imaged politics of the mass media.

NOTES

1. *The Writings of Thomas Jefferson*, 10 vols, Paul L. Ford (ed.) (New York: Putnam, 1892–9): 286.
2. *The Federalist*, Jacob E. Cooke (ed.) (Middletown, CT: Wesleyan University Press, 1961), no. 23, p. 147.

SECTION 4
LIBERALISM

The section on Liberalism opens with another modern classic, Louis Hartz's *The Liberal Tradition in America*. In many ways this book can be read as an alternative explanation to Pocock's study on republicanism. In his study Hartz argued that the genuine American liberal tradition developed because of the non-existence of a significant counterforce. The very fact that America knew no feudalism left a void in the American political spectrum. In a situation where all citizens are 'born equal' and where positions are not inherited as in feudal societies or in aristocratic and monarchic regimes, no genuine conservatism could develop and the hegemony of liberal ideas was assured. According to Hartz, the South (and with it slavery) was the closest thing to the old European regimes that America had. But even the South never had been in a position in terms of developing ideas that could in principle become hegemonic.

Hartz's argument has been criticised for not discussing any other influences, influences which have been known to exist. One of the responses, which sympathised with Hartz's overall intention to study the hegemony of liberal ideas but which was also critical of how Hartz had pursued the project, came from James P. Young. In his study *Reconsidering American Liberalism* Young provides a revisionist multivariant account of the liberal paradigm in which other influences such as political theology, republicanism and a variety of liberalisms are integrated.

A very different, less historically founded, attempt to give liberalism a proper foundation comes from political philosophy. Although John Rawls' *Political Liberalism* does not refer directly to American experiences, Rawls' model is less neutral than it purports to be. In many ways Rawls' attempt could also be read and interpreted as an attempt to universalise the positive experiences and achievements of American liberalism. In particular his wish to provide an inclusive model for a pluralist society hints to an American theme. Also, the idea of 'public reason' could easily be seen as generalising the principle of American judicial review. There are other ideas in Rawls such as the 'overlapping consensus', 'democratic citizenship', and the whole idea of constitutionalism that could easily be identified as having an American background. However, the abstractness and the neutral tone in which *Political Liberalism* is kept can also have positive effects. It is in the very nature of the philosophical enterprise to abstract from concrete backgrounds – with the purpose of making the theory more universally applicable.

In contrast to Rawls, two other political scientists are more open when it comes to stating the peculiarly American context they are working from. Judith N. Shklar's groundbreaking essay 'The Liberalism of Fear' (published in her *Political Thought and Political Thinkers* collection) is the attempt to historicise American liberalism but without the Hartzian motive of writing it large. According to Shklar, liberalism in the United States is a much more recent achievement than has been thought. Shklar sees a genuine American contribution to liberalism in that it was 'invented' out of the fear of repeating the bad experiences associated with the old regimes of Europe. Stephen Holmes' search for a proper theoretical foundation of liberalism in his *Passions and Constraints* leads him to an analysis that stresses the differences between a European, negative model of freedom ('freedom from') and a more positive model of enabling rights as it is known in America ('freedom to'). Stephen Holmes, in his attempt to promote liberal ideas and liberal political philosophy, indirectly also criticises liberalism's antidote. It is indeed remarkable how willing not only European but also American thinkers have been to construct a straw man of liberalism that is then easily demolished.

24

THE LIBERAL TRADITION IN AMERICA

Louis Hartz

One of the central characteristics of a nonfeudal society is that it lacks a genuine revolutionary tradition, the tradition which in Europe has been linked with the Puritan and French revolutions: that it is 'born equal', as Tocqueville said. And this being the case, it lacks also a tradition of reaction: lacking Robespierre it lacks Maistre, lacking Sydney it lacks Charles II. Its liberalism is what Santayana called, referring to American democracy, a 'natural' phenomenon. But the matter is curiously broader than this, for a society which begins with Locke, and thus transforms him, stays with Locke, by virtue of an absolute and irrational attachment it develops for him, and becomes as indifferent to the challenge of socialism in the later era as it was unfamiliar with the heritage of feudalism in the earlier one. It has within it, as it were, a kind of self-completing mechanism, which insures the universality of the liberal idea. Here, we shall see, is one of the places where Marx went wrong in his historical analysis, attributing as he did the emergence of the socialist ideology to the objective movement of economic forces. Actually socialism is largely an ideological phenomenon, arising out of the principles of class and the revolutionary liberal revolt against them which the old European order inspired. It is not accidental that America which has uniquely lacked a feudal tradition has uniquely lacked also a socialist tradition. The hidden origin of socialist thought everywhere in the West is to be found in the feudal ethos. The *ancien régime* inspires Rousseau; both inspire Marx.

From: Louis Hartz, *The Liberal Tradition in America* (San Diego, New York and London: Harcourt Brace & Co., 1955).

[...]

The moral unanimity of a liberal society reaches out in many directions.

At bottom it is riddled with paradox. Here is a Lockian doctrine which in the West as a whole is the symbol of rationalism, yet in America the devotion to it has been so irrational that it has not even been recognized for what it is: liberalism. There has never been a 'liberal movement' or a real 'liberal party' in America: we have only had the American Way of Life, a nationalist articulation of Locke which usually does not know that Locke himself is involved; and we did not even get that until after the Civil War when the Whigs of the nation, deserting the Hamiltonian tradition, saw the capital that could be made out of it. This is why even critics who have noticed America's moral unity have usually missed its substance. Ironically, 'liberalism' is a stranger in the land of its greatest realization and fulfillment. But this is not all. Here is a doctrine which everywhere in the West has been a glorious symbol of individual liberty, yet in America its compulsive power has been so great that it has posed a threat to liberty itself. Actually Locke has a hidden conformitarian germ to begin with, since natural law tells equal people equal things, but when this germ is fed by the explosive power of modern nationalism, it mushrooms into something pretty remarkable. One can reasonably wonder about the liberty one finds in Burke.

I believe that this is the basic ethical problem of a liberal society: not the danger of the majority which has been its conscious fear, but the danger of unanimity, which has slumbered unconsciously behind it: the 'tyranny of opinion' that Tocqueville saw unfolding as even the pathetic social distinctions of the Federalist era collapsed before his eyes.

[...]

It raises the question of whether a nation can compensate for the uniformity of its domestic life by contact with alien cultures outside it. It asks whether American liberalism can acquire through external experience that sense of relativity, that spark of philosophy which European liberalism acquired through an internal experience of social diversity and social conflict. But if the final problem posed by the American liberal community is bizarre, this is merely a continuation of its historic record. That community has always been a place where the common issues of the West have taken strange and singular shape.

[...]

America represents the liberal mechanism of Europe functioning without the European social antagonisms, but the truth is, it is only through these antagonisms that we recognize the mechanism. We know the European liberal, as it were, by the enemies he has made: take them away in American fashion and he does not seem like the same man at all.

[...]

Technically we are actually dealing with two factors: the absence of feudalism and the presence of the liberal idea. The escape from the old European order could be accompanied by other ideas, as for instance the Chartist concept which had some effect in the settlement of Australia.[1] But in terms of European history itself the abstraction of the feudal force implies the natural development of liberalism, so that for all practical purposes we are dealing with a single factor.

Now there is nothing wrong with this, provided we do not claim for our factor any more than it can actually account for on the basis of comparative analysis. It is reasonable to reject the essentially religious claims of ultimate causality that single factor theories such as those of Marx and Hobbes advance. There is no 'secret' or 'key' to the historical process, or if there is, we certainly cannot know it. But we must not, because of this, brand as fruitless any attempt to isolate a significant historical variable and to study it by consistently comparing cases. If we do, we shall have thrown out, along with the bath water of false monisms, the very baby of scientific analysis. Granted that a single factor cannot illuminate all situations, it can still illuminate many. And these, given what we want to know at any moment, may be very relevant indeed.

[...]

Now a sense of community based on a sense of uniformity is a deceptive thing. It looks individualistic, and in part it actually is. It cannot tolerate internal relationships of disparity, and hence can easily inspire the kind of advice that Professor Nettels once imagined a colonial farmer giving his son: 'Remember that you are as good as any man – and also that you are no better'.[2] But in another sense it is profoundly anti-individualistic, because the common standard is its very essence, and deviations from that standard inspire it with an irrational fright. The man who is as good as his neighbors is in a tough spot when he confronts all of his neighbors combined. Thus William Graham Sumner looked at the other side of Professor Nettels' colonial coin and did not like what he saw: 'public opinion' was an 'impervious mistress ... Mrs Grundy held powerful sway and Gossip was her prime minister'.[3]

Here we have the 'tyranny of the majority' that Tocqueville later described in American life; here too we have the deeper paradox out of which it was destined to appear. Freedom in the fullest sense implies both variety and equality; but history, for reasons of its own, chose to separate these two principles, leaving the one with the old society of Burke and giving the other to the new society of Paine. America, as a kind of natural fulfillment of Paine, has been saddled throughout its history with the defect which this fulfillment involves, so that a country like England, in the very midst of its ramshackle class-ridden atmosphere, seems to contain an indefinable germ of liberty, a respect for the privacies of life, that America cannot duplicate. At the bottom of the American experience of freedom, not in antagonism to it but as a constituent element of it, there has always lain the inarticulate premise of conformity, which critics from the time of Cooper to the time of Lewis have sensed and furiously attacked. 'Even what is best in America is compulsory,' Santayana once wrote, 'the idealism, the zeal, the beautiful happy unison of its great moments'.[4] Thus while millions of Europeans have fled to America to discover the freedom of Paine, there have been a few Americans, only a few of course, who have fled to Europe to discover the freedom of Burke. The ironic flaw in American liberalism lies in the fact that we have never had a real conservative tradition.

[...]

When we study national variations in political theory, we are led to semantic considerations of a delicate kind, and it is to these, finally, that we must turn if we wish to get at the basic assumption of American thought. We have to consider the peculiar meaning that American life gave to the words of Locke.

There are two sides to the Lockian argument: a defense of the state that is implicit, and a limitation of the state that is explicit. The first is to be found in Locke's basic social norm, the concept of free individuals in a state of nature. This idea untangled men from the myriad associations of class, church, guild, and place, in terms of which feudal society defined their lives; and by doing so, it automatically gave to the state a much higher rank in relation to them than ever before. The state became the only association that might legitimately coerce them at all. That is why the liberals of France in the eighteenth century were able to substitute the concept of absolutism for Locke's conclusions of limited government and to believe that they were still his disciples in the deepest sense. When Locke came to America, however, a change appeared. Because the basic feudal oppressions of Europe had not taken root, the fundamental social norm of Locke ceased in large part to look like a norm and began, of all things, to look like a sober description of fact. The effect was significant enough. When the Americans moved from that concept to the contractual idea of organizing the state, they were not conscious of having already done anything to fortify the state, but were conscious only that they were about to limit it. One side of Locke became virtually the whole of him. Turgot ceased to be a modification of Locke and became, as he was for John Adams, the destruction of his very essence.

It was a remarkable thing – this inversion of perspectives that made the social norms of Europe the factual premises of America. History was on a lark, out to tease men, not by shattering their dreams, but by fulfilling them with a sort of satiric accuracy. In America one not only found a society sufficiently fluid to give a touch of meaning to the individualist norms of Locke, but one also found letter-perfect replicas of the very images he used. There was a frontier that was a veritable state of nature. There were agreements, such as the Mayflower Compact, that were veritable social contracts. There were new communities springing up *in vacuis locis*, clear evidence that men were using their Lockian right of emigration, which Jefferson soberly appealed to as 'universal' in his defense of colonial land claims in 1774. A purist could argue, of course, that even these phenomena were not enough to make a reality out of the presocial men that liberalism dreamed of in theory. But surely they came as close to doing so as anything history has ever seen. Locke and Rousseau themselves could not help lapsing into the empirical mood when they looked across the Atlantic. 'Thus, in the beginning,' Locke once wrote, 'all the world was America...'[5]

In such a setting, how could the tremendous, revolutionary social impact that liberalism had in Europe be preserved? The impact was not, of course, missing entirely; for the attack on the vestiges of corporate society in America that began in 1776, the disestablishment of the Anglican church, the abolition of quitrents and primogeniture, the breaking up of the Tory estates, tinged American liberalism with its own peculiar fire. Nor must we therefore assume that the Americans had wider political objectives than the Europeans, since even their new governmental forms were, as Becker once said, little more than the 'colonial institutions with the Parliament and king left out'.[6] But after these cautions have been taken, the central point is clear. In America the first half of Locke's argument was bound to become less a call to arms than a set of pre-liminary remarks essential to establishing a final conclusion: that the power of the state must be limited. Observe how it is treated by the Americans in their great debate with England, even by original thinkers like Otis and Wilson. They do not lavish upon it the fascinated inquiry that we find in Rousseau or Priestley. They advance it mechanically, hurry through it, anxious to get on to what is really bothering them: the limits of the British Parliament, the power of taxation. In Europe the idea of social liberty is loaded with dynamite; but in America it becomes, to a remarkable degree, the working base from which argument begins.

Here, then, is the master assumption of American political thought, the assumption from which all of the American attitudes discussed in this essay flow: the reality of atomistic social freedom.

[...]

No one can deny that conscious purpose went into the making of the colonial world, and that the men of the seventeenth century who fled to America from Europe were keenly aware of the oppressions of European life. But they were revolutionaries with a difference, and the fact of their fleeing is no minor fact: for it is one thing to stay at home and fight the 'canon and feudal law', and it is another to leave it far behind.[7] It is one thing to try to establish liberalism in the Old World, and it is another to establish it in the New. Revolution, to borrow the words of T. S. Eliot, means to murder and create, but the American experience has been projected strangely in the realm of creation alone. The destruction of forests and Indian tribes-heroic, bloody, legendary as it was – cannot be compared with the destruction of a social order to which one belongs oneself. The first experience is wholly external and, being external, can actually be completed; the second experience is an inner struggle as well as an outer struggle, like the slaying of a Freudian father, and goes on in a sense forever.[8]

Moreover, even the matter of creation is not in the American case a simple one. The New World, as Lord Baltimore's ill-fated experiment with feudalism in the seventeenth century illustrates, did not merely offer the Americans a virgin ground for the building of a liberal system: it conspired itself to help that system along. The abundance of land in America, as well as the need for a lure to settlers, entered it so completely at every point, that Sumner was actually ready to say, 'We have not made America, America has made us.'[9]

It is this business of destruction and creation which goes to the heart of the problem. For the point of departure of great revolutionary thought everywhere else in the world has been the effort to build a new society on the ruins of an old one, and this is an experience America has never had. We are reminded again of Tocqueville's statement: the Americans are 'born equal'.

That statement, especially in light of the strange relationship which the revolutionary Americans had with their admirers abroad, raises an obvious question. Can a people that is born equal ever understand peoples elsewhere that have become so? Can it ever lead them? Or to turn the issue around, can peoples struggling for a goal understand those who have inherited it? This is not a problem of antitheses such, for example, as we find in Locke and Filmer. It is a problem of different perspectives on the same ideal. But we must not for that reason assume that it is any less difficult of solution; it may in the end be more difficult since antitheses define each other and hence can understand each other, but different perspectives on a single value may, ironically enough, lack this common ground of definition. Condorcet might make sense out of Burke's traditionalism, for it was the reverse of his own activism, but what could he say about Otis, who combined both concepts in a synthesis that neither had seen? America's experience of being born equal has put it in a strange relationship to the rest of the world.

NOTES

1. What is needed here is a comparative study of new societies which will put alongside the European institutions left behind the positive cultural concepts brought to the various frontier settings. There are an infinite variety of combinations possible, and an infinite variety of results. Veblen, in a sentence he never followed up, caught some of the significance of this problem when he said that 'it was the fortune of the American people to have taken their point of departure from the European situation when the system of Natural Liberty was still "obvious and simple"' while other colonial enterprises 'have had their institutional point of departure blurred with a scattering of the holdovers that were brought in again by the return wave of reaction in Europe, as well as by these later-come stirrings of radical discontent that have questioned the eternal fitness of the system of Natural Liberty itself'. *What Veblen Taught*, W. Mitchell (ed.) (New York, 1947), pp. 368–9.
2. G. Netiels, *Roots of American Civilization* (New York, 1938), p. 315.
3. Quoted in A. G. Keller (ed.), *The Challenge of Facts and Other Essays* (New Haven, 1914), p. 318.
4. G. Santayana, *Character and Opinion in the United States* (New York, 1924), p. 210.
5. J. Locke, *Second Treatise on Civil Government* (Oxford, 1947), p. 29.
6. C. L. Becker, *Freedom and Responsibility in the American Way of Life* (New York, 1945), p. 16.

7. In a real sense physical flight is the American substitute for the European experience of social revolution. And this, of course, has persisted throughout our national history, although nothing in the subsequent pattern of flight, the 'safety-valve' notwithstanding, has approximated in significance the original escape from Europe. It is interesting how romance has been thrown alike around the European liberals who stayed home to fight and the American liberals who fled their battle. There are two types of excitement here, that of changing familiar things and that of leaving them, which both involve a trip into the unknown. But though one may find a common element of adventure in flight and revolution, it is a profound mistake to confuse the perspectives they engender. They are miles apart – figuratively as well as literally.

8. Note the words of Goethe:

> *Amerika, du hast es besser*
> *Als unser Kontinent, das Alte*
> *Hast keine verfallene Schloesser*
> *Und keine Basalte.*
> *Dich stoert nicht im Innern*
> *Zu lebendiger Zeit*
> *Unnuetzes Erinnern*
> *Und vergeblicher Streit.*

9. W. G. Sumner, *The Challenge of Facts and Other Essays*, p. 304.

25

RECONSIDERING AMERICAN LIBERALISM

James P. Young

The contribution of Louis Hartz was to cast the argument in more explicitly political and more general, theoretical terms; at the same time he tried to explain the origins of consensus. Hartz proposed that we should take seriously the often repeated observation that America is a historically unique nation. Fruitfully using Marxian categories to arrive at Tocquevillian conclusions,[1] Hartz contended that America has experienced a kind of inverted Law of Combined Development, skipping the feudal stage of history, as Leon Trotsky had argued that Russia had leaped over the bourgeois, middle-class interlude. The latter is, by contrast, the heart of the American worldview. Since we have not had a history of an organic, hierarchically organized, feudal society, Hartz, following Tocqueville, noted that the result was that Americans were 'born equal' rather than having had to become so.[2]

Consequently, American thought is profoundly middle-class liberal in its basic orientation. Americans have never seriously considered any ideological or philosophical alternatives, a fact that has led to a certain intellectual rigidity – noticed particularly by Tocqueville – and that has raised the specter of massive pressures to conform to the universally held tenets of liberal culture. Hartz described this consensus as deeply, even irrationally, 'Lockean' in character. As he put it: 'Locke dominates American political thought, as no thinker anywhere dominates the political thought of a nation. He is a massive national cliché.' It is not, of course, that the political theory of John Locke as such was irrational; it

From: James P. Young, *Reconsidering American Liberalism* (Boulder, CO: Westview Press, 1995).

is rather the way in which it was absorbed into the American mind without conscious thought that Hartz found notable and also troubling. Still, the meaning of 'Lockeanism' was never precisely defined in Hartz's book, although he did refer to 'the reality of atomistic social freedom' as the 'master assumption' of American political thought.[3] This last point, I will argue, is a great overstatement, though such a concept of freedom is a powerful recurrent force in US politics. However, to insist on this concept as the essence of the tradition is to give way to a misleading simplification. But beyond this very contestable and contested theory of human nature, liberalism clearly stood in Hartz's work for such basic ideas as constitutionalism, capitalism, and a formal commitment to political and legal, if not economic, equality. Moreover, at least in Hartz's version, liberalism was clearly democratic in character. Surely these ideas are near the heart of American political thought.

According to Hartz, the depth of these attachments has frozen American thought and politics at the center of the political and ideological continuum. The result is that America has not experienced the development of a traditionalist, European-style conservatism or, still less, any politically significant form of socialism. Further, American politics has been notable for a distinctively lower level of class conflict than has been typical of other advanced capitalist, industrial societies. These are compelling considerations, and there is no doubt that the Hartz thesis explains a great deal about the politics and history of the United States. At the minimum, the liberal tradition, if it does not cause the peculiarities of American politics, acts as a powerful limiting factor on its development.[4] If we cannot seriously contemplate ideas or policies that fall outside the liberal framework, then the system has a powerful tendency toward self-perpetuation, both politically and economically, though the rigidities inherent in the narrow range of allowable ideas may well threaten that perpetuation in the long run.

However, in spite of its power, the Hartz thesis is flawed and has not gone without critical scrutiny. First, Hartz began his analysis with the Revolution, thus leaving out 168 years of colonial history. The result, of course, was that the profoundly formative experience of Puritanism was almost entirely ignored. This is unfortunate because, although it can be argued that Puritanism, in a nice example of the law of unintended consequences, might well have contributed to the development of liberalism, it certainly was not in itself liberal and therefore did not fit easily with the thesis of the absolute dominance of the liberal creed.

Second, although it is certainly true that the United States never passed through a feudal period, an analysis of colonial life suggests that there were significant vestiges of hierarchy. Those vestiges, which took particularly deep root in the slave South, were a source of some tension.

Third, according to significant research carried out in the years since Hartz wrote, the ideas of neoclassical republicanism were very important in the Revolution and perhaps for a considerable time thereafter. This theory stemmed ultimately from Aristotle and reached these shores by way of Machiavelli, the English republicans of the seventeenth century, and the 'Country' opposition to the Walpole government in eighteenth-century England. Like Puritan thought, neoclassical republicanism, in its rejection of individualism and the pursuit of self-interest, is not a liberal theory. Proponents of Hartz's view must take republicanism into account, even if, in the end, they treat it as less important than the 'republican synthesis', which has been advanced by some as a fundamental alternative to the thesis of liberal dominance. Although I believe that the significance of the republican synthesis has been much exaggerated, it nonetheless provides an interesting complication for the theory of liberal ideological hegemony.

Fourth, a theory of consensus must face the fact of the ubiquity of conflict in American history. There are severe limits to a model that offers a consensual interpretation of the history of a nation, when the central event of that history is a civil war. And the Civil War is not the only problem, for, as Robert Dahl has pointed out, there has been intense, seriously disruptive conflict approximately once a generation through the course of US history. Aside from the Civil War, the Revolution, and the framing of the Constitution, the disruptive events include the struggle over the Alien and Sedition Acts in the Washington administration, the crisis over the Hartford convention in 1815, the battle over the tariff and nullification during the Jackson presidency, the trauma of Reconstruction, the adjustment to the rapid post-Civil War emergence of large-scale industrial capitalism that transformed the structure of the economy, the Great Depression of the 1930s, and the civil rights revolution of the 1960s.[5] And to those must be added the deeply wounding conflict over the Vietnam War and the continuing crisis in race relations, which has now taken on a new dimension as part of the controversy over multiculturalism. Because the particularist advocates of the latter have claimed that the universalism of liberalism was a sham – merely empty words – the idea of multiculturalism is not easy to reconcile with the individualism of liberal principles. Nor should the deep conflicts over the 'social issues' – abortion, crime, drugs, the family, sexual orientation – be ignored. This is a long list of conflicts for a 'consensual' society to display.

Surely Richard Hofstadter was right when he argued that 'consensus, to be effective, must be a matter of behavior as well as thought, of institutions as well as theories'.[6] Further, if, as in Wolin's term, it is events such as these and their assimilation into the culture that constitute the 'birthright' of Americans, the historical inheritance that shapes the national identity,[7] then conflict as much as consensus appears to be central to the tradition of American politics. Put differently, it is obvious that major conflict can occur within a framework of widely shared ideas.

Two other points require further notice. The first is that although Americans may have the social attitudes of a people 'born equal', the nation is by no means egalitarian as a matter of empirical reality, regardless of how one understands equality. However, if one looks at the question in the comparative perspective of a Tocqueville, the point behind his observation about Americans being born equal becomes clear. Nonetheless, the manifest inequalities in American society have been, and no doubt will continue to be, sources of serious political conflict.

The second point is that for Hartz, liberalism and democracy were so closely intertwined as to be virtually indistinguishable. However, this is a somewhat problematic assumption. Liberalism and democracy are terms and movements that have separate histories. Essentially, as Russell Hanson succinctly pointed out, democracy has to do with a conception of the people as the ultimate authority, whereas liberalism is concerned with limitations on that authority. The suggested opposition is by no means necessary or absolute, but there is a potential tension here.[8] For example, Hanson argued that at the present time democracy is threatened by an excess of liberalism in the area of economics. In contrast, Jennifer Hochschild, in her study of contemporary race relations, argues very forcefully that our difficulties lie in democratically based hostility to blacks, which could be curbed only by the imposition of liberal controls over the inclinations of racist white majorities.[9] Here is not the place to enter into that interesting dispute, which fully illustrates the complexities inherent in the compound notion of liberal democracy. To the extent that the United States is somehow ineradicably liberal and also aspires to be more democratic, a reconciliation of democracy and liberalism is of continuing theoretical and political importance.

Hanson argues that democracy is an essentially contested concept, that is, not only that its meaning was, in fact, in dispute, but that in principle there could be no resolution to the argument.[10] Much of the history of American politics can be told in terms of a struggle to control the meaning of this central notion. The side in a political dispute that can successfully claim the democratic label has a tremendous rhetorical advantage. I would suggest that something analogous can be said about liberalism. At this writing *liberalism* is surely not an honorific term on a par with *democracy*. Still, even when there has been the most conflict in American history, liberalism broadly conceived has been a vital, even if not the only, tradition in American thought.

One thing that is clearly illustrated by Hartz's *Liberal Tradition in America* is the great plasticity of its central term. The history he recounted in his book was a tale of the 'pragmatic' adaptation of the liberal tradition while politics remained within the framework outlined by the basic ideas of individualism, capitalism, constitutionalism, and some measure of a rather vaguely defined and often formulaic or even mythological equality. In this perspective, the meaning of the essential elements of liberalism has been a source of much contestation. Given the high level of abstraction of such terms as *liberty*, *equality* and *democracy*, the specification of their meaning is in itself a significant source of conflict. Further, a good deal of what is at stake in American politics today is rooted in the question of the continued adaptability of the liberal tradition. In the view of many, liberal ideas have exhausted whatever vitality they might have had. If that is true, then the basic character of US politics is due for a profound change.

Perhaps it is useful to suggest more fully than Hartz the range of meanings attached to the idea of liberalism. At least three major currents of thought have been fitted under the rubric. Common to all is an image of human beings as essentially equal, rights-bearing, interest-oriented individuals–individuals who are entitled to have those rights defended, particularly against governmental intrusion. I call this the liberal idea. It is the foundation of the liberalism of constitutional limitations; its patron saint, so to speak, is John Locke, and its contemporary advocates range from Robert Bork on the 'conservative' Right to Lawrence Tribe on the liberal Left. The centrality of this image of human nature is a major part of what allowed Hartz to argue for the critical role of Lock-eanism in American political culture.

A second form of liberal theory is economic, free market, or laissez-faire liberalism; its lineage may be traced back to Adam Smith, and its best-known contemporary advocate is economist Milton Friedman, not to mention former president Ronald Reagan. That is the intellectual source of much of the opposition to government regulation of the economy in the Republican Party. This theory is also individualistic and rests on the assumption that the economic laws of the market – supply and demand and so on – will lead to benign outcomes through the self-equilibrating guidance of a 'hidden hand'. Those outcomes will develop only if government does not interfere with the pursuit of self-interest, on which the system supposedly rests. That is also the version of liberalism that most clearly rests on a theory of 'atomistic social freedom'.

The third form can be called reform liberalism; its intellectual roots can be seen in the work of John Stuart Mill and Thomas Hill Green in England, and in the thought of John Dewey and the political ideas of the populist and Progressive movements late in the nineteenth and early in the twentieth centuries, the New Deal, Fair Deal, New Frontier, and Great Society programs, and then on to contemporary philosophers such as John Rawls and political leaders such as Edward Kennedy and Bill Clinton. The focus continues to be on the free, equal, rights-bearing individual, but now, it is argued, those individuals may best be served by an active government, though one that, in economics, still adheres to the theory of the market, albeit in regulated form. That view often generates conflict with laissez-faire liberals, who, much to the despair of those who prize neat ideological labels, have come to be known as 'conservatives'. In any case, the reform tradition dominated American politics for most of this century and lasted until the onset of the Reagan revolution.

It is important to remember that to insist on the relative narrowness of the ideological spectrum is not to assert the unimportance of ideas in the United States. On the contrary, in fact. On one level, as I have argued, the absence of both traditionalist conservatism and any politically viable form of socialism serves as a profoundly limiting factor on the permissible range of sociopolitical alternatives that may plausibly be discussed. On another level, as Hartz observed, 'law has flourished on the corpse of philosophy in America'.[11] It is that which helps to explain the striking tendency of Americans to turn political questions into matters of constitutional law, to the extent that law often becomes a form of applied political theory. American law is permeated by sometimes confining assumptions rooted in liberal thought, and law is often a major focus of ideological debate, as can be illustrated by the sometimes fierce confirmation battles over nominations to the Supreme Court.

Finally, more important still, Samuel Huntington argues persuasively that the tenacity with which we hold to the liberal creed is, in itself, a major source of political conflict, because when values are so widely held, any deviation from them is bound to receive critical attention.[12] The civil rights movement, for example, certainly gained much of its moral and political force from its ability to appeal to what were presumably among the most deeply held values in the culture, even, or perhaps especially, when they were largely being observed in the breach. One need not share Huntington's distrust of what he rather disdainfully refers to as political 'moralism' to feel the force of much of his analysis of American history. In fact, our finest hours probably come when we ask ourselves to live up to the highest principles in liberalism. It is precisely that sort of criticism Walzer has in mind when he tries to show how the 'shared values' of a society become powerful weapons in the quest for justice.

A further note of caution must be introduced. Huntington is certainly correct to insist on the importance of the 'liberal creed'. However, as Rogers Smith observed, he overestimated both the unchanging nature of the consensus and the highly abstract nature of the ideas that it included.[13] Much of this critique, as I have already implied, can be applied to Hartz as well. Although Hartz was fully aware of the continual transformations of the liberal tradition, he did overstress, I think, a politics of 'pragmatic' adaptation and, as Dahl and Wolin suggest, downplayed the significance of intense conflict in the course of US history. Once again, one reason for conflict is surely the abstract nature of the principles that make up the liberal tradition. It is one thing, for example, to endorse liberty and equality, but many will argue that there is an inevitable tension, if not direct conflict, between the two ideas when we try to implement them. I would prefer to argue, as does Michael Walzer, that liberty and equality stand best when they stand together,[14] but that argument only reinforces the point that these concepts are highly abstract and that the attempt to apply them is likely to breed conflict and debate. I am not denying the earlier assertion that liberalism acts as a powerful limiting force on US politics, but rather insisting that there is ample room for serious conflict even within the confines of the tradition.

A few general thoughts on the relation of conflict and consensus in politics and culture are in order. There can be no perfectly consensual politics; the very idea of politics implies conflict. An essential aspect of the political problem is to find a way to resolve those conflicts peacefully, generally within a framework of rules that are part of a regime's consensus. Theorists may differ over the source of the rules. For those with ancestors as diverse as Thomas Hobbes and Karl Marx, the focus is on conflict. Either by nature or because of the structure of the preexisting society, society is seen to be essentially noncooperative, so that it is force rather than a system of shared values that ultimately holds it together. Any apparent consensus reflects the power of the dominant elites to impose their will on others so as to create a system of ideas supportive of the status quo. A second view, often associated with the implicitly conservative Parsonian sociology that was dominant in the 1950s, and before Parsons, with turn-of-the-century French sociologist Emile Durkheim, finds it impossible to imagine a society held together largely by force, so that consensus rests on a more or less spontaneously generated set of commonly held values. A social system without such a set of social values would be seen by theorists of the consensus school to be in danger of self-destruction.[15]

Neither of these views is entirely adequate by itself, and thus the mix between consensus and coercion is one of the defining characteristics of any political regime. This mixture is one of the theoretical issues at stake in the attempt to ascertain the broad outlines of American politics and history. Richard Hofstadter, who in some sense started it all, drew back from many of the implications of the consensus model. There surely can be no doubt, he wrote in one of his last works, that the consensus theory was a needed corrective to the Progressive model, since even the most devoted Marxist should be able to perceive the 'pervasively liberal-bourgeois character of American society in the past'. (In fact, some Marxists have come to insist on this point.) And yet, Hofstadter went on, the consensus framework has some 'intrinsic limitations *as history*'. He said that the proposition was essentially negative in that its primary use was to outline the limits of conflict in US history.[16] The criticism is fair, but such a use is still an important, though sometimes overlooked, function of a historical theory. Louis Hartz displayed his own sense of this when he wrote, apropos the relation between conflict and consensus, 'You do not get closer to the significance of an earthquake by ignoring the terrain on which it takes place.'[17]

Hartz was fully aware that his was a single-factor analysis of the American tradition. Such an analysis can have great utility. It is like sitting in a darkened room and aiming a flashlight at the wall. If the beam is direct, it will illuminate a small area with great clarity, though leaving much of the wall in darkness. If the beam is aimed at an angle, the area covered will be greater, though the light will be less intense. So it is in the use of a theory. *The Liberal Tradition in America* illuminates some important aspects of our politics with great intensity, but nevertheless, and with all due respect to Hartz's masterpiece, conflict recedes into the background and what often seem to be intricate but rather arcane variations on the consensus theme come to the fore. There is no question of the great, perhaps unique, importance of liberalism in US politics and history, but surely there is more to be said.

NOTES

1. Samuel Huntington, *American Politics: The Promise of Disharmony* (Cambridge, MA: Harvard University Press, 1981), p. 7.
2. Louis Hartz, *The Liberal Tradition in America* (New York: Harcourt Brace, 1955), p. 6. For a similar analysis by Richard Hofstadter, see *The Age of Reform* (New York: Knopf, 1955), p. 9. Long before the Marxists, Europeans began to see that something unusual was happening in the American colonies. See Jack P. Greene, *The Intellectual Construction of America: Exceptionalism and Identity from 1648 to 1800* (Baltimore: Johns Hopkins University Press, 1993). See also *Is America Different? A New Look at American Exceptionalism*. Byron E. Shafer (ed.) (New York: Oxford University Press, 1991). This analysis may make the consensus theory appear to be a celebration of the unique virtues of American democracy. However, Hofstadtet clearly wrote *The American Political Tradition* from a position well to the left of the ideas he described, and Hartz, who was, like Hofsendter, influenced by Marx, clearly managed to achieve enough critical distance from the dominant liberalism to be troubled by its narrowness. Not all consensus theorists managed this detachment. See Daniel Boorstin. *The Genius of American Politics* (Chicago: University of Chicago Press, 1953). Boorstin rejoiced in what he took to be the absence of serious ideological conflict in American history. For a discussion of some of the possible conservative implications of consensus see John Higham, 'The Cult of the "American Consensus": Homogenizing American History.' *Commentary* (February 1959), pp. 93–100, and 'Beyond Consensus: The Historian as Moral Critic', *American Historical Review* (April 1962), pp. 609–25.
3. Hartz, *Liberal Tradition*, pp. 140, 62.
4. J. David Greenstone, 'Political Culture and American Political Development: Liberty, Union, and the Liberal Bipolarity', *Studies in American Political Development*, vol. 1 (New Haven: Yale University Press, 1987), pp. 1–49. This is perhaps the most important critical study of the Hartz thesis. I cannot here go into the discussion Greenstone offers of the distinction between the liberal tradition as a limiting versus a causal factor. The article now appears in a fine book, J. D. Greenstone, *The Lincoln Persuation: Remaking American Liberalism* (Princeton: Princeton University Press, 1993). Without denying the importance of Hartz of the centrality of liberalism in US politics, Greenstone significantly amends the Hartz thesis. He reaches conclusions, particularly on Lincoln, that are complementary to mine, though by following a quite different analytical path. For another significant discussion, see John P. Diggins, 'Knowledge and Sorrow: Louis Hartz's Quarrel with American History', *Political Theory* (August 1988), pp. 355–76. Diggins's *The Lost Soul of American Politics* (New York: Basic Books, 1984) is the most extended attempt to restate the central importance of the liberal ideology at length and in depth. For other discussions, see the Symposium on Hartz in *Comparative Studies in Society and History* (1963), pp. 261–84. Hartz made a further contribution to this debate in the same issue of that journal: 'American Historiography and Comparative Analysis: Further Reflections', pp. 65–78.
5. Robert A. Dahl, 'The American Oppositions: Affirmation and Denial'. In *Political Oppositions in Western Democracies*, ed. Dahl (New Haven: Yale University Press, 1966), pp. 51–3.
6. Richard Hofstader, *The Progressive Historians* (New York: Knopf, 1963), p. 457.
7. Wolin, 'Contract and Birthright', *Political Theory* (May 1986), p. 182.
8. Russell Hanson, *The Democratic Imagination in America* (Princeton, NJ: Princeton University Press, 1985), p. 13. In many ways Hanson's book is parallel to this one, though in writing of liberal democracy, he focused on the democratic component, whereas I am more concerned with the liberal side. However, in a discussion of US politics, the two can never be entirely separated. For my review of Hanson's book, see *Political Theory* (May 1987), pp. 265–9. On the relationship between

democracy and liberalism, see also Amy Gutmann, 'How Liberal Is Democracy?' In Douglas MacClean and Claudia Mills (eds), *Liberalism Reconsidered* (Totowa, NJ: Rowman and Allanheld, 1983), pp. 25–50; and Don Herzog, 'Up Toward Liberalism', *Dissent* (Summer 1989), pp. 356–7.

9. Jennifer Hochschild, *The New American Dilemma* (New Haven: Yale University Press, 1984).

10. On the idea of essential contestability, see also William Connolly, *The Terms of Political Discourse*, 2nd ed. (Princeton, NJ: Princeton University Press, 1982).

11. Hartz, *Liberal Tradition*, p. 10. This observation provided the theme of Rogers Smith, *Liberalism and American Constitutional Law* (Cambridge: Harvard University Press, 1985). More recently, H. Jefferson Powell argued a similar point, extending it by saying that not only do political issues get transformed into legal questions, but they also become moral issues, so that the law defines the American identity. This may overstate the case, but the insight is important. See Powell, *The Moral Tradition of American Constitutionalism* (Durham, NC: Duke University Press, 1993), pp. 3–4. Note also George Kateb's remark that the two centuries of judicial interpretation of the Bill of Rights constitute the richest, most subtle and ingenious body of thinking on rights – 'a unique contribution to the meaning of human dignity'. See Kateb, *The Inner Ocean: Individualism and Democratic Culture* (Ithaca, NY: Cornell University Press, 1992), p. 3. In this perspective there may be more important American thought than Hartz recognized.

12. Samuel H. Huntington, *American Politics: The Promise of Disharmony* (Cambridge, MA: Harvard University Press, 1980). The recent work of Michael Walzer has drawn extensively on this conflict between ideals and social reality as a major factor in the development of social criticism.

13. Rogers Smith, 'The "American Creed" and Constitutional Theory', *Harvard Law Review* (May 1982), pp. 1696–1700, 1697. Smith develops his reservations on the Hartz thesis in 'Beyond Tocqueville, Myrdal, and Hartz: The Multiple Traditions in America'. *American Political Science Review* (September 1993), pp. 549–66.

14. Michael Walzer, 'In Defense of Equality', in *Radical Principles* (New York: Basic Books, 1980), p. 256.

15. I have drawn here on my introduction to J. P. Young, *Consensus and Conflict: Readings in American Politics* (New York: Dodd, Mead, 1972), pp. 2–3. See also the literature cited therein.

16. Hofstadter, *Progressive Historians*, pp. 451, 452. I have been helped in these reflections on consensus history by Andrew Delbanco, *The Puritan Ordeal* (Cambridge, MA: Harvard University Press, 1989), pp. 3–7. The concluding chapter of *Progressive Historians* is one of the most brilliant explorations of the consensus question. See pp. 437–66. The most extended treatment is Sternsher, *Consensus, Conflict, and American Historians*.

17. Hartz, *Liberal Tradition*, p. 20.

26

POLITICAL LIBERALISM

John Rawls

Now the serious problem is this. A modern democratic society is characterized not simply by a pluralism of comprehensive religious, philosophical, and moral doctrines but by a pluralism of incompatible yet reasonable comprehensive doctrines. No one of these doctrines is affirmed by citizens generally. Nor should one expect that in the foreseeable future one of them, or some other reasonable doctrine, will ever be affirmed by all, or nearly all, citizens. Political liberalism assumes that, for political purposes, a plurality of reasonable yet incompatible comprehensive doctrines is the normal result of the exercise of human reason within the framework of the free institutions of a constitutional democratic regime. Political liberalism also supposes that a reasonable comprehensive doctrine does not reject the essentials of a democratic regime. Of course, a society may also contain unreasonable and irrational, and even mad, comprehensive doctrines. In their case the problem is to contain them so that they do not undermine the unity and justice of society.

The fact of a plurality of reasonable but incompatible comprehensive doctrines – the fact of reasonable pluralism – shows that, as used in *Theory of Justice*, the idea of a well-ordered society of justice as fairness is unrealistic.

[...]

The problem of political liberalism is: how is it possible that there may exist over time a stable and just society of free and equal citizens profoundly divided

From: John Rawls, *Political Liberalism* (New York: Columbia University Press, 1993).

by reasonable though incompatible religious, philosophical, and moral doctrines? Put another way: how is it possible that deeply opposed though reasonable comprehensive doctrines may live together and all affirm the political conception of a constitutional regime? What is the structure and content of a political conception that can gain the support of such an overlapping consensus? These are among the questions that political liberalism tries to answer.

[...]

The problem of political liberalism is to work out a conception of political justice for a constitutional democratic regime that the plurality of reasonable doctrines – always a feature of the culture of a free democratic regime – might endorse. The intention is not to replace those comprehensive views, nor to give them a true foundation. Indeed, that intention would be delusional, but that is not the point. Rather, doing that is not the business of political liberalism.

Part of the seeming complexity of political liberalism – shown, say, in its having to introduce a further family of ideas – arises from accepting the fact of reasonable pluralism. For once we do this, then we assume that, in an ideal overlapping consensus, each citizen affirms both a comprehensive doctrine and the focal political conception, somehow related. In some cases the political conception is simply the consequence of, or continuous with, a citizen's comprehensive doctrine; in others it may be related as an acceptable approximation given the circumstances of the social world. In any case, since the political conception is shared by everyone while the reasonable doctrines are not, we must distinguish between a public basis of justification generally acceptable to citizens on fundamental political questions and the many nonpublic bases of justification belonging to the many comprehensive doctrines and acceptable only to those who affirm them.

[...]

Given the fact of the reasonable pluralism of democratic culture, the aim of political liberalism is to uncover the conditions of the possibility of a reasonable public basis of justification on fundamental political questions. It should, if possible, set forth the content of such a basis and why it is acceptable. In doing this, it has to distinguish the public point of view from the many nonpublic (not private) points of view. Or, alternatively, it has to characterize the distinction between public reason and the many nonpublic reasons and to explain why public reason takes the form it does.

[...]

The historical origin of political liberalism (and of liberalism more generally) is the Reformation and its aftermath, with the long controversies over religious toleration in the sixteenth and seventeenth centuries.[1] Something like the modern understanding of liberty of conscience and freedom of thought began then. As Hegel saw, pluralism made religious liberty possible, certainly not

Luther's and Calvin's intention.[2] Of course, other controversies are also of crucial importance, such as those over limiting the powers of absolute monarchs by appropriate principles of constitutional design protecting basic rights and liberties.

Yet despite the significance of other controversies and of principles addressed to settling them, the fact of religious division remains. For this reason, political liberalism assumes the fact of reasonable pluralism as a pluralism of comprehensive doctrines, including both religious and nonreligious doctrines. This pluralism is not seen as disaster but rather as the natural outcome of the activities of human reason under enduring free institutions. To see reasonable pluralism as a disaster is to see the exercise of reason under the conditions of freedom itself as a disaster. Indeed, the success of liberal constitutionalism came as a discovery of a new social possibility: the possibility of a reasonably harmonious and stable pluralist society.[3] Before the successful and peaceful practice of toleration in societies with liberal institutions there was no way of knowing of that possibility. It is more natural to believe, as the centuries-long practice of intolerance appeared to confirm, that social unity and concord requires agreement on a general and comprehensive religious, philosophical, or moral doctrine. Intolerance was accepted as a condition of social order and stability. The weakening of that belief helps to clear the way for liberal institutions. Perhaps the doctrine of free faith developed because it is difficult, if not impossible, to believe in the damnation of those with whom we have, with trust and confidence, long and fruitfully cooperated in maintaining a just society.

As I noted earlier, then, the problem of political liberalism is: how is it possible that there may exist over time a stable and just society of free and equal citizens profoundly divided by reasonable religious, philosophical, and moral doctrines? This is a problem of political justice, not a problem about the highest good. For the moderns the good was known in their religion; with their profound divisions, the essential conditions of a viable and just society were not. The problem of understanding these conditions moves to the center of the stage. Part of this problem is: What are the fair terms of social cooperation between citizens characterized as free and equal yet divided by profound doctrinal conflict? What is the structure and content of the requisite political conception, if, indeed, such a conception is even possible? This is not the problem of justice as it arose in the ancient world. What the ancient world did not know was the clash between salvationist, creedal and expansionist religions. That is a phenomenon new to historical experience, a possibility realized by the Reformation. Of course, Christianity already made possible the conquest of people, not simply for their land and wealth, and to exercise power and dominion over them, but to save their souls. The Reformation turned this possibility inward upon itself.

What is new about this clash is that it introduces into people's conceptions of their good a transcendent element not admitting of compromise. This element forces either mortal conflict moderated only by circumstance and exhaustion, or equal liberty of conscience and freedom of thought. Except on the basis of these last, firmly founded and publicly recognized, no reasonable political conception of justice is possible. Political liberalism starts by taking to heart the absolute depth of that irreconcilable latent conflict.

[...]

HOW IS POLITICAL LIBERALISM POSSIBLE?

1. One of the deepest distinctions between conceptions of justice is between those that allow for a plurality of reasonable though opposing comprehensive doctrines each with its own conception of the good, and those that hold that there is but one such conception to be recognized by all citizens who are fully reasonable and rational. Conceptions of justice that fall on opposite sides of this divide are distinct in many fundamental ways. Plato and Aristotle, and the Christian tradition as represented by Augustine and Aquinas, fall on the side of the one reasonable and rational good. Such views hold that institutions are justifiable to the extent that they effectively promote that good. Indeed, beginning with Greek thought the dominant tradition seems to have been that there is but one reasonable and rational conception of the good. The aim of political philosophy – always viewed as part of moral philosophy, together with theology and metaphysics – is then to determine its nature and content. The classical utilitarianism of Bentham, Edgeworth and Sidgwick belongs to this dominant tradition.[4]

By contrast, we have seen that political liberalism supposes that there are many conflicting reasonable comprehensive doctrines with their conceptions of the good, each compatible with the full rationality of human persons, so far as that can be ascertained with the resources of a political conception of justice.[5] As noted before, this reasonable plurality of conflicting and incommensurable doctrines is seen as the characteristic work of practical reason over time under enduring free institutions. So the question the dominant tradition has tried to answer has no answer: no comprehensive doctrine is appropriate as a political conception for a constitutional regime.[6]

2. Before asking how political liberalism is possible let us note that the political relationship in a constitutional regime has these two special features: first, it is a relationship of persons within the basic structure of society, a structure of basic institutions we enter only by birth and exit only by death (or so we may appropriately assume). To us it seems that we have simply materialized, as it were, from nowhere at this position in this social world with all its advantages and disadvantages, according to our good or bad fortune. I say from nowhere because we have no prior public or nonpublic identity: we have not come from somewhere else into this social world. Political society is closed: we come to be within it and we do not, and indeed cannot, enter or leave it voluntarily.[7]

Second, political power is always coercive power backed by the government's use of sanctions, for government alone has the authority to use force in upholding its laws. In a constitutional regime the special feature of the political relation is that political power is ultimately the power of the public, that is, the power of free and equal citizens as a collective body. This power is regularly imposed on citizens as individuals and as members of associations, some of whom may not accept the reasons widely said to justify the general structure of political authority – the constitution – or when they do accept that structure, they may not regard as justified many of the statutes enacted by the legislature to which they are subject.

3. This raises the question of the legitimacy of the general structure of authority with which the idea of public reason is intimately connected. The background of this question is that, as always, we view citizens as reasonable and rational, as well as free and equal, and we also view the diversity of reasonable religious, philosophical and moral doctrines found in democratic societies as a permanent feature of their public culture. Granting this, and seeing political power as the power of citizens as a collective body, we ask: when is that power appropriately exercised? That is, in the light of what principles and ideals must we, as free and equal citizens, be able to view ourselves as exercising that power if our exercise of it is to be justifiable to other citizens and to respect their being reasonable and rational?

To this political liberalism says: our exercise of political power is fully proper only when it is exercised in accordance with a constitution the essentials of which all citizens as free and equal may reasonably be expected to endorse in the light of principles and ideals acceptable to their common human reason. This is the liberal principle of legitimacy. To this it adds that all questions arising in the legislature that concern or border on constitutional essentials, or basic questions of justice, should also be settled, so far as possible, by principles and ideals that can be similarly endorsed. Only a political conception of justice that all citizens might be reasonably expected to endorse can serve as a basis of public reason and justification.[8]

Let us say, then, that in a constitutional regime there is a special domain of the political identified by the two features above described, among others. The political is distinct from the associational, which is voluntary in ways that the political is not; it is also distinct from the personal and the familial, which are affectional, again in ways the political is not. (The associational, the personal and the familial are simply three examples of the nonpolitical; there are others.)

4. Given the existence of a reasonably well-ordered constitutional regime, two points are central to political liberalism. First, questions about constitutional essentials and matters of basic justice are so far as possible to be settled by appeal to political values alone. Second, again with respect to those same fundamental questions, the political values expressed by its principles and ideals normally have sufficient weight to override all other values that may come in conflict with them.

Now in holding these convictions we clearly imply some relation between political and nonpolitical values. If it is said that outside the church there is no salvation, and therefore a constitutional regime cannot be accepted unless it is unavoidable, we must make some reply. We say that such a doctrine is unreasonable: it proposes to use the public's political power – a power in which citizens have an equal share – to enforce a view bearing on constitutional essentials about which citizens as reasonable persons are bound to differ uncompromisingly. When there is a plurality of reasonable doctrines, it is unreasonable or worse to want to use the sanctions of state power to correct, or to punish, those who disagree with us.

Here it is important to stress that this reply does not say, for example, that the doctrine *extra ecclesia nullam salus* is not true. Rather, it says that those who want to use the public's political power to enforce it are being unreasonable. That does not mean that what they believe is false. A reply from within a comprehensive view – the kind of reply we should like to avoid in political discussion – would say that the doctrine in question is a misapprehension of the divine nature, and hence not true. However, there may be no way to avoid entirely implying its lack of truth, even when considering constitutional essentials.

A basic point, however, is that in saying it is unreasonable to enforce a doctrine, while we may reject that doctrine as incorrect, we do not necessarily do so. Quite the contrary: it is vital to the idea of political liberalism that we may with perfect consistency hold that it would be unreasonable to use political power to enforce our own comprehensive view, which we must, of course, affirm as either reasonable or true.

5. Finally, we come to the question of how, as I have characterized it, political liberalism is possible. That is, how can the values of the special domain of the political – the values of a subdomain of the realm of all values – normally outweigh whatever values may conflict with them? Put another way, how can we affirm our comprehensive doctrine and yet hold that it would not be reasonable to use state power to gain everyone's allegiance to it?

The answer to this question, the various aspects of which we shall discuss from now on, has two complementary parts. The first part says that values of the political are very great values and hence not easily overridden: these values govern the basic frame-work of social life – the very groundwork of our existence[9] – and specify the fundamental terms of political and social cooperation. In justice as fairness some of these great values – the values of justice – are expressed by the principles of justice for the basic structure: among them, the values of equal political and civil liberty; fair equality of opportunity; the values of economic reciprocity; the social bases of mutual respect between citizens.

Other great political values – the values of public reason – are expressed in the guidelines for public inquiry and in the steps taken to make such inquiry free and public, as well as informed and reasonable. An agreement on a political conception of justice is to no effect without a companion agreement on guidelines of public inquiry and rules for assessing evidence. The values of public reason not only include the appropriate use of the fundamental concepts of judgment, inference, and evidence, but also the virtues of reasonableness and fairmindedness as shown in abiding by the criteria and procedures of common-sense knowledge and accepting the methods and conclusions of science when not controversial. We also owe respect to the precepts governing reasonable political discussion.

Together these values express to the liberal political ideal that since political power is the coercive power of free and equal citizens as a corporate body, this power should be exercised, when constitutional essentials and basic questions of justice are at stake, only in ways that all citizens can reasonably be expected to endorse in the light of their common human reason.

6. Political liberalism tries, then, to present an account of these values as those of a special domain – the political – and hence as a freestanding view. It is left to citizens individually – as part of liberty of conscience – to settle how they think the values of the political domain are related to other values in their compre-hensive doctrine. For we always assume that citizens have two views, a comprehensive and a political view; and that their overall view can be divided into two parts, suitably related. We hope that by doing this we can in working political practice ground the constitutional essentials and basic institutions of justice solely in those political values, with these values understood as the basis of public reason and justification.

But for this to hold, we need the second, and complementary, part of the answer as to how political liberalism is possible. This part says that the history of religion and philosophy shows that there are many reasonable ways in which the wider realm of values can be understood so as to be either congruent with, or supportive of, or else not in conflict with, the values appropriate to the special domain of the political as specified by a political conception of justice. History tells of a plurality of not unreasonable comprehensive doctrines. This makes an overlapping consensus possible, thus reducing the conflict between political and other values.

NOTES

1. Judith Shklar, in her *Ordinary Vices* (Cambridge, MA: Harvard University Press, 1984), speaks of the liberalism of fear, represented by Montaigne and Montesquieu, and described in that work as born out of the cruelties of the religious civil wars. See p. 5.
2. See *Grundlinien der Philosophie des Rechts* (1821), §270, near the end of the long comment.
3. Hume remarks on this in para. 6 of 'Liberty of the Press' (1741). See also A. G. Dickens, *The English Reformation* (London: Fontana Press, 1967), pp. 440f.
4. So likewise do the recent forms of ethical liberalism as expressed by Joseph Raz in *The Morality of Freedom* (Oxford: Clarendon Press, 1986) and Ronald Dworkin, 'The Foundations of Liberalism', in *The Tanner Lectures on Human Values* (Salt Lake City: University of Utah Press, 1991), vol. XI.
5. The point here is that while some would want to claim that given the full resources of philosophical reason, there is but one reasonable conception of the good, that cannot be shown by the resources of a reasonable political conception of justice.
6. This conclusion does not mean that the liberalisms of Kant and Mill are not reasonable and appropriate doctrines which lead one to support democratic

institutions. But they are two such doctrines among others, and so but two of the philosophical views likely to persist and to gain adherents in a reasonably just democratic regime. Indeed, their liberalisms have a certain historical preeminence as being among the first and most important doctrines to affirm modern constitutional democracy and to develop ideas that have been significant in its justification and defense.

7. The appropriateness of this assumption rests in part on a fact I shall only mention here: namely, that the right of emigration does not make the acceptance of political authority voluntary in the way that freedom of thought and liberty of conscience make the acceptance of ecclesiastical authority voluntary. This brings out a further feature of the domain of the political, one that distinguishes it from the associational. Immigration is also a common fact but we can abstract from it to get an uncluttered view of the fundamental question of political philosophy. Of course, immigration is an important question and must be discussed at some stage. I surmise this is best done in discussing the appropriate relations between peoples, or the law of peoples, which I don't consider in these lectures.

8. This paragraph can be stated more rigorously if we wished. One way to do this is to look at the question of legitimacy from the point of view of the original position. We suppose the parties to know the facts of reasonable pluralism and of oppression along with other relevant general information. We then try to show that the principles of justice they would adopt would in effect incorporate this principle of legitimacy and would justify only institutions it would count legitimate.

9. The phrase is from J. S. Mill, *Utilitarianism* ch. 5, para. 25.

27

THE LIBERALISM OF FEAR

Judith N. Shklar

Every adult should be able to make as many effective decisions without fear or favor about as many aspects of her or his life as is compatible with the like freedom of every other adult. That belief is the original and only defensible meaning of liberalism. It is a political notion, because the fear and favor that have always inhibited freedom are overwhelmingly generated by governments, both formal and informal. And while the sources of social oppression are indeed numerous, none has the deadly effect of those who, as the agents of the modern state, have unique resources of physical might and persuasion at their disposal.

Apart from prohibiting interference with the freedom of others, liberalism does not have any particular positive doctrines about how people are to conduct their lives or what personal choices they are to make. It is not, as so many of its critics claim, synonymous with modernity. Not that the latter is a crystal clear historical concept. Generally it does not refer to simply everything that has happened since the Renaissance, but to a mixture of natural science, technology, industrialization, skepticism, loss of religious orthodoxy, disenchantment, nihilism, and atomistic individualism. This is far from being a complete list, but it covers the main characteristics of modernity as it is perceived by those who believe that the word stands for centuries of despair and that liberalism is its most characteristic political manifestation.

It is by no means necessary to engage in disputes about the quality of the historiography or factual validity of this sort of discourse in general, but for the

From: Nancy Rosenblum (ed.), *Liberalism and the Moral Life* (Cambridge, MA: Harvard University Press, 1989).

student of political theory at least one point must be noted. That is that liberalism has been very rare both in theory and in practice in the last two hundred odd years, especially when we recall that the European world is not the only inhabited part of the globe. No one could ever have described the governments of eastern Europe as liberal at any time, though a few briefly made a feeble effort in that direction after the First World War. In central Europe it has been instituted only after the Second World War, and then it was imposed by the victors in a war that we forget at our peril. Anyone who thinks that fascism in one guise or another is dead and gone ought to think again. In France liberalism under the three Republics flickered on and off and is only now reasonably secure, though it is still seriously challenged. In Britain it has enjoyed its longest political success, but not in the vast areas, including Ireland, that England ruled until recently. Finally, let us not forget that the United States was not a liberal state until after the Civil War, and even then often in name only. In short, to speak of a liberal era is not to refer to anything that actually happened, except possibly by comparison to what came after 1914.

The state of political thought was no more liberal than that of the reigning governments, especially in the years after the French Revolution. And we should not forget the deeply illiberal prerevolutionary republican tradition of which John Pocock has reminded us so forcefully. It is in any case difficult to find a vast flow of liberal ideology in the midst of the Catholic authoritarianism, romantic corporatist nostalgia, nationalism, racism, proslavery, social Darwinism, imperialism, militarism, fascism, and most types of socialism which dominated the battle of political ideas in the last century. There was a current of liberal thought throughout the period, but it was hardly the dominant intellectual voice. In the world beyond Europe it was not heard at all. It was powerful in the United States only if black people are not counted as members of its society.

Why then, given the actual complexity of the intellectual history of the past centuries, is there so much easy generalizing about modernity and its alleged liberalism? The reason is simple enough: liberalism is a latecomer, since it has its origins in post-Reformation Europe. Its origins are in the terrible tension within Christianity between the demands of creedal orthodoxy and those of charity, between faith and morality. The cruelties of the religious wars had the effect of turning many Christians away from the public policies of the churches to a morality that saw toleration as an expression of Christian charity. One thinks of Sebastien Castellion among Calvinists, for example.[1] Others, torn by conflicting spiritual impulses, became skeptics who put cruelty and fanaticism at the very head of the human vices; Montaigne is the most notable among them. In either case the individual, whether the bearer of a sacred conscience or the potential victim of cruelty, is to be protected against the incursions of public oppression.

Later, when the bond between conscience and God is severed, the inviolability of personal decisions in matters of faith, knowledge, and morality is still defended on the original grounds that we owe it to each other as a matter of mutual respect, that a forced belief is in itself false and that the threats and bribes used to enforce conformity are inherently demeaning. To insist that individuals must make their own choices about the most important matter in their lives – their religious beliefs – without interference from public authority, is to go very far indeed toward liberalism. It is, I think, the core of its historical development, but it would be wrong to think of principled toleration as equivalent to political liberalism. Limited and responsible government may be implicit in the claim for personal autonomy, but without an explicit political commitment to such institutions, liberalism is still doctrinally incomplete. Montaigne was surely tolerant and humanitarian but he was no liberal. The distance between him and Locke is correspondingly great. Nevertheless, liberalism's deepest grounding is in place from the first, in the conviction of the earliest defenders of toleration, born in horror, that cruelty is an absolute evil, an offense against God or humanity. It is out of that tradition that the political liberalism of fear arose and continues amid the terror of our time to have relevance.[2]

There are of course many types of liberalism that remain committed to the primacy of conscience, whether in its Protestant or Kantian versions. There is Jeffersonian liberalism of rights, which has other foundations; and the Emersonian quest for self-development has its own liberal political expression. Liberalism does not in principle have to depend on specific religious or philosophical systems of thought. It does not have to choose among them as long as they do not reject toleration, which is why Hobbes is not the father of liberalism. No theory that gives public authorities the unconditional right to impose beliefs and even a vocabulary as they may see fit upon the citizenry can be described as even remotely liberal. Of all the cases made against liberalism, the most bizarre is that liberals are really indifferent, if not openly hostile, to personal freedom. This may follow from the peculiar identification of *Leviathan* as the very archetype of liberal philosophy, but it is a truly gross misrepresentation which simply assures that any social contract theory, however authoritarian intentions, and any anti-Catholic polemic add up to liberalism.[3]

The convoluted genealogy of liberalism that insists on seeing its origins in a theory of absolutism is not in itself interesting. More common is a sort of free association of ideas that perceives a danger to traditional revealed religion in toleration and hence assumes that liberalism is of necessity atheistic, agnostic, relativistic and nihilistic. This catalogue of accusations is worth mentioning, because it is commonplace and because it is easily and usefully refuted. The original mistake is the failure to distinguish psychological affinities from logical consequences. As a result, these critics cannot grasp that the liberalism of fear as a strictly political theory is not necessarily linked to any one religious or scientific doctrine, though it is psychologically more compatible with some rather than with others. It must reject only those political doctrines that do not recognize any difference between the spheres of the personal and the public. Because of the primacy of toleration as the irreducible limit on public agents, liberals must always draw such a line. This is not historically a permanent or unalterable boundary, but it does require that every public policy be considered with this separation in mind and be consciously defended as meeting its most severe current standard.

The important point for liberalism is not so much where the line is drawn, as that it be drawn, and that it must under no circumstances be ignored or forgotten. The limits of coercion begin, though they do not end, with a prohibition upon invading the private realm, which originally was a matter of religious faith, but which has changed and will go on changing as objects of belief and the sense of privacy alter in response to the technological and military character of governments and the productive relationships that prevail. It is a shifting line, but not an erasable one, and it leaves liberals free to espouse a very large range of philosophical and religious beliefs.

The liberalism of fear is thus not necessarily tied to either skepticism or to the pursuit of the natural sciences. There is, however, a real psychological connection between them. Skepticism is inclined toward toleration, since in its doubts it cannot choose among the competing beliefs that swirl around it, so often in murderous rage. Whether the skeptic seeks personal tranquility in retreat or tries to calm the warring factions around her, she must prefer a government that does nothing to increase the prevailing levels of fanaticism and dogmatism. To that extent there is a natural affinity between the liberal and the skeptic. Madison's discussion in the *Federalist* of how to end sectarian and similar factional conflicts through freedom is the perfect example of the fit between skepticism and liberal politics.[4] Nevertheless, a society of believers who choose never to resort to the use of the agencies of government to further their particular faith is imaginable, though not usual.

The intellectual flexibility of skepticism is psychologically more adapted to liberalism, but it is not a necessary element of its politics. A society governed by extremely oppressive skeptics can be easily imagined if, for example, they were to follow Nietzsche's political notions energetically. That is also true of the natural sciences. These tend to flourish most in freedom, quite unlike the fine arts and literature in this respect, but it is not impossible to imagine a science-friendly dictatorship. The publicity and the high standards of evidence, as well as the critical cast of mind which the natural sciences ideally require, again may suggest a psychological bond between the inner life of science and liberal politics. That is, however, far from being necessarily or even normally the case. There are many thoroughly illiberal scientists, in fact. The alliance between science and liberalism was one of convenience at first, as both had much to fear from the onslaughts of religion. With this shared enemy of censorship and persecution in abeyance, the identity of attitudes tended to fade. Science and liberalism were not born together; the former is far older. Nothing, however, can erase the chief difference between the two. The natural sciences live to change, while liberalism does not have to take any particular view of tradition.

To the extent that the European past was utterly hostile to freedom and that the most ancient of Indo-European traditions is the caste society, liberals must reject particular traditions. No society that still has traces of the old tripartite division of humanity into those who pray, those who fight, and those who labor can be liberal.[5] To turn one's back on some or even most traditions does not, however, mean that one must forego all tradition as a matter of intellectual honesty. Liberalism need not decide among traditions that are not hostile to its aspirations, nor does it have to regard the claims of any traditions as inherently false, simply because they do not meet scientific standards of rational proof. It all depends on the content and tendencies of the tradition. Clearly representative government is impregnated with traditions in Britain and in the United States. The habits of voluntarism depend on a variety of traditions. These are surely more than merely compatible with liberalism.

Intellectual modesty does not imply that the liberalism of fear has no content, only that it is entirely nonutopian. In that respect it may well be what Emerson called a party of memory rather than a party of hope.[6] And indeed there are other types of liberalism that differ from it sharply in this respect. First of all there is the liberalism of natural rights which looks to the constant fulfillment of an ideal preestablished normative order, be it nature's or God's, whose principles have to be realized in the lives of individual citizens through public guarantees. It is God's will that we preserve ourselves, and it is our own and society's duty to see that we are protected in our lives, liberties, and property and all that pertains to them. To that end we have a duty to establish protective public agencies and the right to demand that they provide us with opportunities to make claims against each and all.

If we take rights seriously we must see to it that principles such as those of *The Declaration of Independence* be made effective in every aspect of our public life. If the agencies of government have a single primary function it is to see to it that the rights of individuals be realized, because our integrity as God's or nature's creations requires it. Conceivably one might argue that a perfect or optimal society would be composed solely of rights-claiming citizens. In all cases, therefore, the liberalism of natural rights regards politics as a matter of citizens who actively pursue their own legally secured ends in accordance with a higher law. The paradigm of politics is the tribunal in which fair rules and decisions are made to satisfy the greatest possible number of demands made by individual citizens against one another individually, and against the government and other socially powerful institutions. The liberalism of natural rights envisages a just society composed of politically sturdy citizens, each able and willing to stand up for himself and others.

Equally given to hope is the liberalism of personal development. Freedom, it argues, is necessary for personal as well as social progress. We cannot make the best of our potentialities unless we are free to do so. And morality is impossible unless we have an opportunity to choose our courses of action. Nor can we benefit from education unless our minds are free to accept and reject what we are told and to read and hear the greatest variety of opposing opinions. Morality and knowledge can develop only in a free and open society. There is even reason to hope that institutions of learning will eventually replace politics and govern-ment. It would not be unfair to say that these two forms of liberalism have their spokesmen in Locke and John Stuart Mill respectively, and they are of course perfectly genuine expressions of liberal doctrine. It must be said, however, that neither one of these two patron saints of liberalism had a strongly developed historical memory, and it is on this faculty of the human mind that the liberalism of fear draws most heavily.

The most immediate memory is at present the history of the world since 1914. In Europe and North America torture had gradually been eliminated from the practices of government, and there was hope that it might eventually disappear everywhere. With the intelligence and loyalty requirements of the national warfare states that quickly developed with the outbreak of hostilities torture returned and has flourished on a colossal scale ever since.[7] We say 'never again', but somewhere someone is being tortured right now, and acute fear has again become the most common form of social control. To this the horror of modern warfare must be added as a reminder. The liberalism of fear is a response to these undeniable actualities, and it therefore concentrates on damage control.

Given the inevitability of that inequality of military, police, and persuasive power which is called government, there is evidently always much to be afraid of. And one may, thus, be less inclined to celebrate the blessings of liberty than to consider the dangers of tyranny and war that threaten it. For this liberalism the basic units of political life are not discursive and reflecting persons, nor friends and enemies, nor patriotic soldier-citizens, nor energetic litigants, but the weak and the powerful. And the freedom it wishes to secure is freedom from the abuse of power and intimidation of the defenseless that this difference invites. This apprehension should not be mistaken for the obsessive ideologies which concentrate solely on the notion of totalitarianism. This is a shorthand for only the extremity of institutionalized violence and almost implies that anything less radically destructive need not concern us at all.

The liberalism of fear, on the contrary, regards abuses of public powers in all regimes with equal trepidation. It worries about the excesses of official agents at every level of government, and it assumes that these are apt to burden the poor and weak most heavily. The history of the poor compared to that of the various elites makes that obvious enough. The assumption, amply justified by every page of political history, is that some agents of government will behave law-lessly and brutally in small or big ways most of the time unless they are prevented from doing so.

The liberalism inspired by these considerations does resemble Isaiah Berlin's negative liberty, but it is not exactly the same. Berlin's negative liberty of 'not being forced' and its later version of 'open doors' is kept conceptually pure and separate from 'the conditions of liberty', that is, the social and political insti-tutions that make personal freedom possible. That is entirely necessary if nega-tive liberty is to be fully distinguished from what Berlin calls 'positive liberty', which is the freedom of one's higher from one's lower self. It cannot be denied, moreover, that this very clear demarcation of negative liberty is the best means of avoiding the slippery slope that can lead us to its threatening opposite.

Nevertheless, there is much to be said for not separating negative liberty from the conditions that are at least necessary to make it possible at all. Limited government and the control of unequally divided political power constitute the minimal condition without which freedom is unimaginable in any politically organized society. It is not a sufficient condition, but it is a necessary prerequisite. No door is open in a political order in which public and private intimidation prevail, and it requires a complex system of institutions to avoid that. If negative freedom is to have any political significance at all, it must specify at least some of the institutional characteristics of a relatively free regime. Socially that also means a dispersion of power among a plurality of politically empowered groups, pluralism, in short, as well as the elimination of such forms and degrees of social inequality as expose people to oppressive practices. Otherwise the 'open doors' are a metaphor – and not, politically, a very illuminating one at that.

Moreover, there is no particular reason to accept the moral theory on which Berlin's negative freedom rests. This is the belief that there are several inherently incompatible moralities among which we must choose, but which cannot be reconciled by reference to a common criterion – paganism and Christianity being the two most obvious examples.[8] Whatever the truth of this metapolitical assumption may be, liberalism can do without it. The liberalism of fear in fact does not rest on a theory of moral pluralism. It does not, to be sure, offer a *summon bomon* toward which all political agents should strive, but it certainly does begin with a *summum malum*, which all of us know and would avoid if only we could. That evil is cruelty and the fear it inspires, and the very fear of fear itself. To that extent the liberalism of fear makes a universal and especially a cosmopolitan claim, as it historically always has done.

What is meant by cruelty here? It is the deliberate infliction of physical, and secondarily emotional, pain upon a weaker person or group by stronger ones in order to achieve some end, tangible or intangible, of the latter. It is not sadism, though sadistic individuals may flock to occupy positions of power that permit them to indulge their urges. But public cruelty is not an occasional personal inclination. It is made possible by differences in public power, and it is almost always built into the system of coercion upon which all governments have to rely to fulfill their essential functions. A minimal level of fear is implied in any system of law, and the liberalism of fear does not dream of an end of public, coercive government. The fear it does want to prevent is that which is created by arbitrary, unexpected, unnecessary, and unlicensed acts of force and by habitual and pervasive acts of cruelty and torture performed by military, paramilitary, and police agents in any regime.

Of fear it can be said without qualification that it is universal as it is physiological. It is a mental as well as a physical reaction, and it is common to animals as well as to human beings. To be alive is to be afraid, and much to our advantage in many cases, since alarm often preserves us from danger. The fear we fear is of pain inflicted by others to kill and maim us, not the natural and healthy fear that merely warns us of avoidable pain. And, when we think politically, we are afraid not only for ourselves but for our fellow citizens as well. We fear a society of fearful people.

Systematic fear is the condition that makes freedom impossible, and it is aroused by the expectation of institutionalized cruelty as by nothing else. However, it is fair to say that what I have called 'putting, cruelty first' is not a sufficient basis for political liberalism. It is simply a first principle, an act of moral intuition based on ample observation, on which liberalism can be built, especially at present. Because the fear of systematic cruelty is so universal, moral claims based on its prohibition have an immediate appeal and can gain recognition without much argument. But one cannot rest on this or any other naturalistic fallacy. Liberals can begin with cruelty as the primary evil only if they go beyond their well-grounded assumption that almost all people fear it and would evade it if they could. If the prohibition of cruelty can be universalized and recognized as a necessary condition of the dignity of persons, then it can become a principle of political morality.

NOTES

1. W. Allen, *A History of Political Thought in the Sixteenth Century* (London: Methuen, 1941), pp. 89–97, 370–7. Quentin Skinner, *The Foundations of Political Thought*, 2 vols (Cambridge: Cambridge University Press, 1978), II, pp. 241–54.
2. See Judith Shklar, *Ordinary Vices* (Cambridge, MA: Harvard University Press, 1984).
3. See, for instance, Laurence Berns, 'Thomas Hobbes', in Leo Strauss and Joseph Cropsey (eds), *A History of Political Philosophy* (Chicago: Rand McNally, 1972), pp. 370–94. C. B. Macpherson, *The Political Theory of Possessive Individualism* (Oxford: Clarendon, 1962). These interpretations depend on seeing Locke as very similar to Hobbes, as Leo Strauss did in *Natural Right and History* (Chicago: University of Chicago Press, 1953), pp. 202–51.
4. Alexander Hamilton et al., *The Federalist Papers*, Clinton Rossiter (ed.) (New York: New American Library, 1961), nos 10, 51.
5. Georges Duby, *The Chivalrous Society*, trans. Cynthia Postan (Berkeley: University of California Press, 1977), pp. 81–7.
6. Ralph Waldo Emerson, 'The Conservative', *Essays and Lectures*, Joel Porte (ed.) (New York: Library of America, 1983), p. 173.
7. Edward Peters, *Torture* (Oxford: Basil Blackwell, 1985), pp. 103–40.
8. Isaiah Berlin, 'Introduction' and 'Two Concepts of Liberty', *Four Essays on Liberty* (Oxford: Oxford University Press, 1982), pp. xxxvii–ixiii, 118–72. Isaiah Berlin, 'The Originality of Machiavelli', *Against the Current* (New York: Viking, 1980), pp. 25–79.

28

PASSIONS AND CONSTRAINT – ON THE THEORY OF LIBERAL DEMOCRACY

Stephen Holmes

Paine and Jefferson took comfort from the observation that no generation had the ability to bind its successors irreversibly. After witnessing the 'suicides' of several democratic regimes, we cannot revive their complacency, their naive trust in the good sense of the present generation, once unleashed from the vexatious commitments of the past.[1] The admittedly real difficulty of binding the future is not always a cause for celebration for the simple reason that our incapacity to commit successors in a semiautocratic manner may lead to the destruction of a fragile system of representative democracy. True, the collapse of the Weimar Republic was due more to the disloyalty of its elites than to Article 48 or defective constitutional design. Still the catastrophe of 1933 suggests, once again, that constitutional precommitment and democratic politics may not be so antagonistic as Jefferson and Paine sometimes believed. There is paradox but no contradiction here. Theorists who recognized the paradox, such as Madison, also embraced it.

A preceding generation cannot use legal entrenchment to prevent a succeeding generation from saying: 'No more freedom!' No constitutional arrangement, however well-designed, can protect reliably against a 'violent popular paroxysm'.[2] But this factual incapacity does not imply that predecessors have no right or reason to design institutions with an eye to inhibiting the future destruction of electorally accountable government. When attempting to bind the future, constitution makers are not simply trying to exercise domination and

From: Stephen Holmes, *Passions and Constraint – On the Theory of Liberal Democracy* (Chicago: University of Chicago Press, 1995).

control. Precommitment is justified because, rather than merely foreclosing options, it holds open possibilities that would otherwise lie beyond reach.

The Paine-Jefferson formula, in truth, is convincing only if we restrict our view to the short run, to relations between two generations. A wider perspective changes the equation. By means of a constitution, generation *a* can help generation *c* protect itself from being sold into slavery by generation *b*. To safeguard the choices available to distant successors, constitution makers restrict the choices available to proximate successors. Ultimately, therefore, Hume was wrong to discern a self-contradiction at the heart of republican theory. Our ancestors *did* have the right to contract away our freedom to contract away the freedom of our descendants. The framers strove to create not merely a popular government but a popular government that (unlike the turbulent Greek republics) might endure. They had a right to bind subsequent generations minimally to prevent them from binding *their* successors maximally. In practice, to be sure, this arrangement will function only if latecomers, currently alive, acknowledge its essential fairness. But this is not an unreasonable expectation. Recognizing the rights of its posterity, a current generation may voluntarily limit its own power over the future; and the easiest way for a large and diverse community to do so may be to submit to the univocal authority of the past. Seen in this light, Madisonian precommitments appear, in principle, both democratic and majoritarian. To grant power to all future majorities, of course, a constitution must limit the power of any given majority. Liberal constitutions, in fact, consist largely of metaconstraints: rules that *compel* each decision-making authority to expose its decisions to criticism and possible revision, rules that *limit* each generation's ability to rob its own successors of significant choices.

Paine and Jefferson shuddered at the idea of binding the future because they could not conceive of 'binding' in a positive or emancipatory way. They did not grasp clearly that constraints can enhance freedom, that rigidities can create flexibilities. Their blind spot was due partly to a naive belief in progress. But it also resulted from their overly conservative conception of how constitutions function. The common metaphors of checking, blocking, limiting, and restraining all suggest that constitutions are, in the main, negative devices used to prevent abuses of power. But rules are also creative. They organize new practices and generate new possibilities which would not otherwise exist.

Constitutions may be usefully compared to the rules of a game and even to the rules of grammar. While *regulative* rules (for instance, 'no smoking') govern preexistent activities, *constitutive* rules (for instance, 'bishops move diagonally') make a practice possible for the first time. Rules of the latter sort should not be thought of as hindrances or chains. Grammatical principles do not merely restrain a speaker, repressing his unruly impulses while permitting orderly ones to filter through. Far from simply handcuffing people, linguistic rules allow interlocutors to do many things they would not otherwise have been able to do or even have thought of doing. Flexibility should not be contrasted with rigidity, therefore, for the simple reason that rigidities can create flexibilities. A democratic constitution, by analogy, does not merely hobble majorities and officials. The American Constitution helped create the Union. It also assigns powers (gives structure to the government, guarantees electoral accountability, protects the rights of the opposition, and so forth), and regulates the way in which these powers are employed (in accord, for example, with principles such as due process and equal treatment). To say that constitutional rules are enabling, not disabling, is to reject the notion that constitutionalism is exclusively concerned with limitations on power.

We can begin the move from negative to positive constitutionalism simply by rethinking our concept of *limitations*. Limits do not necessarily weaken; they can also strengthen. For one thing, 'that ill deserves the Name of Confinement, which hedges us in only from Bogs and Precipices'.[3] Constitutions, moreover, can be binding in a way that engenders unprecedented possibilities. By having himself bound to the mast, Ulysses could enjoy an event (song without shipwreck) that he could not otherwise have experienced. His strategy of preventive self-incapacitation, however, is not precisely analogous to the designing and ratification of a constitution. In America, if the framers had not 'bound' their successors, there would have been no country. That is why the framers are often assimilated to the Founders. Constitutions do not merely limit power; they can create and organize power as well as give it direction. Most important of all, limited government can subserve self-government by helping create the 'self' (or national unity) which does the governing. That constitutionalism can contribute to nation building provides powerful evidence that it has a positive, not merely a negative, function.

[...]

Although 'the rights of the Constitution' are much discussed in Great Britain, Parliament's authority over the form of government remains 'transcendent and uncontrollable'.[4] Constitutional amendment by a simple parliamentary majority, obviously enough, is incompatible with constitutionalism as Madison and Hamilton understood it. As a popularly ratified document that the government cannot redesign by ordinary means, the constitution is an instrument of self-government, a technique whereby the citizenry rules itself. How else could a large democratic community manage its own affairs? A collectivity cannot formulate coherent purposes apart from all decision-making procedures. 'The people' cannot act as an amorphous blob.

Carl Schmitt, an ardent opponent of liberal constitutionalism, loftily spurned such down-to-earth considerations. Like many less cynical theorists, he subscribed to the legendary opposition between constitutional limitations and democratic government.[5] Because *das Volk* is the ultimate constituent power, he claims, it must be conceived as an unstructured 'Urgrund' or even as 'das "formlos Formende"' which cannot be precommitted by constitutional procedures.[6] But Schmitt's democratic mysticism, not to mention its practical consequences, suffices to discredit this approach. It is meaningless to speak about popular government apart from some sort of legal framework which enables the electorate to express a coherent will. For this reason, democratic citizens require some organizational support from regime-founding fore-fathers.[7] Unless they tie their own hands, with the help of their predecessors, 'the people' will be unable to deliberate effectively and act consistently.

Decisions are made on the basis of predecisions. Electoral choices are made on the basis of constitutional choices. When they enter the voting-booth, for instance, voters decide who shall be president, but not how many presidents there shall be.[8] Similarly, they do not decide, at that moment, the date when the election is to be held. (As Locke recognized, 'this power of chusing must also be exercised by the People, either at certain appointed seasons, or else when they are summoned to it'.)[9] Arguing that constitutionalism was an American innovation, alien to Great Britain, Madison noted that British parliamentarians had 'actually changed, by legislative acts, some of the most fundamental articles of the government'. His principal example of a higher-order law that ought not to depend upon the discretion of elected deputies is electoral law itself. 'They have in particular, on several occasions, changed the period of election; and, on the last occasion, not only introduced septennial in place of triennial elections, but by the same act, continued themselves in place four years beyond the term for which they were elected by the people'. Under the system developed at Philadelphia, by contrast, the legislature cannot, of its own sweet will, rewrite the rules of the electoral game. For the House of Repre-sentatives, for instance, 'biennial elections' are 'unalterably fixed by such a Constitution'.[10]

Fixed-calendar elections, which may well be constitutionally prescribed, deny discretion to both public officials and present-day electoral majorities on a very important question. In practice, liberal democracy is never simply the rule of the people but always the rule of the people within certain predetermined channels, according to certain prearranged procedures, following certain preset criteria of enfranchisement, and on the basis of certain predrawn electoral districts. The last example is revealing, even though districting schemes are not usually entrenched in the constitution. (As a product of federalism, the American Senate is an exception.) While placing supreme authority in an elected legislature,[11] Locke granted the power to reapportion the elected assembly to the unselected executive.[12] Population shifts make it undemocratic to fix electoral districts in an unalterable charter. But the authority periodically to readjust the system to unforeseen demographic changes can be constitutionally assigned. It would be unwise, Locke thought, to ascribe the task of remedying gross malappor-tionment to the very assembly created by gross malapportionment. Such a negligent allocation of oversight power would make legislators judges in their own cause.[13]

Citizens can enforce their will only through elections held on the basis of a preexistent apportionment plan, a plan which may be unfair or obsolete. As a result, the responsibility for flexible redistricting must be lodged outside the popularly elected legislature (for instance, in the courts). To preserve democracy, in this case, voters must partially *abdicate* the power of apportionment, that is, must remove it from the hands of elected and accountable representatives. Here we encounter the paradox of democracy not as a theoretical puzzle but as a functioning institutional arrangement: citizens can increase their power by tying their own hands. Limited dedemocratization subserves continuing democratic rule.

[. . .]

Is Milton Friedman the legitimate heir to Adam Smith? Did Locke's antagonism to cruel and arbitrary tyranny imply a repudiation of public provision for the needs of the poor? Does T. H. Marshall's famous sequence of legal rights, political rights, and social rights map the smooth unfolding of an initial promise or a step-by-step disavowal of the past? What is the relation between the old liberalism and the new liberalism, between the *Rechtsstaat* and the *Sozialstaat*, between constitutional rights and welfare rights?

These questions are neither uninteresting nor unanswerable. But the point of asking them is not immediately clear. Even if we could announce that public assistance represented a betrayal or a consummation of classical liberal principles, no political consequences would necessarily follow, one way or the other. The perpetuation of traditional orientations and commitments may be a sign of heroic tenacity, but 'fidelity to the sources' may also be a symptom of mental rigidity and moral sclerosis. Some adversaries of the welfare state try to make us feel derelict for having abandoned our noble libertarian heritage. Contrariwise, friends of the welfare state commend us for having thrown off the shameful inheritance of Social Darwinism. Depending on one's perspective, in other words, historical continuity can deserve praise or blame.

I stress this admittedly obvious consideration to avoid a misconstrual of my objectives in this chapter. While aiming to highlight some neglected similarities and interconnections between eighteenth-century liberal rights and twentieth-century welfare rights, I remain conscious that such an exercise has limited value. Policy debates, for one thing, cannot be sensibly conducted as legacy disputes. The liberal movement, moreover, was complex and diffuse. It evolved over the course of centuries and assumed different forms in different national contexts. Even when studying a single country during one and the same period, we can employ 'liberalism' (which, when used to describe pre-nineteenth-century political thought, is something of an anachronism) only as an umbrella term covering a variety of political tendencies and outlooks. As a result, diverse historical perspectives on liberal thought remain possible; different interpreters of the canon will inevitably produce divergent answers to the continuity question. Furthermore, a similarity or correspondence of beliefs, which is all I shall attempt to document, does not constitute proof of historical continuity. Evidence of transmission and reception would be required to support any kind of stronger claim.

Normative continuity, the bequeathing and inheriting of a system of moral values, moreover, even if it could be established, would not constitute a *causal explanation* of the emergence and stabilization of contemporary welfare regimes. General affluence, a dramatic increase in state revenues during wartime, socially accepted obligations toward veterans, the need to secure political stability in the face of boom-and-slump cycles in the economy, the growing bargaining power of previously disenfranchised groups – these and many other factors played a decisive role in the emergence of contemporary economic rights. Public relief programs, moreover, have sometimes been embraced by political elites for purely self-interested reasons: because, for example, 'Rebellions of the Belly are the worst', or because indigence provides a breeding ground for contagious diseases that might eventually infect the rich, or because 'poverty in the midst of plenty is likely to increase the incidence of crime'.[14] Recognition that the castle is not safe unless the cottage is well-fed was no doubt conducive to the enactment of modern redistributionist legislation. If normative continuity out-weighed normative discontinuity, as I think it did, it was only one element among the many that contributed to the rise of the welfare state. The erroneous assumption that classical liberals would have been utterly hostile to transfer programs remains such a commonplace, however, that a succinct refutation can still be useful.

FOUR RIVAL VIEWS

A two-by-two table is the most economical way to survey possible responses to the continuity question. We can distinguish, along a *descriptive* dimension, between those who assert a sharp rupture between liberal rights and welfare rights and those who discern an unbroken continuity linking the two. Along an *evaluative* dimension, we can then contrast those who view continuity with approval and discontinuity with disapproval and those who take the opposite approach (see Figure 1).

1. In the first cell, we can locate what I have been calling *negative constitutionalism*, the standard Hayekian view that liberalism was a basically

	disapproval	approval
discontinuity	1	2
continuity	3	4

Figure 1. Possible Responses to the Continuity Question

antistatist philosophy, concerned solely with limiting abusive government – that is, with preventing tyranny and straitjacketing political power. Liberalism, from this austere perspective, is wholly incompatible with positive programs of public provision, all of which require confiscatory taxation, a 'taking' from A in order to give to B, and other 'stultifying' acts of governmental intervention into a sphere of otherwise spontaneous and voluntary relations. In a free society, according to this view, all individuals must look after their own material welfare as well as their souls. Liberal citizens can be prevented from harming each other but never forced to make one another prosper or even to relieve each other's distress.

2. The second possibility is equally well known. To build the welfare state, it is said, modern citizens had to leave behind the anticommunal, privatistic, beggar-thy-neighbor and devil-take-the-hindmost attitudes purportedly typical of classical liberalism. Social provision depends on forms of solidarity and civic friendship that liberalism purportedly aims to destroy. It fits poorly into a society where all human relations are meant to be voluntary and instrumental, and where contractual freedom cannot be limited by norms of justice and fairness. Before they could endorse the welfare state, therefore, rulers and ruled alike had to be weaned from a morally impoverished *sauve qui peut* liberalism and converted to morally robust, samaritan values and traditions.

3. Third, and quite distinctly, many theorists and publicists have perceived a continuity between liberalism and the welfare state but have gone on to argue that this continuity is morally deplorable – indeed, that it discloses either the original sin of liberalism or the phoniness of welfare rights. This third category is probably the most interesting because it encourages us to ponder the disconcerting bedfellowship of far-left and far-right critics of economic rights. Remember that both Marxists and Reaganites (the former inhabiting cell 3, and the latter cell 1) blame the dole for weakening the moral fiber of recipients, for infantilizing them into dependency – defusing their revolutionary potential in the one case, destroying their frontiers-manlike self-reliance in the other. A different coincidence of opposites is contained within cell 3 itself. Both radicals and ultraconservatives[15] passionately assail the bourgeois individualism and materialistic euphoria of liberal society – as an obstacle to the classless society on the one hand and as an extinction of deference and hierarchy on the other. Neither sees anything in welfare states that fundamentally changes the picture, anything transcending the limits that, in their view, hideously deform the liberal tradition.

However it is judged politically, the position identified by cell 1 is both historically inaccurate and conceptually confused. Above all, it exaggerates the discontinuity between classical and contemporary liberals. Modern liberalism is best understood as a rethinking of the principles of classical liberalism, an adaptation of these principles to a new social context where individual freedom is threatened in new ways. Hence, even those who sympathize with some of the policy implications of the view represented by cell 2 may find it dissatisfying as a historical account. Cell 3 should evoke a contrary response: even those who find it morally and politically unpalatable may concede that it is historically on the right track, since it recognizes the continuum between the classical liberalism of the seventeenth and eighteenth centuries and redistributionist liberalism today.

4. Having signaled the existence of these three alternatives, I turn now directly to the fourth and, I am convinced, superior claim that there is a demonstrable historical continuity, or at least compatibility, between classical liberalism and the values embodied in the welfare state, and that this common ground is, by and large, a moral and political advantage. If we wished to attach a name to this final position, we would probably be justified in citing John Rawls, a defender of welfarist redistribution as well as a self-proclaimed theoretical descendant of Locke and Kant. (While Rawls's own arguments for welfarist redistribution are not strengthened philosophically by citing such a pedigree, the attacks of those critics who accuse him of betraying the spirit of liberalism *can* be definitively refuted thereby.)

In any case, the evidence favoring cell 4, or at least suggesting some kind of historical continuity, is bountiful. Consider, as a randomly chosen example, Montesquieu's unambiguous affirmation of the state's duty to relieve poverty: 'The alms given to a naked man in the street do not fulfill the obligations of the state, which owes to every citizen a certain subsistence, a proper nourishment, convenient clothing, and a kind of life not incompatible with health.'[16] No series of such quotations, of course, would demonstrate the compatibility of welfare measures with the principles of classical liberalism, much less the logical derivation or historical emergence of the former from the latter. Montesquieu may well have been an inconsistent or incomplete liberal, unable to free himself from vestigial strains of aristocratic paternalism or Christian almsgiving. Perhaps if he had thought through the implications of the 'rule of law', he would have written more like A. V. Dicey. I think not, however. To make my position credible, I must now show how redistributionist conclusions are not merely consistent with but, in a changed context, follow directly from liberal principles themselves.

THE PRIMACY OF JUSTICE

In this chapter, I continue to adopt a nominalist approach to the concept of liberalism, taking as my benchmark the cluster of views advanced and defended by, among others, Locke, Montesquieu, Hume, Smith, Madison, Kant, and Mill.[17] This list allows us to register skepticism, at the very outset, about the Hayekian assumption that classical liberals were fiercely hostile to social planning. One of the theorists mentioned actually wrote a constitution; all the others recognized the benefits of shrewd constitutional design; and a constitution, although it does not involve a central allocation of most goods and services, *is* a 'plan' with significant allocative implications.[18] The writings of those theorists listed, moreover, provide virtually no evidence that liberalism is deeply incompatible with democratic or majoritarian politics (which may have further redistributive consequences). All of them believed that choices made collectively by communities were a form of *freedom* that rivaled in importance choices made severally by individuals. When Locke wrote that people should freely choose their form of government, for example, he had collective decision making in mind, not the uncoordinated choices of individual consumers in an economic marketplace.[19]

Claimants to the mantle of Adam Smith, such as Milton Friedman, typically paint welfare measures as profoundly illiberal: 'The central defect of these measures is that they seek through government to force people to act against their own immediate interests in order to promote a supposedly general interest.'[20] But is there anything particularly illiberal about the realization that, in the absence of coercion, self-love will induce individuals to exempt themselves from generally useful rules? Liberal constitutions, it is worth recalling, are designed to do precisely what Friedman apparently deplores: to *force* officeholders, at least, to act against their own immediate interests in order to promote the general interest. And what does Friedman think is the purpose of criminal law?

As our list of representative liberal theorists suggests, liberalism should not be considered principally an antistatist philosophy of limited government.[21] The fact is, liberals were as wary of anarchy as of tyranny. They advocated not merely freedom from government, but also order through government. Security is impossible without a state monopoly on the legitimate use of violence. To the extent that he defined freedom as security, a definition to which I shall return, even Montesquieu conceived sovereign power, organized along liberal lines, as an indispensable instrument of freedom.[22]

The order that liberals admired, moreover, was not just any kind of order, not simply the suppression of random violence and civil war. Instead, it was a certain kind of order, an order qualified in a specific way: *a just order*. The primacy of justice in liberal thought, alas, is often underestimated. According to Friedman, again, 'the egalitarian ... will defend taking from someone to give to others ... on grounds of "justice". At this point equality comes sharply into conflict with freedom; one must choose. One cannot be both an egalitarian, in this sense, and a liberal.'[23] But why should a conflict between freedom and equality, even assuming that one exists, require an either/or choice?

There is nothing so melodramatic about normative dissonance, after all. To put Friedman's liberty-equality conflict into perspective, let us consider the conflict, say, between liberty of the press and the right to privacy. This is a *conflict between freedom and freedom*. It requires not an either/or decision but rather a rough balancing of important but rival interests. The conflict between freedom and equality, which Friedman and other libertarians magnify into a final showdown between the forces of good and evil (where one will emerge triumphant while the other is extinguished) is no different. It is just another example of the everyday moral conflict characterizing all liberal societies and requiring pragmatic compromise. By juxtaposing the conflict between freedom and equality – stressed by libertarians – to the many conflicts between freedom and freedom, we de-dramatize the former and put it into perspective. And we show how we can remain simultaneously egalitarians and liberals, perhaps along Rawlsian lines.

Classical liberals, it should be said, never placed *justice* in disdainful quotation marks; they never sacrificed or subordinated justice to freedom, as Friedman's litmus test would require. On the contrary, Hume urges us 'to look at the vast apparatus of government, as having ultimately no other object or purpose but the distribution of justice'.[24] In a similar spirit, Montesquieu asserted that 'we must therefore acknowledge relations of justice [*des rapports d'equité*] antecedent to the positive law by which they are established'.[25] According to Adam Smith, too, justice was the 'main pillar' of society. He was committed not simply to the natural system of liberty but to 'the natural system of perfect liberty *and justice*'. Every man should be free to follow his own interests in his own way, he argued, but only 'as long as he does not violate the laws of justice'.[26] Interest-governed behavior can enhance social stability and security, by an invisible hand, but only if the interests propelling action are just.[27] Madison agreed: 'Justice is the end of government. It is the end of civil society.'[28]

Justice, to be sure, is a slippery and polysignificant concept, difficult to define in a univocal way. Perhaps the theorists cited above were thinking about *just retribution* and not *just distribution*. Perhaps they meant to affirm 'the limits of justice', confining the term *just* to the giving and receiving of what individuals voluntarily contract to give and receive. According to a preliberal such as Hobbes, for example, 'The definition of INJUSTICE, is no other than *the not Performance of Covenant*' and 'the nature of Justice, consisteth in keeping of valid Covenants'.[29] Even this restrictive definition of justice, however, includes an explicit entitlement to affirmative state action to protect individuals from harm by third parties.

We can say with some confidence, moreover, that liberals did *not* uniformly conceive justice in this narrow 'Hobbesian' fashion, as a simple matter of enforcing contracts. For one thing, they universally associated justice with a more substantive idea of impartiality: *all* individuals must be protected *equally* from third-party injury. They explicitly advocated *equal access to the law*, a norm incompatible in principle with many ostensibly 'contractual' relations (such as those involving indentured servitude). An underlying egalitarian norm explains, for instance, Madison's advocacy of 'a government which will protect all parties, the weaker as well as the more powerful'.[30] Access to the court must not be distributed according to merit, contribution, inherited social status, or even prior consent. A jury trial must be made available to *all* similar offenders. A just distribution of the community's legal resources is, in principle, an equal or universal distribution – not conditional, for example, on the quantity of taxes paid. One might even argue that a just distribution of, say, trial by jury was conceived by liberals as a distribution according to need.

NOTES

1. I am thinking, for instance, of the Second French Republic and, especially, of the Weimar Republic.
2. *The Federalist Papers* (New York: Mentor, 1961), no. 16 (Hamilton), p. 118.
3. John Locke, *Two Treatises of Government*, (Cambridge: Cambridge University, Press, 1988), 11, §57.
4. *Federalist Papers*, no. 53 (Madison), p. 331.
5. Carl Schmitt, *Verfassungslehre* (Berlin: Duncker & Humblot, 1928), p. 41.
6. We might translate 'das formlos Formende' as 'the shaping power that itself has no shape'. Seizing the chance to dismay his legalistically minded colleagues, Schmitt wrote, quite unrealistically: 'Ein geregeltes Verfahren, durch welches die Betätigung der Verfassungsgebenden Gewalt gebunden wäre, kann es nicht geben.' [There can be no regulated procedure through which the activity of the constituent power would be bound. (Ibid., pp. 81–2).
7. *Federalist Papers*, no. 40 (Madison), p. 253.
8. Again, the election itself is carried out on the basis of a preselection of the candidates – which itself can be made more or less democratically.
9. Locke, *Two Treatises of Government*, II, §154.
10. *Federalist Papers*, no. 53 (Madison), pp. 331, 332.
11. Strictly speaking, Locke's 'legislative' was King-in-Parliament, and therefore only partially elective.
12. Locke, *Two Treatises of Government*, II, §§ 157–8.
13. Locke's argument, interestingly enough, was echoed by Chief Justice Warren in his majority opinion in *Reynolds v. Sims*, 377 US 533 (1964), whereby the Court compelled Alabama to revise an absolete districting scheme that had granted some citizens forty times greater influence on the choice of representatives than others.
14. Francis Bacon, 'Of Seditions and Troubles'. In *The Essayes or Counsels Civill and Morall*. M. Kiernan (ed.) (Cambridge, MA: Harvard University Press, 1985), pp. 45–6; Richard Posner, *Economic Analysis of Law*, 4th ed. (Boston: Little, Brown, 1992), pp. 463–4.
15. *Unlike* Reaganites, the latter repudiate the market for traditionalist reasons, as a violation of inherited customs and attachments.
16. Montesquieu, *The Spirit of the Laws*, trans. Thomas Nugent (New York: Hafner, 1949), vol. 2, p. 25.
17. I shall again be discussing Hobbes as well – the preliberal whose thinking left the most lasting traces on the liberal tradition.
18. *Federalist Papers* no. 37 (Madison), p. 225; no. 38, p. 233.
19. Locke, *Two Treatises of Government* 11, § 102.
20. Milton Friedman, *Capitalism and Freedom* (Chicago: University of Chicago Press, 1962), p. 200.
21. This view is advanced by, among others, Friedrich Hayek, *The Constitution of Liberty* (Chicago: University of Chicago Press, 1960), pp. 176–92.
22. Montesquieu, *Spirit of the Laws*, vol. 1, p. 183; for a contrary view, see the one-sided argument of Franz Neumann, *The Democratic and Authoritarian State* (New York: Free Press, 1957), pp. 96–148.
23. Friedman, *Capitalism and Freedom*, p. 195.
24. David Hume, 'Of the Origin of Government', in *Essays: Moral, Political and Literary* (Indianapolis: Liberty Classics, 1985), p. 37.
25. Montesquieu, *Spirit of the Laws*, vol. 1, p. 2.
26. Adam Smith, *The Theory of Moral Sentiments*, D. D. Raphael and A. L. Macfie (eds) (Oxford: Oxford University Press, 1976), p. 86; Smith, *An Inquiry into the Nature and Causes of the Wealth of Nations* (New York: Modern Library, 1937), p. 572, my emphasis; ibid., p. 651.

27. A concern for the welfare of others, in other words, was built into the liberal definition of legitimate private action. Locke, in a passage cited above, distinguished *proper interests* from improper ones on the grounds that the former were those compatible with the public good (see *Two Treatises of Government*, II, § 57). Selfinterest is subordinate to the just, the right, and the proper, and that means: to the general good. Improper or sinister interests, those violating the norm of justice, must be legally repressed. An ascriptive, hierarchical, demeaning and oppressive social system, where a few reaped all the benefits and the majority bore all the burdens, might be 'peaceful' enough, but it would not qualify as a liberal social order for the simple reason that it would not be just. However orderly, slavery remains a vile and miserable, and therefore unacceptable, estate of man.
28. *Federalist Papers*, no. 51 (Madison), p. 324.
29. Thomas Hobbes, *Leviathan* (Harmondsworth: Penguin, 1968), pp. 202–3.
30. *Federalist Papers*, no. 51 (Madison), p. 325.

SECTION 5
PRAGMATISM

The contributions to the Pragmatism section could in many ways be summarised as an attempt to pin down precisely what it is that is unique about American public philosophy. It was Ralph Waldo Emerson who in his *Essays and Lectures* first considered these uniquely American aspects and preconditions which helped to create a different kind of knowledge, a knowledge that was not based on the 'aristocracy of the minds' as in Europe but a knowledge that responded to democratic conditions and needs. Where Emerson prepared the ground, William James turned pragmatism into a well-respected philosophical and public enterprise. He was the first one to coin the term 'pragmatism' and to popularise it. James had an astute sense of how to turn a rather complicated method – Peirce's philosophical papers are for example not that accessible and easy to understand – into a public philosophy. James made a conscious decision to get rid of most of the old philosophical ballast from Europe – be it the metaphysical component, the essentialism, the formalities or the system-building aspects. His essay 'What Pragmatism means' constitutes an attempt to get rid of dogmas and doctrines and to open the mind for the new. It is, in the words of James, an 'attitude of orientation' in pursuit of multiple truths.

John Dewey, together with Peirce and James the representative of the 'first pragmatism', continued where James had left off. Dewey's book *The Public and its Problems* must be seen as the biggest attempt to turn pragmatism into a coherent public philosophy. He was convinced that developments at the beginning of the twentieth century had led to a loss in terms of the sharing of common experiences. In other words, the great society that was the United States was fragmenting into little publics which didn't communicate with each other. Because no integrated whole seemed to be available, Dewey attempted to argue for a radical change in which better dissemination, the communication of the results of social inquiry, the formation of public opinion and informed judgement would form the backbone of a renewed and reformed great public.

These early statements of pragmatism, however, must be distinguished from a later pragmatism which is broader in its intellectual aspirations in that it includes more sociological and political thought. The work of C. Wright Mills, Cornell West and Richard Rorty are representative of this 'broader church' of American pragmatism.

In many ways C. Wright Mills' *The Power Elite*, published thirty years after Dewey's *The Public and its Problem*, can be interpreted as an updated version of Dewey's original criticism. Mills criticises the transformation of the public into an apathetic mass that was governed by a powerful elite. Modern mass communication and the media market had almost eliminated primary publics and the free competition and exchange of opinions. The new and increased manipulation of symbols and signs made it necessary to rethink the role of intellectuals in modern mass society. Thus Mills also indirectly indicates that in times of great challenge and risk, the time for alternative solutions and rescue is also imminent. In Mills' imagination this would be a new 'cultural worker' working in the new cultural apparatus, deciphering, dissecting and 'translating' the powerful messages of second-hand worlds.

In many ways Cornel West's programme for the renewal of pragmatism, as outlined in his *The American Evasion of Philosophy* continues the task of creating the great public that has first been described by Dewey and that Mills has called cultural apparatus. His 'prophetic pragmatism' continues with an unfinished task and despises and deconstructs ideologies and old truths.

The philosopher Richard Rorty is currently regarded as the intellectual who is most outspoken when it comes to the tasks of the 'second Pragmatism'. In an important essay entitled 'The priority of democracy to philosophy' (published in *Objectivity, relativism, and truth*) Rorty makes it clear that the pragmatists' position and affiliation should be first and foremost with democracy – not with philosophic truth. This critique, which was mainly directed against communitarian thinking, can also be read as a critique of the later multicultural, Foucauldian left that seems to dominate American campuses these days. Against their relativist values, Rorty emphasises democratic values, that is the competition of minds in which the better argument should prevail – not the silent or uncritical acceptance of difference in the multicultural zoo.

29

TWO ESSAYS: THE AMERICAN SCHOLAR AND THE YOUNG AMERICAN

Ralph Waldo Emerson

THE AMERICAN SCHOLAR

The scholar is that man who must take up into himself all the ability of the time, all the contributions of the past, all the hopes of the future. He must be an university of knowledges. If there be one lesson more than another, which should pierce his ear, it is: the world is nothing, the man is all; in yourself is the law of all nature, and you know not yet how a globule of sap ascends; in yourself slumbers the whole of Reason; it is for you to know all, it is for you to dare all. Mr President and Gentlemen, this confidence in the unsearched might of man belongs, by all motives, by all prophecy, by all preparation, to the American Scholar. We have listened too long to the courtly muses of Europe. The spirit of the American freeman is already suspected to be timid, imitative, tame. Public and private avarice make the air we breathe thick and fat. The scholar is decent, indolent, complaisant. See already the tragic consequence. The mind of this country, taught to aim at low objects, eats upon itself. There is no work for any but the decorous and the complaisant. Young men of the fairest promise, who begin life upon our shores, inflated by the mountain winds, shined upon by all the stars of God, find the earth below not in unison with these – but are hindered from action by the disgust which the principles on which business is managed inspire, and turn drudges, or die of disgust – some of them suicides. What is the remedy? They did not yet see, and thousands of young men as hopeful now crowding to the barriers for the career, do not yet see, that, if the single man

From: Ralph Waldo Emerson, *Essays and Lectures* (New York: The Library of America, 1983).

plant himself indomitably on his instincts, and there abide, the huge world will come round to him. Patience, patience; with the shades of all the good and great for company; and for solace, the perspective of your own infinite life; and for work, the study and the communication of principles, the making those instincts prevalent, the conversion of the world. Is it not the chief disgrace in the world, not to be an unit – not to be reckoned one character – not to yield that peculiar fruit which each man was created to bear, but to be reckoned in the gross, in the hundred, or the thousand, of the party, the section, to which we belong; and our opinion predicted geographically, as the north, or the south? Not so, brothers and friends – please God, ours shall not be so. We will walk on our own feet; we will work with our own hands; we will speak our own minds. The study of letters shall be no longer a name for pity, for doubt and for sensual indulgence. The dread of man and the love of man shall be a wall of defence and a wreath of joy around all. A nation of men will for the first time exist, because each believes himself inspired by the Divine Soul which also inspires all men.

THE YOUNG AMERICAN

Gentlemen, the development of our American internal resources, the extension to the utmost of the commercial system, and the appearance of new moral causes which are to modify the state, are giving an aspect of greatness to the Future, which the imagination fears to open. One thing is plain for all men of common sense and common conscience, that here, here in America, is the home of man. After all the deductions which are to be made for our pitiful politics, which stake every gravest national question on the silly die, whether James or whether Jonathan shall sit in the chair and hold the purse; after all the deduction is made for our frivolities and insanities, there still remains an organic simplicity and liberty, which, when it loses its balance, redresses itself presently, which offers opportunity to the human mind not known in any other region.

It is true, the public mind wants self-respect. We are full of vanity, of which the most signal proof is our sensitiveness to foreign and especially English censure. One cause of this is our immense reading, and that reading chiefly confined to the productions of the English press. It is also true, that, to imaginative persons in this country, there is somewhat bare and bald in our short history, and unsettled wilderness. They ask, who would live in a new country, that can live in an old? and it is not strange that our youths and maidens should burn to see the picturesque extremes of an antiquated country. But it is one thing to visit the pyramids, and another to wish to live there. Would they like tithes to the clergy, and sevenths to the government, and horse-guards, and licensed press, and grief when a child is born, and threatening, starved weavers, and a pauperism now constituting one-thirteenth of the population? Instead of the open future expanding here before the eye of every boy to vastness, would they like the closing in of the future to a narrow slit of sky, and that fast contracting to be no future? One thing, for instance, the beauties of aristocracy, we commend to the study of the travelling American. The English, the most conservative people this side of India, are not sensible of the restraint, but an American would seriously resent it. The aristocracy, incorporated by law and education, degrades life for the unprivileged classes. It is a questionable compensation to the embittered feeling of a proud commoner, the reflection that a fop, who, by the magic of title, paralyzes his arm, and plucks from him half the graces and rights of a man, is himself also an aspirant excluded with the same ruthlessness from higher circles, since there is no end to the wheels within wheels of this spiral heaven. Something may be pardoned to the spirit of loyalty when it becomes fantastic; and something to the imagination, for the baldest life is symbolic. Philip II of Spain rated his ambassador for neglecting serious affairs in Italy, whilst he debated some point of honor with the French ambassador; 'You have left a business of importance for a ceremony'. The ambassador replied, 'Your majesty's self is but a ceremony'. In the East, where the religious sentiment comes in to the support of the aristocracy, and in the Romish church also, there is a grain of sweetness in the tyranny; but in England, the fact seems to me intolerable, what is commonly affirmed, that such is the transcendent honor accorded to wealth and birth, that no man of letters, be his eminence what it may, is received into the best society, except as a lion and a show. The English have many virtues, many advantages, and the proudest history of the world; but they need all, and more than all the resources of the past to indemnify a heroic gentleman in that country for the mortifications prepared for him by the system of society, and which seem to impose the alternative to resist or to avoid it. That there are mitigations and practical alleviations to this rigor, is not an excuse for the rule. Commanding worth, and personal power, must sit crowned in all companies, nor will extraordinary persons be slighted or affronted in any company of civilized men. But the system is an invasion of the sentiment of justice and the native rights of men, which, however decorated, must lessen the value of English citizenship. It is for Englishmen to consider, not for us; we only say, let us live in America, too thankful for our want of feudal institutions. Our houses and towns are like mosses and lichens, so slight and new; but youth is a fault of which we shall daily mend. This land, too, is as old as the Flood, and wants no ornament or privilege which nature could bestow. Here stars, here woods, here hills, here animals, here men abound, and the vast tendencies concur of a new order.

30

WHAT PRAGMATISM MEANS

William James

The pragmatic method is primarily a method of settling metaphysical disputes that otherwise might be interminable. Is the world one or many? Fated or free? Material or spiritual? Here are notions either of which may or may not hold good of the world; and disputes over such notions are unending. The pragmatic method in such cases is to try to interpret each notion by tracing its respective practical consequences. What difference would it practically make to any one if this notion rather than that notion were true? If no practical difference whatever can be traced, then the alternatives mean practically the same thing, and all dispute is idle. Whenever a dispute is serious, we ought to be able to show some practical difference that must follow from one side or the other's being right.

A glance at the history of the idea will show you still better what pragmatism means. The term is derived from the same Greek word πρᾶγμα meaning action, from which our words 'practice' and 'practical' come. It was first introduced into philosophy by Mr Charles Peirce in 1878. In an article entitled 'How to Make Our Ideas Clear' in the *Popular Science Monthly* for January of that year.[1] Mr Peirce, after pointing out that our beliefs are really rules for action, said that, to develop a thought's meaning, we need only determine what conduct it is fitted to produce: that conduct is for us its sole significance. And the tangible fact at the root of all our thought distinctions, however subtle, is that there is no one of them so fine as to consist in anything but a possible difference of practice. To attain perfect clearness in our thoughts of an object, then, we need only

From: William James (ed. Russell B. Goodman), *Pragmatism: A Contemporary Reader* (London: Routledge, 1995).

consider what conceivable effects of a practical kind the object may involve – what sensations we are to expect from it, and what reactions we must prepare. Our conception of these effects, whether immediate or remote, is then for us the whole of our conception of the object, so far as that conception has positive significance at all.

This is the principle of Peirce, the principle of pragmatism.

[. . .]

There is absolutely nothing new in the pragmatic method. Socrates was an adept at it. Aristotle used it methodically. Locke, Berkeley and Hume made momentous contributions to truth by its means. Shadworth Hodgson keeps insisting that realities are only what they are 'known as'. But these forerunners of pragmatism used it in fragments: they were a prelude only. Not until in our time has it generalized itself, become conscious of a universal mission, pretended to a conquering destiny. I believe in that destiny, and I hope I may end by inspiring you with my belief.

Pragmatism represents a perfectly familiar attitude in philosophy, the empiricist attitude, but it represents it, as it seems to me, both in a more radical and in a less objectionable form than it has ever yet assumed. A pragmatist turns his back resolutely and once for all upon a lot of inveterate habits dear to professional philosophers. He turns away from abstraction and insufficiency, from verbal solutions, from bad *a priori* reasons, from fixed principles, closed systems, and pretended absolutes and origins. He turns towards concreteness and adequacy, towards facts, towards action and towards power. That means the empiricist temper regnant and the rationalist temper sincerely given up. It means the open air and possibilities of nature, as against dogma, artificiality, and the pretence of finality in truth.

At the same time it does not stand for any special results. It is a method only. But the general triumph of that method would mean an enormous change in what I called the 'temperament' of philosophy. Teachers of the ultra-rationalistic type would be frozen out, much as the courtier type is frozen out in republics, as the ultramontane type of priest is frozen out in protestant lands. Science and metaphysics would come much nearer together, would in fact work absolutely hand in hand.

Metaphysics has usually followed a very primitive kind of quest. You know how men have always hankered after unlawful magic, and you know what a great part in magic *words* have always played. If you have his name, or the formula of incantation that binds him, you can control the spirit, genie, afrite, or whatever the power may be. Solomon knew the names of all the spirits, and having their names, he held them subject to his will. So the universe has always appeared to the natural mind as a kind of enigma, of which the key must be sought in the shape of some illuminating or power-bringing word or name. That word names the universe's *principle*, and to possess it is after a fashion to possess the universe itself. 'God', 'Matter', 'Reason', 'the Absolute',

'Energy', are so many solving names. You can rest when you have them. You are at the end of your metaphysical quest.

But if you follow the pragmatic method, you cannot look on any such word as closing your quest. You must bring out of each word its practical cash-value, set it at work within the stream of your experience. It appears less as a solution, then, than as a program for more work, and more particularly as an indication of the ways in which existing realities may be *changed*.

Theories thus become instruments, not answers to enigmas in which we can rest. We don't lie back upon them, we move forward, and, on occasion, make nature over again by their aid. Pragmatism unstiffens all our theories, limbers them up and sets each one at work. Being nothing essentially new, it harmonizes with many ancient philosophic tendencies. It agrees with nominalism, for instance, in always appealing to particulars; with utilitarianism in emphasizing practical aspects; with positivism in its disdain for verbal solutions, useless questions and metaphysical abstractions.

All these, you see, are *anti-intellectualist* tendencies. Against rationalism as a pretension and a method pragmatism is fully armed and militant. But, at the outset, at least, it stands for no particular results. It has no dogmas, and no doctrines save its method.

[...]

But as the sciences have developed farther, the notion has gained ground that most, perhaps all, of our laws are only approximations. The laws themselves, moreover, have grown so numerous that there is no counting them; and so many rival formulations are proposed in all the branches of science that investigators have become accustomed to the notion that no theory is absolutely a transcript of reality, but that any one of them may from some point of view be useful. Their great use is to summarize old facts and to lead to new ones. They are only a man-made language, a conceptual shorthand, as someone calls them, in which we write our reports of nature; and languages, as is well known, tolerate much choice of expression and many dialects.

Thus human arbitrariness has driven divine necessity from scientific logic. If I mention the names of Sigwart, Mach, Ostwald, Pearson, Milhaud, Poincaré, Duhem, Ruyssen, those of you who are students will easily identify the tendency I speak of, and will think of additional names.

Riding now on the front of this wave of scientific logic Messrs Schiller and Dewey appear with their pragmatistic account of what truth everywhere signifies. Everywhere, these teachers say, 'truth' in our ideas and beliefs means the same thing that it means in science. It means, they say, nothing but this, *that ideas (which themselves are but parts of our experience) become true just in so far as they help us to get into satisfactory relation with other parts of our experience*, to summarize them and get about among them by conceptual short-cuts instead of following the interminable succession of particular phenomena. Any idea upon which we can ride, so to speak; any idea that will carry us prosperously from any one part of our experience to any other part, linking things satisfactorily, working securely, simplifying, saving labor; is true for just so much, true in so far forth, true *instrumentally*. This is the 'instrumental' view of truth taught so successfully at Chicago.

[...]

I need not multiply instances. A new opinion counts as 'true' just in proportion as it gratifies the individual's desire to assimilate the novel in his experience to his beliefs in stock. It must both lean on old truth and grasp new fact; and its success in doing this is a matter for the individual's appreciation. When old truth grows, then, by new truth's addition, it is for subjective reasons. We are in the process and obey the reasons. That new idea is truest which performs most felicitously its function of satisfying our double urgency. It makes itself true, gets itself classed as true, by the way it works; grafting itself then upon the ancient body of truth.

NOTE

1. Translated in the *Revue Philosophique* for January 1879 (vol. vii).

31

THE PUBLIC AND ITS PROBLEMS

John Dewey

We have inherited local town-meeting practices and ideas. But we live and act and have our being in a continental national state. We are held together by non-political bonds, and the political forms are stretched and legal institutions patched in an *ad hoc* and improvised manner to do the work they have to do. Political structures fix the channels in which non-political, industrialized currents flow. Railways, travel and transportation, commerce, the mails, telegraph and telephone, newspapers, create enough similarity of ideas and sentiments to keep the thing going as a whole, for they create interaction and interdependence. The unprecedented thing is that states, as distinguished from military empires, can exist over such a wide area. The notion of maintaining a unified state, even nominally self-governing, over a country as extended as the United States and consisting of a large and racially diversified population would once have seemed the wildest of fancies. It was assumed that such a state could be found only in territories hardly larger than a city-state and with a homogeneous population. It seemed almost self-evident to Plato – as to Rousseau later – that a genuine state could hardly be larger than the number of persons capable of personal acquaintance with one another. Our modern state-unity is due to the consequences of technology employed so as to facilitate the rapid and easy circulation of opinions and information, and so as to generate constant and intricate interaction far beyond the limits of face-to-face communities. Political and legal forms have

From: John Dewey, *The Public and its Problems* (Athens, OH: Swallow Press/Ohio University Press, 1980).

only piecemeal and haltingly, with great lag, accommodated themselves to the industrial transformation. The elimination of distance, at the base of which are physical agencies, has called into being the new form of political association.

[...]

The resulting political integration has confounded the expectations of earlier critics of popular government as much as it must surprise its early backers if they are gazing from on high upon the present scene. The critics predicted disintegration, instability. They foresaw the new society falling apart, dissolving into mutually repellent animated grains of sand. They, too, took seriously the theory of 'Individualism' as the basis of democratic government. A stratification of society into immemorial classes within which each person performed his stated duties according to his fixed position seemed to them the only warrant of stability. They had no faith that human beings released from the pressure of this system could hold together in any unity. Hence they prophesied a flux of governmental régimes, as individuals formed factions, seized power, and then lost it as some newly improvised faction proved stronger. Had the facts conformed to the theory of Individualism, they would doubtless have been right. But, like the authors of the theory, they ignored the technological forces making for consolidation.

In spite of attained integration, or rather perhaps because of its nature, the Public seems to be lost; it is certainly bewildered.[1] The government, officials and their activities, are plainly with us. Legislatures make laws with luxurious abandon; subordinate officials engage in a losing struggle to enforce some of them; judges on the bench deal as best they can with the steadily mounting pile of disputes that come before them. But where is the public which these officials are supposed to represent?

[...]

What, after all, is the public under present conditions? What are the reasons for its eclipse? What hinders it from finding and identifying itself? By what means shall its inchoate and amorphous estate be organized into effective political action relevant to present social needs and opportunities? What has happened to the public in the century and a half since the theory of political democracy was urged with such assurance and hope?

Previous discussion has brought to light some conditions out of which the public is generated. It has also set forth some of the causes through which a 'new age of human relationships' has been brought into being. These two arguments form the premises which, when they are related to each other, will provide our answer to the questions just raised. Indirect, extensive, enduring and serious consequences of conjoint and interacting behavior call a public into existence having a common interest in controlling these consequences. But the machine age has so enormously expanded, multiplied, intensified and complicated the scope of the indirect consequences, have formed such immense and consolidated unions in action, on an impersonal rather than a community basis, that the resultant public cannot identify and distinguish itself. And this discovery is obviously an antecedent condition of any effective organization on its part. Such is our thesis regarding the eclipse which the public idea and interest have undergone. There are too many publics and too much of public concern for our existing resources to cope with. The problem of a democratically organized public is primarily and essentially an intellectual problem, in a degree to which the political affairs of prior ages offer no parallel.

Our concern at this time is to state how it is that the machine age in developing the Great Society has invaded and partially disintegrated the small communities of former times without generating a Great Community.

[…]

The local face-to-face community has been invaded by forces so vast, so remote in initiation, so far-reaching in scope and so complexly indirect in operation, that they are, from the standpoint of the members of local social units, unknown. Man, as has been often remarked, has difficulty in getting on either with or without his fellows, even in neighborhoods. He is not more successful in getting on with them when they act at a great distance in ways invisible to him. An inchoate public is capable of organization only when indirect consequences are perceived, and when it is possible to project agencies which order their occurrence. At present, many consequences are felt rather than perceived; they are suffered, but they cannot be said to be known, for they are not, by those who experience them, referred to their origins. It goes, then, without saying that agencies are not established which canalize the streams of social action and thereby regulate them. Hence the publics are amorphous and unarticulated.

There was a time when a man might entertain a few general political principles and apply them with some confidence. A citizen believed in states' rights or in a centralized federal government; in free trade or protection. It did not involve much mental strain to imagine that by throwing in his lot with one party or another he could so express his views that his belief would count in government. For the average voter to-day the tariff question is a complicated medley of infinite detail, schedules of rates specific and *ad valorem* on countless things, many of which he does not recognize by name, and with respect to which he can form no judgment. Probably not one voter in a thousand even reads the scores of pages in which the rates of toll are enumerated and he would not be much wiser if he did. The average man gives it up as a bad job. At election time, appeal to some time-worn slogan may galvanize him into a temporary notion that he has convictions on an important subject, but except for manufacturers and dealers who have some interest at stake in this or that schedule, belief lacks the qualities which attach to beliefs about matters of personal concern. Industry is too complex and intricate.

Again the voter may by personal predilection or inherited belief incline towards magnifying the scope of local governments and inveigh against the evils of centralization. But he is vehemently sure of social evils attending the liquor traffic. He finds that the prohibitory law of his locality, township, county or state, is largely nullified by the importation of liquor from outside, made easy by modern means of transportation. So he becomes an advocate of a national amendment giving the central government power to regulate the manufacture and sale of intoxicating drinks. This brings in its train a necessary extension of federal officials and powers. Thus to-day, the south, the traditional home of the states' rights doctrine, is the chief supporter of national prohibition and Volstead Act. It would not be possible to say how many voters have thought of the relation between their professed general principle and their special position on the liquor question: probably not many. On the other hand, life-long Hamiltonians, proclaimers of the dangers of particularistic local auton-omy, are opposed to prohibition. Hence they play a tune *ad hoc* on the Jeffersonian flute. Gibes at inconsistency are, however, as irrelevant as they are easy. The social situation has been so changed by the factors of an industrial age that traditional general principles have little practical meaning. They persist as emotional cries rather than as reasoned ideas.

[...]

It is not that there is no public, no large body of persons having a common interest in the consequences of social transactions. There is too much public, a public too diffused and scattered and too intricate in composition. And there are too many publics, for conjoint actions which have indirect, serious and enduring consequences are multitudinous beyond comparison, and each one of them crosses the others and generates its own group of persons especially affected with little to hold these different publics together in an integrated whole.

[...]

Conditions have changed, but every aspect of life, from religion and education to property and trade, shows that nothing approaching a transformation has taken place in ideas and ideals. Symbols control sentiment and thought, and the new age has no symbols consonant with its activities. Intellectual instrumen-talities for the formation of an organized public are more inadequate than its overt means. The ties which hold men together in action are numerous, tough and subtle. But they are invisible and intangible. We have the physical tools of communication as never before. The thoughts and aspirations congruous with them are not communicated, and hence are not common. Without such communication the public will remain shadowy and formless, seeking spas-modically for itself, but seizing and holding its shadow rather than its substance. Till the Great Society is converted into a Great Community, the Public will remain in eclipse. Communication can alone create a great community. Our

Babel is not one of tongues but of the signs and symbols without which shared experience is impossible.

[...]

Regarded as an idea, democracy is not an alternative to other principles of associated life. It is the idea of community life itself. It is an ideal in the only intelligible sense of an ideal: namely, the tendency and movement of some thing which exists carried to its final limit, viewed as completed, perfected. Since things do not attain such fulfillment but are in actuality distracted and interfered with, democracy in this sense is not a fact and never will be. But neither in this sense is there or has there ever been anything which is a community in its full measure, a community unalloyed by alien elements. The idea or ideal of a community presents, however, actual phases of associated life as they are freed from restrictive and disturbing elements, and are contemplated as having attained their limit of development. Wherever there is conjoint activity whose consequences are appreciated as good by all singular persons who take part in it, and where the realization of the good is such as to effect an energetic desire and effort to sustain it in being just because it is a good shared by all, there is in so far a community. The clear consciousness of a communal life, in all its implications, constitutes the idea of democracy.

Only when we start from a community as a fact, grasp the fact in thought so as to clarify and enhance its constituent elements, can we reach an idea of democracy which is not utopian. The conceptions and shibboleths which are traditionally associated with the idea of democracy take on a veridical and directive meaning only when they are construed as marks and traits of an association which realizes the defining characteristics of a community. Fraternity, liberty and equality isolated from communal life are hopeless abstractions. Their separate assertion leads to mushy sentimentalism or else to extravagant and fanatical violence which in the end defeats its own aims. Equality then becomes a creed of mechanical identity which is false to facts and impossible of realization. Effort to attain it is divisive of the vital bonds which hold men together; as far as it puts forth issue, the outcome is a mediocrity in which good is common only in the sense of being average and vulgar. Liberty is then thought of as independence of social ties, and ends in dissolution and anarchy. It is more difficult to sever the idea of brotherhood from that of a community, and hence it is either practically ignored in the movements which identify democracy with Individualism, or else it is a sentimentally appended tag. In its just connection with communal experience, fraternity is another name for the consciously appreciated goods which accrue from an association in which all share, and which give direction to the conduct of each. Liberty is that secure release and fulfillment of personal potentialities which take place only in rich and manifold association with others: the power to be an individualized self making a distinctive contribution and enjoying in its own way the fruits of association. Equality denotes the unhampered share which each individual member of the community has in the consequences of associated action. It is equitable because it is measured only by need and capacity to utilize, not by extraneous factors which deprive one in order that another may take and have. A baby in the family is equal with others, not because of some antecedent and structural quality which is the same as that of others, but in so far as his needs for care and development are attended to without being sacrificed to the superior strength, possessions and matured abilities of others. Equality does not signify that kind of mathematical or physical equivalence in virtue of which any one element may be substituted for another. It denotes effective regard for whatever is distinctive and unique in each, irrespective of physical and psychological inequalities. It is not a natural possession but is a fruit of the community when its action is directed by its character as a community.

Associated or joint activity is a condition of the creation of a community. But association itself is physical and organic, while communal life is moral, that is emotionally, intellectually, consciously sustained. Human beings combine in behavior as directly and unconsciously as do atoms, stellar masses and cells.

[...]

Human associations may be ever so organic in origin and firm in operation, but they develop into societies in a human sense only as their consequences, being known, are esteemed and sought for. Even if 'society' were as much an organism as some writers have held, it would not on that account be society. Interactions, transactions, occur *de facto* and the results of interdependence follow. But participation in activities and sharing in results are additive concerns. They demand *communication* as a prerequisite.

Combined activity happens among human beings; but when nothing else happens it passes as inevitably into some other mode of interconnected activity as does the interplay of iron and the oxygen of water. What takes place is wholly describable in terms of energy, or, as we say in the case of human interactions, of force. Only when there exist *signs* or *symbols* of activities and of their outcome can the flux be viewed as from without, be arrested for consideration and esteem, and be regulated. Lightning strikes and rives a tree or rock, and the resulting fragments take up and continue the process of interaction, and so on and on. But when phases of the process are represented by signs, a new medium is interposed. As symbols are related to one another, the important relations of a course of events are recorded and are preserved as meanings. Recollection and foresight are possible; the new medium facilitates calculation, planning, and a new kind of action which intervenes in what happens to direct its course in the interest of what is foreseen and desired.

Symbols in turn depend upon and promote communication. The results of conjoint experience are considered and transmitted. Events cannot be passed from one to another, but meanings may be shared by means of signs. Wants and impulses are then attached to common meanings. They are thereby transformed into desires and purposes, which, since they implicate a common or mutually understood meaning, present new ties, converting a conjoint activity into a community of interest and endeavor.

[...]

A thing is fully known only when it is published, shared, socially accessible. Record and communication are indispensable to knowledge. Knowledge cooped up in a private consciousness is a myth, and knowledge of social phenomena is peculiarly dependent upon dissemination, for only by distribution can such knowledge be either obtained or tested. A fact of community life which is not spread abroad so as to be a common possession is a contradiction in terms. Dissemination is something other than scattering at large. Seeds are sown, not by virtue of being thrown out at random, but by being so distributed as to take root and have a chance of growth. Communication of the results of social inquiry is the same thing as the formation of public opinion. This marks one of the first ideas framed in the growth of political democracy as it will be one of the last to be fulfilled. For public opinion is judgment which is formed and entertained by those who constitute the public and is about public affairs.

[...]

Signs and symbols, language, are the means of communication by which a fraternally shared experience is ushered in and sustained. But the winged words of conversation in immediate intercourse have a vital import lacking in the fixed and frozen words of written speech. Systematic and continuous inquiry into all the conditions which affect association and their dissemination in print is a precondition of the creation of a true public. But it and its results are but tools after all. Their final actuality is accomplished in face-to-face relationships by means of direct give and take. Logic in its fulfillment recurs to the primitive sense of the word: dialogue. Ideas which are not communicated, shared, and reborn in expression are but soliloquy, and soliloquy is but broken and imperfect thought.

NOTE

1. See Walter Lippmann's 'The Phantom Public'. To this as well as to his 'Public Opinion'. I wish to acknowledge my indebtedness, not only as to this particular point, but for ideas involved in my entire discussion even when it reaches conclusions diverging from his.

32

THE POWER ELITE

C. Wright Mills

The transformation of public into mass is of particular concern to us, for it provides an important clue to the meaning of the power elite. If that elite is truly responsible to, or even exists in connection with, a community of publics, it carries a very different meaning than if such a public is being transformed into a society of masses.

The United States today is not altogether a mass society, and it has never been altogether a community of publics. These phrases are names for extreme types; they point to certain features of reality, but they are themselves constructions; social reality is always some sort of mixture of the two. Yet we cannot readily understand just how much of which is mixed into our situation if we do not first understand, in terms of explicit dimensions, the clear-cut and extreme types:

At least four dimensions must be attended to if we are to grasp the differences between public and mass.

1. There is first, the ratio of the givers of opinion to the receivers, which is the simplest way to state the social meaning of the formal media of mass communication. More than anything else, it is the shift in this ratio which is central to the problems of the public and of public opinion in latter-day phases of democracy. At one extreme on the scale of communication, two people talk personally with each other; at the opposite extreme, one spokesman talks impersonally through a network of communications to millions of listeners and viewers. In between these extremes there are

From: C. Wright Mills, *The Power Elite* (New York and London: Oxford University Press, 1956).

assemblages and political rallies, parliamentary sessions, law-court debates, small discussion circles dominated by one man, open discussion circles with talk moving freely back and forth among fifty people, and so on.

2. The second dimension to which we must pay attention is the possibility of answering back an opinion without internal or external reprisals being taken. Technical conditions of the means of communication, in imposing a lower ratio of speakers to listeners, may obviate the possibility of freely answering back. Informal rules, resting upon conventional sanction and upon the informal structure of opinion leadership, may govern who can speak, when, and for how long. Such rules may or may not be in congruence with formal rules and with institutional sanctions which govern the process of communication. In the extreme case, we may conceive of an absolute monopoly of communication to pacified media groups whose members cannot answer back even 'in private'. At the opposite extreme, the conditions may allow and the rules may uphold the wide and symmetrical formation of opinion.

3. We must also consider the relation of the formation of opinion to its realization in social action, the ease with which opinion is effective in the shaping of decisions of powerful consequence. This opportunity for people to act out their opinions collectively is of course limited by their position in the structure of power. This structure may be such as to limit decisively this capacity, or it may allow or even invite such action. It may confine social action to local areas or it may enlarge the area of opportunity; it may make action intermittent or more or less continuous.

4. There is, finally, the degree to which institutional authority, with its sanctions and controls, penetrates the public. Here the problem is the degree to which the public has genuine autonomy from instituted authority. At one extreme, no agent of formal authority moves among the autonomous public. At the opposite extreme, the public is terrorized into uniformity by the infiltration of informers and the universalization of suspicion. One thinks of the late Nazi street-and-block-system, the eighteenth-century Japanese kumi, the Soviet cell structure. In the extreme, the formal structure of power coincides, as it were, with the informal ebb and flow of influence by discussion, which is thus killed off.

By combining these several points, we can construct little models or diagrams of several types of societies. Since 'the problem of public opinion' as we know it is set by the eclipse of the classic bourgeois public, we are here concerned with only two types: public and mass.

In a *public*, as we may understand the term, (1) virtually as many people express opinions as receive them; (2) public communications are so organized that there is a chance immediately and effectively to answer back any opinion expressed in public. Opinion formed by such discussion (3) readily finds an outlet in effective action, even against – if necessary – the prevailing system of authority. And (4) authoritative institutions do not penetrate the public, which is thus more or less autonomous in its operations. When these conditions prevail, we have the working model of a community of publics, and this model fits closely the several assumptions of classic democratic theory.

At the opposite extreme, in a *mass*, (1) far fewer people express opinions than receive them; for the community of publics becomes an abstract collection of individuals who receive impressions from the mass media. (2) The communications that prevail are so organized that it is difficult or impossible for the individual to answer back immediately or with any effect. (3) The realization of opinion in action is controlled by authorities who organize and control the channels of such action. (4) The mass has no autonomy from institutions; on the contrary, agents of authorized institutions penetrate this mass, reducing any autonomy it may have in the formation of opinion by discussion.

The public and the mass may be most readily distinguished by their dominant modes of communication: in a community of publics, discussion is the ascendant means of communication, and the mass media, if they exist, simply enlarge and animate discussion, linking one *primary public* with the discussions of another. In a mass society, the dominant type of communication is the formal media, and the publics become mere *media markets*: all those exposed to the contents of given mass media.

From almost any angle of vision that we might assume, when we look upon the public, we realize that we have moved a considerable distance along the road to the mass society. At the end of that road there is totalitarianism, as in Nazi Germany or in Communist Russia. We are not yet at that end. In the United States today, media markets are not entirely ascendant over primary publics. But surely we can see that many aspects of the public life of our times are more the features of a mass society than of a community of publics.

What is happening might again be stated in terms of the historical parallel between the economic market and the public of public opinion. In brief, there is a movement from widely scattered little powers to concentrated powers and the attempt at monopoly control from powerful centers, which, being partially hidden, are centers of manipulation as well as of authority. The small shop serving the neighborhood is replaced by the anonymity of the national corporation: mass advertisement replaces the personal influence of opinion between merchant and customer. The political leader hooks up his speech to a national network and speaks, with appropriate personal touches, to a million people he never saw and never will see. Entire brackets of professions and industries are in the 'opinion business', impersonally manipulating the public for hire.

In the primary public the competition of opinions goes on between people holding views in the service of their interests and their reasoning. But in the mass society of media markets, competition, if any, goes on between the manipulators with their mass media on the one hand, and the people receiving their propaganda on the other.

Under such conditions, it is not surprising that there should arise a conception of public opinion as a mere reaction – we cannot say 'response' – to the content of the mass media. In this view, the public is merely the collectivity of individuals each rather passively exposed to the mass media and rather helplessly opened up to the suggestions and manipulations that flow from these media. The fact of manipulation from centralized points of control constitutes, as it were, an expropriation of the old multitude of little opinion producers and consumers operating in a free and balanced market.

In official circles, the very term itself, 'the public' – as Walter Lippmann noted thirty years ago – has come to have a phantom meaning, which dramatically reveals its eclipse. From the standpoint of the deciding elite, some of those who clamor publicly can be identified as 'Labor', others as 'Business', still others as 'Farmer'. Those who can *not* readily be so identified make up 'The Public'. In this usage, the public is composed of the unidentified and the non-partisan in a world of defined and partisan interests. It is socially composed of well-educated salaried professionals, especially college professors; of non-unionized employees, especially white-collar people, along with self-employed professionals and small businessmen.

In this faint echo of the classic notion, the public consists of those remnants of the middle classes, old and new, whose interests are not explicitly defined, organized or clamorous. In a curious adaptation, 'the public' often becomes, in fact, 'the unattached expert', who, although well informed, has never taken a clear-cut, public stand on controversial issues which are brought to a focus by organized interests. These are the 'public' members of the board, the commission, the committee. What the public stands for, accordingly, is often a vagueness of policy (called open-mindedness), a lack of involvement in public affairs (known as reasonableness), and a professional disinterest (known as tolerance).

Some such official members of the public, as in the field of labor-management mediation, start out very young and make a career out of being careful to be informed but never taking a strong position; and there are many others, quite unofficial, who take such professionals as a sort of model. The only trouble is that they are acting as if they were disinterested judges but they do not have the power of judges; hence their reasonableness, their tolerance, and their open-mindedness do not often count for much in the shaping of human affairs.

All those trends that make for the decline of the politician and of his balancing society bear decisively upon the transformation of public into mass.[1] One of the most important of the structural transformations involved is the decline of the voluntary association as a genuine instrument of the public. As we have already seen, the executive ascendancy in economic, military, and political institutions has lowered the effective use of all those voluntary associations which operate between the state and the economy on the one hand, and the family and the individual in the primary group on the other. It is not only that institutions of power have become large-scale and inaccessibly centralized; they have at the same time become less political and more administrative, and it is within this great change of framework that the organized public has waned.

In terms of *scale*, the transformation of public into mass has been under-pinned by the shift from a political public decisively restricted in size (by property and education, as well as by sex and age) to a greatly enlarged mass having only the qualifications of citizenship and age.

In terms of *organization*, the transformation has been underpinned by the shift from the individual and his primary community to the voluntary associa-tion and the mass party as the major units of organized power.

Voluntary associations have become larger to the extent that they have become effective; and to just that extent they have become inaccessible to the individual who would shape by discussion the policies of the organization to which he belongs. Accordingly, along with older institutions, these voluntary associations have lost their grip on the individual. As more people are drawn into the political arena, these associations become mass in scale; and as the power of the individual becomes more dependent upon such mass associations, they are less accessible to the individual's influence.[2]

Mass democracy means the struggle of powerful and large-scale interest groups and associations, which stand between the big decisions that are made by state, corporation, army, and the will of the individual citizen as a member of the public. Since these middle-level associations are the citizen's major link with decision, his relation to them is of decisive importance. For it is only through them that he exercises such power as he may have.

The gap between the members and the leaders of the mass association is becoming increasingly wider. As soon as a man gets to be a leader of an asso-ciation large enough to count he readily becomes lost as an instrument of that association. He does so (1) in the interests of maintaining his leading position in, or rather over, his mass association and (2) because he comes to see himself not as a mere delegate, instructed or not, of the mass association he represents, but as a member of 'an elite' composed of such men as himself. These facts, in turn, lead to (3) the big gap between the terms in which issues are debated and resolved among members of this elite, and the terms in which they are presented to the members of the various mass associations. For the decisions that are made must *take into account* those who are important – other elites – but they must be *sold* to the mass memberships.

The gap between speaker and listener, between power and public, leads less to any iron law of oligarchy than to the law of spokesmanship: as the pressure group expands, its leaders come to organize the opinions they 'represent'. So elections, as we have seen, become contests between two giant and unwieldy parties, neither of which the individual can truly feel that he influences, and neither of which is capable of winning psychologically impressive or politically decisive majorities. And, in all this, the parties are of the same general form as other mass associations.[3]

When we say that man in the mass is without any sense of political belonging, we have in mind a political fact rather than merely a style of feeling. We have in mind a certain way of belonging to a certain kind of organization. The way of belonging here implied rests upon a belief in the purposes and in the leaders of an organization, and thus enables men and women freely to be at home within it. To belong in this way is to make the human association a psychological center of one's self, to take into our conscience, deliberately and freely, its rules of conduct and its purposes, which we thus shape and which in turn shape us. We do not have this kind of belonging to any political organization.

The kind of organization we have in mind is a voluntary association which has three decisive characteristics: first, it is a context in which reasonable opinions may be formulated; second, it is an agency by which reasonable activities may be undertaken; and third, it is a powerful enough unit, in comparison with other organizations of power, to make a difference.

It is because they do not find available associations at once psychologically meaningful and historically effective that men often feel uneasy in their political and economic loyalties. The effective units of power are now the huge corporation, the inaccessible government, the grim military establishment. Between these, on the one hand, and the family and the small community on the other, we find no intermediate associations in which men feel secure and with which they feel powerful. There is little live political struggle. Instead, there is administration from above, and the political vacuum below. The primary publics are now either so small as to be swamped, and hence give up; or so large as to be merely another feature of the generally distant structure of power, and hence inaccessible.

Public opinion exists when people who are not in the government of a country claim the right to express political opinions freely and publicly, and the right that these opinions should influence or determine the policies, personnel, and actions of their government.[4] In this formal sense there has been and there is a definite public opinion in the United States. And yet, with modern developments this formal right – when it does still exist as a right – does not mean what it once did. The older world of voluntary organization was as different from the world of the mass organization, as was Tom Paine's world of pamphleteering from the world of the mass media.

Notes

1. See, especially, the analysis of the decline of the independent middle classes.
2. At the same time – and also because of the metropolitan segregation and distraction – the individual becomes more dependent upon the means of mass communication for his view of the structure as a whole.
3. On elections in modern formal democracies, E. H. Carr has concluded: 'To speak today of the defence of democracy as if we were defending something which we knew and had possessed for many decades or many centuries is self-deception and sham –

mass democracy is a new phenomenon – a creation of the last half-century – which it is inappropriate and misleading to consider in terms of the philosophy of Locke or of the liberal democracy of the nineteenth century. We should be nearer the mark, and should have a far more convincing slogan, if we spoke of the need, not to defend democracy, but to create it.' *The New Society* (London: Macmillan, 1951), pp. 75–6.

4. Cf. Hans Speier, *Social Order and The Risks of War* (New York: George Stewart, 1952), pp. 323–39.

33

THE AMERICAN EVASION OF DEMOCRACY

Cornel West

Prophetic pragmatism denies Sisyphean pessimism and utopian perfectionism. Rather, it promotes the possibility of human progress and the human impossibility of paradise. This progress results from principled and protracted Promethean efforts, yet even such efforts are no guarantee. And all human struggles – including successful ones – against specific forms of evil produce new, though possibly lesser, forms of evil. Human struggle sits at the center of prophetic pragmatism, a struggle guided by a democratic and libertarian vision, sustained by moral courage and existential integrity, and tempered by the recognition of human finitude and frailty. It calls for utopian energies and tragic actions, energies and actions that yield permanent and perennial revolutionary, rebellious, and reformist strategies that oppose the *status quos* of our day. These strategies are never to become ends-in-themselves, but rather to remain means through which are channeled moral outrage and human desperation in the face of prevailing forms of evil in human societies and in human lives. Such outrage must never cease, and such desperation will never disappear, yet without revolutionary, rebellious, and reformist strategies, credible and effective opposition wanes. Prophetic pragmatism attempts to keep alive the sense of alternative ways of life and of struggle based on the best of the past. In this sense, the praxis of prophetic pragmatism is tragic action with revolutionary intent, usually reformist consequences, and always visionary outlook. It concurs with Raymond Williams' tragic revolutionary perspective:

From: Cornel West, *The American Evasion of Philosophy* (Madison, WI: University of Wisconsin Press, 1989).

The tragic action, in its deepest sense, is not the confirmation of disorder, but its experience, its comprehension and its resolution. In our own time, this action is general, and its common name is revolution. We have to see the evil and the suffering, in the factual disorder that makes revolution necessary, and in the disordered struggle against the disorder. We have to recognize this suffering in a close and immediate experience, and not cover it with names. But we follow the whole action: not only the evil, but the men who have fought against evil; not only the crisis, but the energy released by it, the spirit learned in it. We make the connections, because that is the action of tragedy, and what we learn in suffering is again revolution, because we acknowledge others as men and any such acknowledgement is the beginning of struggle, as the continuing reality of our lives. Then to see revolution in this tragic perspective is the only way to maintain it.[1]

This oppositional consciousness draws its sustenance principally from a tradition of resistance. To keep alive a sense of alternative ways of life and of struggle requires memory of those who prefigured such life and struggle in the past. In this sense, tradition is to be associated not solely with ignorance and intolerance, prejudice and parochialism, dogmatism and docility. Rather, tradition is also to be identified with insight and intelligence, rationality and resistance, critique and contestation. Tradition *per se* is never a problem, but rather those traditions that have been and are hegemonic over other traditions. All that human beings basically have are traditions – those institutions and practices, values and sensibilities, stories and symbols, ideas and metaphors that shape human identities, attitudes, outlooks, and dispositions. These traditions are dynamic, malleable and revisable, yet all changes in a tradition are done in light of some old or newly emerging tradition. Innovation presupposes some tradition and inaugurates another tradition. The profound historical consciousness of prophetic pragmatism shuns the Emersonian devaluing of the past. Yet it also highlights those elements of old and new traditions that promote innovation and resistance for the aims of enhancing individuality and expanding democracy. This enhancement and expansion constitute human progress. And all such progress takes place within the contours of clashing traditions. In this way, just as tragic action constitutes resistance to prevailing *status quos*, the critical treatment and nurturing of a tradition yield human progress. Tragedy can be an impetus rather than an impediment to oppositional activity; tradition may serve as a stimulus rather than a stumbling block to human progress.

Prophetic pragmatism understands the Emersonian swerve from epistemology – and the American evasion of philosophy – not as a wholesale rejection of philosophy but rather as a reconception of philosophy as a form of cultural criticism that attempts to transform linguistic, social, cultural, and political traditions for the purposes of increasing the scope of individual development and democratic operations. Prophetic pragmatism conceives of philosophy as a historically circumscribed quest for wisdom that puts forward new interpretations of the world based on past traditions in order to promote existential sustenance and political relevance. Like Emerson and earlier pragmatists, it views truth as a species of the good, as that which enhances the flourishing of human progress. This does not mean that philosophy ignores the ugly facts and unpleasant realities of life and history. Rather, it highlights these facts and realities precisely because they provoke doubt, curiosity, outrage, or desperation that motivates efforts to overcome them. These efforts take the forms of critique and praxis, forms that attempt to change what is into a better what can be.

Prophetic pragmatism closely resembles and, in some ways, converges with the metaphilosophical perspectives of Antonio Gramsci. Both conceive of philosophical activity as 'a cultural battle to transform the popular "mentality" '[2] It is not surprising that Gramsci writes:

> What the pragmatists wrote about this question merits re-examination . . . they felt real needs and 'described' them with an exactness that was not far off the mark, even if they did not succeed in posing the problems fully or in providing a solution.[3]

Prophetic pragmatism is inspired by the example of Antonio Gramsci principally because he is the major twentieth-century philosopher of praxis, power and provocation without devaluing theory, adopting unidimensional conceptions of power, or reducing provocation to Clausewitzian calculations of warfare. Gramsci's work is historically specific, theoretically engaging, and politically activistic in an exemplary manner. His concrete and detailed investigations are grounded in and reflections upon local struggles, yet theoretically sensitive to structural dynamics and international phenomena. He is attuned to the complex linkage of socially constructed identities to human agency while still convinced of the crucial role of the ever-changing forms in class-ridden economic modes of production. Despite his fluid Leninist conception of political organization and mobilization (which downplays the democratic and libertarian values of prophetic pragmatists) and his unswerving allegiance to sophisticated Marxist social theory (which is an indispensable yet ultimately inadequate weapon for prophetic pragmatists), Gramsci exemplifies the critical spirit and oppositional sentiments of prophetic pragmatism.

This is seen most clearly in Gramsci's view of the relation of philosophy to 'common sense.' For him, the aim of philosophy is not only to become worldly by imposing its elite intellectual views upon people, but to become part of a social movement by nourishing and being nourished by the philosophical views of oppressed people themselves for the aims of social change and personal meaning.

[...]

Prophetic pragmatism purports to be not only an oppositional cultural criticism but also a material force for individuality and democracy. By 'material force' I simply mean a practice that has some potency and effect or makes a difference in the world. There is – and should be – no such thing as a prophetic pragmatist movement. The translation of philosophic outlook into social motion is not that simple. In fact, it is possible to be a prophetic pragmatist and belong to different political movements, for example feminist, Chicano, black, socialist, left-liberal ones. It also is possible to subscribe to prophetic pragmatism and belong to different religious and/or secular traditions. This is so because a prophetic pragmatist commitment to individuality and democracy, historical consciousness and systemic social analyses, and tragic action in an evil-ridden world can take place in – though usually on the margin of – a variety of traditions. The distinctive hallmarks of a prophetic pragmatist are a universal consciousness that promotes an all-embracing democratic and libertarian moral vision, a historical consciousness that acknowledges human finitude and con-ditionedness, and a critical consciousness which encourages relentless critique and self-criticism for the aims of social change and personal humility.

[...]

I hold a religious conception of pragmatism. I have dubbed it 'prophetic' in that it harks back to the Jewish and Christian tradition of prophets who brought urgent and compassionate critique to bear on the evils of their day. The mark of the prophet is to speak the truth in love with courage – come what may. Prophetic pragmatism proceeds from this impulse. It neither requires a religious foundation nor entails a religious perspective, yet prophetic pragmatism is compatible with certain religious outlooks.

The severing of ties to churches, synagogues, temples, and mosques by the left intelligentsia is tantamount to political suicide; it turns the pessimism of many self-deprecating and self-pitying secular progressive intellectuals into a self-fulfilling prophecy. This point was never grasped by C. Wright Mills, though W. E. B. Du Bois understood it well.

[...]

Prophetic pragmatism worships at no ideological altars. It condemns oppression anywhere and everywhere, be it the brutal butchery of third-world dictators, the regimentation and repression of peoples in the Soviet Union and Soviet-bloc countries, or the racism, patriarchy, homophobia and economic injustice in the first-world capitalist nations. In this way, the precious ideals of individuality and democracy of prophetic pragmatism oppose all those power structures that lack public accountability, be they headed by military generals, bureaucratic party bosses, or corporate tycoons. Nor is prophetic pragmatism confined to any preordained historical agent, such as the working class, black people, or women. Rather, it invites all people of goodwill both here and abroad to fight for an Emersonian culture of creative democracy in which the plight of the wretched of the earth is alleviated.

[...]

Prophetic pragmatism is a deeply American response to the end of the Age of Europe, the emergence of the United States as the world power, and the decolonization of the third world. The response is 'American' not simply because it appropriates and promotes the major American tradition of cultural criticism, but also because it is shaped by the immediate American intellectual situation. This situation is not a 'closing of the American mind', as nostalgically and tendentiously understood by Allan Bloom's popular work. Rather, it is a complex configuration of the effects on American intellectual life of the decentering of Europe, the centering of the United States and the decolonizing of Asia and Africa.

NOTES

1. Raymond Williams, *Modern Tragedy*, (Stanford: Stanford University Press, 1966), pp. 83–4.
2. Antonio Gramsci, *Selections from the Prison Notebooks*, ed. and trans. Quintin Hoare and Geoffrey Nowell Smith (New York: International Publishers, 1971), p. 348.
3. Ibid., pp. 348, 349.

34

THE PRIORITY OF DEMOCRACY TO PHILOSOPHY

Richard Rorty

To refuse to argue about what human beings should be like seems to show a contempt for the spirit of accommodation and tolerance, which is essential to democracy. But it is not clear how to argue for the claim that human beings ought to be liberals rather than fanatics without being driven back on a theory of human nature, on philosophy. I think that we must grasp the first horn. We have to insist that not every argument need to be met in the terms in which it is presented. Accommodation and tolerance must stop short of a willingness to work within any vocabulary that one's interlocutor wishes to use, to take seriously any topic that he puts forward for discussion. To take this view is of a piece with dropping the idea that a single moral vocabulary and a single set of moral beliefs are appropriate for every human community everywhere, and to grant that historical developments may lead us to simply *drop* questions and the vocabulary in which those questions are posed.

Just as Jefferson refused to let the Christian Scriptures set the terms in which to discuss alternative political institutions, so we either must refuse to answer the question 'What sort of human being are you hoping to produce?' or, at least, must not let our answer to this question dictate our answer to the question 'Is justice primary?'[1] It is no more evident that democratic institutions are to be measured by the sort of person they create than that they are to be measured against divine commands. It is not evident that they are to be measured by anything more specific than the moral intuitions of the particular historical

From: Richard Rorty, *Objectivity, Relativism, and Truth* (Cambridge: Cambridge University Press, 1988).

community that has created those institutions. The idea that moral and political controversies should always be 'brought back to first principles' is reasonable if it means merely that we should seek common ground in the hope of attaining agreement. But it is misleading if it is taken as the claim that there is a natural order of premises from which moral and political conclusions are to be inferred – not to mention the claim that some particular interlocutor (for example, Nietzsche or Loyola) has already discerned that order. The liberal response to the communitarians' claim must be, therefore, that even if the typical character types of liberal democracies *are* bland, calculating, petty and unheroic, the prevalence of such people may be a reasonable price to pay for political freedom.

The spirit of accommodation and tolerance certainly suggests that we should seek common ground with Nietzsche and Loyola, but there is no predicting where, or whether, such common ground will be found. The philosophical tradition has assumed that there are certain topics (for example, 'What is God's will?', 'What is man?', 'What rights are intrinsic to the species?') on which everyone has, or should have, views and that these topics are prior in the order of justification to those at issue in political deliberation. This assumption goes along with the assumption that human beings have a natural center that philosophical inquiry can locate and illuminate. By contrast, the view that human beings are centerless networks of beliefs and desires and that their vocabularies and opinions are determined by historical circumstance allows for the possibility that there may not be enough overlap between two such networks to make possible agreement about political topics, or even profitable discussion of such topics.[2] We do not conclude that Nietzsche and Loyola are crazy because they hold unusual views on certain 'fundamental' topics; rather, we conclude this only after extensive attempts at an exchange of political views have made us realize that we are not going to get anywhere.[3]

One can sum up this way of grasping the first horn of the dilemma sketched earlier by saying that Rawls puts democratic politics first and philosophy second. He retains the Socratic commitment to free exchange of views without the Platonic commitment to the possibility of universal agreement – a possibility underwritten by epistemological doctrines like Plato's Theory of Recollection[4] or Kant's theory of the relation between pure and empirical concepts. He disengages the question of whether we ought to be tolerant and Socratic from the question of whether this strategy will lead to truth. He is content that it should lead to whatever intersubjective reflective equilibrium may be obtainable, given the contingent make-up of the subjects in question. Truth, viewed in the Platonic way, as the grasp of what Rawls calls 'an order antecedent to and given to us', is simply not relevant to democratic politics. So philosophy, as the explanation of the relation between such an order and human nature, is not relevant either. When the two come into conflict, democracy takes precedence over philosophy.

This conclusion may seem liable to an obvious objection. It may seem that I have been rejecting a concern with philosophical theories about the nature of men and women on the basis of just such a theory. But notice that although I have frequently said that Rawls *can be content* with a notion of the human self as a centerless web of historically conditioned beliefs and desires, I have not suggested that he *needs* such a theory. Such a theory does not offer liberal social theory a *basis*. If one *wants* a model of the human self, then this picture of a centerless web will fill the need. But for purposes of liberal social theory, one can do without such a model. One can get along with common sense and social science, areas of discourse in which the term 'the self' rarely occurs.

If, however, one has a taste for philosophy – if one's vocation, one's private pursuit of perfection, entails constructing models of such entities as 'the self', 'knowledge', 'language', 'nature', 'God', or 'history', and then tinkering with them until they mesh with one another – one *will* want a picture of the self. Since my own vocation is of this sort, and the moral identity around which I wish to build such models is that of a citizen of a liberal democratic state, I commend the picture of the self as a centerless and contingent web to those with similar tastes and similar identities. But I would not commend it to those with a similar vocation but dissimilar moral identities – identities built, for example, around the love of God, Nietzschean self-overcoming, the accurate representation of reality as it is in itself, the quest for 'one right answer' to moral questions, or the natural superiority of a given character type. Such persons need a more complex and interesting, less simple-minded model of the self – one that meshes in complex ways with complex models of such things as 'nature' or 'history'. Nevertheless, such person may, for pragmatic rather than moral reasons, be loyal citizens of a liberal democratic society. They may despise most of their fellow citizens, but be prepared to grant that the prevalence of such despicable character types is a lesser evil than the loss of political freedom. They may be ruefully grateful that their private senses of moral identity and the models of the human self that they develop to articulate this sense – the ways in which they deal with their aloneness – are not the concern of such a state. Rawls and Dewey have shown how the liberal state can ignore the difference between the moral identities of Glaucon and of Thrasymachus, just as it ignores the difference between the religious identities of a Catholic archbishop and a Mormon prophet.

There is, however, a flavor of paradox in this attitude toward theories of the self. One might be inclined to say that I have evaded one sort of self-referential paradox only by falling into another sort. For I am presupposing that one is at liberty to rig up a model of the self to suit oneself, to tailor it to one's politics, one's religion or one's private sense of the meaning of one's life. This, in turn, presupposes that there is no 'objective truth' about what the human self is *really* like. That, in turn, seems a claim that could be justified only on the basis of a metaphysico-epistemological view of the traditional sort. For surely if anything is the province of such a view, it is the question of what there is and is not a 'fact of the matter' about. So my argument must ultimately come back to philosophical first principles.

Here I can only say that if there were a discoverable fact of the matter about what there is a fact of the matter about, then it would doubtless be metaphysics and epistemology that would discover that meta-fact. But I think that the very idea of a 'fact of the matter' is one we would be better off without. Philosophers like Davidson and Derrida have, I think, given us good reason to think that the *physis – nomos, in se–ad nos* and objective – subjective distinctions were steps on a ladder that we can now safely throw away. The question of whether the reasons such philosophers have given for this claim are themselves metaphysico-epistemological reasons, and if not, what sort of reasons they are, strikes me as pointless and sterile. Once again, I fall back on the holist's strategy of insisting that reflective equilibrium is all we need try for – that there is no natural order of justification of beliefs, no predestined outline for argument to trace. Getting rid of the idea of such an outline seems to me one of the many benefits of a conception of the self as a centerless web. Another benefit is that questions about whom we need justify ourselves to – questions about who counts as a fanatic and who deserves an answer – can be treated as just further matters to be sorted out in the course of attaining reflective equilibrium.

I can, however, make one point to offset the air of light-minded aestheticism I am adopting toward traditional philosophical questions. This is that there is a moral purpose behind this light-mindedness. The encouragement of light-mindedness about traditional philosophical topics serves the same purposes as does the encouragement of light-mindedness about traditional theological topics. Like the rise of large market economies, the increase in literacy, the proliferation of artistic genres and the insouciant pluralism of contemporary culture, such philosophical superficiality and light-mindedness helps along the disenchantment of the world. It helps make the world's inhabitants more pragmatic, more tolerant, more liberal, more receptive to the appeal of instrumental rationality.

If one's moral identity consists in being a citizen of a liberal polity, then to encourage light-mindedness may serve one's moral purposes. Moral commitment, after all, does not require taking seriously all the matters that are, for moral reasons, taken seriously by one's fellow citizens. It may require just the opposite. It may require trying to josh them out of the habit of taking those topics so seriously. There may be serious reasons for so joshing them. More generally, we should not assume that the aesthetic is always the enemy of the moral. I should argue that in the recent history of liberal societies, the willingness to view matters aesthetically – to be content to indulge in what Schiller called 'play' and to discard what Nietzsche called 'the spirit of seriousness' – has been an important vehicle of moral progress.

I have now said everything I have to say about the communitarian claims that I distinguished at the outset: the claim that the social theory of the liberal state rests on false philosophical presuppositions. I hope I have given reasons for thinking that insofar as the communitarian is a critic of liberalism, he should drop this claim and should instead develop either of the first two claims: the empirical claim that democratic institutions cannot be combined with the sense of common purpose prodemocratic societies enjoyed, or the moral judgment that the products of the liberal state are too high a price to pay for the elimination of the evils that preceded it. If communitarian critics of liberalism stuck to these two claims, they would avoid the sort of terminal wistfulness with which their books typically end. Heidegger, for example, tells us that 'we are too late for the gods, and too early for Being'. Unger ends *Knowledge and Politics* with an appeal to a *Deus absconditus*. MacIntyre ends *After Virtue* by saying that we 'are waiting not for a Godot, but for another – doubtless very different – St Benedict'.[5] Sandel ends his book by saying that liberalism 'forgets the possibility that when politics goes well, we can know a good in common that we cannot know alone', but he does not suggest a candidate for this common good.

Instead of thus suggesting that philosophical reflection, or a return to religion, might enable us to re-enchant the world, I think that communitarians should stick to the question of whether disenchantment has, on balance, done us more harm than good, or created more dangers than it has evaded. For Dewey, communal and public disenchantment is the price we pay for individual and private spiritual liberation, the kind of liberation that Emerson thought characteristically American. Dewey was as well aware as Weber that there is a price to be paid, but he thought it well worth paying. He assumed that no good achieved by earlier societies would be worth recapturing if the price were a diminution in our ability to leave people alone, to let them try out their private visions of perfection in peace. He admired the American habit of giving democracy priority over philosophy by asking, about any vision of the meaning of life, 'Would not acting out this vision interfere with the ability of others to work out their own salvation?' Giving priority to that question is no more 'natural' than giving priority to, say, MacIntyre's question 'What sorts of human beings emerge in the culture of liberalism?' or Sandel's question 'Can a community of those who put justice first ever be more than a community of strangers?' The question of which of these questions is prior to which others is, necessarily, begged by *everybody*. Nobody is being any more arbitrary than anybody else. But that is to say that nobody is being arbitrary at all. Everybody is just insisting that the beliefs and desires they hold most dear should come first in the order of discussion. That is not arbitrariness, but sincerity.

The danger of re-enchanting the world, from a Deweyan point of view, is that it might interfere with the development of what Rawls calls 'a social union of social unions',[6] some of which may be (and in Emerson's view, should be) very small indeed. For it is hard to be both enchanted with one version of the world and tolerant of all the others. I have not tried to argue the question of whether Dewey was right in this judgment of relative danger and promise. I have merely argued that such a judgment neither presupposes nor supports a theory of the self. Nor have I tried to deal with Horkheimer and Adorno's prediction that the 'dissolvent rationality' of the Enlightenment will eventually cause the liberal democracies to come unstuck.

The only thing I have to say about this prediction is that the collapse of the liberal democracies would not, in itself, provide much evidence for the claim that human societies cannot survive without widely shared opinions on matters of ultimate importance – shared conceptions of our place in the universe and our mission on earth. Perhaps they cannot survive under such conditions, but the eventual collapse of the democracies would not, in itself, show that this was the case – any more than it would show that human societies require kings or an established religion, or that political community cannot exist outside of small city-states.

Both Jefferson and Dewey described America as an 'experiment'. If the experiment fails, our descendants may learn something important. But they will not learn a philosophical truth, any more than they will learn a religious one. They will simply get some hints about what to watch out for when setting up their next experiment. Even if nothing else survives from the age of the democratic revolutions, perhaps our descendants will remember that social institutions *can* be viewed as experiments in cooperation rather than as attempts to embody a universal and ahistorical order. It is hard to believe that this memory would not be worth having.

NOTES

1. This is the kernel of truth in Dworkin's claim that Rawls rejects 'goal-based' social theory, but this point should not lead us to think that he is thereby driven back on a 'rights-based' theory.
2. But one should not press this point so far as to raise the specter of 'untranslatable languages'. As Donald Davidson has remarked, we would not recognize other organisms as actual or potential language users – or, therefore, as persons – unless there were enough overlap in belief and desire to make translation possible. The point is merely that efficient and frequent communication is only a necessary, not a sufficient, condition of agreement.
3. Further, such a conclusion is *restricted* to politics. It does not cast doubt on the ability of these men to follow the rules of logic or their ability to do many other things skillfully and well. It is thus not equivalent to the traditional philosophical charge of 'irrationality'. That charge presupposes that inability to 'see' certain truths is evidence of the lack of an organ that is essential for human functioning generally.
4. In Kierkegaard's *Philosophical Fragments*, to which I have referred earlier, we find the Platonic Theory of Recollection treated as the archetypal justification of 'Socratism' and thus as the symbol of all forms (especially Hegel's) of what Bernard Williams has recently called 'the rationalist theory of rationality' – the idea that one is rational only if one can appeal to universally accepted criteria, criteria whose truth and applicability all human beings can find 'in their heart'. This is the philosophical core of the Scriptural idea that 'truth is great, and will prevail', when the idea is dissociated from the idea of 'a New Being' (in the way that Kierkegaard refused to dissociate it).
5. See Jeffrey Stout's discussion of the manifold ambiguities of this conclusion in 'Virtue Among the Ruins: An Essay on MacIntyre'. *Neue Zeitschrift für Systematische Theologie und Religionsphilosophie* 26 (1984): pp. 256–73, especially p. 269.

6. This is Rawls's description of 'a well-ordered society (corresponding to justice as fairness)' (*Theory of Justice*, p. 527). Sandel finds these passages metaphorical and complains that 'intersubjective and individualistic images appear in uneasy, sometimes unfelicitous combination, as if to betray the incompatible commitments contending within' (*Liberalism and the Limits of Justice*, pp. 150 ff.). He concludes that 'the moral vocabulary of community in the strong sense cannot in all cases be captured by a conception that [as Rawls has said his is] "in its theoretical bases is individualistic"'. I am claiming that these commitments will look incompatible only if one attempts to define their philosophical presuppositions (which Rawls himself may occasionally have done too much of), and that this is a good reason for not making such attempts. Compare the Enlightenment view that attempts to sharpen up the theological presuppositions of social commitments had done more harm than good and that if theology cannot simply be discarded, it should at least be left as fuzzy (or, one might say, 'liberal') as possible. Oakeshott has a point when he insists on the value of theoretical muddle for the health of the state.

Elsewhere Rawls has claimed that 'there is no reason why a well-ordered society should encourage primarily individualistic values if this means ways of life that lead individuals to pursue their own way and to have no concern for the interest of others' ('Fairness to Goodness', *Philosophical Review* 84 [1975]: p. 550). Sandel's discussion of this passage says that it 'suggests a deeper sense in which Rawls' conception is individualistic', but his argument that this suggestion is correct is, once again, the claim that 'the Rawlsian self is not only a subject of possession, but an antecedently individuated subject' (*Liberalism and the Limits of Justice*, pp. 61 ff.). This is just the claim I have been arguing against by arguing that there is no such thing as 'the Rawlsian self and that Rawls does not want or need a 'theory of the person'. Sandel says (p. 62) that Rawls 'takes for granted that every individual consists of one and only one system of desires', but it is hard to find evidence for this claim in the texts. At worst, Rawls simplifies his presentation by imagining each of his citizens as having only one such set, but this simplifying assumption does not seem central to his view.

PART II: THINKING THE SOCIAL: MODERN APPLICATIONS OF AMERICAN SOCIAL AND POLITICAL THOUGHT

SECTION I
DEMOCRACY AND POWER

Part II concentrates more on the applications of the ideas that have been presented in preceding chapters. The section concerned with Democracy and Power introduces the writing of another modern scholar, Barrington Moore. In his classic work *Social Origins of Dictatorship and Democracy*, Moore looks at the various historical routes from pre-modern to modern times. While the first road, taken by English, French and American societies led to capitalism and western democracy, the second path to modernisation followed by Germany and Japan led to fascism; the third path, that of China and Russia, led to Communism. What was crucial in each path was the coming to terms with the decline of the peasantry in conjunction with the creation or development of a social group that could trigger and accelerate the industrialisation process. In societies that took the first road, events such as the Puritan Revolution, the French Revolution and the American Civil War helped to radically accelerate the process. Societies that would in the course of the twentieth century turn to either fascism or communism had delayed the modernisation process and had difficulties with the transition from an agriculture-dominated society to industrialisation to fascism and communism. Fascism and communism here functioned as catalysts that helped to jump-start the modernisation process. However, as Moore also tries to show, America was also in some ways a latecomer. The American Revolution and Independence had left some unfinished business that was only completed by the Civil War.

In this section of the Reader, Moore's pioneering work is followed by an important debate on the contemporary state of American democracy. The two extremes of the debate are represented by two modern classics, by the radical sociologist C. Wright Mills and the political scientist Robert A. Dahl. In his seminal study, *The Power Elite*, Mills maintains that the US is now governed by a powerful tripartite elite, consisting of the political directorate, the higher business class and the military. Robert A. Dahl could not disagree more. As he has pointed out in *A Preface to Democratic Theory*, the US represents a hybrid form of democracy in which the rise to power is much more complex than Mills describes. Dahl further argues in his own empirical study *Who Governs?* that power in America still needs consent from below and is successfully moderated by democratic forces.

The other contributions in this section are variations on the theme. They spell out what democracy and power mean in the twentieth and twenty-first centuries. Amy Gutmann and Dennis Thompson's study *Democracy and Disagreement* looks at deliberative models of democracy. Their book can be seen as an attempt to look at the substance of deliberation, the moral choices that citizens make and the moral dilemmas they are sometimes confronted with. Benjamin Barber's attempt to argue for *Strong Democracy* follows a slightly different path. Although Barber is in general support of deliberative efforts, his argument goes more into the direction of improved and new institutionalised options in which citizens can fully participate. It is, in other words, an attempt to argue for the choice to have more democratic choices. In contrast, Samuel Bowles and Herbert Gintis' study *Democracy and Capitalism* is an attempt to come to terms with the undemocratic nature of capitalism. Genuine democracy, they argue, is concerned with both democratic means and ends, not just means as the old left would have it. More specifically, Bowles and Gintis ask us to rethink the way we think about rights, particularly the subversive role that liberal rights can play when dealing with the more undemocratic features of capitalism. Robert Bellah et al. opt again for another way of deepening democracy. In their study *Habits of the Heart* Bellah and his fellow communitarians argue for the strengthening of community ties. The communitarian effort would redress the balance between a currently rather overdeveloped individualism and a civic society in decline. Finally, Sheldon S. Wolin asks us to seek those rare moments in which the political could again become prominent and to question current institutional arrangements. In his essay 'Fugitive Democracy' he argues that the democratic view of the citizen-as-actor is somehow incompatible with the existing arrangements in which the state has become the fixed centre.

35

SOCIAL ORIGINS OF DICTATORSHIP AND DEMOCRACY

Barrington Moore

In the range of cases examined here one may discern three main historical routes from the preindustrial to the modern world. The first of these leads through what I think deserve to be called bourgeois revolutions. Aside from the fact that this term is a red flag to many scholars because of its Marxist connotations, it has other ambiguities and disadvantages. Nevertheless, for reasons that will appear in due course I think it is a necessary designation for certain violent changes that took place in English, French and American societies on the way to becoming modern industrial democracies and that historians connect with the Puritan Revolution (or the English Civil War as it is often called as well), the French Revolution and the American Civil War. A key feature in such revolutions is the development of a group in society with an independent economic base, which attacks obstacles to a democratic version of capitalism that have been inherited from the past. Though a great deal of the impetus has come from trading and manufacturing classes in the cities, that is very far from the whole story. The allies this bourgeois impetus has found, the enemies it has encountered, vary sharply from case to case. The landed upper classes, our main concern at the start, were either an important part of this capitalist and democratic tide, as in England, or if they opposed it, they were swept aside in the convulsions of revolution or civil war. The same thing may be said about the peasants. Either the main thrust of their political efforts coincided with that toward capitalism and political democracy, or else it was negligible. And it was

From: Barrington Moore, Jr., *Social Origins of Dictatorship and Democracy* (Harmondsworth: Penguin Books, 1966).

negligible either because capitalist advance destroyed peasant society or because this advance began in a new country, such as the United States, without a real peasantry.

The first and earlier route through the great revolutions and civil wars led to the combination of capitalism and Western democracy. The second route has also been capitalist, but culminated during the twentieth century in fascism. Germany and Japan are the obvious cases. I shall call this the capitalist and reactionary form. It amounts to a form of revolution from above. In these countries the bourgeois impulse was much weaker. If it took a revolutionary form at all, the revolution was defeated. Afterward sections of a relatively weak commercial and industrial class relied on dissident elements in the older and still dominant ruling classes, mainly recruited from the land, to put through the political and economic changes required for a modern industrial society, under the auspices of a semi-parliamentary regime. Industrial development may proceed rapidly under such auspices. But the outcome, after a brief and unstable period of democracy, has been fascism. The third route is of course communism, as exemplified in Russia and in China. The great agrarian bureaucracies of these countries served to inhibit the commercial and later industrial impulses even more than in the preceding instances. The results were twofold. In the first place these urban classes were too weak to constitute even a junior partner in the form of modernization taken by Germany and Japan, though there were attempts in this direction. And in the absence of more than the most feeble steps toward modernization a huge peasantry remained. This stratum, subject to new strains and stresses as the modern world encroached upon it, provided the main destructive revolutionary force that overthrew the old order and propelled these countries into the modern era under communist leadership that made the peasants its primary victims.

Finally, in India we may perceive still a fourth general pattern that accounts for the weak impulse toward modernization. In that country so far there has been neither a capitalist revolution from above or below, nor a peasant one leading to communism. Likewise the impulse toward modernization has been very weak. On the other hand, at least some of the historical prerequisites of Western democracy did put in an appearance. A parliamentary regime has existed for some time that is considerably more than mere façade. Because the impulse toward modernization has been weakest in India, this case stands somewhat apart from any theoretical scheme that it seems possible to construct for the others. At the same time it serves as a salutary check upon such generalizations. It is especially useful in trying to understand peasant revolutions, since the degree of rural misery in India where there has been no peasant revolution is about the same as in China where rebellion and revolution have been decisive in both premodern and recent times.

To sum up as concisely as possible, we seek to understand the role of the landed upper classes and the peasants in the bourgeois revolutions leading to capitalist democracy, the abortive bourgeois revolutions leading to fascism, and the peasant revolutions leading to communism. The ways in which the landed upper classes and the peasants reacted to the challenge of commercial agriculture were decisive factors in determining the political outcome.

[...]

By 1860 the United States had developed three quite different forms of society in different parts of the country: the cotton-growing South; the West, a land of free farmers; and the rapidly industrializing Northeast.

The lines of cleavage and cooperation had by no means always run in these directions. To be sure, from the days of Hamilton and Jefferson there had been a tug-of-war between agrarians and urban commercial and financial interests. The expansion of the country westward made it seem for a moment, under President Jackson in the 1830s, that the principles of agrarian democracy, in practice an absolute minimum of central authority and a tendency to favor debtors over creditors, had won a permanent victory over those of Alexander Hamilton. Even in Jackson's own time, however, agrarian democracy had severe difficulties. Two closely related developments were to destroy it: the further growth of industrial capitalism in the Northeast and the establishment of an export market for Southern cotton.

[...]

The ultimate causes of the war are to be found in the growth of different economic systems leading to different (but still capitalist) civilizations with incompatible stands on slavery. The connection between Northern capitalism and Western farming helped to make unnecessary for a time the characteristic reactionary coalition between urban and landed elites and hence the one compromise that could have avoided the war. (It was also the compromise that eventually liquidated the war.) Two further factors made compromise extremely difficult. The future of the West appeared uncertain in such a way as to make the distribution of power at the center uncertain, thus intensifying and magnifying all causes of distrust and contention. Secondly, as just noted, the main forces of cohesion in American society, though growing stronger, were still very weak.

[...]

One sense of revolution is a violent destruction of political institutions that permits a society to take a new course. After the Civil War, industrial capitalism advanced by leaps and bounds. Clearly that was what Charles Beard had in mind when he coined the famous phrase 'the Second American Revolution'. But was the burst of industrial capitalist growth a consequence of the Civil War? And how about the contribution to human freedom that all but the most conservative associate with the word revolution? The history of the Fourteenth Amendment, prohibiting the states from depriving any person of life, liberty or property, epitomizes the ambiguity on this score. As every educated person knows, the Fourteenth Amendment has done precious little to protect Negroes and a tremendous amount to protect corporations. Beard's thesis that such was the original intent of those who drafted the amendment has been rejected by some.[1] That in itself is trivial. About the consequence, there is no doubt. Ultimately the way one assesses the Civil War depends on the assessment of freedom in modern American society and the connection between the institutions of advanced industrial capitalism and the Civil War.

[...]

The inquiry leads back toward political questions and incompatibilities between two different kinds of civilizations: in the South and in the North and West. Labor-repressive agricultural systems, and plantation slavery in particular, are political obstacles to a *particular kind* of capitalism, at a specific historical stage: competitive democratic capitalism we must call it for lack of a more precise term. Slavery was a threat and an obstacle to a society that was indeed the heir of the Puritan, American, and French Revolutions. Southern society was based firmly on hereditary status as the basis of human worth. With the West, the North, though in the process of change, was still committed to notions of equal opportunity. In both, the ideals were reflections of economic arrangements that gave them much of their appeal and force. Within the same political unit it was, I think, inherently impossible to establish political and social institutions that would satisfy both. If the geographical separation had been much greater, if the South had been a colony for example, the problem would in all probability have been relatively simple to solve at that time – at the expense of the Negro.

That the Northern victory, even with all its ambiguous consequences, was a political victory for freedom compared with what a Southern victory would have been seems obvious enough to require no extended discussion. One need only consider what would have happened had the Southern plantation system been able to establish itself in the West by the middle of the nineteenth century and surrounded the Northeast. Then the United States would have been in the position of some modernizing countries today, with a latifundia economy, a dominant antidemocratic aristocracy, and a weak and dependent commercial and industrial class, unable and unwilling to push forward toward political democracy. In rough outline, such was the Russian situation, though with less of a commercial emphasis in its agriculture in the second half of the nineteenth century. A radical explosion of some kind or a prolonged period of semireactionary dictatorship would have been far more probable than a firmly rooted political democracy with all its shortcomings and deficiencies.

Striking down slavery was a decisive step, an act at least as important as the striking down of absolute monarchy in the English Civil War and the French Revolution, an essential preliminary for further advances. Like these violent upheavals, the main achievements in our Civil War were political in the broad sense of the term. Later generations in America were to attempt to put economic content into the political framework, to raise the level of the people toward some conception of human dignity by putting in their hands the material means to determine their own fate. Subsequent revolutions in Russia and China have had the same purpose even if the means have in large measure so far swallowed up and distorted the ends. It is in this context, I believe, that the American Civil War has to be placed for its proper assessment.

NOTE

1. J. G. Randall and David Donald, *The Civil War and Reconstruction* (Boston: Heath, 1961), p. 83.

36

THE POWER ELITE

C. Wright Mills

Changes in the American structure of power have generally come about by institutional shifts in the relative positions of the political, the economic, and the military orders. From this point of view, and broadly speaking, the American power elite has gone through four epochs, and is now well into a fifth.

1. During the first – roughly from the Revolution through the administration of John Adams – the social and economic, the political and the military institutions were more or less unified in a simple and direct way: the individual men of these several elites moved easily from one role to another at the top of each of the major institutional orders. Many of them were many-sided men who could take the part of legislator and merchant, frontiersman and soldier, scholar and surveyor.[1]

Until the downfall of the Congressional caucus of 1824, political institutions seemed quite central; political decisions, of great importance; many politicians, considered national statesmen of note. 'Society, as I first remember it,' Henry Cabot Lodge once said, speaking of the Boston of his early boyhood, 'was based on the old families; Doctor Holmes defines them in the "Autocrat" as the families which had held high position in the colony, the province and during the Revolution and the early decades of the United States. They represented several generations of education and standing in the community . . . They had ancestors who had filled the pulpits, sat upon the bench, and taken part in the government

From: C. Wright Mills, *The Power Elite* (New York and London: Oxford University Press, 1956).

under the crown; who had fought in the Revolution, helped to make the State and National constitutions and served in the army or navy; who had been members of the House or Senate in the early days of the Republic, and who had won success as merchants, manufacturers, lawyers, or men of letters.'[2]

Such men of affairs, who – as I have noted – were the backbone of Mrs John Jay's social list of 1787, definitely included political figures of note. The important fact about these early days is that social life, economic institutions, military establishment, and political order coincided, and men who were high politicians also played key roles in the economy and, with their families, were among those of the reputable who made up local society. In fact, this first period is marked by the leadership of men whose status does not rest exclusively upon their political position, although their political activities are important and the prestige of politicians high. And this prestige seems attached to the men who occupy Congressional position as well as the cabinet. The elite are political men of education and of administrative experience, and, as Lord Bryce noted, possess a certain 'largeness of view and dignity of character'.[3]

2. During the early nineteenth century – which followed Jefferson's political philosophy, but, in due course, Hamilton's economic principles – the economic and political and military orders fitted loosely into the great scatter of the American social structure. The broadening of the economic order which came to be seated in the individual property owner was dramatized by Jefferson's purchase of the Louisiana Territory and by the formation of the Democratic-Republican party as successor to the Federalists.

In this society, the 'elite' became a plurality of top groups, each in turn quite loosely made up. They overlapped to be sure, but again quite loosely so. One definite key to the period, and certainly to our images of it, is the fact that the Jacksonian Revolution was much more of a status revolution than either an economic or a political one. The metropolitan 400 could not truly flourish in the face of the status tides of Jacksonian democracy; alongside it was a political elite in charge of the new party system. No set of men controlled centralized means of power; no small clique dominated economic, much less political, affairs. The economic order was ascendant over both social status and political power; within the economic order, a quite sizable proportion of all the economic men were among those who decided. For this was the period – roughly from Jefferson to Lincoln – when the elite was at most a loose coalition. The period ended, of course, with the decisive split of southern and northern types.

Official commentators like to contrast the ascendancy in totalitarian countries of a tightly organized clique with the American system of power. Such comments, however, are easier to sustain if one compares mid-twentieth-century Russia with mid-nineteenth-century America, which is what is often done by Tocqueville-quoting Americans making the contrast. But that was an America of a century ago, and in the century that has passed, the American elite have not remained as patrioteer essayists have described them to us. The 'loose cliques' now head institutions of a scale and power not then existing and, especially since World War I, the loose cliques have tightened up. We are well beyond the era of romantic pluralism.

3. The supremacy of corporate economic power began, in a formal way, with the Congressional elections of 1866, and was consolidated by the Supreme Court decision of 1886 which declared that the Fourteenth Amendment protected the corporation. That period witnessed the transfer of the center of initiative from government to corporation. Until the First World War (which gave us an advanced showing of certain features of our own period) this was an age of raids on the government by the economic elite, an age of simple corruption, when Senators and judges were simply bought up. Here, once upon a time, in the era of McKinley and Morgan, far removed from the undocumented complexities of our own time, many now believe, was the golden era of the American ruling class.[4]

The military order of this period, as in the second, was subordinate to the political, which in turn was subordinate to the economic. The military was thus off to the side of the main driving forces of United States history. Political institutions in the United States have never formed a centralized and autonomous domain of power; they have been enlarged and centralized only reluctantly in slow response to the public consequence of the corporate economy.

In the post-Civil-War era, that economy was the dynamic; the 'trusts' – as policies and events make amply clear – could readily use the relatively weak governmental apparatus for their own ends. That both state and federal governments were decisively limited in their power to regulate, in fact meant that they were themselves regulatable by the larger moneyed interests. Their powers were scattered and unorganized; the powers of the industrial and financial corporations concentrated and interlocked. The Morgan interests alone held 341 directorships in 112 corporations with an aggregate capitalization of over $22 billion – over three times the assessed value of all real and personal property in New England. With revenues greater and employees more numerous than those of many states, corporations controlled parties, bought laws and kept Congressmen of the 'neutral' state. And as private economic power overshadowed public political power, so the economic elite overshadowed the political.

Yet even between 1896 and 1919, events of importance tended to assume a political form, foreshadowing the shape of power which after the partial boom of the twenties was to prevail in the New Deal. Perhaps there has never been any period in American history so politically transparent as the Progressive era of President-makers and Muckrakers.

4. The New Deal did *not* reverse the political and economic relations of the third era, but it did create within the political arena, as well as in the corporate world itself, competing centers of power that challenged those of the corporate directors. As the New Deal directorate gained political power, the economic elite, which in the third period had fought against the growth of 'government' while raiding it for crafty privileges, belatedly attempted to join it on the higher

levels. When they did so they found themselves confronting other interests and men, for the places of decision were crowded. In due course, they did come to control and to use for their own purposes the New Deal institutions whose creation they had so bitterly denounced.

But during the thirties, the political order was still an instrument of small propertied farmers and businessmen, although they were weakened, having lost their last chance for real ascendancy in the Progressive era. The struggle between big and small property flared up again, however, in the political realm of the New Deal era, and to this struggle there was added, as we have seen, the new struggle of organized labor and the unorganized unemployed. This new force flourished under political tutelage, but nevertheless, for the first time in United States history, social legislation and lower-class issues became important features of the reform movement.

In the decade of the thirties, a set of shifting balances involving newly instituted farm measures and newly organized labor unions – along with big business – made up the political and administrative drama of power. These farm, labor and business groups, moreover, were more or less contained within the framework of an enlarging governmental structure, whose political direc-torship made decisions in a definitely political manner. These groups pressured, and in pressuring against one another and against the governmental and party system, they helped to shape it. But it could not be said that any of them for any considerable length of time used that government unilaterally as their instru-ment. That is why the thirties was a *political* decade: the power of business was not replaced, but it was contested and supplemented: it became one major power within a structure of power that was chiefly run by political men, and not by economic or military men turned political.

The earlier and middle Roosevelt administrations can best be understood as a desperate search for ways and means, within the existing capitalist system, of reducing the staggering and ominous army of the unemployed. In these years, the New Deal as a system of power was essentially a balance of pressure groups and interest blocs. The political top adjusted many conflicts, gave way to this demand, sidetracked that one, was the unilateral servant of none, and so evened it all out into such going policy line as prevailed from one minor crisis to another. Policies were the result of a political act of balance at the top. Of course, the balancing act that Roosevelt performed did not affect the funda-mental institutions of capitalism as a type of economy. By his policies, he subsidized the defaults of the capitalist economy, which had simply broken down; and by his rhetoric, he balanced its political disgrace, putting 'economic royalists' in the political doghouse.

The 'welfare state', created to sustain the balance and to carry out the subsidy, differed from the 'laissez-faire' state: 'If the state was believed neutral in the days of T. R. because its leaders claimed to sanction favors for no one,' Richard Hofstadter has remarked, 'the state under F. D. R. could be called neutral only in the sense that it offered favors to everyone'. The new state of the corporate commissars differs from the old welfare state. In fact, the later Roosevelt years – beginning with the entrance of the United States into overt acts of war and preparations for World War II – cannot be understood entirely in terms of an adroit equipoise of political power.

[...]

The shape and meaning of the power elite today can be understood only when these three sets of structural trends are seen at their point of coincidence: the military capitalism of private corporations exists in a weakened and formal democratic system containing a military order already quite political in outlook and demeanor. Accordingly, at the top of this structure, the power elite has been shaped by the coincidence of interest between those who control the major means of production and those who control the newly enlarged means of violence; from the decline of the professional politician and the rise to explicit political command of the corporate chieftains and the professional warlords; from the absence of any genuine civil service of skill and integrity, independent of vested interests.

The power elite is composed of political, economic, and military men, but this instituted elite is frequently in some tension: it comes together only on certain coinciding points and only on certain occasions of 'crisis'. In the long peace of the nineteenth century, the military were not in the high councils of state, not of the political directorate, and neither were the economic men – they made raids upon the state but they did not join its directorate. During the thirties, the political man was ascendant. Now the military and the corporate men are in top positions.

Of the three types of circle that compose the power elite today, it is the military that has benefited the most in its enhanced power, although the corporate circles have also become more explicitly intrenched in the more public decision-making circles. It is the professional politician that has lost the most, so much that in examining the events and decisions, one is tempted to speak of a political vacuum in which the corporate rich and the high warlord, in their coinciding interests, rule.

NOTES

1. For points used to characterize the first and second of these phases, I have drawn from Robert Lamb, 'Political Elites and the Process of Economic Development'. *The Progress of Underdeveloped Areas* (Edited by Bert Hoselitz) (Chicago: University of Chicago Press, 1952).
2. Henry Cabot Lodge, *Early Memoirs*, cited by Dixon Wecter, *The Saga of American Society* (New York: Scribner's, 1937), p. 206.
3. Lord James Bryce, *The American Commonwealth* (New York: Macmillan, 1918), vol. I, pp. 84–5. In pre-revolutionary America, regional differences were of course important; but see William E. Dodd, *The Cotton Kingdom* (Vol. 27 of the Chronicles of America Series, edited by Allen Johnson) (New Haven: Yale University Press, 1919), p. 41; Louis B. Wright, *The First Gentlemen of Virginia* (Huntington Library, 1940), Ch. 12; Samuel Morison and Henry S. Commager, *The Growth of the*

American Republic (New York: Oxford University Press, 1950), pp. 177–8; James T. Adams, *Provincial Society, 1690–1763* (New York: Macmillan, 1927), p. 83.

4. Cf., for example, David Riesman, in collaboration with Reuel Denney and Nathan Glazer, *The Lonely Crowd* (New Haven: Yale University Press, 1950).

37

A PREFACE TO DEMOCRATIC THEORY

Robert A. Dahl

Few Americans who look upon our political process attentively can fall, at times, to feel deep frustration and angry resentment with a system that on the surface has so little order and so much chaos.

For it is a markedly decentralized system. Decisions are made by endless bargaining; perhaps in no other national political system in the world is bargaining so basic a component of the political process. In an age when the efficiencies of hierarchy have been re-emphasized on every continent, no doubt the normal American political system is something of an anomaly, if not, indeed, at times an anachronism. For as a means to highly integrated, consistent decisions in some important areas – foreign policy, for example – it often appears to operate in a creaking fashion verging on total collapse.

Yet we should not be too quick in our appraisal, for where its vices stand out, its virtues are concealed to the hasty eye. Luckily the normal system has the virtues of its vices. With all its defects, it does nonetheless provide a high probability that any active and legitimate group will make itself heard effectively at some stage in the process of decision. This is no mean thing in a political system.

It is not a static system. The normal American system has evolved, and by evolving it has survived. It has evolved and survived from aristocracy to mass democracy, through slavery, civil war, the tentative uneasy reconciliation of North and South, the repression of Negroes and their halting liberation;

From: Robert A. Dahl, *A Preface to Democratic Theory* (Chicago: University of Chicago Press, 1956).

through two great wars of worldwide scope, mobilization, far-flung military enterprise, and return to hazardous peace; through numerous periods of economic instability and one prolonged depression with mass unemployment, farm 'holidays', veterans' marches, tear gas and even bullets; through two periods of postwar cynicism, demagogic excesses, invasions of traditional liberties, and the groping, awkward, often savage, attempt to cope with problems of subversion, fear, and civil tension.

Probably this strange hybrid, the normal American political system, is not for export to others. But so long as the social prerequisites of democracy are substantially intact in this country, it appears to be a relatively efficient system for reinforcing agreement, encouraging moderation, and maintaining social peace in a restless and immoderate people operating a gigantic, powerful, diversified, and incredibly complex society.

This is no negligible contribution, then, that Americans have made to the arts of government – and to that branch, which of all the arts of politics is the most difficult, the art of democratic government.

38

WHO GOVERNS? DEMOCRACY AND POWER IN AN AMERICAN CITY

Robert A. Dahl

Leaving to one side as a doubtful case the elected oligarchy that governed New Haven during its first century and a half, public officials in New Haven have been selected for the last century and a half through democratic institutions of a rather advanced sort. For more than a century, indeed, New Haven's political system has been characterized by well-nigh universal suffrage, a moderately high participation in elections, a highly competitive two-party system, opportunity to criticize the conduct and policies of officials, freedom to seek support for one's views, among officials and citizens, and surprisingly frequent alternations in office from one party to the other as electoral majorities have shifted. (Hereafter, when I speak of the political system of New Haven, I will assume what I have just enumerated to be the defining characteristics of that system: 'stability' will mean the persistence of these characteristics.)

During this period New Haven has not, so far as I can discover, fallen at any time into the kind of semi-dictatorship occasionally found in other American communities. Violence is not and seems never to have been a weapon of importance to New Haven's rulers. Party bosses have existed and exist today; the parties tend to be highly disciplined, and nominations are centrally controlled. But despite occasional loose talk to the contrary, today the parties are too competitive and the community too fragmented for a party boss to be a community boss as well.

Like every other political system, of course, the political system of New Haven falls far short of the usual conceptions of an ideal democracy; by almost

From: Robert A. Dahl, *Who Governs? Democracy and Power in an American City* (New Haven: Yale University Press, 1961).

any standard, it is obviously full of defects. But to the extent that the term is ever fairly applied to existing realities, the political system of New Haven is an example of a democratic system, warts and all. For the past century it seems to have been a highly stable system.

Theorists have usually assumed that so much stability would be unlikely and even impossible without widespread agreement among citizens on the key ideas of democracy, including the basic rights, duties, and procedures that serve to distinguish democratic from nondemocratic systems. Tocqueville, you will recall, concluded that among the three causes that maintained democracy among the people of the United States – their physical, social, and economic conditions, their laws, and their customs – it was the customs that constituted 'the peculiar cause which renders that people the only one of the American nations that is able to support a democratic government'. By 'customs', he explained, he meant 'the whole moral and intellectual condition of a people'. Considering his remarkable eye for relevant detail, Tocqueville was uncharacteristically vague as to the specific nature of these customs. But the general import of his argument is perfectly clear. 'Republican notions insinuate themselves,' as he says at one place, 'into all the ideas, opinions, and habits of the Americans and are formally recognized by the laws; and before the laws could be altered, the whole community must be revolutionized.'[1]

Before the days of the sample survey it was difficult to say with confidence how widely shared various ideas of democracy actually were in the United States, or even in New Haven. The data are still inadequate. However, some recent findings[2] cast doubt on the validity of the hypothesis that the stability of the American democratic system depends, as Tocqueville and others seem to argue, on an almost universal belief in the basic rules of the democratic game. These studies offer support for some alternative hypotheses. First, although Americans almost unanimously agree on a number of general propositions about democracy, they disagree about specific applications to crucial cases. Second, a majority of voters frequently hold views contrary to rules of the game actually followed in the political system. Third, a much higher degree of agreement on democratic norms exists among the political stratum than among voters in general. Fourth, even among the political stratum the amount of agreement is hardly high enough to account by itself for the stability of the system.

I propose, therefore, to examine some alternative explanations. Because my data on New Haven are not wholly adequate for the task at hand, the theory I shall sketch out might properly be regarded more as reflections on the process of creating consensus than as a testing of theory by a hard examination of the facts in New Haven. But New Haven will provide a convenient reference point.

SOME ALTERNATIVE EXPLANATIONS

There are at least five alternative ways (aside from denying the validity or generality of recent findings) to account for the stability of the political system in New Haven.

First, one may deny that New Haven is 'democratic' and argue that it is in fact run by a covert oligarchy of some sort. Thus the problem, it might be said, is illusory. Yet even in the absence of comparable studies our findings argue strongly that New Haven is not markedly *less* democratic than other supposedly democratic political systems. Some of these, we know, have proved to be unstable; hence the problem does not vanish after all.

Second, one might argue that things were different in the good old days. Yet it is hardly plausible to suppose that in 1910, when slightly less than half the population of New Haven consisted of first- and second-generation immigrants (many of them from countries with few democratic traditions), democratic beliefs were more widespread than they are now. In any case, the main characteristics of the political system – majority rule, the legitimacy of opposition, and so on – do not show any signs of disappearing.

Third, it might be said that the political system of New Haven is scarcely autonomous enough to furnish us with adequate explanations of its own stability, for stability may depend much less on the beliefs of citizens locally than on state and national institutions. There is much truth in this objection, but it does not altogether explain why some American towns, cities, and counties have at various times moved a good deal farther from democratic norms than New Haven has.

Fourth, one might argue that the system has not been entirely stable, that in fact most seemingly stable democratic systems are constantly in transition. Surely this is a valid point, but it is one that cuts both ways. In New Haven, as elsewhere, the rules of the game have altered in quite important, one is tempted to say fundamental, ways over the past century and a half. For example, organized, overt political competition, which was anathema to the patrician oligarchy, seems to have been fully legitimate since about 1840. Consider the electorate – the active voters. Partly as a result of the abolition of property qualifications in 1845, but probably more as a result of party organization and competition, the proportion of voting adults shot up and then stabilized at a moderate level. In most elections from 1800–33 the voters comprised less than a quarter of the adult males and sometimes less than ten per cent; since 1834, however, they have made up from a half to three-quarters of the adult male (and since 1920, female) population. A final example: throughout the nineteenth century, an implicit norm excluded persons of foreign birth or non-Yankee origins from nomination or election to the mayoralty; since the mayoralty election of 1899, the norm has very nearly come to operate in reverse.

Because of, or in spite of, these changes, however, the essential characteristics of the political system as I described them have remained substantially intact for the past century. With appropriate techniques, probably one could detect and describe significant fluctuations in the 'intensity', 'degree' or 'magnitude' of the various characteristics, but this line of inquiry would not help much in the present problem.

Fifth, one might argue that the stability of New Haven's political system does not depend on a widespread belief that certain democratic norms, rules, or procedures are highly desirable or intrinsically preferable to other rules; in some circumstances a democratic system could be highly stable if a substantial part of the electorate merely *accepted* them. A majority of voters who do not really believe in extending freedom of speech to individuals and groups beyond the pale of popular morality – and who would readily say so during an interview – might nonetheless acquiesce in such extensions on a variety of pragmatic grounds.

NOTES

1. Alexis de Tocqueville, *Democracy in America* (New York: Vintage Books, 1955), pp. 310, 334, 436.
2. Especially Samuel Stouffer, *Communism, Conformity and Civil Liberties* (New York: Doubleday, 1955) and James W. Prothro and Charles M. Grigg, 'Fundamental Principles of Democracy: Bases of Agreement and Disagreement', *Journal of Politics*, 22 (1960), pp. 276–94.

39

DEMOCRACY AND DISAGREEMENT

Amy Gutmann and Dennis Thompson

Of the challenges that American democracy faces today, none is more formidable than the problem of moral disagreement. Neither the theory nor the practice of democratic politics has so far found an adequate way to cope with conflicts about fundamental values. We address the challenge of moral disagreement here by developing a conception of democracy that secures a central place for moral discussion in political life.

Along with a growing number of other political theorists, we call this conception deliberative democracy. The core idea is simple: when citizens or their representatives disagree morally, they should continue to reason together to reach mutually acceptable decisions. But the meaning and implications of the idea are complex. Although the idea has a long history, it is still in search of a theory. We do not claim that this book provides a comprehensive theory of deliberative democracy, but we do hope that it contributes toward its future development by showing the kind of deliberation that is possible and desirable in the face of moral disagreement in democracies.

Some scholars have criticized liberal political theory for neglecting moral deliberation. Others have analyzed the philosophical foundations of deliberative democracy, and still others have begun to explore institutional reforms that would promote deliberation. Yet nearly all of them stop at the point where deliberation itself begins. None has systematically examined the substance of deliberation – the theoretical principles that should guide moral argument and

From: Amy Gutmann and Dennis Thompson, *Democracy and Disagreement* (Cambridge, MA: Belknap Press of Harvard University Press, 1996).

their implications for actual moral disagreements about public policy. That is our subject, and it takes us into the everyday forums of democratic politics, where moral argument regularly appears but where theoretical analysis too rarely goes.

Deliberative democracy involves reasoning about politics, and nothing has been more controversial in political philosophy than the nature of reason in politics. We do not believe that these controversies have to be settled before deliberative principles can guide the practice of democracy. Since on occasion citizens and their representatives already engage in the kind of reasoning that those principles recommend, deliberative democracy simply asks that they do so more consistently and comprehensively.

[...]

Although the ideal of deliberative democracy has long been recognized, it has been imperfectly realized both in practice and in theory. The fragments of dialogue with which this book began signal not only the prevalence of moral argument in politics but also its inadequacy. Neither of the parties in the several disputes seemed to be looking for any common moral ground. The president was mistaken in implying that government has no moral responsibility to women who cannot afford abortions, but his critics failed to see the moral force of his point that having a right does not necessarily mean that the government should fund the exercise of it. The white male employee at AT&T who feared losing out to a less qualified woman or black with no experience in the company did not appreciate that he may owe his position to a system that has been unfair in the past. But neither did AT&T or the government give sufficient weight to the moral objection that he and other employees, including some women, were unfairly denied promotions. Dianna Brown's advocate overstated her case by equating capital punishment with the state's failure to fund her transplant, but the doctor who denied her claim by appealing mainly to overall costs and benefits did not recognize the state's responsibility to respect her basic opportunities. Throughout this book we have encountered citizens and officials similarly engaged in serious moral argument, sometimes reaching agreement, sometimes maintaining mutual respect, but often falling short of both.

Conventional theories of democracy have not been friendly to the ideal of deliberative democracy. Some have simply neglected it, implying by their silence that it does not matter. Others have put obstacles in its path, creating frameworks that leave little or no room for deliberation in everyday politics. One obstacle is a proceduralism that tells citizens to agree on some neutral rules of fair play and keep their moral disagreements to themselves, safely confined to their private lives, categorically removed from the public agenda. Another obstacle is a constitutionalism in which the tasks of moral deliberation and the defense of rights are assigned to an institution that is supposed to be above politics – the Supreme Court. Constitutionalism of this kind neglects the way in which other institutions can contribute to a more deliberative public policy as well as a better understanding of rights. Since both of these obstacles find counterparts in the thinking of many public officials and citizens, conventional theory and practice combine to make moral deliberation in politics less than it could be. One of our aims has been to show how these obstacles might be overcome, and democracy might be made safe for deliberation.

Moral argument in politics can be socially divisive, politically extremist, and morally inconclusive, but avoiding it for these reasons would be self-defeating. The divisions, the extremism, and the inconclusiveness would persist, while the prospects of finding better terms of social cooperation would deteriorate. The need for deliberation originates in the human condition, in circumstances that are not likely to disappear: scarcity, limited generosity, incompatible values, and incomplete understanding. Moral argument will almost certainly intrude into politics no matter what our theories say or what our practices imply. The important question is what kind of moral argument our democracy should foster – what its content should be, and under what conditions it should be conducted.

The answer we have given is a conception of deliberative democracy constituted by six principles. The first three – reciprocity, publicity, and accountability – are the chief conditions that regulate deliberation. The other three – basic liberty, basic opportunity, and fair opportunity – are the key components of the content of deliberation. This content includes claims that could be offered by a wide variety of moral theories, including libertarianism and egalitarianism. Even if what goes into the process of deliberation can be derived from these theories, what comes out is quite different. The claims lose their distinctive identity when they are required to reach some accommodation with one another and with the claims that express other fundamental values.

We distinguish the set of principles that refer to conditions from that which relates to the content because each set plays a different role in deliberation. One difference is that citizens and officials are more likely to make the content than the conditions of deliberation the subject of their actual deliberations. When Dianna Brown challenged Arizona's health care policy that denied her a liver transplant, she implicitly appealed to the principle of opportunity: 'I would like a *chance for a chance*' Neither she nor the officials to whom she appealed referred to a principle of publicity, but the policy of defunding organ transplants to which she objected could be criticized for having violated that principle. The two kinds of principles in this way typically operate on different levels: the conditions as a guide to how deliberation should be conducted, the content as part of the deliberation itself.

This difference between the two kinds of principles should not be identified with the distinction between process and substance in any of its conventional forms – such as procedure and outcome, rights and utility, or policy and principle. Neither the conditions of deliberative democracy nor its content are privileged in the way that one or the other of the terms in the standard dichotomies is.

[...]

The gap between the theory and practice of deliberative democracy is narrower than in most other conceptions of democracy. To be sure, its highest ideals make demands that actual politics may never fulfill. But its principles modulate their demands in response to the limits of political necessity: they speak in the idiom of 'insofar as' or 'to the degree that'.

Even more important, the theory of deliberative democracy partly constitutes its own practice: the arguments with which democratic theorists justify the theory are of the same kind that democratic citizens use to justify decisions and policies in practice. In contrast to some forms of utilitarianism, deliberative democracy does not create a division between reasons that are appropriate in theory and those that are appropriate in practice. In contrast to some other conceptions of democracy, deliberative democracy does not divide institutions into those in which deliberation is important and those in which it is not. This continuity of theory and practice has implications for the design of institutions in modern democracies.

In the course of analyzing the principles in the context of cases, we mentioned a number of institutions that could make democracy more deliberative. We did not undertake to provide an inventory of institutional changes because the design of the institutions of deliberative democracy depends critically on developing principles to assess them. That is the prior task on which this book has concentrated. Once the principles of deliberative democracy are better understood, the search for their most suitable institutional expression can become more productive. The best forum for considering the design of deliberative institutions is likely to be one in which deliberation, however nascent, has a prominent place.

Without trying to propose specific institutional reforms, we can set out some implications of the continuity of theory and practice that should influence institutional design in a deliberative democracy. Each implication may be understood as expressing a caution against dividing deliberative labor in ways that check that continuity. The essential idea is that all institutions of government have a responsibility for deliberation. Institutions should be arranged so as to provide opportunities and incentives for officials and citizens to engage in moral reasoning. Institutions should also be transparent in the sense that their actual purposes should coincide with their publicly acknowledged purposes.

The first implication tells against the tendency to designate some institutions as forums for reason and others as arenas of power. It challenges those constitutional democrats who see courts as the agents of deliberation and legislatures as the brokers of interests. In a democracy in which citizens are governed on the basis of values adopted and refined through collective deliberations, all the makers of public policy – legislators as well as judges – should give reasons based on principles that reflect these values. Legislatures as well as courts, then, should be designed to encourage these reason-giving practices.

Second, deliberative labor should not be divided so that representatives give reasons while citizens merely receive them. Representation is necessary in modern democracies, but exclusive specialization in moral reasoning about their policies is neither necessary nor desirable. Some citizens already make remarkably good use of the limited opportunities for deliberation that exist. Deliberation may not have produced the best possible solution to health care priorities in Oregon or environmental risks in Tacoma, but its results were probably no worse than less deliberative means would have achieved, and they surely advanced public understanding further. Forums like these could be designed to consider a far wider range of issues; they could also play a role in the consideration of national issues, perhaps even in political campaigns.

Third, the practice of deliberation should not be confined to the institutions of government. Unless citizens have the experience of reasoning together in other institutions in which they spend more of their time they are not likely to develop either the interest or the skill that would enable them to deliberate effectively in politics. That is why it is so important that the processes of decision making that citizens encounter at work and at leisure should seek to cultivate the virtues of deliberation. The discussion that takes place in these settings not only is a rehearsal for political action, but also is itself a part of citizenship in deliberative democracy. Deliberative democracy does not demand that all social institutions primarily serve its ends, but its success does depend on the support of the whole range of intermediary institutions – those that act on citizens (such as the media, health care organizations, professional sports), those in which they act (interest groups, private clubs, trade unions, professional associations), as well as those in which they work (corporations, small businesses, government agencies, military services).

In any effort to make democracy more deliberative, the single most important institution outside government is the educational system. To prepare their students for citizenship, schools must go beyond teaching literacy and numerary, though both are of course prerequisites for deliberating about public problems. Schools should aim to develop their students' capacities to understand different perspectives, communicate their understandings to other people, and engage in the give-and-take of moral argument with a view to making mutually acceptable decisions. These goals, which entail cultivating moral character and intellectual skills at the same time, are likely to require some significant changes in traditional civics education, which has neglected teaching this kind of moral reasoning about politics.

Finally, deliberative democracy should avoid any rigid division between the structure and the culture of institutions. Political reformers tend to pay more attention to structure than to culture. Certainly it is important to consider changes in the formal rules and the informal incentives that could influence how officials and citizens act. But the attitudes that institutions cultivate are also critical. In tracing the ways that deliberation can help resolve various controversies, we have repeatedly noted how dispositions can promote deliberative practices in political institutions. Among the most notable dispositions of this kind are the virtues of civic integrity and civic magnanimity, which express the essential value of mutual respect. To flourish – sometimes even to survive – in the face of fundamental moral disagreement, institutions need to cultivate these virtues in citizens.

A deliberative culture in an institution not only helps citizens develop the virtues of civic integrity and magnanimity but also enables those who already have these virtues to act in accordance with them. Practicing civic virtues, moreover, can in turn improve the practices of democratic institutions. Even without changing the structure of legislative debate, members of Congress who concentrate on the substance of issues contribute to developing a culture more favorable to deliberation. By contrast, when a culture encourages the practice of impugning the motives of one's opponents instead of assessing the merits of their positions, deliberation withers. When the 'imputation of bad motive' dominates an institutional culture, citizens do not reason together so much as they reason against one another. They reflexively attack persons instead of policies, looking for what is behind policies rather than what is in them. In a culture where moral disagreement turns so readily into general distrust, citizens are not disposed to think and act in a reciprocal frame of mind.

A reciprocal perspective is important not only to enable citizens to resolve disagreement but also to enable them to learn to live with it. Certainly citizens should welcome agreement when they can agree that what they can agree on is morally right. But given the intractable sources of disagreement, citizens cannot expect to reach mutually justifiable agreement over the whole range of significant issues in politics.

Many theorists of democracy refuse to face up to this moral fact of political life. They assume that it is simply the result of misunderstanding, which could be overcome if citizens would only adopt the correct philosophical view or cultivate the proper moral character. Among secular views, utilitarianism is the most prominent example, but many other comprehensive moralities also fail to take disagreement seriously. Other theorists accept the persistence of disagreement but try to defuse it by redrawing the boundaries of political communities so that more public policy is made by like-minded citizens. This is the strategy of some communitarians. Still other theorists suggest that disagreement could be overcome if communities cultivated the right virtues of character in their citizens. But important as cultivating good character is, it cannot promise to dissolve the moral disagreements at the heart of the kind of controversies we have been considering. Bad character certainly exacerbates many political disagreements, but good character is hardly sufficient to resolve controversies over subsidizing abortion, giving preference to blacks and women, or funding organ transplants.

Proceduralism and constitutionalism recognize that moral disagreement is here to stay, but in different ways try to keep it in check. Many proceduralists hope that if citizens agree on some basic rules of the game, they will be able to domesticate the remaining disagreement by leaving it to political bargaining or by moving it off the political agenda into private life. Many constitutionalists hope that after carving out a sphere of agreement on fundamental values and protecting it from the pressures of ordinary politics, they can safely let the remaining disagreement simmer. Again, the important moral questions are to be settled at the borders of democratic politics.

The conception of deliberative democracy defended here puts moral reasoning and moral disagreement back at the center of everyday politics. It reinforces and refines the practices of moral argument that prevail in ordinary political life – the ways in which citizens deal with moral disagreement in middle democracy. Its principles show citizens and their representatives how to live with moral disagreement in a morally constructive way. Deliberative democracy is more idealistic than other conceptions because it demands more than democratic politics normally delivers. It is more realistic because it expects less than moral agreement would promise. While acknowledging that we are destined to disagree, deliberative democracy also affirms that we are capable of deciding our common destiny on mutually acceptable terms.

40

STRONG DEMOCRACY

Benjamin Barber

We suffer, in the face of our era's manifold crises, not from too much but from too little democracy. This Jeffersonian conviction lies at the heart of the argument that unfolds here. From the time of de Tocqueville, it has been said that an excess of democracy can undo liberal institutions. I will try to show that an excess of liberalism has undone democratic institutions: for what little democracy we have had in the West has been repeatedly compromised by the liberal institutions with which it has been undergirded and the liberal philosophy from which its theory and practice have been derived.

In implicating liberalism in the insufficiencies of democracy, I do not mean to attack liberalism. There is little wrong with liberal institutions that a strong dose of political participation and reactivated citizenship cannot cure. In pointing to liberal philosophy as a source of democratic weakness, I do not mean to attack philosophy. I wish only to endorse Saul Bellow's observation that 'history and politics are not at all like the notions developed by intelligent, informed people.[1] Liberal philosophy has attracted a great many intelligent, informed people to its ranks; their work has yielded powerful notions of right, freedom and justice – notions so coherent and well-grounded in philosophy as to be untainted by the political world in which men are condemned to live.[2]

Unlike many of the books written by these intelligent metaphysicians of the political, this study does not address problems of truth or justice or the

From: Benjamin Barber, *Strong Democracy: Participatory Politics for a New Age* (Berkeley: University of California Press, 1984).

antecedents of politics in nature or science. I begin rather with Graham Greene's belief that in the realm of human relations 'Truth . . . has never been of any real value to any human being – it is a symbol for mathematicians and philosophers to pursue.[3] Democratic politics is a form of human relations, and does not answer to the requirements of truth. My task in this book has been to try to find an approach to democracy suitable to human relations rather than to truth. I have been much helped by the tradition of American pragmatism. It is an oddity of American political thinking that it has turned to English and Continental modes of thought to ground a political experience notable for its radical break with the English and Continental ways of doing politics; at the same time it has neglected indigenous sources that have a natural affinity for the American way of doing politics – as anybody who reads Peirce or James or Dewey will recognize.

The English-inflected language of liberalism has left the rhetoric of democracy pallid and unaffecting; I hope to restore and revivify not so much the rhetoric as the practice of democracy – which, however, turns out to be in part a matter of the language and the rhetoric. As will become evident, the crisis of liberal democracy is very much a crisis in language and theory.

That there is a crisis probably does not require demonstration. Crisis has become the tedious cliché with which we flaunt our hardpressed modernity. From the very inception of the idea of modernity, we have portrayed ourselves in the vivid terms of crisis: the crisis of the modern state, the crisis of liberal institutions, the crisis of leadership, the crisis of party government, and the crisis of democracy. These phrases seem so banal only because the realities to which they point are so familiar.

The crisis in liberal democracy is expressed most pungently in the claim that the world has become 'ungovernable', that no leader or party or constitutional system can cope with the welter of problems that afflict large-scale industrial societies. Like Mary Shelley's good Dr. Frankenstein, modern man has created an artificial world he cannot control. The modern monsters are machines, computers, bureaucracies, corporations and constitutions; their monstrosity lies less in their wilfullness than in their emancipation from all will and purpose. If the world has become ungovernable, how can men be expected to govern themselves? How can they ask that their representatives govern them well? 'Ungovernability' permits presidents who cannot govern to excuse themselves and presidents who will not govern to justify themselves.

If the leaders cannot govern, the people increasingly refuse to be governed. Alienation has become a central indicator of modern political crisis, whether it is measured by plummeting electoral participation figures, widespread distrust of politicians, or pervasive apathy about things public and political. Mean voter turnout in America since World War II hovers around fifty percent for presidential elections – lower than every other noncompulsory democracy in the West. In a country where voting is the primary expression of citizenship, the refusal to vote signals the bankruptcy of democracy.

Political scientists continue to hope that the crisis in participation is a function of party realignment of the kind that occurs in twenty-or thirty-year cycles in most democratic societies. But there is evidence that the party system is breaking down or breaking up, and that representative party democracy may be being replaced by dangerous new variants of neodemocracy – the politics of special interests, the politics of neopopulist fascism, the politics of image (via television and advertising), or the politics of mass society.[4]

As fewer and fewer Americans participate in public affairs, more and more public affairs are being relegated to the private sector. If politics can be redefined as the public airing of private interests, public goods can be redefined as private assets. Thus, soldiers are now 'hired' on the private market, public lands are sold off into private hands to be maintained by charging the public for goods and services once deemed to belong to the public, and private 'incentive' systems are used to get private corporations to live up to public responsibilities. This pervasive privatization of the *res publica* (things public) has deep roots in liberal thinking, although finally it corrupts even the most liberal and indirect forms of democracy. Indeed, it is a major theme of this book that cynicism about voting, political alienation, a preference for things private, and the growing paralysis of public institutions are more than the consequences of modernity. They are symptoms of a malaise that is inseparable from liberal ways of thinking about and doing politics. They are dark mirror images of liberalism's strengths. The major devices by which liberal theory contrives to guarantee liberty while securing democracy – representation, privacy, individualism, and rights, but above all representation – turn out neither to secure democracy nor to guarantee liberty. Representation destroys participation and citizenship even as it serves accountability and private rights. Representative democracy is as paradoxical an oxymoron as our political language has produced; its confused and failing practice make this ever more obvious.

The position I take here asserts that liberalism serves democracy badly if at all, and that the survival of democracy therefore depends on finding for it institutional forms that loosen its connection with liberal theory. Bluntly expressed, my claim is that strong democracy is the only viable form modern democratic politics can take, and that unless it takes a participatory form, democracy will pass from the political scene along with the liberal values it makes possible.

Liberal democracy was, to be sure, an attempt to adapt pure democracy to the realities of governing in a large-scale nation state. Pure democracy suggested a form of government in which all of the people governed themselves in all public matters all of the time; such a form could hardly be expected to function efficiently in a nation of continental proportions with millions of citizens. Representative democracy therefore substituted for the pure principle a defini- tion of democracy as a form of government in which some of the people, chosen by all, govern in all public matters all of the time. This approach purchased efficiency without sacrificing accountability, but it did so at an enormous cost to participation and to citizenship. Strong democracy tries to revitalize citizenship without neglecting the problems of efficient government by defining democracy as a form of government in which all of the people govern themselves in at least some public matters at least some of the time. To legislate and to implement laws at least some of the time is to keep alive the meaning and function of citizenship in all of us all of the time; whereas to delegate the governing power, even if only to representatives who remain bound to us by the vote, is to give away not power but civic activity, not accountability but civic responsibility, not our secondary rights against government but our primary right to govern. If democracy entails the right to govern ourselves rather than to be governed in accordance with our interests, then liberal democratic institutions fall short of being democratic.

In reading Hobbes, Locke and the American founders and in trying to live as citizens in the institutions fashioned from their ideas, we have persuaded ourselves that democracy is a vital means to other, prior human ends; that liberty, equality, justice and human rights have a natural existence; and that our governing institutions gain their legitimacy only insofar as they serve these values. But democracy understood as self-government in a social setting is not a terminus for individually held rights and values; it is their starting place. Autonomy is not the condition of democracy, democracy is the condition of autonomy. Without participating in the common life that defines them and in the decision-making that shapes their social habitat, women and men cannot become individuals. Freedom, justice, equality and autonomy are all products of common thinking and common living; democracy creates them. Jefferson observed that the origin of property from nature was 'a moot question' since 'stable ownership is the gift of social law, and is given late in the progress of society.'[5]

Our most deeply cherished values are all gifts of law and of the politics that make law possible. We are born in chains – slaves of dependency and insufficiency – and acquire autonomy only as we learn the difficult art of governing ourselves in common; we are born inferior or superior as measured by natural endowment or hereditary status; we acquire equality only in the context of socially sanctioned political arrangements that spread across naturally unequal beings a civic mantle of artificial equality. The rights we often affect to hurl impudently into the face of government are rights we enjoy only by virtue of government. The private sphere we guard so jealously from the encroachments of the public sector exists entirely by dint of law, which is the public sector's most significant creation.

The rights we claim title to and the values we live by are, then, legitimate only as the politics from which they issue is legitimate. My argument here is that strong democracy is the only fully legitimate form of politics; as such, it constitutes the condition for the survival of all that is most dear to us in the Western liberal tradition. To be free we must be self-governing; to have rights we must be citizens. In the end, only citizens can be free. The argument for strong democracy, though at times deeply critical of liberalism, is thus an argument on behalf of liberty.

The problem of human freedom is hardly peculiar to America alone. Yet America has always carried a special responsibility for freedom in the West – a last best hope of our civilization's democratic aspirations. Consequently, I will perhaps be forgiven for dwelling on the American system of government and using its democratic politics as an archetype for the benefits and the ills of the liberal tradition. To restore democracy to America – or to create it where it has never existed – is a cosmopolitan project even if it is constrained by American parochialism.

[...]

A Strong Democratic Program for the Revitalization of Citizenship:

1. A national system of NEIGHBORHOOD ASSEMBLIES of from one to five thousand citizens; these would initially have only deliberative functions but would eventually have local legislative competence as well.
2. A national CIVIC COMMUNICATIONS COOPERATIVE to regulate and oversee the civic use of new telecommunications technology and to supervise debate and discussion of referendum issues.
3. A CIVIC VIDEOTEX SERVICE and a CIVIC EDUCATION POSTAL ACT to equalize access to information and promote the full civic education of all citizens.
4. Experiments in DECRIMINALIZATION and INFORMAL LAY JUSTICE by an engaged local citizenry.
5. A national INITIATIVE AND REFERENDUM PROCESS permitting popular initiatives and referenda on congressional legislation, with a multichoice format and a two-stage voting plan.
6. Experimental ELECTRONIC BALLOTING, initially for educational and polling purposes only, under the supervision of the Civic Communications Cooperative.
7. Selective local elections to local office by LOTTERY, with pay incentives.
8. Experiments with an INTERNAL VOUCHER SYSTEM for selected schools, public housing projects and transportation systems.
9. A program of UNIVERSAL CITIZEN SERVICE, including a military-service option for all citizens.
10. Public sponsorship of LOCAL VOLUNTEER PROGRAMS in 'common work' and 'common action'.
11. Public support of experiments in WORKPLACE DEMOCRACY, with public institutions as models for economic alternatives.
12. A new ARCHITECTURE OF CIVIC AND PUBLIC SPACE.

This program does not illustrate strong democracy; it is strong democracy. Implemented, it will give to the theory developed above the life and breath of a genuine practice.

INSTITUTIONALIZING REGRET

Even the most sympathetic reader may scan this panoply of novel institutions and procedural innovations and conclude that proposals so varied, novel, and uncertain pose too many risks. More democracy, even if achieved, will surely mean more legislation, more interference, more encroachment, and thus less liberty. A more competent citizenry may feel impelled to do more and so grow in time to be less tolerant of resistance to its wisdom and of deviation from its common judgments. Democratic tinkerers may start by making minor changes and end by scrapping the Constitution. Such a reader, like so many democratic liberals, will finally come to see Burke as the ally of Locke – to think it more prudent to keep what we have, however incomplete it is, than to gamble it away for what we might have, however attractive.

The uncertainty of all knowledge and the foibles of women and men – which may but do not necessarily lessen with their transformation into citizens – impose on the strong democrat a responsibility to institutionalize regret: to build into his reforms limits on the will to change and to build into mechanisms of public choice limits on all political will.

[...]

The case for democracy has two advocates: one speaks from human weakness and, pointing to the sand on which every claim to knowledge finally must rest, says with regret, 'We must govern ourselves together; there is no one else who can govern for us'. It is that voice to which the call for limits responds.

But there is another, more affirmative advocate – one who perceives in speech itself, in the Greek faculty of reason called *logos*, the distinctive feature that sets humankind off from the animal kingdom and bestows the twin gifts of self-consciousness and other-consciousness. To this advocate the right of every individual to speak to others, to assert his being through the act of communication, is identified with the precious wellspring of human autonomy and dignity. Thus it was that in Greece *Isegoria* – the universal right to speak in the assembly – came to be a synonym not merely for democratic participation but for democracy itself. Thus it is that democracy, if it is to survive the shrinking of the world and the assaults of a hostile modernity, will have to rediscover its multiple voices and give to citizens once again the power to speak, to decide and to act; for in the end human freedom will be found not in caverns of private solitude but in the noisy assemblies where women and men meet daily as citizens and discover in each other's talk the consolation of a common humanity.

NOTES

1. Saul Bellow, *To Jerusalem and Back* (New York: Viking, 1976), p. 8.

2. Like every modern writer, I have been torn by the requirements of gender-blind usage and the requirements of style, particularly in a field dominated by the language of 'political man', 'man's nature', and 'mankind'. Although I have tried where possible to refer to women and men or to use neutral terms such as 'humankind' or 'persons'. I have frequently reverted to traditional usage and simply written 'man' or 'men'. I hope readers will understand that I intend a generic meaning even where I use masculine terms and that the political equality of women and men is an unstated premise throughout my book.

3. Graham Greene, *The Heart of the Matter* (London: Pelican Books, 1948), p. 58.

4. Political scientists such as Walter Dean Burnham who might once have subscribed to the realignment theory now take a much bleaker view; see Burnham, *The Current Crisis in American Politics* (New York: Oxford University Press, 1983). Others write skeptically about the autonomy of the federal bureaucracy from any form of genuine democratic control; see Eric A. Nordlinger, *On the Autonomy of the Democratic State* (Cambridge, MA: Harvard University Press, 1983).

5. Thomas Jefferson, *Writings*, cited in R. Schlatter, *Private Property* (New Brunswick, NJ: Rugters University Press, 1951), p. 198.

41

DEMOCRACY AND CAPITALISM

Samuel Bowles and Herbert Gintis

In principle there is no reason why a democratically organized economy could not be considerably more innovative than its capitalist rival. Indeed, capitalist societies would seem to be in many ways hostile to innovation: credit, essential to innovation, is generally available in large amounts only to the wealthy; highly selective educational systems further limit the potential number of innovators; widespread unemployment fosters worker resistance to new methods of production; profit seekers often avoid research the benefits of which cannot be appropriated and sold. The challenge to a democratic economy will be to maintain existing (or design new) systems of economic competition, entrepreneurial reward and credit availability, fostering innovation and protecting economically creative individuals and groups against the rule of the majority.

The promise of the extension of personal rights over property rights is not merely feasible and abstractly desirable. Indeed, the shift in the terms of debate on economic organization is more than matched by the vast change in economic and political conditions facing democratic social movements in the advanced capitalist countries. Three underlying trends seem particularly germane to this development.

First, the costs of producing, storing and processing information have fallen drastically in the past two decades and will continue to fall. The information revolution now vastly enhances the power of citizens and workers to control

From: Samuel Bowles and Herbert Gintis, *Democracy and Capitalism* (New York: Basic Books, 1986).

production and resource allocation in a decentralized manner. Yet at the same time it augments the capacity of states, businesses and other hierarchical organizations to monitor the activities and invade the privacy of citizens. Democratization may be the only effective means of protecting privacy and directing the information revolution in socially benevolent directions.

Second, production is increasingly carried out on a global scale. The assembly in one country of parts produced elsewhere to fabricate a commodity to be sold in yet another corner of the globe is still the exception. But in many industries it is already much more than a gleam in a corporate planner's eye. The information revolution and the associated reduction in transportation costs have contributed strongly to this trend. In the absence of social control over investment, the globalization of production challenges the sovereignty of the nation state. In effect, it forces democrats to choose between the private control of investment, entailing ineffectual economic policy and a democratic impotence, on the one hand, and the development of democratic institutions for the social accountability of investment on the other.

Finally, the twentieth century has rightly been called the epoch of revolution. But the Chinese, Russian and other upheavals are matched by a silent revolution in the advanced capitalist countries: the disappearance of the peasant and the housewife as the principal occupations in society. At the turn of the century in most of Europe and North America, well over half the adult working population were either farmers or homemakers (or both). These two occupations constituted a vast labor reserve for capitalist expansion, allowing the accumulation process to proceed through boom and depression without encountering the labor scarcity that would enhance the aspirations and the bargaining power of workers.

These two great labor pools – the home and the farm – are now substantially depleted. The prospect then is for a weakening of capitalist power at the center and perhaps another retreat of profit-seekers into the labor-abundant capitalist periphery reminiscent of Europe's fifteenth- and sixteenth-century expansion into Africa, Asia, and Latin America following the labor shortage resulting from the decimation of the European population in the later Middle Ages.

If a depletion of internal labor reserves makes the stick of unemployment increasingly costly for employers to wield, their control of work processes in Europe, North America, and Japan will depend more on the carrot of commitment and participation or perhaps on the development of new sources of labor supply or forms of domination less dependent on labor abundance.

All three of these trends – the globalization of production, the information revolution and the demise of the home and the farm as labor reserves for capitalist employment – will shape not only the debate on economic democracy, but the evolution of the ongoing clash between citizen rights and property rights.

[. . .]

Our vision of a postliberal democracy is based on the following propositions, each derived from the reasoning of earlier chapters. First, the capitalist economy – and indeed virtually any feasible alternative – is a public arena whose structure regulates the distributional, appropriative, political, cultural, and other projects of various social actors. No coherent conception of democracy can escape the conclusion that the powers thus conferred on individual and collective actors in the economy ought to be subject to democratic accountability.

Second, lack of secure access to one's livelihood is a form of dependency, one that confers power on those who control the means of life. Economic dependency – whether in the form of the financial dependence of women on men, unemployment induced deliberately by macroeconomic policy to discipline the labor force, or the instrumental use of the threat of capital flight – arbitrarily limits individual choices and erodes democratic accountability even where it is formally secured. Economic dependency is thus antithetical to both liberty and popular sovereignty.

Third, the economy, the state, and the family produce people. The lifelong development of the capacities, preferences, sentiments, and identities of individuals results from an interaction between genetic potential and structured social practices. The impact of social structure on human development ranges from the relationship between the sexual division of labor and what Nancy Chodorow calls 'feminine personality,' to the connection between the hierarchical structure of work and the value that parents place on obedience in their children, and to the effect of the decline of residential neighborhoods on civic orientations. Because the growth and effectiveness of democratic institutions depend on the strength of democratic capacities, a commitment to democracy entails the advocacy of institutions that promote rather than impede the development of a democratic culture. Further, because learning, or more broadly, human development, is a central and lifelong social activity of people, there is no coherent reason for exempting the structures that regulate learning – whether they be schools, families, neighborhoods, or workplaces – from the criteria of democratic accountability and liberty.

Fourth, the power of unaccountable authority and the limitations of personal choice in liberal democratic capitalist societies derive in part from the manner in which our personal identities are intimately bound up with unaccountable collectivities, whether they be the nation-state, the patriarchal family, or the modern corporation. The near-monopoly exercised by these institutions on our sense of social identity is rivaled only by equally anti-democratic invidious distinctions of class, race, and gender. But the modern ideal of universalist values, by leaving the autonomous individual face-to-face with the abstract state, is more likely to exacerbate than to solve the problem. Both liberty and popular sovereignty would be served by the vitality of democratic communities standing between the individual and the state, and by the related possibility of a proliferation of noninvidious distinctions among people.

One cannot derive specific institutional prescriptions from these four quite general propositions. But they do point unmistakably toward the democratization of the economy, the attenuation of economic inequality, the democratization of the learning process, and the promotion of what Hannah Arendt calls 'new public spaces for freedom.' On balance, these objectives are complementary, yet none is without its dilemmas and contradictions.

[...]

Our commitment to democracy is both to a means and to an end, although in both cases the commitment is an admittedly minimal and insufficient basis for a fully articulated philosophy of education. Our commitment implies that people ought to learn what they choose to learn when they make choices in a general environment of liberty and popular sovereignty. We do not know what people would choose to become under these conditions: our moral and political commitment is to try it and see. Many, indeed most, educational choices are not now made under these conditions. But to the extent that some are made under conditions approximating liberty and accountability we see the possibility of a democratic learning dynamic, one that would inhabit the imperfect realms of democracy and choice in our society and progressively transform ever-wider circles of social life toward democratic ends.

The economic institutions and commitments required to make good the promise of postliberal democracy – the displacement of profit-driven capital markets by the democratically accountable planning of investment and resource allocation, the organization of workplaces and other communities by means of representative and participatory institutions, and the attenuation of economic inequality – are all familiar objectives of democratic socialist movements over the past century. We have chosen to term our visionary-historical alternative postliberal democracy rather than socialism simply because we regard those time-honored commitments of socialists not as ends in themselves but as means toward securing an expanded conception of liberty and popular sovereignty. Our treatment of socialism – and the elimination of class exploitation – as means toward the achievement of democracy in no way diminishes our commitment to these objectives, though it does express our rejection of the not uncommon tendency of socialists to relegate democracy to the status of a means, however indispensable, for the achievement of classlessness.

Our insistence on the priority of the terms 'democracy' and its constituent elements – 'popular sovereignty' and 'liberty' – over more traditional economic phrases of the socialist lexicon, such as the 'abolition of exploitation' and 'public ownership of the means of production,' thus expresses our conception of the political nature of economic concerns, not their unimportance. For example, we have addressed the central issue of economic inequality not primarily from the standpoint of distributive justice but rather as a form of dependency that limits personal freedom. And we have advocated social control over investment not primarily to achieve a more efficient allocation of resources but as a necessary means toward securing popular sovereignty in the face of the threat of capital strike.

Our choice of terms reflects a recognition of both the hegemony of liberal democratic discourse as the virtually exclusive medium of political communication in the advanced capitalist nations and the profoundly contradictory, malleable, and potentially radical nature of this discourse. No less important, the privileged status of democracy in our discourse reflects our central moral commitment and political project: to the creation of a new social order in which people – individuals and communities – are more nearly the authors of their own individual and collective histories.

42

HABITS OF THE HEART – INDIVIDUALISM AND COMMITMENT IN AMERICAN LIFE

Robert Bellah et al.

We are divided, we are told, by race, by culture, by creed, by differing views of the national identity. But we are united, as it turns out, in at least one core belief, even across lines of color, religion, region and occupation: the belief that economic success or misfortune is the individual's responsibility, and his or hers alone.

How can we account for this overwhelming value consensus which seems to fly in the face of our usual picture of America as a contentious, deeply divided society? The fact becomes even more puzzling once we notice that this common American belief is shared by the population of no other industrial nation, either in Europe or in East Asia. Those nations too are experiencing the disorienting shocks of the new global economy. Yet the gap in income between the best-off and the worst-off is vastly greater in the United States than in any of them, and we continue to tolerate significantly higher rates of economic deprivation than they do. Why are we paying a higher cost, as a society, for economic change? Is this high cost related to the decline of trust and confidence? Could these developments share a common source in some of our unquestioned beliefs about individuals and their responsibilities? In other words, is this conundrum rooted in cultural values which are so taken for granted as to be nearly invisible to Americans?

INDIVIDUALISM AGAIN

In *Habits of the Heart* we attempted to understand this cultural orientation. Following Alexis de Tocqueville, we called it individualism. Individualism, the

From: Robert Bellah et al., *Habits of the Heart: Individualism and Commitment in American Life* (Berkeley: University of California Press, 1996).

first language in which Americans tend to think about their lives, values independence and self-reliance above all else. These qualities are expected to win the rewards of success in a competitive society, but they are also valued as virtues good in themselves. For this reason, individualism places high demands upon every person even as the open nature of American society entices with chances of big rewards.

American individualism, then, demands personal effort and stimulates great energy to achieve, yet it provides little encouragement for nurturance, taking a sink-or-swim approach to moral development as well as to economic success. It admires toughness and strength and fears softness and weakness. It adulates winners while showing contempt for losers, a contempt that can descend with crushing weight on those considered, either by others or by themselves, to be moral or social failures.

In *Habits* we explored this American individualism. We asked where it came from and sought to describe its anatomy. We found that it took both a 'hard' utilitarian shape and a 'soft' expressive form. One focused on the bottom line, the other on feelings, which often were viewed therapeutically. Most critically, we questioned whether individualism in either form serves us well as a society, whether it serves even the most successful among us, that educated upper middle class which has historically been most devoted to many of the values of individualism. Our answer then was a qualified no. We argued, again inspired by Tocqueville, that individualism has been sustainable over time in the United States only because it has been supported and checked by other, more generous moral understandings.

In times of economic prosperity, Americans have imagined individualism as a self-sufficient moral and political guide. In times of social adversity such as the present, they are tempted to say that it is up to individuals to look after their own interests. Yet many of us have felt, in times both of prosperity and of adversity, that there is something missing in the individualist set of values, that individualism alone does not allow persons to understand certain basic realities of their lives, especially their interdependence with others. These realities become more salient as individual effort alone proves inadequate to meet the demands of living. At such times in the past Americans have turned to other cultural traditions, particularly those we termed the biblical and civic republican understandings of life. These two traditions have served the nation well when united action to address common problems has been called for.

The biblical tradition, a second language familiar to most Americans through a variety of communities of faith, teaches concern for the intrinsic value of individuals because of their relationship to the transcendent. It asserts the obligation to respect and acknowledge the dignity of all. This tradition has played a crucial political role since the beginning of the republic, especially at moments of national crisis and renewal such as the Civil War, by insisting that the nation rests on a moral foundation. At such times currents in biblical religion have made common cause with the civic republicanism which guided the nation's founders, to insist that the American experiment is a project of common moral purpose, one which places upon citizens a responsibility for the welfare of their fellows and for the common good.

The key point of connection between these traditions, one which sets them off form radical individualism, is their appreciation for the social dimensions of the human person. These voices have contested individualism's mistaken identification of individuality with the typical virtues of adolescence, initiative and independence, along with their less savory concomitants of adulation of success and contempt for weakness. Civic republicanism and biblical religion remind us that being an individual – being one's own person – does not entail escaping our ties to others, and that real freedom lies not in rejecting our social nature but in fulfilling it in a critical and adult loyalty, as we acknowledge our common responsibility to contribute to the wider fellowship of life. It was these voices above all which we sought to amplify in the public conversation even as we feared that our national discourse was being impoverished by the monotones of a strident and ultimately destructive individualism.

Strongly though we emphasized the importance of individualism when we published *Habits*, we perhaps understated the ambiguity of its relationship to the biblical and republican traditions, which in some ways mitigate individualism but in other ways significantly contribute to it. As Ernst Troeltsch pointed out, ascetic Protestantism, the form of biblical religion most pervasive in our formative period and still widely influential, has a strongly anti-political, even anti-civic, side.[1] The state and the larger society are considered unnecessary because the saved take care of themselves. Even more problematic is the tendency in this same strand of Protestantism to exclude those who are considered morally unworthy – unworthiness often being determined by their lack of economic success (the undeserving poor) – from the social body altogether. This attitude is countered by other Protestants and particularly by the Catholic tradition, in which an emphasis on the common good precludes the exclusion of anyone from society's care and concern. As opposed to that strand in Protestantism which looks at work as a way individuals prove themselves, this other view sees work as a contribution to a common endeavor in which all do what they can but none is rejected because of inability. Still, we cannot forget that one influential strand of biblical religion in America encourages secession from public life rather than civic engagement, and is even tempted to condemn the most vulnerable as morally unworthy.

Further, one influential type of republicanism that we inherited from the eighteenth century, our version of the English Whig tradition, best known in its early form as anti-federalism, was anti-state and anti-urban, idealizing the yeoman farmer in all his independence. Jefferson's insistence on putting the nation's capital in a swamp was not accidental. Jefferson-Madison republicanism viewed with hostility not only cities but also taxation and virtually any functions for the state. A paranoid fear of the state is not something new, but can be seen from the earliest days of the republic.[2]

We also underestimated the *moral* meaning of the individualism we called utilitarian. In at least one version of utilitarian individualism the real focus is on moral self-discipline and self-help, not primarily on extrinsic rewards. Worldly rewards are simply signs of good moral character – an idea that developed gradually in the Calvinist tradition. The individualist focus on adolescent independence, which we certainly emphasized, involves enduring fears of a meddling, powerful father who might push one back to childish dependence, fears easily transferred to a paternalistic state seen as threatening to reduce free citizens to helpless subjects.[3] This moral utilitarianism works out in class terms: the rich are independent adults and the poor are dependent children, and both have only themselves to thank or blame. American individualism resists more adult virtues, such as care and generativity, let alone wisdom, because the struggle for independence is all-consuming.

This complex culture of individualism was much more functional on the frontier (though it certainly had destructive consequences there as well) than it can be in the complex, interdependent society we have become today. If some readers of *Habits* saw us as nostalgic for an idealized past, we would now like to disabuse them. We still believe that the biblical and republican traditions are in many ways preferable to utilitarian and expressive individualism, but there is no form of them that we can appropriate uncritically or affirm without reservation.

THE CRISIS OF CIVIC MEMBERSHIP

The consequences of radical individualism are more strikingly evident today than they were even a decade ago, when *Habits of the Heart* was published. In *Habits* we spoke of commitment, of community, and of citizenship as useful terms to contrast to an alienating individualism. Properly understood, these terms are still valuable for our current understanding. But today we think the phrase 'civic membership' brings out something not quite captured by those other terms. While we criticized distorted forms of individualism, we never sought to neglect the central significance of the individual person or failed to sympathize with the difficulties faced by the individual self in our society. 'Civic membership' points to that critical intersection of personal identity with social identity. If we face a crisis of civic identity, it is not just a social crisis, it is a personal crisis as well.

[...]

When we wrote *Habits* the term communitarianism had not yet come into vogue, nor had the concern with civil society, sparked as it was by the fall of Communism and the concern for the bases of democracy in post-Communist societies. *Habits* got pulled into the debate in ways beyond our anticipation. As we pointed out in the preface to *The Good Society*, if communitarianism means opposition to the neocapitalist agenda and to a theoretical liberalism for which autonomy is almost the only virtue, then we are communitarians. But if it means a primary emphasis on small-scale and face-to-face relations, with the nineteenth-century small town as its exemplar, we are not communitarians.[4] As we argued in *The Good Society* and reiterate here, only effective institutions – economic political, and social – make complex modern societies livable.

Granted that small-scale communities alone cannot solve our problems, a tension still exists over where to look for solutions. In contemporary republicanism or even nationalism, as represented by Michael Lind's *The Next American Nation*, national consensus and national action are deemed essential to transcend our present difficulties. In opposition stands a sophisticated communitarianism or associationalism that argues for a primary emphasis on devolving functions onto lower-level associations (although not avoiding the responsibility of the state), as represented by Jonathan Boswell's *Community and the Economy*[5] or Paul Hirst's *Associative Democracy*.[6] We refuse, however, to see the two sides as antithetical, for we believe that only a national consensus could devolve responsibility onto associations in a way that does not weaken public provision.

We are impressed by the vigor of the civil society discussion even though it is inconclusive with respect to policy implications.[7] What makes us sympathetic to democratic communitarianism and democratic associationalism as represented by the proposals of Boswell and Hirst is that they do not imagine civil society to be hermetically sealed off from the state and the economy. Rather, they see community and associational life as interpenetrating government and the economy. They would give associations governance functions in both spheres. Hirst foresees associations as actually taking on the function of social welfare provision, as already happens to some degree in our society. Both of them wish to see democratic governance functions operating within the economy. They assume that the state and the economy are supposed to serve people rather than the other way around, as seems all too often to be the case today.

NOTES

1. On page 810 of Vol. II of *The Social Teaching of the Christian Churches* (London: Allen and Unwin, 1931 [1911]), Ernst Troeltsch writes that ascetic Protestantism 'regards the State from a purely utilitarian standpoint' and denies that 'the State [is] an ethical end in itself, which was self-evident to the Ancient World, and has reappeared within the modern world.' This is 'the natural result of the transference of all true life-values into the religious sphere, which means that even in the most favorable light the rest of the life-values are only regarded as means to an end'. Although this is a 'common Christian idea, ... Calvinism goes much farther than Lutheranism or Catholicism'.
2. Stanley Elkins and Eric McKitrick, *The Age of Federalism: The Early American Republic, 1788–1800* (New York: Oxford University Press, 1993), passim, but particularly ch. 4.
3. George Lakoff, *Moral Politics* (Chicago: University of Chicago Press, 1996).
4. We believe this regressive notion of communitarianism is largely the product of its critics; those who call themselves communitarians are not motivated by nostalgia or by fear of the modern world. See Amitai Etzioni, *The Spirit of Community* (New York: Touchstone, 1993).

5. Jonathan Boswell, *Community and the Economy: The Theory of Public Cooperation* (London: Routledge, 1990).

6. Paul Hirst, *Associative Democracy: New Forms of Economic and Social Governance* (Amherst: University of Massachusetts Press, 1994).

7. The emerging literature on civil society is vast. Important theoretical statements include: Ernst Gellner, *Conditions of Liberty: Civil Society and Its Rivals* (New York: Penguin, 1994); John Keane, *Democracy and Civil Society* (New York: Verso, 1988); Adam B. Seligman, *The Idea of Civil Society* (New York: Free Press, 1992); and Jean Cohen and Andrew Arato, *Civil Society and Political Theory* (Cambridge, MA: MIT Press, 1992). For an explicitly religious perspective see the publications of the Corresponding Academy on Civil Society, sponsored by the German Protestant Academies, the Vesper Society, the Ecumenical Foundation of Southern Africa, and the World Council of Churches.

43

FUGITIVE DEMOCRACY

Sheldon S. Wolin

I shall take the *political* to be an expression of the idea that a free society composed of diversities can nonetheless enjoy moments of commonality when, through public deliberations, collective power is used to promote or protect the well-being of the collectivity. *Politics* refers to the legitimized and public contestation, primarily by organized and unequal social powers, over access to the resources available to the public authorities of the collectivity. Politics is continuous, ceaseless, and endless. In contrast, the political is episodic, rare.

Democracy is one among many versions of the political, but it is peculiar in being the one idea that most other versions pay lip service to. I am reluctant, for reasons to be discussed later, to describe democracy as a 'form' of government or as a type of politics distinguished by its 'experimentalism'.[1] In my understanding, democracy is a project concerned with the political potentialities of ordinary citizens, that is, with their possibilities for becoming political beings through the self-discovery of common concerns and of modes of action for realizing them.

[...]

Democracy has no continuous history following the absorption of Athens into the Macedonian empire. From 322 BCE to the political experiments launched by the American and French revolutions of the eighteenth century, there were examples of city-state republics in which the 'people' sometimes had

From: Sheldon S. Wolin, *Essays on Theory and Democracy* (Princeton, NJ: Princeton University Press, 1996).

a small share, but the evidence over-whelmingly indicates that these were oligarchies dominated by the rich and well-born. That hiatus ends in the destruction of democratic hopes by the failure of modern revolutions and in the creation, instead, of the modern representation of democracy, the nation-state organization. Today democracy is universally acclaimed as the only true criterion of legitimacy for political systems, and its real presence is said to consist of free elections, free political parties and free press. And, of course, the free market. The specifications are so precise that the United States periodically dispatches experts to Central America to determine whether those requirements have been met.

Paradoxically, while hardly anyone questions that the self-styled 'advanced industrialized democracies' really are democracies, fewer still care to argue that 'the people' actually rule in any one of them, or that it would be a good idea if it did. For in societies where managerial rule is widely practised, democracy appears as inherently crude and hence unsuited for the task of governing complex and rapidly changing societies. At the same time in those quarters, it is often declared that democracy demands such a high level of political sophistication from citizens as to make it doubtful that it can be mastered by Third World peoples. Thus democracy is too simple for complex societies and too complex for simple ones.

What is actually being measured by the claim of democratic legitimacy is not the vitality of democracy in those nations but the degree to which democracy is attenuated so as to serve other ends. The most fundamental of these is the establishment and development of the modernizing state. The so-called problem of contemporary democracy is not, as is often alleged, that the ancient conception of democracy is incompatible with the size and scale of modern political societies. Rather it is that any conception of democracy grounded in the citizen-as-actor and politics-as-episodic is incompatible with the modern choice of the state as the fixed center of political life and the corollary conception of politics as continuous activity organized around a single dominating objective, control of or influence over the state apparatus.

Democracy in the late modern world cannot be a complete political system, and given the awesome potentialities of modern forms of power and what they exact of the social and natural world, it ought not to be hoped or striven for. Democracy needs to be reconceived as something other than a form of government: as a mode of being that is conditioned by bitter experience, doomed to succeed only temporarily, but is a recurrent possibility as long as the memory of the political survives. The experience of which democracy is the witness is the realization that the political mode of existence is such that it can be, and is, periodically lost. Democracy, Polybius remarks, lapses 'in the course of time' (6:39). Democracy is a political moment, perhaps *the* political moment, when the political is remembered and re-created. Democracy is a rebellious moment that may assume revolutionary, destructive proportions, or may not.

Today it is no longer fashionable to appeal to cycles of government or to states of nature. Yet it might be argued that a belief in the restorative power of democracy is still part of the American political consciousness. Certain events support that belief: the recurrent experience of constituting political societies and political practices, beginning with colonial times and extending through the Revolution and beyond to the westward migrations where new settlements and towns were founded by the hundreds; the movement to abolish slavery and the abortive effort at reconstructing American life on the basis of racial equality; the Populist and agrarian revolts of the nineteenth century; the struggle for autonomous trade unions and for women's rights; the civil rights movement of the 1960s and the antiwar, antinuclear and ecological movements of recent decades.

Just what constitutes a restorative moment is a matter of contestation. Ancient historians claimed that the hegemony which Athens established over Greece as a result of her leadership in the war against Persia was due to the energies and talents encouraged by democracy. In the most recent Persian war, American leaders hailed the triumph of American arms as a new restorative moment. 'Desert Storm' was represented not as the restoration of democracy, nor as the taking back of power by the people, but as a certain kind of healing, one that meant 'kicking the Vietnam syndrome' and thus restoring America's unity and its status as Number One. That understanding of the restorative moment represents a perfect inversion in which the state of war, rather than the state of nature, serves as the condition of renewal.

'Desert Storm', or constitutional democracy's Persian War, demonstrates the futility of seeking democratic renewal by relying on the powers of the modern state. The possibility of renewal draws on a simple fact: that ordinary individuals are capable of creating new cultural patterns of commonality at any moment. Individuals who concert their powers for low income housing, worker ownership of factories, better schools, better health care, safer water, controls over toxic waste disposals and a thousand other common concerns of ordinary lives are experiencing a democratic moment and contributing to the discovery, care and tending of a commonality of shared concerns. Without necessarily intending it, they are renewing the political by contesting the forms of unequal power that democratic liberty and equality have made possible and that democracy can eliminate only by betraying its own values.

But renewal also must draw on a less simple fact: a range of problems and atrocities exists that a locally confined democracy cannot resolve. Like pluralism, interest group politics, and multicultural politics, localism cannot surmount its limitations except by seeking out the evanescent homogeneity of a broader political. Recall the remarkable phenomenon of Polish Solidarity, a movement composed of highly disparate elements – socialists, artists, teachers, priests, believers, atheists, nationalists and so on. Yet one of the literal meanings of solidarity is 'community or perfect coincidence of (or between) interests'.[2] Clearly homogeneity was not then and need not now be equated with dreary uniformity, any more than equality need be mere leveling. What it does require is understanding what is truly at stake politically: heterogeneity, diversity, and multiple selves are no match for modern forms of power.

NOTES

1. I have discussed this topic at greater length in 'Norm and Form', in J. Peter Euben, John R. Wallach, and Josiah Ober (eds), *Athenian Political Thought and the Reconstruction of American Democracy* (Ithaca, NY: Cornell University Press, 1994).
2. *Oxford English Dictionary*, entry 2 s.v. 'solidarity'.

SECTION 2
JUSTICE AND INJUSTICE

In his *Reflections on the Causes of Human Misery* (not contained in this collection) Barrington Moore has tried to identify the common historical patterns of injustice. Moore encourages us to think about the unity of misery: nobody enjoys suffering. Additionally, suffering is obviously not a value in its own right nor is it limited to certain 'national' cultures and experiences. In contrast to Moore's *ex negativo* attempt to reflect on the unity of human misery, John Rawls' philosophical attempt to promote a theory of justice works more on the constructive or 'positive' side of human experiences. Like his attempt to theorise political liberalism, John Rawls' attempt to conceptualise justice as fairness has a hidden American strand. The 'American' theme is the rejection of 'European' models of an overall notion of equality as a precondition or outcome – not only in terms of distribution, but also of production (very often for the cost of liberty) – and the stressing of mainly distributive justice, equal opportunity and fairness in which individual liberty is both precondition and (an improved) outcome. Rawls' heroic attempt is now regarded as one of the most astute twentieth-century attempts to revive the field of political philosophy. However, this attempt also provoked reactions, as can be seen in the responses from Robert Paul Wolff and in Michael Walzer's alternative attempt to theorise justice. In *Understanding Rawls* Wolff takes issue with the abstractness of Rawls' theory. He criticises Rawls for not taking into account the concrete facts of 'actually existing' society based on welfare-state capitalism.

However, Wolff sympathises with Rawls' intent, that is, the need to have an overall and up-to-date model of justice. Michael Walzer goes a step further than Wolff and argues against the one-dimensional view of Rawls' conception of

---

justice. For Walzer, a truly pluralist society needs to address the question of complex equality. There is no single vantage point from which to talk about distributive justice. What Walzer does, then, is to elaborate a theory of complex equality in which there are many vantage points from which to address the question of equality.

Ronald Dworkin and Judith N. Shklar's contributions must be viewed as further attempts to clarify or sketch out the particularly American dimensions of the justice debate. In his book *Sovereign Virtue*, Dworkin sets up the theoretical framework, which would allow him to re-address the relationship between liberty and equality. As he explains, the starting point is to accept equality of resources as the leading idea. Working with such a model of distributive justice, the old debates between two opposed ideas, liberty vs. justice/equality, are replaced by a model in which liberty is discussed in the context of justice/equality only. Having relieved us of a philosophical burden, Dworkin then goes on to argue how a conception of equality that is based on equality of resources can enrich our understanding of liberty.

Although most theories of justice and equality that are presented here have an American background, this background – being a member i.e. a citizen – is often implicitly taken for granted. It is Judith N. Shklar's unique contribution to have highlighted the long American path that led to a state where theories of justice and equality could actually be discussed in a theoretical format. In other words, American society and politics must have made some historical advances in terms of practical belonging before addressing justice issues in theory. In her book *American Citizenship* Shklar discusses two strands that played a major role in American debates of justice – 'voting' and 'earning'. What Shklar also shows in her study is the complex relationship between political and social rights that has developed in the US.

44

A THEORY OF JUSTICE

John Rawls

My aim is to present a conception of justice which generalizes and carries to a higher level of abstraction the familiar theory of the social contract as found, say, in Locke, Rousseau, and Kant.[1] In order to do this we are not to think of the original contract as one to enter a particular society or to set up a particular form of government. Rather, the guiding idea is that the principles of justice for the basic structure of society are the object of the original agreement. They are the principles that free and rational persons concerned to further their own interests would accept in an initial position of equality as defining the fundamental terms of their association. These principles are to regulate all further agreements; they specify the kinds of social cooperation that can be entered into and the forms of government that can be established. This way of regarding the principles of justice I shall call justice as fairness.

Thus we are to imagine that those who engage in social cooperation choose together, in one joint act, the principles which are to assign basic rights and duties and to determine the division of social benefits. Men are to decide in advance how they are to regulate their claims against one another and what is to be the foundation charter of their society. Just as each person must decide by rational reflection what constitutes his good, that is, the system of ends which it is rational for him to pursue, so a group of persons must decide once and for all what is to count among them as just and unjust. The choice which rational men would make in this hypothetical situation of equal liberty, assuming for the

From: John Rawls, *A Theory of Justice* (Cambridge, MA: Belknap Press of Harvard University Press, 1999).

present that this choice problem has a solution, determines the principles of justice.

In justice as fairness the original position of equality corresponds to the state of nature in the traditional theory of the social contract. This original position is not, of course, thought of as an actual historical state of affairs, much less as a primitive condition of culture. It is understood as a purely hypothetical situation characterized so as to lead to a certain conception of justice.[2] Among the essential features of this situation is that no one knows his place in society, his class position or social status, nor does any one know his fortune in the distribution of natural assets and abilities, his intelligence, strength and the like. I shall even assume that the parties do not know their conceptions of the good or their special psychological propensities. The principles of justice are chosen behind a veil of ignorance. This ensures that no one is advantaged or disadvantaged in the choice of principles by the outcome of natural chance or the contingency of social circumstances. Since all are similarly situated and no one is able to design principles to favor his particular condition, the principles of justice are the result of a fair agreement or bargain. For given the circumstances of the original position, the symmetry of everyone's relations to each other, this initial situation is fair between individuals as moral persons, that is, as rational beings with their own ends and capable, I shall assume, of a sense of justice. The original position is, one might say, the appropriate initial status quo, and thus the fundamental agreements reached in it are fair. This explains the propriety of the name 'justice as fairness': it conveys the idea that the principles of justice are agreed to in an initial situation that is fair. The name does not mean that the concepts of justice and fairness are the same, any more than the phrase 'poetry as metaphor' means that the concepts of poetry and metaphor are the same.

Justice as fairness begins, as I have said, with one of the most general of all choices which persons might make together, namely, with the choice of the first principles of a conception of justice which is to regulate all subsequent criticism and reform of institutions. Then, having chosen a conception of justice, we can suppose that they are to choose a constitution and a legislature to enact laws, and so on, all in accordance with the principles of justice initially agreed upon. Our social situation is just if it is such that by this sequence of hypothetical agreements we would have contracted into the general system of rules which defines it. Moreover, assuming that the original position does determine a set of principles (that is, that a particular conception of justice would be chosen), it will then be true that whenever social institutions satisfy these principles those engaged in them can say to one another that they are cooperating on terms to which they would agree if they were free and equal persons whose relations with respect to one another were fair. They could all view their arrangements as meeting the stipulations which they would acknowledge in an initial situation that embodies widely accepted and reasonable constraints on the choice of principles. The general recognition of this fact would provide the basis for a public acceptance of the corresponding principles of justice. No society can, of course, be a scheme of cooperation which men enter voluntarily in a literal sense; each person finds himself placed at birth in some particular position in some particular society, and the nature of this position materially affects his life prospects. Yet a society satisfying the principles of justice as fairness comes as close as a society can to being a voluntary scheme, for it meets the principles which free and equal persons would assent to under circumstances that are fair. In this sense its members are autonomous and the obligations they recognize self-imposed.

One feature of justice as fairness is to think of the parties in the initial situation as rational and mutually disinterested. This does not mean that the parties are egoists, that is, individuals with only certain kinds of interests, say in wealth, prestige and domination. But they are conceived as not taking an interest in one another's interests. They are to presume that even their spiritual aims may be opposed, in the way that the aims of those of different religions may be opposed. Moreover, the concept of rationality must be interpreted as far as possible in the narrow sense, standard in economic theory, of taking the most effective means to given ends. I shall modify this concept to some extent, as explained later, but one must try to avoid introducing into it any controversial ethical elements. The initial situation must be characterized by stipulations that are widely accepted.

In working out the conception of justice as fairness one main task clearly is to determine which principles of justice would be chosen in the original position. To do this we must describe this situation in some detail and formulate with care the problem of choice which it presents. These matters I shall take up in the immediately succeeding chapters. It may be observed, however, that once the principles of justice are thought of as arising from an original agreement in a situation of equality, it is an open question whether the principle of utility would be acknowledged. Offhand it hardly seems likely that persons who view themselves as equals, entitled to press their claims upon one another, would agree to a principle which may require lesser life prospects for some simply for the sake of a greater sum of advantages enjoyed by others. Since each desires to protect his interests, his capacity to advance his conception of the good, no one has a reason to acquiesce in an enduring loss for himself in order to bring about a greater net balance of satisfaction. In the absence of strong and lasting benevolent impulses, a rational man would not accept a basic structure merely because it maximized the algebraic sum of advantages irrespective of its permanent effects on his own basic rights and interests. Thus it seems that the principle of utility is incompatible with the conception of social cooperation among equals for mutual advantage. It appears to be inconsistent with the idea of reciprocity implicit in the notion of a well-ordered society. Or, at any rate, so I shall argue.

I shall maintain instead that the persons in the initial situation would choose two rather different principles: the first requires equality in the assignment of basic rights and duties, while the second holds that social and economic inequalities, for example inequalities of wealth and authority, are just only if they result in compensating benefits for everyone, and in particular for the least advantaged members of society. These principles rule out justifying institutions on the grounds that the hardships of some are offset by a greater good in the aggregate. It may be expedient but it is not just that some should have less in order, that others may prosper. But there is no injustice in the greater benefits earned by a few provided that the situation of persons not so fortunate is thereby improved. The intuitive idea is that since everyone's well-being depends upon a scheme of cooperation without which no one could have a satisfactory life, the division of advantages should be such as to draw forth the willing cooperation of everyone taking part in it, including those less well situated. The two principles mentioned seem to be a fair basis on which those better endowed, or more fortunate in their social position, neither of which we can be said to deserve, could expect the willing cooperation of others when some workable scheme is a necessary condition of the welfare of all.[3] Once we decide to look for a conception of justice that prevents the use of the accidents of natural endowment and the contingencies of social circumstance as counters in a quest for political and economic advantage, we are led to these principles. They express the result of leaving aside those aspects of the social world that seem arbitrary from a moral point of view.

The problem of the choice of principles, however, is extremely difficult. I do not expect the answer I shall suggest to be convincing to everyone. It is, therefore, worth noting from the outset that justice as fairness, like other contract views, consists of two parts: (1) an interpretation of the initial situation and of the problem of choice posed there, and (2) a set of principles which, it is argued, would be agreed to. One may accept the first part of the theory (or some variant thereof), but not the other, and conversely. The concept of the initial contractual situation may seem reasonable although the particular principles proposed are rejected. To be sure, I want to maintain that the most appropriate conception of this situation does lead to principles of justice contrary to utilitarianism and perfectionism, and therefore that the contract doctrine provides an alternative to these views. Still, one may dispute this contention even though one grants that the contractarian method is a useful way of studying ethical theories and of setting forth their underlying assumptions.

Justice as fairness is an example of what I have called a contract theory. Now there may be an objection to the term 'contract' and related expressions, but I think it will serve reasonably well. Many words have misleading connotations which at first are likely to confuse. The terms 'utility' and 'utilitarianism' are surely no exception. They too have unfortunate suggestions which hostile critics have been willing to exploit; yet they are clear enough for those prepared to study utilitarian doctrine. The same should be true of the term 'contract' applied to moral theories. As I have mentioned, to understand it one has to keep in mind that it implies a certain level of abstraction. In particular, the content of the relevant agreement is not to enter a given society or to adopt a given form of government, but to accept certain moral principles. Moreover, the undertakings referred to are purely hypothetical: a contract view holds that certain principles would be accepted in a well-defined initial situation.

The merit of the contract terminology is that it conveys the idea that principles of justice may be conceived as principles that would be chosen by rational persons, and that in this way conceptions of justice may be explained and justified. The theory of justice is a part, perhaps the most significant part, of the theory of rational choice. Furthermore, principles of justice deal with conflicting claims upon the advantages won by social cooperation; they apply to the relations among several persons or groups. The word 'contract' suggests this plurality as well as the condition that the appropriate division of advantages must be in accordance with principles acceptable to all parties. The condition of publicity for principles of justice is also connoted by the contract phraseology. Thus, if these principles are the outcome of an agreement, citizens have a knowledge of the principles that others follow. It is characteristic of contract theories to stress the public nature of political principles. Finally there is the long tradition of the contract doctrine. Expressing the tie with this line of thought helps to define ideas and accords with natural piety. There are then several advantages in the use of the term 'contract'. With due precautions taken, it should not be misleading.

A final remark. Justice as fairness is not a complete contract theory. For it is clear that the contractarian idea can be extended to the choice of more or less an entire ethical system, that is, to a system including principles for all the virtues and not only for justice. Now for the most part I shall consider only principles of justice and others closely related to them; I make no attempt to discuss the virtues in a systematic way.

NOTES

1. As the text suggests, I shall regard Locke's *Second Treatise of Government*, Rousseau's *The Social Contract* and Kant's ethical works beginning with *The Foundations of the Metaphysics of Morals* as definitive of the contract tradition. For all of its greatness, Hobbes' *Leviathan* raises special problems. A general historical survey is provided by J. W. Gough, *The Social Contract*, 2nd ed. (Oxford: The Clarendon Press, 1957), and Otto Gierke, *Natural Law and the Theory of Society*, trans. with an introduction by Ernest Barker (Cambridge, The University Press, 1934). A presentation of the contract view as primarily an ethical theory is to be found in G. R. Grice, *The Grounds of Moral Judgment* (Cambridge: Cambridge University Press, 1967).

2. Kant is clear that the original agreement is hypothetical. See *The Metaphysics of Morals*, pt. I (*Rechtslehre*, especially §§47, 52; and pt. II of the essay 'Concerning the Common Saying: This May Be True in Theory but It Does Not Apply in Practice, in *Kant's Political Writings*, ed. Hans Reiss and trans. by H. B. Nisbet (Cambridge: Cambridge University Press, 1970), pp. 73–87. See Georges Vlachos, *La Pensée politique de Kant* (Paris: Presses Universitaires de France, 1962), pp. 326–35: and J. G. Murphy, *Kant: The Philosophy of Right* (London: Macmillan, 1970), pp. 109–12, 133–36, for a further discussion.

3. For the formulation of this intuitive idea I am indebted to Allan Gibbard.

45

UNDERSTANDING RAWLS

Robert Paul Wolff

Rawls says little or nothing about the concrete facts of social, economic, and political reality. For all the reasons I have chronicled throughout this essay, *A Theory of Justice* can be placed historically in the tradition of utopian liberal political economy of the late nineteenth and early twentieth centuries. One could characterize it briefly, even brusquely, as a philosophical *apologia* for an egalitarian brand of liberal welfare-state capitalism. And yet the device of the bargaining game and the veil of ignorance, while preserving the political, psychological and moral presuppositions of such a doctrine, raise the discussion to so high a level of abstraction that the empirical specificity needed to lend any plausibility to it are drained away. What remains, it seems to me, is ideology, which is to say prescription masquerading as value-neutral analysis.

[...]

Some critics have complained – I think with justification – that by ruling out micro-tests in which our intuitions are strong and the multiplicity of factors conceptually manageable, Rawls has overprotected his theory to the point of vacuity.[1] Nevertheless, I agree with Rawls that the principles of social justice must be conceived, in the first instance, as applying to society as a whole rather than to small-scale practices from which a society can be aggregated. I am willing, therefore, to follow his lead, and to think about the two principles in their society-wide application.

From: Robert Paul Wolff, *Understanding Rawls* (Princeton, NJ: Princeton University Press, 1977 and Gloucester, MA: Peter Smith, 1990).

Consider contemporary American society. The basic facts of income and wealth distribution are well-known and have been widely discussed in recent years. Putting it very roughly (since, for our purposes, nothing is to be gained by a straining after precision), the lowest fifth of households, in terms of income, receives about five per cent of the income distributed in a year, while the highest fifth receives about forty per cent – an eightfold spread. Even taking into account such mitigating facts as the larger number of single-person 'households' in the lower fifths, it remains true that income is very unevenly distributed. Wealth, of course, is much more unevenly distributed than income. The wealthiest one-half of one per cent of all families own perhaps one-quarter of all the wealth, while the holdings of the lower fifty per cent are negligible. The data on income and wealth taken together, incidentally, dramatically show that it is income inequality rather than wealth inequality that accounts for the basic pattern of distribution in America. Save for the special case of large accumulations of capital, whose primary significance is as sources of economic power rather than as sources of private satisfaction, what matters most in America is how much your job pays, not how big your portfolio is or how much land you have inherited.[2]

I believe that the pattern of distribution of income and wealth in America is unjust (although I and my family are clearly winners in it, not losers); and the tenor of Rawls' occasional remarks suggests that he agrees. How would he have us think about that injustice? How would he have us compare the present set of economic arrangements to other possible arrangements?

Presumably, we are to look at the reasonable expectations of the least advantaged representative household in our society and ask whether there is some other set of arrangements that would increase those expectations. Now, I have made much of Rawls' unclarity with regard to the indexing of primary goods, the defining of 'least advantaged representative man', the lexical priority of political 'goods', and so forth. But I propose to ignore any rhetorical advantage that might be gained by reactivating those criticisms here, because I believe that the problems in Rawls' social philosophy go a good deal deeper.

The first question to ask is whether there is an undistributed inequality surplus being generated in our economy by the existing set of economic arrangements.[3] If we assume that plumbers must be paid more than department store clerks in order to encourage young men (and women) to train as plumbers, and in order to draw into plumbing those with a hydraulic turn of mind, must they be paid *as much more* than clerks as they now are? Speaking generally, could our present division of labor and pattern of wages be altered in the direction of equalizing rewards without making it unmanageable? Are there significant categories of higher paid workers whose income is greater than would be required to attract them to, sort them into, and hold them in, those better rewarded occupations?

Let us suppose that the answer to these questions is, and is known by us to be, yes. I believe it is, I think Rawls believes so too; and since my quarrel with him turns on other questions, I propose to avoid the treacherous quicksand of econometric estimations.

The second question we must ask, following the guidance of Rawls' principles, is whether there are other, entirely different sets of economic arrangements that, while serving the fundamental purposes of production and reproduction of goods and services, will generate inequality surpluses, the feasible distribution of which would raise the expectations of the least advantaged representative man above the level that can be achieved under our present arrangements by redistributing the existing inequality surplus. I apologize to the reader for the complexity of that sentence, but the question Rawls' theory requires us to ask is very complicatedly hypothetical. I can think of a number of different ways to organize the growing of wheat or the assembling of automobiles – both of which, however, are merely smallscale or micro-examples from Rawls' point of view. But when I try to form a usable notion of alternatives to our present total set of economic arrangements, my mind can do no better than to rehearse the arrangements that have actually existed in some society or other – feudalism, slave-labor farming, hunting and gathering, state capitalism, collectivist socialism and so forth. After eliminating those arrangements (slavery, for example) that violate portions of Rawls' principles other than the difference principle, I am to imagine how each of the remaining candidates would work out under the conditions of technology, resource availability and actual or potential labor skill level obtaining in America today. Then I must gauge the size (if any) of the inequality surplus thus generated, and estimate the effect of the most favorable feasible redistribution on the reasonable expectations of the least advantaged representative man. Finally, Rawls tells me to order all of the alternative sets of arrangements under consideration according to the magnitude of the expectations of the least advantaged. I now presumably know which alternatives are more just, and which less just, than present-day America, and the last step is simply to shift to the number-one candidate on the list.

The manifest vagueness of these calculations and estimations has a very important consequence for Rawls's theory. Inevitably, one finds oneself construing the difference principle as a pure distribution principle. One simply stops asking *how* the goods to be distributed actually come into existence.

[...]

Rawls seems to have no conception of the generation, deployment, limitations or problems of political power. In a word, he has no theory of the *state*.

When one reflects that *A Theory of Justice* is, before all else, an argument for substantial redistributions of income and wealth, it is astonishing that Rawls pays so little attention to the institutional arrangements by means of which the redistribution is to be carried out. One need not know many of the basic facts of society to recognize that it would require very considerable political power to enforce the sorts of wage rates, tax policies, transfer payments and job regulation called for by the difference principle. The men and women who apply the principle, make the calculations and issue the redistribution orders will be the most powerful persons in the society, be they econometricians, elected representatives, or philosopher-kings. How are they to acquire this power? How will they protect it and enlarge it once they have it? Whose interests will they serve, and in what way will the serving of those interests consolidate them and strengthen them vis-à-vis other interests? Will the organization of political power differ according to whether the principal accumulations of productive resources are privately owned rather than collectively owned?

Questions of this sort have been the stock in trade of the political economist, political sociologist and political philosopher for at least the two centuries since the publication of *The Wealth of Nations*, and, in a slightly different form, they constitute the conceptual skeleton for such classic works as Plato's *Republic*. Laissez-faire liberals, welfare-state neo-classicals and democratic socialists will dispute about the answers, but all would agree that any theory of social justice must include some coherent account of the sources, organization, distribution, and workings of political power. Rawls, so far as I can see, has no such account.

[...]

There is a deep ambivalence in Rawls' thought, running through his characterization of the bargaining game, his analysis of the difference principle and even his moral psychology. On the one hand, as we have already seen, Rawls erects his entire theory on the notion of an inequality surplus, which requires some conception of the way in which goods and services are produced and even – rudimentarily – of the social relationships into which workers enter in the activity of production. On the other hand, the notion of a bargaining game, particularly of a game of fair division, treats the goods to be distributed as exogenously given. So far as the theory of games of fair division is concerned, no difference exists between dividing a pie that one or another of the players has baked and dividing a pie that has drifted gently down from the sky. That is what Nozick means when he alludes to 'manna from heaven'. The economic models employed by Rawls exhibit the same concern with distribution to the exclusion of production. Nothing in the notion of Pareto optimality, or in the formalism of an indifference map, requires us to distinguish between the ongoing distribution of goods and services produced in the daily reproduction of social life, and the parceling out of free gifts miraculously come upon. Welfare economics, we might say, is the pure theory of the cargo cult.

Not even the full panoply of neo-classical economics, with its theories of marginal productivity, its production functions, and its theorems of general equilibrium, tells us anything about the ways in which the organization of production determines the distribution of power and thereby establishes systematic patterns of exploitation and domination. Rawls does not deny the reality of political power, nor does he claim that it has its roots elsewhere than in the economic arrangements of a society. But by employing the models of analysis of the classical liberal tradition and of neo-classical economics, he excludes that reality from the pages of his book. Precisely because he has inflated his exposition enormously in pursuit of systematic wholeness, the absence has the effect of a denial, with consequences that are not merely false but ideological.

[...]

Rawls' failure grows naturally and inevitably out of his uncritical acceptance of the socio-political presuppositions and associated modes of analysis of classical and neo-classical liberal political economy. By focusing exclusively on distribution rather than on production, Rawls obscures the real roots of that distribution. As Marx says in his *Critique of the Gotha Program*, 'Any distribution whatever of the means of consumption is only a consequence of the distribution of the conditions of production themselves. The latter distribution, however, is a feature of the mode of production itself.'

Is Rawls right? Because his two principles of justice abstract from the real foundations of any social and economic order, the question has no useful answer. Has Rawls sought the principles of justice in the right way? No, for his theory, however qualified and complicated, is in the end a theory of pure distribution. Rawls' enormous sophistication and imaginativeness shows us that the failure is due not to any inadequacies of execution, but rather to the inherent weaknesses of that entire tradition of political philosophy of which *A Theory of Justice* is perhaps the most distinguished product.

NOTES

1. On this point, see Robert Nozick, *Anarchy, State, and Utopia*, pp. 204ff.
2. Since one often hears of sheltered millions on which little tax is paid, and proposals for income redistribution manage always to make it sound as though a few rich families are all that keep the other two hundred million of us down, it might be worth nothing some of the actual dollar figures at which different fractions of the population divide from one another. In 1974, for example, a young husband and wife, each with a new PhD and a job as an assistant professor at $14,500 could by teaching summer school just scrape into the top five per cent of all American families (cutoff point: $31,948). If a union carpenter earning $7 an hour and his waitress wife pulling in $2.50 an hour in wages and tips could persuade their teenage son to mow lawns and bag groceries, and if their thirteen year old daughter did some regular babysitting one evening a week, the four of them would find themselves in the top fifth of American families (cutoff point $20,445). When we speak of soaking the rich, neither of these families comes readily to mind. In light of the actual figures (which may be found, for example, in the *Statistical Abstract of the United States*), it is difficult to see why Rawls imputes life-plans to parties in the original position that are of such a nature that they care little for what they may obtain, in the way of primary goods, above what they can secure through the difference principle. Anyone living in the United States today should have a keen sense of the difference in quality of life purchasable with, say $20,445 per family as against $14,916 (the top, or cutoff point, of the third fifth).
3. In order to avoid begging any methodological or theoretical questions, I am using this neutral, and rather vague, locution, 'set of economic arrangements', instead of such loaded phrases as 'social relationships of production'. Eventually, I shall want to argue that Rawls' way of talking abstracts from most of what is causally significant in the economic and political life of a society.

46

SPHERES OF JUSTICE – A DEFENSE OF PLURALISM AND EQUALITY

Michael Walzer

Distributive justice is a large idea. It draws the entire world of goods within the reach of philosophical reflection. Nothing can be omitted; no feature of our common life can escape scrutiny. Human society is a distributive community. That's not all it is, but it is importantly that: we come together to share, divide, and exchange. We also come together to make the things that are shared, divided, and exchanged; but that very making – work itself – is distributed among us in a division of labor. My place in the economy, my standing in the political order, my reputation among my fellows, my material holdings: all these come to me from other men and women. It can be said that I have what I have rightly or wrongly, justly or unjustly; but given the range of distributions and the number of participants, such judgments are never easy.

The idea of distributive justice has as much to do with being and doing as with having, as much to do with production as with consumption, as much to do with identity and status as with land, capital, or personal possessions. Different political arrangements enforce, and different ideologies justify, different distributions of membership, power, honor, ritual eminence, divine grace, kinship and love, knowledge, wealth, physical security, work and leisure, rewards and punishments, and a host of goods more narrowly and materially conceived – food, shelter, clothing, transportation, medical care, commodities of every sort and all the odd things (paintings, rare books, postage stamps) that human beings collect. And this multiplicity of goods is matched by a multiplicity of

From: Michael Walzer, *Spheres of Justice: A Defense of Pluralism and Equality* (New York: Basic Books, 1983).

distributive procedures, agents and criteria. There are such things as simple distributive systems – slave galleys, monasteries, insane asylums, kindergartens (though each of these, looked at closely, might show unexpected complexities); but no full-fledged human society has ever avoided the multiplicity. We must study it all, the goods and the distributions, in many different times and places.

There is, however, no single point of access to this world of distributive arrangements and ideologies. There has never been a universal medium of exchange. Since the decline of the barter economy, money has been the most common medium. But the old maxim according to which there are some things that money can't buy is not only normatively but also factually true. What should and should not be up for sale is something men and women always have to decide and have decided in many different ways. Throughout history, the market has been one of the most important mechanisms for the distribution of social goods; but it has never been, it nowhere is today, a complete distributive system.

Similarly, there has never been either a single decision point from which all distributions are controlled or a single set of agents making decisions. No state power has ever been so pervasive as to regulate all the patterns of sharing, dividing and exchanging out of which a society takes shape. Things slip away from the state's grasp; new patterns are worked out – familial networks, black markets, bureaucratic alliances, clandestine political and religious organizations. State officials can tax, conscript, allocate, regulate, appoint, reward, punish, but they cannot capture the full range of goods or substitute themselves for every other agent of distribution. Nor can anyone else do that: there are market coups and cornerings, but there has never been a fully successful distributive conspiracy.

And finally, there has never been a single criterion, or a single set of interconnected criteria, for all distributions. Desert, qualification, birth and blood, friendship, need, free exchange, political loyalty, democratic decision: each has had its place, along with many others, uneasily coexisting, invoked by competing groups, confused with one another.

In the matter of distributive justice, history displays a great variety of arrangements and ideologies. But the first impulse of the philosopher is to resist the displays of history, the world of appearances, and to search for some underlying unity: a short list of basic goods, quickly abstracted to a single good; a single distributive criterion or an interconnected set; and the philosopher himself standing, symbolically at least, at a single decision point. I shall argue that to search for unity is to misunderstand the subject matter of distributive justice. Nevertheless, in some sense the philosophical impulse is unavoidable. Even if we choose pluralism, as I shall do, that choice still requires a coherent defense. There must be principles that justify the choice and set limits to it, for pluralism does not require us to endorse every proposed distributive criteria or to accept every would-be agent. Conceivably, there is a single principle and a single legitimate kind of pluralism. But this would still be a pluralism that encompassed a wide range of distributions. By contrast, the deepest assumption of most of the philosophers who have written about justice, from Plato onward, is that there is one, and only one, distributive system that philosophy can rightly encompass.

Today this system is commonly described as the one that ideally rational men and women would choose if they were forced to choose impartially, knowing nothing of their own situation, barred from making particularist claims, confronting an abstract set of goods.[1] If these constraints on knowing and claiming are suitably shaped, and if the goods are suitably defined, it is probably true that a singular conclusion can be produced. Rational men and women, constrained this way or that, will choose one, and only one, distributive system. But the force of that singular conclusion is not easy to measure. It is surely doubtful that those same men and women, if they were transformed into ordinary people, with a firm sense of their own identity, with their own goods in their hands, caught up in everyday troubles, would reiterate their hypothetical choice or even recognize it as their own. The problem is not, most importantly, with the particularism of interest, which philosophers have always assumed they could safely – that is, uncontroversially – set aside. Ordinary people can do that too, for the sake, say, of the public interest. The greater problem is with the particularism of history, culture, and membership. Even if they are committed to impartiality, the question most likely to arise in the minds of the members of a political community is not, What would rational individuals choose under universalizing conditions of such-and-such a sort? But rather, What would individuals like us choose, who are situated as we are, who share a culture and are determined to go on sharing it? And this is a question that is readily transformed into, What choices have we already made in the course of our common life? What understandings do we (really) share?

Justice is a human construction, and it is doubtful that it can be made in only one way. At any rate, I shall begin by doubting, and more than doubting, this standard philosophical assumption. The questions posed by the theory of distributive justice admit of a range of answers, and there is room within the range for cultural diversity and political choice. It's not only a matter of implementing some singular principle or set of principles in different historical settings. No one would deny that there is a range of morally permissible implementations. I want to argue for more than this: that the principles of justice are themselves pluralistic in form; that different social goods ought to be distributed for different reasons, in accordance with different procedures, by different agents; and that all these differences derive from different understandings of the social goods themselves – the inevitable product of historical and cultural particularism.

[...]

Complex equality might look more secure if we could describe it in terms of the harmony, rather than the autonomy, of spheres. But social meanings and distributions are harmonious only in this respect: that when we see why one good has a certain form and is distributed in a certain way, we also see why another must be different. Precisely because of these differences, however, boundary conflict is endemic. The principles appropriate to the different spheres are not harmonious with one another; nor are the patterns of conduct and feeling they generate. Welfare systems and markets, offices and families, schools and states are run on different principles: so they should be. The principles must somehow fit together within a single culture; they must be comprehensible across the different companies of men and women. But this doesn't rule out deep strains and odd juxtapositions. Ancient China was ruled by a hereditary divine-right emperor and a meritocratic bureaucracy. One has to tell a complex story to explain that sort of coexistence. A community's culture is the story its members tell so as to make sense of all the different pieces of their social life – and justice is the doctrine that distinguishes the pieces. In any differentiated society, justice will make for harmony only if it first makes for separation. Good fences make just societies.

We never know exactly where to put the fences; they have no natural location. The goods they distinguish are artifacts; as they were made, so they can be remade. Boundaries, then, are vulnerable to shifts in social meaning, and we have no choice but to live with the continual probes and incursions through which these shifts are worked out. Commonly, the shifts are like sea changes, very slow. But the actual boundary revision, when it comes, is likely to come suddenly, as in the creation of a national health service in Britain after the Second World War: one year, doctors were professionals and entrepreneurs; and the next year, they were professionals and public servants. We can map a program of such revisions, based on our current understanding of social goods. We can set ourselves in opposition, as I have done, to the prevailing forms of dominance. But we can't anticipate the deeper changes in consciousness, not in our own community and certainly not in any other. The social world will one day look different from the way it does today, and distributive justice will take on a different character than it has for us. Eternal vigilance is no guarantee of eternity.

It isn't likely, however, that we (or our children or grandchildren) will live through changes on such a scale as to call into doubt the fact of differentiation and the argument for complex equality. The forms of dominance and domination, the precise ways in which equality is denied, may well change. Indeed, it is a common argument among social theorists today that education and technical knowledge are increasingly the dominant goods in modern societies, replacing capital and providing the practical base for a new ruling class of intellectuals.[2] That argument is probably wrong, but it nicely suggests the possibility of large-scale transformations that still leave intact the range of goods and social meaning. For even if technical knowledge takes on a new importance, we have no reason to think that it will be so important as to require us to dispense with all the other distributive processes in which it currently plays no part at all – and then to give people exams, for example, before allowing them to serve on juries, or raise children, or take vacations, or participate in political life. Nor will the importance of knowledge be such as to guarantee that only intellectuals can make money or receive divine grace or win the respect of their fellow citizens. We can assume, I think, that social change will leave more or less intact the different companies of men and women.

And that means that complex equality will remain a lively possibility even if new opponents of equality take the place of old ones. The possibility is, for all practical purposes, permanent . . . and so is the opposition. The establishment of an egalitarian society will not be the end of the struggle for equality. All that one can hope for is that he struggle might get a little easier as men and women learn to live with the autonomy of distributions and to recognize that different outcomes for different people in different spheres make a just society. There is a certain attitude of mind that underlies the theory of justice and that ought to be strengthened by the experience of complex equality: we can think of it as a decent respect for the opinions of mankind. Not the opinions of this or that individual, which may well deserve a brusque response: I mean those deeper opinions that are the reflections in individual minds, shaped also by individual thought, of the social meanings that constitute our common life. For us, and for the foreseeable future, these opinions make for autonomous distributions; and every form of dominance is therefore an act of disrespect. To argue against dominance and its accompanying inequalities, it is only necessary to attend to the goods at stake and to the shared understandings of these goods. When philosophers do this, when they write out of a respect for the understandings they share with their fellow citizens, they pursue justice justly, and they reinforce the common pursuit.

In his *Politics*, Aristotle argued that justice in a democracy requires the citizens to rule and be ruled in turn. They take turns governing one another.[3] That is not a likely picture of a political community that includes tens of millions of citizens. Something like it might be possible for many of them, ruling not only in the state but also in cities and towns, companies and factories. Given the number of citizens, however, and the shortness of life, there simply is not time enough, even if there is will and capacity enough, for everyone to have his turn. If we consider the sphere of politics by itself, inequalities are bound to appear. Politicians, orators, activists, and militants – subject, we can hope, to constitutional limits – will exercise more power than the rest of us do. But politics is only one (though it is probably the most important) among many spheres of social activity. What a larger conception of justice requires is not that citizens rule and are ruled in turn, but that they rule in one sphere and are ruled in another – where 'rule' means not that they exercise power but that they enjoy a greater share than other people of whatever good is being distributed. The citizens cannot be guaranteed a 'turn' everywhere. I suppose, in fact, that they cannot be guaranteed a 'turn' any-where. But the autonomy of spheres will make for a greater sharing of social goods than will any other conceivable arrangement. It will spread the satisfaction of ruling more widely; and it will establish what is always in question today – the compatibility of being ruled and of respecting oneself. For rule without domination is no affront to our dignity, no denial of our moral or political capacity. Mutual respect and a shared self-respect are the deep strengths of complex equality, and together they are the source of its possible endurance.

NOTES

1. See John Rawls, *A Theory of Justice* (Cambridge, MA, 1971); Jürgen Habermas, *Legitimation Crisis*, trans. Thomas McCarthy (Boston, 1975), esp. p. 113; Bruce Ackerman, *Social Justice in the Liberal State* (New Haven, 1980).
2. See, for example, Alvin W. Gouldner, *The Future of Intellectuals and the Rise of the New Class* (New York, 1979).
3. Aristotle, *The Politics*, 1283, trans. Ernest Barker (Oxford, 1948), p. 157.

47

SOVEREIGN VIRTUE – THE THEORY AND PRACTICE OF EQUALITY

Ronald Dworkin

I argued for a conception of equality according to which ideal equality consists in circumstances in which people are equal not in their welfare but in the resources at their command. What are the implications for liberty of that claim about equality?

The question is limited in two ways. First, I mean by liberty what is sometimes called negative liberty – freedom from legal constraint – not freedom or power more generally. Second, I am interested not in liberty generally, but only in the connection between liberty and distributional equality. So though I shall defend a characteristic thesis of liberalism, that people's liberty over matters of great personal concern should not be infringed, I shall defend that thesis only against challenges grounded in distributional arguments. I shall not consider moralistic or paternalistic challenges to liberalism; I shall not consider the argument, for example, that liberty in matters of religion must be abolished in order to ensure everyone's salvation. There are, of course, fundamentalist political movements, like the Moral Majority, that oppose liberalism on grounds of that sort. But distributional challenges to liberalism are, I believe, of greater political importance now than moralistic or political ones. It is a popular opinion that certain liberties, including freedom of choice in education, must be limited in order to achieve true economic equality, for example. It is also a popular opinion, though in different quarters, that other liberties, including freedom of sexual choice, must be limited in order to give the majority the moral environment it

From: Ronald Dworkin, *Sovereign Virtue – The Theory and Practice of Equality* (Cambridge, MA: Harvard University Press, 2000).

wishes to have and is entitled to have as a matter of distributional justice. I do consider arguments against liberalism of that character.

I try to defend, however, a much more general claim: that if we accept equality of resources as the best conception of distributional equality, liberty becomes an aspect of equality rather than, as it is often thought to be, an independent political ideal potentially in conflict with it. My argument for that thesis is complex, and it might be well to provide, in advance, an informal description of the main ideas the argument develops. Many of us believe that what we consider the morally important liberties – freedom of speech, religion, and conviction, and freedom of choice in important personal matters, for example – should be protected except in the most extreme circumstances, and we would be reluctant to think that these liberties should be abridged even for the sake of gains in equality. But the latter view is very hard to defend. We are willing to limit even important liberties for the sake of other goals, after all. We limit freedom of speech in various ways to protect ourselves from unwanted noise at inconvenient times, and we limit freedom of choice in education to ensure that children receive competent schooling. But if these important liberties yield to competing values of that sort, why should they not yield to the normally more imperative requirements of distributional justice?

If liberty were valuable in the way some people think art can be valuable – for its own sake, quite apart from its impact on those who enjoy it – then we might be able to understand, if not to approve, the view that liberty is of such fundamental metaphysical importance that it must be protected whatever the consequences for people. But liberty seems valuable to us only because of the consequences we think it does have for people: we think lives led under circumstances of liberty are better lives just for that reason. Can it really be more important that the liberty of some people be protected, to improve the lives those people lead, than that other people, who are already worse off, have the various resources and other opportunities that *they* need to lead decent lives? How could we defend that view? We might be tempted to dogmatism: to declare our intuition that liberty is a fundamental value that must not be sacrificed to equality, and then claim that no more can or needs to be said. But that is hollow, and too callous. If liberty is transcendently important we should be able to say something, at least, about why.

Those are among my reasons for thinking that any appealing defense of the morally important liberties must proceed in a different, less conventional way: not by insisting that liberty is more important than equality, but by showing that these liberties must be protected according to the best view of what distributional equality is, the best view of when a society's distribution of property treats each citizen with equal concern. That claim seems plausible if we accept equality of resources as the best view. Other conceptions of equality define an equal distribution through a metric that is insensitive to the distinct quality and value of liberty. Equality of welfare understood as the satisfaction of tastes and preferences, for example, defines an equal distribution as one in which people's preferences are equally satisfied, and since it is a contingent matter how much people prefer liberty to other resources they might secure by its sacrifice, it seems dubious that protecting the morally important liberties will always be justified as improving equality of welfare.

Equality of resources, on the other hand, provides an account of distributional equality that is immediately and obviously sensitive to the special character and importance of liberty. It makes an equal distribution depend not on a bare outcome that can be measured directly, like preference-satisfaction, but on a process of coordinated decisions in which people who take responsibility for their own ambitions and projects, and who accept, as part of that responsibility, that they belong to a community of equal concern, are able to identify the true costs of their own plans to other people, and so design and redesign these plans so as to use only their fair share of resources in principle available to all. Whether an actual society approaches equality of resources depends, then, on the adequacy of the process of discussion and choice it provides for that purpose. A substantial degree of liberty is necessary to make any such process adequate because the true cost to others of one person's having some resource or opportunity can be discovered only when people's ambitions and convictions are authentic and their choices and decisions reasonably well tailored to those ambitions and convictions. Neither is possible unless liberty is ample. So liberty is necessary to equality, according to this conception of equality, not on the doubtful and fragile hypothesis that people really value the important liberties more than other resources, but because liberty, whether or not people do value it above all else, is essential to any process in which equality is defined and secured. That does not make liberty instrumental to distributional equality any more than it makes the latter instrumental to liberty: the two ideas rather merge in a fuller account of when the law governing the distribution and use of resources treats everyone with equal concern.

It follows that equality of resources requires us to take a different view of political controversies, like the controversy over private education and private medicine, that are widely thought to present a stark choice between liberty and equality. If limiting freedom of choice in education and medicine really would improve equality of resources – as some limitations plainly would – then no defensible ideal of liberty would be compromised, and liberals should have no objection. But not every infringement of liberty that is said to promote equality of resources really does so, and infringing the liberties liberals are most concerned to protect – the morally most important liberties – could rarely, if ever, count as a contribution to equality so understood. Equality of resources provides a more convincing explanation of our intuitive convictions about the importance of liberty than any theory according to which liberty and equality are independent and sometimes conflicting virtues.

48

AMERICAN CITIZENSHIP – THE QUEST FOR INCLUSION

Judith N. Shklar

There is no notion more central in politics than citizenship, and none more variable in history, or contested in theory. In America it has in principle always been democratic, but only in principle. From the first the most radical claims for freedom and political equality were played out in counterpoint to chattel slavery, the most extreme form of servitude, the consequences of which still haunt us. The equality of political rights, which is the first mark of American citizenship, was proclaimed in the accepted presence of its absolute denial. Its second mark, the overt rejection of hereditary privileges, was no easier to achieve in practice, and for the same reason. Slavery is an inherited condition. I shall try to show, however briefly, the enormous impact that not merely the institution of black chattel slavery but servitude as an integral part of a modern popular representative republic, dedicated to 'the blessings of liberty', has had on the way Americans think about citizenship.

The dignity of work and of personal achievement, and the contempt for aristocratic idleness, have since Colonial times been an important part of American civic self-identification. The opportunity to work and to be paid an earned reward for one's labor was a social right, because it was a primary source of public respect. It was seen as such, however, not only because it was a defiant cultural and moral departure from the corrupt European past, but also because paid labor separated the free man from the slave. The value of political rights was enhanced for the same reason. The ballot has always been a

From: Judith N. Shklar, *American Citizenship: The Quest for Inclusion* (Cambridge, MA: Harvard University Press, 1991).

certificate of full membership in society, and its value depends primarily on its capacity to confer a minimum of social dignity.

Under these conditions citizenship in America has never been just a matter of agency and empowerment, but also of social standing as well. I shun the word *status* because it has acquired a pejorative meaning; I shall speak of the standing of citizens instead. To be sure, standing is a vague notion, implying a sense of one's place in a hierarchical society, but most Americans appear to have a clear enough idea of what it means, and their relative social place, defined by income, occupation and education, is of some importance to them. They also know that their concern for their social standing is not entirely compatible with their acknowledged democratic creed. Often they tend to resolve the conflict between conduct and ideology by assuring themselves that really there is less exclusiveness and status-consciousness than there used to be in the past[1] Nevertheless, standing as a place in one of the higher or lower social strata and the egalitarian demand for 'respect' are not easily reconciled. The claim that citizens of a democracy are entitled to respect unless they forfeit it by their own unacceptable actions is not a triviality. On the contrary, it is a deeply cherished belief, and to see just how important it has always been, one has to listen to those Americans who have been deprived of it through no fault of their own.

The significance of the two great emblems of public standing, the vote and the opportunity to earn, seems clearest to these excluded men and women. They have regarded voting and earning not just as the ability to promote their interests and to make money but as the attributes of an American citizen. And people who are not granted these marks of civic dignity feel dishonored, not just powerless and poor. They are also scorned by their fellow-citizens. The struggle for citizenship in America has, therefore, been overwhelmingly a demand for inclusion in the polity, an effort to break down excluding barriers to recognition, rather than an aspiration to civic participation as a deeply involving activity.

I do not intend to imply that citizenship as standing is the only meaning that the very idea of citizenship has in American history. Quite the contrary. The word *citizenship* has at least four quite distinct though related meanings, and what I have called standing is only one of these. Three equally significant meanings are citizenship as nationality, as active participation or 'good' citizenship and finally, ideal republican citizenship. These other ways of considering citizenship are so important that I want to make sure I do not give the impression of having ignored or neglected them.

In any modern state and especially in an immigrant society, citizenship must always refer primarily to nationality. Citizenship as nationality is the legal recognition, both domestic and international, that a person is a member, native-born or naturalized, of a state. Such citizenship is not trivial. To be a stateless individual is one of the most dreadful political fates that can befall anyone in the modern world. And the possession of an American passport particularly is profoundly valued, especially by naturalized citizens. Few indeed are the new American citizens who have chosen to throw their naturalization papers away.

American citizenship as nationality has its own history of exclusions and inclusions, in which xenophobia, racism, religious bigotry, and fear of alien conspiracies have played their part. In the years before the Civil War the civic position of alien residents of the United States was, moreover, dependent upon the conflicting interests of the various states and of the federal government. Its history has, therefore, been extremely complicated. For instance, at one time Midwestern states were so starved for labor that they offered any alien white male the vote immediately upon declaring his intention eventually to become a citizen. At the same time the citizens of New England were contemplating ways and means to exclude their Irish neighbors from full citizenship.[2] The history of immigration and naturalization policies is not, however, my subject. It has its own ups and downs, but it is not the same as that of the exclusion of native-born Americans from citizenship. The two histories have their parallels, since both involve inclusion and exclusion, but there is a vast difference between discriminatory immigration laws and the enslavement of a people.

[...]

I also want to remind political theorists that citizenship is not a notion that can be discussed intelligibly in a static and empty social space. Whatever the ideological gratifications that the mnemonic evocation of an original and pure citizenry may have, it is unconvincing and ultimately an uninteresting flight from politics if it disregards the history and present actualities of our institutions. Citizenship has changed over the years, and political theorists who ignore the best current history and political science cannot expect to have anything very significant to contribute to our political self-understanding.[3] They stand in acute danger of theorizing about nothing at all except their own uneasiness in a society they have made very little effort to comprehend. Neither Supreme Court opinions, which at times serve to structure our public debates, nor the writings of other philosophers, however distinguished, can act as a substitute for a genuinely historical and politically informed understanding of what citizenship has been and now is in America.[4]

The reasons for imagining that American citizenship has never altered are curious. It may well be that because America's basic institutions seem to have changed so little since 1787, we often discuss citizenship as if it existed in an institutional deep freeze. The unchanging permanence of the political structure is simply being taken for granted because of its formal continuity, even by those who do remember the significance of the constitutional amendments that followed the Civil War. Moreover, the longevity of the ideology that goes under the entirely appropriate name of 'the American Dream' is indeed an extraordinary phenomenon.[5] Its roots lie far back in the first decades of the last century, and I hope to explore them in these essays. The endurance of much of the original Constitution and of the faith in its promise does not, however, justify the assumption that nothing significant has happened to American citizenship since the eighteenth century. To be sure, like the ancient Romans, we too may find the stability of authority and the gratifying support of tradition in acts of ancestor worship.[6] Nothing, however, would have mortified the actual founders of the republic more deeply. Every page of *The Federalist Papers* is a call to the people of America to take its fate into its own hands and to fashion its institutions in the light of the best political science of the present, rather than to look timidly to the past. The good citizen of today can do no less.

[...]

America has not marched single file down a single straight liberal highway as both the lamenters and the celebrators of its political life have claimed, either in despair or in complacency.[7] What has been continuous is a series of conflicts arising from enduring anti-liberal dispositions that have regularly asserted themselves, often very successfully, against the promise of equal political rights contained in the Declaration of Independence and its successors, the three Civil War amendments. It is because slavery, racism, nativism and sexism, often institutionalized in exclusionary and discriminatory laws and practices, have been and still are arrayed against the officially accepted claims of equal citizenship that there is a real pattern to be discerned in the tortuous development of American ideas of citizenship. If there is permanence here, it is one of lasting conflicting claims.

[...]

One way to undertake a historically rich inquiry into American citizenship is therefore to investigate what citizenship has meant to those women and men who have been denied all or some of its attributes, and who ardently wanted to be full citizens. Their voices not only put the question of citizenship on the public agenda from the Revolution to the present; they also defined what was unique about American citizenship: voting and earning. Because exclusion was so much more common and so much easier than inclusiveness, citizenship was, moreover, always something that required prolonged struggle, and this also has molded its character. Citizenship so gained lost much of its urgency once it was attained. The years of denial have left their paradoxical marks upon this constitutional right.

The American Constitution does not mention citizenship at all until the Fourteenth Amendment, but Americans had quite clear ideas about what the social meaning of citizenship was, and when they were denied it, they protested.

NOTES

1. Richard P. Coleman and Lee Rainwater, *Social Standing in America* (New York: Basic Books, 1978), passim.
2. Kirk H. Porter, *A History of Suffrage in the United States* (Chicago: University of Chicago Press, 1918), pp. 112–34. Leon E. Aylesworth, 'The Passing of Alien Suffrage,' *American Political Science Review*, 25 (1931), 114–16.
3. As an example of the right way to discuss citizenship I would cite Dennis F. Thompson, *The Democratic Citizens* (Cambridge: Cambridge University Press, 1970), a model of how to integrate political theory and political science.

4. See Cass R. Sunstein, 'Beyond the Republican Revival', *Yale Law Journal*, 97 (1988), pp. 1539–90, for an example of how remote from anything concrete even the best of the legalistic republicanism now is.

5. See Kay Lehman Schlozman and Sidney Verba, *Insult to Injury* (Cambridge, MA: Harvard University Press, 1979), pp. 103–38, 346–51, for an account of its hold even on the unemployed and working poor.

6. Hannah Arendt, 'What Is Authority?' in *Between Past and Future* (New York: Viking, 1961), pp. 91–141.

7. Louis Hartz, *The Liberal Tradition in America* (New York: Harcourt, Brace, 1954) and Samuel P. Huntington, *American Politics: The Promise of Disharmony* (Cambridge, MA: Harvard University Press, 1981). I have been very careful not to follow their tendency to even out the discontinuities in America's past, and especially to exaggerate American liberalism. In this I have been particularly helped by Rogers M. Smith, 'The "American Creed" and American Identity: The Limits of Liberal Citizenship in the United States', *Western Political Quarterly*, 41 (1988), pp. 225–51, and 'One United People: Second Class Female Citizenship and the American Quest for Community', *Yale Journal of Law and the Humanities*, I (1989), pp. 229–93.

SECTION 3
PLURALISM AND MULTICULTURALISM

'Pluralism and Multiculturalism' contains the most varied range of contributions. This section starts with an article that W. E. B. Du Bois wrote in 1906 ('The Color Line Belts the World') and which contains the classic formulation of the 'color line' as being the problem of the future. Since Du Bois' prediction there has been a stream of attempts to grasp and conceptualise the multicultural dimensions of modern American society. Du Bois made his statement at the beginning of the twentieth century; almost a hundred years later the sociologist Nathan Glazer is convinced – as he writes in his book – that we are all multiculturalists now. Glazer's perception is that Americans now pay far more attention to minorities and to difference. However, he also warns us that too much emphasis is given to the recognition of difference.

Charles Taylor made an attempt to ground multiculturalism philosophically. In his widely discussed book *Multiculturalism and 'The Politics of Recognition'* Taylor looks back to the philosophical origins and sees Rousseau as being the philosopher who first discovered the idea of a new subjectivity. However, it was Herder who first discussed the idea of the cultural origins of such subjectivity and authenticity. The problem in modern times, as Taylor sees it, is how to balance rights and cultural difference. Taylor, who is a Canadian citizen, also proposes a rather 'Canadian' solution. He suggests formally acknowledging difference, as in, for example, the case of Quebec. However, such 'Canadian' solutions might not work in the US context. It is another philosopher, Michael Walzer, who takes a closer look into American multiculturalism and pluralism in his book *What it means to be an American*. Walzer refers to the political meaning of 'E pluribus unum' – 'Out of many – one' but he also refers to 'manyness-in-one' – as represented by the famous symbol of the American eagle holding a sheaf containing many arrows. Walzer argues that hyphenation allows for both cultural and political identities, that is to say, in the United States the manyness of ethnic backgrounds is usually defined culturally while the oneness refers to political identity.

In their study *Color Conscious* Anthony Appiah and Amy Gutmann also provide an account of the uniquely American dimensions of multiculturalism and pluralism, but it seems that their theoretical tools are more elaborated and refined than Walzer's – at least when it comes to the treatment of such topics as racism, racial identity and racial identification. Appiah and Gutmann argue that one has to distinguish between a normative and a descriptive level when it comes to these subjects. Against racism we normatively have to stress our common humanity. However, this should not prevent us from looking at the internal pluralism of our humanity. The problem here is one of finding the right perspective on how to do so. Appiah in particular stresses that studying the various signifiers such as 'African', 'colored', 'black' and so on we not only can trace the history of these signifiers but can also learn something about their effects.

The last part of the section contains a selection from current debates. While agreeing with the finding that race still matters, bell hooks' *killing rage: ending racism* looks at some neglected dimensions in the current debates on multiculturalism. In particular she is concerned with the feminist side of the struggle against racism and prejudice. In his essay collection *Loose Canons – Notes on the Cultural Wars* Henry Louis Gates takes issue with the essentialism that often creeps into the theoretical and practical treatment of ethnic and cultural diversity. Like Ralph Ellison's work, Gates' contribution can be seen as an attempt to avoid all essentialisation without forgetting that prejudice and racism do exist. His intriguing answer to the American identity problem resembles Ellison's statement that America's identity is indeed 'jazz-shaped'.

49

THE COLOR LINE BELTS THE WORLD

W. E. B. Du Bois

We have a way in America of wanting to be 'rid' of problems. It is not so much a desire to reach the best and largest solution as it is to clean the board and start a new game. For instance, most Americans are simply tired and impatient over our most sinister social problem, the Negro. They do not want to solve it, they do not want to understand it, they want to simply be done with it and hear the last of it. Of all possible attitudes this is the most dangerous, because it fails to realize the most significant fact of the opening century, namely the Negro problem in America is but a local phase of a world problem. 'The problem of the twentieth century is the problem of the Color Line.' Many smile incredulously at such a proposition, but let us see.

The tendency of the great nations of the day is territorial, political and economic expansion, but in every case this has brought them in contact with darker peoples, so that we have today England, France, Holland, Belgium, Italy, Portugal and the United States in close contact with brown and black peoples, and Russia and Austria in contact with the yellow. The older idea was that the whites would eventually displace the native races and inherit their lands, but this idea has been rudely shaken in the increase of American Negroes, the experience of the English in Africa, India and the West Indies, and the development of South America. The policy of expansion, then, simply means world problems of the Color Line. The question enters into European imperial politics and floods our continents from Alaska to Patagonia.

From: W. E. B. Du Bois (ed. David Levering Lewis), *W. E. B. Du Bois: A Reader* (New York: Henry Holt, 1995).

This is not all. Since 732, when Charles Martel beat back the Saracens at Tours, the white races have had the hegemony of civilization – so far so that 'white' and 'civilized' have become synonymous in every-day speech; and men have forgotten where civilization started. For the first time in a thousand years a great white nation has measured arms with a colored nation and been found wanting. The Russo–Japanese War has marked an epoch. The magic of the word 'white' is already broken, and the Color Line in civilization has been crossed in modern times as it was in the great past. The awakening of the yellow races is certain. That the awakening of the brown and black races will follow in time, no unprejudiced student of history can doubt. Shall the awakening of these sleepy millions be in accordance with, and aided by, the great ideals of white civilization, or in spite of them and against them? This is the problem of the Color Line. Force and Fear have hitherto marked the white attitude toward darker races; shall this continue or be replaced by Freedom and Friendship?

50

WE ARE ALL MULTICULTURALISTS NOW

Nathan Glazer

When one finds affirmative action encompassed in multicultralism, one feels that the malleability of words has been taken to a useless extreme. The two developments are different in their origins. They are different in their objectives: justice for individuals and groups in one case, respect for the group in the other. They are different in the ways they were instituted: by government action in one case, by faculties and school boards and textbook publishers in the other.

It is not necessary to make 'multiculturalism' cover every aspect of racial and ethnic and gender policy in the United States, and to turn it into a universal epithet denouncing every policy in regard to racial and ethnic groups one deplores. We have other perfectly good words, some predating 'multicultural-ism', such as the 'balanced ticket', to describe the appointment of members of minority groups or of women to the slates of political parties; there is nothing new about the fact that politicians make appointments to show responsiveness to voting blocs.

Even though multiculturalism now has spread far beyond the schools, and far beyond its prime sense of respect for other cultures, for the purposes of this book I will confine it to this more restricted meaning. When I say multi-culturalism has won, and that 'we are all multiculturalists now', I mean that we all now accept a greater degree of attention to minorities and women and their role in American history and social studies and literature classes in schools. Those few who want to return American education to a period in which the

From: Nathan Glazer, *We Are All Multiculturalists Now* (Cambridge, MA: Harvard University Press, 1997).

various subcultures were ignored, and in which America was presented as the peak and end-product of civilization, cannot expect to make any progress in the schools.

Multiculturalism is, in its own way, a universalistic demand: all groups should be recognized. Some groups, however, have fallen below the horizon of attention, and other groups, defined by neither language nor ethnic or racial culture, have risen above it. So we find, for example, that multiculturalism is indifferent to the variety of ethnic groups of European origin but has come to encompass women and gays and lesbians. It is not easy to understand how this has happened.

Of course some limits had to be set on the multiculturalist demand for universal recognition and respect for group difference. There are, after all, thousands of cultures, if we associate a distinctive culture with every ethnic and racial group, and hundreds of them are present, to some degree, in the United States. The limit multiculturalism imposes on who will be recognized is set by the degree of prejudice and discrimination, or in stronger terms, 'oppression', these groups have faced in the United States. Indeed, the opponents of multiculturalism label it 'oppression studies'. But even after one has confined the beneficiaries of multiculturalism to the oppressed, there is the problem of just who is oppressed, and there is still the tension with multiculturalism's universalistic claim that all groups must be recognized. At the University of California, Berkeley, when multiculturalists demanded that students should take a required course dealing with a number of major American ethnic and racial groups, the opponents of the required course riposted, 'And what about Europeans?' The advocates of the requirement had to reluctantly concede. Europeans were added to the African Americans, Hispanics, Asian Americans and Native Americans on the list of groups that could serve to fulfill the requirements of the course.

What was lost in that victory was any distinctions among the Europeans, some of whom had earlier been dominant, and some of whom had been subdominant. Indeed, one group of Europeans, Jews, were at one time considered the model of a minority group, and were so considered in all textbooks on American minorities. Italians, Greeks, Poles and other Slavic groups could also have made a claim to victim status at one time or another, and certainly a claim to distinctiveness, whatever their degree of victimization. But in fact, few have made the claim in recent years. Except for Jews, who are also a religious group and have a long and important tradition of religious writings, no European group has been able to make much of a mark in ethnic and racial studies and programs. (Jews are dominantly but not exclusively European.) These groups had become American under the old regime of assimilation. To now demand recognition went against the grain of their experience, their expectations, their hopes for themselves in America. So they were all merged, for the purposes of ethnic studies at Berkeley, into the new category of Europeans.

If one explores the demands of multiculturalists, one discovers that, even among victims of oppression, not all groups are entitled to multicultural attention. Long before we became multiculturalists, the challenge to a monolithic and uniform American history celebrating its goodness and its triumphs came from those who emphasized not ethnic and racial division but class division. They explored the life of workers, their struggles, the bloody conflicts in which they were often engaged to improve their working conditions. This interest was undoubtedly stimulated by the Great Depression and the rise of new, powerful unions. The history of the working class and its organizations, such as the trade unions, became an important topic of interest to historians, and in time the volume of work on such matters among scholars began to filter down to the high schools and to affect modestly the history curriculum. So there were new sections in textbooks on the rise of the city, industrialism and manufacturing, mass immigration.

But the contrast between this revision of American history and the victory of multiculturalism is striking. Even though one hears the phrase 'race, class, and gender' used to describe the new emphases being promoted in colleges – that was the rallying cry of those who fought the required Western Civilization course at Stanford University and replaced it with one giving more attention to race, class, and gender – class has certainly come in third, if it is evident at all, in the revision of curricula. The poor get into the new curriculum only if their poverty is associated with being female or nonwhite. Class as such plays little role in multiculturalism, an oddity that is worth some passing consideration. One suspects that the main reason is that 'workers' are no longer seen as a deprived and oppressed and victimized group. It is rather the nonworking lower class that now takes the bottom victim position in the social ladder of class, and the worker and his institutions, such as trade unions, if not further specified by gender and race, are considered suspect and very likely prejudiced against minorities and women.

If it is not easy to understand how class came to be excluded from multiculturalism, similarly it is not easy to understand how women's studies came to be included. Women have been discriminated against in jobs and have been the victims of sexual harassment both on and off the job, but these civil rights issues are not part of multiculturalism if we take it to refer to culture. Women share, indeed shape, the culture of their families and their racial or ethnic group. To think of women as a uniformly deprived group because of their culture and regardless of their income, their race or ethnicity, their fathers, husbands, sons, requires something of a wrenching exercise in perspective. This exercise was not undertaken by earlier movements for the deprived and oppressed, such as socialist movements, or anticolonial movements.

Certainly one can speak of women's culture, as one can apply the term to almost any group, from a men's club and corporation to the entire West. There are some things that are held in common across vast stretches of population and area. Perhaps a distinctive women's language, a variant of the common tongue, is one. Multiculturalism in its origins – in Canada, for example – was thinking of language groups and cultural groups. When women's studies exploded, both women's studies and the new ethnic and racial studies could trace a common history, arising in the same decades, drawing on similar resentments, and a common new awareness of inequality. These similarities between racial and ethnic emphases in education and women's perspectives overweighed the enormous differences as categories between racial and ethnic groups on the one hand, and the entire female sex on the other.

Women's studies is part of multiculturalism, so large a part that it often outweighs all the rest. In the canon of received outrages perpetrated by multi-culturalists – which has been put together by the opponents of multiculturalism to make their case – a hefty segment deals with offences to the sensitivities of women. That women and racial and ethnic studies advocates are united is in one sense surprising. Women have fared much better in establishing large and respected fields in the humanities and social sciences, for example, than the racial and ethnic groups have. They have also done better in getting their view-point into elementary and high school texts. They have been more successful in getting academic jobs. (Asian American scholars also get a good number of jobs in a variety of fields, particularly in science and technology, but not because of their race or their expertise in Asian American studies.)

[...]

If multiculturalism already extends beyond race and ethnic differences to include women's studies, why not the 'cultures' of different 'life-style' groups? It makes sense within the multicultural perspective. History moves toward ever greater equality, recognizing equality in ever new spheres, from the civil, to the political, to the economic, to the cultural. We have discovered and tried to make good the inequality in all these respects of the female sex. If progress is the spread of equality and liberty, one does not see how any good argument can be made against gay and lesbian claims. Behind the victory of multiculturalism, whatever the discomforts it brings, lie these two great principles, equality and liberty, and few want to be in the position of opposing their claims.

'Multiculturalism' is a term which many of us who have studied immigration and ethnic groups might have found perfectly satisfactory to cover our sense, some decades back, that American history and social studies should incorporate a larger recognition of American diversity. But terms take on a life of their own, totally unexpected by their original users. Multiculturalism has now become a contested term, an epithet to some, a banner to others. Multiculturalism of some kind there is, and there will be. The fight is over how much, what kind, for whom, at what ages, under what standards. To say one is 'for' or 'against' multiculturalism without going through all this effort is not to say much. The work of defining what kind, how much, for whom, and all the rest will continue to be done in national and state commissions, in state agencies, in local school boards, in individual schools by individual teachers, by textbook publishers and test makers. Having had some experience with a state commission reviewing a social studies curriculum, I have discovered how hard such work is, how various are our conceptions of America, how surprisingly we can disagree on what seem to me to be simple truths.

But overall I believe that short of the extremes there is a good deal of commonality. The new America that multiculturalism, in its principal variants, envisages and is trying to establish as the America we learn about in schools will not, like the old, take it for granted that this is the best of all countries, as well as the strongest and the richest. We will become more self-conscious about making any claim to a distinctive virtue and superiority, and that is all for the best. There is much, after all, in the education of the old America that would grate on us today. The question that disturbs so many of us is whether the new multi-culturalism will establish as a norm in education an all-embracing denunciation of the old America, will spread a sense of resentment among many students, will lead to conflict greater than now exists between minorities and majorities. Will multiculturalism undermine what is still, on balance, a success in world history, a diverse society that continues to welcome further diversity, with a distinctive and common culture of some merit? I believe things will not come to that pass because the basic demand of the multiculturalists is for inclusion, not separation, and inclusion under the same rules – stretching back to the Constitution – that have permitted the steady broadening of what we under-stand as equality.

51

MULTICULTURALISM AND
'THE POLITICS OF RECOGNITION'

Charles Taylor

We can distinguish two changes that together have made the modern preoccupation with identity and recognition inevitable. The first is the collapse of social hierarchies, which used to be the basis for honor. I am using *honor* in the *ancien régime* sense in which it is intrinsically linked to inequalities. For some to have honor in this sense, it is essential that not everyone have it. This is the sense in which Montesquieu uses it in his description of monarchy. Honor is intrinsically a matter of 'préférences'.[1] It is also the sense in which we use the term when we speak of honoring someone by giving her some public award, for example, the Order of Canada. Clearly, this award would be without worth if tomorrow we decided to give it to every adult Canadian.

As against this notion of honor, we have the modern notion of dignity now used in a universalist and egalitarian sense, where we talk of the inherent 'dignity of human beings', or of citizen dignity. The underlying premise here is that everyone shares in it.[2] It is obvious that this concept of dignity is the only one compatible with a democratic society, and that it was inevitable that the old concept of honor was superseded. But this has also meant that the forms of equal recognition have been essential to democratic culture.

[...]

But the importance of recognition has been modified and intensified by the new understanding of individual identity that emerges at the end of the

From: Charles Taylor (ed. Amy Gutmann), *Multiculturalism and the Politics of Recognition* (Princeton, NJ: Princeton University Press, 1992).

eighteenth century. We might speak of an *individualized* identity, one that is particular to me, and that I discover in myself. This notion arises along with an ideal, that of being true to myself and my own particular way of being. Following Lionel Trilling's usage in his brilliant study, I will speak of this as the ideal of 'authenticity'.[3] It will help to describe in what it consists and how it came about.

One way of describing its development is to see its starting point in the eighteenth-century notion that human beings are endowed with a moral sense, an intuitive feeling for what is right and wrong. The original point of this doctrine was to combat a rival view, that knowing right and wrong was a matter of calculating consequences, in particular, those concerned with divine reward and punishment. The idea was that understanding right and wrong was not a matter of dry calculation, but was anchored in our feelings.[4] Morality has, in a sense, a voice within.

The notion of authenticity develops out of a displacement of the moral accent in this idea. On the original view, the inner voice was important because it tells us what the right thing to do is. Being in touch with our moral feelings matters here, as a means to the end of acting rightly. What I'm calling the displacement of the moral accent comes about when being in touch with our feelings takes on independent and crucial moral significance. It comes to be something we have to attain if we are to be true and full human beings.

To see what is new here, we have to see the analogy to earlier moral views, where being in touch with some source – for example, God, or the Idea of the Good – was considered essential to full being. But now the source we have to connect with is deep within us. This fact is part of the massive subjective turn of modern culture, a new form of inwardness, in which we come to think of ourselves as beings with inner depths. At first, this idea that the source is within doesn't exclude our being related to God or the Ideas; it can be considered our proper way of relating to them. In a sense, it can be seen as just a continuation and intensification of the development inaugurated by Saint Augustine, who saw the road to God as passing through our own self-awareness. The first variants of this new view were theistic, or at least pantheistic.

The most important philosophical writer who helped to bring about this change was Jean-Jacques Rousseau. I think Rousseau is important not because he inaugurated the change; rather, I would argue that his great popularity comes in part from his articulating something that was in a sense already occurring in the culture. Rousseau frequently presents the issue of morality as that of our following a voice of nature within us. This voice is often drowned out by the passions that are induced by our dependence on others, the main one being *amour propre*, or pride. Our moral salvation comes from recovering authentic moral contact with ourselves. Rousseau even gives a name to the intimate contact with oneself, more fundamental than any moral view, that is a source of such joy and contentment: 'le sentiment de l'existence'.[5]

The ideal of authenticity becomes crucial owing to a development that occurs after Rousseau, which I associate with the name of Herder – once again, as its major early articulator, rather than its originator. Herder put forward the idea that each of us has an original way of being human: each person has his or her own 'measure'.[6] This idea has burrowed very deep into modern consciousness. It is a new idea. Before the late eighteenth century, no one thought that the differences between human beings had this kind of moral significance. There is a certain way of being human that is *my* way. I am called upon to live my life in this way, and not in imitation of anyone else's life. But this notion gives a new importance to being true to myself. If I am not, I miss the point of my life; I miss what being human is for *me*.

This is the powerful moral ideal that has come down to us. It accords moral importance to a kind of contact with myself, with my own inner nature, which it sees as in danger of being lost, partly through the pressures toward outward conformity, but also because in taking an instrumental stance toward myself, I may have lost the capacity to listen to this inner voice. It greatly increases the importance of this self-contact by introducing the principle of originality: each of our voices has something unique to say. Not only should I not mold my life to the demands of external conformity; I can't even find the model by which to live outside myself. I can only find it within.[7]

Being true to myself means being true to my own originality, which is something only I can articulate and discover. In articulating it, I am also defining myself. I am realizing a potentiality that is properly my own. This is the background understanding to the modern ideal of authenticity, and to the goals of self-fulfillment and self-realization in which the ideal is usually couched. I should note here that Herder applied his conception of originality at two levels, not only to the individual person among other persons, but also to the culture-bearing people among other peoples. Just like individuals, a *Volk* should be true to itself, that is, its own culture. Germans shouldn't try to be derivative and (inevitably) second-rate Frenchmen, as Frederick the Great's patronage seemed to be encouraging them to do. The Slavic peoples had to find their own path. And European colonialism ought to be rolled back to give the peoples of what we now call the Third World their chance to be themselves unimpeded. We can recognize here the seminal idea of modern nationalism, in both benign and malignant forms.

This new ideal of authenticity was, like the idea of dignity, also in part an offshoot of the decline of hierarchical society. In those earlier societies, what we would now call identity was largely fixed by one's social position. That is, the background that explained what people recognized as important to themselves was to a great extent determined by their place in society, and whatever roles or activities attached to this position. The birth of a democratic society doesn't by itself do away with this phenomenon, because people can still define themselves by their social roles. What does decisively undermine this socially derived identification, however, is the ideal of authenticity itself. As this emerges, for instance, with Herder, it calls on me to discover my own original way of being. By definition, this way of being cannot be socially derived, but must be inwardly generated.

But in the nature of the case, there is no such thing as inward generation, monologically understood. In order to understand the close connection between identity and recognition, we have to take into account a crucial feature of the human condition that has been rendered almost invisible by the overwhelmingly monological bent of mainstream modern philosophy.

This crucial feature of human life is its fundamentally *dialogical* character. We become full human agents, capable of understanding ourselves, and hence of defining our identity, through our acquisition of rich human languages of expression. For my purposes here, I want to take *language* in a broad sense, covering not only the words we speak, but also other modes of expression whereby we define ourselves, including the 'languages' of art, of gesture, of love and the like. But we learn these modes of expression through exchanges with others. People do not acquire the languages needed for self-definition on their own. Rather, we are introduced to them through interaction with others who matter to us – what George Herbert Mead called 'significant others'.[8] The genesis of the human mind is in this sense not monological, not something each person accomplishes on his or her own, but dialogical.

Moreover, this is not just a fact about *genesis*, which can be ignored later on. We don't just learn the languages in dialogue and then go on to use them for our own purposes. We are of course expected to develop our own opinions, outlook, stances toward things and to a considerable degree through solitary reflection. But this is not how things work with important issues, like the definition of our identity. We define our identity always in dialogue with, sometimes in struggle against, the things our significant others want to see in us. Even after we outgrow some of these others – our parents, for instance – and they disappear from our lives, the conversation with them continues within us as long as we live.[9]

[...]

There is a form of the politics of equal respect, as enshrined in a liberalism of rights, that is inhospitable to difference, because (a) it insists on uniform application of the rules defining these rights, without exception and (b) it is suspicious of collective goals. Of course, this doesn't mean that this model seeks to abolish cultural differences. This would be an absurd accusation. But I call it inhospitable to difference because it can't accommodate what the members of distinct societies really aspire to, which is survival. This is (b) a collective goal, which (a) almost inevitably will call for some variations in the kinds of law we deem permissible from one cultural context to another, as the Quebec case clearly shows.

I think this form of liberalism is guilty as charged by the proponents of a politics of difference. Fortunately, however, there are other models of liberal society that take a different line on (a) and (b). These forms do call for the invariant defense of *certain* rights, of course. There would be no question of cultural differences determining the application of *habeas corpus*, for example. But they distinguish these fundamental rights from the broad range of immunities and presumptions of uniform treatment that have sprung up in modern cultures of judicial review. They are willing to weigh the importance of certain forms of uniform treatment against the importance of cultural survival, and opt sometimes in favor of the latter. They are thus in the end not procedural models of liberalism, but are grounded very much on judgments about what makes a good life – judgments in which the integrity of cultures has an important place.

Although I cannot argue it here, obviously I would endorse this kind of model. Indisputably, though, more and more societies today are turning out to be multicultural, in the sense of including more than one cultural community that wants to survive. The rigidities of procedural liberalism may rapidly become impractical in tomorrow's world.

NOTES

1. 'La nature de l'honneur est de demander des préférences et des distinctions ...' Montesquieu, *De l'esprit des lois*, Bk 3, ch. 7.
2. The significance of this move from 'honor' to 'dignity' is interestingly discussed by Peter Berger in his 'On the Obsolescence of the Concept of Honour', in *Revisions: Changing Perspectives in Moral Philosophy*, Stanley Hauerwas and Alasdair MacIntyre (eds) (Notre Dame, IN: University of Notre Dame Press, 1983), pp. 172–81.
3. Lionel Trilling, *Sincerity and Authenticity* (New York: Norton, 1969).
4. I have discussed the development of this doctrine at greater length, at first in the work of Francis Hutcheson, drawing on the writings of the Earl of Shaftesbury, and its adversarial relation to Locke's theory in *Sources of the Self* (Cambridge, MA: Harvard University Press, 1989), ch. 15.
5. Le sentiment de l'existence dépouillé de toute autre affection est par lui-même un sentiment précieux de contentement et de paix qui suffiroit seul pour rendre cette existence chère et douce à qui sauroit écarter de soi toutes les impressions sensuelles et terrestres qui viennent sans cesse nous en distraire et en troubler ici bas la douceur. Mais la plupart des hommes agités de passions continuelles connoissent peu cet état et ne l'ayant goûté qu'imparfaitement durant peu d'instans n'en conservent qu'une idée obscure et confuse qui ne leur en fait pas sentir le charme.' Jean-Jacques Rousseau, *Les Rêveries du promeneur solitaire*, 'Cinquième Promenade,' in *Œuvres complètes* (Paris: Gallimard, 1959), 1:1047.
6. 'Jeder Mensch hate in eigenes Maass, gleichsam eine eigne Stimmung aller seiner sinnlichen Gefühle zu einander.' Johann Gottlob Herder, *Ideen*, ch. 7, sec. 1, in *Herders Sämtliche Werke*, Bernard Suphan (ed.) (Berlin: Weidmann, 1877–1913), 13: 291.
7. John Stuart Mill was influenced by this Romantic current of thought when he made something like the ideal of authenticity the basis for one of his most powerful arguments in *On Liberty*. See especially chapter 3, where he argues that we need something more than a capacity for 'ape-like imitation': 'A person whose desires and impulses are his own – are the expression of his own nature, as it has been developed and modified by his own culture – is said to have a character.' 'If a person possesses any tolerable amount of common sense and experience, his own mode of laying out his existence is the best, not because it is the best in itself, but because it is his own mode.' John Stuart Mill, *Three Essays* (Oxford: Oxford University Press, 1975), pp. 73, 74, 83.

8. George Herbert Mead, *Mind, Self, and Society* (Chicago: University of Chicago Press, 1934).
9. This inner dialogicality has been explored by M. M. Bakhtin and those who have drawn on his work. See, of Bakhtin, especially *Problems of Dostoyevsky's Poetics*, trans. Caryl Emerson (Minneapolis: University of Minnesota Press, 1984). See also Michael Holquist and Katerina Clark, *Mikhail Bakhtin* (Cambridge, MA: Harvard University Press, 1984); and James Wertsch, *Voices of the Mind* (Cambridge, MA: Harvard University Press, 1991).

52

WHAT IT MEANS TO BE AN AMERICAN

Michael Walzer

Immigration is a genuine problem in countries with ancient majorities – as it is not, or ought not to be, in immigrant societies like ours. For the members of the majority nation or religion won't want to be overwhelmed in their own country. They will favor immigrants who resemble themselves and seem likely to blend into the established culture. The arguments about immigration in contemporary Europe regularly exhibit a xenophobic or racist character. But this isn't the necessary character of every argument in favor of restrictions on the admission of foreigners. We can test the men and women who defend restrictions by asking them how they mean to treat those foreigners already admitted and how they want to deal with the countries from which the immigrants come: are they ready for political cooperation and serious economic assistance? Americans expand their solidarity by taking new nations into their state (Slavs, Italians, and Jews in the late nineteenth and early twentieth centuries, Hispanics and Asians today). Europeans are more likely to expand their solidarity by forming economic unions or political federations with other nation-states. In the first case, the politics of difference produces new, hyphenated identities (Asian-American) in place of the old singularities. In the second, it produces a new singular identity (European, say) alongside and in addition to the old one.

The United States is not most importantly a union of states but of nations, races, and religions, all of them dispersed and inter-mixed, without ground of their own. The European Community is (or is on its way to becoming) a more

From: Michael Walzer, *What it Means to be an American* (New York: Marsilio, 1996).

literal 'United States', for it is precisely a union of states – or of nations on their own ground. Immigration among these states, like the existence of national or religious minorities within them, produces something more like an American society. But the fundamental contrast between Europe and America is likely to remain: we might think of it as a contrast between territorially grounded ('tribal') and groundless ('multicultural') difference. The two require dissimilar negotiations, which give rise in turn to dissimilar unions. Nonetheless, they reflect a common moral and political imperative.

[...]

The United States is less importantly a union of states than it is a union of ethnic, racial and religious groups – a union of otherwise unrelated 'natives'. What is the nature of this union? The Great Seal of the United States carries the motto *E pluribus unum*, 'From many, one', which seems to suggest that manyness must be left behind for the sake of oneness. Once there were many, now the many have merged or, in Israel Zangwell's classic image, been melted down into one. But the Great Seal presents a different image: the 'American' eagle holds a sheaf of arrows. Here there is no merger or fusion but only a fastening, a putting together: many-in-one. Perhaps the adjective 'American' describes this kind of oneness. We might say, tentatively, that it points to the citizenship, not the nativity or nationality, of the men and women it designates. It is a political adjective, and its politics is liberal in the strict sense: generous, tolerant, ample, accommodating – it allows for the survival, even the enhancement and flourishing, of manyness.

On this view, appropriately called 'pluralist', the word 'from' on the Great Seal is a false preposition. There is no movement from many to one, but rather a simultaneity, a coexistence – once again, many-in-one. But I don't mean to suggest a mystery here, as in the Christian conception of a God who is three-in-one. The language of pluralism is sometimes a bit mysterious – thus Kallen's description of America as a 'nation of nationalities' or John Rawls' account of the liberal state as a 'social union of social unions' – but it lends itself to a rational unpacking.[1] A sheaf of arrows is not, after all, a mysterious entity. We can find analogues in the earliest forms of social organization: tribes composed of many clans, clans composed of many families. The conflicts of loyalty and obligation, inevitable products of pluralism, must arise in these cases too. And yet, they are not exact analogues of the American case, for tribes and clans lack Kallen's 'anonymity'. American pluralism is, as we shall see, a peculiarly modern phenomenon – not mysterious but highly complex.

In fact, the United States is not a literal 'nation of nationalities' or a 'social union of social unions'. At least, the singular nation or union is not constituted by, it is not a combination or fastening together of, the plural nationalities or unions. In some sense, it includes them; it provides a framework for their coexistence; but they are not its parts. Nor are the individual states, in any significant sense, the parts that make up the United States. The parts are individual men and women. The United States is an association of citizens. Its 'anonymity' consists in the fact that these citizens don't transfer their collective name to the association. It never happened that a group of people called Americans came together to form a political society called America. The people are Americans only by virtue of having come together. And whatever identity they had before becoming Americans, they retain (or, better, they are free to retain) afterward. There is, to be sure, another view of Americanization, which holds that the process requires for its success the mental erasure of all previous identities – forgetfulness or even, as one enthusiast wrote in 1918, 'absolute forgetfulness'.[2] But on the pluralist view, Americans are allowed to remember who they were and to insist, also, on *what else they are.*

They are not, however, bound to the remembrance or to the insistence. Just as their ancestors escaped the old country, so they can if they choose escape their old identities, the 'inwardness' of their nativity. Kallen writes of the individual that 'whatever else he changes, he cannot change his grandfather'.[3] Perhaps not; but he can call his grandfather a 'greenhorn', reject his customs and convictions, give up the family name, move to a new neighborhood, adopt a new 'life-style'.

He doesn't become a better American by doing these things (though that is sometimes his purpose), but he may become an American simply, an American and nothing else, freeing himself from the hyphenation that pluralists regard as universal on this side, though not on the other side, of the Atlantic Ocean. But, free from hyphenation, he seems also free from ethnicity: 'American' is not one of the ethnic groups recognized in the United States census. Someone who is only an American is, so far as our bureaucrats are concerned, ethnically anonymous. He has a right, however, to his anonymity; that is part of what it means to be an American.

[...]

America is very different, and not only because of the eclipse of republicanism in the early nineteenth century. Indeed, republicanism has had a kind of afterlife as one of the legitimating ideologies of American politics. The Minute Man is a republican image of embodied citizenship. Reverence for the flag is a form of republican piety. The Pledge of Allegiance is a republican oath. But emphasis on this sort of thing reflects social disunity rather than unity; it is straining after oneness where oneness doesn't exist. In fact, America has been, with severe but episodic exceptions, remarkably tolerant of ethnic pluralism (far less so of racial pluralism).[4] I don't want to underestimate the human difficulties of adapting even to a hyphenated Americanism, nor to deny the bigotry and discrimination that particular groups have encountered. But tolerance has been the cultural norm.

Perhaps an immigrant society has no choice; tolerance is a way of muddling through when any alternative policy would be violent and dangerous. But I would argue that we have, mostly, made the best of this necessity, so that the virtues of toleration, in principle though by no means always in practice, have supplanted the singlemindedness of republican citizenship. We have made our peace with the 'particular characteristics' of all the immigrant groups (though not, again, of all the racial groups) and have come to regard American nationality as an addition to rather than a replacement for ethnic consciousness. The hyphen works, when it is working, more like a plus sign. 'American', then, is a name indeed, but unlike 'French' or 'German' or 'Italian' or 'Korean' or 'Japanese' or 'Cambodian', it can serve as a second name. And as in those modern marriages where two patronymics are joined, neither the first nor the second name is dominant: here the hyphen works more like a sign of equality.

We might go further than this: in the case of hyphenated Americans, it doesn't matter whether the first or the second name is dominant. We insist, most of the time, that the 'particular characteristics' associated with the first name be sustained, as the Know-Nothings urged, without state help – and perhaps they will prove unsustainable on those terms. Still, an ethnic-American is someone who can, in principle, live his spiritual life as he chooses, *on either side of the hyphen*.

[...]

One step more is required before we have fully understood this strange America: it is not the case that Irish-Americans, say, are culturally Irish and politically American, as the pluralists claim (and as I have been assuming thus far for the sake of the argument). Rather, they are culturally Irish-American and politically Irish-American. Their culture has been significantly influenced by American culture; their politics is still, both in style and substance, significantly ethnic. With them, and with every ethnic and religious groups except the American-Americans, hyphenation is doubled. It remains true, however, that what all the groups have in common is most importantly their citizenship and what most differentiates them, insofar as they are still differentiated, is their culture. Hence the alternation in American life of patriotic fevers and ethnic revivals, the first expressing a desire to heighten the commonality, the second a desire to reaffirm the difference.

At both ends of this peculiarly American alternation, the good that is defended is also exaggerated and distorted, so that pluralism itself is threatened by the sentiments it generates. The patriotic fevers are the symptoms of a republican pathology. At issue here is the all-important ideological commitment that, as Gleason says, is the sole prerequisite of American citizenship. Since citizenship isn't guaranteed by oneness all the way down, patriots or superpatriots seek to guarantee it by loyalty oaths and campaigns against 'un-American' activities. The Know-Nothing party having failed to restrict naturalization, they resort instead to political purges and deportations. Ethnic revivals are less militant and less cruel, though not without their own pathology. What is at issue here is communal pride and power – a demand for political recognition without assimilation, an assertion of interest-group politics against republican ideology, an effort to distinguish this group (one's own) from all the others. American patriotism is always strained and nervous because hyphenation makes indeed for dual loyalty but seems, at the same time, entirely American. Ethnic revivalism is also strained and nervous, because the hyphenates are already Americans, on both sides of the hyphen.

[...]

On the basis of some decades of experience, one can reasonably argue that ethnic pluralism is entirely compatible with the existence of a unified republic. Kallen would have said that it is simply the expression of democracy in the sphere of culture. It is, however, an unexpected expression: the American republic is very different from that described, for example, by Montesquieu and Rousseau. It lacks the intense political fellowship, the commitment to public affairs, that they thought necessary. 'The better the constitution of a state is,' wrote Rousseau, 'the more do public affairs encroach on private in the minds of the citizens. Private affairs are even of much less importance, because the aggregate of the common happiness furnishes a greater proportion of that of each individual, so that there is less for him to seek in particular cares.' This is an unlikely description unless ethnic culture and religious belief are closely interwoven with political activity (as Rousseau insisted they should be). It certainly misses the reality of the American republic, where both have been firmly relegated to the private sphere. The emotional life of US citizens is lived mostly in private – which is not to say in solitude, but in groups considerably smaller than the community of all citizens. Americans are communal in their private affairs, individualist in their politics. Civil society is a collection of groups; the state is an organization of individual citizens. And society and state, though they constantly interact, are formally distinct. For support and comfort and a sense of belonging, men and women look to their groups; for freedom and mobility, they look to the state.

Still, democratic participation does bring group members into the political arena where they are likely to discover common interests. Why has this not caused radical divisiveness as in the European empires? It certainly has made for conflict, sometimes of a frightening sort, but always within limits set by the nonterritorial and socially indeterminate character of the immigrant communities and by the sharp divorce of state and ethnicity. No single group can hope to capture the state and turn it into a nation-state. Members of the group are citizens only as Americans, not as Germans, Italians, Irishmen, Jews, or Hispanics.

[...]

Distributive justice among groups is bound to be relative to the vitality of their centers and of their committed members. Short of corporatism, the state cannot help groups unable or unwilling to help themselves. It cannot save them from ultimate Americanization. Indeed, it works so as to permit individual escape (assimilation and intermarriage) as well as collective commitment. The primary function of the state, and of politics generally, is to do justice to individuals, and in a pluralist society ethnicity is simply one of the background conditions of this effort. Ethnic identification gives meaning to the lives of many men and women, but it has nothing to do with their standing as citizens. This distinction seems worth defending even if it makes for a world in which there are no guarantees of meaning. In a culturally homogeneous society the government can foster a particular identity, deliberately merging culture and politics. This the US government cannot do. Pluralism is thus still an experiment, still to be tested against the long-term historical and theoretical power of the nation-state.

NOTES

1. Horace Kallen, *Culture and Democracy in the United States* (New York: Boni and Liveright, 1924), p. 122 (cf. 116); John Rawls, *A Theory of Justice* (Cambridge, MA: Harvard University Press, 1971), p. 527.
2. Quoted in Kallen, *Culture and Democracy*, p. 138; the writer was superintendent of New York's public schools.
3. Kallen, *Culture and Democracy*, p. 94.
4. The current demand of (some) black Americans that they be called African-Americans represents an attempt to adapt themselves to the ethnic paradigm – imitating, perhaps, the relative success of various Asian-American groups in a similar adaptation. But names are no guarantees; nor does antinativist pluralism provide sufficient protection against what is all too often an *ethnic*-American racism. It has been argued that this racism is the necessary precondition of hyphenated ethnicity: the inclusion of successive waves of ethnic immigrants is possible only because of the permanent exclusion of black Americans. But I don't know what evidence would demonstrate *necessity* here. I am inclined to reject the metaphysical belief that all inclusion entails exclusion. A historical and empirical account of the place of blacks in the 'system' of American pluralism would require another essay, a different book.

53

COLOR CONSCIOUS

K. Anthony Appiah

If we follow the badge of color from 'African' to 'Negro' to 'colored race' to 'black' to 'Afro-American' to 'African-American' (and this ignores such fascinating detours as the route by way of 'Afro-Saxon') we are thus tracing the history not only of a signifier, a label, but also a history of its effects. At any time in this history there was, within the American colonies and the United States that succeeded them, a massive consensus, both among those labeled black and among those labeled white, as to who, in their own communities, fell under which labels. (As immigration from China and other parts of the 'Far East' occurred, an Oriental label came to have equal stability.) There was, no doubt, some 'passing'; but the very concept of passing implies that, if the relevant fact about the ancestry of these individuals had become known, most people would have taken them to be traveling under the wrong badge.

The major North American exception was in southern Louisiana, where a different system in which an intermediary Creole group, neither white nor black, had social recognition; but *Plessy v. Fergusson* reflected the extent to which the Louisiana Purchase effectively brought even that state gradually into the American mainstream of racial classification. For in that case Homer Adolph Plessy – a Creole gentleman who could certainly have passed in most places for white – discovered in 1896, after a long process of appeal, that the Supreme Court of the United States proposed to treat him as a Negro and

From: K. Anthony Appiah and Amy Gutmann, *Color Conscious* (Princeton, NJ: Princeton University Press, 1996).

therefore recognize the State of Louisiana's right to keep him and his white fellow citizens 'separate but equal'.

The result is that there are at least three sociocultural objects in America – blacks, whites and Orientals – whose membership at any time is relatively, and increasingly, determinate. These objects are historical in this sense: to identify all the members of these American races over time, you cannot seek a single criterion that applies equally always; you can find the starting point for the race – the subcontinental source of the population of individuals that defines its initial membership – and then apply at each historical moment the criteria of intertemporal continuity that apply at that moment to decide which individuals in the next generation count as belonging to the group. There is from the very beginning until the present, at the heart of the system, a simple rule that very few would dispute even today: where both parents are of a single race, the child is of the same race as the parents.

The criteria applicable at any time may leave vague boundaries. They certainly change, as the varying decisions about what proportion of African ancestry made one black or the current uncertainty as to how to assign the children of white-yellow 'miscegenation' demonstrate. But they always definitely assign some people to the group and definitely rule out others; and for most of America's history the class of people about whom there was uncertainty (are the Florida Seminoles black or Indian?) was relatively small.[1]

Once the racial label is applied to people, ideas about what it refers to, ideas that may be much less consensual than the application of the label, come to have their social effects. But they have not only social effects but psychological ones as well; and they shape the ways people conceive of themselves and their projects. In particular, the labels can operate to shape what I want to call 'identification': the process through which an individual intentionally shapes her projects – including her plans for her own life and her conception of the good – by reference to available labels, available identities.

Identification is central to what Ian Hacking has called 'making up people'.[2] Drawing on a number of examples, but centrally homosexuality and multiple personality syndrome, he defends what he calls a 'dynamic nominalism', which argues that 'numerous kinds of human beings and human acts come into being hand in hand with our invention of the categories labeling them'.[3] I have just articulated a dynamic nominalism about a kind of person that is currently usually called 'African-American'.

Hacking reminds us of the philosophical truism, whose most influential formulation is in Elizabeth Anscombe's work on intention, that in intentional action people act 'under descriptions'; that their actions are conceptually shaped. It follows, of course, that what people can do depends on what concepts they have available to them; and among the concepts that may shape one's action is the concept of a certain kind of person and the behavior appropriate to that kind.

[…]

We *can* ask whether someone is really of a black race, because the constitution of this identity is generally theoretically committed: we expect people of a certain race to behave a certain way not simply because they are conforming to the script for that identity, performing that role, but because they have certain antecedent properties that are consequences of the label's properly applying to them. It is because ascription of racial identities – the process of applying the label to people, including ourselves – is based on more than intentional identification that there can be a gap between what a person ascriptively is and the racial identity he performs: it is this gap that makes passing possible.

Race is, in this way, like all the major forms of identification that are central to contemporary identity politics: female and male; gay, lesbian and straight; black, white, yellow, red and brown; Jewish-, Italian-, Japanese- and Korean-American; even that most neglected of American identities, class. There is, in all of them, a set of theoretically committed criteria for ascription, not all of which are held by everybody, and which may not be consistent with one another even in the ascriptions of a single person; and there is then a process of identification in which the label shapes the intentional acts of (some of) those who fall under it.

It does not follow from the fact that identification shapes action, shapes life plans, that the identification itself must be thought of as voluntary. I don't recall ever choosing to identify as a male;[4] but being male has shaped many of my plans and actions. In fact, where my ascriptive identity is one on which almost all my fellow citizens agree, I am likely to have little sense of choice about whether the identity is mine; though I *can* choose how central my identification with it will be – choose, that is, how much I will organize my life around that identity. Thus if I am among those (like the unhappily labeled 'straight-acting gay men', or most American Jews) who are able, if they choose, to escape ascription, I may choose not to take up a gay or a Jewish identity; though this will require concealing facts about myself or my ancestry from others.

If, on the other hand, I fall into the class of those for whom the consensus on ascription is not clear – as among contemporary so-called biracials, or bisexuals, or those many white Americans of multiple identifiable ethnic heritages[5] – I may have a sense of identity options: but one way I may exercise them is by marking myself ethnically (as when someone chooses to wear an Irish pin) so that others will then be more likely to ascribe that identity to me.

Differences among Differences

Collective identities differ, of course, in lots of ways; the body is central to race, gender, and sexuality but not so central to class and ethnicity. And, to repeat an important point, racial identification is simply harder to resist than ethnic identification. The reason is twofold. First, racial ascription is more socially salient: unless you are morphologically atypical for your racial group, strangers, friends, officials are always aware of it in public and private contexts, always notice it, almost never let it slip from view. Second – and again both in intimate settings and in public space – race is taken by so many more people to be the basis for treating people differentially. (In this respect, Jewish identity in America strikes me as being a long way along a line toward African-American identity: there are ways of speaking and acting and looking – and it matters very little whether they are 'really' mostly cultural or mostly genetic – that are associated with being Jewish; and there are many people, white and black, Jewish and Gentile, for whom this identity is a central force in shaping their responses to others.)

This much about identification said, we can see that Du Bois' analytical problem was, in effect, that he believed that for racial labeling of this sort to have the obvious real effects that it did have – among them, crucially, his own identification with other black people and with Africa – there must be some real essence that held the race together. Our account of the history of the label reveals that this is a mistake: once we focus, as Du Bois almost saw, on the racial badge – the signifier rather than the signified, the word rather than the concept – we see both that the effects of the labeling are powerful and real and that false ideas, muddle and mistake and mischief, played a central role in determining both how the label was applied and to what purposes.

This, I believe, is why Du Bois so often found himself reduced, in his attempts to define race, to occult forces: if you look for a shared essence you won't get anything, so you'll come to believe you've missed it, because it is super-subtle, difficult to experience or identify: in short, mysterious. But if, as I say, you understand the sociohistorical process of construction of the race, you'll see that the label works despite the absence of an essence.

Perhaps, then, we can allow that what Du Bois was after was the idea of racial identity, which I shall roughly define as a label, *R*, associated with *ascriptions* by most people (where ascription involves descriptive criteria for applying the label); and *identifications* by those that fall under it (where identification implies a shaping role for the label in the intentional acts of the possessors, so that they sometimes act *as an R*), where there is a history of associating possessors of the label with an inherited racial essence (even if some who use the label no longer believe in racial essences).

In fact, we might argue that racial identities could persist even if nobody believed in racial essences, provided both ascription and identification continue.

There will be some who will object to my account that it does not give racism a central place in defining racial identity: it is obvious, I think, from the history I have explored, that racism has been central to the development of race theory. In that sense racism has been part of the story all along. But you might give an account of racial identity in which you counted nothing as a racial essence unless it implied a hierarchy among the races;[6] or unless the label played a role in racist practices. I have some sympathy with the former strategy; it would fit easily into my basic picture. To the latter strategy, however, I make the philosopher's objection that it confuses logical and causal priority: I have no doubt that racial theories grew up, in part, as rationalizations for mistreating blacks, Jews, Chinese and various others. But I think it is useful to reserve the concept of racism, as opposed to ethnocentrism or simply inhumanity, for practices in which a race concept plays a central role. And I doubt you can explain racism without first explaining the race concept.

I *am* in sympathy, however, with an animating impulse behind such proposals, which is to make sure that here in America we do not have discussions of race in which racism disappears from view. As I pointed out, racial identification is hard to resist in part because racial ascription by others is so insistent; and its effects – especially, but by no means exclusively, the racist ones – are so hard to escape. It is obvious, I think, that the persistence of racism means that racial ascriptions have negative consequences for some and positive consequences for others – creating, in particular, the white-skin privilege that it is so easy for people who have it to forget; and it is clear, too, that for those who suffer from the negative consequences, racial identification is a predictable response, especially where the project it suggests is that the victims of racism should join together to resist it.

[...]

Cultural Identity in an Age of Multiculturalism

Most contemporary racial identification – whether it occurs in such obviously regressive forms as the white nationalism of the Aryan Nation or in an Afrocentrism about which, I believe, a more nuanced position is appropriate – most naturally expresses itself in forms that adhere to modified (and sometimes unreconstructed) versions of the old racial essences. But the legacy of the Holocaust and the old racist biology has led many to be wary of racial essences and to replace them with cultural essences. Before I turn to my final cautionary words about racial identifications, I want to explore, for a moment, the substitution of cultures for races that has occurred in the movement for multiculturalism.

In my dictionary I find as a definition for 'culture' 'the totality of socially transmitted behavior patterns, arts, beliefs, institutions and all other products of human work and thought'.[7] Like most dictionary definitions, this is, no doubt, a proposal on which one could improve. But it surely picks out a familiar constellation of ideas. That is, in fact, the sense in which anthropologists largely use the term nowadays. The culture of the Asante or the Zuni, for the anthropologist, includes every object they make – material culture – and everything they think and do.

The dictionary definition could have stopped there, leaving out the talk of 'socially transmitted behavior patterns, arts, beliefs, institutions' because these *are* all products of human work and thought. They are mentioned because they are the residue of an older idea of culture than the anthropological one; some-thing more like the idea we might now express with the word 'civilization': the 'socially transmitted behavior patterns' of ritual, etiquette, religion, games, arts; the values that they engender and reflect; and the institutions – family, school, church, state – that shape and are shaped by them.[8] The habit of shaking hands at meetings belongs to culture in the anthropologist's sense; the works of Sandro Botticelli and Martin Buber and Count Basie belong to culture also, but they belong to civilization as well.

There are tensions between the concepts of culture and of civilization. There is nothing, for example, that requires that an American culture should be a totality in any stronger sense than being the sum of all the things we make and do.

American civilization, on the other hand, would have to have a certain coherence. Some of what is done in America by Americans would not belong to American civilization because it was too individual (the particular bedtime rituals of a particular American family); some would not belong because it was not properly American, because (like a Hindi sentence, spoken in America) it does not properly cohere with the rest.

The second, connected, difference between culture and civilization is that the latter takes values to be more central to the enterprise, in two ways. First, civilization is centrally defined by moral and aesthetic values: and the coherence of a civilization is, primarily, the coherence of those values with each other and, then, of the group's behavior and institutions with its values. Second, civiliza-tions are essentially to be evaluated: they can be better and worse, richer and poorer, more and less interesting. Anthropologists, on the whole, tend now to avoid the relative evaluation of cultures, adopting a sort of cultural relativism, whose coherence philosophers have tended to doubt. And they do not take values as more central to culture than, for example, beliefs, ideas and practices.

The move from 'civilization' to 'culture' was the result of arguments. The move away from evaluation came first, once people recognized that much evaluation of other cultures by the Europeans and Americans who invented anthropology had been both ignorant and biased. Earlier criticisms of 'lower' peoples turned out to involve crucial misunderstandings of their ideas; and it eventually seemed clear enough, too, that nothing more than differences of upbringing underlay the distaste of some Westerners for unfamiliar habits. It is a poor move from recognizing certain evaluations as mistaken to giving up evaluation altogether, and anthropologists who adopt cultural relativism often preach more than practice it. Still, this cultural relativism was a response to real errors. That it is the wrong response doesn't make the errors any less erroneous.

The arguments against 'civilization' were in place well before the midcentury. More recently, anthropologists began to see that the idea of the coherence of a civilization got in the way of understanding important facts about other societies (and, in the end, about our own). For even in some of the 'simplest' societies, there are different values and practices and beliefs and interests

337

associated with different social groups (for example, women as opposed to men). To think of a civilization as coherent was to miss the fact that these different values and beliefs were not merely different but actually opposed. Worse, what had been presented as the coherent unified worldview of a tribal people often turned out, on later inspection, to be merely the ideology of a dominant group or interest.

But the very idea of a coherent structure of beliefs and values and practices depends on a model of culture that does not fit our times.

[...]

A COMMON CULTURE

There is an ideal – and thus to a certain extent imaginary – type of small-scale, technologically uncomplicated, face-to-face society, where most interactions are with people whom you know, that we call 'traditional'. In such a society every adult who is not mentally disabled speaks the same language. All share a vocabulary and a grammar and an accent. While there will be some words in the language that are not known by everybody – the names of medicinal herbs, the language of some religious rituals – most are known to all normal adults. To share a language is to participate in a complex set of mutual expectations and understandings: but in such a society it is not only linguistic behavior that is coordinated through universally known expectations and understandings. People will share an understanding of many practices – marriages, funerals, other rites of passage – and will largely share their views about the general workings not only of the social but also of the natural world. Even those who are skeptical about particular elements of belief will nevertheless know what everyone is supposed to believe, and they will know it in enough detail to behave very often as if they believed it, too.

A similar point applies to many of the values of such societies. It may well be that some people, even some groups, do not share the values that are enunciated in public and taught to children. But, once more, the standard values are universally known, and even those who do not share them know what it would be to act in conformity with them and probably do so much of the time.

In such a traditional society we may speak of these shared beliefs, values, signs and symbols as the common culture; not, to insist on a crucial point, in the sense that everyone in the group actually holds the beliefs and values but in the sense that everybody knows what they are and everybody knows that they are widely held in the society.

Now, the citizens of one of those large 'imagined communities' of modernity we call 'nations' need not have, in this sense, a common culture. There is no single shared body of ideas and practices in India, or, to take another example, in most contemporary African states. And there is not now and there has never been a common culture in the United States, either. The reason is simple: the United States has always been multilingual, and has always had minorities who did not speak or understand English. It has always had a plurality of religious traditions; beginning with American Indian religions and Puritans and Catholics and Jews and including now many varieties of Islam, Buddhism, Jainism, Taoism, Bahai and so on. And many of these religious traditions have been quite unknown to one another. More than this, Americans have also always differed significantly even among those who do speak English, from North to South and East to West, and from country to city, in customs of greeting, notions of civility and a whole host of other ways. The notion that what has held the United States together historically over its great geographical range is a common culture, like the common culture of my traditional society, is – to put it politely – not sociologically plausible.

The observation that there is no common American national culture will come as a surprise to many: observations about American culture, taken as a whole, are common. It is, for example, held to be individualist, litigious, racially obsessed. I think each of these claims is actually true, because what I mean when I say there is no common culture of the United States is not what is denied by someone who says that there is an American culture.

Such a person is describing large-scale tendencies within American life that are not necessarily participated in by all Americans. I do not mean to deny that these exist. But for such a tendency to be part of what I am calling the *common culture* they would have to derive from beliefs and values and practices (almost) universally shared and known to be so. And *that* they are not.

At the same time, it has also always been true that there was a dominant culture in these United States. It was Christian, it spoke English and it identified with the high cultural traditions of Europe and, more particularly, of England. This dominant culture included much of the common culture of the dominant classes – the government and business and cultural elites – but it was familiar to many others who were subordinate to them. And it was not merely an effect but also an instrument of their domination.

The United States of America, then, has always been a society of many common cultures, which I will call, for convenience, subcultures, (noting, for the record, that this is not the way the word is used in sociology).

It would be natural, in the current climate, with its talk of multiculturalism, to assume that the primary subgroups to which these subcultures are attached will be ethnic and racial groups (with religious denominations conceived of as a species of ethnic group). It would be natural, too, to think that the characteristic difficulties of a multicultural society arise largely from the cultural differences between ethnic groups. I think this easy assimilation of ethnic and racial subgroups to subcultures is to be resisted.

First of all, it needs to be argued, and not simply assumed, that black Americans, say, taken as a group, *have* a common culture: values and beliefs and practices that they share and that they do not share with others. This is equally true for, say, Chinese-Americans; and it is *a fortiori* true of white Americans. What seems clear enough is that being an African-American or an

Asian-American or white is an important social identity in the United States. Whether these are important social identities because these groups have shared common cultures is, on the other hand, quite doubtful, not least because it is doubtful whether they *have* common cultures at all.

The issue is important because an analysis of America's struggle with difference as a struggle among cultures suggests a mistaken analysis of how the problems of diversity arise. With differing cultures, we might expect misunderstandings arising out of ignorance of each others' values, practices, and beliefs; we might even expect conflicts because of differing values or beliefs. The paradigms of difficulty in a society of many cultures are misunderstandings of a word or a gesture; conflicts over who should take custody of the children after a divorce; whether to go to the doctor or to the priest for healing.

Once we move from talking of cultures to identities whole new kinds of problems come into view. Racial and ethnic identities are, for example, essentially contrastive and relate centrally to social and political power; in this way they are like genders and sexualities.

Now, it is crucial to understanding gender and sexuality that women and men and gay and straight people grow up together in families, communities, denominations. Insofar as a common culture means common beliefs, values and practices, gay people and straight people in most places have a common culture: and while there are societies in which the socialization of children is so structured by gender that women and men have seriously distinct cultures, this is not a feature of most 'modern' societies. And it is perfectly possible for a black and a white American to grow up together in a shared adoptive family – with the same knowledge and values – and still grow into separate racial identities, in part because their experience outside the family, in public space, is bound to be racially differentiated.

I have insisted that we should distinguish between cultures and identities; but ethnic identities characteristically have cultural distinctions as one of their primary marks. That is why it is so easy to conflate them. Ethnic identities are created in family and community life. These – along with mass-mediated culture, the school, and the college – are, for most of us, the central sites of the social transmission of culture. Distinct practices, ideas, norms go with each ethnicity in part because people *want* to be ethnically distinct: because many people want the sense of solidarity that comes from being unlike others. With ethnicity in modern society, it is often the distinct identity that comes first, and the cultural distinction that is created and maintained because of it – not the other way around. The distinctive common cultures of ethnic and religious identities matter not simply because of their contents but also as markers of those identities.

[...]

Many African-Americans, on the other hand, have cultural lives in which the ways they eat, the churches they go to, the music they listen to, and the ways they speak *are* marked as black: their identities are marked by cultural differences.

I have insisted that African-Americans do not have a single culture, in the sense of shared language, values, practices, and meanings. But many people who think of races as groups defined by shared cultures, conceive that sharing in a different way. They understand black people as sharing black culture *by definition*: jazz or hip-hop belongs to an African-American, whether she likes it or knows anything about it, because it is culturally marked as black. Jazz belongs to a black person who knows nothing about it more fully or naturally than it does to a white jazzman.

[…]

The connection between individual identity, on the one hand, and race and other collective identities, on the other, seems to be something like this: each person's individual identity is seen as having two major dimensions. There is a collective dimension, the intersection of her collective identities; and there is what I will call a personal dimension, consisting of other socially or morally important features of the person – intelligence, charm, wit, cupidity – that are not themselves the basis of forms of collective identity.

The distinction between these two dimensions of identity is, so to speak, a sociological rather than a logical distinction. In each dimension we are talking about properties that are important for social life. But only the collective identities count as social categories, kinds of person. There is a logical category but no social category of the witty, or the clever, or the charming, or the greedy: people who share these properties do not constitute a social group, in the relevant sense. The concept of authenticity is central to the connection between these two dimensions; and there is a problem in many current understandings of that relationship, a misunderstanding one can find, for example, in Charles Taylor's recent (brilliant) essay *Multiculturalism and the Politics of Recognition*.

[…]

BEYOND IDENTITY

The large collective identities that call for recognition come with notions of how a proper person of that kind behaves: it is not that there is *one* way that blacks should behave, but that there are proper black modes of behavior. These notions provide loose norms or models, which play a role in shaping the life plans of those who make these collective identities central to their individual identities; of the identifications of those who fly under these banners.[9] Collective identities, in short, provide what we might call scripts: narratives that people can use in shaping their life plans and in telling their life stories. In our society (though not, perhaps, in the England of Addison and Steele) being witty does not in this way suggest the life script of 'the wit'. And that is why

341

what I called the personal dimensions of identity work differently from the collective ones.

This is not just a point about modern Westerners: cross-culturally it matters to people that their lives have a certain narrative unity; they want to be able to tell a story of their lives that makes sense. The story – my story – should cohere in the way appropriate by the standards made available in my culture to a person of my identity. In telling that story, how I fit into the wider story of various collectivities is, for most of us, important. It is not just gender identities that give shape (through, for example, rites of passage into woman – or manhood) to one's life: ethnic and national identities too fit each individual story into a larger narrative. And some of the most 'individualist' of individuals value such things. Hobbes spoke of the desire for glory as one of the dominating impulses of human beings, one that was bound to make trouble for social life. But glory can consist in fitting and being seen to fit into a collective history: and so, in the name of glory, one can end up doing the most social things of all.

How does this general idea apply to our current situation in the multicultural West? We live in societies in which certain individuals have not been treated with equal dignity because they were, for example, women, homosexuals, blacks, Catholics. Because, as Taylor so persuasively argues, our identities are dialogically shaped, people who have these characteristics find them central – often, negatively central – to their identities. Nowadays there is a widespread agreement that the insults to their dignity and the limitations of their autonomy imposed in the name of these collective identities are seriously wrong. One form of healing of the self that those who have these identities participate in is learning to see these collective identities not as sources of limitation and insult but as a valuable part of what they centrally are. Because the ethics of authenticity requires us to express what we centrally are in our lives, they move next to the demand that they be recognized in social life as women, homosexuals, blacks, Catholics. Because there was no good reason to treat people of these sorts badly, and because the culture continues to provide degrading images of them nevertheless, they demand that we do cultural work to resist the stereotypes, to challenge the insults, to lift the restrictions.

These old restrictions suggested life scripts for the bearers of these identities, but they were negative ones. In order to construct a life with dignity, it seems natural to take the collective identity and construct positive life scripts instead.

An African-American after the Black Power movement takes the old script of self-hatred, the script in which he or she is a nigger, and works, in community with others, to construct a series of positive black life scripts. In these life scripts, being a Negro is recoded as being black: and this requires, among other things, refusing to assimilate to white norms of speech and behavior. And if one is to be black in a society that is racist then one has constantly to deal with assaults on one's dignity. In this context, insisting on the right to live a dignified life will not be enough. It will not even be enough to require that one be treated with equal dignity despite being black: for that will require a concession that being black counts naturally or to some degree against one's dignity. And so one will end up asking to be respected *as a black*.

I hope I seem sympathetic to this story. I *am* sympathetic. I see how the story goes. It may even be historically, strategically necessary for the story to go this way.[10] But I think we need to go on to the next necessary step, which is to ask whether the identities constructed in this way are ones we can all be happy with in the longer run. What demanding respect for people *as blacks* or *as gays* requires is that there be some scripts that go with being an African-American or having same-sex desires. There will be proper ways of being black and gay: there will be expectations to be met; demands will be made. It is at this point that someone who takes autonomy seriously will want to ask whether we have not replaced one kind of tyranny with another. If I had to choose between Uncle Tom and Black Power, I would, of course, choose the latter. But I would like not to have to choose. I would like other options. The politics of recognition requires that one's skin color, one's sexual body, should be politically acknowledged in ways that make it hard for those who want to treat their skin and their sexual body as personal dimensions of the self. And 'personal' doesn't mean 'secret' but 'not too tightly scripted', 'not too constrained by the demands and expectations of others'.

In short, so it seems to me, those who see potential for conflict between individual freedom and the politics of identity are right.

[…]

Collective identities have a tendency, if I may coin a phrase, to 'go imperial', dominating not only people of other identities, but the other identities, whose shape is exactly what makes each of us what we individually and distinctively are.

In policing this imperialism of identity – an imperialism as visible in racial identities as anywhere else – it is crucial to remember always that we are not simply black or white or yellow or brown, gay or straight or bisexual, Jewish, Christian, Moslem, Buddhist or Confucian but that we are also brothers and sisters; parents and children; liberals, conservatives and leftists; teachers and lawyers and auto-makers and gardeners; fans of the Padres and the Bruins; amateurs of grunge rock and lovers of Wagner; movie buffs; MTV-holics, mystery-readers; surfers and singers; poets and pet-lovers; students and teachers; friends and lovers. Racial identity can be the basis of resistance to racism; but even as we struggle against racism – and though we have made great progress, we have further still to go – let us not let our racial identities subject us to new tyrannies.

IN CONCLUSION

Much of what I have had to say in this essay will, no doubt, seem negative. It is true that I have defended an analytical notion of racial identity, but I have gone to worry about too hearty an endorsement of racial identification. Let me quote Matthew Arnold: 'I thought, and I still think, that in this [Celtic] controversy, as in other controversies, it is most desirable both to believe and to profess that the work of construction is the fruitful and important work, and that we are demolishing only to prepare for it.'[11] So here are my positive proposals: live with fractured identities; engage in identity play; find solidarity, yes, but recognize contingency, and, above all, practice irony.[12] In short I have only the proposals of a banal 'postmodernism'. And there is a regular response to these ideas from those who speak for the identities that now demand recognition, identities toward which so many people have struggled in dealing with the obstacles created by sexism, racism, homophobia. 'It's all very well for you. You academics live a privileged life; you have steady jobs; solid incomes; status from your place in maintaining cultural capital. Trifle with your own identities, if you like; but leave mine alone.'

To which I answer only: my job as an intellectual is to call it as I see it. I owe my fellow citizens respect, certainly, but not a feigned acquiescence. I have a duty to reflect on the probable consequences of what I say; and then, if I still think it worth saying, to accept responsibility for them. If I am wrong, I say, you do not need to plead that I should tolerate error for the sake of human liberation; you need only correct me. But if I am right, so it seems to me, there is a work of the imagination that we need to begin.

And so I look forward to taking up, along with others, the fruitful imaginative work of constructing collective identities for a democratic nation in a world of democratic nations; work that must go hand in hand with cultivating democracy here and encouraging it everywhere else. About the identities that will be useful in this project, let me say only this: the identities we need will have to recognize *both* the centrality of difference within human identity *and* the fundamental moral unity of humanity.

NOTES

1. See Kevin Mulroy, *Freedom on the Border: The Seminole Maroons in Florida, the Indian Territory, Coahuila, and Texas* (Lubbock, TX: Texas Tech University Press, 1993).
2. Ian Hacking, 'Making Up People' reprinted from *Reconstructing Individualism: Autonomy, Individuality and the Self in Western Thought*, Thomas Heller, Morton Sousa, and David Wellbery (eds) (Stanford: Stanford University Press, 1986), in *Forms of Desire: Sexual Orientation and the Social Constructionist Controversy*, Edward Stein (ed.) (New York: Routledge, 1992), pp. 69–88 (page references are to this version).
3. Hacking, 'Making Up People', p. 87.
4. That I don't recall it doesn't *prove* that I didn't, of course.
5. See Mary C. Waters, *Ethnic Options: Choosing Identities in America* (Berkeley and Los Angeles: University of California Press, 1990).
6. This is the proposal of a paper on metaphysical racism by Berel Lang at the New School for Social Research seminar 'Race and Philosophy' in October 1994, from which I learned much.
7. *American Heritage Dictionary III for DOS* (3rd ed.) (Novato, CA: Wordstar International Incorporated, 1993).

8. The distinction between culture and civilization I am marking is not one that would have been thus marked in nineteenth-century ethnography or (as we would now say) social anthropology: culture and civilization were basically synonyms, and they were both primarily used in the singular. The distinctions I am making draw on what I take to be the contemporary resonances of these two words. If I had more time, I would explore the history of the culture concept the sort of way we have explored 'race'.

9. I say 'make' here not because I think there is always conscious attention to the shaping of life plans or a substantial experience of choice but because I want to stress the antiessentialist point that there are choices that can be made.

10. Compare what Sartre wrote in his 'Orphée Noir', in *Anthologie de la Nouvelle Poésie Nègre et Malagache de Langue Francaise*, L. S. Senghor (ed.), p. xiv. Sartre argued, in effect, that this move is a necessary step in a dialectical progression. In this passage he explicitly argues that what he calls an 'antiracist racism' is a path to the 'final unity ... the abolition of differences of race'.

11. Arnold, *On the Study of Celtic Literature*, p. ix.

12. See, for example, Richard Rorty, *Contingency, Irony and Solidarity* (New York: Cambridge University Press, 1989), and my review of it: 'Metaphys. Ed', *Village Voice*, 19 September 1989 p. 55.

54

KILLING RAGE: ENDING RACISM

bell hooks

Nationalist appeals for a unitary representation of blackness tend to emphasize notions of authenticity that uphold a vision of patriarchal family life and of nationhood as the only possible structures wherein the crisis in black identity can be resolved. Studies of patriarchal black families or anti-racist organizations structured on the same hierarchical model would reveal that these structures reinscribe patterns of domination rather than disrupt or alter them. Yet even in the face of overwhelming evidence that the patriarchal family is not a site of redemption and healing, many African Americans desperately cling to the assumption that the pain in black life can be healed by establishing patriarchy and black nationalist identity. Those black folks who attempt to question the tropes of nation and family tend to be dismissed as traitors to the race, as assimilationists. This is especially true for black women who critique black nationalism from a feminist standpoint.

So far all expressions of black nationalism in the United States deploy a rhetoric of redemption that valorizes patriarchal thinking and male domination. Embedded in all forms of nationalist thought is the acceptance and affirmation of sexist exploitation and oppression. To build nations and 'pure' races the bodies of women must be controlled, our sexual activities policed and our reproductive rights curtailed. Since so many black females have been conscious of the need to resist sexist thinking, contemporary black nationalist groups can no longer recruit black women by overtly announcing their support

From: bell hooks, *killing rage: ending racism* (London: Penguin Books, 1995).

of patriarchal thinking. To appeal to black females much contemporary black nationalist writing attempts to incorporate gender in ways that superficially appear to be progressive. However, like the patriarchal Eurocentric model of social organization it critiques and repudiates, within Afrocentric scholarship black women writers frame their discourse in relation to knowledge received from patriarchal black male elders. Gender relations are talked about in much the same way as a Eurocentric thinker like Ivan Illich presents them in his work when he evokes a nostalgic precapitalist world where men and women had their separate but equal domains, respected one another, and lived in harmony with the natural world. Similarly, Afrocentric constructions of a utopian all-black world where men and women share power equally are evoked to counter critiques that call attention to the link between patriarchal thinking and black nationalism. In the black separatist imagination, feminism is reinvented as always and only a white woman's issue. Setting the boundaries in this way constructs another essentialist paradigm wherein black women who embrace feminist thinking can be deemed inauthentic, traitors to the race.

Feminist critique is particularly threatening to black nationalism precisely because it highlights the contradictory relation to structures of domination in the black imagination. Black folks who can speak eloquently about racism, opposing exploitation and dehumanization, deny the value of these same critiques when they are raised within a discourse of gender. The correlations between the structures of racist oppression and exploitation and patriarchal domination are so obvious that to ignore them requires the closing off of the mind. Significantly, nationalist black spokespersons who recognize Malcolm X as a leader and teacher tend to disregard the progressive thinking about gender that is present in the writings and conversations completed shortly before his death. The inability of black nationalist thinkers to conceive of any paradigm for nation and family life that is not patriarchal reveals the depths of black male longing to assert hierarchical control and power. Though critical of white cultural imperialism, nationalist black males see no contradiction between that analysis and their support of hierarchical models of social organization that affirm coercive control and domination of others. Ideas of nation and family that surface in contemporary black nationalist writing mirror the white supremacist nation-state that is benevolently patriarchal. A distinction must be made between overt brutal domination of women by men, which most Afrocentric thinkers clearly repudiate as do their white counterparts, and the Enlightenment vision of a world where men are inherently the protectors and caretakers of women and children that evokes a benevolent model of patriarchal organization of society that is assumed to be directly mirroring a 'natural' order.

At its best, black nationalist thought seeks to revise and redress white Western biases, especially as they overdetermine ways of knowing, critique white supremacy, and offer black folks grounding in an oppositional worldview that promotes black self-determination. Within the framework of an institutionalized patriarchal theory and practice of black nationalism, these positive dimensions are undermined. It is the failure of black nationalism to offer an inclusive complex understanding of black identity, one that is not sexist, homophobic, patriarchal, or supportive of capitalism, that renders it suspect and politically problematic.

[...]

The contemporary crisis of identity is best resolved by our collective willingness as African Americans to acknowledge that there is no monolithic black community, no normative black identity. There is a shared history that frames the construction of our diverse black experiences. Knowledge of that history is needed by everyone as we seek to construct self and identity. In *Race Matters*, Cornel West suggests that it is only as we critically interrogate notions of black authenticity, closed-ranks mentality, and black cultural conservatism that we can begin to really theorize complex understandings of black subjectivity. Insisting that we need new frameworks, West declares:

> This new framework should be a prophetic one of moral reasoning with its fundamental ideas of a mature black identity, coalition strategy, and black cultural democracy. Instead of cathartic appeals to black authenticity, a prophetic viewpoint bases mature black self-love and self-response on the moral quality of black responses to undeniable racist degradation in the American past and present. These responses assume neither a black essence that all black people share nor one black perspective to which all black people should adhere.

While the insights West shares should guide African Americans in our collective effort to retheorize black identity, like many nationalist thinkers with whom he does not agree, his concern with black response to whiteness seems to undermine his insistence on a complex understanding of black identity. West asserts: 'Mature black identity results from an acknowledgement of the specific response to white supremacist abuses and a moral assessment of these responses such that the humanity of black people does not rest on deifying or demonizing others.' Penetrating critiques of narrow nationalism like the one West offers are necessary. However, we need to make those critiques within a prophetic discursive framework where we insist on theorizing black identity from multiple locations, not simply in relation to white supremacy.

A fundamental characteristic of being black in white supremacist capitalist patriarchy is that we are all socialized to believe that only race matters. Hence black folks often do not accord other aspects of experience such as class, sexual practice, etc. serious regard as we think about constructing self and identity. While it certainly is important for black folks to foreground discussions of white supremacy, it is equally important for us to affirm that liberation takes place only in a context where we are able to imagine subjectivities that are diverse, constantly changing, and always operating in states of cultural contingency. To embrace and accept fluid black subjectivities, African-American attachment to a notion of the unitary self must be broken. African Americans must embrace the progressive political understanding of diasporic black identity.

55

LOOSE CANONS – NOTES ON THE CULTURAL WARS

Henry Louis Gates

'Race' as a meaningful criterion within the biological sciences has long been recognized to be a fiction. When we speak of the 'white race' or the 'black race', the 'Jewish race' or the 'Aryan race', we speak in misnomers, biologically, and in metaphors, more generally. Nevertheless, our conservations are replete with usages of *race* which have their sources in the dubious pseudo-science of the eighteenth and nineteenth centuries.

[. . .]

Race has become a trope of ultimate, irreducible difference between cultures, linguistic groups or practitioners of specific belief systems, who more often than not have fundamentally opposed economic interests. Race is the ultimate trope of difference because it is so very arbitrary in its application. The sanction of biology contained in sexual difference, simply put, does not and can never obtain when one is speaking of 'racial difference'. Yet, we carelessly use language in such a way as to *will* this sense of *natural* difference into our formulations. To do so is to engage in a pernicious act of language, one which exacerbates the complex problem of cultural or 'ethnic' difference, rather than assuages or redresses it. This is especially the case at a time when racism has become fashionable, once again. That, literally every day, scores of people are killed in the name of differences ascribed to 'race' only makes even more imperative this gesture to 'deconstruct', if you will, the ideas of difference

From: Henry Louis Gates, Jr., *Loose Canons: Notes on the Cultural Wars* (New York and Oxford: Oxford University Press, 1992).

inscribed in the trope of race, to take discourse itself as our common subject to be explicated to reveal the latent relations of power and knowledge inherent in popular and academic usages of 'race'.

[...]

To say that ethnic identity is socially constructed is not to say that it is somehow unreal, to deny the complexities of our own positionality, to claim that these are not differences that make a difference.

We cannot, finally, succumb to the temptation to resurrect our own version of the Thought Police, who would determine who, and what, is 'black'. 'Mirror, Mirror on the Wall, Who's the Blackest One of All?' is a question best left behind in the sixties. If we allow ourselves to succumb to the urge to build an academic discipline around this perverse question, we will, like the fairy-tale witch, die from our own poison. For if the coming century in this country is multicolored, it is a blackness without blood that *we* must pass on.

[...]

As a humanist, I am just as concerned that so many of my colleagues, on the one hand, feel that the prime motivation for a diverse curriculum is population shifts, as I am that those opposing diversity see it as fore-closing the possibility of a shared 'American' identity. Both sides quickly resort to a grandly communitarian rhetoric. Both think they're struggling for the very soul of America. But if academic politics quickly becomes a *bellum omnium contra omnes*, perhaps it's time to wish a *pax* on both their houses.

What is multiculturalism, and why are they saying such terrible things about it? We've been told it threatens to fragment American culture into a warren of ethnic enclaves, each separate and inviolate. We've been told that it menaces the Western tradition of literature and the arts. We've been told it aims to politicize the school curriculum, replacing honest historical scholarship with a 'feel good' syllabus designed solely to bolster the self-esteem of minorities. The alarm has been sounded, and many scholars and educators – liberals as well as conservatives – have responded to it. After all, if multiculturalism is just a pretty name for ethnic chauvinism, who needs it?

There is, of course, a liberal rejoinder to these concerns, which says that this isn't what multiculturalism is – or at least not what it ought to be. The liberal pluralist insists that the debate has been miscast from the beginning and that it is worth setting the main issues straight.

There's no denying that the multicultural initiative arose, in part, because of the fragmentation of American society by ethnicity, class, and gender. To make it the culprit for this fragmentation is to mistake effect for cause. Mayor Dinkins's metaphor about New York as a 'gorgeous mosaic' is catchy but unhelpful, if it means that each culture is fixed in place and separated by grout. Perhaps we should try to think of American culture as a conversation among different voices – even if it's a conversation that some of us weren't able to join until recently. Perhaps we should think about education, as the conservative philosopher Michael Oakeshott proposed, as 'an invitation into the art of this conversation in which we learn to recognize the voices', each conditioned, as he says, by a different perception of the world. Common sense says that you don't bracket ninety per cent of the world's cultural heritage if you really want to learn about the world.

To insist that we 'master our own culture' before learning others only defers the vexed question: What gets to count as 'our' culture? What makes knowledge worth knowing? Unfortunately, as history has taught us, an Anglo-American regional culture has too often masked itself as universal, passing itself off as our 'common culture', and depicting different cultural traditions as 'tribal' or 'parochial'. So it's only when we're free to explore the complexities of our hyphenated American culture that we can discover what a genuinely common American culture might actually look like. Common sense (Gramscian or otherwise) reminds us that we're *all* ethnics, and the challenge of transcending ethnic chauvinism is one we all face.

Granted, multiculturalism is no magic panacea for our social ills. We're worried when Johnny can't read. We're worried when Johnny can't add. But shouldn't we be worried, too, when Johnny tramples gravestones in a Jewish cemetery or scrawls racial epithets on a dormitory wall? It's a fact about this country that we've entrusted our schools with the fashioning and refashioning of a democratic polity; that's why the schooling of America has always been a matter of political judgment. But in America, a nation that has theorized itself as plural from its inception, our schools have a very special task.

The society we have made simply won't survive without the values of tolerance. And cultural tolerance comes to nothing without cultural understanding. In short, the challenge facing America in the next century will be the shaping, at long last, of a truly common public culture, one responsive to the long-silenced cultures of color. If we relinquish the ideal of America as a plural nation, we've abandoned the very experiment that America represents.

SECTION 4
CIVIL SOCIETY, SOCIAL THEORY
AND THE TASK OF INTELLECTUALS

This section opens with an excerpt from Jean L. Cohen and Andrew Arato's discussion of the concept and idea of civil society in their groundbreaking book *Civil Society and Political Theory*. What made Cohen and Arato's book so important was not only their discussion of the various streams of the civil society concept but also their own attempt to re-conceptualise the very idea. In particular they argue against a one-dimensional concept of civil society. However, as in other civil society theories, the idea of a revival of the public sphere is crucial for injecting new life into civil society, thus helping to 'democratise democracy'.

After the fall of the Berlin Wall and against the backdrop of an American political science suffering from self-congratulatory complacency, the call for a renewal of civil society was badly needed. In his essay 'The Strange Silence of Political Theory' (published in his *Democracy in Dark Times*) the political scientist Jeffrey C. Isaac argued against the 'deafening silence' of American political theory. While in the past there used to be an open exchange of ideas between Europe and America – Isaac reminds the reader of such figures as Jefferson, Madison, Paine and Burke, who all had a vivid interest in what was going on in the world – there is now no listening and little learning. However, how and what exactly Americans can learn from '1989' and the collapse of Communism remained an unanswered question in Isaac's piece. In this respect the contributions of Jeffrey C. Goldfarb prove to be more specific. In his study *Civility and Subversion*, Goldfarb explores a wide range of possibilities on how American society can learn from '1989'. Goldfarb looks at the possibilities of renewing the public sphere through the development of genuine space for deliberation that is not limited to the few. He makes clear that the task of intellectuals in 'democratising democracy' is complicated and marked by the paradox that intellectual argument is usually elitist, while democracy strives generally towards maximum involvement and participation. The problem, as Goldfarb sees it, is to get the balance right.

Crucial in all the debates on modern civil society is the role of the public sphere and, within it, the question of maximum participation. As the following readings show, the situation of and full participation from women is something to be desired. However, how exactly women should contribute in the public sphere is hotly debated. In her essay 'Antigone's Daughters' Jean Bethke Elshtain elaborates on a classic theme – Antigone representing the 'private' female multilayered identity-in-process that throws sand into the public machine. Such 'social feminism' that attributes the private with the good and the public as its bad antithesis is criticised by Mary G. Dietz. She argues that 'good mothers' (and other female characters) can of course be good citizens but that being good mothers doesn't necessarily qualify them automatically as good citizens.

What needs to be studied especially is the concrete history, that is the shifts between the public and the private spheres. Re-interpreting Habermas' seminal work *The Structural Transformation of the Public Sphere* with critical feminist eyes, the historian Mary P. Ryan has attempted to write the history of the American public sphere by looking at the role and participation of women.

The last contribution from Jeffrey C. Alexander is an attempt to synthesise some of the ideas that are related to the very idea of civil society. One of the achievements of Alexander's efforts is to integrate some of the criticism that has been voiced against the usefulness of the civil society concept, particularly by looking at some of the uncivil elements that still prevail in modern civil society.

56

CIVIL SOCIETY AND POLITICAL THEORY

Jean L. Cohen and Andrew Arato

Those aspects of contemporary institutions that contribute to the autonomy and further rationalization of civil society constitute the positive side; the reified structures that promote colonization, the negative. Here we can only indicate the outlines of the conception that would have to be developed for a theory of the institutional dynamics of contemporary civil society. Our evidence is constituted at this stage only by the tradition of social and political theory that seeks to contest the opposing theses of one-dimensionality and system integration. Even from such a preliminary point of view, we believe that it is possible to claim that the institutional developments of the modern family, of political and cultural public spheres, and of associations are all similarly dualistic.

1. With respect to the family, we support Habermas' challenge to the old Frankfurt thesis (which he used to share) that the assumption of socialization by the schools and the mass media and the loss of the property base of the middle-class patriarchal family entails, along with the abolition of the father's authority, the end of ego autonomy. From the standpoint of the system/lifeworld distinction, the picture looks rather different. The freeing of the family from many economic functions and the diversification of the agencies of socialization create a potential for egalitarian interfamilial relations and liberalized socialization processes. The rationality potential of communicative interaction in this sphere is thereby released. Of course, new types of conflicts and even pathologies appear when these potentials are blocked and when the demands of the

From: Jean L. Cohen and Andrew Arato, *Civil Society and Political Theory* (Cambridge, MA: MIT Press, 1992).

formally organized subsystems in which the adult must participate conflict with the capacities and expectations of those who have experienced these emancipatory socialization processes.[1]

2. The principles of democratic legitimacy and representation imply the free discussion of all interests within institutionalized public spheres (parliaments) and the primacy of the lifeworld with respect to the two subsystems. As we have seen in Luhmann, however, uncoupling the centralized public sphere from genuine participation leads to a screening out of a wide range of interests and issues from general discussion. The role of political parties and the electoral process is to aggregate certain important social constellations of interest and to limit, in time and space, more general societal inputs to politics to the narrowest channels of privatized, depoliticized individuals. The political organizations that are to mediate between civil society and politics become bureaucratic organizations of the political system itself, and they defuse rather than actualize democratic participation. Parliaments in this view specialize in the show of decision making; they are smokescreens for decisions made outside all public discussion. Finally, the political public sphere is merely the extension of a commercialized mass culture and is equally manipulated.

But this is not the whole story. Luhmann, for example, is never able to show how elite democracy can avoid both the repoliticization and republicization of spheres outside the political system and the spread of dysfunctional forms of apathy with respect to politics Nor does he satisfactorily explain why elite democracies are forced not only to propagate the official conception of the classical theory of democracy but also to structure important parts of the dramaturgy of political process accordingly. He does not consider the reversal of power relations made possible by this dramaturgy that can easily be played out 'for real'. The empirical case for the predominant, almost exclusive, process of political communication filtering downward is not convincing. Large structural shifts such as the creation of welfare states, but also the current neoliberal turn, seem to respond to many grass-roots initiatives Moreover, the bureaucratic catch-all party form presupposed by elite theorists does not seem to provide sufficient centers of social identification, nor is it able to respond well to the emergence of new issues of great urgency. Thus, some countries have experienced the emergence of extraparliamentary oppositions or parties with a new type of relation to movements. These phenomena have affected the structure of the political public sphere as well. While the central political public sphere, constituted by parliaments and the major media, remains rather (but not everywhere equally!) closed and inaccessible, a plurality of alternative publics, differentiated but interrelated, time and again revives the processes and the quality of political communication. With the emergence of new types of political organizations, even the public discussion in parliaments and party conventions tends to be affected, as has been the case in West Germany. It seems, therefore, that along with the elite democratic, oligarchic tendencies toward the drying up of political public life, we should postulate a contrary, if weaker, trend of redemocratization, based on the new cultural (practical, aesthetic, and cognitive) potentials of the lifeworld.

3. Nor can one construe the development of the mass media as a purely negative sign of the commodification or administrative distortion of communication. This point is especially important because, in Habermas's early thesis on the public sphere, the fusion argument, implying the obliteration of the bridges between state and civil society, works only if the cultural substance of mediation is 'commodified', and 'industrialized'. There is little reason to deny the immense role in our societies of a top-to-bottom, center-to-periphery model of mass communications. Yet generalized forms of communication also deprovincialize, expand and create new publics. In the area of general communications, what we said about the differentiation and pluralization of political publics is even more true. From subcultures to great educational institutions, from political to scientific publics, from social movements to microinstitutions, the spaces for consequential, critical communication have immensely expanded along with the growth of the commercialized and manipulated frameworks of public relations, advertising, and industrial culture. Since the project of an enlightened public sphere was first articulated, we have had neither a single history of decline (the rise of mass culture) nor a process of 'democratization', but two simultaneous histories made possible by democratization: one of the penetration of culture through money and power and another of the renewal of a more universal inclusive, and pluralistic public life made possible by the modernization of the lifeworld. While the first of these processes often seems to be dominant, this is not due to an inevitability latent in the technical means of communication. The technical development of the electronic media does not necessarily lead to centralization; it can involve horizontal, creative, autonomous forms of media pluralism.[2]

4. The problem of associations, which is excluded from Habermas's analysis,[3] is parallel to that of culture, to which it is linked through the structures of the public sphere. As Durkheim and Gramsci realized, the hostility of the modern state and economy to corporate bodies and associations could not block their reemergence and modernization. In this context, the bureaucratization of associations and the emergence of pseudo-pluralist and corporatist forms of interest representation and aggregation, a key dimension of the fusion argument, cannot be considered the only tendency in contemporary associational life. The existence of an immense number of voluntary associations in all liberal democracies,[4] the emergence of new ones in the context of corporatist bargaining, and their role in citizen initiatives and social movements[5] may not demonstrate the somewhat one-sided Parsonian point that ours is the age of association and not bureaucracy; but it is clear that legitimate left criticisms of a pluralist thesis that occludes the highly differential access of various types of associations to the political system should not close our eyes to the validity of this thesis against all claims of atomization and massification in our societies. The resilience of associations and the periodic revival of their

dynamism can be explained through the modernization of the lifeworld and its normative contribution to the scarce resource of solidarity.

5. Finally, the development of legality up to the contemporary democratic welfare state involves both the modernization of civil society and its penetration by administrative agencies. It is, moreover, in the double nature of law itself that one must locate the ambiguous character of the contemporary juridification of society. According to Habermas, as a 'medium', law functions as an organizational means together with money and/or power to *constitute* the structure of economy and administration in such a way that they can be coordinated independently of direct communication. As an 'institution', on the other hand, law is 'a societal component of the lifeworld ... embedded in a broader political, cultural and social context ... in a continuum with moral norms and superimposed communicatively structured areas of action'.[6] Juridification in this sense plays a regulative rather than a constitutive role, expanding and giving a binding form to (the ethical principles of) communicatively coordinated areas of action. This empowering dimension of at least some types of legal regulation is fostered by juridification itself. Foucault's error in this regard, typical of all anarchist postures, is to have focused exclusively on the role of law as medium, while dismissing the freedom-securing, empowering institutional moment as mere show. Both dimensions are present in Luhmann, but by definition they are always present, and thus the tension between the two options and the possibility of choosing between them cannot arise. The distinction between system and lifeworld allows us to contrast and choose (in some areas of life at least) between two forms of legal regulation, only one of which is compatible with the autonomy of the institutional life of civil society.[7]

At first sight, law as institution seems like a weak competitor for law as medium, with the latter expressing the extension of the purposive-regulative activity of welfare-state administrations primarily. The fact that this activity interferes with the reproduction of the lifeworld may appear as an irrelevant externality. However, the reduction of law entirely to a medium, most complete in the political instrumentalization of modern law, is not only an inefficient form of intervention in many life spheres, including the economy, but also leads to that weakening of the normative in law that Luhmann at one time considered to be the function of the positivization of law.[8] This outcome would affect the binary code of right–wrong through which law must operate and would weaken the legitimacy of the legal system as a whole. Law as medium, despite its tendency to replace law as institution, is possible only if law is also an institution. At least a partial choice for law as institution is necessary if the steering functions of law are to be protected.

The choice between law as medium and law as institution does not help with another pressing problem: the legal regulation of the subsystems themselves. Like Habermas' analysis in *The Theory of Communicative Action* of the other alternatives within the structures of existing civil societies, the idea of law as institution tells us only what we should defend against colonization. Hence his inclination, later reversed, to see new social movements as primarily defensive reactions to colonization, hardly constitutive of a politics. It may very well be that the absence of the concept of association, both within the institutional analysis of civil society and with respect to the dynamics of social movements, led Habermas to revive the classical breakdown thesis that understands movements merely as reactions to normative disintegration or other types of dislocations accompanying modernization.[9] Our task is to prove that the recovery of the concept of association, when linked to new ideas of publics and legal regulation, allows the formulation of a new politics of civil society.

THE POLITICS OF CIVIL SOCIETY

We have reconstructed the concept of civil society in terms of the categories of system and lifeworld in order to develop a political theory that might contribute to contemporary democratic projects in both the West and the East. We are concerned, to say the least, about the emergence of three, increasingly dominant, interpretations of the reconstruction of civil society: a neoliberal model that identifies the civil with the bourgeois; an antipolitical model that rigidly juxtaposes society to the state, and an antimodern interpretation that seeks to absorb the modern economy in a less differentiated society. These approaches all have in common a dichotomous model of civil society and state, albeit in different forms. In opposition to state socialism in the East and the welfare state in the West, the neoliberals, the antipoliticians, and the antimoderns variously seek to rebuild a market society, a society animated by cultural or social movements yet free of interest-group and party politics, or a nondifferentiated, socially embedded economy.

Only a model that differentiates civil society from both state and economy, and analyzes the mediations among them, can avoid such misinterpretations of the projects of its reconstruction.

[...]

Societal self-organization, associations, and the public sphere are, of course, the categories of civil society that we have inherited and developed. Initially, it seemed fully acceptable for Habermas to link these categories to each other (and, presumably, to legal institutions) only on the horizontal level, and even then on the basis of an explicit theory not of civil society but of the dimension of the lifeworld that institutionalizes stored-up meanings, solidarities, and competences. However the concept of civil society, unlike that of lifeworld, also involves *vertical* linkages, which can be conceived either as mediations, between individuals and groups, between groups and social institutions, and between social institutions and global political (and presumably economic) institutions, or, in the case of the latter set, as an analytically separate but complementary political (and economic) society. In the Hegelian system, this role is played by family, corporation, estates, and estate parliaments; in Habermas' book on the public sphere, it is played by the family, the literary public sphere, and the political public sphere. In Tocqueville's analysis, many of these mediations are located on the separate analytical level of political society, which in the three-part model must be logically supplemented by economic society.

Whichever of the two basic variants we choose, Hegelian or Tocquevillian, it seems to us that Habermas' current theory of system and lifeworld, which we want to defend on the most abstract level, does not easily allow for either mediations between society and the subsystems or for analytically separated spheres of political and economic society playing analogous roles. Nevertheless, one can use Habermas's analytical framework in a different way than he himself has done.[10]

The abstract categories of system and lifeworld indicate only where the *weight of coordination* lies in a given institutional framework. Cultural, social and personality-reproducing institutions have their center of gravity in com-municative/normative forms of action coordination. Nevertheless, it becomes possible to locate strategic dimensions as well as forms of administration and monetarization in lifeworld institutions (a point that has unduly disturbed critics such as Axel Honneth and Nancy Fraser) without pathological consequences, as long as they remain subordinated to communicative coordination and goal definition and as long as they are not allowed to develop their own logics – the proper meaning of colonization. Whenever pertinent, normatively speaking, this framework allows us (as well as Habermas) to speak of decolonization on the basis of the immanent possibilities within such lifeworld institutions. But we go further, insisting on the possibility of democratizing political and economic institutions.

NOTES

1. For an interesting historical analysis that supports this thesis, see Carl Degler, *At Odds: Women and the Family in America from the Revolution to the Present* (Oxford: Oxford University Press, 1980). Degler argues that the development of the intimate sphere of the family, together with the doctrine of separate spheres and the new conception of childhood, opened up the terrain on which women were able to experience the beginnings of a sense of self, despite the fact that it was tied to the role of wife and mother. It was this new conception that projected them into the 'public' sphere and ultimately led to claims for autonomy and individuality in all spheres of life, thus challenging the patriarchal character of the first form of the companionate family and, ultimately, the doctrine of separate spheres itself.
2. Interpreters from Walter Benjamin to Hans-Magnus Enzensberger have stressed this against the contrary view of Adorno.
3. Habermas may exclude them because of an exaggerated fear of all corporatism and particularism; see 'The New Obscurity'. In this context, the medicine suggested – a combination of universal normative justifications and the pluralism of subcultures – is justified. The fear that these subcultures merely constitute 'a mirror image of the neocorporatistic gray zone' is not justified, however, given the relation of the associations to anything but gray forms of alternative publics.
4. The discussion in Gabriel A. Almond and Sidney Verba, *Civic Culture: Political Attitudes and Democracy in Five Nations* (Princeton, NJ: Princeton University Press, 1953), is still impressive on this point, and they were proved correct by the new movements of the period that followed publication of their book.

5. See chapter 10 of our book (Boston: Beacon Press, 1987).

6. Jürgen Habermas, *Theory of Communicative Action*, vol. 2, ch. 8.

7. The idea of law as a medium does not mean that we conceive of law as a medium of communication like money and power but, rather, that we understand law in some of its capacities, the dominant ones in contemporary society, as functionalized to facilitate the operation of the media of the administrative state and the market economy. In this view, law represents the code through which the genuine medium of power would operate, to use Luhmann's term. The distinction between law as institution and law as medium, moreover, may refer to the same legal code operating in two different ways; for example, the same statute might be applied by administrative courts and also by trial (jury) courts. We might, of course, regard the complete political instrumentalization of law as its reduction to a medium, but this would be identical to the medium of power, which in order to operate must be represented in a code that is, if no longer genuinely legal, then perhaps moral or historical-philosophical or religious. There are, unfortunately, sufficient examples of each of these options today.

Our notion that there are alternatives in contemporary legal processes could be derived by means other than the distinction between law as medium and law as institution. In particular, Unger's distinction among formal, substantive, and procedural law represents a fruitful alternative starting point. Parsons was the first to note an elective affinity between formal law and economic society, between substantive law and state administration, and between procedural law and civil society. It might in fact be better to treat formal and substantive law themselves, in analogy to liberal and welfare-state juridification, as ambiguous from the point of view of civil society, as empowering groups and individuals while also promoting new forms of dependence and unfreedom. As a form of reflexive law, procedural law (that is, procedures applied to other procedures) cannot replace the other types of modern law. The meta level presupposes levels to which it must be applied, in this case in a reflexive manner. However, the increased use of procedural law can reinforce the empowering dimension of substantive and formal law. This could, of course, also be seen as reinforcing the dimension, aspect, or application of law as an institution. While we shall argue later that reflexive law helps introduce a new form of postregulatory regulation of state and economy, it may also represent an important bulwark of the lifeworld against colonization operating through legal codes.

8. See R.M. Unger, *Law in Modern Society* (New York Free Press, 1976), pp. 192–200; F. Ewald, 'A Concept of Social law', and G. Teubner, 'After Legal Instrumentalism? Strategic Models of Post-regulatory Law', both in Teubner (ed.) *Dilemmas of Law in the Welfare State*. Even Luhmann now seems more inclined to accept this historicized position, pointing to the politicization of law in welfare states; see 'The Self-Reproduction of Law and Its Limits', in *Dilemmas of Law in the Welfare State*. He makes the mistake though, of considering the project of 'reflexive law' to be even more destructive of norms than instrumentalization. At times, Unger seems to make a similar mistake, treating substantive and procedural law in an undifferentiated way as both expressive of purposive legal reasoning and destructive of the rule of law; see, for example, *Law in Modern Society*, 195. Elsewhere, though, he rightly notes the incorporation of formality in procedural law, which thus becomes a compromise between formal and substantive law; see, for example, *Law in Modern Society*, 212.

9. See chapter 10 of our book.

10. Habermas employs his own framework in a way that is at times precariously close to Gorz's dualistic schemes, which he nevertheless rejects on a more concrete political level.

57

THE STRANGE SILENCE OF POLITICAL THEORY

Jeffrey C. Isaac

The 'Revolutions of 1989' took the world by storm. Even their participants failed to anticipate how quickly the power of Communist regimes would dissolve in the face of mounting crisis and determined opposition.[1] In a few months the face worn by world politics for five decades was transformed. The Cold War was over, and the dramatic ideological antagonism between communism and liberalism, which had defined the politics of the twentieth century, was concluded with a Communist plea of 'no contest' and the exultant triumph of Western liberalism.[2]

One would have expected that such dramatic and consequential events would have been grist for the mill of American political theorists. The power of ideas in a world of cynicism and manipulation. The relevance of an avowedly humanistic vocabulary in a postmodern age. The nature of democratic movements, the strategies they employ, the choices they face, the kinds of politics they aspire to construct. The emphatic political revival of liberalism at a time of deep philosophical skepticism, a renewed preoccupation with political foundations at a time of anti-foundationalism. The 'meanings' of the revolutions of 1989. The possibilities are virtually endless. And yet, surprisingly, American political theory responded to these events with a deafening silence.

[...]

Historical caution, a determination to let time pass and truly, 'deeply' process events, never deterred the 'great' theorists of the past upon whom we

From: *Political Theory* 23, November 1995.

worshipfully comment again and again. Recall Kant's observation on the French Revolution:

> even if the end viewed in connection with this event should not now be attained, even if the revolution or reform of a national constitution should finally miscarry, or, after some time had elapsed, everything should relapse into its former rut ... that event is too important, too much inter-woven with the interest of humanity, and its influence too widely propagated in all areas of the world to not be recalled on any favorable occasion by the peoples which would then be roused to a repetition of new efforts of this kind.[3]

What R. R. Palmer has called the age of democratic revolutions – 1776–89 – was one of the founding moments of modern political thought.[4] Current events, unprecedented revolutions, provided the raw material, the inspiration behind some of the most seminal theorists of the period – Jefferson and Madison, Paine and Wollstonecraft, de Maistre and Burke, Kant and later Hegel. How to classify such writers? Are they philosophers, politicians, essayists, journalists? Does the classification 'political theorist', with its heavily academic connota-tions, really suffice? There is a striking discrepancy between the passionate engagement in current events that characterized most of the foundational writers of contemporary political theory and the disconnection of contempor-ary political theorists themselves.

[...]

The writings of Havel, Konrad, Michnik and others offer pioneering treatments of important contemporary problems – the nature of civil, non-violent resistance to post-totalitarian dictatorship, the character of self-limiting radicalism in a post-Marxist age, the importance of civil society, the role of the intellectual in the modern world.[5]

But even if it were true that these writers were wholly unoriginal and their politics entirely derivative, this claim could be established only on the basis of a serious engagement with their writings and their politics. It would con-stitute an *interpretation* of the revolutions of 1989, an *argument* that could be supported by evidence and might be debated.[6] What is most striking about recent American political theory is not that it lacks sufficient admiration for these revolutions but that it seems bereft of any interpretation or argument whatsoever.

And absence of originality, the rearticulation of anachronistic themes, in any case, can hardly be considered a reason for dismissal by a discipline marked by a preoccupation with historical texts. Have we stopped writing about Mill because he is a historical figure whose views are no longer modish, his conceptions of subjectivity surpassed by the latest Paris fashions about the constitution of the self? Do we ignore Locke because he is derivative of Hobbes, or Rousseau because he is derivative of Locke? As we of course all know and commonly acknowledge, no theory is wholly original, all theory is derivative, building upon prior idioms, expanding, enriching, reconstituting languages and themes already a part of the cultural and political landscape. So even if the revolutions of 1989 simply reinstated earlier idioms of democratic liberalism, this history would be a reason not to ignore them but to explore their links with earlier idioms and the reasons for them. What are the connections, for example, between Michnik's fascinating writings on the role of the Church in the Polish movement toward democracy and the thinking of early liberal tolerationists such as Locke and Voltaire?[7] What are the linkages between the rhetoric and practices of cosmopolitan federalism being advocated by figures such as Havel and the writings of Montesquieu, Jefferson or Madison?

[...]

Perhaps the fact is that the silence of American political theory is due to an insularity that characterizes American society as a whole. It certainly seems that British, French and German theorists have paid more attention to recent events in Central Europe than have their American counterparts. America has always been apart from the Old World, separated by thousands of miles of ocean, but also by a distinctive political history. While certainly fractious and violent in its own right, American history has always lacked the kind of ideological polarization that has characterized Europe. Our shores and our unique constitutional history have spared us two world wars, the ascendancy of totalitarianism, fifty years in which half of Europe was dominated by Communist dictatorship and all of Europe threatened to become a nuclear battlefield. Americans are far removed from and in some ways blithely indifferent to what is currently going on in Europe.

Daniel Boorstin has suggested that the peculiar genius of America is that it lacks any political theory, that Americans have been able to live liberal democracy while others have had to argue about it.[8] This is of course a controversial and in many ways flawed thesis, but it also highlights a truth, one discerned long ago by Tocqueville. The American Revolution was dramatically unlike the French Revolution that followed it, and American political history has thus been spared the trials and tribulations of having to struggle with the legacies of Jacobinism and anti-Jacobinism that have dominated modern European politics. In this sense American intellectual life has lacked the ideological anchoring so powerful across the Atlantic.

As Emerson, William James and Dewey noted, this lack has been in many ways a blessing, creating opportunities for forms of eclectic, experimental, *pragmatic* political thought unencumbered by ideological orthodoxy.[9] And yet, through a strange twist of fate, this opportunity has largely been squandered. This is a complex matter. Part of the explanation surely lies in the bureaucratic model of university life, imported from Germany in the early part of the twentieth century, which helped to stifle creativity and promote intellectual professionalization.[10] Part of the explanation lies in the intellectual habits of mind that have acquired prominence among American political theorists. One thing is clear: the most dramatic development of contemporary history has been the defeat of the Jacobin revolutionary model by the revolutions of 1989. The Central European democrats have turned for guidance to the United States, to its history of federalism and political pluralism, and to writers, including Tocqueville and Arendt, who have emphasized the unique virtues of American democratic traditions and American forms of political improvisation. And yet, irony of ironies, American political theorists seem transfixed by the French and German philosophical *reactions* to the Jacobin model and its failure. While exciting and also portentous political upheavals proceed in Central Europe, many American theorists remain curiously caught in the orbit of Heidegger and Habermas, Foucault and Derrida, working through the offshoots of a critique of a Marxism that is now for all practical purposes dead. Others remain wedded to a monumental history of ideas that has its roots in German Romanticism, while few remain attentive to political developments taking place before their very eyes.[11]

Almost forty years ago C. Wright Mills published a book, called *The Sociological Imagination*, about the failure of social science to present intelligible and powerful accounts of the intersections between personal experience and political history. Mills demonstrated a variety of ways in which the intellectual habits of modern American academics – hyperempiricism and hyperabstraction, conceptual grandiosity, the use of jargon, the dismissal of historical materials – obstructed clear thinking about politics and abetted the evasion of significant political issues and relations. He argued that social science needed a new vision of intellectual craftsmanship and political vocation, a vision that attended to what was significant, and whose standards of significance transcended the narrow boundaries of academic and professional respectability and convention. In the spirit of Deweyan pragmatism, perhaps the richest idiom of distinctively American theory, Mills endorsed modes of inquiry that illuminated the historical experiences of our time in intellectually serious and morally *relevant* ways.[12]

Postwar American political theory was born in a revolt against many of the academic conventions Mills criticized, yet political theory today is susceptible to much the same criticism.[13] It lacks what we might call a political imagination, a sense of what is significant and a commitment to addressing it in illuminating and accessible ways. In some respects Sheldon Wolin's *Politics and Vision*, published in 1960, clarifies such an imagination, especially in its view of theory as a way of grappling with pressing political issues. But in other ways Wolin's seminal book is the forerunner of today's academicized political theory. For its vision of 'the political' is too highly mediated not by positivistic methodologies but by a series of reflections on classic political thinkers and their contribution to a distinctive vocation of political theory with its own distinctive pedagogy. The result is a high-minded view of theory as a nobler kind of inquiry into an especially virtuous reality, a view that is one of the chief causes of the irrelevance that motivates my discussion.[14]

Wolin's book was perhaps the most important contribution to the effort to establish and defend a distinctive identity for political theory at a time of impending encroachment by behavioral political science. As I see it, the problem with political theory today is exactly the opposite – not that it lacks its own identity but that it is too wedded to its identity as a distinctive, *profound* enterprise, that it values theoretical ingenuity and philosophical declamation over empirical insight or historical relevance.[15]

The world is witnessing drastic and dramatic changes, promising hope but also danger and disaster. The 'end of history' loudly proclaimed in 1989 has given way to a decade of bitter ethno-national conflicts. Political theorists ought to address these changes and to make them intelligible. Just as the American and French revolutions inaugurated an age of democratic reform and conservative counterrevolution, the developments known as the revolutions of 1989 have posed the possibility of new forms of democratic citizenship and new forms of authoritarian reaction. The failure of political theory to address these possibilities represents a missed opportunity for important intellectual work, and indeed belies the field's claim to do serious *political* theory. It also constitutes a grave ethical abdication. For current events present serious choices regarding moral responsibility, political membership and constitutional foundations, choices that political theory might truly help to illuminate. The nondecisions of political theorists in this matter – the decisions to attend to other things – do have ethical consequences. Political theory fiddles while the fire of freedom spreads, and perhaps the world burns.

NOTES

1. See Timothy Garton Ash. *The Magic Lantern* (New York: Random House, 1991).
2. See Francis Fukuyama, 'The End of History', *National Interest* 16 (Summer 1989); Jean-François Revel, *Democracy against Itself: The Future of the Democratic Impulse* (New York: Free Press, 1993); and Larry Diamond and Marc Plattner (eds), *The Global Resurgence of Democracy* (Baltimore: Johns Hopkins University Press, 1993).
3. Immanuel Kant, *On History*, Lewis White Beck (ed.) (Indianapolis: Bobbs-Merrill, 1963), p. 148.
4. R. R. Palmer. *The Age of the Democratic Revolution* (Princeton, NJ: Princeton University Press, 1959).
5. See my 'Civil Society and the Spirit of Revolt', *Dissent* (Summer 1993), pp. 356–61; Jean Elshtain, 'Politics without Cliche', *Social Research* 60 (Fall 1993), pp. 433–44; Jeffrey C. Goldfarb, *Beyond Glasnost: The Post-Totalitarian Mind* (Chicago: University of Chicago Press, 1989) and *After the Fall: The Pursuit of Democracy in Central Europe* (New York: Basic Books, 1992); and especially Jean Cohen and Andrew Arato, *Civil Society and Political Theory* (Cambridge, MA: MIT Press, 1992).
6. Ralf Dahrendorf offers such an interpretation in *Reflections on the Revolution in Europe* (New York: Random House, 1990). A similar though more nuanced interpretation is presented in Jürgen Habermas, 'What Does Socialism Mean Today? The Revolutions of Recuperation and the Need for New Thinking', in Robin Blackburn (ed.) *After the Fall: The Failure of Communism and the Future of Socialism* (London: Verso, 1991), pp. 25–46.

7. I briefly address this theme in 'Adam Michnik: Politics and the Church', *Salmagundi*, no. 103 (Summer 1994), pp. 198–212, an essay on Michnik's pathbreaking *The Church and the Left*, ed. and trans. David Ost (Chicago: University of Chicago Press, 1992).

8. Daniel J. Boorstin, *The Genius of American Politics* (Chicago: University of Chicago Press, 1953).

9. The writing of George Kateb seeks to capture this spirit. See *The Inner Ocean: Individualism and Democratic Culture* (Ithaca, NY: Cornell University Press, 1992).

10. See Peter T. Manicas, *A History and Philosophy of Science* (London: Blackwell, 1989), and C. Wright Mills, *Sociology and Pragmatism* (London: Oxford University Press, 1948).

11. I am not claiming that either the critique of Marxism or the history of ideas has been rendered pointless, but only that it is astonishing how much more powerfully they seem to concern political theorists than recent events that certainly place a different coloration on these pursuits.

12. C. Wright Mills, *The Sociological Imagination* (London: Oxford University Press, 1959).

13. On this score see John G. Gunnell, *The Descent of Political Theory* (Chicago: University of Chicago Press, 1993).

14. While Wolin's book has helped to license an excessive preoccupation with 'the tradition of political philosophy' among many political theorists, his own work has always been marked by an engagement with current political concerns, from his interventions during the Berkeley Free Speech Movement (see Seymour Martin Lipset and Sheldon S. Wolin (eds), *The Berkeley Student Revolt* [New York: Anchor, 1965]), to his editorship of the journal *democracy*, to some of the essays published in *The Presence of the Past* (Baltimore: Johns Hopkins University Press, 1989).

15. For some indications of this concern with subdisciplinary identity, see William E. Connolly. 'From the Editor', *Political Theory* 17 (February 1989), pp. 3–7; and Tracy Strong, 'From the Editor'. *Political Theory* 18 (February 1990), pp. 3–5, and 'From the Editor', *Political Theory* 20 (February 1992), pp. 4–7.

58

CIVILITY AND SUBVERSION: THE INTELLECTUAL IN DEMOCRATIC SOCIETY

Jeffrey C. Goldfarb

Intellectuals have a paradoxical status in democratic societies. On the one (enlightened) hand, democracy requires the cultural excellence intellectuals do contribute, their special knowledge, their creative capacities and their communicative skills. On the other hand, the egalitarian one, in democracies intellectuals and their 'cultural excellence' are viewed with suspicion. Intellectual position is established through hierarchies of judgment. There is such a thing as a good and a bad argument, a fine and a mediocre piece of work, and intellectual power depends upon such judgment. Yet, democracy inculcates an inherent suspicion of hierarchy as a matter of fundamental principle. This conflict, it seems to me, is an ongoing part of the democratic experience, a central problematic of democratic life, making the intellectual's position in democratic society a perpetually uncertain one. Intellectuals have a love-hate relationship with democracy, and democracy has a love-hate relationship with intellectuals.[1]

On the side of love, or at least mutual dependence: democracy is the rule of the people, and to be a viable form of governance it requires an informed and critical citizenry. Democrats need both the expertise and the normative insights provided by the cultural activities of intellectuals in order to pursue the ideal of wise governance. Further and more importantly, they need the opportunity for public deliberations that intellectual contestation opens. In a democracy, an informed public must be capable of making critical judgments, sometimes about complicated matters. Thus intellectuals should take part in public life,

From: Jeffrey C. Goldfarb, *Civility and Subversion: The Intellectual in Democratic Society* (Cambridge: Cambridge University Press, 1998).

and their fellow citizens, or at least their representatives, ought to be informed about the fruits of intellectual activities. Otherwise, some form of tyranny or oligarchy is likely to be more powerful and pervasive. For, if a democratic polity does not draw upon all the sources of available information and good judgment, it will be weakened. The makers of the American Revolution and Constitution – the founding political elite – clearly adhered to such a republican vision, as Gordon Wood has brilliantly underscored.[2]

But Wood has just as clearly demonstrated the instability of the elite's vision. Democracies may not hate intellectuals, but they are often deeply suspicious of them. The American founders expected a natural aristocracy, an intellectual elite (themselves), to lead in public affairs, replacing the corruption and incompetency of the old hierarchy with a new, i.e. definitely late eighteenth century, sort of meritocracy. Instead, an egalitarian dynamic, described by Tocqueville as a 'providential force', overturned both the old hierarchy and the republican dreams of a new, democratically sanctioned one. When push came to shove, the yeoman farmers, mechanics, and craftsmen chose from among themselves, or from among others, people like Andrew Jackson or Martin Van Buren, who most clearly represented their interests, judgments and prejudices. The democratic tension between enlightened intellectual ideals and egalitarian ideals, then, dates back to at least the early years of the world's oldest democracy, and it has been with us ever since.

[...]

Many potential intellectuals have misunderstood their relationship with politics. Central to this misunderstanding and to an abdication of intellectual responsibilities, in my judgment, is a confusion of political commitment with ideology.

Some intellectuals over-commit in their ideological engagement, while others attempt to avoid ideology at all costs, turning away from public responsibilities in the name of disinterested science, art and scholarship. Both in the case of the overly committed, the tendentious partisans, such as those condemned by Julian Benda in his classic *The Treason of the Intellectuals*, and in the case of the scientists, artists and scholars who believe that they must remain confined in their specialized realm, the intellectual flees from public responsibility. While the ideologist confuses theory with politics,[3] the disengaged intellectual fears such confusion and retreats to insignificance or to apology for the way things are. They both contribute, even if in very different ways, to the 'de-intellectualization' of public life. The ideologist imagines that all political problems can be solved with the help of the true theory, i.e. his or her ideology. The disengaged intellectual either imagines that the fruits of science will, in some unforeseeable future, solve political problems in an objective way, or withdraws from general public concerns, acquiescing to the status quo.

I realize I am raising controversial issues here. My position, following the insights of Hannah Arendt, depends upon making a strong distinction between political ideas and principles on the one hand and ideology and its politics of coercion on the other.[4] It is predicated on a conviction that between ideology and indifference there is a possibility of principled critical action. This is not the conventional position. Usually people either imagine that all political ideas are in a sense ideological, or they believe that ideologies are bad ideas associated with a political-intellectual position to which they are opposed. The potential contribution of the intellectual to democratic society becomes apparent, in my judgment, only when we distance ourselves from both of these positions.

[. . .]

Roles are the subject matter of the sociological literature on intellectuals, a literature which strangely over-looks a major achievement and promise of modernity, to wit, democracy. The partisan intellectual argues for a party position, often as an ideologist in the name of a 'superior' theory, archetypically Marxism. The detached intellectual, in the name of a superior objective understanding, promises a resolution of political conflict through scientific means. The expert promises to substitute science for political conflicts and deliberations. Oddly, public deliberation and the rule of the people are absent from these accounts.

I am pointing to two problems: the inadequate self-understanding of intellectuals regarding their role in society and the same misunderstanding on the part of professional observers regarding the intellectual world. All the discussion of intellectuals as the new class, whether it is viewed with hope (e.g. in some of the work of Alvin Gouldner) or with dismay (e.g. in Konrad and Szelenyi on Eastern Europe), sees the intellectual project as that of legislation, as Zygmunt Bauman has put it.[5] Bauman maintains that with postmodernity comes the new role of interpretation, which he seems to understand as being a diminished task. I believe, to the contrary, that the new task is neither new nor less preferable to legislation, and it involves a lot more than interpretation. We observe it in the life of Socrates, and we can observe it in our own times. It is most apparent among intellectuals who seek to support democracy.

It is at this point that the special role of the intellectual to foster deliberation in democratic society becomes clear. The democratic intellectual addresses the paradox of democracy and culture, between democracy's egalitarianism and culture's hierarchy. Seen from this point of view, partisan, detached and expert intellectuals have mistakenly come down strongly on the side of hierarchy rather than democracy. What appears to be simply a description of a social role is, in fact, an anti-democratic political stance. For anti-democrats, such as Socrates and Plato, this would not be a problem. In our democratic age, it is. The vanguard Marxist claims a superior knowledge based on Marxism's special insights into history's subject, the proletariat. The more open, detached intellectual claims special knowledge based on his or her power of scientific synthesis, and the policy expert makes similar claims for his or her objective science. Missing from each of these positions is an appreciation of the intellectual's contribution to democratic deliberations.

[...]

There is, at the end of the twentieth century, a fundamental confusion of political perspective, a general uncertainty about what's left and what's right.[6] Intellectuals in democratic societies attempt to face this changed situation, at the same time that they face the problems of diversity. The great modern political traditions of liberalism, conservatism and socialism, the bread and butter of political intellectuals in the modern era, have been undermined by the collapse of communism and anti-communism, and by the crises of the welfare states of Europe and North America. This does provide the opportunity to avoid the stale ideological clichés of the recent past, to rediscover the discursive responsibilities of intellectuals, avoiding ideological temptations, but it does, as well, lead to political confusions. Making sense in public has become extremely difficult, not only because it is always difficult to be an intellectual, especially in a democracy, and these difficulties have become even more pronounced with the confrontation of the other, but also because the repertoire of political ideas which we have inherited has become strikingly stale.

Staleness is especially a problem for the political left. My specific concern about Said's position on the role of the intellectual and his self-understanding of his role as an intellectual, his reflexive support of the oppressed, his simpleminded leftism, is that it does not take into account the fact that it is the left in the former free world, in the former anti-communist domain, that has been most weakened by the political confusions of our fissured political traditions. Said, and others of his critical disposition, proceed as if these changes have not occurred. Post-modernists, post-structuralists, radical feminists and queer theorists, among others of the academic cultural left, proceed ignoring the dimensions of the change in the global political culture after the fall of communism. On the global stage and in the arena of domestic politics of Europe and North America, and probably beyond these regions as well, the right makes sense, while the left engages in cultural controversies and a cultural status hierarchy that function apart from the fields of consequential political and societal life. Many may not like the right-wing packages being presented by neo – and not so neo – conservatives, but the projects of privatization, global markets, fundamentalist religious positions, and nationalism are understandable to significant portions of the world's citizenries. Intellectuals of the left have thought their way into an apparently permanent marginality.

Said is an intellectual celebrity on the American left. He shares this status with such figures as Noam Chomsky, bell hooks and Cornell West. They all have a tendency to preach to the convinced: to declare the rightness of their position, to exhort the righteous to act well, to denounce those who act poorly, to be 'for all the good things and against all the bad ones', as Saul Bellow once satirically put it,[7] without presenting an argument to the unconvinced, the non-partisan. The common sense of their positions, as they have influenced the life of academe, has come to be labeled political correctness. Right-wing critics of the so-called academic left caricaturize concerns about sexism, racism, Western hegemony, and the injustices of free market economies, and these criticisms are not countered in ways that make sense beyond academic left enclaves. Thus, the right prevails in the broader public arena, as the left celebrates the marginal and denounces the central for its oppression. But because the center is not being challenged directly from the left, and it continues to function in and through the mass media, it is dominated by the positions of the right. Balanced budgets, prayer in schools, the privatization of public concerns, from social security to schooling, are the central items on the post-cold war political agenda, not the injustices of race, class, and gender, and the problems of de-industrialization and the devastation of the environment.

I, therefore, am not persuaded by much of the argument against a public life by the doyens of political correctness: the post-modernists, multiculturalists, and advocates of identity politics, even as I am quite aware that their concerns for the problems of diversity are pressing. I think they often substitute ideology for principled politics. Marginalized philosopher kings imagine that, through a magical intellectual slight of hand, they solve real political problems by withdrawing from ongoing political life. Academic politics have become more real to some post-modern critics than the consequential democratic politics of the general society.

Yet, I do not want to suggest that there is nothing to post-modern, multicultural and identity-based criticism. On the contrary, because the politics of our times are fundamentally different from those of the times of Lippmann, Dewey, and Mills, these forms of criticism have a great deal to say about our public culture. This is because of the problems raised by diversity and the impact of the other, to be sure, as the cogency of Said's position indicates, but it is no less a result of our radically changed geopolitical and geocultural situation. The politics of culture on the world stage lends cogency to post-modern deliberations.

[...]

No simple post-modern master narratives will replace those of the modern era, but minor narratives, dealing with concrete pressing problems, being written and read by intellectuals, ... related to the old political traditions. These can and should be coordinated in and through discussion in public, not through a theoretical sleight of hand. In fact, the minor narratives can help form the public sphere beyond the control of the state and the direct influence of economic logic. This is a key, perhaps the key, critical intellectual role of our times.

NOTES

1. Alexis de Tocqueville explored this tension in the second volume of his *Democracy in America*, trans. George Lawrence, ed. J. P. Mayer; (New York: Anchor Books, 1969), see specifically the first book of this volume.
2. Gordon Wood, *The Radicalness of the American Revolution*, (New York: Knopf, 1992)

3. For a cogent argument against this confusion see Richard Rorty, 'The Priority of Democracy to Philosophy', in his *Objectivity, Relativism, and Truth*, (New York: Cambridge University Press, 1991), pp. 175–96.

4. See Hannah Arendt, *The Origins of Totalitarianism*, pp. 460–82, and 'Truth and Politics', in *Between Past and Future*, (New York: Penguin, 1980) pp. 227–64. For a more recent set of reflections that parallel the ones presented here see Jean Bethke Elshtain, *Democracy on Trial*, (New York: Basic Books, 1995).

5. Gouldner, *The Future of the Intellectuals and the Rise of the New Class*, George Konrad and Ivan Szelenyi, *The Intellectuals on the Road to Class Power: A Sociological Study of the Role of the Intelligentsia in Socialism*, (New York: Harcourt, Brace, Jovanovich, 1979), Zygmunt Bauman, *Legislators and Interpreters* (Cambridge, MA: Polity Press, 1987).

6. There are by now a whole series of works that deal with the fact that our political culture no longer makes sense in the way it did even in the most recent past. My contribution to these reflections can be found in Jeffrey C. Goldfarb, *After the Fall* (New York: Basic Books, 1992). Noteworthy contributions to this genre include: Ralf Dahrendorf, *Reflections on the Revolution in Europe: In a letter intended to have been sent to a Gentleman in Warsaw*, (New York: Times Books, 1990); Hans Magnus Enzensberger, *Civil Wars: From L.A. to Bosnia*, (New York: The New Press, 1990), and Anthony Giddens, *Beyond Left and Right: The Future of Radical Politics*, (Stanford: Stanford University Press, 1994).

7. In Saul Bellow, *It All Adds Up: From the Dim Past to the Uncertain Future*, (New York: Penguin, 1995); p. 170.

59

ANTIGONE'S DAUGHTERS

Jean Bethke Elshtain

How does one hold on to a social location for contemporary daughters of Antigone without simultaneously insisting that women accept traditional terms of political quiescence? The question answers itself: the standpoint of Antigone is of a woman who dares to challenge public power by giving voice to familial and social imperatives and duties. Hers is not the world of the *femme couverte*, the delicate lady, or the coy sex-kitten. Hers is a robust voice, a bold voice: woman as guardian of the prerogatives of the *oikos*, preserver of familiar duty and honour, protector of children, if need be their fierce avenger. To recapture that voice and to reclaim that standpoint, and not just for women alone, it is necessary to locate the daughters of Antigone where, shakily and problematically, they continue to locate themselves: in the arena of the social world where human life is nurtured and protected from day to day. This is a world women have not altogether abandoned, though it is one both male-dominant society and some feminist protest have devalued as the sphere of 'shit-work', 'diaper talk' and 'terminal social decay'. This is a world that women, aware that they have traditions and values, can bring forward to put pressure on contemporary public policies and identities.

Through a social feminist awareness, women can explore, articulate and reclaim this world. To reaffirm the standpoint of Antigone for our own time is to portray women as being able to resist the imperious demands and overweening claims of state power when these run roughshod over deeply rooted

From: Anne Phillips (ed.), *Feminism and Politics* (Oxford: Oxford University Press, 1998).

values. Women must learn to defend without defensiveness and embrace without sentimentality the perspective that flows from their experiences in their everyday material world, 'an actual local and particular place in the world'.[1] To define this world simply as the 'private sphere' in contrast to the 'public sphere' is to mislead. For contemporary Americans, 'private' conjures up images of narrow exclusivity. The world of Antigone, however, is a *social* location that speaks of, and to, identities that are unique to a particular family, on the one hand; but, on another and perhaps even more basic level, it taps a deeply buried human identity, for we are first and foremost not political or economic men but family men and women. Family imagery goes deep and runs strong, and all of us, for better or worse, sporadically or consistently, have access to that imagery, for we all come from families even if we do not go on to create our own. The family is that arena that first humanizes us or, tragically, damages us. The family is our entry point into the wider social world. It is the basis of a concept of the social for, as Hegel recognized, 'the family is a sort of training ground that provides an understanding of another-oriented and public-oriented action'.[2]

What is striking about political theory in the Western tradition is the very thin notion of the social world so much of that theory describes. All aspects of social reality that go into making a person what he or she is fall outside the frame of formal, abstract analyses. In their rethinking of this tradition, many feminist thinkers, initially at least, locked their own formulations into an overly schematic public-private dichotomy, even if their intention was to challenge or to question it.[3] Those feminists who have moved in the direction of 'social feminism' have, in their rethinking of received categories, become both more historical and more interpretive in their approach to social life. One important female thinker whose life and work form a striking contrast to the classical vision and to overly rigid feminist renderings of the public and private, particularly those who disdain anything that smacks of the traditionally 'feminine', is Jane Addams. Addams embodies the standpoint of Antigone. A woman with a powerful public identity and following, who wielded enormous political power and influence, Addams' life work was neither grandly public nor narrowly private. Instead, she expressed the combined values of centuries of domestic tradition, and the dense and heady concoction of women's needs, and she brought these to bear on a political world that held human life very cheap indeed.

Addams recognized, in uncritical celebrations of heroic male action, a centuries-long trail of tears. What classical political theorists dismissed as ignoble – the sustenance of life itself – Addams claimed as truly heroic. Rather than repudiating human birth and the world surrounding it as a possible source of moral truth and political principle, Addams spoke from the standpoint of the 'suffering mothers of the disinherited', of 'women's haunting memories', which, she believed, 'instinctively challenge war as the implacable enemy of their age-long undertaking'.[4] At one point she wrote:

Certainly the women in every country who are under a profound imperative to preserve human life, have a right to regard this maternal impulse as
important now as the compelling instinct evinced by primitive woman
long ago, when they made the first crude beginnings of society by refusing
to share the vagrant life of man because they insisted upon a fixed abode in
which they might cherish their children. Undoubtedly women were then
told that the interests of the tribe, the diminishing food supply, the honour
of the chieftain, demanded that they leave their particular caves and go
out in the wind and weather without regard to the survival of their
children. But at the present moment the very names of the tribes and of
the honors and the glories which they sought are forgotten, while the basic
fact that the mothers held the lives of their children above all else, insisted
upon staying where the children had a chance to live, and cultivate the
earth for their food, laid the foundations of an ordered society.[5]

A feminist rethinking of Addams' category of the social, resituating it as an
alternative to privatization and public self-interestedness, would allow us to
break out of the rigidities into which current feminist discourse has fallen.
Seeing human beings through the prism of a many-layered, complex social
world suffused with diverse goods, meanings and purposes opens up the
possibility for posing a transformed vision of the human community against
the arid plain of bureaucratic statism. This communitarian ideal involves a
series of interrelated but autonomous social spheres. It incorporates a vision of
human solidarity that does not require uniformity and of cooperation that
permits dissent. The aim of all social activity would be to provide a frame
within which members of a diverse social body could attain both individual
and communal ends and purposes, without, however, presuming some final
resolution of these ends and purposes; a social world featuring fully public
activities at one end of a range of possibilities and intensely private activities at
the other.

If this communal ideal is to be claimed as a worthy ideal for our time, a first
requirement is a feminist framework that locates itself in the social world in
such a way that our current public, political realities can be examined with a
critical and reflective eye. One alternative feminist perspective, a variation on
both 'difference' and 'social' feminism that helps us to do this is called 'maternal
thinking' by its author, Sara Ruddick.[6] According to Ruddick, mothers have
had a particular way of thinking that has largely gone unnoticed – save by
mothers themselves. That is, women in mothering capacities have developed
intellectual abilities that wouldn't otherwise have been developed; made judgements they wouldn't otherwise have been called upon to make; and affirmed
values they might not otherwise have affirmed. In other words, mothers engage
in a discipline that has its own characteristic virtues and errors and that
involves, like other disciplines, a conception of achievement. Most important
for the purposes of feminist theory, these concepts and ends are dramatically at

odds with the prevailing norms of our bureaucratic, and increasingly techno-logical, public order.

Ruddick claims that one can describe maternal practices by a mother's interest in the preservation, the growth and the social acceptability of her child. These values and goods may conflict, for preservation and growth may clash with the requirements for social acceptability. Interestingly, what counts as a failure within the frame of maternal thinking, excessive control that fails to give each unique child room to grow and develop, is the *modus operandi* of both public and private bureaucracies. Were maternal thinking to be taken as the base for feminist consciousness, a wedge for examining an increasingly over-controlled public world would open up immediately. For this notion of maternal thought to have a chance to flourish as it is brought to bear upon the larger world, it must be transformed in and through social feminist awareness.

To repeat: the core concepts of maternal achievement put it at odds with bureaucratic manipulation. Maternal achievement requires paying a special sort of attention to the concrete specificity of each child; it turns on a special kind of knowledge of this child, this situation, without the notion of seizure, appropriation, control or judgement by impersonal standards. What maternal thinking could lead to, though this will always be problematic as long as mothers are socially subordinated, is the wider diffusion of what attentive love to all children is about and how it might become a wider social imperative.

Maternal thinking opens up for reflective criticism the paradoxical juxta-positions of female powerlessness and subordination, in the overall social and political sense, with the extraordinary psycho-social authority of mothers. Maternal thinking refuses to see women principally or simply as victims, for it recognizes that much good has emerged from maternal practices and could not if the world of the mother were totally destructive. Maternal thinking transformed by feminist consciousness, hence aware of the binds and con-straints imposed on mothers, including the presumption that women will first nurture their sons and then turn them over to sacrifice should the gods of war demand human blood, offers us a mode of reflection that links women to the past yet offers up hope of a future. It makes contact with the strengths of our mothers and grandmothers; it helps us to see ourselves as Antigone's daughters, determined, should it be necessary, to chasten arrogant public power and resist the claims of political necessity. For such power, and such claims, have, in the past, been weapons used to trample upon the deepest yearnings and most basic hopes of the human spirit.

Maternal thinking reminds us that public policy has an impact on real human beings. As public policy becomes increasingly impersonal, calculating, and technocratic, maternal thinking insists that the reality of a single human child be kept before the mind's eye. Maternal thinking, like Antigone's protest, is a rejection of amoral statecraft and an affirmation of the dignity of the human person.

NOTES

1. Smith, 'A Sociology for Women', in Julia A. Sterman and Evelyn Torton Beck (eds), *The Prism of Sex: Essays in the Sociology of Knowledge* (Madison, WI: University of Wisconsin Press, 1979), p. 168.
2. Bennett, 'Feminism and Civic Virtue', unpublished paper (1981).
3. I consider myself guilty on this score. See one of my earlier formulations on the public – private dilemma, 'Moral Woman/Immoral Man: The Public/Private Distinction and its Political Ramifications', *Politics and Society*, 4 (1974), 453–73. I try to restore a richness this initial foray dropped out in *Public Man, Private Woman: Women in Social and Political Thought* (Princeton, NJ: Princeton University Press, 1981).
4. Jane Addams, *The Long Road of Woman's Memory* (New York: Macmillan, 1916), p. 40.
5. Ibid. pp. 126–7.
6. Sara Ruddick, 'Maternal Thinking', typescript. A shortened version has appeared in *Feminist Studies* (Summer 1980), but I draw upon the original full-length draft.

60

CITIZENSHIP WITH A FEMINIST FACE: THE PROBLEM WITH MATERNAL THINKING

Mary G. Dietz

The hallmark of Elshtain's 'social feminism' is her attempt to 'make a case for family ties' and the practice of mothering.[1] Her case proceeds both historically (by reconsidering episodes in the history of political thought from the standpoint of the treatment of women) and programmatically (by criticizing current feminist theories and by offering her own 'reconstructive ideal of public and private').[2] Elshtain wants to show that the family is neither the reactionary and repressive institution of feminist and leftist critics nor the perfectly harmonious world of Filmerian patriarchs and the New Right. In the face of these critics and apologists, both Left and Right, Elstain insists that 'the family remains the locus of the deepest and most resonant human ties, the most enduring hopes, the most intractable conflicts, the most poignant tragedies and the sweetest triumphs human life affords'.[3]

Making short work of the Right, Elshtain levels criticism mainly at past feminist thought. In her view, previous feminism threatens to demean or destroy women's most powerful experiences, perhaps their very identities. What survives the demeaning or the destruction are some unacceptable alternatives: the distortion of identity and the obliteration of the private (the way radical feminists see women as 'hags' and 'witches'); the juridical levelling of identity and the elevation of the 'social' (the way liberal feminists see women and men merely as equal legal entities); or the reduction of identity and instrumentalization of the private (the way Marxist feminists see women as reproducers).

From: *Political Theory* 13/1, February 1985.

Social feminism is expressly designed to overcome these liabilities and to supplant these other feminist alternatives. For the sake of new feminist politics, it seeks to foster the identity of 'women-as-mothers' and to establish the moral primacy of the family, and so the private realm of human life.

[...]

For social feminism, then, the family is the most elevated and primary realm of human life. It has existential priority, and moral superiority, over the public realm of politics. To dramatize the radicalness of this position, Elshtain contrasts social feminism with the entire 2,500-year tradition of political thought.

> Aristotle and all the other political theorists down through the centuries who asserted the primacy of politics and viewed man (the male, at any rate, if not generic humanity) as pre-eminently a political animal even as they downgraded or simply took for granted the private sphere, were guilty of a serious distortion.[4]

To remedy this Aristotelian distortion, social feminists not only must reject the political priority of men over women; they must also reverse the existential priority of the public realm over the private realm.

[...]

Social feminism, guided by maternal thinking, also chastens what Elshtain calls the 'article of faith' of the contemporary feminist movement: 'The personal is the political.'[5] She reads this credo as a theoretical justification to politicize, criticize and manipulate the private world of the family and personal life. Social feminism would seek to protect the private sphere from this sort of desecration. By preserving and protecting its 'moral imperatives', social feminism would purge feminism's soul of its antifamilial and matriphobic spectre and restore an authentic and unique identity to women.

From such an identity would emerge a vital public-moral consciousness and a renewed vision of citizenship. This is the more constructive – or rather, recon-structive – vision of social feminism. Drawing upon the 'private virtues' and the 'humanizing imperative' that emerge from the social practice of mothering, social feminism promotes a 'politics of compassion' and seeks to create an 'ethical polity'.[6] Although this reconstructive politics is not (yet) fully elabor-ated, it would appear that an 'ethical polity' would embody or forward: (1) privacy and the protection of the private realm from politicization; (2) individual freedom ('from some all-encompassing public imperative'); (3) equality (because all individuals are 'irreplaceable beings and immortal souls'); (4) pluralism (of 'diverse spheres and competing ideals'); (5) non-violence; (6) civic virtue (based on a 'devotion to public, moral responsibilities and ends'); and (7) an active citizenry (in which 'men and women alike partake of the public sphere on an equal basis for participatory dignity and equality').[7]

This, in a word, is democracy by social feminist means.

[...]

Social feminism is open to a number of criticisms, most of which cannot be developed here, and some of which can only be mentioned.[8] Many of these criticisms seize upon the incompleteness of Elshtain's accounts of the family, of the social practice of mothering, or of maternal thinking. There is, for example, the definitional problem of just what sorts of relationship count as a 'family'. With some justification, perhaps, Elshtain does not want 'to throw the honourable mantle "family" over every ad hoc collection of persons who happen to be under one roof at the same time'.[9] But where legitimately to throw the mantle is not clear. This is especially troubling, given the great diversity of what have been and continue to be taken in different cultures and eras as families. Contemporary feminists and women generally may rightly wonder whether an extended non-nuclear family, a kibbutz, an ashram, a cooperative, or a lesbian household display (or do not display) the right sort of 'genuine commitment of family men and women who retained their commitments to and for one another'.[10]

Women with empirical and sociological sensibilities may also call attention to the lack of caring and love often displayed in modern families (however defined). Such lack may range from professional or upper-class families in which children are not in fact 'kept before the mind's eye', though they are otherwise well treated, to those tragic cases of families with battered wives and abused children. Should not actual families be investigated before we place women's and feminists' ideals and hopes on the material basis of the family and the social practice of mothering? Some critics might contend that the family is still generally the scene of women's housework, unpaid labour, or of their second shift. First-wave and socialist – not social – feminists were not, I think, so wide of the mark that these features of family life do not impinge upon what it is to engage in 'maternal thinking'. Even setting aside the family as an institution, women and feminists may also wonder upon what basis we are 'maternal thinkers'. Are we that as mothers, as potential future mothers, as women generally, even if, individually, some of us cannot or choose not to have children?

These may or may not prove insuperable problems, but until they are addressed and overcome we must judge the case for social feminism as incomplete, at the least. But there are more serious problems with social feminism, problems that threaten to undermine the political relevance of maternal thinking and so Elshtain's hopes for a new feminist political consciousness. Social feminism reinforces an abstract split between the public and private realms that cannot or should not be maintained; and no theoretical connection is provided for linking maternal thinking and the social practice of mothering with the kind of 'ethical polity' Elshtain envisions, namely one informed by democratic thinking and the political practices of citizenship.

I want to begin my criticism of social feminism indirectly by considering what might seem to be two unlikely figures – Aristotle and (Sophocles') Antigone. I begin here because Elshtain herself considers Aristotle and Antigone to be important episodes in a reconstructed history of feminist political thought. Her interpretations of them – in *Public Man, Private Woman*, and in 'Antigone's Daughters' – are illustrative of social feminism: its critical powers in the case of Aristotle; its praise and prescriptions in the case of Antigone. I think both interpretations are misguided, however, and symptomatic of the general difficulties of social feminism, difficulties I will turn to more directly in the following section.

Aristotle can be approached in two very different ways, one we might call 'deprecative', the other 'generous'. According to the former approach, one that Elshtain endorses, Aristotle consigns the private realm to insignificance. He leaves no doubt as to who occupies the private realm, where 'mere life' is preserved, and who acts in the public realm in pursuit of the 'good life.' Preserving 'mere life' is the task of women, slaves and certain kinds of labourers. Children also exist in this realm, though young males are liberated from it when they come of age. The private realm is mute: 'a modest silence is a woman's crown'. It is functional in that it serves to satisfy primary needs: 'First house, and wife, and ox to draw the plough'. And it is hierarchic by nature: 'the relation of male to female is naturally that of the superior to the inferior – of the ruling to the ruled'.[11] Aristotle allows that rule of this familial sort is of a higher nature than, say, rule over an animal, but the fact that in his view women or slaves rank only slightly above oxen is not particularly comforting. Conversely, women and slaves cannot partake or participate in the 'good life' of the polis where Greek males, 'naturally fitter to command', bask in heroic admiration of themselves and each other and 'aim at being equal' as public citizens.[12]

In Elshtain's reading, Aristotle is elitist because women are privatized, slaves oppressed and aliens condemned as barbarians. Here she rightly calls attention to the oppressive institutions that Aristotle accepts and ardently justifies as 'given' by nature. But Elshtain's criticisms go deeper still, to Aristotle's theoretical foundations. It is the split between the public and the private realms, and Aristotle's glorification of the former, to which she objects. 'It is important to remember', Elshtain argues, 'that most of the debates in the "public space" had little to do with great or noble ends, and much to do with jockeying for position and pelf, raising money by any means necessary'.[13] The 'public space', in short, is a deceptive notion, a relic of a distant past and a way of demeaning the private and familial concerns of everyday life. Conversely, the social feminist response to Aristotelian elitism is to resurrect the family, establish it as the primary realm of human life, and declare that the private virtues of love and humility, for example, are the bases for public consciousness. And when Elshtain accuses Aristotle of distorted thinking and seeks to reclaim the 'family man and woman' as primary over 'political and economic man,' she plainly wants us to reject Aristotle's mute, functional and hierarchic view of the family and of women, and his adulation and mystification of the polis and of men. In effect, social feminism stands Aristotle on his head. The virtues of private woman are lauded over the vices of public man, but social feminism remains locked in the same public/private perspective that it espies in Aristotelianism.

The consequences of standing Aristotle on his head are clear. The private realm of the family takes on an aura of holiness – a social feminist holiness – that radiates from loving and attentive mothers who personify specific 'moral imperatives'. The public realm becomes a dark and ominous antithesis to the virtuous private. Indeed, all that is public, in Elshtain's view, is statist, cold, brutal, uncompromisingly arrogant, eminently in need of maternal chastening. The political conclusion is obvious: feminists must embrace 'the perspective that flows from their experiences' (that is, family life and mothering) and resist 'the imperious demands and overweening claims of state power' and a public life 'created by men'

[...]

My point about Aristotle is this: the questions of who we are allowed to be and what rights we are allowed to exercise, even in the supposed sanctity of the family, have always been and will continue to be governed by political determinations. This governance stretches across the whole range of our lives and sets the conditions for what we consider to be 'private' and what we deem to be 'public' pursuits. And this is why, according to Aristotle, politics is existentially prior to all other human activities and practices.[15]

There is a second and more moral way in which politics is primary. In this activity, human beings can collectively and inclusively relate to one another not as strong over weak, fast over slow, master over apprentice, or mother over child, but as equals who render judgements on matters of shared importance, deliberate over issues of common concern and act in concert with one another. As Aristotle puts it, 'the members of a political association aim by their very nature at being equal and differing in nothing'.[16] Aristotle's shorthand for this activity is 'citizenship'. He calls the experience of citizenship, of simultaneously ruling and being ruled, the good life.[17] For it is when human beings act as citizens that they, and not a king or a parliament or a phalanx of faceless bureaucrats, have the power to determine the conditions of their 'mere' lives. Aristotle's point is not that citizens are the warrior-heroes of some fixed public realm, but rather that citizenship is a qualitatively distinct form of activity in which individuals collectively and perpetually determine the forever shifting boundaries of what is private and public. This endless collective self-determination is what it means to be free. Without question, Aristotle was wrong to restrict women to the household and render them eternally subject to natural and familial inequalities. But this forms no necessary part of his argument concerning politics and citizenship. Surely his vision of the good life, as one in which citizens relate to one another as equals, collectively determine their lives, and strive to be free, remains a compelling one. When compared to fascist terror, communist collectivizations, and liberal interest-group politics, it is a noble vision and one for which democracy still strives.[18]

What I am suggesting, in short, is that we learn different lessons from Aristotle about the political – not those based on an abstract split between the public and private realms, nor on the necessary consignment of women to the household. These different lessons will help us better understand the nature of a feminist political consciousness than will the deprecatory reading.

Related lessons follow if we read *Antigone* differently and more carefully. Rather than viewing the tension in the drama, as Elshtain does, as one of public (male) versus private (female), as one between the vices of public power and the virtues of private familial love, we might read *Antigone* as illustrative of two opposing *political* viewpoints. One is of Creon, who represents the state and centralized power, and the other is of Antigone, who represents the customs and traditions of a collective civil life, an entire political ethos, which Creon's mandate and he himself threaten. If we interpret *Antigone* this way, the character of the heroine deepens immensely, for she emerges not simply as a 'sister' whose familial loyalties pit her against a king, but as a citizen of Thebes whose defence of her brother is rooted in a devotion to the gods and to the ways and laws of her city. Likewise, Creon is not simply a man – a king of the public realm who besmirches a family's honour and trivializes private loyalties. He is the manifestation of a particular kind of politics, authoritarian rulership, to which Antigone, as citizen, is in opposition.

For Elshtain to read Antigone's loyalty as 'private' or 'familial' is not only anachronistic (for the defence of the 'private' against the 'state' is a later, liberal construct), but also unpolitical, for she misses the very thing that makes Antigone such a strikingly unusual Greek character (and Sophocles, despite his views on women's silence, such a visionary tragedian). She is a political person (that is, neither a 'private woman' nor a 'public man'). Antigone transcends the public/private split because she embodies the personal made political. Through her speech and her action, she transforms a matter of private concern into a public issue. In the Aristotelian idiom, Antigone realizes her human and distinctively political potentiality when she refuses to maintain a 'modest silence'. Indeed, if anyone in the drama symbolizes the sort of commitment to the private that Elshtain would have feminists adopt, it is Ismene, who shares Antigone's horror of the treatment of Polynices, but nevertheless begs her sister not to challenge Creon, to stay at home and remain silent. Of the two sisters surely Ismene is by far the more fierce defender of *oikos* [the household], for she tries her utmost to preserve the household and family peace between her sister and their uncle. She wants to save her sister from destruction. It is Antigone who insults and then deserts Ismene.

The reason why Antigone is a heroine and Ismene is not has nothing to do with 'private' or 'familial' virtues, for both sisters loved their brother. The difference between them has to do with political consciousness. Antigone understands that Creon's refusal to allow Polynices' burial is not just a singular personal insult but a collective political threat. The former may be countered with a 'modest silence' or supplication; the latter demands decisive political action. Antigone takes such action; Ismene does not.

There is more here than mere interpretative disputes in the history of political ideas. Feminist political consciousness, not just Aristotle or Antigone, are at issue. Because Elshtain envisions a world divided naturally and abstractly into dual realms, and human beings as either virtuous private or arrogant public creatures, feminist political consciousness is perilously close to becoming politically barren. To understand more precisely why this is so, we must recall the values of the private realm – intimacy, love, and attentiveness – and the defining aim of social feminism – 'the preservation of life' – and determine why these are inadequate bases for feminist political consciousness.

Without question, the protection of life is a necessary prerequisite for any political order. Who would not argue that the growth and preservation of children are vital social imperatives, or that the protection of vulnerable human life is important? But surely a movement or a political consciousness committed simply to caring for 'vulnerable human existence', as Elshtain's social feminism is, offers no standards – indeed, it can only echo the silence of Ismene – when it comes to judging between political alternatives or establishing political values that are worthy of feminist support. An enlightened despotism, a welfare state and a democratic republic may all protect children's lives or show compassion for the poor. But what standards for judging further among these political orders can social feminism offer us? Its moral imperative – the preservation and growth of children – has been fulfilled. This should be a matter of considerable concern for social feminists because, as we have seen, Elshtain intimates that social feminists are indeed committed to a particular kind of political order – namely, a democratic community. And in a generous acknowledgement, she applauds 'those aspects of Aristotelian thought that turn on the imperative that acting in common together with others to agreed upon ends is a worthy form of human life'.[19] But Elshtain fails to provide a theoretical argument which links maternal thinking and the social practice of mothering *to* democratic values and a democratic politics.

In order to link these successfully, she would have to show that maternal virtues are conceptually connected to, or that the social practice of mothering causally brings about, democratic values – particularly active citizenship, self-government, egalitarianism and the exercise of freedom. But this Elshtain cannot do. Maternal virtues cannot be political in the required sense because, as Elshtain herself acknowledges, they are connected to and emerge out of an activity that is special, distinctive, unlike any other. We must conclude, then, that this activity is unlike the activity of citizenship; the two cannot be viewed as somehow encompassing the same attributes, abilities and ways of knowing. Thus, to be a mother is not in itself to have the requisite capacity for citizenship. (Good) mothers may also be (good) citizens, but their being (good) mothers does not make them (good) citizens. The two descriptions of women are not interchangeable.

We must press this point further by considering the actual relationship between a mother and her child. It is not analogous to the relationship among citizens even when (and that is, as yet, empirically undetermined) it displays the ideal virtues Elshtain praises. The mother and the child are in radically different positions in terms of power and control. The child is subordinate to the mother, and the need relations are highly differentiated as well. The infant's is absolute; the mother's relative. A mother experiences her infant as continuous with self, not separate.[20] In other words, the special and distinctive aspects of mothering emerge out of a decidedly unequal relationship, even if benign or loving, in which one person is responsible for a given period of time for the care and preservation of another. This is an intimate, exclusive and particular activity, and mothers preserve their children, not mothering itself. Following Elshtain, we might call this the condition of attentive love.

Democratic citizenship, on the other hand, is collective, inclusive, and generalized. Because it is a condition in which individuals aim at being equal, the mother-child relationship is a particularly inappropriate model. For citizenship is an active condition, in which many persons share the responsibility of ruling and concern themselves not only with matters of general public policy but also with perpetuating the very activity of citizenship itself. Following Aristotle, we might call this the condition of freedom.

Furthermore, the bond among citizens is not like the love between a mother and child, for citizens are, not intimately, but politically involved with each other. Looked at in this way, social feminism commits a version of one of the ideological extravagances of the French Revolution, namely, the demand that democratic citizenship reflect the 'brotherhood of man'. But citizens do not, because they cannot, relate to one another as brother does to brother, or mother does to child. We look in the wrong place for a model of democratic citizenship if we look to the family (even when we have carefully defined the family).[21] We would do better to look at friendship in Aristotle's sense, or, better still, at mutual respect in Hannah Arendt's sense, for a model of the kind of bond we might expect from, or hope to nurture in, democratic citizens.

[. . .]

The need to challenge 'arrogant public power' and an 'amoral political order' – to use Elshtain's words – remains a crucial feminist task. But the only effective challenge to a corrupt or unjust state is one that is itself expressly political. Not the language of love and compassion, but only the language of freedom and equality, citizenship and justice, will challenge non-democratic and oppressive political institutions. Accordingly, what feminist political consciousness must draw upon is the potentiality of women-as-citizens and their historical reality as a collective and democratic power, not upon the 'robust' demands of motherhood. In practice, we might expect such consciousness to take shape not in the silent procession of empty baby strollers, nor in acquiescence to interest-group and party politics, but in public speeches and debates, organized movements with expressly political goals, and democratic activities in which feminist citizens challenge the 'givens' and seek to revitalize democratic values with a view toward the generations of citizens to come.

NOTES

1. Jean Bethke Elshtain, 'Feminism, Family and Community', Dissent, 29/4 (Fall 1982), p. 447.
2. Elshtain, *Public Man, Private Woman*, (Princeton, NJ: Princeton University Press, 1981), pp. 337, 343.
3. Elshtain, 'On "the Family Crisis"', Democracy, 3/1 (Winter 1983), p. 183.
4. Elshtain, *Public Man, Private Woman*, p. 327.
5. Elshtain, 'Feminists Against the Family', *The Nation* (Nov. 1979), p. 1.
6. This may account for Elshtain's extremely curious statement in *Public Man, Private Woman*: 'I shall spend somewhat less time discussing a reconstructive notion of the public because it stands in less need of a defense and reaffirmation within feminist political discourse than our besieged sphere of the private'. (p. 337) This is surprising for at least three reasons: first, because we have been led to believe that one of Elshtain's major goals is the reconstruction of the public; second, because she has argued that previous feminist discourse has been woefully inadequate in its attempt to formulate a political (public) consciousness; and third (and most important), it reconfirms that Elshtain thinks the 'public' and 'private' are distinct entities that can be split apart and examined separately – as if changing or 'reconstructing' one has nothing to do with the other.
7. This is a reconstruction of Elshtain's very brief sketch in the final chapter of *Public Man, Private Women*, esp. pp. 349–53.
8. See esp. Barbara Ehrenreich's comments in *Dissent*, 30/1 (Winter 1983); and Marshall Berman, 'Feminism, Community, Freedom', *Dissent*, 30/2 (Spring 1983).
9. Elshtain, *Public Man, Private Woman*, p. 448, p. 322, n. 30, where Elshtain acknowledges, but does not pursue, the problem of defining 'family'. For an analysis that captures the conceptual and material complexities of the family, see Philippe Ariès, *Centuries of Childhood: A Social History of Family Life* (New York: Vintage Books, 1962).
10. Elshtain, *Public Man, Private Woman*, p. 441.
11. Aristotle, *Politics*, E. Barker (ed.) (New York: Oxford University Press, 1962), I. xiii, p. 36; I. ii, p. 4; I. xiii, pp. 34–6.
12. Ibid. I. xii, p. 32. See discussion in Elshtain, *Public Man, Private Woman*, p. 346.
13. Ibid.
14. Elshtain, 'Antigone's Daughters', *Democracy*, 2/2 (April 1982), p. 56; 'Feminism, Family, and Community', p. 447.
15. Aristotle, *Politics*, I. ii, p. 6,
16. Ibid. I. xii, p. 32.
17. Ibid. I. ii, pp. 4–5; and III. vi, pp. 110–13.
18. For a 'generous' view of the *vita activa* that has none of the sexist characteristics of Aristotelian thought, see Hannah Arendt, *The Human Condition* (Chicago: University of Chicago Press, 1958).
19. Elshtain, *Public Man, Private Woman*, 351.
20. For a more detailed analysis of the mother–child relationship, see Nancy Chodorow, *The Reproduction of Mothering: Psychoanalysis and the Sociology of Gender* (Berkeley: University of California Press, 1978). For an analysis of mother–child relations that acknowledges the problems of maternal authority, see Dorothy Dinnerstein, *The Mermaid and the Minotaur* (New York: Harper

Colophon, 1977). Dinnerstein's conclusion implies that we should be concerned not with 'familizing' the polity, but with democratizing the family. Hence she argues for 'dual parenting', a subject neither Ruddick nor Elshtain addresses. Nor do they consider, as does Dinnerstein, the possibilities and meaning of 'fathering'.

21. Though this issue cannot be discussed here in the detail it deserves, familial metaphors are inappropriate for understanding political arrangements. Those who are tempted to think otherwise would do well to return to Locke's arguments against Filmer's *Patriarcha*. For a modern view, see Martha Acklesberg, ' "Sisters" or "Comrades"? The Politics of Friends and Families', in Irene Diamond (ed.), *Families, Politics, and Public Policy: A Feminist Dialogue on Women and the State* (New York: Longman, 1983), pp. 339–56.

61

GENDER AND PUBLIC ACCESS: WOMEN'S POLITICS IN 19TH-CENTURY AMERICA

Mary P. Ryan

I do not intend to enter the discussion on this theoretical plane, however, and will leave it to others to identify the gendered assumptions that underwrite public philosophy from Aristotle through Habermas.[1] Rather, I will engage the subject of women and the public sphere on the ground of history. From the vantage point of a historian of the United States, I will sketch a counter-narrative to Habermas' depiction of the chronological decline from an idealized bourgeois public sphere. Starting at approximately the same time and place where Habermas commences his story of the eviscerating transformation of the public sphere (Western republics in the eighteenth and nineteenth centuries), feminist historians plot out the ascension of women into politics. This discrepancy cannot be ironically dismissed with the painful observation that when women finally won the franchise and official access to the public, they found themselves the conquerers of a hollow fortress. Although female suffrage did not swiftly lead to gender equality, it did remove a major constitutional impediment to public access and in the process undermined a gender division that had both hamstrung women as political subjects and blemished the whole doctrine of the public sphere. Moreover, in a critical slice of history that postdates the writing of *Structural Transformation*, the new women's movement injected considerable feminist substance into public discourse, articulating concerns once buried in the privacy of one sex as vital matters of public interest. Even the barest outlines of women's political history are sufficient to call into question a

From: Craig Calhoun (ed.), *Habermas and the Public Sphere* (Cambridge, MA: MIT Press, 1992).

characterization of the last century as a blanket, undifferentiated decline of public life. I propose to outline in a very sketchy and condensed way how this feminist-inspired history of the public deviates from Habermas' account. From a woman's perspective this history starts out from different premises, evolves through a different and more problematic relationship to the public sphere, and presents a distinctive projectory into the future.

The geographical location and temporal parameters of my abbreviated history, the United States between 1825 and 1880, introduce additional contrasts with Habermas' model, based largely in Western Europe. The public as built on American soil in the nineteenth century was structured around different political possibilities and challenges. The relatively painless and rapid expansion of suffrage to adult white males circumvented the intense, abrasive encounter between the bourgeois public sphere and French revolutionaries or English Chartists. Subsequently the American polity was divided more fractiously by ethnic, racial and sectional differences than on the Continent. These divisions, along with more mottled class differences, were organized swiftly and in a bipolar fashion into two mass political parties. Perhaps most decisive of all, the American Republic, stepchild of the parliament of Great Britain, was not born in a ferocious struggle against absolutism, nor in close conjunction with a strong mercantilist state. The limited government of confederated states endured through the Civil War. As Stephen Showronek has recently pointed out and as Tocqueville observed long ago, antebellum public life was intensely focused at the local and municipal level. It is at this historical site that I (drawing evidence especially from New York, New Orleans and San Francisco) have based my search for women in public.[2]

Since I share Habermas' premiss that no prototype of the public sphere can be 'abstracted to any number of historical situations that represent formally similar constellations', my search for an American public spotlights different times, institutions, forms and locations as the markings of the public. First of all, from my historical vantage-point the most robust expressions of American publicness date from the 1820s and 1830s, not the eighteenth century. Second, this public spirit flourished in distinctive spaces, not primarily in literary and political clubs and in the culture of print but in outdoor assemblages, in open, urban spaces, along the avenues, on street corners and in public squares. Third, American citizens enacted publicness in an active, raucous, contentious and unbounded style of debate that defied literary standards of rational and critical discourse. Fourth, the practice of publicness in nineteenth-century America took shape in a distinctive class and social context. Although elite merchants dominated local public offices, convened their own public meetings, set up their own literary clubs and were treated deferentially in the public press, this American garden variety of the bourgeoisie was not the major staging ground of public politics. Nor could the most exuberant public formations of Jacksonian America be characterized as plebian. Rather, this urban public found its social base in amorphous groupings of citizens aggregated according to ethnicity, class, race, pet cause and party affiliation. These widespread, diverse and intersecting political conventions were a popular enactment of the principle of open access to public debate on matters of general interest. Not the ideal bourgeois public sphere but this variegated, decentred and democratic array of public spaces will be the setting of my story and serve as my historical standard of publicness.

Although this pivot of my history is quite remote from the starting-point of Habermas' chronology, it provides the best American approximation of the optimal function of the public sphere as he presents it: 'a process in which the exercise of social power and political domination is effectively subjected to the mandate of democratic publicity'. Moreover, these social, political, and cultural practices of the American public resemble Western European publicness in critical ways.

[...]

Public access put women in a position to ponder their own political identity and to formulate the claims of their sex on the public good. In political skirmishes like the campaign against prostitution legislation, some women even forged an ad hoc gender identity that bridged class divisions. Still, the politics of prostitution, like female moral reform, was but one rather prickly way to generate gender identity. It placed the woman citizen in a defensive position and identified her by her sexual and reproductive biology. To contemporary feminists, this is an invitation to essentialism and a narrow base on which to mount gender politics. Fortunately, at the time of the anti-prostitution campaign, women were also assembling in the public sphere on an altogether broader and more radical principle, that of women's rights. The women's rights conventions first convened in 1848 and meeting irregularly through the next decade did not cohere as a national and sustained organization until the Civil War. The National Loyal Women's League and subsequently the Equal Rights Association, both headquartered in New York and presided over by Elizabeth Cady Stanton, were the crucible of an independent women's movement that would appropriate the ideal of the public sphere for the second sex.

The Loyal Women's League was founded as an appendage of the anti-slavery movement with the specific goal of pushing the Lincoln administration toward emancipating the slaves. Its postwar, post-emancipation sequel, the Equal Rights Association, championed the civil and political liberties of African-Americans. At the very first meeting of the LWL, however, Stanton and her partner in feminism, Susan B. Anthony, placed women's public interest on the same agenda, forcing through a resolution in favour of women's suffrage. In a now familiar story, the alliance between African-Americans and women was broken when the 'negro first' policy of Radical Republicans secured suffrage and the privileges of citizenship for African-American men and simultaneously wrote a gender restriction into the Constitution. Stanton and Anthony promptly founded a national association for the single and explicit purpose of securing the rights of women. Stanton, Anthony and their colleagues across the country decided forthwith to form a women's suffrage association and to build their politics on the solid, independent base of their own gender position. As this autonomous public, the women's rights movement proceeded to identify a broad agenda of gender issues for black and white women, not just suffrage but also marriage reform, equal pay, sexual freedom and reproductive rights.[3]

For veteran politicians like Stanton, the time had come to purge the public sphere of gender distinctions. She turned to the Republican tradition, 'the birth right of the revolution', and 'the rights of man' to legitimate women's direct assault on the public sphere. But Stanton had learned through more than thirty years' experience in every sector of politics open to her sex that to win rights for those who occupied the social position of women required the explicit acknowledgement of gender difference. Only by taking up a political position explicitly as feminists, rather than trusting in formal commitments to abstract principles of public discourse, could women escape from the obfuscation, occlusion and manipulation that had hitherto characterized their place in American public life. From this position Stanton slightly but critically revised the concept of the public handed down by her forefathers. Her goal was that 'government may be republican in fact as well as form; a government by the people, and the whole people; for the people and the whole people'. To Stanton, the whole was made up of separate parts, and especially excluded populations like African-Americans and women. Stanton was still a lonely voice in the American public, still likely to be ridiculed in the public press and scarcely heard in the citadels of power. But at a time when public ideology and deep-rooted social structures sentenced women to privacy, she had taken a critical step toward the longest yet incomplete revolution.[4]

Even at a time when the public was supposedly in decline and as avenues to power seemed to narrow, women like Stanton laid claim to a public space for their sex. Late in the nineteenth century, in the face of a more powerful state apparatus and amid the cacophony of mass politics, women had found multiple points of access to the public. They won state funds for their private welfare schemes, lobbied for their sex-specific interests, and prohibited state bureaucracies from trampling on the liberties of their sex. By occupying these scattered public places, nineteenth-century women worked out their own political identities, opened up the public to a vast new constituency, and enlarged the range of issues that weighed into the 'general interest'.

These peregrinations through gender politics are but one illustration of the transformation of American public life that progressed outside the bourgeois public sphere during the nineteenth century. Much of this critical history was located in democratic public spaces, at proliferating points of access to political discussion where established authority could be challenged. Whether the occupants of these dispersed public spaces were working men, immigrants, African-Americans or women, each fought their way into the public from a distinctive position in civil society, usually a place of political marginality and social injustice. Like the bourgeoisie before them, these social groups gave definition to their own particular stakes in the public interest as they expanded the domain of the public. The imperfect public they constituted was grounded in a historical construction and political articulation of diverse, malleable and separate identities and interests. In a complex and far from egalitarian society like the nineteenth-century United States, this method of broadening access to public space proved to be the vehicle for democratizing public discourse and public policy.

Women's politics is a powerful example of this democratizing process and a critical index of publicness. Gender restrictions patently contradicted public ideology and had built exclusion into the very foundation of the public sphere. Denied public, formal and direct legitimacy, gender issues found their way into politics in corrupted forms, like the cloying feminine symbols used in electoral campaigns or the periodic, partisan-inspired crackdowns on prostitution. Denied admission to the public sphere directly and in their own right, women found circuitous routes to public influence. The ways women manoeuvred around the gender restrictions of the public are stocked with meaning for those who cherish the public. As sex reformers, for example, women exposed the fictions of privacy on which the segregation of gender and politics was supposedly based, while female-run charities built up a private system of meeting public needs that presaged the welfare state and some of its more anti-democratic features. Before 1880 it was only a small group of women's rights advocates who saw through all the obfuscations and contradictions of this largely clandestine gender politics and made their claim for full citizenship in the public sphere. Yet the tenacious efforts of women to subvert these restrictions and to be heard in public testify to the power of public ideals, that persistent impulse to have a voice in some space open and accessible to all where they could be counted in the general interest.

Each of the many ways whereby nineteenth-century women became political tells us something important about that privileged space called the public sphere. I will suggest just a few implications we might draw from the experience of our foremothers. First, the public as read through women's history spotlights the simple colloquial meaning of 'public', that of open access to the political sphere. The women's politics of the last century warns against a spatial or conceptual closure that constrains the ideal of the public to a bounded sphere with *a priori* rules about appropriate behaviour therein. Feminists and female citizens played for high stakes in a real world of politics, and would find far more comfort in a plural and decentred concept of the public.

Second, women's assiduous efforts to win and exercise the right of public access is an example of the practical ways in which the public ideal has maintained its resilience over time, that is, through a progressive incorporation of once-marginalized groups into the public sphere. As long as the distributive issues of justice remain unachieved civic goals, this proliferation of publics is a particularly significant measure of the public wellbeing. Furthermore, as

Andrew Arato and Jean Cohen have pointed out, demands for public access by once marginalized groups or insurgent social movements serve over time to accumulate and expand the rights of all citizens.[5]

Third, the history of women in and on the way to the public sphere suggests that the notions of interest and identity need not be antithetical to the public good. From the vantage-point of women's history, the identification of a political interest of one's own was not a fall from public virtue but a step toward empowerment. Because the second sex, like many marginalized populations, was socially dependent on their politically dominant superiors, their empowerment necessitated the construction of a separate identity and the assertion of self-interest. In practice, inclusive representation, open confrontation and full articulation of social and historical differences are as essential to the public as is a standard of rational and disinterested discourse.

Finally, the history of women in public challenges us to listen carefully and respectfully for the voices of those who have long been banished from the formal public sphere and polite public discourse. Those most remote from public authorities and governmental institutions and least versed in their language sometimes resort to shrill tones, civil disobedience and even violent acts in order to make themselves heard. Therefore, my chronicle would not be complete without reference to those women least likely to find a voice in the formal public sphere and those most likely, therefore, to express their interests in loud, coarse and, yes, abrasive ways. These women citizens are represented by the participants in the New York Draft Riots of 1863. The women rioters, mostly poor Irish-Americans, were found looting businesses, physically assaulting policemen, helping to set the Colored Orphan Asylum afire, and committing ugly, violent acts on the corpses of their adversaries. There was no civility, virtue or logic in their political acts, yet their grievances against a draft policy that exacted an excessive cost of war from their class and sex were both just and reasoned, if tragically misdirected. However we draw the normative or procedural boundaries of the public sphere, they must be permeable to even distorted voices of people like these, many of whom still remain outside its reach.

These stray morals of my story might be drawn together in a simple public sentiment. Because everyday politics inevitably falls short of standards of perfect rational discourse, a chimera even in the heyday of the bourgeois public sphere, the goal of publicness might best be allowed to navigate through wider and wilder territory. That is, public life can be cultivated in many democratic spaces where obstinate differences in power, material status and hence interest can find expression. The proliferation of democratic publics that posed a major counter-force to the escalating dominance of the state and capitalism in the nineteenth-century United States is carried forward in our own time by feminist movements. The movement of women into the public is a quantum leap in our public life; it both expands membership in the public and articulates vital aspects of the general interest that have hitherto been buried in gender restrictions and disguised as privacy. In the late twentieth century, women's historically problematic relationship to the public has become transformed into a public asset, both a practical and theoretical boon to the utopian aspirations that Jürgen Habermas set before us twenty-five years ago.

NOTES

1. See, for example, Nancy Fraser, 'What's Critical about Critical Theory? The Case of Habermas and Gender', *New German Critique* (1985): pp. 97–133; Iris Marion Young, 'Impartiality and the Civic Public: Some Implications of Feminist Critiques of Moral and Political Theory', in Seyla Benhabib and Drucilla Cornell (eds), *Feminism as Critique* (Minneapolis, 1987); Pateman, *The Sexual Contract* (Stanford, 1988).
2. Stephen Skowronek, *Building a New American State* (Cambridge, 1982).
3. Carroll Smith-Rosenberg, *Disorderly Conduct: Visions of Gender in Victorian America* (New York, 1985); Barbara Meil Hobson, *Uneasy Virtue: The Politics of Prostitution and the American Reform Tradition* (New York, 1987).
4. Anne Douglas, *The Feminization of American Culture* (New York, 1979); Gillian Brown, *Domestic Individualism* (Berkeley, 1991); Mary P. Ryan, *The Empire of the Mother* (New York, 1981).
5. *New York Tribune*, 25 December 1844; Edward Crapsey, *The Netherside of New York* (Montclair, NJ, 1969, repr. of 1872 ed.), preface, pp. 9, 120; Revd E. H. Chapin, *Humanity in the City* (New York, 1854), pp. 11–45.

62

CIVIL SOCIETY I, II, III

Jeffrey C. Alexander

Civil society and capitalism must be conceptualized in fundamentally different terms. Civil society should be conceived as a solidary sphere in which a certain kind of universalizing community comes gradually to be defined and to some degree enforced. To the degree this solidary community exists, it is exhibited by 'public opinion', possesses its own cultural codes and narratives in a democratic idiom, is patterned by a set of peculiar institutions, most notably legal and journalistic ones, and is visible in historically distinctive sets of interactional practices like civility, equality, criticism and respect. This kind of civil community can never exist as such; it can exist only 'to one degree or another'. One reason is that it is always interconnected with, and interpenetrated by, other more and less differentiated spheres which have their own criteria of justice and their own system of rewards. There is no reason to privilege any one of these non-civil spheres over any others. The economy, the state, religion, science, the family – each differentiated sphere of activity is a defining characteristic of modern and post-modern societies. We are no more a capitalist society than we are a bureaucratic, secular, rational one, or indeed a civil one.

Rather than try to reduce the contemporary social system to the identity of one of its spheres, I would suggest that we acknowledge social differentiation both as a fact and as a process and that we study the boundary relationships between spheres.

[...]

From: Jeffrey C. Alexander, *Real Civil Societies* (London: Sage, 1998).

One can speak of civil and non-civil boundary relationships in terms of facilitating inputs, destructive intrusions and civil repairs. Boundary tensions can seriously distort civil society, threatening the very possibility for an effective and democratic social life. These distorting forces are destructive intrusions; in the face of them, the actors and institutions of civil society can make repairs by seeking to regulate and reform what happens in such non-civil spheres. Yet such subsystem interpenetration can also go the other way. Some of the goods and the social forms produced by other spheres actually facilitate the realization of a more civil life. Conservative theorists and politicians, not to mention the elites in these non-civil spheres themselves, are inclined to emphasize the facilitating inputs of non-civil spheres to the creation of a good social life. Those on the liberal and radical left are more inclined to emphasize the destructive intrusions that these interpenetrations entail, and the repairs that must be made as a result. Neither side of this argument can be ignored in the effort to theorize the relation between civil society and other kinds of social institutions in a general way.

That the economic sphere in its capitalist form facilitates the construction of a civil society in important ways is a historical and sociological fact that should not be denied. When an economy is structured by markets, behavior is encouraged that is independent, rational and self-controlled. It was for this reason that the early intellectuals of capitalism, from Montesquieu to Adam Smith, hailed market society as a calming and civilizing antidote to the militaristic glories of aristocratic life. It is in part for this same reason that societies which have recently exited from communism have staked their emerging democracies on the construction of market societies in turn. Yet, quite apart from markets, industrialization itself can be seen in a positive vein. By creating an enormous supply of cheap and widely available material media, mass production lessens the invidious distinctions of status markers that separated rich and poor in more restricted economies. It becomes increasingly possible for masses of people to express their individuality, their autonomy and their equality through consumption and, in so doing, to partake of the common symbolic inheritance of cultural life. Facilitating inputs are produced from the production side as well. As Marx was among the first to point out, the complex forms of teamwork and cooperation that are demanded in productive enterprises can be considered forms of socialization, in which persons learn to respect and trust their fellow partners in the civil sphere.

In so far as the capitalist economy supplies the civil sphere with facilities like independence, self-control, rationality, equality, self-realization, cooperation and trust, the boundary relations between these two spheres are frictionless; structural differentiation thus seems to produce integration and individuation in turn. It is clear to all but the most diehard free marketers, however, that an industrializing, market economy also has put roadblocks in the way of civil society. In the everyday language of social science, these blockages are expressed purely in terms of economic inequalities, that is, as class divisions, housing differentials, dual labor markets, poverty and unemployment. These facts only become crystallized in social terms – as social problems produced by the dynamics of public opinion and social movements – because they are viewed as destructive intrusions into the civil realm. Economic criteria are, as it were, interfering with civil ones.

The stratification of economic products, both human and material, narrows and polarizes civil society. It provides a broad field for the 'discourse of repression', which pollutes and degrades economic failure. Despite the fact that there is no inherent relationship between failure to achieve distinction in the economic realm and failure to sustain expectations in civil society – the lack of connection being the very point of the construction of an independent civil realm – this connection is continually made.

[...]

To the degree that civil society exists as an independent force, economically underprivileged actors have dual memberships. They are not just unsuccessful or dominated members of the capitalist economy; they have the ability to make claims for respect and power on the basis of their only partially realized membership in the civil realm. On the basis of the implied universalism of solidarity in civil society, moreover, they believe these claims should find a response. They broadcast appeals through the communicative institutions of civil society; organize such social movements demanding socialism or simply economic justice through its networks and public spaces; and create voluntary organizations, such as trade unions, that demand fairness and freedom of expression to wage employees. Sometimes they employ their space in civil society to confront economic institutions and elites directly, winning concessions in face-to-face negotiations. At other times, they make use of regulatory institutions, like law and the franchise, to force the state to intervene in economic life on their behalf. While these efforts at repairs often fail, they often succeed in institutionalizing 'workers' rights'. In this situation, civil criteria might be said to have entered directly into the economic, capitalist sphere. Dangerous working conditions are prohibited; discrimination in labor markets is outlawed; arbitrary economic authority is curtailed; unemployment is controlled and humanized; wealth itself is redistributed according to criteria that are antithetical to those of a strictly economic kind.

The kinds of tense and permeable boundary relationships I have described here cannot be conceptualized if capitalism and civil society are conflated with one another. Only if these realms are separated analytically can we gain some empirical purchase not only on the wrenching economic strains of the last two centuries but on the extraordinary 'repairs' that have been made to the social fabric in response. There is no doubt, indeed, that in the boundary relations of capitalist economy and civil society the interplay of facilitating input, destructive intrusions, and repairs will continue in the future. In the process, new economically related civil issues, workplace democracy for example, will become the focus of public spotlight.

I have tried to separate civil society and capitalism, however, not only better to conceptualize economic strains but to challenge the identification of 'capitalism' with 'society', that is, to challenge the very notion that the society we live in can be understood under the rubric of capitalism. Markets are not, after all, the only threats, or even the worst threats, that have been levied against democratic civil life. Each of the other non-civil spheres has also fundamentally undermined civil society in different times and different ways. In Catholic countries, Jews and Protestants have often been construed as uncivil and prevented from fully entering the civil life. For most of the history of civil societies, patriarchal power in the family transferred directly into the lack of civil status for women. Scientific and professional power has empowered experts and excluded ordinary persons from full participation in vital civil discussions. Political oligarchies, whether in private organizations or in national governments themselves, have used secrecy and manipulation to deprive members of civil society of access to information about crucial decisions affecting their collective life. The racial and ethic structuring of primordial communities has distorted civil society in terrible ways.

In fact, the identification of capitalism and civil society is just one example of the reductive and circumscribing conflation of civil society with a particular kind of non-civil realm. Indeed, in the course of Western history the anti-civil intrusions I have referred to above have been so destructive that the social movements organized for repair, and the theorists who articulate their demands, have sometimes come to believe that these blockages are intrinsic to civil society itself. Socialists have argued that civil society is essentially and irrevocably bourgeois; that, as long as there are markets and private property, participants in the economic realm can never be treated in a respectful and egalitarian way. In a homologous manner, radical feminists have argued that civil societies are inherently patriarchal, that the very idea of a civil society is impossible to realize in a society that has families which allow men to dominate women. Zionists, similarly, have argued that European societies are fundamentally antisemitic. Black nationalists have claimed that racism is essential, and that the civil realm in white settler societies will always, and necessarily, exclude blacks.

On the basis of arguments I have presented here, I would suggest that these radical arguments for emancipation from civil society are neither empirically accurate nor morally compelling. They generalize from particular historical instances of highly distorted and oppressive boundary relations, drawing the illegitimate conclusion that the civil sphere must always be distorted in this particular way. On this faulty basis, they project utopian societies, communism for example, which deny the necessity for a universalistic civil sphere, utopian projects which claim to abolish boundary conflicts altogether. What they really deny, however, is the pluralism, complexity and inevitably conflict-ridden nature of democratic social life. The separation of capitalism and civil society points, then, to the need to recognize the relative autonomy that exists between civil society and other kinds of social spheres, a relative autonomy which sometimes manifests itself in highly destructive interpenetrations but can also allow highly effective repairs.

SECTION 5
AMERICAN SOCIAL AND POLITICAL
THOUGHT AT THE DAWN OF
THE 21ST CENTURY

This section starts with Michael J. Sandel's study *Democracy's Discontent* in which he criticises the hegemonic liberal paradigm that he sees as prevalent in American society and politics. Sandel's main contention is that the formative project in which civic virtues, republican freedom and the idea of the common good were of prime importance has been abandoned for the procedural and individualist conception of freedom in which solely the idea of individual interests and ends prevails. Sandel's main intention is to promote an up-to-date version of American civic republicanism, in other words a public philosophy in which there is neither a soulless, storyless and somewhat anonymous citizenry nor room for ambiguity and self-doubt. Sandel's formulation of his own 'fusion republicanism' has provoked criticism, as can be seen from a collection entitled *Debating Democracy's Discontent* which gathers various contributions of well-known American intellectuals. Nancy L. Rosenblum locates Sandel's contribution between 'fusion republicanism', a mingling or a mindset of political ideas of a rather disparate sort – sometimes with conservative overtones – and the liberalism he criticises. Richard Rorty defends his own 'minimalist liberalism' against Sandel's all embracing republicanism. He sees no need for America to develop a common set of ideas. What America needs is a modern moral identity – something Rorty has trouble in detecting in Sandel's republicanism. As Richard Sennett points out, on reflection one can actually detect enlightening disagreements between Sandel and Rorty's ideas. When juxtaposed they actually offer two versions – not necessarily mutually exclusive – of how to come to terms with modern citizenship.

However, some of the more important aspects of Sandel's work are those of the discovery of a new 'civic epistemology', that is the development of the capacity to communicate political ideas about the common good. With Sandel's critique it becomes again possible to have a language and an understanding of the common good that is not just motivated by the interests of individuals (as it is in liberalism).

In his book *Whose Keeper?* Alan Wolfe takes the argument a step further and discusses the moral obligation of the social sciences and whether the modern social sciences in the US are conceptually prepared and up for the difficult task of finding a common moral language that civil society finds appealing. Very similar questions are being asked by Albert O. Hirschman in his essay 'Morality and the social sciences: a durable tension'.

The section ends with two readings that discuss the public role of intellectuals. In his book *The Company of Critics* Michael Walzer suggests that in most modern societies criticism has to come 'from within', that is to say no longer does the critic stand above or outside what he criticises. As C. L. R. James has further demonstrated in his *Mariners, Renegades and Castaways*, the role that intellectuals in the United States play has been very different if one compares it to the role intellectuals played in Europe. James demonstrates this very clearly in his discussion of the work of Herman Melville.

63

DEMOCRACY'S DISCONTENT – AMERICA IN SEARCH OF A PUBLIC PHILOSOPHY

Michael J. Sandel

If there were a way to secure freedom without attending to the character of citizens, or to define rights without affirming a conception of the good life, then the liberal objection to the formative project might be decisive. But is there such a way? Liberal political theory claims that there is. The voluntarist conception of freedom promises to lay to rest, once and for all, the risks of republican politics. If liberty can be detached from the exercise of self-government and conceived instead as the capacity of persons to choose their own ends, then the difficult task of forming civic virtue can finally be dispensed with. Or at least it can be narrowed to the seemingly simpler task of cultivating toleration and respect for others.

On the voluntarist conception of freedom, statecraft no longer needs soul-craft, except in a limited domain. Tying freedom to respect for the rights of freely choosing selves would dampen old disputes about how to form the habits of self-rule. It would spare politics the ancient quarrels about the nature of the good life. Once freedom is detached from the formative project, 'the problem of setting up a state can be solved even by a nation of devils', in Kant's memorable words. 'For such a task does not involve the moral improvement of man'.[1]

But the liberal attempt to detach freedom from the formative project confronts problems of its own, problems that can be seen in both the theory and the practice of the procedural republic. The philosophical difficulty lies in the liberal conception of citizens as freely choosing, independent selves,

From: Michael J. Sandel, *Democracy's Discontent: America in Search of a Public Philosophy* (Cambridge, MA: Belknap Press of Harvard University Press, 1996).

unencumbered by moral or civic ties antecedent to choice. This vision cannot account for a wide range of moral and political obligations that we commonly recognize, such as obligations of loyalty or solidarity. By insisting that we are bound only by ends and roles we choose for themselves, it denies that we can ever be claimed by ends we have not chosen – ends given by nature or God, for example, or by our identities as members of families, peoples, cultures, or traditions.

Some liberals concede we may be bound by obligations such as these, but insist they apply to private life alone and have no bearing on politics. But this raises a further difficulty. Why insist on separating our identity as citizens from our identity as persons more broadly conceived? Why should political deliberation not reflect our best understanding of the highest human ends? Don't arguments about justice and rights unavoidably draw on particular conceptions of the good life, whether we admit it or not?

The problems in the theory of procedural liberalism show up in the practice it inspires. Over the past half-century, American politics has come to embody the version of liberalism that renounces the formative ambition and insists government should be neutral toward competing conceptions of the good life. Rather than tie liberty to self-government and the virtues that sustain it, the procedural republic seeks a framework of rights, neutral among ends, within which individuals can choose and pursue their own ends.

But the discontent that besets American public life today illustrates the inadequacy of this solution. A politics that brackets morality and religion too completely soon generates its own disenchantment. Where political discourse lacks moral resonance, the yearning for a public life of larger meaning finds undesirable expression. Groups like the Moral Majority seek to clothe the naked public square with narrow, intolerant moralisms. Fundamentalists rush in where liberals fear to tread. The disenchantment also assumes more secular forms. Absent a political agenda that addresses the moral dimension of public questions, attention becomes riveted on the private vices of public officials. Political discourse becomes increasingly preoccupied with the scandalous, the sensational and the confessional as purveyed by tabloids, talk shows and eventually the mainstream media as well. In cannot be said that the public philosophy of contemporary liberalism is wholly responsible for these tendencies. But its vision of political discourse is too spare to contain the moral energies of democratic life. It creates a moral void that opens the way for intolerance and other misguided moralisms.

A political agenda lacking substantive moral discourse is one symptom of the public philosophy of the procedural republic. Another is the loss of mastery. The triumph of the voluntarist conception of freedom has coincided with a growing sense of disempowerment. Despite the expansion of rights in recent decades, Americans find to their frustration that they are losing control of the forces that govern their lives. This has partly to do with the insecurity of jobs in the global economy, but it also reflects the self-image by which we live. The liberal self-image and the actual organization of modern social and economic life are sharply at odds. Even as we think and act as freely choosing, independent selves, we confront a world governed by impersonal structures of power that defy our understanding and control. The voluntarist conception of freedom leaves us ill equipped to contend with this condition. Liberated though we may be from the burden of identities we have not chosen, entitled though we may be to the range of rights assured by the welfare state, we find ourselves overwhelmed as we turn to face the world on our own resources.

The inability of the reigning political agenda to address the erosion of self-government and community reflects the impoverished conceptions of citizenship and freedom implicit in our public life. The procedural republic that has unfolded over the past half-century can now be seen as an epic experiment in the claims of liberal as against republican political thought. Our present predicament lends weight to the republican claim that liberty cannot be detached from self-government and the virtues that sustain it, that the formative project cannot be dispensed with after all. The procedural republic, it turns out, cannot secure the liberty it promises because it cannot inspire the moral and civic engagement self-government requires.

If the public philosophy of contemporary liberalism fails to answer democracy's discontent, it remains to ask how a renewed attention to republican themes might better equip us to contend with our condition. How would a political agenda informed by the civic strand of freedom differ from the one that now prevails? Is self-government in the republican sense even possible under modern conditions? If so, what economic and political arrangements would it require, and what qualities of character would be necessary to sustain them?

How American politics might recover its civic voice is not wholly a speculative matter. Although the public philosophy of the procedural republic predominates in our time, it has not extinguished the civic understanding of freedom. Around the edges of our political discourse and practice, hints of the formative project can still be glimpsed. As the reigning political agenda lost energy in the 1980s and 1990s, these residual civic impulses quickened. Americans of various ideological persuasions groped to articulate a politics that reached beyond the terms of the procedural republic and spoke to the anxieties of the time.

These groupings, however partial and inchoate, gesture nonetheless toward the kind of political debate that would accord greater attention to republican themes. These expressions of Americans' persisting civic aspirations have taken two forms; one emphasizes the moral, the other the economic prerequisites of self-government. The first is the attempt, coming largely but not wholly from the right, to revive virtue, character-formation and moral judgment as considerations in public policy and political discourse. The second involves a range of efforts, coming mostly though not entirely from the left, to contend with economic forces that disempower communities and threaten to erode the social fabric of democratic life.

[...]

Even a politics that engaged rather than avoided substantive moral discourse, that attended to the civic consequences of economic inequality, that strengthened the mediating institutions of civil society – even such a politics would confront a daunting obstacle. This obstacle consists in the formidable scale on which modern economic life is organized and the difficulty of constituting the democratic political authority necessary to govern it.

This difficulty actually involves two related challenges. One is to devise political institutions capable of governing the global economy. The other is to cultivate the civic identities necessary to sustain those institutions, to supply them with the moral authority they require. It is not obvious that both these challenges can be met.

In a world where capital and goods, information and images, pollution and people, flow across national boundaries with unprecedented ease, politics must assume transnational, even global forms, if only to keep up. Otherwise, economic power will go unchecked by democratically sanctioned political power. Nation-states, traditionally the vehicles of self-government, will find themselves increasingly unable to bring their citizens' judgments and values to bear on the economic forces that govern their destinies. The disempowering of the nation-state in relation to the global economy may be one source of the discontent that afflicts not only American politics but other democracies around the world.

If the global character of the economy suggests the need for transnational forms of governance, however, it remains to be seen whether such political units can inspire the identification and allegiance – the moral and civic culture – on which democratic authority ultimately depends. In fact there is reason to doubt that they can. Except in extraordinary moments, such as war, even nation-states find it difficult to inspire the sense of community and civic engagement self-government requires. Political associations more expansive than nations, and with fewer cultural traditions and historical memories to draw upon, may find the task of cultivating commonality more difficult still.

Even the European Community, one of the most successful experiments in supranational governance, has so far failed to cultivate a common European identity sufficient to support its mechanisms of economic and political integregation. Advocates of further European integration worry about the 'democratic deficit'.

[...]

The cosmopolitan ideal is flawed, both as a moral ideal and as a public philosophy for self-government in our time. The notion that universal identities must always take precedence over particular ones has a long and varied history. Kant tied morality to respect for persons as rational beings independent of their particular characteristics, and Marx identified the highest solidarity as that of man with his species-being. Perhaps the clearest statement of the cosmopolitan ethic as a moral ideal is the one offered by the Enlightenment philosopher Montesquieu:

> If I knew something useful to me, but prejudicial to my family, I would reject it from my soul. If I knew something useful to my family but not to my country, I would try to forget it. If I knew something useful to my country, but prejudicial to Europe, or useful to Europe but prejudicial to humankind, I would regard it as a crime ... [For] I am a man before I am a Frenchman, or rather ... I am necessarily a man, while I am a Frenchman only by chance.[2]

If our encompassing loyalties should always take precedence over more local ones, then the distinction between friends and strangers should ideally be overcome. Our special concern for the welfare of friends would be a kind of prejudice, a measure of our distance from universal human concern. Montesquieu does not shrink from this conclusion. 'A truly virtuous man would come to the aid of the most distant stranger as quickly as to his own friend,' he writes. 'If men were perfectly virtuous, they wouldn't have friends'.[3]

It is difficult to imagine a world in which persons were so virtuous that they had no friends, only a universal disposition to friendliness. The problem is not simply that such a world would be difficult to bring about but that it would be difficult to recognize as a human world. The love of humanity is a noble sentiment, but most of the time we live our lives by smaller solidarities. This may reflect certain limits to the bounds of moral sympathy. More important, it reflects the fact that we learn to love humanity not in general but through its particular expressions.

[...]

The cosmopolitan ethic is wrong, not for asserting that we have certain obligations to humanity as a whole but rather for insisting that the more universal communities we inhabit must always take precedence over more particular ones.

Most of us find ourselves claimed, at one time or another, by a wide range of different communities, some overlapping, others contending. When obligations conflict, there is no way of deciding in advance, once and for all, which should prevail. Deciding which of one's identities is properly engaged – as parent or professional, follower of a faith or partisan of a cause, citizen of one's country or citizen of the world – is a matter of moral reflection and political deliberation that will vary according to the issue at stake. The best deliberation will attend to the content of the claims, their relative moral weight and their role in the narratives by which the participants make sense of their lives. Montesquieu to the contrary, such claims cannot simply be ranked according to the size or scope of the community that gives rise to them. No general principle of much practical use can rank obligations in advance, and yet some responses to moral and political dilemmas are better – more admirable or worthy or fitting – than others. Unless this were so, there would be no point, and no burden, in deliberation itself.

The moral defect of the cosmopolitan ethic is related to its political defect. For even as the global economy demands more universal forms of political identity, the pull of the particular reasserts itself. Even as nations accede to new institutions of global governance, they confront rising demands from ethnic, religious and linguistic groups for various forms of political recognition and self-determination. These demands are prompted in part by the dissolution of the empires that once contained them, such as the Soviet Union. But the growing aspiration for the public expression of communal identities may also reflect a yearning for political identities that can situate people in a world increasingly governed by vast and distant forces.

For a time, the nation-state promised to answer this yearning, to provide the link between identity and self-rule. In theory at least, each state was a more or less self-sufficient political and economic unit that gave expression to the collective identity of a people defined by a common history, language or tradition. The nation-state laid claim to the allegiance of its citizens on the ground that its exercise of sovereignty expressed their collective identity.

In the contemporary world, however, this claim is losing its force. National sovereignty is eroded from above by the mobility of capital, goods and information across national boundaries, the integration of world financial markets, the transnational character of industrial production. At the same time, national sovereignty is challenged from below by the resurgent aspirations of subnational groups for autonomy and self-rule. As their effective sovereignty fades, nations gradually lose their hold on the allegiance of their citizens.

[...]

The cosmopolitan vision is wrong to suggest that we can restore self-government simply by pushing sovereignty and citizenship upward. The hope for self-government lies not in relocating sovereignty but in dispersing it. The most promising alternative to the sovereign state is not a one-world community based on the solidarity of humankind, but a multiplicity of communities and political bodies – some more, some less extensive than nations – among which sovereignty is diffused. The nation-state need not fade away, only cede its claim as sole repository of sovereign power and primary object of political allegiance. Different forms of political association would govern different spheres of life and engage different aspects of our identities. Only a regime that disperses sovereignty both upward and downward can combine the power required to rival global market forces with the differentiation required of a public life that hopes to inspire the reflective allegiance of its citizens.

In some places, dispersing sovereignty may entail according greater cultural and political autonomy to subnational communities – such as Catalans and

Kurds, Scots and Québecois – even while strengthening and democratizing transnational structures, such as the European Union. Or it may involve modes of devolution and subsidiarity along geographic rather than ethnic and cultural lines. Arrangements such as these may ease the strife that arises when state sovereignty is an all-or-nothing affair, absolute and indivisible, the only meaningful form of self-determination.

In the United States, which never was a nation-state in the European sense, proliferating sites of political engagement may take a different form. America was born of the conviction that sovereignty need not reside in a single place. From the start, the Constitution divided power among branches and levels of government. Over time, however, we too have pushed sovereignty and citizenship upward, in the direction of the nation.

The nationalizing of American political life occurred largely in response to industrial capitalism. The consolidation of economic power called forth the consolidation of political power. Present-day conservatives who rail against big government often ignore this fact. They wrongly assume that rolling back the power of the national government would liberate individuals to pursue their own ends instead of leaving them at the mercy of economic forces beyond their control.

Conservative complaints about big government find popular resonance, but not for the reasons conservatives articulate. The American welfare state is politically vulnerable because it does not rest on a sense of national community adequate to its purpose. The nationalizing project that unfolded from the Progressive era to the New Deal to the Great Society succeeded only in part. It managed to create a strong national government but failed to cultivate a shared national identity. As the welfare state developed, it drew less on an ethic of social solidarity and mutual obligation and more on an ethic of fair procedures and individual rights. But the liberalism of the procedural republic proved an inadequate substitute for the strong sense of citizenship the welfare state requires.

If the nation cannot summon more than a minimal commonality, it is unlikely that the global community can do better, at least on its own. A more promising basis for a democratic politics that reaches beyond nations is a revitalized civic life nourished in the more particular communities we inhabit. In the age of NAFTA, the politics of neighborhood matters more, not less. People will not pledge allegiance to vast and distant entities, whatever their importance, unless those institutions are somehow connected to political arrangements that reflect the identity of the participants.

This is reason to consider the unrealized possibilities implicit in American federalism. We commonly think of federalism as a constitutional doctrine that, once dormant, has recently been revived by conservatives who would shift power from the federal government to the states. But federalism is more than a theory of intergovernmental relations. It also stands for a political vision that offers an alternative to the sovereign state and the univocal political identities such states require. It suggests that self-government works best when sovereignty is dispersed and citizenship formed across multiple sites of civic engagement. This aspect of federalism informs the pluralist version of republican politics. It supplies the differentiation that separates Tocqueville's republicanism from Rousseau's, that saves the formative project from slipping into coercion.

[...]

The formative aspect of republican politics requires public spaces that gather citizens together, enable them to interpret their condition and cultivate solidarity and civic engagement. For the civil rights movement, these public spaces were provided by the black churches of the South. They were the sites of the mass meetings, the civic education, the prayer and song, that equipped blacks to join in the boycotts and the marches of the movement.[4]

We commonly think of the civil rights movement as finding its fruition in the civil rights and voting rights laws passed by Congress. But the nation would never have acted without a movement whose roots lay in more particular identities and places.

[...]

The global media and markets that shape our lives beckon us to a world beyond boundaries and belonging. But the civic resources we need to master these forces, or at least to contend with them, are still to be found in the places and stories, memories and meanings, incidents and identities, that situate us in the world and give our lives their moral particularity.

The public philosophy by which we live bids us to bracket these attachments, to set them aside for political purposes, to conduct our political debates without reference to them. But a procedural republic that banishes moral and religious argument from political discourse makes for an impoverished civic life. It also fails to answer the aspiration for self-government; its image of citizens as free and independent selves, unencumbered by moral or civic ties they have not chosen, cannot sustain the public spirit that equips us for self-rule.

Since the days of Aristotle's polis, the republican tradition has viewed self-government as an activity rooted in a particular place, carried out by citizens loyal to that place and the way of life it embodies. Self-government today, however, requires a politics that plays itself out in a multiplicity of settings, from neighborhoods to nations to the world as a whole. Such a politics requires citizens who can think and act as multiply-situated selves. The civic virtue distinctive to our time is the capacity to negotiate our way among the sometimes overlapping, sometimes conflicting obligations that claim us, and to live with the tension to which multiple loyalties give rise. This capacity is difficult to sustain, for it is easier to live with the plurality between persons than within them.

The republican tradition reminds us that to every virtue there corresponds a characteristic form of corruption or decay. Where civic virtue consists in holding together the complex identities of modern selves, it is vulnerable to corruption of two kinds. The first is the tendency to fundamentalism, the response of those who cannot abide the ambiguity associated with divided sovereignty and multiply-encumbered selves. To the extent that contemporary politics puts sovereign states and sovereign selves in question, it is likely to provoke reactions from those who would banish ambiguity, shore up borders, harden the distinction between insiders and outsiders and promise a politics to 'take back our culture and take back our country', to 'restore our sovereignty' with a vengeance.[5]

The second corruption to which multiply-encumbered citizens are prone is the drift to formless, protean, storyless selves, unable to weave the various strands of their identity into a coherent whole. Political community depends on the narratives by which people make sense of their condition and interpret the common life they share; at its best, political deliberation is not only about competing policies but also about competing interpretations of the character of a community, of its purposes and ends. A politics that proliferates the sources and sites of citizenship complicates the interpretive project. At a time when the narrative resources of civic life are already strained – as the soundbites, factoids and disconnected images of our media-saturated culture attest – it becomes increasingly difficult to tell the tales that order our lives. There is a growing danger that, individually and collectively, we will find ourselves slipping into a fragmented, storyless condition. The loss of the capacity for narrative would amount to the ultimate disempowering of the human subject, for without narrative there is no continuity between present and past, and therefore no responsibility, and therefore no possibility of acting together to govern ourselves.

Since human beings are storytelling beings, we are bound to rebel against the drift to storylessness. But there is no guarantee that the rebellions will take salutary form. Some, in their hunger for story, will be drawn to the vacant, vicarious fare of confessional talk shows, celebrity scandals, and sensational trials. Others will seek refuge in fundamentalism. The hope of our time rests instead with those who can summon the conviction and restraint to make sense of our condition and repair the civic life on which democracy depends.

NOTES

1. Immanuel Kant, 'Perpetual Peace' (1795), in *Kant's Political Writings*, Hans Reiss (ed.) (Cambridge: Cambridge University Press, 1970), pp. 112–13.
2. Montesquieu, *Mes pensées*, in *Œuvres complètes*, Roger Chaillois (ed.) (Paris: Gallimard, 1949), nos 10, 11, pp. 980–1.
3. Ibid., no. 604, pp. 1129–30.
4. See Aldon D. Morris, *The Origins of the Civil Rights Movement* (New York: Free Press, 1984).
5. The quoted phrases are from Patrick J. Buchanan, Speech to Republican National Convention, August 12 1992, and from Buchanan as quoted in Richard L. Berke, 'A Conservative Sure His Time Has Come', *New York Times*, May 30 1995, p. A1.

64

FUSION REPUBLICANISM

Nancy L. Rosenblum

'Fusion republicanism' is my name for the fluid mix of democratic ideology, potential militancy and invocation of civic virtue prevalent in American political life. It is not a consistent ideology much less a systematic political philosophy. Rather, as 'fusion' suggests, it is a conglomeration of disparate elements of political thought and practice that coalesce around certain unifying republican themes. Fusion republicanism covers a broad spectrum of positions, from respectable democratic theory to civic fundamentalism promulgated by extremists. It is manifest in many quarters of political life: it is institutionalized in 'our localism', for example; it is latent in the conduct of juries with their potential for nullification – a characteristically republican form of opposition to proceduralism; and it is overt in self-styled citizen militias permanently poised for armed resistance. The elements of fusion republicanism are mutually reinforcing, even if their proponents are not always allies.

[...]

It is as important to locate Sandel's public philosophy in the company of fusion republicanism as to discriminate it from the liberalism he rejects; republicanism is, after all, his avowed ideological framework. Like any much-used political concept, it gives rise to John Adams' lament that republicanism 'may signify any thing, every thing, or nothing'. Still, as Gordon Wood explains, from its first applications in America, it signified more than popular

From: Anita K. Allen and Milton C. Regan, Jr. (ed.), *Debating Democracy's Discontent* (Oxford: Oxford University Press, 1998).

elections, more even than a form of government. Republicanism was celebrated for 'its spirit, its morality, its freedom, its sense of friendship and duty, and its vision of society'.[1] That is the bright side of republicanism, which also exhibits grimmer faces. If liberalism has excesses and errant strands, so does republicanism. The elements of fusion republicanism, including its pathologies, recur throughout American history and are exhibited plainly in contemporary public life. Republicanism as well as liberalism is 'a tale fraught with moral complexity, replete with strange ideological bed-fellows'.[2] I intend to follow Sandel in bringing to the foreground the 'often unreflective background' of our current political discourse. To the extent that Sandel would affirm or disavow contemporary expressions of republicanism, it should shed light on where he is positioned on the spectrum and may, secondarily, illuminate his relation to liberalism. In any case, it is necessary to fill out his map of the terrain.

Democracy's Discontent is a sober consideration of certain facets of republicanism in American political thought. Most importantly, Sandel describes the shift from an approach to political economy guided by considerations of the conditions of self-government to one directed mainly by the imperatives of growth and distributive justice. In doing so he adds an important dimension to the standard repertoire of the civic uses of property. Sandel takes us beyond the Jeffersonian insistence on real property as an aspect of personal identity and bulwark against influence and corruption, and beyond the notion that productive labor reflects republican virtue and marks the earner as a citizen in contrast to a slave on the one hand and the idle aristocrat on the other. Moreover, he sets out to provide a political, not just intellectual, history of this theme: identifying the strains of American public philosophy that relate to collective economic self-control, the politicians that promulgate them and the associations (like the Knights of Labor) that have been its chief carriers.

This is a perceptive but selective account of the historical strands of republicanism in American political thought. It draws attention to vital subjects for democratic deliberation, but it also disregards much of the terrain of fusion republicanism, historical and contemporary. There is nothing wrong with selectivity, particularly if the principles of selection are pronounced. But the limited contours of Sandel's account are bound to affect our assessment of his diagnosis of the American political condition overall. His thesis – propounded with severe certainty – that the eclipse of republican public philosophy by a dominant procedural liberalism is the source of democracy's discontent may need modification if there are other contributing sources to discontent, among them arrant elements of republicanism.

[...]

The scale of self-government is a standard democratic theme, and republicanism militates in favor of localism. It is driven by concern that political representatives not be at such a distance from constituents that they are unaccountable; concern for a community's ability to control its own character;

and concern for cultivating civic engagement. The assumption is that political loyalties affix most securely to this level of government, where residents can be consulted on particulars and representation is 'actual'. 'As the republican tradition taught', Sandel advises, 'local attachments can serve self-government by engaging citizens in a common life beyond their private pursuits, by forming the habit of attending to public things'.[2]

[...]

Sandel's historical sympathies lie with decentralizing rather than nationalizing versions of economic reform and with movements aimed at 'protecting local communities and independent producers from the effects of massive concentrations of economic power'.[3] That said, his claims for the present are cautious. He is less interested in policy prescriptions than in simply urging that public deliberation take account of the civic consequences of political economy. His illustration of exemplary local self-organization is the community development corporation, which mixes self-help with federal and business support.[4] This sort of effort, while commendable, is a modest and typically short-lived 'pocket of political activism'.[5] It does not speak to the structural obstacles to casting cities as an alternative form of decentralized power with the capacity to moderate economic instability, say, or transform workplaces into scenes of civic education.

On the larger question of political authority, it is unclear under what conditions Sandel would favor local or state measures – either legal constraints or moral and material incentives – to prevent businesses from down-sizing or relocating, for example. It is also unclear how he judges the ceaseless competition among cities and suburbs to lure enterprises there. Is this a selfish scramble to advance private interests (corruption)? Or the lively expression of healthy localism on the part of equally civic-minded communities concerned about the social conditions of citizenship?[6]

Republicanism faces the challenge of determining *which* level of political community in a complex, pluralistic polity should regulate specific activities, and for whose benefit. Localism replicates the debate about business: whether corporate responsibility is to shareholders, stakeholders or the wider public. The question of allocating authority is more acute when the principal consideration is promoting civic engagement by making self-government effective. For virtual authority without actual control is more likely to frustrate expectations for self-government than repair democracy's discontent.

[...]

The usual response to any suggestion that the elements of fusion republicanism converge and are mutually reinforcing in practice is fierce denial. Understandably, even leaders who indulge in republican charges against their political opponents do not want to be held to account for excesses and abominations committed in the name of democratic discontent: 'the attempt to locate in society's political discourse the cause of a lunatic's action is ... contemptible'; the connection between political speech and hateful crime is 'grotesque and offensive'.[7]

The trouble is, in daily political life it is not always easy to draw a bright line separating points on the spectrum. When is militant republican rhetoric calculated to exploit popular feelings, or the exaggerated pose of partisans charging one another with disregard for the common good? When does it reflect the deep beliefs and herald the potentially violent action of civic fundamentalists? When is it the considered judgment of virtuous citizens? Is Alabama Governor Jones' threat to use state troops to resist a court order rhetorical defiance in the name of civic renewal, or extremism? Is the Governor safely ensconced on the civil side of democracy's discontent? In individual instances we try to sort out principled antifederalists, say, from true believers in some fantastic conspiracy. Despite the difficulty, as a practical matter we must insist strongly on drawing these distinctions.

From the standpoint of political theory, dissecting the elements of fusion republicanism and separating out proponents in a way that does not taint sober public philosophy or assign guilt by association is even more complicated. It is beyond the scope of this short chapter, but I want to conclude by briefly suggesting two areas where work needs to be done.

In part, the difficulty is a function of the genuinely perplexing relationships among political theory, 'public philosophy', and popular ideology. What is the direction of intellectual influence? Bits and pieces of ideas from political theory, public philosophy and ideology are exchanged. Bits and pieces are appropriated unsystematically in popular political discourse and as rationales for political action. Understanding these relationships involves a sociology of knowledge to explain how concepts move out into general circulation and are taken up. Karl Mannheim's writing on conservatism is a model, but this sort of study has not been applied to republicanism. How do ideas move out, become used and misused? What are the principal carrier groups? Contemporary citizen militias claim to be part of a long-standing civic tradition, but are they? Or are they *sui generis*, recent American originals? The ideology of localism, say, or the mechanisms of direct popular resistance have not been uncovered as well as the intellectual high ground Sandel recalls for us in his discussion of the political economy of citizenship. Tracing the lines of influence requires an exhaustive history of the strands of fusion republicanism.

The second difficulty concerns the political anatomy of the elements of fusion republicanism. The polemical objective behind labels of 'extremism' applied to any ideological spectrum – left or right, liberal or republican – is to designate advocates as an insignificant 'fringe' and to disavow any gradual continuum. We should not permit ourselves the comforting assumption that fringe groups are responsible for the climate of hostility that transforms democratic discontent into anti-government hatred. Again, 'extremists' are the *beneficiaries* of a diffuse climate of hostility and of widespread agitation to correct the sense of disempowerment.

However, an accurate identification of a particular position as core and others as 'extremist' is an empirical matter. It is particularly difficult when the center is shifting, as it appears to be in the USA.[8] Sandel sees a moving center to American political ideology overall, away from procedural liberalism toward some form of republicanism. As I have tried to show, the elements of fusion republicanism are fluid, and republicanism may have its own moving center.

Subtitled 'America in search of a public philosophy', *Democracy's Discontent* suggests that Sandel's account of republicanism articulates widespread sentiment and addresses commonly felt needs. Do social science studies of public attitudes and beliefs sustain this assumption? Does Sandel track what Americans think? Are his examples of republican discontent and his model correctives representative? Sandel's public philosophy claims the intellectual high ground of republicanism, but it is an empirical question whether it is republicanism's current center. It may be that shifts along the spectrum of fusion republicanism – the real limits on local autonomy, say, or the experience of jury nullification, or the strengthening of civic fundamentalism – push Sandel's position closer to the edge of the republican spectrum, and closer to liberalism, even to the legalistic, procedural face of liberalism.

In any case, this sort of anatomy lesson is the responsibility of political theorists who advocate a public philosophy. Sandel should acknowledge the spectrum of fusion republicanism. He should be at least as attentive to its current expressions, including pathologies, as he is to liberalism's. He should indicate which expressions earn his enthusiastic support? Which are unfaithful to his understanding of republican principles? Which are aberrant? What institutions of self-government are vulnerable to abuse? What ideological alliances does he think are in the best interests of civic renewal? This responsibility is made more urgent to the extent that fusion republicanism is a real force in American political life.

NOTES

1. Gordon S. Wood, *The Radicalism of the American Revolution* (New York: Vintage, 1991), pp. 95–6, 99.
2. Michael J. Sandel, *Democracy's Discontent: American in Search of a Public Philosophy* (Cambridge, MA: Harvard University Press, 1996), p. 314.
3. Ibid., p. 227.
4. Ibid., pp. 303–4.
5. Ibid., p. 333.
6. Suburbs compete with cities and with one another for businesses and affluent residents that add to the tax base with minimal fiscal impact. (The boroughs of New York City compete with one another to lure businesses or get them to expand there. 'The Wrong Way to Lure Business', *New York Times*, editorial, 8 September 1996, sec. 4, p. 16).
7. Columnist George Will, cited in Lewis H. Lapham, 'Seen But Not Heard: The Message of the Oklahoma Bombing', *Harper's Magazine*, July 1995, p. 32; Newt Gingrich, Speaker of the House of Representatives, cited in Lapham, p. 34.
8. Alan Wolfe, 'Sociology, Liberalism, and the Radical Right', *New Left Review*, p. 28 (1987), pp. 3–27.

65

A DEFENSE OF MINIMALIST LIBERALISM

Richard Rorty

Sandel sees liberals and republicans as disagreeing about the nature of freedom, or liberty. Republicans believe that liberty 'depends on sharing in self-government'.[1] Liberals believe that it consists in 'the capacity of persons to choose their values and ends'. On Sandel's account,

> The voluntarist conception of freedom promises to lay to rest, once and for all, the risks of republican politics. If liberty can be detached from the exercise of self-government and conceived instead as the capacity of persons to choose their own ends, then the difficult task of forming civic virtue can finally be dispensed with.[2]

The way Sandel sets up the quarrel between liberals and republicans seems to me factitious. Most people nowadays believe *both* that a free society is one in which citizens participate in government *and* that it is one in which people are, within the limits Mill defined, left alone to choose their own values and ends. They see no need to choose between these two definitions. Any society that does not meet *both* requirements, they think, hardly deserves to be called 'free'.

Another problem I have with the passage I have quoted is that I cannot think of a liberal who would want either to 'detach liberty from the exercise of self-government', or to 'dispense with the difficult task of forming civic virtue'. Kant, Mill and Dewey do not fit either description. Rawls, I assume, wants the state to do its best to inculcate the civic virtue of taking the right to be prior to

From: Anita K. Allen and Milton C. Regan, Jr. (ed.), *Debating Democracy's Discontent* (Oxford: Oxford University Press, 1998).

the good. I cannot imagine any of these thinkers claiming that the risks of republican politics can ever be avoided.

My main reaction to this passage, however, is that the level of abstraction at which we pose questions like 'in what does liberty consist?' or 'what does "freedom" really mean?' is too high to do us any good. I think that philosophers and political scientists should resist the temptation to ascend to that level. Unlike Sandel, I do not think that America is 'in search of a public philosophy'. It is certainly in search of a moral identity. But I do not think that such an identity can be acquired by getting clearer about the meanings of terms like 'liberty'.

[. . .]

Sometimes people cannot live with themselves unless they draw a line in the sand. Their moral identity demands that if their community begins to tolerate heresy, or to permit slavery, then they must emigrate, or foment a revolution or otherwise break off their participation in the political process. Sometimes a whole segment of society needs to draw a line in the sand. Then we get civil war, or secession.

I take the pragmatist, minimalist liberal, position to be: try to educate the citizenry in the civic virtue of having as few such compelling interests, beliefs and desires as possible. Try, for example, to get them to change the subject from 'When does human life begin?' to 'How can some unprincipled and wishy-washy consensus about abortion be hammered out?' Try to get them to be as flexible and wishy-washy as possible, and to value democratic consensus more than they value almost anything else. Try to make them as little inclined to emigrate or secede as possible, by encouraging them to tolerate compromise on matters which they previously thought uncompromisable.

Notice that this position has nothing to do with the nature or the extent of truth. It does not say that there is no truth about moral and religious questions. It does not say that they are matters of opinion rather than knowledge. It says instead: try to raise as few moral and religious questions as you can manage. Try to replace as many such questions as possible with political questions. Minimalist liberalism does not say that morality and religion are noncognitive, or somehow epistemologically or metaphysically second-rate. It just tries to deflect attention from all questions other than 'what sort of compromise might we be able freely to agree upon?' The procedural republic tries to instill in its citizens the virtues of compromise and tolerance, and to educate them out of other virtues (those of the warrior or the nun, for example) – the kind of virtues which might get in the way of compromise and tolerance.

Sandel is of course right that there are some questions, such as slavery, about which we twentieth-century Americans cannot tolerate compromise. Rawls would agree that any procedural republic has to have some moral backbone: agreement on procedure cannot be all that keeps the community together. But Rawls wants this moral backbone to be, so to speak, as thin and flexible as possible. We minimalists think that there is no point in asking philosophers to figure out how thin is too thin, nor how flexible is too flexible. For those too are practical questions. Democracies make political decisions about what principles to compromise. Philosophers then clean up the mess by formulating new principles which justify having compromised the old principles.

[...]

The United States, in the decades after the Second World War, offered one of the very rare peacetime examples of a huge industrialized democracy living a very intense 'common life at the level of the nation'. For those decades witnessed the rise and the triumph of the civil rights movement. Limited as that triumph was, it amounted to the greatest single set of changes in the manners and morals of the Americans ever accomplished by peaceful political consensus. Each of these changes was intensely discussed in almost every bar, union hiring-hall, board-room and locker-room in the country. If, as Sandel says, 'the republican tradition taught that to be free is to share in governing a political community that controls its own fate,[3] then republicans should rejoice in what America accomplished between 1950 and 1970.

Sandel does, in fact, rejoice. He describes the civil rights movement as 'the finest expression of republican politics in our time'.[4] But I do not see why it could not equally well be described as the finest expression of *liberal* politics in our time. Certainly we who call ourselves 'liberals' think of it that way. It seems to me that only Sandel's attempt to encumber political liberalism with philosophical voluntarism prevents him from accepting this alternative description.

If thirty years ago the USA was still capable of pulling itself up by its own moral bootstraps, can it be accurate to describe postwar America as gradually coming to despair over its ability to govern itself? Sandel thinks of postwar America this way partly because he thinks that 'the liberal self-image and the actual organization of modern social and economic life are sharply at odds'. But, once again, I do not think that what he calls 'the liberal self-image', the image of the self as pure unencumbered will, exists outside the minds of philosophers and political theorists. I do not think that the average American's self-image has shifted from republican to liberal. The farthest I can go toward agreement with Sandel's sense that things are getting worse is to agree that Americans were more trusting, tolerant and self-confident during the King years than they are now.

But this seems explicable by the fact that during those years the gap between rich and poor was narrowing, whereas more recently it has been widening. In the last twenty-five years, most Americans have lost the sense of economic security which the previous twenty produced. The change in national mood seems to me sufficiently accounted for by economic facts. I see no need to appeal, as Sandel does, to changes in moral sensibility. Sandel thinks that:

The sense of disempowerment that afflicts citizens of the procedural republic may reflect the loss of agency that results when liberty is detached from self-government and located in the will of an independent self, unencumbered by moral and communal ties it has chosen.[5]

I think that notions like 'loss of agency' and 'the will of an independent self' are much too abstract, much too philosophical, to explain what is going on.

More concrete stories than Sandel's are told by Edward Luttwak and Michael Lind. These stories are about what Lind calls the 'Brazilianization' of America: the increasing power of a conspicuously consuming oligarchy, the increasing social and cultural distance between that oligarchy and everybody else, and the consequent loss of assurance that most American children can look forward to a satisfying and secure future. The stories Luttwak and Lind tell, concentrating on money rather than self-image, seem to me more plausible than Sandel's. Granted that nowadays there is a lot of disenchantment with politics and a lot of fear for the possibility of self-government, I do not think this is because of an increasingly voluntarist self-image. I suspect that it has the same banal causes as gave rise to disenchantment with politics during the Gilded Age: the rise of a self-enclosed oligarchy, increasing economic insecurity in the bottom half of the population, and the increasing shamelessness of elected officials in accepting bribes.

I have no idea whether we shall see, in the next century, the sort of re-enchantment with politics that gave us the Progressive era and, later, the civil rights movement. Maybe this time around the oligarchs will win, and democratic government be reduced to a farce once and for all. But in trying to estimate the chances that this tragedy will occur, I do not think it helps to look for changes in our understanding of the nature of liberty or of selfhood.

By way of conclusion, let me say that I quite agree with Sandel when he says that 'a politics that brackets morality and religion too completely soon generates its own disenchantment'.[6] But I think it important to remember that what emerges from Rawlsian attempts to put the search for consensual compromise above moral and religious conviction is not an *absence* of morality and religion, but new moralities and new religions. The morality of America was different after the King years than before, but it was no less a morality, and no less cohesive a bond between citizens. The religion of many American Protestants became different in the decades after the theologians of the Progressive era proclaimed the Social Gospel. But the resulting version of Protestantism – a version that paid less attention to sex and more to love – was still a religion, and was no less efficacious in the lives of believers.

Politics will always be bound up with morality and religion, but morality and religion are as much subject to historical mutation as is politics. In the past it was assumed that they provided a framework within which to discuss politics. I read Dewey, and try to read Rawls, as taking democratic politics as a framework within which to discuss morality and religion.

NOTES

1. Michael J. Sandel, *Democracy's Discontent: America in Search of a Public Philosophy* (Cambridge, MA: Harvard University Press, 1996), p. 5.
2. Ibid., p. 10.
3. Ibid., p. 2.
4. Ibid., p. 348.
5. Ibid., p. 4.
6. Ibid., p. 12.

66

MICHAEL SANDEL AND RICHARD RORTY: TWO MODELS OF THE REPUBLIC

Richard Sennett

Michael Sandel's *Democracy's Discontent* is an inspired and deeply disturbing polemic about citizenship. It asks if our very ways of thinking about political activity can address these expanded demands, particularly in the economic realm, and answers that our political understanding is too impoverished and arid to do so. Sandel's book has aroused great debate in the United States, most trenchantly an attack by the philosopher Richard Rorty. But the issue Sandel raises is so basic that it transcends the confines of scholarly argument or indeed of American society. (As a reader's weather advisory, I should note that both writers are known to me; in this chapter, I want to make clear, as impartially as I can, why they are in conflict.)

Sandel's target is liberal politics, not in its ordinary American sense as championship of the welfare state, but in the more classical usage of the word 'liberal' in political theory; this is a tradition which begins with Locke, follows one path in the writings of Kant, another, utilitarian direction in the work of John Stuart Mill and finds one denouement in such modern philosophers as John Rawls.

In Sandel's view, this liberal tradition has erred in imagining citizens ideally as 'unencumbered selves', members of the genus *citizen* without, in Sandel's words 'any special obligations to their fellow citizens, apart from the universal, natural duty not to commit injustice.'[1] Such a view seems to Sandel wrong in principle:

From: *The Times Literary Supplement*, 18 October 1996.

> It fails to capture those loyalties and responsibilities whose moral force
> consists partly in ... understanding ourselves as the particular persons we
> are – as members of this family or city or nation or people. As bearers of
> that history. As citizens of this republic.[2]

Such a minimalist view of citizenship, he maintains, cannot provide people
with the will and energy they need to fight for the common good, particularly
when that shared well-being is challenged, as it is, today, by economic forces
which threaten to crack apart community and isolate people in individual
struggles for survival. The 'encumbrances' of religious faith, family feeling,
communal identity are instead the ingredients of the political will to fight for a
better common fate.

For Sandel, formal politics ought to orchestrate these social relations. It can
only perform this sovereign task if it makes substantive judgments of value:
rather than affirm the right of homosexuals to live in a married state, for
instance, the polity has to affirm that homosexual unions share family virtues
kindred to heterosexual ones; rather than simply affirm the private right of a
woman to choose, the polity in dealing with abortion has actually to decide
when life begins.[3]

Sandel's is a politics of commitment. He calls it 'republican', again not to
identify his views with the American Republican Party – if that institution has
any firm views beyond the sponsorship of greed – but in order to make common
cause with American political leaders like James Madison or Abraham Lincoln
who believed the State should serve as the place of judgment for society, rather
than more passively as society's umpire. Sandel thus does not dwell in Clintonia,
that other America in which words speak louder than deeds. Sandel's version of
republican democracy focuses on surmounting the hesitancy that impedes
acting together; democracy means making and keeping mutual commitments.
More largely, *Democracy's Discontent* affirms the pursuit of the common good
in republican democracy in contrast to the pursuit of procedural rights in liberal
democracy.

Most of Sandel's critics have attacked this general account of liberalism and
republicanism, but it occupies only the first third of his book. The last two-
thirds of *Democracy's Discontent*, called 'The Political Economy of Citizenship', explores with great historical acumen just how these two principles have
become manifest in the real world of labor, class, and capitalist development.
Sandel earns his theory by this history.

At the risk of brutally simplifying, this history could be summarized as the
unintended triumph of liberal democracy in the course of capitalism's evolution
in America.

[...]

Words like 'duty' and 'loyalty' do contain in themselves a coercive undertow,
and it is that current in Sandel's thinking which his most serious critics, such as

Richard Rorty, have contested. Rorty's politics are as left-leaning as Sandel's, but he leans in that direction from a different position.

First, Rorty does not think the public is 'in search of a public philosophy', as Sandel's subtitle proclaims, because for Rorty, there is no need to choose between liberal and republican goals. The public wants both rights and common goods; it deserves both, and it gets too little of each.

Second, Rorty rejects the characterization of liberalism in terms of its belief in a 'minimalist self', at least liberalism of a pragmatic sort. 'All selves are always already equally encumbered, but some of them are encumbered with good beliefs and desires and some with bad ones.'[4] For instance, Rorty argues, membership in an American fundamentalist church makes a person less apt to search for the common democratic good 'than does an affiliation with an extended family, a trade union, or a bowling league'.[5] 'Take your own views seriously, he says to Sandel, and you really will have to judge between good and bad, or even more perilously, true and false beliefs; your polity will shrink radically once you start to do so, the Christian Coalition will be expelled beyond the pale, the local trade union and bowling league within it. The anti-democratic character of this ultimate judgment is why Rorty wants to change the subject, in the case of abortion, 'from "when does human life begin?" to "how can some unprincipled and wishy-washy consensus about abortion be hammered out?"'

Finally, the two disagree about what Richard Rorty calls 'sentiment' but what seems to me a much broader intellectual issue.

One of the most moving passages in Sandel's book is his depiction of the Southern general Robert E. Lee on the eve of the Civil War, torn between fighting in the name of his native Virginia or for the principle of the American Union. Sandel contemplates Lee's moral dilemma in deciding to 'stand with his people, even to lead them in a cause which he opposed'.[6] For Sandel this is a telling instance of the sense of obligation which creates commitment. When he writes of Lee as an example of 'the disposition to see and bear one's life circumstance as a reflectively situated being',[7] the key word in that phrase is 'bear'. Politics is not about the pursuit of happiness; it addresses shared experiences which weigh heavily on those who do their duty by one another. Sandel's use of the word 'encumbered' evokes this same weight. Lee's plight resonates with other forms of republican sentiment; the necessity of making commitments to a particular collective good, if not always tragic, more often than not entails an arduous, painful sacrifice.

Rorty looks at Lee's dilemma as an instance of what he calls 'irony'. By this he does not intend any frou-frou lightness. Rather, he means the capacity for distancing oneself from circumstances so as to judge well whether and how to act; Lee was possessed of that ironic distance, though I imagine Rorty believes Lee's tragedy lay in accepting the more local rather than the larger common good. But the capacity for ironic distance seems to Rorty a genuine moral sentiment, and it leads him to a particular political credo: 'I do not think that the state can do much to instill irony in its citizens ...'[8] That moral temper has more to do with culture and the habits of everyday life.

So this debate is really about the relation between civil society and political activity. Sandel sees civil society culminating in political action – or it should move in that direction if we are to do battle with an ever more corrosive capitalism. For Rorty, civil society, whether strong or weak, ironic or blind, stands beyond the reach of politics. Moreover, the 'network of beliefs and desires' that Rorty calls the self is too complicated a map to have a single destination. While, for Sandel, the more weighted, encumbered with commitment, the more consequent and dignified the self becomes. As a result, what I detect in this debate is that Sandel is more likely, and Rorty less likely, to believe political activity is cathartic.

This is a philosophical disagreement about the nature of citizenship, but one with historical resonances and practical consequences. John Winthrop's arguments in favor of a Puritan commonwealth eerily foreshadow Michael Sandel's views on democracy, while colonial Quakers sounded a more Rortian note. Those Quakers worried about 'the immoderate desire for the good', in William Sharples' words, fearing the personal disappointment and political confusion that immoderate desire for the good inevitably produces. So does Richard Rorty. But Sandel, like Winthrop, sees matters differently. Both the Puritan and the republican-socialist have worried about the lack of will and energy in the polity – if only our difficulties lay in an excess of fervor. Michael Sandel's is the most compelling, if troubling, account I have read of how citizens might draw on the energies of everyday life and the ties of civil society to reinvigorate the public realm.

NOTES

1. Michael J. Sandel, *Democracy's Discontent: America in Search of a Public Philosophy* (Cambridge, MA: Harvard University Press, 1996), p. 14.
2. Ibid.
3. Ibid., pp. 100–8.
4. Richard Rorty, 'Comments on Michael Sandel's *Democracy's Discontent*', American Political Science Association symposium (1 September 1996), p. 2.
5. Ibid., p. 3.
6. Sandel, p. 40.
7. Ibid.
8. Rorty, p. 6.

67

WHOSE KEEPER? SOCIAL SCIENCE AND MORAL OBLIGATION

Alan Wolfe

In looking to religion, philosophy, literature or politics to find the rules of moral obligation, we look in the wrong place. There is an arena in which modern liberal democrats discuss problems of moral obligation, and often with surprising vigor. I will argue that liberal democracies have done away neither with moral codes nor with institutions and practices that embody them. The gap between the need for codes of moral obligation and the reality of societies that are confused about where these codes can be found is filled, however uncomfortably, by the contemporary social sciences.[1] Even those social sciences that pride themselves on rigorous value neutrality, insisting that they are only describing how people do act, not advocating how they should, contain implicit (and often explicit) statements of what people's obligations to one another should be. (The reliance on numbers, statistical techniques and algebraic reasoning so common in modern social science journals is not, in my opinion, an alternative to moral philosophy but its continuation, an extension of an effort that began with Hobbes and Hume to systematize moral reasoning, greatly aided, these days, by a host of new technologies.) Adam Smith, the founder of modern economics, was by trade a professor of moral philosophy. His followers, though themselves often unwilling to admit it, have the same calling.

For all their tendency toward jargon and abstraction, the ideas of social scientists remain the most common guideposts for moral obligation in a secular,

From: Alan Wolfe, *Whose Keeper? Social Science and Moral Obligation* (Berkeley and Los Angeles: University of California Press, 1989).

nonliterary age. (Witness the popularity of Milton Friedman's ideas on television or on the best-seller lists, let alone the constant attempts of mass media to find academic experts to comment on one social trend after another.) Moreover, the social sciences contain not only a moral theory of how people should act toward one another, but also a large body of empirical information about how they actually do.

[...]

The contemporary social sciences, despite occasional claims to the contrary, have not done especially well as predictive sciences. One reason they nonetheless continue to flourish is because they are a particularly modern form of secular religion, involving, in their own idiosyncratic language, fundamental questions of what kind of people we who are modern are.

If the social sciences are taken as the theater of moral debate in modern society, the problem facing modern liberal democrats is not a lack of moral guidelines but a plentitude. Instead of having one source for their moral codes, they have at least three: economics, political science and sociology. (I have not included anthropology in this list, not out of lack of respect – quite the contrary, actually – but because its focus on modern societies tends to be indirect.) Corresponding to each are three sets of institutions or practices charged with the maintenance of moral responsibility: those of the market, the state and what was once called civil society. When the theory of each social science is linked to the practices it favors, quite distinct approaches to the problem of how to structure obligations to the self and others emerge.

[...]

In the face of approaches to moral regulation that no longer seem as promising as they once were, it makes sense to try to find a way of thinking about obligations to others that puts into better balance individual needs and collective restraints. Such an approach – to the degree that it calls on individuals to rely on self-restraint, ties of solidarity with others, community norms, and voluntary altruism – finds its roots in a historic concern with civil society. What was once a three-sided debate has become, as markets and states have both expanded, two-sided. Sociology itself has contributed to this narrowing of options, because it has found in markets and states seeming solutions to its own moral ambivalence. A third way to think about moral obligation cannot overcome the discontents of modernity, but it can give to people a moral code that, unlike those stressing either individualism or collective obligations, enriches a decision-making process that too often leaves modern people feeling incomplete. To revive notions of moral agency associated with civil society is to begin the development of a language appropriate to addressing the paradox of modernity and to move us away from techniques that seek to displace moral obligations by treating them purely as questions of economic efficiency or public policy.

THE WITHERING AWAY OF CIVIL SOCIETY

Learning how to behave in modern society is not only difficult, but there are also few trusted signposts to guide the way. No one can ever be sure in advance how behavior in one part of society will affect behavior in any other. So great is the potential for unanticipated consequences and perverse outcomes that any effort to regulate society directly seems cumbersome, if not utopian. The uncertainty of the moral choices we must make every day enhances the attraction of the market and the state. (Simultaneously, this uncertainty makes economics and political science seem far more realistic and in greater accord with modern people's understanding of human nature than sociology.)

The market responds to the sense that consequences are best managed when left unanticipated, while the state offers to take choice out of individual hands and give it to the experts. Thus, if housing and other costs are allowed to rise because there are no controls on the market, women must go to work to earn extra income, and the question of how they should treat their obligations to the next generation is decided, without anyone really seeming to decide it. Similarly, if fiduciary experts tell us we need to raise the social security tax to keep the fund from going bankrupt, our obligation to the previous generation is resolved for us, and we need neither praise nor blame ourselves for whatever results. To the degree that the market and the state offer relief to the complexity of social coordination, they promise the possibility of reconciling the paradox of modernity behind the scenes. Both make the whole business of moral regulation seem easier than, in fact, it is.

Because they are conspicuously less demanding, the state and the market eventually come to be viewed as the only forms of regulation that modern people have at their disposal, especially in the economic organization of their society. As one sociologist puts it,

> Under modern conditions . . . the options are sharply reduced. Specifically, the basic option is whether economic processes are to be governed by market mechanisms or by mechanisms of political allocation. In social-scientific parlance, this is the option between market economies and command economies.[2]

Yet there did exist, at the very start of the modern period, an alternative to both the market and the state. That alternative was called 'civil society', a term with so many different meanings and used in so many different contexts that, before it can be used again, some clarification is in order.

In the eighteenth century, thinkers who unleashed modern bourgeois consciousness, such as Adam Smith, Adam Ferguson and David Hume, believed that civil society was the realm that protected the individual against the (monarchical or feudal) state. Society was, in their view, a precious – and precarious – creation. 'It is here that a man is made to forget his weakness, his cares of safety and his subsistence, and to act from those passions which make him discover his force,' wrote Adam Ferguson.[3] Modern people, taking advantage of what Ferguson called 'the gift of society to man',[4] were no longer at the mercy of nature. All progress, not only in commercial affairs but also in the possibility of curbing the passions and creating mutual sympathy, hinged on the mutual interdependence that men could obtain by leaving a state of nature. When Durkheim wrote of society as a secular god, he was reiterating a notion that found its first expression in the Scottish Enlightenment.

Like any god, society could be demanding. In return for the benefits it offers, it imposes obligations. 'The general obligation,' Hume wrote, 'which binds us to government, is the interest and necessities of society; and this obligation is very strong'.[5] Therefore, in addition to our 'natural' obligations, such as loving children, Hume wrote of justice and morality, obligations undertaken 'from a sense of obligation when we consider the necessities of human society'.[6] But how, if we are to be as secular as Hume was on his deathbed,[7] do we come to appreciate these necessities? The hopes of the theorists of civil society lay in a rational understanding of what made society work – what today we would call social science. In the writings of Montesquieu, for example, who has been called 'the first moralist with a sociological perspective',[8] we witness the idea that a science of society can help us use modern intelligence to organize our obligations to others. The thinkers of the Scottish Enlightenment, who were deeply influenced by Montesquieu, were confident that 'constant and universal principles of human nature', as Hume called them, would make possible a modern moral order:

> The mutual dependence of men is so great in all societies that scarce any human action is entirely complete in itself, or is performed without some reference to the actions of others, which are requisite to make it answer fully the intention of the agent ... In proportion as men extend their dealings and render their intercourse with others more complicated, they always comprehend in their schemes of life a greater variety of voluntary actions which they expect from the proper motives to cooperate with their own.[9]

For the thinkers of the Scottish Enlightenment, civil society was coterminous with what today we call 'the private sector', a realm of personal autonomy in which people could be free to develop their own methods of moral accounting. The ethical superiority of what would come to be called capitalism was due to the moral energy unleashed by the idea that people are responsible for their own actions. Yet it was also clear to these thinkers that to the degree that capitalism encouraged pure selfishness, it ran the risk of destroying this very moral potential. The new economic order being created during the late eighteenth and early nineteenth centuries strengthened individual freedom, but it also made obvious the degree to which people in civil society were interdependent. Hegel, for example, like Ferguson and Hume, argued that the selfish energies unleashed by the market create 'a system of complete interdependence, wherein the livelihood, happiness and legal status of one man is interwoven with the livelihood, happiness and rights of all'.[10] Freedom, from this point of view, did not exist in opposition to society; rather, civil society, by forcing people to recognize the reality of their interdependence, made freedom possible. Freedom was a social, not a natural, phenomenon, something that existed only through the recognition, rather than the denial, of obligations to others.

Given this understanding of the relationship between civil society and moral potential, the development of capitalism through the nineteenth century – although seen by most theorists, including Marx, as a progressive force – also contained the potential to destroy the very civil society it helped create. In the eighteenth century the greatest threat to civil society was the old order symbolized by the state, against which both liberalism and the market were allies. By the mid-nineteenth century the old order was passing, and the moral autonomy of civil society began to be threatened from a new direction. Because the market, capitalism's greatest achievement, placed a monetary value on all things, it increasingly came to be viewed as undermining the ability of people to find and protect an authenticity that was uniquely their own. If an eighteenth-century theorist of civil society were to have appeared in the middle of the nineteenth century looking for a place where individuals could create their own moral rules, he would have found it neither in the private sector nor in the public.

In the nineteenth century, as a result of these developments, the meaning of civil society began to change. No longer a dualistic conception, it became tripartite, standing between the market and the state, embodying neither the self-interest of the one nor the coercive authority of the other. This idea was already implicit, if in somewhat different form, in Hegel, who viewed civil society as a place of transition from the realm of particularism to that of the universal. Other thinkers found in civil society an alternative to both markets and states. Alexis de Tocqueville, for example, anxious to guard against the centralizing power of the state, did not look to 'industrial callings' (which, he felt, might reproduce the aristocracy of old) but instead paid attention to ideas of voluntarism and localism. Late-nineteenth-century liberals, wanting to reject laissez-faire but suspicious of governmental collectivism, discovered in pluralism a modified notion of civil society. Certain Marxists, especially Antonio Gramsci, were attracted to the idea of civil society as an alternative to Leninism. And the classical thinkers in the sociological tradition all used civil society as the focal point of their critique of modernity. Emile Durkheim and Max Weber were both strongly influenced by Hegel, and the notion of civil society lay also at the heart of Tönnies' notion of *Gemeinschaft*, Simmel's fear of the influence of large numbers, Cooley's concept of the primary group, the emphasis on local communities in the Chicago school sociology of Robert A. Park and the concept of a lifeworld developed by Jürgen Habermas. If there is one underlying theme that unifies the themes in sociology that never developed the resiliency of concepts such as the market or the state – such as organic solidarity, the collective conscience, the generalized other, sociability and the gift relationship – it would be the idea of civil society.

Although civil society seems to have all but disappeared from the modern political imagination, it has in recent years begun once again to attract attention.[11] No doubt the reason for this appeal is an increasing feeling that modernity's two greatest social instruments, the market and the state, have become more problematic. Under extreme conditions of state oppression there can be no question of the power of the ideal of civil society. In Eastern Europe especially, where, in the words of Claude Lefort, 'the new society is thought to make the formation of classes or groups with antagonistic interests impossible',[12] the pluralistic vision associated with civil society seeks to protect an autonomous social realm against political authority.[13] Georg Konrad suggests that 'civil society is the antithesis of military society' and that 'antipolitics' – his name for morality – 'is the ethos of civil society'.[14] Adam Michnik writes of Solidarity in Poland:

> The essence of the spontaneously growing Independent and Self-governing Labor Union Solidarity lay in the restoration of social ties, self-organization aimed at guaranteeing the defense of labor, civil and national rights. For the first time in the history of communist rule in Poland 'civil society' was being restored, and it was reaching a compromise with the state.[15]

One need not equate the oppression that exists in Eastern Europe with the imperfections of capitalism in the West to argue that the tripartite theory of civil society can serve as an alternative both to the market under capitalism and to the state under socialism. Contemporary capitalist societies bear little resemblance to the moral world of the Scottish Enlightenment. Composed more of bureaucratic firms than self-motivated individuals, these societies rationalize away personal responsibility rather than extend its realm. Instead of broadening the recognition of mutual interdependence, they deny it, arguing that capitalism is not the product of society but the result of a natural order determined by animalistic instincts. Rather than understanding that economic self-interest is made possible only because obligations are part of a preexisting moral order, they increasingly organize the moral order by the same principles that organize the economy. The more extensively capitalism develops, the more the social world that makes capitalism possible comes to be taken for granted rather than viewed as a gift toward which the utmost care ought to be given. Societies organized by the market need a theory of civil society as much as societies organized by the state, or else their social ecologies will become as damaged as their natural ecologies.[16]

But given the confused meanings associated with the term, how ought civil society be understood? There is certainly a temptation, when faced with the limits of the market and the state as moral codes, to reject both in favor of some preexisting moral community that may never have existed or, if it did exist, was so oppressive that its members thought only of escape. That meaning of civil society is emphatically *not* the one that will be discussed here. Not only is it unrealistic to expect that modern liberal democracies will somehow stop relying on the market and the state, but it is also unfair to ask modern liberal democrats to do without these organizing structures. The market, for all its problems, does promote individual choice, thereby enabling people to act as the creators of their own moral rules. The state, no matter how critical one may be of its authority, not only creates a certain level of security without which modern life would be impossible but, as the Scandinavian societies show, also promotes equality and generally creates a better life for most. Markets and states are here to stay, and it is not my intention to say otherwise.

[...]

My aim is to make three points that I hope will contribute to a revival of a sociological approach to moral regulation. The first is a theoretical one: to recall that neither the market nor the state was ever expected to operate without the moral ties found in civil society. Markets flourish in a moral order defined by noneconomic ties of trust and solidarity; markets are necessary for modernity, but they tend to destroy what makes them work. Similarly, the liberal theory of the state was neither purely liberal, for its originators relied on preexisting moral ties to temper the bleakness of the social contract, nor purely statist, because it assumed a strong society. Like the market, the liberal state survives by basing itself on other things than its theory demands.

There has never existed, until the present, a pure theory of either the market or the state. When we look more closely at recent efforts to develop both – such as the effort by the Chicago school of economics to extend the principle of rational choice to all social realms, not just to those we understand as economic; the cognitive treatments of moral obligation found in the work of John Rawls or Lawrence Kohlberg; the justification for state authority associated with conservative political theorists such as Lawrence Mead; or modern forms of the social democratic welfare state that organize moral relations as well as economic ones – we find that markets and states organized without civil society tend to develop in ways quite contrary to their original intentions.

The second point I wish to make is that as modern societies come to rely ever more thoroughly on either the market or the state to organize their codes of moral obligation, living with the paradoxes of modernity will become increasingly difficult. What makes modern liberal democracy such a frustrating condition is that the less we live in tightly bound communities organized by strong social ties, the greater is our need to recognize our dependence on others, even perfect strangers. To be modern, in short, requires that we extend the 'inward' moral rules of civil society 'outward' to the realm of nonintimate and distant social relations. Yet states and markets – both of which are 'outward' moral codes organizing obligations to distant others – operate in exactly the opposite fashion in their codification of the business of moral obligation, for they have begun to organize 'inward' relationships once associated with civil society, such as matters involving the family, the local community and friendship and other informal networks. (In Jürgen Habermas' language, this process represents the colonization of the lifeworld by system logics.)[17] Civil society is increasingly squeezed from two directions, raising the question of whether, as a result, people are more confused about how to balance obligations to those they love with obligations to strangers and distant others.

Being modern will always require some way of linking both intimate and distant obligations. Although in theory that balance could just as easily be found by extending outward obligations inward, the proper balance will more realistically be found by extending inward obligations outward. The contribution that a sociological approach can make to discussions of moral obligation is to emphasize that no abstract and formal rules exist specifying what we owe others and others owe us. Instead, moral obligation ought to be viewed as a socially constructed practice, as something we learn through the actual experience of trying to live together with other people. It is for this reason that we ought to worry about the weakness of civil society vis-à-vis the market and the state, for the more we rely on impersonal mechanisms of moral obligation, the more out of practice we become as moral agents capable of finding our own ways to resolve the paradoxes of modernity. We need civil society – families, communities, friendship networks, solidaristic workplace ties, voluntarism, spontaneous groups and movements – not to reject, but to complete the project of modernity.

[...]

Both the acceptance and the rejection of modernity lead sociology toward its own abolition. Sociology without society will be the fate of any attempt to formulate an approach toward moral regulation that without reservation either rejects or accepts both the market and the state.

One could, of course, view the gradual disappearance of a specifically sociological approach to moral obligation as a good thing. After all, what has been taking place in the social sciences is a genuinely interdisciplinary movement. The creative energy of much of contemporary social-scientific research lies in what Albert Hirschman calls 'trespassing', an art at which Hirschman himself is a master. Subject matter no longer counts for much in identifying any individual social science discipline, for each has become more concerned with the purview of what used to be thought of as the others' proper domain. Nor is technique the primary differentiation, since increasingly the formal rigor of economics has drawn all the social sciences. What began in the eighteenth century as a unified endeavor may again become one in the twenty-first.

There are obvious benefits to this intermingling of the social sciences, yet from a moral, as opposed to a scientific, point of view something will be lost if sociology drops its search for a distinctive approach to the problem of moral regulation. Modern liberal democracy needs a way of thinking about moral obligations that expresses the same ambivalence about modernity that modern liberal democrats so often feel. What Robert Merton, in a different context, has called 'sociological ambivalence' should be the defining characteristic of a sociological approach to moral obligation.[18] Unlike romantic, nostalgic longings for an earlier time, sociology ought to accept modernity and, with it, markets and states. But sociology ought also to accept them critically, by pointing out their limits and reminding people of the assumptions on which they are premised.

It is important that this same ambivalence toward markets and states be carried over into an ambivalence toward civil society. Civil society should not be viewed, as it is by those who reject modernity, as a moral paradise of the past. But neither should it be rejected out of hand in favor of rational choice on the one hand or the determining power of large-scale collective structures on the other. Civil society is indeed vulnerable to both the state and the market, as I have argued to this point. But that means neither that its disappearance is inevitable nor that it will be protected automatically and passively. It is possible for social ties to complement, and even strengthen, the ties of the economic and political system, but only if people develop their own capacity as moral agents and work actively and deliberately at protecting what is social about themselves. Understood in this way, civil society is the proper subject matter of sociology, but civil society viewed as the process by which individuals construct together with others the social meanings through which they interpret reality – including the reality of moral obligation itself.

Sociology, by retaining an ambivalence toward modernity, will possess a distinctive temperament or style. Each of the social sciences has, in fact, a style. What Donald McClosky has argued for economics – that it is a specific form of rhetoric – is also true of political science and sociology.[19] The modern economic temperament, especially in the Chicago school of economics, is spunky, irreverent and brash. Convinced that they have discovered the dirty little secret of modern society, the ubiquity of self-interest behind the respectable bourgeois cloak of do-goodish rhetoric, Chicago school theorists approach their subject avidly. Enthusiastic in their task, respectful of one another's work and distrustful of their antagonists in this struggle for moral souls, their temperament is lodgelike in its ritualism and bonding patterns. It is a distinctively New World tone, *arriviste* and impatient, distrustful of settled customs, raw. Chicago – the natural location for writers like Theodore Dreiser who also worked to strip the politeness from bourgeois conventionality – is the perfect home for a temperament so vigorous yet so lacking in nuance and irony.

In contrast, much of the defense of the state that one finds in the political approach to moral obligation, especially in the writings of Morris Janowitz, Samuel Huntington and Lawrence Mead, is characterized by a tragic vision of society. Its temperament is essentially puritanical, holding out a vision of redemption in which people are expected to take responsibility for their own actions but where it is recognized that, in the world we (unfortunately) live in, only discipline and authority can keep society functioning. High-minded, serious, worried – the distinctive temperament of the political approach to moral regulation is as Bostonian (and therefore Jamesian) as the economic is Midwestern (and therefore Dreiserian). Its temperament is reflective of a WASP elite in decline, a touch of *noblesse oblige* matched by a tinge of resentment that those who ought to be grateful for the elite's advice are not paying any attention.

The temperament of contemporary sociology, in contrast to both these approaches, ought to be marked by respect for ambiguity and a willingness to live with paradox. Sociology should be the liminal science, concerned as much with the outcasts of society as with either the older aristocracy or the newly rich. Its sense of the moral order ought therefore to be fluid, unlike the political approach, but not so fluid that, like the economic approach, it will be generally unable to locate institutions. Sociology should be less high-minded and serious than the political approach, reminding us that morality is not so strict and unforgiving that it stands ready to condemn all who do not meet its strictures. But it should also be far more morally conscious than the economic approach, reminding us that the individualism and freedom that markets give us carry with them a responsibility to be aware of the effects our actions have on others. The concerns of sociology should be with feelings and emotions rather than instincts and preferences (in this sense, it is not surprising that two of the most important works in contemporary sociology use the word *heart* in their titles).[20] Tending more to the literary and cultural than to the scientific and analytical, sociology has a style that emphasizes the expressive rather than the utilitarian strand of American culture – Ginsberg and Didion, these are its appropriate literary cousins. In short, the sociological temperament is neither Bostonian nor Midwestern; its essence, and much of its best work, is inspired by California and by the underside of New York.

Ambivalent toward its subject matter and ambiguous in its style, sociology would be best off retaining a certain awkwardness in its political perspective as well. Classical sociology was unsure of its political heritage, counting among its founders radicals like Marx as well as conservatives like Tocqueville. It is difficult to classify the politics of most of the major thinkers in the sociological tradition. Was Durkheim a conservative, a liberal or even a radical?[21] Was Tönnies a reactionary or a reformer? Were Simmel and Weber apologists for capitalism, as Georg Lukács once argued, or among its foremost critics?[22] Sociology began as a debate between conservatives and radicals; it ignored, as best it could, most of the political positions in between.

[...]

Whatever the moral issues that will define the social fabric of the future, their resolution will be smoother if individuals have a place in society that allows them to take personal responsibility for the moral decisions they make. The contribution of sociologists to an understanding of moral obligation in modern society should be to facilitate the process by which individuals come to recognize and appreciate the importance of civil society. Because the intimate sphere of society is fragile, modern liberal democrats need to think more about how they can preserve it. They will be better able to do so if they think about three aspects of the groups to which they belong: Who should and who should not be members, since membership brings in its wake obligation? How ought groups to establish rules for distributing the benefits they offer? And what are one's obligations to a group that one wishes to leave in order to join another? A sociological approach to moral obligation requires that we think about what can be called entrance rules, waiting rules and exit rules.

Some people feel an obligation to all humanity, and sometimes even to all animals as well, but for most people moral obligation is more meaningful when obligations are limited in scope. Communities, Michael Walzer has written, 'must have boundaries'.[23] One of the most difficult issues in the business of defining moral obligation is deciding on *entrance rules*, criteria for determining who should belong to the group to which one is presumably obligated.

[...]

When the satisfaction of self-interest becomes difficult to resist, reliance on common services – even when self-interest might dictate an exit – improves everyone else's capacity to rely on common services. When reliance on government to provide services becomes difficult to resist, individuals who can and want to provide for themselves can ease the fiscal burden involved in having government provide services for those who cannot. When people know that they share with others a common culture, restraints on self-interest (in market-oriented societies) or on claims to rights (in state-oriented societies) are more likely to exist. When, in short, civil society exists as a sphere alongside the market and the state, it contributes to the more effective working of both of them; when the market and the state exist without civil society, neither can work as promised. If the question is whether we use abstract rules that regulate our relationships with strangers to organize our relationships with intimates or we rely on the recognition of our dependency on intimates to help us codify our relationships with strangers, the latter seems to make more sense. Most people find it easier to move from the particular to the general than the reverse.

Still, when all is said and done there is not and can never be any guarantee that stronger relations in civil society will create the practices that enable people to take personal responsibility for the fate of abstract others. All the social scientist can do in such a circumstance is to remind modern liberal democrats that they do not live in tribal clans. If people are not aware of a world outside the intimate sphere, social science must make them aware of it. Sociology in particular ought to reinforce the idea that moral obligation can become a social practice only when – as the thinkers of the Scottish Enlightenment proposed and the classical tradition in sociology carried forward – society is understood as a gift. Moreover, it is a gift that we give to ourselves, since no one put it in place for us. It is difficult for modern people to remember these things, because we take for granted society's independence from nature in a way that eighteenth-century theorists never could. A social bond, now in place, is simply assumed to be. Society has become part of the scenery of modern life, the backdrop in front of which economics and politics play their roles.

If modern liberal democrats are going to learn to live with the difficulties of moral obligation, they will need to put behind them the temptations of Rousseau. We are not born free and corrupted by our institutions. If anything, we are born as selfish egoists, and only our institutions and practices save us from ourselves. A long tradition in social theory holds that individuals are anything but angels. Put them together with no rules to help them define their moral obligations – in prisons or market situations lacking any moral restraint – and they will act as pure market theorists or neo-Hobbesians assume. That they do not act that way all the time is because they have accepted the gift of society – which is why it is so risky to flirt with the idea of taking the gift back. Having rules to regulate our social interaction is what makes everything else possible.

It is only because modern liberal democrats take society for granted that they can even consider relying on the market or the state to structure rules of moral obligation. What makes the approach of the Chicago school of economics so tantalizing is its suggestion that we can do without society and all its difficulties. The issue is not that Chicago school theories are wrong in their description of how ubiquitous self-interest can become; it is the disturbing possibility that they may be right. When we make self-interest the guide to all our moral decisions, we are in a sense proclaiming that we no longer wish to enjoy the gift of society but wish instead to be ruled by something called human 'nature', as if society were not put in place to prevent us from acting like selfish genes. To the degree that Chicago school economics describes what is taking place in society, it describes a society that is in decline because its members are not willing to adhere to the rules that make it work. The problem with the Chicago school recommendations is that if we choose to go back to 'nature', it will take a social decision to do so. Nature, as Karl Polanyi emphasized, looks different when it is socially created.[24]

Much the same is true of neo-Hobbesian approaches to politics. The conditions of modern life are nowhere near the state they were at the time of the English civil war, when Hobbes was prompted to call for sovereign authority. But numerous reminders of the fragility of the social bond exist, even in the most modern of liberal democracies. The 'normal accidents' of complex technology, the precariousness of the compromises between labor and capital, racial and ethnic hostilities, increasing homelessness and marginality, the savagery of urban life and the transmission of AIDS (which shows that we are capable of killing each other through love just as Hobbes' Englishmen killed each other through war) are just a few reminders of how thin the line is between the natural and the social.[25]

The promise of the Hobbesian approach to social order is that government will protect us from our own animalistic instincts. To some degree, of course, this is true: instill enough fear in people, and they may well obey. Yet no society can rely on the police forever. In fact, it is not government that separates us from a state of nature, but society, the invisible links of trust and reliance on others that enable us not to carry guns whenever we face unknown others. When society makes civilized life possible we tend, as with the market, to assume its existence. We are thereby tempted to take the shortcut of keeping order through use of the state instead, forgetting that the state is a product of society, that substituting the former for the latter is to return us to the state of nature from which we have emerged. It is at this point that pure statists and pure market theorists recognize the need for each other: since both take society for granted, each reinforces the distrust that proves the other's view of human nature correct.[26]

Society and nature are radically different ecologies. It is a serious mistake to believe that respect for nature can help us develop rules for respecting society.[27] The common response of people concerned with protecting the natural environment is laissez-faire: intervention – to alter genes or re-direct rivers, for example – is best not done, for who can tell what the consequences will be if we tamper? When the same notion is applied to society, however, the social order is understood to be so self-regulating that any effort to give it a conscious direction will be self-defeating. Yet while there is evolution in nature, there is no evolution in society – except in those movements that are the product of will and deliberation. By applying the rules of laissez-faire to society, we strip ourselves of the capacity to engage in social growth: we are forced to sit and watch as our social ecology crumbles. Then, when it seems almost too late to stop the process, we call on the authority of government to save us from our worst instincts; yet because government intervention is premised on the notion that our nature drives us to escape our obligations, we thereby acknowledge our inability to trust one another instead.

It seems strange to justify modernity on the basis of a premodern conception of moral agency in which individuals can control everything in society except their own natures, but that is essentially what we do when we rely on the rules of markets and states to codify our obligations for us. Under the rules of contemporary economics and politics, society, modernity's greatest invention, is brought into being to regulate our interactions with one another but then is stripped of its power to do so through deemphasis of the social skills we have at our disposal. In the constant shifting between economic and political rules, society has little role to play at all; the dialectic of freedom and constraint is fought out between individuals whose nature impels them to want more on the one hand and a Hobbesian source of authority that once in a while has to call a halt to the process on the other.

The gift society has given us lies in the benefits we receive – including high rates of economic growth, large and centralized economies, a government capable of delivering services, and rapid social and economic mobility – by coordinating our actions with those of others. Yet all gifts, even when altruistically offered, are given in the expectation that the receiver will reciprocate. In return for the gift of society, modern liberal democrats are asked only one thing: to recognize that in return for these benefits they relinquish 'pure' freedom, the ability to do anything they want in any way at any time. It is in this sense that the constraints on freedom imposed by modernity are social, not natural; it is not our inability to transcend gravity or overcome the anarchy of a state of nature that restricts our freedom to do what we like, but our inability to transcend our dependence on others.

When we recognize society as a gift, we realize that we are free because our preferences can change through interaction with others, not because they are constant. We are free because we can give meaning to the way our situations are defined. We are free because we recognize that the condition of being modern sets internal limits on free-ridership, even if there were no external obstacles to impede us. We are free because we elevate loyalty over exit and voice, because we have strong intimate relations that enable us to resist mass society's pressure to conform. We are free because we fulfill our obligations to society because we want to, not because government does it for us. We are free, not to express our nature, but to create it. We are free because we accept the regulation and discipline needed to make social cooperation work but then challenge that regulatory process to take account of real people in real situations of time and space. We are free because we can grow and develop. We are free only when others are also free, and they are free only when we are.

The message that sociology offers modern liberal democrats is neither complacent nor apocalyptic. It is commonsensical: here is society; you have given it to yourself as a gift; if you do not take care of it, you should not be surprised when you can no longer find it. That message by itself cannot tell people how to satisfy their obligations to intimate and distant others simultaneously, but it at least makes it clear that if people themselves do not continue to try to meet those obligations, no one else will do it for them.

NOTES

1. Various explorations of the relationship between morality and the social sciences have recently begun to appear. See, for example, Norma Haan, Robert Bellah, Paul Rabinow and William M. Sullivan, *Social Science as Moral Inquiry* (New York: Columbia University Press, 1983) and Amartya Sen, *On Ethics and Economics* (Oxford: Basil Blackwell, 1987).
2. Peter L. Berger, *The Capitalist Revolution: Fifty Propositions About Prosperity, Equality, and Liberty* (New York: Basic Books, 1986), p. 20.
3. Adam Ferguson, *An Essay on the History of Civil Society* (Philadelphia: Wm. Fry, 1819), p. 32.
4. Ibid., p. 33.
5. Quoted in David Frisby and Derek Sayer, *Society* (London: Tavistock, 1986), p. 23.

6. Quoted in Michael Ignatieff, *The Needs of Strangers: An Essay on Privacy, Solidarity and the Politics of Being Human* (New York: Penguin Books, 1985) p. 92.

7. Ignatieff (ibid., pp. 83–7) recounts the story of Hume's secular death as told by Boswell and Adam Smith.

8. Alasdair MacIntyre, *A Short History of Ethics* (New York: Collier Books, 1966), p. 179.

9. David Hume, 'An Inquiry Concerning Human Understanding', in *Essays: Moral, Political, and Literary*, T.H. Greene and T.H. Grose (eds) (London: Longmans Green, 1875), 2: pp. 72–3.

10. T. M. Knox, *Hegel's Philosophy of Right* (New York: Oxford University Press, 1967), p. 123.

11. Among conservatives, for example, the concept of 'mediating structures' bears some resemblance to civil society. See Peter Berger and Richard John Neuhaus, *To Empower People: The Role of Mediating Structures in Public Policy* (Washington, DC: American Enterprise Institute, 1977); for a left perspective, see John Keane, *Democracy and Civil Society* (London: Verso, 1988). Also relevant to this discussion are Torben Hviid Nielsen, 'The State, the Market, and the Individual', *Acta Sociologica* 29, no. 4 (1986): pp. 283–302, and Nielsen, *Samfund og magt* (Copenhagen: Akademisk Forlag, 1988), pp. 81–101.

12. Claude Lefort, *The Political Forms of Modern Society* (Cambridge, MA: MIT Press, 1986), p. 285.

13. For a collection of writings emphasizing this point, see John Keane (ed.), *Civil Society and the State* (London: Verso, 1988).

14. Georg Konrad, *Antipolitics* (London: Quarter Books, 1984), p. 92.

15. Adam Michnik, *Letters from Prison and Other Essays* (Berkeley and Los Angeles: University of California Press, 1985), p. 124.

16. For a review of a large body of literature showing the importance of social support networks organized by neither the market nor the state, see Marc Pilisuk and Susan Hillier Parks, *The Healing Web: Social Networks and Human Survival* (Hanover, NH: University Press of New England, 1986).

17. Jürgen Habermas, *Theory of Communicative Action*, vol. I: *Reason and the Rationality of Society*, trans. Thomas McCarthy (Boston: Beacon Press, 1984).

18. Robert K. Merton, *Sociological Ambivalence and Other Essays* (New York: Free Press, 1976).

19. Donald McCloskey, *The Rhetoric of Economics* (Madison: University of Wisconsin Press, 1985).

20. Arlie Russell Hochschild, *The Managed Heart: Commercialization of Human Feeling* (Berkeley and Los Angeles: University of California Press, 1983); and Robert Bellah et al., *Habits of the Heart: Individualism and Commitment in American Life* (Berkeley and Los Angeles: University of California Press, 1985).

21. For the first position, see Robert Nisbet, *Emile Durkheim* (Englewood Cliffs, NJ: Prentice-Hall, 1963), for the second, Stephen Seidman, *Liberation and the Origins of European Social Theory* (Berkeley and Los Angeles: University of California Press, 1983); and for the third, Steve Fenton, *Durkheim and Modern Social Theory* (Cambridge: Cambridge University Press, 1985).

22. For Lukács's views, see his *The Destruction of Reason*, trans. Peter Palmer (Atlantic Highlands, NJ: Humanities Press, 1981).

23. Michael Walzer, *Spheres of Justice: A Defense of Pluralism and Equality* (New York: Basic Books, 1983), p. 50.

24. Karl Polanyi, *The Great Transformation: The Political and Economic Origin of Our Times* (Boston: Beacon Press, 1957), p. 141.

25. The term *normal accidents* comes from Charles Perrow, *Normal Accidents: Living with High-Risk Technologies* (New York: Basic Books, 1984).

26. On how free-market economics can be linked to strong government, especially in the British context, see Andrew Gamble, *The Free Economy and the Strong State* (Durham, NC: Duke University Press, 1988).
27. For a different point of view, see William R. Catton, Jr., Gerhard Lenski and Frederick H. Buttel, 'To What Degree Is a Social System Dependent on Its Resource Base?' in *The Social Fabric*, James F. Short (ed.) (Beverly Hills, CA: Sage, 1986), p. 166.

68

MORALITY AND THE SOCIAL SCIENCES

Albert O. Hirschman

The tension between the 'warm' heart and the 'cold' or, at best, 'cool' head is a well-known theme in Western culture, especially since the Romantic Age. But I am speaking here not only of tension, but of an existential incompatibility between morality and moralizing, on the one hand, and analytical-scientific activity, on the other. This incompatibility is simply a fact of experience. Our analytical performance becomes automatically suspect if it is openly pressed into the service of moral conviction; and conversely, moral conviction is not dependent on analytical argument and can actually be weakened by it, just as religious belief has on balance been undermined rather than bolstered by the proofs of God and their intellectual prowess. The matter has been best expressed by the great German poet Hölderlin in a wonderfully pithy, if rather plaintive, epigram. Entitled '*Guter Rat*' (Good Advice), it dates from about 1800 and, in my free translation, reads:

> If you have brains and a heart, show only one or the other, You will not get credit for either should you show both at once.[1]

The mutual exclusiveness of moralizing and analytical understanding may be nothing but a happenstance, reflecting the particular historical conditions under which scientific progress in various domains was achieved in the West. These conditions have of course left strong marks on cultural attitudes, marks so well identified by Hölderlin.

From: Albert O. Hirschman, *Essays in Trespassing* (Cambridge: Cambridge University Press, 1981).

But the hostility to morality is more than a birthmark of modern science. With regard to the social sciences in particular, there are some more specific reasons to think that antimoralist petulance will frequently recur, because of the very nature of the social scientific enterprise and discourse. Let me briefly explain.

In all sciences fundamental discovery often takes the form of paradox. This is true for some of the principal theorems of physics, such as the Copernican proposition about the earth moving around the sun rather than vice versa. But it can be argued that social science is peculiarly subject to the compulsion to produce paradox.

The reason is that we all know so much about society already without ever having taken a single social science course. We live in society; we often contribute to social, political and economic processes as actors; and we think – often mistakenly, of course – that we know roughly what goes on not only in our own minds, but also in those of others. As a result, we have considerable intuitive, commonsense understanding of social science 'problems' such as crime in the streets, corruption in high places and even inflation, and everyone stands forever ready to come forward with his or her own 'solution' or nostrum. Consequently, for social science to *enhance* our considerable, untutored knowledge of the social world it must come up with something that has not been apparent or transparent before or, better still, with something that shows how badly commonsense understanding has led us astray.[2] Important social science discoveries are therefore typically counterintuitive, shocking and concerned with *unintended* and unexpected consequences of human action.

With the commonsense understanding of social science problems having usually a strong moral component (again much more so than in the natural sciences), the immoralist vocation of the social sciences can in good measure be attributed to this compulsion to produce shock and paradox. Just as one of social science's favorite pastimes is to affirm the hidden rationality of the seemingly irrational or the coherence of the seemingly incoherent, so does it often defend as moral, or useful, or at least innocent, social behavior that is widely considered to be reprehensible. In economics, examples of this sort of quest for the morally shocking come easily to mind. Following the early lead of Mandeville and his rehabilitation of luxury, many an economist has carved out a reputation by extolling the economic efficiency functions of such illegal or unsavory activities as smuggling, or black marketeering, or even corruption in government.

[...]

There is a notable instance of what Veblen called a 'trained incapacity'. It is so strong, in fact, that we will often not avow to ourselves the moral source of our scientific thought processes and discoveries. As a result, quite a few of us are *unconscious* moralists in our professional work. I have a personal story to illustrate this point, and here is how I told it in the special preface I wrote – for reasons that will be apparent – for the *German* edition of *Exit, Voice, and Loyalty*:

As is related in my book, its intellectual origin lies in an observation I made some years ago in Nigeria. But quite a while after the book had been published in the United States, it dawned on me that my absorption with its theme may have deeper roots. A large part of the book centers on the concern that exit of the potentially most powerful carriers of voice prevents the more forceful stand against decline that might otherwise be possible. This situation is not altogether unrelated to the fate of the Jews who were still in Germany after 1939. Most of the young and vigorous ones, like myself, got out in the early years after Hitler took over, leaving a gravely weakened community behind. Of course, the possibilities of any effective voice were zero in the circumstances of those years no matter who left and who stayed. Nevertheless, the real fountainhead of the book may well lie in some carefully repressed guilt feelings that, even though absurd from the point of view of any rational calculus, are simply there.[3]

At this point, a further afterthought suggests itself: it was probably fortunate that I was *not* aware of those deeper moral stirrings when I wrote the book; otherwise the presentation of my argument might have been less general, less balanced as between the respective merits of exit and voice, and less scientifically persuasive. My excursion into autobiography thus points to an odd conclusion: one, perhaps peculiarly effective, way for social scientists to bring moral concerns into their work is to do so unconsciously! This bit of advice is actually not quite as unhelpful as it sounds. For the reasons given, it seems to me impractical and possibly even counterproductive to issue guidelines to social scientists on how to incorporate morality into their scientific pursuits and how to be on guard against immoral 'side effects' of their work. Morality is not something like pollution abatement that can be secured by slightly modifying the design of a policy proposal. Rather, it belongs into the center of our work; and it can get there only if the social scientists are morally alive and make themselves vulnerable to moral concerns – then they will produce morally significant works, consciously or otherwise.

I have a further, more ambitious, and probably utopian thought. Once one has gone through the historical account and associated reasoning of this essay, once we have become fully aware of our intellectual tradition with its deep split between head and heart and its not always beneficial consequences, the first step toward overcoming that tradition and toward healing that split has already been taken. Down the road, it is then possible to visualize a kind of social science that would be very different from the one most of us have been practicing: a moral-social science where moral considerations are not repressed or kept apart, but are systematically commingled with analytic argument, without guilt feelings over any lack of integration; where the transition from preaching to proving and back again is performed frequently and with ease; and where moral considerations need no longer be smuggled in surreptitiously, nor expressed unconsciously, but are displayed openly and disarmingly. Such would be, in part, my dream for a 'social science for our grandchildren'.

NOTES

1. 'Hast Du Verstand und ein Herz, so zeige nur eines von beiden, Beides Verdammen sie Dir, zeigest Du beides zugleich'. Hölderlin's distinction between *Verstand* (reason) and *Herz* (heart) reflects the rehabilitation of the passions in the eighteenth century that led to the 'heart' standing for the many generous moral feelings, impulses and beneficent passions man was now credited with while reason was becoming downgraded; at an earlier time, the contrast, not between the heart and the head, but between the passions and reason, or the passions and the interests, carried a very different value connotation. I have dealt with these matters in *The Passions and the Interests* (Princeton, NJ: Princeton University Press, 1977), pp. 27–8, 43–4 and 63–6.
2. See Gilles Gaston Granger, 'L'explication dans les sciences sociales', *Social Science Information* 10 (1971), p. 38.
3. Original English text of preface to German edition in Albert O. Hirschman, *Abwanderung und Widerspruch* (Tübingen: J.C.B. Mohr, 1974), p. vii.

69

THE COMPANY OF CRITICS

Michael Walzer

Imagine a social critic who breaks his ties with family and country, leaves the cave, discovers True Doctrine, and then returns to measure his former fellows and their common way of life against his new and objective standard. A hero, certainly (wouldn't we want to kill him?), and entirely sufficient for the purposes of criticism: there would be no point in having more than one such person. If he knew the Truth and judged us without passion, impartially, like a total stranger, we could only listen in silence; his criticism would supercede our complaints. Indeed, not only ours – had he time and energy enough, such a critic could serve the whole world, a Hercules among critics. If his standards were objective, no one could deny him global reach.

But there is no Hercules, no single all-sufficient critic, a fact for which we probably have one another to thank. Though the intellectual thrust of Western culture is undoubtedly monistic in character, so that critics are constantly tempted to think of themselves in Herculean terms, cultural practice is very different. We don't agree on which doctrine is True Doctrine, and so we have many social critics; criticism comes at us from all sides. There is no way to define the critical enterprise so that we will always admire its products. Nor is it easy to describe what social critics do. They do all sorts of things; they measure us by different standards, from different vantage points, in different critical languages, at different levels of specialization, with different ends in view. Most generally, they attend to our faults – our individual as well as institutional faults

From: Michael Walzer, *The Company of Critics: Social Criticism and Political Commitment in the 20th Century* (New York: Basic Books, 1988).

because it is always an individual fault, the failing of particular men and women, to tolerate bad institutions. But since our faults are named and numbered in so many different ways, the critics must compete for our attention, and they do that by criticizing one another. Now there is no reason for the rest of us to listen in silence. We participate in the critical enterprise by supporting one critic or group of critics against the others. Participation is especially extensive and especially important under conditions of modernity. A modern democratic society is a confabulation of critics. But then it makes no sense to look for global reach; each society is its own confabulation.

Perhaps there is one common mark of the critical enterprise. It is founded in hope; it cannot be carried on without some sense of historical possibility. Criticism is oriented toward the future: the critic must believe that the conduct of his fellows can conform more closely to a moral standard than it now does or that their self-understanding can be greater than it now is or that their institutions can be more justly organized than they now are. For all his foretellings of doom, a prophet like Amos must hold open the possibility of repentance and reform, else there would be no reason to prophesy; Socrates' claim that he should be paid to criticize his fellow citizens is similarly optimistic – not because he believes that the claim will be accepted but because he believes that his criticism is a real service: it can make Athens a better city. Even the most savage satire of contemporary minds and mores rests upon some hope, however dim or embittered, that minds and mores might be different in the future. The standard conservative lamentation that things are sliding steadily downhill, despite its undertones of melancholy and despair, is written to arrest the slide or, at least, to slow it down. There is no such thing as a strictly backward-looking social criticism, as if criticism were a kind of retributive punishment for past crimes; the critic may take his standards from the past, but he intends those standards to have some future resonance.

It follows that a strict historical determinism is incompatible with critical argument. Even if the one conceptual possibility that history has determined to be the only actual possibility is also the one the critic has chosen, he has no reason to defend that choice or to find fault with a society in which large numbers of men and women resist it. In a determined universe, the resistance is as blameless as it is pointless. I don't mean to suggest that criticism and determinism have never coexisted in a single person's mind and work. Marxism is the classic example of a doctrine that combines the two. The fact that Marx has been read as if he were a universal social critic, a Hercules among critics, probably has something to do with the combination. If history has only one end, then every temporary stopping point, every social formation short of the end, can be measured and found wanting. But this is, as Marx sometimes says, a scientific and not a moral measurement.[1] It is a measurement made from a great distance, and partly for that reason, it isn't critical in character. There is nothing and nobody to criticize: each stop along the track of history is determined in exactly the same way as the track itself. When Marx writes critically of bourgeois society, he simply forsakes his determinist doctrine. And then, though he is a powerful critic indeed, there is no reason to think him a universal critic: he can no longer claim to be applying an objective and necessary standard. He simply explores some of the possibilities, conceptual and practical, that bourgeois society holds open.

Does it take a theory like Marxism to tell us what those possibilities are? One sort of social criticism is theoretical in this special sense. It works from historical or sociological arguments that stress the inner tensions or long-term tendencies of contemporary institutions. Surrendering determinism, the critic looks for a structuralist version of probable cause – or at least some more or less 'scientific' reason to think that his standards don't lie beyond history but are attainable within it. Social criticism, on this view, depends on a critical theory of society.[2] But I don't think that this is an unavoidable dependency. In the long history of criticism, the sense of possibility has more often been assumed than theoretically grounded. Or it has been derived from some theological or philosophical argument about human agency. Men and women must be capable, it is said, of doing what God's covenant commands or what secular morality requires. The truth of that claim depends, of course, on how the critic understands God and morality. The crucial dependency is not theoretical but practical: people are capable of doing only what they believe or can be brought to believe ought to be done. Just as critical theory fails unless it can provide a recognizable account of everyday experience, so criticism generally will fail unless it draws its strength from everyday conceptions of God and morality. The critic starts, say, from the views of justice embedded in the covenantal code or from the bourgeois idea of freedom, on the assumption that what is actual in consciousness is possible in practice, and then he challenges the practices that fall short of these possibilities.

But both the covenantal code and the bourgeois idea of freedom allow for more than one possibility: there are as many possibilities as there are plausible accounts of the code and the idea. And so, again, there are many social critics, many forms of criticism; the orientation to the future is no constraint on critical pluralism. Any given theory of history closes off some possibilities and opens others, but that only means that theories of history will themselves be contested by rival schools of criticism; historical analysis is one possible critical language. Not the only language, for there are critics who dispense with history altogether and there are others who engage it only insofar as they recognize their own historical limits and draw their critical standards from local moralities. There is no plausible way to limit the range and variety of criticism except by repression, which is more likely to be directed at the critical enterprise itself than at the plurality of critics.

THE MOTIVES OF CRITICISM

Social critics are driven by a passion for truth or anger at injustice or sympathy for the oppressed or fear of the masses or ambition for power – and underlying any or all of these, by the imitation of heroism: Socrates dressed up as Achilles.

But the preferred motive, the one most likely to figure in philosophical accounts of criticism and in the critic's own self-description, is benevolence, a disinterested desire for the well-being of humanity. Criticism may be ruthless and painful, but the critic talks to us like Hamlet to his mother: 'I must be cruel only to be kind'.[3] Kindness forces his hand, but since what he says doesn't sound kind, he would be happier to be silent. Hence the myth of the reluctant critic, the prophet called by God who would refuse the call if he could or the citizen who grimly waits until the pain of watching some social evil is greater than that of speaking out against it. In fact, there are many critics who aren't at all reluctant to speak out, who, like the Roman Cato, positively enjoy the castigation of others. And it seems priggish to suggest that since castigation is morally necessary, it must never be enjoyable. Misanthropy is also a motive for the critical enterprise. The critic need not feel kindly toward the people he criticizes.

But he ought to acknowledge his connections to those people: if he were a stranger, really disinterested, it is hard to see why he would involve himself in their affairs. The passion for truth will not be a sufficient reason unless it is matched by a passion to tell the truth to *these* men and women (rather than to discover it for oneself or record it for posterity). Connection is a problem, however, if we believe that only the alienated or willfully detached critic is able to recognize the truth, to penetrate the social masquerade and see the moral ugliness underneath. Perhaps he doesn't love his fellows, but so long as he recognizes them as fellows, doesn't he have a powerful motive to join the masquerade? Even the misanthrope, if he is a local misanthrope, may well stop short of the deepest truths. Certainly, many critics have felt that they had to disconnect themselves, to break the bonds of fellowship; it was this act rather than their subsequent critical words that tested their courage. But I am interested now in a rather different argument: that disconnection is not so much chosen as imposed and that the discomfort of disconnected men and women motivates and enables their criticism. This is what drives the critic and makes his penetration and his cruelty possible. He loves truth or truth-telling, or he hates injustice or whatever, because he is alienated.

The argument has been forcefully made by Christopher Lasch in an essay on Lincoln Steffens, one of the original American 'muckrakers':

> It is time we began to understand radicals like Lincoln Steffens not as men driven by a vague humanitarian idealism but as men *predisposed* to rebellion as the result of an early estrangement from the culture of their own class; as a result, in particular, of the impossibility of pursuing within the framework of established convention the kind of careers they were bent on pursuing. The intellectuals of the early twentieth century were predisposed to rebellion by the very fact of being intellectuals in a society that had not yet learned to define the intellectual's place ... [They] were outsiders by necessity: a new class not yet absorbed into the cultural consensus.[4]

This is a sociological version of the contemporary critic's self-description. It has an obvious weakness: how are we to explain why some intellectuals 'predisposed' to rebellion actually become rebels while others do not? Why Steffens and Randolph Bourne and John Reed but not Walter Lippmann, who was closely associated with all three? And how are we to explain the earlier generation of rebels and critics to whom twentieth-century intellectuals looked for inspiration – Ralph Waldo Emerson, Henry David Thoreau, Walt Whitman? And what about later rebels and critics who found the career framework (the academic ladder) securely in place, like C. Wright Mills, say, or any of a large number of professional dissenters, including Lasch himself?

Lasch also notices, perceptively, I think, that alienation can account for the surrender of critical perspective, the 'treason' of the intellectuals. It is as useful in explaining the end as the beginning of radical criticism, which makes it too useful by half:

> Detachment carried with it a certain defensiveness about the position of intellect (and intellectuals) in American life; and it was this defensiveness ... which sometimes prompted intellectuals to forsake the role of criticism and to identify themselves with what they imagined to be the laws of historical necessity and the working out of the popular will.[5]

But the operative word, again, is 'sometimes'. Sometimes not, and what is it that makes the difference between those who forsake the critical enterprise and those who stick to it? Perhaps this is a matter of individual psychology, but the use of 'forsake' suggests that Lasch is really talking about moral choice. Men and women choose to become critics, and some of those who make the choice are not in any significant sense alienated from the culture of their class (or their city, country, race, or religion) – though they must set themselves in opposition to important aspects of that culture.

Given the general limitations of sociological accounts, the idea of marginality probably does better than Lasch's 'estrangement' in explaining the birth and breeding of social critics. They come from some remote and neglected part of the country (Silone), or from an imperial colony (Camus), or from a declining social class (Orwell), or they are members of or choose to identify themselves with a lowborn, oppressed or pariah group. But this is not alienation or even detachment; it is better described as a kind of antagonistic connection. One of its most common forms is a passionate commitment to cultural values hypocritically defended at the center, cynically disregarded at the margins. Antagonism, not alienation, provides the clearest lead into the critical enterprise. Since criticism derives ultimately from common complaint, it needs to be explained in terms of the ideological contradictions and social conflicts that common complaint reflects, though sometimes only dimly. That explanation may itself require 'scientific' detachment. But criticism requires no such thing: a detached critic may well be insufficiently antagonistic, more ready to analyze the contradictions and conflicts than to take a stand within them.

We should probably be no quicker to admire the benevolence than the detachment of the critic. Benevolence itself can be a mask, as Rousseau suggests when he writes caustically of the philosopher who loves humanity only so as more easily to dislike his neighbors.[6] But this is an easy case, since benevolence here is a piece of deception (possibly self-deception). More often it is genuinely problematic: thus the critic whose benevolent feelings are focused on future generations for whose sake he feels that he must be hard on his contemporaries, or the critic who holds lovingly in his mind an idealized picture of his fellow citizens or coreligionists or comrades in the movement (any movement) and then is forced to tell the particular men and women whom he meets that they don't measure up. As this last example suggests, the critic's involvement in social conflict may bring him allies; it doesn't always bring him allies with whom he is content. His fiercest criticism is often aimed at those individuals and groups to whom he feels closest, who are most likely to disappoint him. Christian preachers castigate the faithful, ignore the infidel; Marxist militants worry about working-class, not bourgeois consciousness.

Disappointment is one of the most common motives for criticism. We have an idea about how institutions ought to function or how people ought to behave. And then something happens, the authorities act with unusual brutality; or something doesn't happen, the people are passive and indifferent; and we feel ourselves thrust into the company of social critics. It takes some further motivation, though, actually to join the company and stick to the critical enterprise. Disappointment isn't enough. Nor does a disinterested desire for the well-being of humanity seem a sufficient motive. A moral tie to the agents or the victims of brutality and indifference is more likely to serve. We feel responsible for, we identify with particular men and women. Injustice is done in my name, or it is done to my people, and I must speak out against it. Now criticism follows from connection.

But the moral tie gets considerably more complicated in modern times, when the victims organize themselves, form a movement or party and defend their interests – often in a language very different from the one the critic has chosen. This is all to the good, certainly, though the critic sometimes finds it hard to surrender his specialized and solitary role. Nor is it clear that he should: movements and parties need criticism as much as societies do. But they also need commitment and support. Would-be critics are warned by movement militants to avoid the sin of pride, urged not to cut themselves off from the political struggle. Imagine the critic pressed by considerations of strategy and tactics – not just ideological movements but practical moves, the political version of feints, ambushes, attacks and encirclements. Should he stand, ever critical, in the way of success or put aside his scruples and follow orders? If he is alienated and defensive in the ways Lasch describes, he may well bow to party discipline, fall silent, march on command. There are many examples, most of them from the twentieth century; these are not problems commonly faced by ancient, medieval or early modern intellectuals (though the Catholic Church has long posed analogous problems for its own internal critics).[7]

The same motives that make for criticism at one moment in time make for silence and acquiescence at another. This is most clearly true of the ambition for political power. Contemporary critics especially, because of their engagement with parties and movements, are drawn by the prospect of power – the most dangerous of critical temptations. They imagine the party as the next government, themselves as office-holders (Lenins, not Stalins), able at last to give their criticism practical force. Political power is in two senses the end of criticism, first because the critic aims at the effectiveness that power makes possible, and second because, having attained power, he can no longer be critical of his own effects. Since these effects will undoubtedly require criticism, other men and women will have to take up the task, driven in turn by their own social connections, their own ambitions and their own imitations of heroism. Every critic who rises to office is succeeded by another critic who claims that office-holding is 'selling out'. One could write the recent history of social criticism as a series of successions of this sort. But there have always been, and there are today, critics who refuse (and critics who never manage) to rise.

SOCIAL CRITICISM AND POPULAR REVOLT

What makes modern criticism both interesting and problematic is not the alienation of the critic but the swelling sound of his accompaniment. Social critics have rarely been solitary or distant figures in this age of popular mobilization, democratic and totalitarian politics, public schooling and mass communication. It is more likely that wherever they go, they go in crowds; they are alone only in solitary confinement. In the past, critics like the Puritan ministers or the orators of the French Revolution might briefly find a popular following, but most of the time criticism was addressed to a narrow audience, the small elite of literate and powerful men. Whatever the critic talked about, these were the people to whom he talked. His situation was not dissimilar from that of more ordinary members of the complaining public who managed – as petitioners or supplicants or even, occasionally, as rebels – to make themselves heard by the elite. There was no one else to talk to, no one else who mattered. In traditional societies, critics necessarily look up. Today many more people matter, and so critics look around. Popular mobilization, whatever its immediate purpose, poses the old questions about language, specialization and distance in a new and urgent way. How does the social critic relate to *these* people, who have found a voice, who claim their rights, who trample on the rights of others, who rush to meetings, who march in the streets, who are herded into camps, who feel pain and rage, who throw bombs, who look for a leader, who accept the discipline of a movement or party – and who, some of them, anyway, are waiting to read his books?

According to the conservative philosopher Ortega y Gasset, popular mobilization demands nothing more from the critic than a shift in direction. The select few can no longer argue with one another or aim their criticism at the even more select and fewer, the rulers of the economy and the state; they must criticize the others, the ascendant mob of mediocre men and women, the 'vertical barbarians' who come not from outside but from within.[8] Ortega's book, *The Revolt of the Masses*, has been published in cheap editions and assigned for many years in college courses, so presumably it is read by the right people: the most ambitious and aggressive of the barbarians. But Ortega seems never to have felt any genuine tie to these people – the tone of his book is less disappointed than sardonic and disdainful – and so his shift in direction is hardly interesting. A decent man, he was willing enough to provide a cultivated voice for common complaint (or for selected common complaints). He only asked that once the cultivated had spoken, the uncultivated should keep quiet. What happens, however, when they are anything but quiet, when the noise level steadily rises, when politics suddenly seems all crudeness and clamor? Now detachment and distance may well be prudent, the conventionally better part of wisdom. Are they also the better part of criticism?

This question is faced most directly by critics who find much to admire or much to hope for in popular politics and culture. Soon enough, some of them will be disappointed, and we will begin to find traces of Ortegan disdain in their writings (Herbert Marcuse provides the clearest example). But I am interested now in the early encounters of critical intellectuals and the 'people' (the working class, the nation, blacks, women and so on). Of course, intellectuals are people too, but they are the ones who draw the line between the two groups – and then set out to cross it. Sometimes the way they draw the line merely anticipates their failure. Thus the Russian radical Dmitry Ivanovich Pisarev, writing in the 1860s:

> Only some sort of material catastrophe ... jolts [the] mass into uneasy movement, into the destruction of its customary, dreamily tranquil, vegetative existence ... The mass does not make discoveries or commit crimes; other people think and suffer, search and find, struggle and err on its behalf – other people eternally alien to it, eternally regarding it with contempt, and at the same time eternally working to increase the amenities of its life.[9]

Here the 'uneasy movement' of the mass serves no social purpose; only the elite of radical critics and revolutionaries acts purposefully; the people are nothing more than the objects of its benevolent activity. But there are two alternative possibilities, both of them sketched in Marx's writing. The first possibility is that the people are the instruments of social criticism or, in Marx's organic image, that critical philosophy is the head and the proletariat the body of the revolution.[10] The philosophical 'negativity' of the critic shapes and directs the rebelliousness of oppressed men and women. It was left to Lenin to argue that the head itself had to be embodied (in the vanguard or party) before it could exercise directive force. One might say that this argument also anticipates failure, whether or not the instrument is 'used' successfully. Human instruments are notoriously recalcitrant, rebellious, ungrateful.

The second possibility is that the people are the subjects of criticism: the revolt of the masses is the mobilization of common complaint.[11] Now the critic participates in an enterprise that is no longer his alone; he agitates, teaches, counsels, challenges, protests *from within*. This is my own view of the proper location and appropriate work of contemporary social critics. I don't mean to suggest that they must bow to the weight of noise and numbers. They have their own voice; they defend their independence; they are still associates of the Ancient and Honorable Company whose trans-historical existence I have tried to evoke. There is only this that is different about them, given the existence of the people as critical subjects: they are newly connected to popular movements and aspirations. Their criticism is auxiliary as well as independent. They can't just criticize, they must also offer advice, write programs, take stands, make political choices, frequently in the harshest circumstances. Alert to the defeats, often self-inflicted, of the mobilized people, they are nonetheless not ready to call for a return to traditional passivity. Critics of this sort must look for a way of talking in tune with but also against their new accompaniment. They need to find a place to stand, close to but not engulfed by their company.

NOTES

1. On the difficult question of Marx's moral views, see Steven Lukes, *Marxism and Morality* (Oxford: Oxford University Press, 1985).
2. Cf. Seyla Benhabib, *Critique, Norm and Utopia: A Study of the Foundations of Critical Theory* (New York: Columbia University Press, 1986).
3. Hamlet, III. iv. 178.
4. Christopher Lasch, *The New Radicalism in America, 1889–1963: The Intellectual as a Social Type*, (New York, 1967), p. 256.
5. Ibid., p. XV.
6. See the first version of Contrat Social in: Jean-Jacques Rousseau, Œuvres Complètes, (Paris, 1964), vol. 3, p. 287.
7. Bertolt Brecht explored this theme in the late twenties and early thirties in a series of dramas of which the best-known is *Die Maßnahme*.
8. José Ortega y Gasset, *The Revolt of the Masses* (Notre Dame, IN: University of Notre Dame Press, 1985).
9. Cited in Joseph Frank, *Dostoevsky: The Stir of Liberation, 1860–1865* (Princeton, NJ: Princeton University Press, 1986) p. 175.
10. Marx, 'Zur Kritik der Hegelschen Rechtsphilosophie. Einleitung', a.a.O., p. 224.
11. This is the standard Marxist view, though how many Marxist intellectuals have actually held it I cannot say. It is the argument of the *Manifesto*: that capitalism teaches the workers who experience it to be social critics and revolutionaries. Intellectuals have little more to do than to elaborate on the meaning of that experience.

70

MARINERS, RENEGADES
AND CASTAWAYS

C. L. R. James

What Melville did was to place within the covers of one book a presentation of a whole civilization so that any ordinary human being today can read it in a few days and grasp the essentials of the world he lived in. To do this a man must contain within his single self, at one and the same time, the whole history of the past, the most significant experiences of the world around him, and a clear vision of the future. Of all this he creates an ordered whole. No philosopher, statesman, scientist or soldier exceeds him in creative effort.

Melville knew how rarely such writers appear, and as usual, he has given the best description of these gigantic efforts of individual human beings.

The great author begins, as we have seen, by seeing the elements of his characters in the world around him. Melville tolerates no nonsense on that question.

But after that an entirely individual personal process begins. The great author has read the great creative works of the past, and it is in this way that he absorbs the great characters and experiences of previous civilizations. He is mature, according to Melville, only when these writings are a part of him, and his own mind, so nourished, functions with complete independence.

Then follows his own original creation. It seems that really new characters with original instincts cannot be developed adequately within the framework of the consciousness of the age. The great author must find in his mind new depths of consciousness, hitherto unprobed, to fill out these original characters.

From: C. L. R. James, *Mariners, Renegades and Castaways* (Detroit: Bewick/ED, 1978).

Melville actually uses the term 'strange stuff' which upheaves and upgushes in the writer's soul. This strange stuff the author has to resolve into its primitive elements. Thus these rare original characters seem to demand for their creation an extension of the range of consciousness of their creators, and through him this extended consciousness is transferred to the rest of mankind, when they are ready to listen.

It is impossible to test whether all this is true or not. All we can do is to examine some other great creative works of the past and great authors of the past and see if any light is thereby thrown upon Melville in this combination of observing actual human character, reading the great works of the past and then digging down into the consciousness.

Two writers immediately come to mind – the great Greek tragedian, Aeschylus, and his *Prometheus Bound*, and the still more famous Shakespeare and his play *King Lear*.

Ahab is a rebel, i.e. a man who is dissatisfied with the old and must have something new. So is Prometheus. So is Lear. Ahab defies science and industrial power, the gods of the nineteenth century. Prometheus was nailed to a rock because he had stolen fire from heaven and given it to primitive, backward, suffering mankind to start them on the road to civilization by means of the arts and sciences. For this, Zeus, King of Gods and men, chained him to a rock for 30,000 years. But still Prometheus defied him. Lear believed that Nature was a beneficent goddess in whose name he ruled, and by whom all his actions were blessed. When he discovered that it was not so, he defied Nature. Then going mad, he denounced the whole society of which he had been ruler and gave a vision of the future.

When Ahab defies the spirit of fire, he is way out in distant seas, thousands of miles away from civilization, standing on the deck of the Pequod, with the meanest mariners, renegades and castaways around him. When Prometheus defies Zeus, he is chained to a rock, on a wild expanse of land at the very ends of the earth. Around him are some young women from all parts of the world who are determined to share his fate. When Lear defies the thunder and the lightning, the most powerful manifestations of the forces of Nature, he is also on an open heath, and with him are a retainer whom he himself had banished; a crazy fool; and another fugitive from justice, disguised as an agricultural vagrant. Zeus hurls Prometheus and his followers into the lower regions with the thunderbolts and lightning of a great storm. Lear is driven mad by the thunder and lightning. These breaking upon him after his grievous experiences seem to be the final culmination of his sufferings. Ahab escapes the lightning and the thunder and the corpusants only to fall victim to his own madness. At times the three characters use almost the same words. These similarities cannot possibly be accidental.

It seems that at very great crises in human history, and they must be very great, an author appears who becomes aware that one great age is passing and another beginning. But he becomes aware of this primarily in terms of new types of human character, with new desires, new needs, new passions. The great writer, at least each of the three greatest writers the author knows, conceives a situation in which this character is brought right up against things that symbolize the old and oppose the new. The scene is set outside the confines of civilization. What is old is established, it has existed for centuries, it is accepted. But the new will not be denied. It is not fully conscious of itself, but it is certain that it is right. A gigantic conflict is inevitable.

It is here that Melville's description of the creative process may help us.

Prometheus, though in the play he is one of the Gods, is an Athenian of the fifth century before Christ. Amidst the surrounding primitiveness and savagery, a wonderful civilization had flowered with almost marvellous suddenness, a civilization based on the development of industry and commerce, practicing democracy, gifted in architecture, sculpture, philosophy and the drama. We have not got the complete drama on Prometheus written by Aeschylus. We have only what amounts to Act II of a play of three acts. But it seems fairly clear that Prometheus stood for the new, the splendid civilization, against the apathy, the ignorance and perhaps the brutal tyranny of the old regime, or more probably the readiness of the first founders of the new regime to compromise with the old and leave things much as they were before. The history of Athens shows us figures who could have served as a model for him. How far he, from this model, was the creation of his author, we cannot at this distance tell. But this much we know. While the ancient Greeks understood the character, to this very day Prometheus is still the prototype of the revolutionary leader, benefactor of humanity, bold, defiant, confident. It would seem that Aeschylus went far beyond his actual model or models, and created the type in such perfection that it lives to this day.

With Lear we can get closer to Melville's theories. Lear was created at the beginning of the seventeenth century about a dozen years before the founding of New England. A new world was on its way, the world of free individualism, of the conquest of Nature, of social revolution against tyrannical monarchy, of open conflicts over the distribution of the national income, when new concepts of justice would be battled over, and scientific explanations would be sought for human crime and error. Now this is what Lear spoke about when, driven mad by the wrongs inflicted upon him, he defied the storm on the heath.

Where did Shakespeare get all this from? How did he conceive of it all in the person of one single character? All we can say is that Melville's explanation is as good as any, and we should not forget that it is a great writer himself speaking. It took literally centuries before the modern world began to understand Lear. Shakespeare, having been given the initial impetus from outside, had to dig deep down into his own consciousness for the new feelings and the new ideas needed to complete his portrayal.

Melville says more than once and with great emphasis that what a great author like Shakespeare writes down is only a partial, inadequate, poor representation of what is in his mind. He says that there are two books, the one the author sees in his mind and the one he writes. And the one in the mind is as sluggish as an elephant, it will not move when called upon, and it sucks away the life-blood of the writer. It is too big and in places too obscure for accurate reproduction. It would seem then that the author does create within himself the character and its world and gives the best account of it he can.

The achievement of a great writer who writes an immortal book now stands before us in all its magnitude. He creates a world of human beings and an environment to correspond. He has read and absorbed how great characters in previous critical situations acted. He recognizes the similarity of emotions. He can use them to help his own structure. But what matters in his work is what is new, and that he must dig out for himself. What matters to us in Ahab is not his heroic determination. It is the sense of purpose, the attitude to science and industry, the defense of individual personality, the attitude to the men around him. There is not, and could not be anything like this in Aeschylus or in Shakespeare.

It is the completeness of the creation in the mind that seems to be the most astonishing thing. Just as from the real world of human beings, one can abstract philosophy, political economy, scientific theory, so from the partial account that is written down of this inherent world, one can deduce scientific theories of which the author was not at all directly conscious. Melville wrote *Moby Dick* in 1851. Yet in it today can be seen the anticipations of Darwin's theory of man's relation to the natural world, of Marx's theory of the relation of the individual to the economic and social structure, of Freud's theory of the irrational and primitive forces which lie just below the surface of human behavior.

He does not only anticipate the work of scientists. He is himself a scientist in human relations. Ahab is of the race of Prometheus. But it seems as if, for Melville, that type was now doomed. Great men, leading their fellows from one stage of civilization to another, there have always been and will always be, but the Promethean individual, containing in himself, his ideas, his plans, the chart of the future, he seems finished. In the world of affairs he leads only to disaster, which is why perhaps in literature he no longer appears at all.

The world of the author's creation is his own world in a very precise sense. Though rooted in reality, it is not a real world. No man ever chased or would chase a White Whale as Ahab did. No intellectual ever followed a totalitarian because of the whiteness of anything. The great writer is dealing in human emotions. The world he creates is designed to portray emotions. Those are real enough. And he will use anything that will bring those emotions vividly before his reader. The White Whale seems infinitely remote from the idea of the master race or the master plan. But within Melville's world the reasoning and feelings and actions and effects of the men who follow this fantasy are as real as those in the actual world of men.

[. . .]

Once the writer has got hold of his characters and their environment, then that world dominates everything, including himself. Structure, style, ideas, phrases fit into or spring from this distinct creation. For convenience we have spoken of characters, then of environment, here of reality, there of logical imagination. But in these great creative works these things are no more separate than, in the real world, a man's political activity can be separated from his personality. The artist's world is a total whole and its effects on the reader is designed to be total. Ahab for example is eaten up inside by his speculations on the nature of the universe and his scientific plans to capture Moby Dick. This is shown on his physical person by the great lines of thought on his forehead which are constantly brought to the notice of the reader. Again, on two dramatic occasions, first Melville and then Ahab himself refer to the weight upon Ahab's back of the countless miseries men have endured since the days of Adam. Ahab's words are worth repeating: 'I feel deadly faint, bowed, and humped, as though I were Adam, staggering beneath the piled centuries since Paradise'.

But on at least twenty-five occasions in the book, from the chapter in which we first see him to the last pages in which he destroys the Pequod, Moby Dick is persistently described for us as a whale with a wrinkled forehead and a hump on his back. Those and his whiteness are his distinguishing features. Thus by degrees it dawns upon us that Moby Dick is the physical embodiment of Ahab's inward crisis. His determination to slay Moby Dick is his determination to slay the demons which are torturing him. But Melville at the same time makes it consistently clear that Moby Dick is actually just a big fish in the sea. It is crazy Ahab who makes of him this fantastic symbol. Similarly the evil effect of the whiteness of the whale is felt by Ishmael who had brought with him from his life on land the vision of a white monster.

If within this world the writer feels that characters or events are needed to make his conception logical, he creates them, often in direct contradiction with ordinary experience and ordinary sense. He is guided by one fact – his world needs them. The writer of this book feels that it is out of some such need that there came figures like Queequeg, Daggoo and Tashtego.

This is the type of world created by the great writer. These are the effects he seeks and these are the means he uses to achieve them. This is his book, his own individual creation, and it is by means of the wrinkled brow and the whiteness of the whale, and the flag streaming forward from Tashtego's own forward-flowing heart that Melville says what he has to say.

And yet at the same time, this most intense individuality of creation is moulded not only out of the general social environment but of the very nationality of the author. Melville establishes in the most unequivocal form that his theme is world civilization. But Aeschylus was in every line of his work an Athenian of the fifth century BC. Similarly Shakespeare was an Elizabethan Englishman, and Melville is the most American of all writers. It is not only his original character that is rooted in the external world. He himself is rooted in that world.

[...]

Structurally *Moby Dick* is one of the most orderly books in the world but orderly in the sociological sense. It is the mark of a man shaped by a civilization where from its foundation the construction and objective classification of material things dominate life and thought to a degree far greater than in any other modern country.

But having once arranged a basic systematic plan, Melville then in his style exhibits all the American exuberance and insatiable grasp at every aspect of life in sight. Ancient and modern history, theology, mythology, philosophy, science, he takes hold of everything and uses it for any purpose he wants. He has in his head the majestic rhythms of the great English prose-writers and he can originate new variations of them. But even within these rhythms he is incurably colloquial and discursive. On occasion some of Ahab's speeches ring slightly hollow. But Melville achieved a harmony between classical English style and the ease of American civilization, which has been managed neither before nor since. He could do whatever he wanted to do, and almost on the same page he could reconcile the most contradictory styles without strain.

And finally he was American, too, not only in structure and in style, but in the deepest content of his great book. No one can really say with any precision what influences shaped a writer's creative imagination. But the period in which Melville wrote was one of the most curious in the history of the United States. On the one hand the mass of the nation in the North, disoriented, cut away from old moorings, hungrily seeking a new basis for a sense of community. On the other – some of the most boundlessly egotistical individual personalities the country has ever known. Some of the men of that period, Stanton, the Secretary of War, Thaddeus Stevens, William Lloyd Garrison, were men of a tempestuous force of character such as have no parallel in contemporary life. The lives of the generals, Grant, Sherman, Sheridan, make equally strange reading.

The Civil War put an end to this torment of a nation. The people found themselves in the formation of the Republican Party, and the struggle for the unity of the nation. The great individualists found their energies disciplined or stimulated in the war itself. But it seems clear that in his ruthless probing to the very end of the problem of individual personality and at the same time the search for a new basis of community, Melville was writing about an America that he knew. When with the end of the Civil War normal life returned, Melville was forgotten. But with the return of crisis in 1914, this time on a world scale, he has been rediscovered.

If this essentially American writer now takes on increasingly the status of the most representative writer of modern civilization, one result of it should be to bring more sharply into prominence the period in which he wrote, the period which preceded the Civil War. That period ushered in the world in which we live. For our world, a world of wars, the fact is neglected that the Civil War was the first great war of modern times. The great Americans of the period preceding it knew that something was wrong, something deeper than slavery, but inasmuch as they lived under democracy and the republic, and had no monarchy nor land-owning aristocracy to contend with, their task was difficult. They probed into strange places and what they found they did not often fully understand. There were no precedents. It is only today when democracies and republics once more have to examine their foundations that the work of Poe, Hawthorne, Whitman, Garrison and Phillips, and Melville can be fully understood. Melville today already towers above his countrymen, and such is the hunger of the world for understanding itself, that the time cannot be far distant when men in every country will know him for what he is – a writer in the great tradition of Aeschylus and Shakespeare and the unsurpassed interpreter of the age in which we live, its past, its present and its uncertain future.

LIST OF AUTHORS

Alexander, Jeffrey C. (1947–): sociologist; *Theoretical Logic in Sociology, Vol. I–IV* (1983), *Twenty Lectures: Sociological Theory Since World War II* (1987), *Fin de Siècle Social Theory* (1995), *Neofunctionalism and After* (1998).

Appiah, K. Anthony (1954–): social philosopher; *Assertion and Conditions* (1958), *In My Father's House* (1992), *Color Conscious* (1996).

Appleby, Joyce (1944–): historian; *Liberalism and Republicanism in the Historical Imagination* (1992), *Inheriting the Revolution – The First Generation of Americans* (2000).

Arato, Andrew (1944–): sociologist; *Civil Society and Political Theory* (1992), *Civil Society, Constitution and Legitimacy* (2000).

Arendt, Hannah (1906–75): political philosopher; *Origins of Totalitarianism* (1951), *The Human Condition* (1958), *On Revolution* (1963).

Barber, Benjamin (1939–): political scientist; *Strong Democracy* (1984), *Jihad vs. McWorld* (1995), *A Passion for Democracy* (1998).

Bellah, Robert (1927–): sociologist; *The Good Society* (1991), *Habits of the Heart* (1985/1996).

Bercovitch, Sacvan (1933–): English literature; *The American Jeremiad* (1978), *The Rites of Assent* (1993).

Bowles, Samuel (1939–): political economist; *Democracy and Capitalism* (1986), *Understanding Capitalism* (1993), *Recasting Egalitarianism* (1998).

Ceaser, James W. (1946–): political scientist; *Reconstructing America* (1997).

Cohen, Jean L. (1946–): political theorist; *Class and Civil Society* (1982), *Civil Society and Political Theory* (1992).

Crèvecoeur, Hector St. John de (1735–1813): farmer and writer; *Letters from an American Farmer* (1793).

Dahl, Robert A. (1915–): political scientist; *A Preface to a Democratic Theory* (1956), *Who Governs?* (1961), *Democracy and Its Critics* (1989), *On Democracy* (1998).

Dewey, John (1859–1952): philosopher; *Democracy and Education* (1916), *The Public and its Problems* (1927), *Reconstruction in Philosophy* (1920/1948).

Dietz, Mary G. (1951–): political scientist; *Between the Human and the Divine* (1988).

Du Bois, W. E. B. (1868–1963): sociologist, writer and civil rights activist; *The Suppression of the African Slave Trade to the United States of America* (1896), *The Philadelphia Negro* (1899), *The Souls of Black Folk* (1903), *Black Reconstruction in America* (1935).

Dworkin, Ronald (1931–): legal theorist; *Taking Rights Seriously* (1978), *Freedom's Law* (1996), *Sovereign Virtue* (2000).

Elshtain, Jean Bethke (1941–): political scientist; *Public Man, Private Woman* (1981), *Democracy on Trial* (1995).

Emerson, Ralph Waldo (1803–82): philosopher and writer; *Essays and Lectures* (1983).

Gates, Henry Louis (1950–): literary critic; *Signifying Monkey* (1988), *Loose Canons* (1992), *Colored People* (1994), *Thirteen Ways of Looking at a Black Man* (1997).

Gintis, Herbert (1940–): political scientist; *Democracy and Capitalism* (1986), *Recasting Egalitarianism* (1998), *Game Theory* (2000).

Glazer, Nathan (1923–): sociologist; *Beyond the Melting Pot* (1970), *Affirmative Discrimination* (1975), *Ethnic Dilemmas* (1983), *We are all Multiculturalists Now* (1997).

Goldfarb, Jeffrey C. (1949–): sociologist; *On Cultural Freedom* (1982), *Civility and Subversion* (1998).

Gutmann, Amy (1949–): philosopher; *Color Conscious* (1996), *Democracy and Disagreement* (1996).

Hamilton, Alexander (1757–1804): politician; *The Federalist Papers* (1788).

Hartz, Louis (1919–68): political scientist; *The Liberal Tradition in America* (1955).

Herberg, Will (1906–77): sociologist; *Protestant, Catholic, Jew* (1955).

Hirschman, Albert O. (1915–): economist; *Exit, Voice and Loyalty* (1970), *The Passions and the Interests* (1977), *Shifting Involvements* (1982), *The Rhetoric of Reaction* (1991).

Hofstadter, Richard (1916–70): historian; *Social Darwinism in America* (1944), *The American Political Tradition* (1948), *Anti-Intellectualism in America* (1962).

Holmes, Stephen (1948–): political scientist; *Passions and Constraints* (1995).

hooks, bell (1952–): writer and cultural critic; *Ain't I A Woman* (1981), *Breaking Bread* (1991), *Black Looks* (1992), *killing rage, ending racism* (1996).

Isaac, Jeffrey C. (1957–): political scientist; *Arendt, Camus and Modern Rebellion* (1994), *Democracy in Dark Times* (1998).

James, C. L. R. (1901–89): social philosopher, literary critic and cricket expert; *Mariners, Renegades and Castaways* (1978), *American Civilisation* (1993).

James, William (1842–1910): psychologist; *The Writings of William James* (1967).

Jay, John (1757–1829): attorney and politician; *The Federalist Papers* (1788).

Jefferson, Thomas (1743–1826): politician and former President of the US; *Notes on the State of Virginia* (1800), *Political Writings* (1999).

Lipset, Seymour Martin (1922–): political sociologist; *Political Man* (1960), *First New Nation* (1963), *Continental Divide* (1990), *American Exceptionalism* (1996).

Madison, James (1751–1836): politician and former President of the US; *The Federalist Papers* (1788).

Mahan, Alfred Thayer (1840–1914): naval officer and historian; *The Influence of Sea Power upon History* (1890).

Miller, Perry (1908–63): historian; *The New England Mind* (1953).

Mills, C. Wright (1916–62): sociologist; *White Collar* (1951), *The Power Elite* (1956), *The Sociological Imagination* (1959).

Moore, Barrington, Jr. (1913–): sociologist; *Social Origins of Dictatorship and Democracy* (1967), *Injustice* (1978).

Paine, Thomas (1737–1809): writer; *Common Sense* (1776), *The Rights of Man* (1791), *The Age of Reason* (1793).

Pocock, John G. A. (1924–): intellectual historian; *The Machiavellian Moment* (1975).

Rawls, John (1921–): philosopher; *A Theory of Justice* (1971/1999), *Political Liberalism* (1993), *Collected Papers* (1999).

Rorty, Richard (1931–): philosopher; *Contingency, Irony, and Solidarity* (1989), *Objectivity, Relativism and Truth* (1991).

Rosenblum, Nancy L. (1947–): political scientist; *Another Liberalism* (1987), *Membership and Morals: The Public Use of Pluralism in America* (1998).

Ryan, Mary P. (1945–): women's historian; *Civic Wars: Democracy and Public Life in the American City during the Nineteenth Century* (1997).

Sandel, Michael J. (1953–): political scientist; *Liberalism and the Limits of Justice* (1982), *Democracy's Discontent* (1996).

Sennett, Richard (1943–): sociologist; *The Hidden Injuries of Class* (1972), *The Fall of Public Man* (1978), *The Corrosion of Character* (1998).

Shklar, Judith N. (1928–92): political scientist; *Ordinary Vices* (1984), *Faces of Injustice* (1990), *American Citizenship* (1991), *Political Thought and Political Thinkers* (1998), *Redeeming American Political Thought* (1998).

Taylor, Charles (1931–): philosopher; *Sources of the Self* (1989), *Multiculturalism and 'The Politics of Disagreement'* (1992).

Thompson, Dennis (1940–): political philosopher; *Democratic Citizen* (1970), *Political Ethics and Public Office* (1987), *Democracy and Disagreement* (1996).

Tocqueville, Alexis de (1805–59): politician and writer; *Democracy in America* (1835), *The Old Regime and the Revolution* (1851).

Turner, Frederick Jackson (1861–1932): historian; *The Frontier in American History* (1920).

Walzer, Michael (1937–): philosopher, *Spheres of Justice* (1983), *The Company of Critics* (1988).

Weber, Max (1864–1920): sociologist; *The Protestant Work Ethic* (1920), *Economy and Society* (1922).

West, Cornel (1953–): social philosopher; *The American Evasion of Philosophy* (1989), *Breaking Bread* (1991).

Wolfe, Alan (1942–): sociologist; *Whose Keeper? Social Science and Moral Obligation* (1989), *One Nation After All* (1998).

Wolff, Robert Paul (1933–): philosopher; *The Ideal of the University* (1969), *About Philosophy* (1976), *Understanding Rawls* (1977).

Wolin, Sheldon S. (1922–): political scientist; *Politics and Vision* (1960), *Tocqueville: Between Two Worlds* (2001).

Young, James P. (1943–): political scientist; *Reconsidering American Liberalism* (1996).

INDEX

abortion, 164, 257, 261, 423, 424
absolutism, 158, 173, 181
accountability, 144, 145, 225, 258, 265, 266
    democratic, 271, 272, 273
activism, 111, 213, 381
Adams, John, 70, 158, 244, 412
Addams, Jane, 375–6
adolescent independence, 277, 278
adversarial political system, 144, 146–7
Aeschylus, 456–60
aestheticism, 230
aethism, 94
African-Americans, 143, 242, 333–4, 335, 339,
    340–1, 342–3, 346–9, 391
Agnew, Spiro, 108
agnosticism, 94
agrarian democracy, 241
agriculture, 247, 271
Alaska, 86
Alien and Sedition Acts, 164
alien residents, 308, 382
alienation, 264–5, 356, 450, 452
ambition, 132, 147
American Civil War, 241–3, 276, 309,
    460–1
American Constitution, 42, 43, 114, 126–34,
    135, 141, 189
    Civil War amendments to, 309
    Fourteenth Amendment, 241–2, 246,
        309
    jeremiad, 106
    separation of power, 409
    American Dream, 24, 41, 42, 86, 87,
        308
American Renaissance literature, 87

American Revolution, 29, 30, 36, 39, 51, 84,
    85, 108
    compared with French Revolution, 119–25,
        364
    ideology and, 113
    neoclassical republicanism, 163
American War of Independence *see* American
    Revolution
American Way of Life, 89, 90, 94, 156
Americanization, 7, 82, 328, 330
ancien régime, 108, 123, 155, 320
ancient Greece, 63, 109, 127, 136, 137, 138,
    139, 283, 382–3,
    456–61
Andros, Sir Edmund, 69
Anglo-Saxon race, 66
anonymity, 328
Anscombe, Elizabeth, 333
Anthony, Susan B., 391–2
anthropology, 116–17, 336–8
anti-federalism, 277
anti-intellectualism, 9–12
anti-Jacobinism, 364
anti-slavery movement, 391
anti-statism, 277
anti-war movements, 41
apportionment, 190–1
Aquinas, St Thomas, 174
Arato, Andrew and Cohen, Jean, 394
Arendt, Hannah, 109, 273, 365, 369, 386
aristocracy, 40, 202–3, 239, 240, 241
aristocratical forms of government, 29, 30, 32,
    34
Aristotle, 114, 163, 174, 205, 300, 380, 382–3,
    386, 410